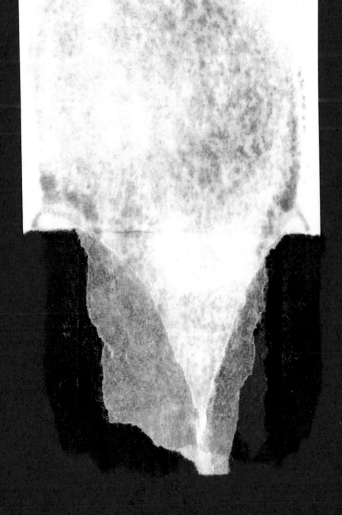

THE VON RICHTHOFEN SISTERS

The Triumphant and the Tragic Modes of Love

Martin Green

The von Richthofen Sisters
The Triumphant and the
Tragic Modes of Love

ELSE *and* FRIEDA VON RICHTHOFEN,

OTTO GROSS, MAX WEBER,

and D. H. LAWRENCE, *in the Years 1870–1970*

BASIC BOOKS, INC., *Publishers*   *New York*

Dedicated to Jim Harvey,

who has shared this enthusiasm with me, and so much else.

Was man, the eternal protagonist, born of woman, with her womb of fathomless emotion? Or was woman, with her deep womb of emotion, born from the rib of active man, the first created? Man, the doer, the knower, the original in *being,* is he lord of life? Or is woman, the great Mother, who bore us from the womb of love, is she the supreme Goddess?

This is the question of all time.

D. H. Lawrence, *Fantasia of the Unconscious*

Contents

Preface

After Bismarck's Prussia defeated France, in 1870, and first nationalized and then imperialized Germany, a new breed began to be born there, of ultra-manly men. The victories of Sedan and Versailles intoxicated German loins to engender a haughty and magnificent race of masters, in whom all the dominant male traits were exaggerated. But some of the daughters and sisters of this breed rebelled and determined to themselves embody other human possibilities—to embody an idea of Woman. Friedrich von Richthofen, one of Bismarck's Prussian officers in the 1870 war, married immediately after the war and his children were all born in the first twelve years of the new German Reich. Two of his daughters rebelled against the world of men, rebelled in competition with and contradiction of each other, following two opposing paths, both of which led to equal heights of glory. Each of these extraordinary women became an inspiration to others; in Germany, England, America; in their lives and in the works they inspired in the men who knew them. Both were beautiful, both were passionate, both were brilliant, but in very different ways. The elder fought her way to a career and independence, to university study and the social sciences, to rational debate and political reform. The younger believed in love and nature, in the life-regenerative powers of her own spontaneous femaleness and unconscious innocence. She married young, but to a man older and unlike herself, and was unhappy with him. The elder married a man with the same intellectual interests as herself, but she too was unhappy. She attached herself to the leading circle of Heidelberg, then Germany's intellectual capital, and to the great sociologist, Max Weber, in discipleship, friendship, and love. Her name was Else Jaffe, and she became a muse of the critical intelligence of our century. The younger ran away from her husband and children with a man younger than herself, who became, under her guidance, one of the world's great Romantic novelists. Her name was Frieda Lawrence, and she became a muse of our erotic imagination.

The main story of this book is told in two parts. Part One (Chapters 1 and 2) discusses the sisters' lives up to 1930 and the ideas of Otto Gross, Max Weber, and D. H. Lawrence. Part Three (Chapters 3 and 4) continues the lives from 1930 to 1970 and discusses the posthumous fate of those men's ideas and the ideas of the men the sisters knew later. Between them is a chronology of the sisters in their century (to be consulted at the reader's convenience), designed to put the main events of their story together with the public events of the century 1870–1970. The Epilogue may be treated to some degree as an appendix since it is in some sense written for readers with a special interest in modern literary history and criticism, though it is my hope and belief that it contains matter of some interest to the general reader as well.

Acknowledgments

First of all, I must acknowledge the editorial work done by Philip Rosenberg who rewrote several passages and supervised the whole manuscript on behalf of my publishers, and the tireless and cheerful collection of photographs done by Carol Vance.

Then I am grateful to the American Philosophical Society for a grant toward research expenses. Also to Professor Roeming and the Center for Twentieth Century Studies at the University of Wisconsin in Milwaukee, where I did the major part of the research for this book. Also to Professor Roberts and the Center for Humanities Research at the University of Texas, which made me welcome and helped me with manuscripts and photographs. Also to the manuscript collections of both the Harvard College Library and the Beinecke Rare Book and Manuscript Library of Yale University, which allowed me to consult and quote from material in their possession. Also to Mr. McGuire and the Princeton University Press, who allowed me to see the references to Otto Gross in the Freud-Jung correspondence while that was still in proof. Also to Claire Oehring, of East Berlin, who sent me a microfilm of Franz Jung's unpublished essay on Otto Gross. Also to Lois Madison Hoffman, who not only let me use her translation of the Gross letters, but also let me see a transcript of her 1967 interview with Frau Jaffe, and sent much other help by mail from Germany. Also to Frau Ellen von Krafft-Delp and Schwester Camilla Ullmann, for the photograph of Otto Gross and for information about Regina Ullmann. Also to many others, in several countries, who are too numerous to mention.

Especially I must thank Frau von Eckardt, who helped me with memories of her mother's life, and with access to her mother's letters; and Professor Baumgarten, who showed me, and allowed me to quote, extracts from other letters confided to his care. (Professor Baumgarten will publish a selection of 300 letters written to and by Max Weber, with Hoffman and Campe of Hamburg, in 1975.)

Finally, I must thank Frau Jaffe, who decided in the spring of 1973 to let me see papers which she had intended to keep private, and thus empowered Frau von Eckardt and Professor Baumgarten to show them to me.

I would also like to thank the following people and institutions for allowing me to reproduce photographs: the von Eckardt family for the pictures of Baroness von Richthofen with Else and Frieda, Else Jaffe, Edgar Jaffe, Else with her son, and Frieda Gross with her son; the Humanities Research Center of the University of Texas at Austin for the pictures of Frieda Weekley and the Lawrence family; Barbara Barr for the picture of Ernest Weekley; Schwester Camilla Ullmann for the picture of Otto Gross as a boy; the Granger Collection for the photographs of D. H. Lawrence, John Middleton Murry, and Wilhelm Reich; Foto Leif Geiges for the picture of Max Weber; J. C. B. Mohr (Paul Siebeck) Tübingen for the photograph of the Weber family; Montague Weekley for the picture of Frieda Weekley with her son; Anna Mahler for the picture of Alma Mahler with her child; Anthony Alpers for the photograph of the young John Middleton Murry; Brown Brothers for the picture of Mabel Luhan; Professor M. Luoma for the photograph of Alfred Weber; F. H. Kerle for the picture of Marianne Weber; Mrs. Erbel Coates for the photograph of Jessie Chambers; the Bettmann Archive, Inc. for the picture of Isadora Duncan; Professor H. F. Peters for the picture of Lou Andreas-Salome; Professor Richard Drinnon for the photograph of Emma Goldman; the Guardian for the picture of F. R. Leavis; Culver Pictures for the photograph of Karl Jaspers; and the Harvard University News Office for the photograph of Talcott Parsons.

Meeting the Sisters

I met Frieda Lawrence in Taos in 1955, the year before she died. I remember mainly her voice, which justified all Lawrence had written about her: so strong, husky, animated, unaffectedly affirmative. It was a *glamorous* voice, except that there were no Celtic twilight suggestions; it was all natural pleasures and natural energies it spoke of, only they promised to be intensified, verified, purified, to the pitch of music.

The voice "justified" her because she seemed small. And though the face I saw must have had the lioness and Viking profile one sees in drawings, and the famous tawny eyes, she didn't really display those to me. She was just an animated little old woman. She devoted all her energy to making conversation, and since I was carrying with me the Pelican paperback on Islam, we had an intensely eager conversation on world religions. It was so intense that when I rose to go I had to offer to leave the book with her, and though she protested, she had made herself out so passionately interested that she more or less had to accept it. So, in due course, I bought myself another copy, while she, a hundred to one, never picked up the book again from where I had left it. Just as I'm sure she turned with a sigh of relief to her husband as I left—he had handsomely bowed himself out on my arrival—and spoke of that quality of *life* of which Lawrence had had so much and his admirers so little. But I like to think that she had both grace enough not to make *much* of that, and wit enough to speculate later, by herself, on who I was.

That half hour is by now mixed up in my memory with anecdotes and photographs. The woman I met was not much like the clear-eyed girl in flounced white satin and flaxen coiffure who looks round and up at the photographer so coyly. Or the glamour shot of her in a big black hood—Frieda as film star. Or her with her son as a baby—the big-eyed Madonna and child. Nor of course the large and busty matron she so soon became and who seems in some photographs an imposture, an imposition by an unkind Fate. But in all of them I feel the same overbearing and yet tender-skinned offering of herself—"here I am . . . it's *me*"—which is yet ready to be terribly hurt if not accepted, and accepted at her own valuation. And along with this spoiled-child quality, a great deal of intelligence, sensitivity, courage, subtlety, only so ill-coordinated with each other and with the fundamental self-assertion. Above all, an assertion that the ill-coordinatedness does not matter—"I may not be saying things right but I *am* right, aren't I?" She is confident (though she demands reassurance) that she has everything that really matters, so why bother about the order of things or the exact phrasing? "You ought to be jolly glad I'm here at all. And you are, aren't you?"

That is the voice I hear coming out of those photographs and memories.

It was in 1971 that I met her sisters, Frau Krug in Munich and Frau Jaffe in Heidelberg. I knew immensely more about Lawrence, and about Frieda, than I had in 1955, but I didn't know much about them. The von Richthofen sisters have always been discreet—even Frieda. She says just about as little as it is possible to say about Otto Gross. And it is my idea that she said very little to each man about his predecessors, revealing at most only *her feelings* about him. All three sisters had a remarkable gift for making men ashamed to say anything commonplace to them, while they never committed themselves, verbally, to anything but the commonplace. Their stimulus was all in their responding, and it was almost entirely ejaculatory, not syntactic.

Frau Krug was still beautiful in a film-starish way, her dark eyes not only bright but clear as old women's eyes aren't, and her skin was without a fleck or a freckle, or a flush or a discoloration, and was wax-white except where it was heavily rouged. She could not move about, but her figure was still straight and slender. And though what she said did not make consistent sense, it still conveyed the magic it was said to have conveyed in her youth. She sparkled her eyes at me and opened her big, painted, cannibal mouth to reveal teeth, her own teeth, still glittering with appetite. She bounced round in her chair and grasped my hand "absent-mindedly" in her animated memories of Boston—which it turned out later she thought was a man she'd known. She was a phenomenon of such stylishness that all potential criticism crept back out of her presence abashed. A lovely lady needs no other justification.

Baron von Richthofen called his daughters the three Graces, Lawrence called them "the goddesses three," and one can indeed feel like Paris awarding the apple of beauty as one looks over their pictures. Their styles of loveliness were so different. Frau Krug, Johanna, was rich and florid and ornamental in her beauty, sumptuous in texture and color, with abundant dark hair and rosy-dusky contours. Her two sisters were both blonde and white-skinned. But whereas Frieda's was a beauty of affirmation—the eager self-affirmation of a self that was more than ego—Else's might almost be called a negation. Hers was a formal beauty, an aesthetic triumph of line and form, her face all purity of feature and clarity of countenance, her figure all slenderness, straightness, ivory-coolness. In her photographs she seems to be submitting to an examination by the camera. She does not give herself to it, nor does she commit herself to being a candidate for beauty, much less a servant of Eros. She is merely there, to be examined by whatever criteria you choose. If Frieda and Johanna challenge you to deny their beauty, Else challenges you to discover hers—or rather, she leaves the whole thing up to you.

I found Frau Jaffe living in an old people's home in Heidelberg, not letting herself be a nuisance to anybody. She was standing, leaning on a cane when I entered the room, but she seemed straight as a wand. Her voice was strikingly like Frieda's, except that *her* vigor of enunciation did not rush on to the next word, but swerved back to the beginning of the phrase, slicing the whole thing cleanly out for your consideration. We had several conversations, in which she refused to tell me what I wanted to know—silently and vigorously refused—and yet entertained me royally. Not with the all-engulfing self-affirmation and life-affirmation of Frieda, but with an ironic challenge and knowingness, a readiness to appreciate a good answer on my part matched with an equal readiness to reprove a bad one and even a challenge to me to reprove her if I could. These were interviews in which she asked me questions—about all kinds of things, but all bearing on who I was. As to who *she* was, she would give me only "classified public" information; but she made sure we should both enjoy that. And in her account of other scholars who came to see her, and of her friend Professor Baumgarten, who was "only seventy years old, only a little one," whom she had to "schimpfen" sometimes, to scold, in these accounts I recognized the organizing image her presence subliminally suggested. She was Queen Elizabeth, and we were all Essexes and Leicesters, there to be teased, challenged, flattered, tested. She wanted to see what we had to teach her, and she was ready to learn, but she also wanted to let us know the limits of our power over her. I think of her as one of the finest conversational ironists I've met. Offering me a bowl of home-baked cookies, just brought her by a young *Freundin,* she remarked on how good they looked, as well as on the kindness of the act. But when I gushingly joined in, she observed, "But yet to eat they are not very good. Taste one." And all the kindness and thoughtfulness of the young *Freundin,* and the appetizing look and smell of her cookies, was zestfully annihilated with a discreet curl of the lip. Not of course that those values had not existed. No one could more unequivocally have affirmed their importance. But they belonged in a different world from a good cookie, didn't they?

With her, too, other images, anecdotes, and photographs complicate the memory. She was such a beautiful girl, so slender and elegantly featured, so proudly drooping her head, so sadly drooping her eyelids. There is so much so wounded, so sorrowful, so renunciatory beneath the sardonic sparkle and below the graceful composure of the posture. She had always to be so careful to defend herself against Frieda's zest, and the men who worshipped it, just as Frieda on her part had to rebel against the elegance and the sorrow of her sister, in order not to feel always wrong in herself. It would never have occurred to Else, after all, to arrive confident that everyone would be "jolly glad" to have her, much less to demand that they should admit it. But certain special people—*bedeutende Männer*—yes, she expected them to recognize her quality, just by the sign of that recognition of them which *she* offered. And she expected their recognition to be respectful. "You needn't think that because I see how clever you are I can't also see when you aren't really saying anything original. And you needn't think I can't see equally well how clever that other man is who is contradicting you rather amusingly. However, we won't have any unpleasantness, will we? Let's spare each other our individual uglinesses, shall we? Let's dispose of those each one by himself."

That is the voice I heard from her.

The two voices were antithetical to each other—each one dominant just in the place the other became hesitant—and so mutually explanatory. The two personalities, if in your mind you brought the one close to the other, clipped together like two pieces of a jigsaw puzzle. And they also belonged in the same picture, in the same life-context, as well as to each other. They were very similar. Despite the difference between what they were "saying," the sisters' voices were alike in their strength, in their vitality, in the force of their demands on life—which is to say, their aggressive response to its demands on them.

Part One

Adventures, 1870–1930

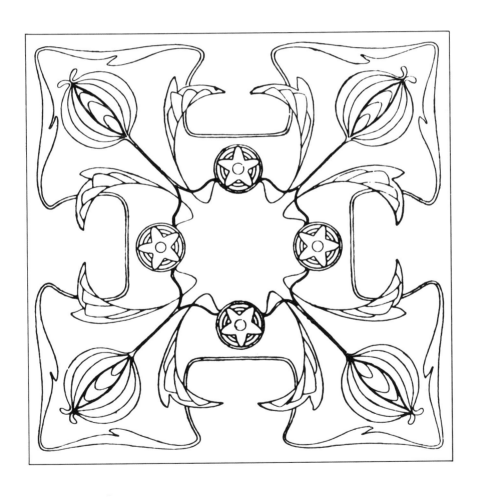

Else and Frieda von Richthofen: Heidelberg and Munich

The German Background

The era in German history that begins in 1870 belongs primarily to Bismarck. It all began with his war, the Franco-Prussian war of 1870–1871, and his empire, the second German Reich. Under Wilhelm I Germany became at last one country, a unified nation capable of defeating France. And this happened under the direction of a brutal, cynical, anti-idealistic, anti-ideological, anti-liberal Junker, actually a pseudo-Junker; a Lermontov or Pushkin hero who dramatized himself as a Junker, that is, as a typical Prussian country squire, a simple and blinkered creature of tradition, all discipline and self-discipline. It had not happened under the direction of the men of principle, the men of advanced ideas, in 1848. But in 1870 Germany became a European power and a world power; it became suddenly rich and strong and self-conscious; it felt itself suddenly a "young giant." And it received all these gifts at the hands of a shameless egotist and a political diabolist, a servant of brute power and a *denier* of every piety of the life of the mind. Bismarck's effect on Germany, and the reaction of that country on the rest of Europe, determined the history of our century.

He created a Germany whose imagination was in thrall to him, and therefore to Junkerism, to Prussianism, to a rankly masculine mode of being. He created a country which intensified, exaggerated, all the patriarchal elements in Western European culture, which made itself a caricature of the patriarchal male. But it expressed many of the values of the rest of Europe even as it caricatured them. There was much that was absurd and tasteless in Bismarck's Germany, judged by European standards, much that was reactionary and old-fashioned, but it was *successful* in economic and industrial terms, it was *powerful* in military and diplomatic terms. It made that exaggerated patriarchalism prevail imaginatively.

A patriarchal family is one in which the husband and father is master; a patriarchal personality is one in which the masterful traits are accentuated; and a patriarchal culture is one in which the institutions of authority, like armies and prisons, bulk large, and the modes of authority in general are military or punitive. So much would suffice to define the idea as I have used it so far, but it is to be a major term in my argument and so more must be said. For modern feeling, patriarchy is also associated with the centralization of power, with the dominant will in our (basically patriarchal) civilization. The centers of resistance to that will are regional, local, or village traditions and life-forms; ultimately, individual homes where the center of life is the mother. This is the world of Woman, which often opposes itself to the world of men, the world of prisons and parliaments and armies and politics. That latter is also the world of public events, of public careers and achievements, in which women play a smaller part than men, and to enter which they must take on to some degree the male mode of being. Else von Richthofen entered that world, the world of academia and social reform, in her protest against patriarchy; Frieda tried academia but fled it to espouse the world of peasants and "primitive" cultures, where even men live in the female mode of being. The world of Woman lives by the values of life and love, the world of men by law and order. But the opposition between the two is not often aggressive. In civilized cultures it is traditional for the world of Woman to subordinate itself to the world of men, and not to seek to control national policy, to direct historical evolution. Only in extreme crises will a group try to make the values of Woman prevail over those of men. Such a crisis was provoked by Bismarck, for he had made a country in which the matriarchal values were almost completely ineffective, a country whose values were based almost entirely on those of the Prussian officer, a country, in short, which was the institutionalization of himself.

Otto von Bismarck was born in 1815 at Schönhausen, just east of the Elbe. The Bismarcks' was a typical Junker estate of wheat and beetroot fields, pastures for sheep and cattle, with woods in the background. Their neighbors, and the Bismarcks themselves, had always lived like eighteenth-century English Tory squires, except that the Junkers were closer than their English counterparts to the practical work of farming, and sometimes themselves milked the cows and sold the wool in the marketplace of the neighboring country town. Their loyalties, to king, to class, and to family, were very strong. The von Richthofens, as Dr. Lucas tells us, held a *Familientag* once every six years to reunite all the male members of that ramified clan and to give them a nostalgic taste of the traditional pastimes of the Junkers, boar- and stag-hunting in the Carpathians, salmon-fishing in the Oder. The Junkers were very Protestant and very German, and very much the feudal lords of their tenants, both in times of war and in times of peace. That is to say, they were patriarchal in a very traditional sense, old-fashioned and small-scale, out of date and harmless. And yet Bismarck identified himself always as a Junker, as a Prussian, and as a soldier in his King's service. Indeed, it was by this means that he built the great new Reich. This Junker ideal, this Junker identity of his, was saved from being passé by being a paradox.

The Bismarck family was not entirely like its neighbors. Otto's mother, Wilhelmine Menken von Bismarck, came of a bureaucratic-professorial family and had fashionably liberal opinions and intellectual ambitions which she was determined to see her son achieve on her behalf. She was not an affectionate mother, however, and it seems clear that Otto von Bismarck determined early on to be like his father—large and masculine, unintellectual and slow-blooded—in revenge upon his mother. He was by natural endowment an extremely clever, irritable, nervous, sentimental, restless soul, but he made his career out of incarnating the opposite qualities, as a coarsely appetitive, crudely violent, tradition-bound simple soul, holding Power in trust for his Master. He was patriarchal by design.

In the world of ideas, then, including political ideas, he was radically perverse. Though superb, even elegant, in his mastery of modern conditions, though a performer, as well as an appreciator, of cosmopolitan and sophisticated style, he set himself in opposition to the taste of his times—its *serious* taste. He was hostile to the enlightened liberal progressivism of the nineteenth century, which aimed at gradually eliminating all conflict, hierarchy, subordination from the world—at making every social opportunity available to every citizen, rich or poor, old or young, man or woman. Bismarck made no effort to live in democratic equality or peace with others. He *served* his master, the man he had made Emperor, and he *ruled* everyone else.

Under his rule Prussia defeated Denmark in 1864, Austria in 1866, France in 1870; under his rule the German Empire was proclaimed in the halls of Versailles itself. During the next twenty years, many of the cities of Germany doubled in size and wealth, so great was the commercial and industrial boom; and from the 1880s on, still under his rule, Germany began to acquire colonies in Africa, the South Seas, the East Indies, imposing its civilization on "primitive" peoples.

Bismarck's personality, including his physique, was legendary in Germany. His powerful corpulence, his strikingly high-pitched voice, "interspersed however with deep-rumbling clearings of his throat," his long-handled lorgnette, through which he stared at both friend and foe with equal impertinence, his wild dogs who terrified all his visitors, and the giant glass of steaming punch which he drank off in great draughts while sitting in the Reichstag—these are details remembered and recited by Heinrich Rickert, the professor of philosophy at Heidelberg, and friend of Max Weber's.

One day, Rickert recalls, when Bismarck was addressing the Reichstag he thought he heard someone call out softly, "Feigheit," cowardice, in protest against the policy he was outlining. He stopped speaking, glared at the deputies, and demanded to know who had spoken. They all remained dumb, and he left the podium and began to pace up and down between the rows, scrutinizing them. Nobody said a word. He took to grabbing likely subjects and shaking them by the shoulders as he repeated the question. Nobody dared to protest. Finally he convinced himself that he had been deceived and returned to the podium to take up his speech again. But still he remained silent awhile, and then said softly, "Give thanks to God that nobody *did* say anything."

A society in which such anecdotes are current is one obsessed with power, patriarchal power. And this anecdote was current in liberal academic Heidelberg, where even the professors were affected by the example of Bismarck and inspired to a kind of imitation. As Alfred Weber, Max's brother, put it, Bismarck infected them with the "power-virus."

Of course, one must be careful to avoid attributing too much to Bismarck. In these years the whole university structure in Germany became immensely more massive than it had been formerly or than it was elsewhere. Professors were much better paid than, for instance, their American counterparts. Their style of life, especially in places like Weber's Heidelberg, was more stately than that of the middle class in general. Their prestige was high, relative both to professors in other countries and to other sectors of German society. The power they exerted over their students was autocratic, patriarchal. Indeed, even the intellectual style of German scholarship was incomparably massive. In all these ways the German professoriate was "typically German," and these ways were not directly attributable to Bismarck's achievement. But they were in harmony with the political facts—or rather, they were all mutually intensifying.

It is important to realize that the Prussianization of Germany was dynamic. It was something that happened in the decades immediately preceeding the beginning of our century. In a sense it *was* the beginning of our century. It was a change from a previous status quo, and all the more dramatic a change for occurring—at least so the liberals thought—in the teeth of historical tendency and in defiance of the spirit of the times.

There had been many Germanies, and Prussia had been one of the least important for men of mind and imagination. There continued to be more than one Germany after 1870, but they ceased to be so alternative and interchangeable. There was now also *one* Germany—that is, the alternatives became hierarchical and Prussia was on top. The liberalism of Badenia and the romanticism of Bavaria became minor national options. In the political sphere, which carried with it commerce, city-building, military training, and so much else, *they* were not Germany; they could hope, at best, to criticize, to modify the thrust of Prussia. Germany was increasingly characterized by Prussianism, with its interdependently feudal, military, and bureaucratic castes. The Junkers dominated the army, and the status of officer became the most prestigious in all Germany, so the Junker style dominated the country. (The armed forces acted directly under the command of the Kaiser, who always wore a uniform in public.) The officers stood for something hostile and superior to the middle class's values and life-style. In order to settle a quarrel honorably, said the officers, you had to fight a duel, and to be eligible to do that, you had to have the right social status, called *Satisfaktionsfähigkeit*. In the Great War, Manfred von Richthofen, a distant cousin of the sisters, translated this dueling style into the terms of mechanized warfare, and so prolonged the Junker tradition yet again. In the years of peace before the war, the dueling corps at the universities produced "feudalized" bourgeois graduates, and there was an efficient machinery for ennobling oneself by purchasing an estate and entailing it. By such means Bismarck's Germany intensified the feudal-patriarchal character of its culture, even among the intellectuals.

Closely linked with the army as a central institution in German life was the Civil Service—that bureaucracy to which Max Weber devoted so much of his attention as a sociologist, because he saw in it both the inevitable future ruler of Western civilization and the death of all spontaneity and freedom. In an essay of 1910, Alfred Weber calculated that Germany then had 150,000 bureaucrats to 500,000 workers in the sphere of commerce; in the sphere of industry there were 860,000 bureaucrats (almost ten times as many as in 1882) to 8,500,000 workers. In 1882 there had been 700,000 bureaucrats in both the private and public spheres of the economy; in 1910 there were nearly 2 million. In the whole nonagricultural economy there was room for only two to three hundred thousand "free" jobs. This is what Max Weber meant by the iron cage, the steel-hard casing, that was enclosing the national life so fast. And it enclosed the personal life too, for the growth of bureaucracy meant that rationality and calculability were intensified a thousandfold, while spontaneity and personal responsibility were correspondingly decreased. To be sure, this bureaucratization was antipathetic to Bismarck personally, for his own style of authority leaned toward the Faustian and the charismatic. But he made use of the bureaucracy, and it was an essential part of his power and his Germany.

In fact, the German bureaucracy was quite specifically a Prussian and military-state phenomenon, having grown up there in the eighteenth century as a means to enforce military conscription and to levy military taxes. (It was said that while every other state was a piece of land with an army attached, Prussia was an army with a piece of land attached.) The administration of the bureaucracy was directly in the hands of the king, but it was quite impersonal in its workings. It was highly professionalized, status-formalized, and divorced from all politics. Entrance was by public examination and it was kept remarkably free from corruption. Its lower ranks were occupied largely by ex-soldiers, and its upper ranks were reserved, as they were in the army, for Junkers—to whom business careers, even in the nineteenth century, were taboo. The top civil servants intermarried with the aristocracy and ruled the most efficient officialdom in the world. Its training linked it very closely with legal studies and the judiciary—with skills in administration, not in debate. Thus the German citizen felt himself always in the presence of state power.

Both the militaristic and the bureaucratic modes of authority were given support in Germany by the Lutheran state religion. Lutheranism assigned politics to the vale of tears, the realm of sin and sorrow which it was hopeless to try to redeem. One left that to "the authorities." This meant that if the authorities, on the one hand, were full of a sense of their own prerogatives, the common people, on the other, were almost religiously bound to accept this state of affairs. What is more, if God had ordained that the world of politics belonged to those in authority, it followed that those in authority were responsible to Him for their political conduct. Thus there arose among the higher state functionaries an extreme devotion to their duties, and even to the concept of duty itself. State Lutheranism was, as it applied to the overwhelming bulk of the population, which was urged to leave politics alone, a "religion for women." We might take Bismarck's own marriage as an emblem of the relationship between this religion and German politics. He took to wife a devout Pietist, who offered him no hint of competition as a personality and no trace of criticism as a moral being. He told his friends that he liked Pietism "in a woman" and praised his Johanna as "facile à vivre." His was a patriarchal marriage par excellence, the kind against which the von Richthofen sisters rebelled.

In political, economic, and domestic life there were similar concentrations of power in the hands of authority figures. Democratic sharing of responsibility was much feebler in Germany than in other European countries. Democratic parliamentary life never rooted itself in the Reichstag, in part because Bismarck took steps to prevent it from doing so, but in part also because German politicians had never learned to cooperate in parties. Moreover, the general orientation of everyone to be sharply for or against authority tended to foster the development of extreme ideologies, so that Marxists and reactionaries could flourish but there was little liberalism. To be sure, the ineffectiveness of German liberalism also had economic causes, for as the British economist R. H. Tawney says, between 1850 and 1900 Germany passed through an economic and industrial revolution that had taken two hundred years in England. As a result the German economy bypassed the stage of small-capitalist economic individualism which elsewhere provided the basis upon which the liberal theories of classical economics were erected. Germany, that is to say, lacked the class which was the bulwark of liberal opinion.

Whatever the causes of the weakness of German liberalism, the fact is that the Reichstag representation of the National Liberal Party, to which Max Weber's father belonged, fell from 152 in 1874 to 45 in 1881. In the Weber home in 1881 there took place the confrontation between Bennigsen and Rickert which fatally split the National Liberal Party. Alfred Weber says that by 1890 it was, "to us young men," a grotesque idea to think of entering that "Schwatzbude," the Parliament, as a career. They joined the academic socialists' union, a German equivalent to the Fabian Society, instead.

In German social life this general illiberalism is nowhere more apparent than in the constant use of titles, their accumulations, and their effect in bringing hierarchical order into private life by means of an elaborate system of occupational and status classifications. This was particularly evident in matters of marriage. Husbands and fathers were allotted much more authority than in Anglo-Saxon cultures, and they played a much larger role in shaping their families' identity; thus wives took on their husbands' occupational titles, and even today the wife of a German professor is addressed as *Frau Professor*.

Obviously connected to this heightened emphasis on the social dimension of marriage is the fact that romantic love, as a sphere of life and feeling, became more independent of, or antithetical to, marriage. Anglo-Saxon romanticism, says Talcott Parsons—from whom I take many of these ideas— was a realistic romanticism, concerned with both love in marriage and success in one's career. (Frieda von Richthofen always felt that D. H. Lawrence's idea of marriage was specifically English.) German romanticism was specifically an escape from marriage, and thus was categorically romantic.

It was also tragic. When they were serious about love at all, the Germans were tragic in their seriousness. In this Germany was only like other European countries in the late nineteenth century. If we take *Tristan und Isolde*, *Anna Karenina*, and *Madame Bovary* as major monuments of passionate love, we see how the celebrations of happiness and fulfillment in them always fade finally before strains of sin and sorrow. This was the role of love in a patriarchal *Weltanschauung*. But at the end of the century, and particularly in Germany, eroticism began to be celebrated as the source of moral value as well as emotional happiness—as the source of all healthy life.

Freud's teaching had such a message at its heart, though that message was severely modified by some of Freud's other ideas. One cannot but be struck by the extent to which the various people in our story suffered from severe neurotic sickness; Marianne Weber's sleeplessness, Frieda Gross's leg pains, Max Weber's headaches and exhaustion when he tried to work, Otto Gross's drug addiction—all these make one feel that Germany was quite especially a place where the strains of nineteenth-century life were becoming intolerable for sensitive people. (The sisters' healthiness time and again set them apart from their friends, making them both attractive and formidable to others.) Outside the Freudian movement there were much more wholehearted celebrations of eroticism to be found.

In his *Religionssoziologie* (*Sociology of Religion*), Max Weber defines eroticism as that glorification of love which arises wherever love "collides with the unavoidably ascetic trait of the vocational specialist type of man." (He thought that modern conditions of life inevitably produced the vocational specialist.) Love outside marriage then seems the only tie left still linking man to "the natural fountain of all life." Such love is a joyful triumph over all rationalism and all salvationism. "This boundless giving of oneself is as radical as possible in its opposition to all functionality, rationality, and generality. . . . The lover realizes himself to be rooted in the kernel of the truly living, which is externally inaccessible to any rational endeavor. He knows himself to be freed from the cold skeleton hands of rational order, just as completely as from the banality of everyday routine." Eroticism of this sort is a religious faith.

The works of art and the lives which expressed this faith in Germany toward the end of the nineteenth century add up to something we may call the erotic movement, and it will claim much of our attention because it carried both von Richthofen sisters with it for a time, and Frieda for all her life. It was a powerful movement in Germany, just because in Germany the patriarchal moralism and cynicism which it attacked was particularly power-ful. Most notably in Bavaria and Munich, there arose a matriarchal rebellion which expressed itself in behavioral terms by idealizing the Magna Mater or Hetaera role, a role in which a woman felt herself "religiously" called to take many lovers and bear many children without submitting to a husband/father/master. This matriarchal rebellion was one of the most sharply characterized forms of the erotic movement, which was in turn an offshoot of the *Lebens-philosophie* movement, the devotion to life-values, to intuition and instinct, which all across Europe then was rebelling against scientific materialism and positivism. In Germany all these movements were unusually active, just because what they were reacting against was unusually solid.

The von Richthofens

Baron Friedrich von Richthofen fought in Bismarck's wars, was wounded in them, and took his life-direction from the rise of the Germany that re-sulted from them. He had become a professional soldier at the age of seven-teen. This was in 1862, the year when Bismarck was granted supreme power by the king of Prussia, and promised in return to rule without a parliamen-tary budget. The parliament had demanded the right to control the army by checking its financial estimates every year, but Bismarck saved the king from this form of democratic control. It was also the year in which the Iron Chancellor said, in a famous speech, that "the great issues of the day will not be decided by speeches and majority resolution . . . but by blood and iron."

Friedrich von Richthofen himself came from an old Prussian Junker family, but he belonged to the Heinersdorfer line, one of its less distinguished branches. He kept up little contact with other members of the family, even his own brother, who was also in the army. The only nationally prominent von Richthofen with whom his daughters seem to have come into contact as they grew up, was Oswald, who served as Colonial Secretary and then For-eign Secretary after the fall of Bismarck. Oswald von Richthofen was one of the earliest German imperialists. Frieda and Johanna were to stay with him in Berlin in the 1890's, when they attended the state balls at which the Kaiser is said to have remarked upon their beauty.

The sisters grew up in Metz, a German garrison town in Lorraine. Before the war it had been French. Their father was an administrator of conquered territory and they belonged to the occupying enemy army. Within two years of the war, a quarter of the original population of Metz had moved across the border to regain French nationality. Those who left were replaced by incoming Germans, most military, so that by 1905 there would be 25,000 soldiers in the town and 35,000 civilians. In the war that made Prussia into the German Empire, Baron von Richthofen had won the Iron Cross but had lost the use of his right hand. Removed from active duty, he was trained as an engineer and sent to work in the administration of the land around Metz. His special responsibility was for the canals around the city. But his former regiment was stationed in the town, and socially he belonged to it still. It was while he was living the life of a garrison officer that he married and his three children were born, in 1874, 1879, and 1882, children of the new Reich.

Many years later, when Frieda eloped with D. H. Lawrence, she took him to Metz, where she unwittingly led him, on a walk, into a military zone. He was arrested as a spy and her father had to intervene to get him released. This was to be Lawrence's first meeting with the Baron and his main brush with Prussian militarism, and it is symbolically significant. Baron von Richthofen was a soldier, a Prussian, an officer, and of the gentleman class. Lawrence was an unemployed schoolteacher, a would-be artist, from a working-class English home. The two men stood for different things, things in opposition to each other, and they gazed at each other across unbridgeable chasms bridged only by the fact that the one man's daughter was the other's wife.

Curiously, Lawrence did not use von Richthofen as his model when in his writings he portrayed a Prussian officer. Frieda's father is sketched, externally, as "the Baron," in the story "The Thorn in the Flesh." But his moral portrait is to be found, rather, in Will of *The Rainbow* and *Women in Love*, and in the young officer of "The Mortal Coil." That is to say, he was fiery, quick, subtle in temperament, an original in his feelings, but limited in all his major ideas to the conventional—to what was conventional for a Prussian officer. He was a courageous man but his courage, all his life, was fatally adolescent—fierce in face-to-face encounters, but easily defeated by official situations and persons of greater weight. Like Will Brangwen, he was a passionate gardener, a skillful modeler, with a great love for animals and birds. Frieda once compared him with Francis of Assisi. In the role of the authoritarian, the man of blood, he seemed to his daughters badly miscast. He played roles assigned to him by society, and would try nothing new, even though the part he must play was fundamentally alien to his nature. Frau Jaffe—Else—showed me a photograph of him glaring at the camera, firing himself at it, eyes blazing, in standard Prussian fashion. "Er scheint streng, aber er war es nicht," she said; he looks severe, but he wasn't. She said it with a tenderness which could well have been significant. The sisters all had a tender condescension for men, which began with their father. They loved him passionately—he was an eminently lovable and distinguished, though difficult, nature—but they pitied him because he was a self-contradiction. This also is part of the symbolism of the confrontation between him and Lawrence (and Frieda). She was confronting her father with a man who lived out the radical sensitiveness and unconventionality which her father contradicted in himself.

For all his unease in the role, however, Baron von Richthofen *was* a Prussian officer, in however external a sense, and that was, in those years, a fate. It was, after all, to his Jubilee as a Prussian officer, to the celebration of his fifty years in Bismarck's army, that Frieda went when she ran away with Lawrence. Those were roughly the fifty years of Bismarck's Reich. And only two years later, in 1914, the fortifications around Metz were the means of tying down large French forces in Lorraine when the Great War broke out.

During his fifty years of service the Baron served Bismarck's Reich well, however little he had served himself. (That contrast, of course, lies behind Ursula's dialogues with Skrebensky in *The Rainbow*. What Ursula says to Anton is what Frieda wanted to say to her father.)

The greater weight of personality which defeated von Richthofen was to be found above all in his wife. But he was also defeated by ordinary moral challenges. Frau Jaffe remembered a day when she was twenty and her father lay in bed and refused to get up, declaring that he was ruined. He had lost a lot of money gambling. He would have to sell their house, but Else, he said, must first go to the commanding general and persuade him to advance the money as a loan, and he would then write an IOU to the general. She did as she was asked.

Besides revealing the crass abdication of responsibility by the father, and the early assumption of the same by the daughter, this anecdote is also striking in what it does not include. The wife and mother plays no part in this crucial transaction, is not involved. She had in some sense washed her hands of her husband, and so her daughter replaced her. What is more, the other daughters were absent, not consulted. This was no Little Women community of sisters; the transaction was solely between Else and her father.

Above all, perhaps, such an anecdote reveals to us a whole genre of experience which was later to enter into a concept that was very important to both Frieda and Lawrence—the concept of "the world of men," an unideological phrase which expresses the patriarchal aspects of society. "The world of men" has, one prime referent, that group of gambling and horse-trading officers in Metz, riding about a "conquered" French landscape, superimposing their bright uniforms on that rich fertility, forever drilling their conscripts for another war; and with nothing better to *do* than to gamble and lose, and then to be afraid to face their wives, and to call on their daughters to save them from the consequences of their folly. This was not the only time that Else had to rescue her father, or her sister's officer-husband, by finding money. On one occasion the scandal seems to have involved the Baron and a mistress, whom Else had to pay off. This incident occurred after Lawrence and Frieda were already living together, but other earlier incidents, dramatized in Frieda's novel, necessitated selling the von Richthofen house and much diminishing their style of living. The psychological effects Frieda describes as follows: "From that day, Anne and Frederick [her mother and father] hated each other, nothing but convention and the children kept them tied together. They lived the life that is so destructive to the best in people, is murderous in its fierce hatred, always newly roused by the contact of daily life. The children vaguely felt the atmosphere of strife without understanding; there is something frightening to children in the war of the sexes. Sex, that thing not understood by children, hidden from them, yet constantly in the air, warps and tortures the life of children. Especially in the sensitive Sybil [Else], the parents' war broke something that never healed in later life."

The Baroness von Richthofen, born Anna Marquier, came from a solid bourgeois family of Donaueschingen, a town in the Black Forest. It was the residential town of the state of Fürstenburg, where the Prince lived, and she grew up in a decidedly eighteenth-century atmosphere. She remained always devoted to that landscape, to nature in general, to reading, and to the provincially aristocratic life with its emphasis on conversation—the conversation of clever and interesting men. Lawrence describes her, in *Women in Love*, as "a country Baroness." She belonged to one of the non-Bismarckian Germanies, but to one rooted in the past. Hers was a pre-Bismarckian, small-state, anti-political, *Kulturstadt* Germany. Her town seems to have been a little Weimar without a Goethe, and Bismarck's Reich she could deal with only by ignoring it.

She is depicted by Lawrence as Anna Brangwen, a stronger personality than her husband, equally fiery and far less vulnerable, never humiliated. Like Lawrence's Anna, Baroness von Richthofen seems to have been forever triumphant in motherhood, housekeeping, friendships, in love of books, flowers, animals, in life-values. Into the world of men she did not venture, for she felt herself vulnerable there. But in her own life area she was, to use Lawrence's phrase, Anna Victrix. She enjoyed society, and even though she needed a set of conventions to control the surface of life, she had a profoundly unconventional temperament. She was a deeply sensual woman, what is loosely called "pagan" and not "Christian." She was a deeply healthy woman; her griefs, her joys, her amusements, her boredom all imposed themselves on others as authentic, even on men of the most refined tastes and developed minds. She had a group of devoted friends, some men and women of distinction in the spheres of literature and painting, but she was royally at its center. And it was a matriarchal world, in the service of life and love, which she created around her.

She and Lawrence became great friends, and she looked forward eagerly to his letters from all over the world. They shared the same values. He admiringly scolded her for her royally domineering ways with the other old ladies in the *Stift* she lived in, and she on her part read *Lady Chatterley's Lover*. (She also read through all of Shakespeare in the last years of her life.) Perhaps one might say that Lawrence got from her more of what he wanted even than from Frieda; or perhaps it was just that he had to pay *her* so much less for what he got from both—which was that sense of abundant health and fertility, of normal life-pleasures intensified to the pitch of a moral-spiritual value.

To her daughters she seemed, in their childhood, heavy-handed and even ruthless. She punished before hearing all the facts and was indifferent to being proven unjust. When the family lost its servant, because of her husband's extravagance, she grew tired of combing her children's long hair and had it all cut off; there is a photograph of all three little girls looking quite forlornly cropped. And they suffered from her attacks on their father, whom they all then preferred, for he was a subtler nature and outside the authority structure of the family. (This situation seems to be reflected in "England, my England.") But as time passed, the sisters' feelings changed. At least in Frieda's case—she was the one most like her mother—it is clear that she came to feel very close to her. We find her signing letters to her mother as "Your Sister in the Lord." And both she and Else came to attach great value to their mother's vigorous "*Schimpfen*" (scolding). This played a large part in Lawrence's idea of the Baroness. In his play *Barbara* he dramatized the occasion when she visited him soon after the elopement and scolded him roundly. Like her daughters, he found her vigor admirable and delightful. They came to pride themselves on similar energies, which expressed life-values without the sickliness of Love.

All three sisters remained close to each other as long as their mother lived. During the twenties they constituted a matriarchy of four. The various husband figures were all external to that grouping, that focus of force. To some degree, one suspects, it acted as a centrifuge, and the men found themselves spun off to circumferential positions. Certainly one is struck by the quantity of personal power generated in the temperamental crucible of the von Richthofen family life. In different ways, all three of the daughters were powerful natures, all three remarkable, indestructible, ruthless. In the simple literal matter of physical health they were all phenomenal (Lawrence describes one of his characters as using her health—the health of a middle-aged woman—like a weapon) and they had something equivalent in the realm of psychological-moral health. The combination of Friedrich and Anna von Richthofen, unhappy as it was, was extremely favorable to "life" in Lawrence's sense. Theirs was a house, like the Brangwens' in *The Rainbow*, where natural dignity, vitality, authenticity, were very highly praised, very acutely discriminated, very richly rewarded. This was of course an opposite sort of power from that served by Bismarck. To be sure, it was still power, and other people suffered from its exercise even as they rejoiced in it. But this was power as the world of woman prizes it, not the world of man. (Lawrence called the Brangwen household a matriarchy.)

Between this mother and this father, then, the three daughters grew up. Else, a precociously clever, precociously responsible girl, seems to have responded in the way that Ursula does in *The Rainbow*. At least, this is Frieda's interpretation, as expressed in her novel. She speaks of the melancholy in Else's cameo face, the droop of her eyelids, her aspiration to be free from home in a world of school, of books and ideas. A good deal of Ursula's early history seems likely to refer primarily to the older sister, both in the social-political criticism and general rebelliousness and particularly in the rebellion against the matriarchy. She was convinced, for instance, that her mother did not love little "Nusch" (Johanna) tenderly enough, and tried to take her mother's place with her younger sister.

She became a schoolteacher at seventeen, made enough money to pay for her own studies at the university, and after taking a doctorate in economics, became an inspector of factories in Karlsruhe. This was in 1900, and she was the first woman ever to be appointed by the state of Badenia to protect the rights of women factory workers. Like Florence Kelley in America, she hoped to be able to do something to control and alleviate, or at least to publicize, the conditions of work of women in factories. It was Max Weber who helped her to get the pioneering position as inspector, and at his house she met the leaders of the Woman's Movement in Germany, Gertrud Bäumler, Helene Lange, Alice Salomon. Her doctoral thesis studied the changes in attitude of the authoritarian political parties in Germany since 1869 toward worker-protection legislation. The subject was suggested to her by Weber, whose first woman student she was, and it aptly symbolizes all the ways she served freedom and justice. Her mode of rebellion against patriarchal oppression was always very much his and Heidelberg's—that is, liberal, reformist, legal, intellectual. She went to Berlin to study when Weber fell ill in 1898, and got to know the Weber family there, including Alfred, but returned to Heidelberg in 1900, and it has been her home ever since—that is, for over seventy years. She lived in Bavaria from 1911 to 1925, but she belonged to Badenia. Her life journey was from Metz to Heidelberg, just as Weber's was from Berlin to Heidelberg. She attended lectures by the sociologist Georg Simmel and the economists Adolph Wagner and Gustav Schmoller in Berlin, among the great names, and took seminars from Paul Hansel and George Jellinek in Heidelberg, but Weber remained her master. This was, of course, a quite extraordinary career for a girl in Germany then. Only four girls matriculated at Heidelberg in 1900; only in February of that year had Badenia made it clear that women could be students in any full sense. Else von Richthofen got her doctorate in 1901. She was the pioneer of a great movement; in 1909, 139 girls matriculated.

The younger sisters, meanwhile, suffered from being thought "not clever like Else." Nusch was young enough to be a pupil in a class of which Else was the teacher; it is a family anecdote that Johanna claimed special privileges as teacher's sister, and was severely denied them. This is easy to believe, for Johanna was always claiming special privileges and Else was always school-mistressy. She was, equally, always a student, and her relations with others were characterized by either or both of those personae. By her own declaration, it was not until she was thirty that she fully acknowledged her sisters—fully realized that they were independent personalities, as opposed to being objects of her care, her protection and correction, her responsibility. With all allowance for playful exaggeration, she was too intelligent to say this without there being some truth in it, and too sensitive for there to have been some truth in it without the cooperation of her sisters. That is to say, Frieda and Johanna must have willingly enacted the roles of being pretty, thoughtless, careless, irresponsible. They were pleasure-loving and pleasure-giving creatures of the world of holiday, and one can trace the effects of this identification in their adult personalities. Johanna may be said to have played such a role all her life, whereas Frieda, though she remained hostile to the world of work, rebelled against the category of non-significance. She determined to prove herself a significant being, a significant *woman*, even in patriarchal Germany, though it had to be by means of a career the opposite of Else's. She did so mainly, of course, by means of the brilliant men who made her the emblematic source of all life within matriarchal or anti-patriarchal *Weltanschauungen*.

Frieda was a wild child—the young Anna of *The Rainbow*. She tells us that the nuns at her convent school would cry after her, "Doucement, douce-ment, ma petite Frieda," and in some sense she determined that everyone should go on forever crying that after her. This sense of herself developed easily, for in the von Richthofen home wild vitality was not held to be in-ferior to orderliness. Thus Frieda, writing after Lawrence's death, describes herself in the character of Paula: "Paula's mother had told her and she had never forgotten: 'You, you are an Atavismus.' Now after a long life Paula knew this was true. She certainly was not modern." Frieda defined herself as "primitive," in her husband's sense of the term, and there was always an element of self-identification in the Lawrences' enthusiasm for the primitive peoples whom they sought out all over the world, those peoples whom Bis-marck's Germany, and England, were stamping out.

It is interesting that Frau Jaffe, at the end of the century we are dis-cussing, also used the word "atavistic" about Lawrence, as a way of describ-ing the total incompatibility of him and Max Weber. Lawrence, she said, was antipathetic to all *"Geist"*; he was atavistic. Else herself, of course, was *not* atavistic. *Geist* is exactly what she devoted her life to.

This contrast between the two sisters expressed itself naturally in their respective attitudes toward Goethe, the embodiment of *Geist*. Else was always quite specially devoted to the bard of Weimar, and during the last years of her life together with Alfred Weber, she always read Goethe aloud to him in the evenings. She even sent Frieda a volume of his letters—in forgetful-ness, for Goethe was a symbol to Frieda of the kind of art and culture she detested. In her manuscripts she returns again and again to Goethe and *Faust*, in order to express her distaste for both. Gretchen seems to her a typical man's woman, a typical heroine of the patriarchal sensibility, and Iphigenie a hateful idealization of self-sacrifice. Thus she criticized Else's marriage by calling it an Iphigenie sacrifice, and conversely she praised Lawrence specifically for being as an artist the antithesis of Goethe, for offering himself only as a man, for offering only what his skin enclosed; there was about him none of the "I-am-everlasting feeling of Goethe," none of Goethe's cultural self-institutionalization and artistic self-marmorealiza-tion. And Lawrence himself echoed her, referring to *Wilhelm Meister* as "a book of peculiar immorality."

In repudiating and cherishing Goethe in this way, Frieda and Else were of course repudiating and cherishing German high culture as a whole. Goethe, *Kultur*, *Geist*, the Apollonian mind—these things are indeed inter-related in the ways that the sisters' symbolic treatment of them implies. Frieda dedicated herself to Eros and renounced *Kultur*, even when it treated erotic themes. *Tristan und Isolde*, the favorite opera of Else and Alfred Weber, was too much under the sway of Thanatos for Frieda.

Eros and Thanatos—love and death—offer only one mythological polarity that can help us understand the two sisters. There are others. Thus Leucus of Lesbos tells of how Aphrodite envied Athene's skill at weaving and flew up from Cyprus to Olympus to sit beside her, to imitate her, and to compete with her. Weaving, even the plaiting of a rope, always symbolizes the creation of matter—hence the idea of the "daedal" earth. The Mothers, at the root of the world, are ever weaving and spinning. But Aphrodite can spin only coarse threads, comparable with willow withes (such rank swamp vegetation always belongs to Aphrodite), and so her fabric unravels as she weaves it. Athene mocks her, and Aphrodite gives up in despair and goes back to Cyprus and to Eros. She is capable of generation only of the imperfect, incomplete, self-undoing kind of this world, where what is done ever needs to be done again, whereas Athene weaves perfect and ideal designs that last for all eternity. There are, as we shall see, many reasons for associating Else with Athene, and Frieda with Aphrodite, the goddess of love, but the myth, we should note, can be read to the advantage of either goddess.

In literal fact, Else could not sew well, nor draw, nor paint. Her mind was "intellectual" rather than "aesthetic," "analytic" rather than "creative." She envied her children, as she had envied her sisters, their talents in these directions. Indeed, her husband, the narrow-seeming Edgar, had far more feeling for art than she, and bought—before 1910—Picassos and Franz Marcs which she scarcely knew how to appreciate. Nor was she by any means always efficient. After the war she sold off her husband's paintings along with his other property at a disastrous loss; and her daughter paid her analyst with a Picasso drawing which she found lying neglected in an attic. But the myth's meaning is all the more poignantly appropriate for these superficial inexactitudes.

Perhaps the most striking effect on Frieda of this conflict with her sister was that renunciation of the intellect which showed itself in self-caricature in all realms of thought, both humble and exalted. Not only was she hopelessly vague in all practical matters—unable even to use the telephone—and fitful at carrying through any systematic work and inefficient at dealing consistently with any scheme of concepts. Even in handling *words*, though she was highly sensitive to them, she was often—recurrently and predictably—childish in her incompetence. A spiritually ambitious woman, and passionately responsive to ideas, she was so devoid of cleverness—that is, of ordinary skill and care in handling the tools of the mind—that she made a fool of herself more often than not. That is why many people who met her set her down for stupid or trivial or vulgar. So marked a pattern of behavior surely demands an explanation which includes intention and will-power. She was caricaturing herself, actively repudiating all competition or comparability with Else—and later, of course, with Lawrence. (Indeed, there is a sense in which Lawrence's mind was much more like Else's than like Frieda's. But it was his intention to be like Frieda.)

We get a glimpse of the early Frieda in an anecdote of the child Ursula in *The Rainbow*, which Frieda claimed as biographical. With great excitement, Ursula tries to help her father in the garden, but, becoming confused and frightened by the task she has taken on, bungles it and abandons it. When her father humorously but roughly reproaches her, she makes no reply but runs away and hides, deeply wounded. Her soul writhes in repudiation, and she makes up her mind that the world of work is not for her.

The significance of this anecdote to Frieda becomes much more comprehensible and much larger when we learn that Else's earliest memories were of happily helping her father in the garden—of the two of them *working* efficiently together. For Frieda to renounce the world of work was, therefore, to renounce among many other things, all competition with or imitation of Else. A powerful factor of wounded pride was concealed beneath the gaiety and spontaneity, the "mere womanhood" with which she met the world; a pride ready to blossom into passionate gratitude and defiant splendor at the touch of a man who would give her at last recognition, appreciation, acknowledgement.

Frieda's own memories of childhood happiness were of running away from domestic troubles to the army drill ground where homesick young conscripts gathered to sing and talk together. She learned the folk songs of each man's native place and sang them, from a table or a flight of steps, to the applause of scores of young men. And when she finally ran home, she was pursued by cries of "Come back again soon." This experience, too, has a clear connection—whether strictly causal or merely symbolic—with her development, for she was always in some sense looking for the acclamation of men. (These are the songs she taught Lawrence and they sang together— we hear of them particularly during the war years—and which she sang beside his bed the night after he died.)

Of the three sisters, Frieda was the first to marry. She was only seventeen when she met Ernest Weekley, a Lector in English at Freiburg University who was fifteen years older than she. He was an academic, a philologist, and a gentleman, though in some sense a self-made man, Victorian in the values he relied on, perhaps Edwardian in those he himself asserted. That is, he left it to society to ensure that the things he cared about most should be maintained. Thus when Frieda broke the rules, by running away with Lawrence, he was destroyed, nervously disintegrated; and his inconsistencies of behavior finally resolved themselves into an ungenerous rigidity not really characteristic of the man he usually was.

The family he came from has been caricatured by Lawrence in *The Virgin and the Gipsy*, and his marriage with Frieda in "New Eve and Old Adam"—though the man there is Lawrence himself rather than Weekley. He was one of nine children in an upward-struggling London family. The early death of a brother left him the oldest, the responsible one, and he became a self-supporting schoolteacher at seventeen, after getting his education free at a school run by a relative. He passed exam after exam by studying at night, and won scholarships to Cambridge and to Bern, but only in 1898, when he was appointed to Nottingham at the age of thirty-four, was his position assured. He then awarded himself a holiday, the first in his life. It was a walking holiday in the Black Forest, and on it he met Frieda. The holiday was a high point in his life, for he was finally receiving the rewards of virtue; that was how his parents and brothers thought about it; he was their hero—he was virtue's hero. And Frieda, he soon recognized, was to be his supreme reward. It was a role to dazzle an imaginative young girl, for it came out of a thousand novels, a thousand dreams, out of the myth of the period.

He married her in 1899 and took her to live in Nottingham, where he had just been appointed lecturer, and where D. H. Lawrence became his student in 1906. An anecdote related by Barbara Barr evokes the atmosphere of the Weekley house, with Frieda thumping out sonatas on the piano in her arty drawing room and Ernest stealing up to lay two pennies on the piano top. Frieda shook her head and went on playing. Irony of so cute a kind was contemptible by her standards, irrelevant to her determination to make herself into something significant, something great. Weekley went on to become a professor and Dean of the Arts Faculty at Nottingham, but he never began to take Frieda's sense of herself seriously.

Why did she marry so unsuitable a man? She says that his attraction for her was his dignity, his solidity. Writing about herself as Paula, she says, "Paula felt firm ground under her feet for the first time in her life. Here was something different from her own home life. There in his English home she felt the solidity of family life, an intimate circle, an ideal to strive after. Her own home life had been such a scattered thing. There was no grit. Only the moment's satisfaction, good times, wanted. Paula wanted more. She had always battled with her parents and their shallow, cynical outlook on life." Moreover, he knew so much, which always meant a lot to Frieda.

Then, too, she may have been influenced by Else's model, for Ernest perhaps seemed to her the husband Else would have wanted. Or even a male version of Else. And she was excited by the sexual power she exerted over him. Her novel's description of her effect on this learned and dignified man is self-excited and self-exciting.

As Paula neared the fountain, [Frieda writes,] she was conscious of her pink and white frock with the pink and white sunbonnet that [he] loved so much. She thought more of her effect on him than of himself. At last she saw him standing on the entrance of a sombre pine-wood, the trees forming a deep archway behind him. He was like a man lifted out of ordinary life. He did not know anything, he was nothing by himself, his sole being was in that approaching pink and white girl. His emotion almost paralysed him. Paula felt slightly uncomfortable, she went up to him. He took her in his arms, gently, tenderly, repressing his passion, so as not to frighten her. "My snowflower," he said.

But the wedding night apparently was hideous, and then Frieda began to discover the limits of her husband's mind. The marriage had much about it that reminds one of Masha and Koolygin in *The Three Sisters.*

Johanna's wedding had come two years after Frieda's. She was seventeen at the time, and at eighteen she bore a child to a man twice her age. Her husband was a staff officer, and she always counted it to have been one of life's great experiences to have ridden at the head of a regiment, on a beautiful horse, before crowds, at that age.

All her life long, moreover, she had the attentions of men, for she was the beauty of the family, and she accepted also the role of being the frivolous one. She was a daughter of Aphrodite. Lawrence wrote once to Frieda, when all three daughters had come to Baden to visit their mother, "Love to you all, the goddesses three," and the phrase was not inappropriate to any of them. But the eldest belonged to Olympus in a special sense.

Heidelberg

Else remained unmarried after both her sisters were settled and had babies. She was an inspector of factories—a job she found exhausting, and she could not be at ease with her working-class clients—but she was, by virtue of her friendship with Max and Marianne Weber, a member of the academic society of Heidelberg. When Friedrich Gundolf, the poet, came to the university there, she was one of the first people to become his friend and to welcome the whole Stefan George circle who came to visit him there. And beyond the literal horizons of Heidelberg, though still in manifestation of Heidelberg's values, stood Friedrich Naumann, the political reformer, whom she also came to know. Naumann was the white hope of the liberal intellectuals in German naitonal politics, and a friend, in some ways a disciple, of Max Weber. Some of the Webers' other friends, like Gertrud Baümer, the feminist, worked with

Naumann on his newspaper, *Die Hilfe*. Marianne Weber, on whom Else to some degree modeled herself, was to become a prominent writer and speaker on feminist topics.

In the sketch of her life which she drew up (in manuscript) later, Else began with the topic sentence, "Dominating influence of Marianne Weber," and this has to be understood in the sense that Marianne demonstrated to her the possibility, the ideal, the duty of a woman to lead a life of intellectual and political activity—to enter the world of men. In the correspondence between the two, the dominant word is *Arbeit*, work; most often this refers to a work which one or the other is writing; sometimes it is their work for a professor or Else's factory inspection, sometimes it is the work of "the workers," but all these meanings blend in a resonance which makes the word a symbol of both their lives. Frieda Gross and Frieda Weekley also spoke of their desire to "work," but they spoke of it to Else, who embodied "work" to them, and their desire was at least kindled by hers. She was, on a small scale, a heroine of the movement. She went on a lecture tour at the end of 1901, and Sophie Riehl, Frieda Gross's aunt, more than once wrote to her for advice in finding study or work opportunities for other women.

Some of her friends in the Woman's Movement were therefore disappointed that she gave up her career so soon. Alice Salomon, for instance, who had also particularly interested herself in women's conditions of work in factories, spoke to Else's daughter many years later of the surprise and regret she then felt. It was as if Else were giving up the life of action, in favor of privacy and retirement. Her life was in fact to be very energetic, but in the form of inspiring others. She became a muse of the intellectual life. She almost certainly felt this as something of a defeat, for there is a letter to her by Sophie Riehl, written early in 1902, in which the latter defends herself against some quasi-accusation of Else's to the effect that she was not exerting herself to be as radically effective as she might, not using her gifts in the service of her social ideals. These reproaches were to be leveled at Else herself soon after, and this guilt may have made her feel even more in moral debt to Marianne Weber.

Whatever the reason, she retreated from her earlier activism into marriage. She had already met Alfred Weber—in Berlin in 1899—and he fell in love with her. And in 1901, briefly, she was engaged. But in 1902, rather suddenly and refusing explanations, she married Edgar Jaffe, also a protégé of Max Weber's and a teacher of Political Economy. Her sisters and friends were shocked by what they felt must be a loveless match on her side, in much the way that Beatrice Potter's friends were shocked by her marriage to Sidney Webb.

In effect, Else von Richthofen married Heidelberg. Whatever her motives at the moment of accepting Edgar Jaffe, it seems clear, when we look over her life as a whole, that the most abiding result and reward for her was that she became permanently a part of Heidelberg, indeed one of the social foci of its intellectual life. She entered the active center of liberal, reformist, resistance Germany, one of the two great nodes of the anti-Bismarck movement. The other centered in Munich, the city to which Frieda von Richthofen was to move, but in the eyes of Heidelberg, in the eyes of Else Jaffe, Munich's politics were dangerous when they were not trivial. It was in Badenia, and above all in its university towns, that all reasonable, useful, responsible, serious resistance to Prussianism seemed to center. Exactly how Heidelberg enacted its resistance will become clear later, when we deal with Max Weber, the great hero of Else Jaffe's party.

If as we observed, Else married Heidelberg "in effect," it was, nonetheless, small, dull, rich Edgar Jaffe whom she married in literal fact. Born in 1865, he was one of fourteen children of a Jewish merchant family centered in Hamburg. Several of the sons were sent abroad to different countries to represent the family firm, which dealt in linen and cotton. Edgar had spent some time in Spain and over ten years in Manchester, England, where he had made a sizable fortune for himself. The Jaffe firm in Manchester had a very good reputation for the fairness and politeness of the employers to their staff; they always gave their Halle tickets to employees for the performances of *The Messiah* and of *Elijah*. When his father died, Edgar Jaffe returned to Germany and took up the academic life.

All the Jaffes of that generation had a lot of money. They tended to retire early—some lived the life of country gentlemen on their estates, breeding horses and trout and growing roses—and were in all respects a fine example of that lavish prosperity which historians associate with the founding years of Bismarck's Reich. Because of their race, they also exemplify that Jewish success in life which so disastrously roused the envy and enmity of less successful Germans.

By becoming an academic, Edgar Jaffe broke with tradition. He was an adventurous person in the same sense as Else von Richthofen was. But both belonged to an intellectual movement of the times. Their break through into academic study, their social science, and their master, Max Weber, were exceptional but also typical of the age. Sociology was sometimes then called the Jewish science. It was the newest field of academic knowledge, and the most Apollonian and scientific in its scrutiny of human culture. It scrutinized the new Prussian Germany, and sought out reasonable ways to resist its excesses.

Being a wealthy man, Jaffe could build for Else a splendid villa; she had several servants and became a hostess to Heidelberg intellectual life. But although Jaffe was intellectually adventurous—indeed, adventurous in many spheres of life—his surface personality was timid, pedantic, precise, insignificant, and dull. (In this, too, as in his marriage, he bears comparison with Sidney Webb.) He was mostly silent and uneasy in company, but if he began to talk it was likely to develop into a lecture, unstoppable, unmodulated, pedantic.

It seems to have been generally agreed that Else never loved him. By marrying him she became a power in that intellectual life which meant so much to her. He built her a four-storied villa high up overlooking all Heidelberg, and visible from all over town. Red-roofed and gabled and many-windowed, some bulging into bays, some recessed into balconies, some with shutters, some with dormers, narrow and vertical, wide and horizontal, it was the very apotheosis of the bourgeois life, in stone and plaster and brick and wood, a fit setting for a muse of the intellectual life then. But it is likely that a large motive was also the power his money gave her—with his full consent— to help out her parents and her sister. We hear of Johanna and her husband, as well as Baron von Richthofen, being lent important sums by Edgar Jaffe in times of crisis. And perhaps most important of all, Else was giving her husband what he wanted. Pity and self-sacrifice were always major motives in Else's life, although the surface of her personality was so cool and ironic, so decisive and incisive. She described her relationship to him, in a letter to Frieda Gross, as "*freundschaftlich,*" a kind of friendship. She even said, at one point, that he was the best possible partner for her in the life she had chosen, with its uneasy mixture of bohemian and bourgeois elements. (She told Frieda Gross that the more their life styles diverged, the more bohemian Frieda became and the more bourgeois Else grew, the closer they would feel.) Edgar was, she said, unfitted for the bourgeois life by his nervousness and his unproductiveness. Events were to prove that his imagination unfitted him for it even more.

Lawrence seems to have been thinking of the Jaffe marriage when he wrote of "Daughters of the Vicar." Mary Lindley is described as "a long slim thing with a fine profile and a proud, pure look of submission to a high fate," which describes Else exactly, while Louisa (who certainly represents Frieda) is short and plump and obstinate-looking. Mary attracts a young clergyman with money, called Massy, who is small, timid, clever, but inhuman and physically repulsive, and Mrs. Lindley, the powerful personality in the family and a woman suggestive of Baroness von Richthofen, cannot bear him. "Quite unable to take part in simple everyday talk, he padded round the house, or sat in the dining-room looking nervously from side to side, always apart in a cold rarefied world of his own. . . . He was unremittingly shy, but perfect in his sense of duty. . . . Seeing his acts, Miss Mary must respect and honour him. In consequence, she must serve him. To do this she had to force herself, shuddering and yet desirous, but he did not perceive it."

Lousia shares her mother's antipathy to Massy, even though she feels humble before her sister's "better attitude." Mary admits that there is something lacking in Massy, but insists that he is "really *good*." When she marries him, Louisa reacts with anger, with a sense of being wounded in her "faith": "Did the real things to her not matter after all?" she asks. Thus Louisa comes to feel that Mary, who has been her ideal, is questionable after all. "How could she be pure—one cannot be dirty in act and spiritual in being. Louisa distrusted Mary's high spirituality. It was no longer genuine for her." She says to herself, "They are wrong—they are all wrong. They have ground out their souls for what isn't worth anything, and there isn't a grain of love in them anywhere. And I *will* have love. They want us to deny it. They've never found it so they want to say it doesn't exist. But I *will* have it. I *will* love—it is my birthright."

In part, Mary married him because with his money she can make life easier for the Lindley family. "She had sold herself, but she had a new freedom. She had got rid of her body. She had sold a lower thing, her body, for a higher thing, her freedom from material things. . . . She had bought her position in the world—that henceforth was taken for granted. There remained only the direction of her activity towards charity and high-minded living." Although Mary is ashamed of her husband before people, she bears him a son, who grows to resemble her and learns to ignore his father, despite the latter's total devotion to him.

Meanwhile Louisa, who "*will* have love," rebels against Mary's spirituality and takes as lover Alfred Durrant, a collier. Though Alfred is no portrait of Lawrence, the marriage of Louisa to a working-class man clearly refers to Frieda's marriage to Lawrence. The story, first called "Two Marriages," is based upon the contrast of the two sisters' directions in life. (Incidentally, it becomes much more interesting when the inhumanly Christian little curate is translated back into Jaffe, the adventurous Jewish ex-businessman turned academic.) Everything to do with Mary's motives, which are most tendenciously and yet sympathetically depicted, bears on Lawrence's and Frieda's feeling about Else. From their point of view, the Jaffes' marriage was a Heidelberg kind of marriage, uniting man and woman on the basis of shared social-moral values—which is to say it was the wrong kind.

Her sister's marriage must have crystallized for Frieda the absolute difference she had long sensed between herself and her sister. It gave energy to her angry rebellion against "spiritual" and "intellectual" values, and the cynicism about life-values which they often concealed—the cynicism of a Winifred Inger or of a Tom Brangwen the younger in *The Rainbow*. What this meant for the sisters' relationship is clear from Lawrence's story: "Mary was wrong, wrong, wrong: she was not superior, she was flawed, incomplete. The two sisters stood apart. They still loved each other, they would love each other as long as they lived. But they had parted ways."

This, I suggest, may be taken as Frieda Weekley's comment on Elsa Jaffe. The fact that she, unlike Louisa, was already married and a mother in 1902 only made her claim for love bolder, angrier, more indignant than it seems in the story. Precisely because she married her professor *before* her sister did, Else's choice must have seemed more deliberate, more responsible, more intentional. All Lawrence's work was to express Frieda's point of view on "spiritual" and "intellectual" marriages.

However, the Lawrences' point of view was very ill-adapted to seeing what was of interest in Edgar Jaffe. He was *very* interesting, and one might say that their failure to see that is one of the most striking condemnations of their point of view. In the world of Woman he was nothing; and that was all they looked at. Though there are wonderful things in "The Daughters of the Vicar," wonderful strokes of art in the best sense, Mr. Massy is not one of them. Compared with Edgar Jaffe, he is bound to seem crudely and even stupidly drawn.

Edgar Jaffe received his Habilitation in 1904 for his thesis on English banking, which he also published. In the same year he bought the *Archiv für Sozialwissenschaft und Sozialpolitik* from Heinrich Braun and in effect presented it to Max Weber. By this act Edgar Jaffe made an important contribution not only to the development of sociology in Germany but also to Max Weber's career in the most personal sense. Since 1897 Weber had been suffering from a neurosis which had incapacitated him as a teacher and writer, and even as a thinker. The activity of the *Archiv* brought him to life again, and was the beginning of his later achievements. Jaffe, Weber, and Werner Sombart were the editors of the journals, but Weber was clearly the dominant figure in the triumvirate. Under his control the *Archiv* had a long and very distinguished career.

One cannot but suspect that Else Jaffe prompted the enterprise, though it is possible that Jaffe's independent admiration of Weber provided all the motive he needed and that she only applauded it after the fact. Jaffe was a man who liked to do good, particularly by smoothing the life-path of more powerful personalities than himself.

In his own works Jaffe emerges as a clear writer and competent expounder of economic questions, though when he touches on political questions it becomes clear that he was not a profound mind. But he is quite interesting. Else, too, was a clear and interesting writer, with perhaps slightly more individuality than her husband, but essentially within the same limits. The writings of both bespeak modest and well-bred minds, well-trained, aware of their own limitations as well as knowing the rules of the intellectual game. He often says something that bears on a theme of Lawrence's, and says it in a humane and unpretentious way. Thus an essay of 1913 on "Die Arbeiterfrage in England" ("The Labor Question in England"), one finds, "The new generation of the upper classes is turning away from crude materialist competition, and wants to enjoy the fruits of their fathers' labors in pleasurable cultural pursuits." Lawrence treats this theme in "England, My England," and in Germany too, one could find the same relaxation of the patriarchal grip on life. Jaffe himself was living out such a loosening of standards in Munich at the time. But he was also interested in a kind of Welfare State Socialism and gives an enthusiastic account of Lloyd George and his social legislation. Although he was somewhat sympathetic to syndicalism and direct action in circumvention of parliaments, his more considered line of thought remained roughly Fabian Socialist—a brand of reformism typical of Heidelberg politics—up to the time of the Revolution. (In 1918 Else translated for publication in revolutionary Munich a Fabian pamphlet, *How Are We Paying for the War?*)

We shall say more about his part in the Revolution at the end of this section, but we should note here the energy and enterprise with which Jaffe committed himself to the life of Schwabing—the Greenwich Village of Munich—after having been at the heart of the infinitely more conscientious and "civilized" society of Heidelberg. He made himself the friend of Otto Gross, perhaps the most brilliant man there, and Fanny zu Reventlow, the most remarkable free woman of her time, was his mistress. He became a patron of modern art, buying new paintings as well as entertaining the painters. During the war he became a pacifist, a socialist, and finally a revolutionary who helped Kurt Eisner drive the King of Bavaria from his throne. However timid his manner, his behavior was bold and colorful. But he was by then separated, informally, from his wife.

All three of the sisters' marriages failed—unless Johanna had aimed in hers only at securing herself the freedom to have affairs with other men. But whereas Frieda was stranded in provincial England, where she found nothing but her children to engage her deepest urges and boldest ambitions, Else had Heidelberg, which was then in the fullest bloom of its career as a center of life and thought. Even her marriage, to begin with, must have seemed a Heidelberg partnership of minds between two of the leading disciples of Max Weber, so that even when the partnership had clearly failed, Heidelberg remained.

The German universities were then the great universities of Europe. In 1895, for instance, there were only thirty American students at the Sorbonne but two hundred at Berlin University. And the two in Badenia, at Heidelberg and Freiburg, were the greatest of all, particularly in philosophy and history and the social sciences. Before 1870 the foreign students, at least the Americans among them, had come to Germany mostly for science and medicine, but in the last three decades of the nineteenth century they came for the liberal arts and the social sciences. At the two Baden universities you could hear more radical social theories put forward and discussed than you could at other German universities. Because the critics naturally felt more comfortable at a distance, radicalism gravitated to Baden while Berlin University became the center of official chauvinism in the Wilhelminian era.

Politically, Badenia was the center of liberalism in Germany. Its ruling dynasty was politically liberal and popular, its government the most constitutionally liberal—the most English—in all of Germany. Prince Max von Baden was made Chancellor of Germany in 1918, as a concession to the liberals, when it became clear that the army—the Prussian army—was defeated.

Moreover, Baden was hospitable to academics; the Prussian Minister of Education Althoff was a tyrant—Max Weber had a brush with him—whereas the Badenian Minister, Sigismund von Reitzenstein, was a great statesman of academia. Then, too, the Grand Duke was Rektor of Heidelberg and the reigning family took an interest in university matters. And finally, professors at Heidelberg got paid considerably more than professors at Berlin did, and had more prestige in the community.

Heidelberg was to German intellectual society what Weimar had been a century before. Some professors held formal dinners as much as once a week, where other *Burgers* did so only once or twice a year. Professor Henry von Thode, for instance, had splendid receptions. His wife, Daniela von Bülow, the daughter of Richard and Cosima Wagner, held an afternoon reception each Monday, after which the guests attended her husband's art history lecture. The conversational tone there was dogmatic and ceremonial, for of the three major intellectual circles of Heidelberg just before the war—von Thode's, Stefan George's, and the Webers'—the first was the most hierarchical while the last was much the simplest in social style.

In the Webers' circle several women were prominent; besides Marianne Weber and Else Jaffe, there were Marie Baum, who succeeded Else as factory inspector of Baden, Gertrud Jaspers, and Gertrud Simmel. The ceremonial social life of the university reached a climax in the summer of 1914, at the Prorektor's Fest, given that year by the Gotheins in Schwetzinger Park. The intellectual life of the place seems to have centered in semi-informal reading groups and discussion groups, of which there were many, rather than in salons. But it was by all accounts a continuous thing, the exchange of ideas, and a part of every social event and every aspect of life. Else Jaffe did not allow her children to read the intellectual pap their cousins read. By the age of ten, her daughter recalls, they were reading the *Odyssey*.

In the Wilhelminian era, there congregated at Heidelberg a large number of brilliant men: Wilhelm Windelband and Heinrich Rickert in philosophy, Ernst Troeltsch in theology, Max and Alfred Weber in sociology, Emil Kraepelin and Karl Jaspers in psychology, Friedrich Gundolf in literature. It was one of the centers of liberalism for the whole world; in 1907 Muhammad Iqbal, philosopher, poet, spiritual leader of Pakistan, lived there. At the Webers' Sunday "jours" Else Jaffe met Simmel, Gundolf, Georg Lukács, Ernest Bloch, Minna Tobler the pianist, and Kläre Schmid-Romberg the actress, along with many Russian revolutionary students. Eugen Levine, for instance, one of the later leaders of the Munich communist regime, was a student at Heidelberg after 1905. Max Weber gave a speech at the opening of these students' *Lesehalle* in 1913 and entertained its members often. He said that if he taught again he would want a seminar made up exclusively of Russians, Poles, and Jews.

Gustav Radbruch mentions among his Russian student-friends there Mathias Kohan-Bernstein, whose father, executed in Siberia, before Mathias was born, had left his unborn son a celebrated letter of revolutionary exhortation. The mother, a doctor, traveled with her son when he went to the university. He was himself later shot by the Bolsheviks. There was Boris Katz, who as Boris Kamkow was imprisoned as a social revolutionary in Bolshevik Russia and then banished. There was Isaiah Steinberg, who became Volkskommissar of Justice briefly; Minna Ostrovsky, who translated important documents from German into Russian; the nonpolitical Osip Bernstein; and others—nearly all Jews. The sad fate of so many of them makes an important part of the sorrowful history of radical Europe, but they were in the prewar years part of the exhilaration of Else Jaffe's Heidelberg.

We get one of the very rare tributes to Frau Jaffe—their rarity testifies to the power of her modesty—in Edgar Salin's memoirs. Salin, an economist of broad intellectual interests, describes her as a member of both the Weber circle in Heidelberg and the George circle in Munich. After she moved to Munich in 1911, her house there became a social center for the disciples of

Stefan George. She was particularly the friend of Karl Wolfskehl among the Georgianer, and helped keep the two so different circles in connection. This was a role typical of much of her life. Salin describes her as "the slender, delicate woman with the expressive features, in which so much friendliness and so much grief had engraved themselves."

But of course her life was not lived completely in either Heidelberg or Munich. She played an important part in her sisters' lives, and her parents' lives, and her friends' lives. In particular, she looked after the children of friends. Peter Gross, the son of Otto and Frieda, lived with the Jaffes for a couple of years after his parents moved to Switzerland; and Camilla, Regina Ullmann's daughter, lived with them after that; and still later came Percy Gothein, the son of Eberhard Gothein and the disciple of Stefan George.

Looking after people was an important part of Else Jaffe's life. In 1918 Otto Gross sent her a message via a woman friend, asking if she would look after him if he came back to Munich. (His health was then endangered, as we shall see.) But Else turned down his appeal, for Otto Gross could not be only looked after. He offered a challenge—a challenge to everything that Heidelberg stood for, that she had committed herself to. At first she had succumbed to his challenge, but then she righted herself and rejected him, repudiated him, in the name of that town's values. For she had built her identity out of these values. They complemented her and in a sense they had created her.

Heidelberg made a life for Else Jaffe which she found deeply, if not completely, satisfying. Not only was she a clever woman, interested in ideas and skillful in drawing out and helping forward clever men. She was also a beautiful and graceful being, who never said a foolish thing nor did a clumsy one. Marianne Weber says that even after Else left Heidelberg for Munich, "in the bloom of her womanhood, and for her grace and intelligence the center of her circle, [she] remained in close inner connection with her Heidelberg friends." Marianne describes her as belonging to the borderland between scholarship and art. Else had a lot to offer such a society—and she also needed it, to give her talents full play. She had something of a passion to be perfect. Not to be triumphant—she was far too modest, too melancholy, too renunciatory, for that—but to be irreproachable, to be complete. The occasions of Heidelberg life offered her opportunities which served her purposes.

Nottingham did not so serve Frieda, who was in those years neither graceful nor complete. In photographs one sees that she has often falsified herself by an overtheatrical posture or expression, assumed just before the camera clicked, or else slumped into defeated dowdiness. She is often either timid or self-consciously triumphant, whereas Else is always "perfect." Her perfection, one assumes, had some causal relation to Frieda's imperfection. Frieda could not achieve her style, her range of expressiveness, by means of the dinner parties and lectures and concerts of a university community, or any other middle-class life style of the English Midlands. She felt trapped there, so that when she ran away with Lawrence in 1912, she walked with him over the Alps into Italy and it is clear from her account of it that this adventure itself—gestures like her throwing away her shoes, for instance— was as important to her as the companion with whom she did it. (She once said that Lawrence and she had had no grand passion for each other when they left England together.) She wanted to get away from Europe entirely, to uncivilized countries. She wanted not merely to see them. She wanted to *be* there, she needed them in order to achieve her "atavistic" self. She had to seek other backdrops before she could achieve *her* style. She needed, ultimately, the mountains and deserts of Taos.

But what she got first was the cafés and studios of Schwabing, perhaps the most Bohemian *quartier* in Germany then. It was a great center of opposition to Bismarck's Germany, and the central figure there, for the von Richthofen sisters, was Otto Gross.

Otto Gross

In her boarding school in Freiburg, Else von Richthofen had become a close friend of Frieda Schloffer, of Graz in Austria; she was a niece of Alois Riehl, the professor of philosophy at Freiburg University, and Sophie Riehl, a woman of education and advanced ideas, called herself the girl's mother. Through this connection with academic society, Else met Marianne Weber, whose close friend she also became. And it was her sardonic fate to become involved with the husbands of both these women. For in 1903 Frieda Schloffer married Dr. Otto Gross, also of Graz, who was then an Assistent at the Neurolog-Psychiatrische Institut there. Gross was a very remarkable man, who had a profound effect on both of the von Richthofen sisters, and indirectly on the men in their lives, notably Weber and Lawrence. (Frieda Schloffer often visited the von Richthofens during school holidays, and she became friends with the other Frieda too. She was in age midway between the two sisters.)

Frieda Schloffer's mother had suffered from "hysterical" illnesses, and the girl herself spent weeks without sleep, had pains in her leg, headaches, and other symptoms she knew to be psychosomatic. She put them down to her unhappiness in Graz society and her rebellion against her fate as a daughter of a bourgeois family there. In 1900 she wrote to Else that the doctor, who came to see her once a week, had forbidden her either to play the piano or to write, and had told her to cultivate calm and cheerfulness. Even her beloved Aunt, or "Maman" Sophie, suffered from nervous eczema and spent much of her life taking cures at one resort or another, so that Frieda came to fear a similar fate for herself. She was a highly romantic and musical girl, very fond of Wagner, and she cherished a very dependent devotion to Else von Richthofen. She admired and feared the latter's independence and determination, and she herself dreamed, rather hopelessly, of working at Toynbee Hall, the social work settlement found in 1884, in the East End of London. She speaks, in a letter written just before her meeting with Otto, of her need to have children and sick people and poor people to help, and of how cut off from them she felt in Graz. When she fell under Gross's spell in 1902, he gave a very different direction to her rebellion and her idealism, but she remained devoted to Else all her life.

Otto Gross, who was ten months younger than she (three years younger than Else), was already a black sheep in Graz society; indeed, he had just taken a cure from morphine addiction when they first met. They married against family opposition and lived in almost total isolation from Graz society, reading together—particularly the Russian novelists and the Old Testament— and developing Otto's theories. Frieda wrote to Else that Otto had two loves, herself and theory, and he clearly was a man for whom ideas had much more substance and personality than they have for most men. He lived in passionate relationship to them. Frieda also wrote that her love for him had much of the mother in it, and that he teased her about how much she liked him to be childish. They both knew that he was to be her task in life.

They were happy with each other in Graz, but unhappy in their social isolation. Otto needed social intercourse, above all with artists, and they decided to go to Munich even though Otto had not yet been granted the permanent teaching position for which they had been waiting. They moved in 1906, and Frieda, who was then expecting a child, invited Else Jaffe to come and stay with them. It must have been almost immediately that Else and Otto became erotically involved with each other. Because eroticism was a moral doctrine, indeed a religion with Otto Gross, their relationship probably should not be described as an "affair," insofar as this term implies something furtive, self-indulgent, amoral. Erotic emancipation was the opposite of all those things; for Otto Gross it was a cause. Though she was by then the mother of two children, Else Jaffe felt, as she noted in a diary, that she was discovering her true nature for the first time.

Otto Gross was the only son of Hanns Gross, the Austrian criminologist, and this man too deserves a few pages of description, for he embodied in his effect on the personal life of his son what Bismarck embodied on the public scene. He was to become famous as a professor of criminology at Graz, but at the time of Otto's marriage he was professor at Prague. The appointment to Graz came in 1905, only one year before his son moved to Munich. Father and son were profoundly hostile to one another, and these relocations were causally interconnected.

Hanns Gross's family on both sides came from Graz, as did his wife's, and as did Otto's wife's. Hanns and Otto both studied there, and Hanns had been judge in the country nearby for thirty years before he took up an academic career. As an examining magistrate, his work entailed cooperating with the local police officers, who were usually ex-army men. They were of course quite untrained scientifically—indeed, untrained in every way except in the rough and ready authoritarianism of military justice. It became Hanns Gross's life work to train first judges like himself, and then police forces, in much more rigorous methods—to rationalize and systemize the enforcement of justice, to introduce all the machinery of "science" into this neglected area of life, to direct it against gypsies, tramps, fortunetellers, vagrants, people on the run of all descriptions. He succeeded finally in making this scientific criminology an academic subject of study at the university of Graz. But we must first say something about that town.

Graz was then the capital city of Styria and the largest city in Austria after Vienna—but a long way after. It was essentially a provincial town, staid and old-fashioned. It had an eleventh-century castle, a fifteenth-century cathedral, a sixteenth-century universty, and the social life seems to have been as petrified as that described by Musil in the third volume of *The Man Without Qualities*. (Musil came from Klagenfurt, a similar town, and from the same social class as Gross.) But the Psychiatrisch-Neurologische Klinik at the university was the best in the country, after those in Vienna. Its head from 1873 to 1889 was Baron Richard von Krafft-Ebing; from then until 1893, Wagner von Jauregg; and both men went from there to head clinics in Vienna. Between 1894 and 1905 the work of the clinic was directed by Gabriel Anton, under whom Otto Gross worked, and to whom he refers gratefully in several of his early papers. They worked in a field that was, in that decade and that country, morally and socially mined with high explosives, for the forces that produced Freudianism were at work in many other people besides Freud himself. In sum, Graz was an old-fashioned and respectable town, with a highly dangerous enclave within it. Otto Gross affiliated himself exclusively to that enclave of psychosexual speculation, and became the most radical of innovators within it.

Hanns Gross was himelf an innovator, in his very different direction. To his German-speaking admirers, he is known as the father of criminology. That is, criminology as an independent academic discipline was brought into existence in German-speaking countries by him more than by anybody else. His *Handbuch für Untersuchungsrichters* (*Handbook for Examining Magistrates*), of 1893, was reissued in 1895, 1898, 1904, 1907, and 1913, was quickly translated into every European language, and is still in use as a standard textbook today. In English, for instance, there have been five editions, in 1906, 1924, 1934, 1950, and 1962—the most recent of which was edited by Richard Leofric Jackson of New Scotland Yard. Indeed, the book tells one how to set up one's own Scotland Yard. It is symbolically apt that nowadays it is of special use to "underdeveloped" countries, telling them how to enter into this particular aspect of the heritage of Western civilization.

A French admirer's praise will indicate its scope. Gross is said to have been "an indefatigable observer; a far-seeking psychologist; a magistrate full of ardour to unearth the truth, whether in favour of the accused or against him; a clever craftsman; in turn, draftsman, photographer, modeller, armourer; having acquired by long experience a profound knowledge of the practices of criminals, robbers, tramps, gypsies, cheats, he opens to us the researches and experiences of many years. His work is no dry or purely technical treatise; it is a living book, because it has lived." For our purposes, perhaps the most significant point made there concerns Gross's profound knowledge of criminals, for his son acquired an equally profound *but sympathetic* knowledge of antisocial types. Indeed, he made *himself* into a criminal, a tramp, a cheat, and so forth.

In *In Search of Criminology* Professor Radzinowicz says that Hanns Gross in fact founded not criminology but criminalistics, the art of criminal investigation. He was not interested in penology, or in the sociology of crime; just in catching criminals and preventing them from committing more crimes. Methodologically, he was a Linnaeus of the field, who collected and classified innumerable cases, but no theorist. He held the quite naïve belief that such work would of itself generate scientifically valid generalizations. Moreover, "his psychological apparatus and interpretations were rudimentary, even allowing for the state of contemporary knowledge upon his subject." In 1926 Hans Gruhle described Gross's *Criminal Psychology* as a "bad bit of popularization." (Gruhle, a friend of Weber's and Else Jaffe's at Heidelberg, was one of the men who found Otto Gross starving, indeed dying, on the streets of Berlin in 1919.) Gruhle's criticism notwithstanding, Professor Radzinowicz nevertheless credits the establishment of the science in Austria to Gross, to "the persistent efforts of one individual, campaigning for a long time in virtual isolation." Moreover, his institute at Graz has continued along the lines which Gross—"this exceptionally strong personality"—laid down for it, and does so today, after two world wars.

Gross did not actually succed in establishing his Criminological Institute, one of the first in the world, until 1912. There was much opposition to it at first, though later much imitation of it. Courses were instituted in the Faculty of Law in criminal psychology, criminal anthropology, criminal statistics, and criminalistics, one per semester. Amassing a collection of the "visible signs of crime," he established a *Kriminalversammlung* which later became a *Kriminalmuseum*, again one of the first in the world. It contained abortion devices, murder weapons, torture-deformed bones, fingerprints, and other memorabilia from the scenes of famous crimes. And in the Institute's criminological laboratory and criminological station, he and an assistant worked at solving actual crime problems sent him by the police, which eventually yielded yet more exhibits for the museum.

His *Criminal Psychology* appeared in 1897. Citing as it did many cases of connection between psychological abnormality, sexual abnormality, and crime, it naturally had its effect in shaping the growing interest in abnormal psychology. Father and son shared that interest. In its second edition of 1905, it twice makes citation of Otto Gross's work, and the American edition of 1911 refers to Otto as a well-known specialist in mental and nervous disorders who collaborated with his father. Hanns also published two volumes of *Collected Criminological Essays*, among many other books. And in 1899 he founded the *Archiv für Kriminalanthropologie und Kriminalistik*, which he edited until his death in 1915. Everything he did was named "criminal" in one way or another.

One feature of his criminology, as distinct from that of others, was its eclectic inclusiveness, the way in which it brought together many different specialized knowledges, ranging from fingerprint and X-ray techniques to psychological theories—even something as speculative as the "psychology of woman." But the spirit, the intention, of his work, was always positivistic. He took the emphasis off eyewitness accounts and put it on "scientific" evidence. And he shifted the focus of attention from the nature of the crime to the nature of the criminal. He used the terms *criminal* and *criminal type* to include those who *would* commit crimes under favoring circumstances. He was scientist, soldier, and policeman, all together. Finally, he loved the royal office of judge, another admirer tells us, and wanted to make the legal process more obedient to authority, less hampered by formal and democratic procedures.

In every way, therefore, Hanns Gross identified himself with the punishing function of the patriarchal culture, both theoretically, by studying that function, and practically, as a judge. He often speaks eloquently of the unappreciated dignity of the work done by the police. "The forces of law and order," he wrote, "are the pride and the reassurance of the working and thriving citizen—if I could bring to the sure processes of this unspeakably hard work some slight easing, then the aim of this book would be achieved."

In an essay of 1905 on "Degeneration and Deportation" one feels the full brutal forcefulness of his thinking. We must deport degenerates in order to save society, he argues. Degenerates are more dangerous than criminals, for some of the latter at least are not lacking in Life-Force. Moreover, there are many degenerates who escape prosecution as criminal—tramps, impostors, the idle, the perverse, revolutionaries—but all are dangerous to the state. Punishment will not work with them. Punishment is something we add to the motivational parallelogram of forces, to make sure that the resultant vector is socially good. But the degenerate's mind is crippled and insusceptible of conviction. The tramp, the revolutionary, the habitual thief, the pederast, these cannot be either dissuaded or cured. It is society's fault; it is culture's curse on civilization. The processes of culture reverse those of Nature, by fostering and propagating the weaker types. So we must remove them from culture—from society. Send them to the colonies for life. Some will go to the wall, and others will be regenerated, as happened in Australia. Southwest Africa is just the place for *our* degenerates, he says. (By 1913 he was writing on "Castration and Sterilization." When he had his son arrested, in the same year, Otto explained his father's action as a retaliation for an essay on the social functions of sadism Otto had just written for a psychoanalytic journal, in which he used his father's life, public and domestic, as his prime example.)

Hanns Gross was a big man, with a dominating personality as well as physique, whose wife, like Bismarck's, played a very subordinate role in the family. Physically pycnic-athletic, with a bull-neck, he was a semi-soldier all his life. His scientific work was done with soldierly precision and punctuality, and his Institute was put at the service of the Fatherland's defence, against internal and external enemies. As a boy he was very active in escapades and very ingenious in mechanical devices—a young Tom Sawyer. He grew up to love the army—his father had been a professional soldier—and he died at the age of sixty-eight of a lung inflammation contracted as a wartime volunteer in the army. His admirers describe him by saying that the three roots of his personality were the military, the judicial, and the scientific. He represents—not only in his son's life, but in all the landscape of this book—the patriarchalism of Bismarck's Germany, and patriarchalism at an extreme. As we shall see, Max Weber's affirmations, like his career and life-style, align themselves with Hanns Gross's only in order to reveal how much more ambivalent and variously human he was.

Otto Gross made himself a living antithesis to his father. He came to stand for total freedom and for the repudiation of patriarchal authority in every possible way. Unlike the other main figures in our story, he grew up in a home where the father was infinitely more impressive than the mother; indeed, his career began in cooperation with his father. He was trained as a doctor and specialized in neurology and psychiatry. He published first—at a very young age—in his father's *Archiv*. He seemed set for a brilliant career, quite different from his father's but still in some sense parallel to his. But even in his first published essay, on the psychology of society's inhibiting mechanisms, we find him wrestling with the emotional problems of justice. Society's punishments are cruel and "unjust," he says, though they will always be necessary. Those unfortunates whose psychology does not provide them with the right inhibitions must suffer, for the good of others. Predestined though they were to commit crime, they must be punished for what they do. And though it is an instinct of revenge which lies at the source of "justice," still justice must be done. The term conceals an irreconcilable contradiction.

It is clear, then, that from the beginning Otto Gross felt himself in profound opposition to what his father stood for. Indeed, in physique, in temperament, in life-style, he was a living antithesis to his father—being all ardent idealism and aesthetic sensibility, all hypersensitivity and emotional extremism.

Thus it comes as no surprise that in his first book, *The Secondary Function of the Brain* (1902), he defined the opposition between himself and his father as psychological, cultural, and historical types. The fifth and last chapter of that work is on differences of individuality between epochs. He has been distinguishing two mental types, recognizable in normal as well as abnormal individuals. On the one hand there is the broad and superficial consciousness, quick to grasp facts of all kinds and to use them to best advantage for short-term ends; and on the other we find the narrow and deep consciousness, slow to grasp facts and use them, powerfully affected by meanings, deeply emotional. These types, we can hardly help noticing, fit Dostoevsky's world; Rogozhin-Dmitri versus Myshkin-Alyosha. (Indeed, Gross often cited Dostoevsky. The antithesis also suggests a traditional way of opposing the male to the female mind—and gives the preference to the latter.)

In the former type, Gross says, the life of emotion is always primitive. Some of these individuals have ideals to which they devote themselves heroically, and in this sense their emotional life can be called idealistic. *"Aber immer ist es banal"* ("But still it is banal"). For one thing, they always lack the richly various and interwoven connection of the upper consciousness with the erotic imagination. The knitting together of the erotic factor with the higher imaginings of aesthetic, ethical, and social matters gives those imaginings their final powerfulness, and their first beauty. But in the broad-consciousness type, the sublimations of the erotic drive never escape the limits of triviality.

In the type characterized by deep consciousness, there is a strong drive toward harmony and unity of experience, toward symbolic abstraction and simplification of the complex. Hence we get what is called the "sensitive" man, who cannot achieve any careless uninhibited self-expression, and who inclines more to the aesthetic than to the socially effective action. The world is apprehended by such men in symbolic and visionary ways, and among the most gifted of them new ideals are born. (It is clear that Gross himself was of this type, as was D. H. Lawrence.)

The opposition of types can be described, he says, in terms of the antithesis between the man of civilization and the man of culture; or between the practical man of affairs and the original man of ideas; or between the realistic man of battle and the solitary shaper of images. The first is proper to stormy eras in which empires are established; the second is the product of the high culture which grows out of empire. (Gross undoubtedly saw this polarity in terms of a contrast between the founding years of Bismarck's Germany and the new era of high culture represented by Rilke and Kafka—two men whom Otto Gross knew later. Max Weber, of course, would have told him that "the stormy era" was never over.)

In the periods of high culture, the old naïve values which had animated society lose their validity, and new ones have to be worked out. Modern art exemplifies this drive. We nowadays want simplicity and depth where earlier ages wanted superficial ornament. They could not immerse themselves, as we can, in a large, simple, single, richly realized image. Thus the old masters of architecture always varied their detail in ornament, but not the new ones; the Wiener Sezession building has a Tonskala allegory in which the same figure appears in twenty different poses. We like that repetition of lines. We respond to the ideal and the symbolic. Through simplicity to harmony—that is the aim of all high-culture art, of all modern art.

Gross was implicitly identifying himself not only with the Wiener Sezession style, a variant of Jugendstil or Art Nouveau, but with art values as a whole—and thereby with Munich-Schwabing, which was the great center of the Jugendstil in Germany, and a great center of modernist art in general. What he says about art is very much like what Kandinski says in *Über das Geistige in der Kunst*, which was written in Munich in 1910 and published in 1912. Kandinsky's is recognized as one of the great manifestoes of modernist art, and Otto Gross's essay anticipates it rather strikingly. As a medical student at the University of Munich in 1897 and 1898, he was in touch with all that was most advanced in its intellectual life. Thus his stress on the erotic means more than it might seem to, because in Schwabing eroticism was a highly elaborated and value-bearing philosophy. Indeed, what is to replace for the new era the old simple values of the patriarchal society will turn out to be something identifiable as the matriarchal values of Schwabing. But we must first give some more detail about Otto Gross's life.

He was, it seems, brilliantly gifted even in childhood, and his father had his only son brought up "like a prince," as Frau Jaffe put it. He was educated by private tutors as well as at schools, and he grew up precociously clever and individualistic. He rejected both wine and meat—"take your carcasses away"—but was early a cocaine and opium addict. He was handsome and athletic looking—several writers describe his springy, loping stride—though he was rejected as unsuitable for military service because of a shoulder dislocation. As a student, he was notably quiet, studious, and refined, avoiding both wine and women. Frieda Schloffer told Else that before Otto got engaged to her he had always drawn back in disgust or disappointment from those intimate relations with women of which he had so ardently dreamed. His intellectual interests were botany and biology. A brilliant talker, though an even better listener, he was very gentle and receptive in manner. After graduating, he went to South America often, as a ship's doctor, and Frau Jaffe still remembered in 1971 his account of standing on the shore at Punta Arenas, looking out over the Pacific, and feeling at the end of everything civilized. He pursued his botanical studies in Patagonia, but before 1900 he seems to have dropped them in favor of psychoanalysis, which led him on to cultural and political theory. Tall, slender, fair-haired, blue-eyed, with soft, parted lips, boyish-looking at forty, his face and manner expressed both great candor and great nobility. His profile suggested to more than one writer the simile of a bird, a bird of prey, a fanatical hawk, for he had a big hooked nose and a retreating chin. But both lines and colors were delicate, and he also suggested porcelain. Many who knew him commented on the gentle earnestness of the gaze he bent upon his companion's face, reading in it with perfect candor and courtesy.

Later in life, his face and manner expressed to some observers also the rigor of fanaticism and the pathos of ruin. This was in part accounted for by the lurid traces of drug addiction—stains on his clothes and blood from his nostrils. He had always dressed untidily. He was, or seemed to be, irresponsible, undisciplined, indifferent to ordinary amenities. He lay in bed all day if he felt no impulse to get up, and would go several days without washing. When he needed money he would ask the nearest friend for it. His wife, according to one witness, went round his haunts every so often and paid his bills. And so on.

One can imagine how much this appealed to Frieda Weekley, who was similarly, and in a similarly principled way, "undisciplined." But her sister, who describing him as "sehr undiszipliniert," refused to believe that he— "*this* Otto Gross"—could have written the books and articles credited to him, for "discipline" was a major category for her and Max Weber. Productivity was one of *their* achievements, and could not be found in the undisciplined.

Of course, Weber made an interpretive as well as evaluative category out of discipline. In "The Meaning of Discipline" he says, ". . . of all those powers that lessen the importance of individual action, the most irresistible is *rational discipline*." Like bureaucracy, its most rational offspring, discipline is impersonal, unfailingly neutral, its ethic a matter of duty. It is something to be associated with Cromwell's Roundhead men of conscience, in opposition to the Cavalier aristocratic men of honor, and Otto Gross was essentially an aristocrat. He himself despised plebeian morality, and everyone who met him seems to have used the word "noble" about him—even Max Weber, who heard much about him from Frau Jaffe. Thus Weber also applied to Gross the word "charisma," which for him defines a mode of power opposite to that of discipline. The charismatic leader, Weber says in "The Sociology of Charismatic Authority," is "recognized" by his followers as their master. He is not guaranteed by any established tests administered by any established authorities; indeed, charismatic authority is, Weber says, "contrary to all patriarchal domination." He lives in but not of the externally given order. He is a revolutionary who transvalues everything. All this applies very well to Otto Gross. We learn from several accounts how total was his authority over his followers, both men and women. He disposed of their lives with their complete assent.

Thus Franz Jung, Gross's disciple, though himself a very powerful personality, writes in his autobiography, *Der Weg Nach Unten*, "For me Otto Gross meant the experience of a first deep and great friendship, and I would have sacrificed myself for him without hesitating. At the same time, I probably stood to him in some quite external relation, to be frank, and never especially close. It was a mixture of respect and faith, the need to believe in and to do honor to something, to take it up and work it through, which he continually hammered into us. For Gross I was probably not much more than a figure on the chessboard of his thoughts, which could be pushed to and fro." This is the way a disciple talks about a charismatic leader.

Despite his lack of conventional discipline, however, Gross seems to have been intellectually not only active but productive. He wrote four books and a flow of articles, only some of which are listed in the Annals later in this volume. There was also a manuscript proposing a new ethics, which seems to have been lost or destroyed at the time of his arrest in 1913. The character of most of this work, moreover, *is* disciplined. He was trained as a scientist, and his psychological essays are very "scientific." He is very alert to the state of research in his subject, and his effort is to reconcile alternative theories. The best example is his *Das Freud'sche Ideogenitätsmoment und seine Beziehung zum Manisch-Depressivem Irresein Kraepelins (Freud's Ideogeneration Factor and its Relation to Kraepelin's Manic-Depressive Insanity)*, which is not only a reconciliation of Freud's theories with Kraepelin's, and thus of psychoanalysis with psychiatry, but also of Wernicke's theories with Anton's, and others. It is also notable that he treated Hans Driesch's vitalism, for instance, with great distrust. This vitalistic or Goethean biology was a natural ally of *Lebensphilosophie*, and was taken up as such by, for instance, Alfred Weber, but Gross was too much the scientist to stomach it. His vocabulary is always abstract, his models mechanical, his philosophy explicitly monistic.

But our interest is primarily with his less technically psychological ideas, and the way he lived them out. They have a very different character from his "scientific" work—work which, according to Franz Jung, Gross came to regret as insincere, as expressing only his intense yearning to be accepted and respected by his colleagues. According to the same source, he destroyed much that he had written of that kind, for he believed in himself as a talker and a practical analyst rather than as a writer—which is to say that he believed in himself as a revolutionary and not as a scientist.

The special character of his psychoanalysis is perhaps best suggested in a review of his book *On Psychopathic Inferiorities* by Simon Guttman; who says that Gross forces the underground tendencies of the patient to surface because he so vitally corroborates them. "Even in the most worm-eaten blockhead Gross recognizes a man, a sphere of meaning, a brain, a metaphysic; so he becomes each patient's philosopher. Every action of Dr. Gross derives from the idea that inside the human being is the place where the world may be taken by the horns." This was written in 1913, and one sees how much he was for that moment what R. D. Laing or Timothy Leary is for us today. Franz Jung's novel *Sophie*, a fictional treatment of Gross's life, corroborates

Guttman's account. One can understand how the hope of so many young people clung to him.

This is not to say that Gross did not receive very high praise also from orthodox psychoanalysts. He was the most brilliant member of the Bohemian set with which Ernest Jones came into contact in Munich in 1908, and Jones described him as "the nearest approach to the romantic idea of a genius I have ever met. . . . Such penetrative powers of divining the inner thoughts of others I was never to see again." Wilhelm Stekel declared that Gross's early work revealed a quality akin to genius. In an obituary—Gross's only obituary, perhaps—he wrote "I only know that I am acquainted with no one who more terribly laid waste his powers, no one who might have done greater things." Erich Mühsam describes Gross as "the most important of Freud's disciples, whom we must thank for psychoanalysis's having escaped the narrow consideration of life from its sexual side exclusively, and having achieved the recognition of the social conditioning of all spiritual experience." Freud himself wrote to Carl Gustav Jung, February 28, 1908, that Gross and Jung himself were the only two among his followers who had original minds. A year later, however, he wrote to Karl Abraham that the extreme attitude represented by Gross was wrong and dangerous to the whole movement; perhaps Gross's cocaine addiction as well as his sexual libertarianism seemed to Freud to be lending substance to society's shadow caricature of his own teachings. Jung's early work also contains much reference to Gross—"On the Psychology of Dementia Praecox" of 1906, and "The Significance of the Father in the Fate of the Individual" of 1909, for example. The latter almost certainly derives from Jung's analysis of Gross—which was in effect a mutual analysis; in its early editions Jung acknowledges a large debt, but later he removed the acknowledgement, just as Freud removed Gross's titles from the bibliography of psychoanalysis. What is more, Jung's *Psychological Types* of 1920 made extensive use of Gross's theory of the two types discussed before; in fact, it is from Gross that Jung derived his famous introvert-extrovert classification.

We know so much about Otto Gross, even though no essay has been written about his work, because he made a strong impression on many imaginative writers, who drew portraits of him in novels. One soon gets to recognize the tall blond doctor with the loping stride, who sits all day in a café with a circle of disciples, psychoanalyzing and philosophizing. Among others, Leonhard Frank, Johannes Becher, Franz Jung, Karl Otten, and especially Franz Werfel described him in fiction. Regina Ullmann also was a close friend of his, and Kafka was at least an acquaintance, although neither of them wrote about him.

From these novels, we can get a picture not only of his appearance and life-style, but even of his ideas.

Franz Werfel describes in his novel *Barbara*, how Otto Gross, (Dr. Gebhart) adopted Babylon as his civilization, in opposition to that of Judaeo-Christian Europe, at least as early as 1917, in Vienna. We meet Gross's literary exposition of this idea in an article entitled "Die Kommunistische Grundidee in der Paradiessymbolik," published in *Sowjet* in 1920. The essay offers a matriarchalist reinterpretation of the story of Genesis, for Gross was addicted to the use of the Bible as a source of anti-Christian myths. Writing to Frieda Weekley, for instance, he deplored Else Jaffe's melancholy moralism by saying that those who had been slaves in Egypt would not be allowed to enter the Promised Land. (All his ancestors had been Protestant but his father was a convert to Catholicism, and he returned to the use of the Bible in repudiation of his father.) If Jezebel had not been defeated by Elijah, he is made to declare in Werfel's novel, world history would have been different and better. Jezebel was Babylon, love-religion, Astarte, Ashtaroth. Jewish monotheistic moralism drove pleasure from the world. (Werfel attributes this myth to Gross again in another, unfinished novel, *The Black Mass*, which was to have centered around Gross.) In the *Sowjet* article, speaking for himself, he describes the expulsion of woman from religion, by Jews, Greeks, and Mohammedans, as the world's first White Terror.

According to Werfel, who follows the facts very closely, insofar as they can be checked, Gross called for sexual revolution in order to save the world in our day. At a meeting of revolutionaries in Vienna in 1918, he demanded a state ministry dedicated to the liquidation of the bourgeois—that is, patriarchalist—family and of bourgeois sexuality. The limitation of sexual life to the orthodox forms of "decent" genital monogamy he regarded as no less a tyranny than marriage itself. Pleasure is the only source of value. Only by reentering into the Paradise Lost of polymorphous perversity can man renew himself, he says in the *Sowjet* article. He believed in, and practiced, an orgiastic therapy which he called the cult of Astarte. He had written a work on the medieval Adamites, according to Werfel, and he was temperamentally one himself. His yellowish but youngish face, his ruined boy's face, was also that of a monk. But a revolutionary monk, who wanted to cancel thousands of years of history. A child between the years of one and three is a genius, he said, and denounced the bourgeois family structure, in which each child is individually owned by its parents. Married domesticity destroys genius.

According to Werfel's Gross, the primitive races made all the great discoveries, and our civilization is corrupt at the roots. The Christian Church is patriarchalism at its crassest. The book of Genesis, however, must have been written by a priest of the old true religion, for it admits that woman was led astray by the Evil Spirit's persuading her to give up her dignity in exchange for ease and comfort. The joint eating of the apple signifies the treaty whereby each man promised to support a woman and her children, in return for that woman's becoming his private property—with the necessary consequences that the children too become his property, that the wives had to promise to be chaste, and that all women had to pretend to be sexually passive, mere prizes and prey to excite man's rapacity. The mastering of women by men brought sin and shame into the world. Gross, a genius but sinister in Werfel's novel, has a vision of the turning point of world history, which came when a horde of ambitious half-apes burst out of the bush and flung themselves upon naked and unsuspecting women. (This is charac-teristically unlike Freud's corresponding vision of the primal sin, in which woman plays no dramatic part.) These half-apes are war-mad creatures with professorial beards and decorations on their breasts—Gross saw his father and perhaps Max Weber in this way—who hang up their tables of the law and their weapons in the innocent temples of sensual love.

It is clear that a man with these ideas was not just "an early Freudian analyst," as Gross is usually described. Freud certainly was a major intellec-tual experience for Gross, both because Freudian theory explained his own problems and because the technique gave him a power over others. Ernest Jones describes Gross as practicing analysis all day long, and all night long, wherever he happened to be. But in matters of ethics and Weltanschauung, Freud was less important to Gross than Nietzsche was. The techniques of Freud and the values of Nietzsche was Gross's formula in 1913. He more than once described Freud's work as being as a whole an extension of, and an application of, Nietzsche's insights.

His relations with Freud were in fact tragic. It is clear, from the Jung-Freud correspondence, that Freud admired Gross's work—enough to be mildly jealous of it and satirical about him. At the Salzburg Conference of Psychoanalysts of 1908, where Gross spoke on the science's "Cultural Per-spectives"—he told Frieda Weekley that these ideas were the first fruits of *their* relationship—Freud reproved him by saying, "We are doctors, and doctors we must remain." Gross believed that they should become philoso-phers and in fact revolutionaries. He believed that the cure of individual neuroses must be rooted in social and cultural change. In the existing state of society, men inevitably must be sick, and the more sensitive the man, the more sick he must be. He himself was sick and did not disguise it from his patients; it was an essential part of his personality. He tried to prevent transference, because he thought that symbolically it must be an endorsement of monogamy, while his patients needed to be helped toward sexual immoralism.

By 1909, Freud had decided that these ideas were dangerous to psychoanalysis. Thereafter, Gross was a heretic to the movement, and his friend Franz Jung says that his difficulties with the authorities in Switzerland in 1912 were caused by orthodox Freudian analysts, who raised a scandal about him and complained to the police. Thus the pattern of Gross's relations with Freud seems to have repeated that of his relations with his father; indeed, C. G. Jung said, after analyzing him, that Gross could not but identify every important man in his life with his father, and every woman with his mother. Thus, once again, enthusiastic admiration, discipleship, and self-subordination were followed by a challenge to the dominant figure, repudiation by him, and finally destruction.

Gross was perfectly aware of his own problems, and of the impotence of conventional analysis to solve them. In Salzburg in 1908, he had told Freud that his earliest memory was of his father telling visitors, "Take care, he bites." With Freud, however, the pattern of his relations was ideological as well as personal. Freud organized insights that were potentially radical or revolutionary in their social effect into a rigorously "scientific" system which was politically neutral, and so in effect conservative. From Gross's point of view, Freud had "gone over to the fathers," had joined the patriarchal side, and we shall see that Max Weber approved of Freud (as a way of disapproving of Gross) precisely for his "scientific" value-neutrality.

But the major figure in Gross's life, from our point of view, remains to be introduced. Freud's work had released him from his bondage to his father. But, as often happened in the psychoanalytic movement, the disciple tried to appropriate these saving truths by becoming more Freud than Freud himself, and then found himself facing another jealous father figure. Who was to save Otto Gross from this new monster? He himself declared that Frieda Weekley had done it, that it was she who "removed the shadow of Freud" from his path. Patriarchy was finally defeated, by matriarchy. Such epigrams are dangerous, but we do find that in his last ten years more of Bachofen than of Freud—perhaps even than of Nietzsche—permeating Gross's conceptual vocabulary.

Otto Gross's mother, to whom he was devoted, seems to have been completely her husband's victim, in the sense that many German wives then were. All the "public" modes of self-assertion were denied them, and they had to be either humble or sly. Several of Gross's literary disciples (Becher, Otten, Hasenclever) were the sons of such families. So, in a very limited sense, was Max Weber. But Frau Gross seems to have been *completely* meek, mild, shy, dim. Frieda Weekley was woman triumphant, Anna Victrix, and it became Gross's mission in life to turn women like his mother into women like Frieda. In part, even Frieda was trumphant only because of the help provided by Otto's endorsement of her. He supplied the ethical-conceptual framework which supported and extended the fitful assertions of her own pride in herself, a pride which was by no means perfectly assured in the fact of her husband's, her sister's, and the world's dissent. Later, Gross's conceptualization of Frieda was to be the ideological dowry she brought to D. H. Lawrence.

Gross's Letters to Frieda Weekley

We know about that conceptualization because a number of his letters to her have survived and found their way to an American university library. They give us all the knowledge we have of their affair, and also of his relationship with Else Jaffe. It is because these letters have never before been published that there is new light to throw on their lives. Frieda Weekley kept them all her life as a prized possession, and also as a document of her identity. When she ran away with D. H. Lawrence in 1912 she sent them to Ernest Weekley in explanation of her action, for they would show to him the real Frieda, who had been stifling in Nottingham. She did not send Lawrence's letters but Gross's.

The letters from Gross that survive now—there may have been others, now lost—are undated, and so purely concerned with ideas and emotions that one cannot even confidently put them in sequence. All we know is that some were written in 1907 and some in 1908, though I guess that some were as late as 1910. However, the ideas and emotions themselves are informative enough to need no more data.

In these letters Gross told Frieda that he had dreamed of "the woman of the future," but that in her he has received the confirmation of his dreams. "My most paralysing *doubts* about mankind's future and my own striving" are over, he writes. "*But now* they can no longer find a vulnerable spot on me—now I know that I have seen and loved the woman I dreamed of for coming generations. . . . I *know* now how people will be who are no longer stained by all the things I hate and fight—I know it through *you*, the only person who *today* has stayed free of chastity as a moral code and Christianity and Democracy and all those heaps of nonsense. . . . How have you managed this miracle, you golden child—kept the curse and the dirt of two gloomy millennia from your soul with your laughter and love?"

Gold and sun and laughter and newness and child—these are all the very images that Lawrence was to apply to Frieda. The central image used by Otto is the sun—the sun seen as the source of all power, and beauty, and majesty. To make her happy, he felt, was to give the world a sun; "Let me see the sun!" he implored. This sun-worship, too, is to be found in Lawrence, particularly in the writings of the New Mexico period, as well as in Klages and Schuler, writers of the Cosmic Circle.

In his letters to Else the tone is rather different. These too are love letters, and eloquent ones, but the eloquence is somewhat more conventional, though his perception of the woman is always acute, as one sees here: "You my unnamable Beloved. You yesterday on the telephone, that was the torture of Tantalus—I fell so desperately in love with your voice—I saw and felt *you*—the magic of the fine nuances and that new clarity, the lovely sureness that has newly come to it—so pure and true your voice was yesterday and in it was a resonance that came from newly unsealed depths. . . . that is the ideal I strive to achieve: that great elemental power of the soul, eroticism, must be like water—blessing, fructifying, loved, mastered—and that is the knowledge I strive to achieve; he who wants to *master* eroticism will be mastered by eroticism—only he who recognizes and assents to eroticism *as it is*—only he masters it and so completely that he can *promise* to be always himself." The ethic and the metaphysic is of course the same as that in the Frieda letters: "Sincerity in our mutual giving—it has not often been known by men—that these were the first blossoms in a new World Spring, that bloom for the beauty of our love? Oh this new spring of a re-awakening newly confident guiltlessness—is not this the kiss that awakens Sleeping Beauty?" But the relationships behind the two sets of letters were different, and the tone to Else, however impassioned and tender, was more hortatory. Otto is often anxious about her, and about her "faith." Above all, he was Else's master in eroticism, whereas Frieda, he implies, was his mistress.

When, in his letters to Frieda, he speaks of Else, he deplores her heaviness and suffering, even as he acknowledges in her so much beauty, so much greatness, so much nobility—even so much freedom from any envy of Frieda. "I can't understand it—that is, I can understand *Else* from *her* life, all the sadness, sunlessness in her and around her—she has always turned toward the suppressed, the bereft of love in her whole life—'social asceticism,' as we said!—she has lived out long years in *pity*—it seems she will still have to learn to be *happy with others*. She probably still doesn't know that the *truly best of all* only *thrives on the heights and in the sun.* . . ."

He loved both sisters, and they both loved him. For Frieda and for Else, though, the affair with Otto Gross must have had, of course, another major dimension, that of sibling rivalry. For the first time, on a scale of any significance, the two sisters had submitted themselves to the same pedagogue and the same examination—and Frieda had triumphed. *She* had been named the woman of the future. The times had changed, and Frieda's qualities were now what particularly excited the imaginations of brilliant men. It was in 1904, when she was thirty, that by her own account Else first realized the independence and significance of her sisters. She was unprepared to compete with them, and on these battlegrounds, the fields of Eros, she was at a disadvantage against Frieda. Their conflict was bitter. "Our last meeting in Heidelberg was completely in the style of "Brünnhild and Krimhild," Frieda wrote to Otto; it had been "dramatic but not good."

But leaving aside for the moment what Gross meant to the relationship between the two sisters, let us consider first the perils and promise held out by Gross to Frieda herself. "You, my bright fire," he wrote her, "don't let yourself be extinguished, keep your glow at all costs, it's so dark on my path—you, my benevolent strength and ardor, *don't* for God's sake, consume yourself in a *smothered* fire. . . ." Frieda is a strong nature, he says, aware of her beauty; she has the freedom of an aristocrat, for she belongs to "an aristocracy of the beautiful and of natural certainty, secure and matter of fact." Frieda, he says, chose him, not he her; "chose me in your great magnificent way." When she sends him a photograph, he replies, "Do you yourself actually know *what* this picture reveals?—that you have been blessed with a great mien (*Gebärde*) and an art which constantly recreates beauty out of your own beauty. . . . The art of bestowing happiness in the greatest simplicity and at the same time in the knowledge that you are giving an invaluable gift. . . . That is so incomparably *great* in the mien of this picture— such an incomparably rich and passionate, exuberant giving of oneself and so much nobility and majesty . . . your bearing so supremely proud and pure . . . —you are exquisite, Beloved . . . so marvelously new—forever new and new again . . . a wonderfully pure soul in you, one kept pure by a genius for *insisting upon yourself*."

The mirror he held up to Frieda was, obviously, one in which she saw herself reflected exactly as she wished to be seen. How much of the image she would have been able to formulate for herself before he did so, how much of it was *true*—that is, to what extent she was able to *enact* that image —we cannot say. But the important thing is clear: because of Otto, she came to Lawrence with a burningly vivid sense of her own value.

In his letters, Gross tells Frieda that she has brought him to the crisis of his life, the test of the value of his existence. He asks her to bring the children to the continent on her next trip so that she need never return to England. "You are the *confirmation* in my life of the flowering and fruitful

yes—the future which has come to me." At one point he thought she was
pregnant by him, and was disappointed to find it not true. But he tells her,
"Don't ever come to me out of pity. . . . My woman of the future . . . *go
with me on my paths*, and your laughter tells me how your abundant
strength and joy spout high into the regions of the sun."

Frieda had given him a ring, on the stone of which were carved three
female figures. These were to symbolize herself, her sister, and his wife, she
said, and she reminded him what remarkable women all three were. The
other two women of the ring ("it has the shimmer of your sunny eyes," he
says) are often discussed in the letters. Through Frieda Gross, he says, he
had learned to believe in the world as a value; through Frieda Weekley he
learned to believe in himself.

Later he writes to Frieda that his wife is with him again, in deep resignation and skepticism, and needing to be won back to flowering life. He
calls on Frieda Weekley to help him by writing her, and she does. "One can
only come to *Frieda*," he writes, by way of explaining his own inability to
help his wife, "as a *strong* and proud person; one simply has to bring it with
one—but with *you* one becomes as one might have been before . . . *you free
one from the past*." Frieda Gross, he complains, never really believed in his
ideas, which he holds so passionately that they are his very self. But Frieda
Weekley, it is clear from her letters as well as his, held them as passionately
as he did. Indeed, we shall see again and again in Frieda's life that she was
capable of loving a man as the incarnation of his ideas.

Gross had not always been troubled by such doubts about the strength
of the conviction with which the three women, compelled by his own conviction, held by his ideas. Certainly in 1906, at the high point of the erotic
movement, he knew no doubts. But when he complained to Frieda about
his wife's lack of belief in his ideas, he already knew that he was losing Else,
too. "Well as I expected, *it's come to an end between Else and me*. And I
have the feeling that my fate isn't finished yet—that this was just the beginning. . . ."

He felt that if he lost one he might lose all three; at least if he lost
Frieda Weekley, he would certainly lose Frieda Gross, for his wife turned
to Else and to Frieda for advice and support when she felt hostile to him.
He becomes extremely depressed. He had had too much happiness—too
much creative energy and too many lofty plans: "There is a sentence from
Heraclitus which is brutally true. The sun may not go beyond the limits of
its orbit or else the Furies will overtake it. . . . They are catching me now,
I feel it. They've already taken *Else* away from me now and have executed
the stroke with a satanic *irony* of means and with *poisoned* weapons. . . . You

have the golden radiance that bans all evil spirits. . . . I feel that this first blow *couldn't have hit me* if *you* had loved me these past few days. . . ."

He describes Else's new affair thus: "An old friend turned up who personifies the *democratic* principle and who has always been infinitely repulsive to me—and to get close to him in any way would be a violation of the most natural and higher precept, the precept of *the separation of the nobility from the common people.* . . . I have to tell her that one can't put master and servant in the same boat—that she can't say *yes to him and me at the same time.*"

She had wanted, or seemed to have wanted, to keep her relationship to Otto as well. Had it been any other man, he would have been delighted. Before he learned who it was, before he knew that this man was the embodiment of "the democratic principle," he had sent her white lilies in congratulation. But when he learned the man's identity, he struggled to get her back into her earlier, higher state of mind, in which she had been his. "But she's completely back in her *democracy* again, considers *it* to be in accord with *her* nature—social asceticism again—all in all, I would have had to come down from my precept and path into the valley and down into the democratic lowland in order to stay with her. . . ." "This misalliance," he says, using the term so central to Victorian concepts of propriety in marriage, expresses Else's hatred of his and Frieda's love; it was an act of "revenge," a "devastating, desolate, crippling act."

One cannot help suspecting that he was right in this suspicion of a revenge motive in Else when one sees the effect the news had on him. (In 1971 Frau Jaffe remembered that at her last meeting with Gross he had asked her for twenty-five marks. She had triumphed in giving him that, as she triumphed again in telling of it.) Frieda had given him his identity when she had told him, *"Du bist Erotik."* She had recognized, before he himself had, that this was the element that gave unity to all his ambitions and aspirations. But ". . . the power of eroticism itself *didn't* give me the strength to secure the aristocratic being in her [Else] . . . that is the poison which weakens me. . . . I was abandoned by *this* particular force, from which basically all goodness comes that I can experience or put into action."

When Else told him she was beginning an affair, he had believed that all her asceticism and envy and negation would disappear in the richness of affirmative living. Then he had a premonition, an icy thought in the night, of who this lover might be. And in fact it was the man who "had seemed to me annoying and obtrusive by his mere presence in the room." Else had rebelled against nobility and aristocracy and *Distanz*—"this refined proud soul who had been Beloved and Sister to me." She must have done this out of hatred, out of jealousy, in revenge for his love of Frieda. "To think that one could have to *choose* between the highest commandment of 'noblesse oblige' and a woman who seemed to personify just *this* commandment in her every movement." Else had entered *his* world in a gay celebration of love, but she was leaving it for a world where he would be a foreigner—for a "person for whom everything valuable to me is unknown and incomprehensible."

In this betrayal, Else had found a way to make him doubt the power of eroticism itself. These were poisoned weapons indeed, and they struck at Frieda too. She said later that the religious approach to sex had been "my feeble contribution" to *Lady Chatterley's Lover*, and between her and Otto, as between her and Lawrence, the faith remained secure, despite Else's attack. Otto told her, in words which Lawrence was to echo later: ". . . you yourself probably have no idea what a genius you are, what wonderful strength and warmth flow so elementally from everything you have breathed something of your life into—it's as though the warmth of your body rushes into me from your letter, so sweet and forceful, like a wave of blissful, liberating sensuality."

If Otto generously credited Frieda with having liberated him, he knew nonetheless that in their relationship it was he who was above all the liberator. "Frieda, it's worth the fight freeing yourself—the world is wide and deep and wonderful in its rejuvenation—especially today, Frieda, especially for *you*—the world rewards a trusting love—what are a thousand 'good people' and all their being and doing against one who gives his innermost becoming to the unknown that is approaching, And *you* and *I* love each other in this secret and passionate love, carried away in this heavy, passionate spring ecstasy of people born too soon.—Come, Frieda, come to me—I love you as I love this time and the signs of the future." Their love was remarkably ideological. They loved each other's identities, and each embraced an idea in the other.

How often they met, and over how long a period, cannot be established, as I said. But they at least laid plans to meet in Amsterdam, at a conference there one summer. Frieda wrote to Else that she and Otto, Edgar Jaffe and a friend of Frieda's named Madge would meet there. She had told Weekley that she was going to meet Edgar and Else. And there are references later in Otto's letters to the night they spent together on the crossing between Amsterdam and England. Presumably then they attended that conference together; and in that case it was probably either the conference of neuropsychiatry, of September 1907, where Gross defended Freud's theory of hysteria against the orthodox interpretations, or the international anarchists' conference of 1907, at which Emma Goldman was one of the American delegates. The anarchists were of course the party most favorable to a matriarchal revolution.

Otto wanted Frieda to run away from her husband, taking her children; to establish a masterless home for them. And there was a moment, though we don't know just what year, when she was on the point of doing so. We know that because of an agitated letter to her, pleading that she shouldn't. It is an unsigned fragment, but it comes from Heidelberg, and has been identified by a family member as written by Else. "You have to see the tremendous shadows around the light—can't you see that he's almost destroyed Frieda's [his wife's] life? that he's not able to constrain himself ever for a quarter of an hour, whether it be for a person or for an objective value?" (That last phrase particularly evokes Else and the world of the Webers.) "As a 'lover' he's incomparable, but a person doesn't consist of that alone. God, it's useless to say anything. You are under that tremendous power of suggestion which emanates from him and which I myself have felt." The writer swears to Frieda that Ernest Weekley's love for her, with all its ineptitudes, is greater than Otto's. That of course is the crucial issue, which man's kind of love is true love, and by saying what she does, Else irrevocably repudiates the erotic movement.

Whatever the decisive arguments were for Frieda—she says in her *Memoirs* that she realized Otto "didn't have his feet on the ground of reality"—she did not leave Ernest Weekley for him. And we have a letter from her to Frieda Gross, written soon after she ran away with Lawrence, in which she declares herself sadly unresponsive to, "unmoved by," a letter she had just received from Otto. She goes on to say that she is eager to meet Ernst Frick again, the painter and disciple of Otto's, to whom the latter had consigned his wife as better for her erotic needs than himself. Frick was, like Lawrence, of the working class by birth, so that the two Friedas had both made love-matches which crossed class boundaries. The two men also were alike in that both lived more or less by Otto Gross's ideas, although in a less risky way than Gross himself. Frieda says in this letter that she and Lawrence have planned a book on which Frick could collaborate with Lawrence.

But although Frieda found herself "unmoved" by Gross's last letters, she kept them, and although she found herself increasingly estranged from their author, she cherished the identity they had given her. She was clearly ready for Lawrence—ready for some man able to recognize that identity, to respond to all its ideological reverberations, and to risk everything on it.

It is appropriate that Otto's affair with Frieda should have had these triumphant consequences, even if the triumphs were in other men's lives. It was, as the letters show, a triumph of the erotic movement. "Du bist Erotik" was a major ideological statement, with behind it a belief in eroticism as a philosophical and metaphysical value, as, above all, a life-creating value. This is the crux of an ideological revolution that seems to have occurred all over Europe between 1890 and 1910, and to have been the major hope of the resistance to patriarchal civilization. Heretofore eroticism had been a fact of nature, to be treated realistically in art and philosophy; or a source primarily of idyll and comedy, not to be taken seriously; or, at its zenith in the nineteenth century, as a source of tragedy, a force intimately connected with death and evil. This is how we see it in *Madame Bovary*, in *Anna Karenina*, and in *Tristan und Isolde*.

Now suddenly eroticism became a force for life and the source of all values. The values of those earlier treatments of love in the tragic mode of death were simply reversed. Thus in 1895 Mabel Ganson (later Mabel Dodge) went to see the play *Iris* in Buffalo and was deeply moved by the tragic fate of the fallen woman, but resolved that, as for *her*, she would never let society either cheat her of fulfillment in love or punish her for taking it illicitly. She didn't see why those had to be the two alternatives.

We may imagine similar moments about that time, when they were all about sixteen, in the lives of Frieda von Richthofen, Alma Schindler, Isadora Duncan—all reacting that way, though secretly, against the tragic erotic art of their times. I will go into this in more detail in Chapter 3. Here let me note only the credal significance of "Du bist Erotik."

The creed had its headquarters in Schwabing, and in 1907, according to Marianne Weber, it reached Heidelberg, arriving there from Munich in the form—though she does not say this—of Gross's conversion of Else Jaffe. Marianne Weber describes this transformation by saying that a new life-style appeared on the horizon of Heidelberg, an anticonventional life-style, hitherto known only in the artist circles of Munich. The Webers—she refers thus to her husband and herself—now met antibourgeois types, servants of Eros, in rebellion against marriage. "Innumerable confrontations took place with the supporters of the 'psychiatric ethic.'" The principal of these was in fact that with Otto Gross, who came to stay with the Jaffes in the spring of 1907 and who converted Edgar to his "faith." Frieda Gross had given birth to a son, Peter, and Else was pregnant with a child by Otto, also to be born in 1907 and also to be called Peter. Both mothers remained devoted to each other, and (later) to the two half-brothers. Frieda sent messages to "You beloved pair" to Heidelberg, when Otto was there with Else. (She was far from equally generous in her attitude to Frieda Weekley, but then she *loved* Else, and she was giving her something.) This was the *Welt Frühling* Otto had spoken of, the triumph of the erotic movement.

Max Weber began to read Freud, to meet the challenge. Both Webers, Marianne says, sympathized with those unhappy in marriage. "In order not to be torn apart by self-reproach, those trapped by fate took over certain ideas of the disciple of Freud, which turned upside down all hitherto received attitudes. However confused all this seemed to the companions [the Webers], they could not turn away in anger. The individuals concerned were too noble beings for that, and too lovable." She was thinking primarily of Else Jaffe. But Else was never easy with eroticism. She wrote to Frieda Gross after the event, "Otto was right to say that I was not made for erotic emancipation." It is clear in his letters that he always felt unsure of her, and in fact quite soon after his stay in Heidelberg she evidently wrote him that she had decided to take up a relationship with a doctor whom she was attracted to. We know very little about this man, and although both the Grosses regarded him as Otto's enemy, this seems to have been because of his temperament, which Otto found "plebeian" and "ignoble." Edgar was on Otto's side in the matter, and even Else, in the sketch of her life, speaks of her "shameful" obsession with this man, and wonders if it arose because he reminded her of her father. Her feeling for him seems to have been quite different in character from what bound her to Otto and to Max, because it was devoid of all relation to the man's *mind*. In all her other relationships the man's achievements, his *Leistungen*, were of first importance to her. In the sketch of her life, she names disappointment in her husband's *Leistungen* as the major emotion of her first years of marriage.

One may also conjecture a motive of self-mortification, or mortification of eroticism and of Otto, in her choice of lover. It is at least striking that again when she became the object of Max Weber's passion, she turned away from him (with ethically noble justification, of course) toward the one man in the world he wanted to deny her—his brother Alfred. This is surely a significant coincidence. And finally one may conjecture—again following a suggestion of Otto's—that she was jealous of her sister Frieda and her success with Otto. The latter praises her extravagantly in one letter for having let him love Frieda, but it is clear that he distrusts the generosity he acclaims.

Weber had been privy, via Marianne, to both sisters' affairs with Gross, and had strongly disapproved. It seems likely that his feelings for Else were already more than friendly. In any case, Gross sent an essay defending the freedom of women against the constraints of patriarchy to Weber's *Archiv* in 1907. Weber rejected it roughly, in a long letter addressed to Edgar Jaffe but sent to Else as an obvious but covert repudiation of Gross as a whole and a pleading with her to reject him also. In this letter Weber distinguishes Gross's work from Freud's, which he finds acceptable, because it is "scientific" and not "prophetic." He has no respect for would-be scientific ideas which are not value-free and do not satisfy the demands of reasonableness and objectivity. He identifies Gross with Nietzsche and the principle of "aristocracy"—though he invidiously insists on the "bourgeois" character, the cowardly self-coddling, of the moral philosophy which Gross allies with that principle. Thus he and Gross identified each other as representatives of "aristocracy" and "democracy" respectively, while Weber claimed to speak for knowledge and Gross for life. Weber then hastens courteously to distinguish the doctrine from the person. "I can recognize, in your accounts of him, the nobility of his nature, which certainly belongs among the most attractive that can be met with today. But how much purer the nobility of his personal charisma would seem, and that unworldliness of love before which I bow profoundly, if it were not distorted by . . ." and the attack goes on.

It seems likely that Else Jaffe had induced Gross to send the article to the *Archiv*; and that she had proposed to Weber a meeting with Gross, for in this letter he elaborately declines such a meeting. Her motives, besides the obvious one of bringing into confrontation these two major figures in her life, may have been the hope that Gross—so brilliant a psychoanalyst—might release Weber from his crippling neurosis. (Weber's letter also directs a good deal of sarcasm, perhaps defensively, against the idea of his lying for months on Freud's couch, remembering infantile misdemeanors.) But with Weber's repudiation of all Gross stood for, she was forced to choose between the two men, and there was obviously no choice for her but Weber. At least, it seems now as if it had to have been him.

At some time in the next year or two she wrote Otto a letter of repudiation and farewell which it may be worth quoting in full. It is very characteristic of her voice, also in that she is here using Max Weber's vocabulary—the idea of the "Prophetic" type was a part of his religious sociology.

> DEAR OTTO,
> I will at least not give you ground for any justified complaint that we never once answered your letters. Of course you won't hear anything from me which will put an end to your condition of not knowing everything, inside and out, for I can only write as a spectator of the situation—about Frieda I can say absolutely nothing. That she herself must do. You know for yourself how hard it is for another person to keep his own feelings clear from hers. So you must take nothing I write as coming from her indirectly—it was because you might do so that up to now I have not written.

But you are quite wrong if you think I so much *want* to find you inconsistent. I only believe that life has not allowed us to live without making compromises. I will however grant you that I at first thought someone must have forced you to give up your relationship to Regina Ullmann*—now I see the conflict differently—that relationship, and your (as it must seem to those of us outside it) ruthlessness toward Frieda, are only symptoms of a development deeply rooted in your nature.

Frieda was quite right when she said to me in the summer "Don't you see that Otto is the Prophet, of whom it must be said, He who is not for me is against me."

Now the Prophet, Otto, burnt more or less all other men in his fire, and took from them the capacity to love a person, an individuated individual, according to his essence. That is an old old story—and that other prophet said of his brothers, "I have no brothers—you (the disciples) are my brothers!" There are for you now—something of this was always there —*only* followers of your teaching, no longer a particular wife, loved according to her *own* essential self. It can scarcely be any other way. Now of course one can imagine a wife giving up all personal needs in love and being equally inflamed by the holy fire, making every sacrifice in order to stay by him in whose mission she completely believes. But if she can't *completely* believe, Otto?

If she can't completely believe, she could perhaps stay with the *man,* giving him her own kind of love—but would the Prophet tolerate that, to wrestle continually with her for her soul, without disintegrating himself in the struggle?

That is the way I see the situation—I don't want dogmatically to declare that you love Frieda less than you used to—though that, as measured by the usual standards, is scarcely to be doubted. The quality of the feeling has anyway changed. (You never give a thought to your little Peter any longer.)

One thing, however, I must say. It also seems quite pointless to make any sacrifice to help you in your cause, because you are destroying your capacity to achieve anything by your senseless attacks on your own health. We cannot know how much of what seems to us indiscriminateness in your ideas, and an entire lack of nuance, and an incapacity to distinguish one individual from another, finally derives from morphine. How the

---

* When Regina Ullmann told Otto Gross that she was pregnant by him, he apparently dropped all connection with her. He seems to have assented, passively, to his father's refusing her the financial support to which she was legally entitled. (Otto himself had no money, and his father sent him out of the country, on yet another cure, to escape the legal obligation.) She even formed the impression that he was encouraging her to kill herself, by leaving poison within her reach. This was a major occasion for Frau Jaffe, who had befriended Regina Ullmann, to decide that Otto Gross was pathologically irresponsible.

external aspects of social life are made difficult by that, you already know.

I am sad, Otto, when I think of you—you are going further and further away, it seems to me, and even the hope of being with you as a friend every now and then grows so small when I think of all you are asking an assent to. And over all that has been life itself settles and kills it quite dead—isn't that terrible?

YOUR ELSE

This letter is not without dignity, or point: According to the testimony of several witnesses, Gross did indeed exert a semi-religious authority over his followers in Munich and Ascona, and that authority was exerted in defiance of major moral values. Nevertheless, his reply is clearly superior in both rhetoric and logic, and it is worth quoting to a certain extent, both because it demonstrates the quality of his mind and because this is the only example we have of a completed exchange between two of our principals. In the passages I have omitted, he more than once cleverly seizes on a point of Else's and turns it against her.

MY ELSE,

It makes me extremely sad to have to realize that you live in this belief, for which you find such gloomy words—that my image in your mind has little by little so transformed itself—Else, that is just not me! Else, just look directly at me—I am not, for God's sake, wearing that gray and misty mantle. It would be far too heavy a load for me—and for a long time I have avoided it. I know I have been through a stage of development which has "verged" pretty much on a kind of Prophecy—and precisely this was, by its essentially alien feeling, perhaps the strongest impression it left on me, to feel that I myself finally needed to be reformed. I realized in myself that every tendency to prophecy is an expression of self-falsification, when one substitutes for oneself, by an illusion, the truth which one knows in principle to be beneficent and powerful. From that conflict I have freed myself, and so am now much further from Prophecy than ever before. Else, I have nothing else to "'announce" except always this one thing—that only through one's consciousness of one's own development does the individuality really free itself. In that way is fulfilled in the individual case what I in my vocation have to do: to free the essential personal style of the individual from all that is alien, destructive, contradictory.—Else, the empowering force, the passion behind this activity can only be joy in individuals, joy in the beauty which belongs to each self-sealed personality. To love this vocation in particular means to love every individuality according to its selfhood. . . . I *was* on such a path—in *Holland*—*there* I made effects with the fatal fanaticism and the fatal gestures of the Prophet—my only success by suggestion*—and that was *possible* because I was *there* so indescribably lonely, so misunderstood, so full of disgust and scorn. . . . Else it is so hard for me—and so unjust—when you write "You go further and further away." . . . I know what binds *me* to people, it is precisely their personality—that is that deepest and essential and unchangeable individuality, which can never be named in words, which can never be analyzed in concepts—the rhythm that moves in a human life, in every least movement of the body and every involuntary expression of fleeting feeling, the indestructible essence that cannot change itself. . . . One person's feeling for another can only *change* itself when the first mistakes the deepest and most abiding in the second. . . . I will from now on accept no assent and no faith in me—but *only* the faith that jusifies so much freedom as is necessary for the development of individuality and insight into one's own individuality. . . . Else, see me as *him,* as the man you once saw me as— I am the same—do not let that which has been die, Else.

YOUR OTTO

In later years, Else looked back to Otto regretfully. He was, she said to Frieda Gross, the only one who "could lift this heavy weight of sadness off my soul"; and when she began to move toward her relationship with Max Weber she—defensively—insisted on her many disagreements with him and wished for a healthy Otto and for *his* kind of ideology. "We shall only little by little realize what was lost with him. And you had him for years. You may well say 'He was worth the trouble he caused.' I often envy you him." And it is notable that she had a special feeling for Peter, Otto's child, among her own family, and that she collected around her other children of his— Peter Gross and Camilla Ullmann, both of whom spent a lot of time with the Jaffes. She felt a special grief, and even guilt, when Peter Jaffe died in 1915. But it is clear that she never repented of her repudiation of him, and always knew that his way and hers were incompatible. She would have had to make herself over completely to have "gone with" Gross.

Frieda Weekley was equally predetermined to choose Gross and Schwabing. But she did not commit herself to them, finally; and the man she did choose was more "reliable," less extreme, and less dangerous to her. (When she introduced Lawrence to her sisters, they approved him as "trustworthy," and they must have been comparing him implicitly with Gross.) Lawrence believed in marriage and the home, which Schwabing denied. He was no revolutionary. But he redefined marriage and home in terms of the eroticism

---

* He is referring to the Psychoanalytic Congress at Amsterdam, at which he spoke as a disciple of Freud.

of the cosmic circle. Although Frieda often rebelled against marriage, she preferred to live with a man who believed in it.

Frieda did *not* leave Weekley for Gross. She knew, she says, that Otto did not "have his feet on the ground of reality." An important trait in her character was a timidity in the face of the outside world. She too was no revolutionary. This trait is emphasized in Lawrence's portraits of both Anna and Ursula Brangwen—and of Harriet Somers and Kate Leslie. The Lawrences were radicals, but radicals of the world of Woman, who wanted to separate themselves from the world of men rather than to take it over. They harnessed the new forces of eroticism to the old forms of domesticity, and in this sense they were very conservative radicals. In this sense, too, they betrayed the heritage of Otto Gross.

The only time Lawrence mentions Otto Gross is in *Twilight in Italy*, which is in many ways the most unguarded and revealing of his books. And even there the allusion is covert. In 1913, walking alone through Switzerland toward Italy, he had tea with two old ladies and told them he was Austrian. "I said I was from Graz; that my father was a doctor in Graz, and that I was walking for my pleasure through the countries of Europe. I said this because I knew a doctor from Graz who was always wandering about, and because I did not want to be myself, an Englishman, to these two old ladies. I wanted to be something else." As is usual in fantasy, the elements in Otto's identity have been jumbled, but they are all there—Graz, a doctor, a father, always wandering—and the elements in Lawrence's relation to him are there too—"I did not want to be myself," "I wanted to be something else," perhaps even "I did not want to be an Englishman."

Just before this passage, Lawrence described meeting some anarchists who were living together in Switzerland. One of them explained their ideas to him and looked to him for approval. "But I did not want him to go on: I did not want to answer. I could feel a new spirit in him, something strange and pure and slightly frightening. He wanted something which was beyond me. And my soul was somewhere in tears, crying helplessly like an infant in the night. I could not respond: I could not answer. He seemed to look at me, me, an Englishman, an educated man, for corroboration. But I could not corroborate him. I knew the purity and new struggling towards birth of a true star-like spirit. But I could not confirm him in his utterance: my soul could not respond. I did not believe in the perfectibility of man. I did not believe in infinite harmony among men. And this was his star, this belief."

It is a curious passage, partly because Lawrence does not, anywhere else, allow himself to be seen in this posture, guiltily passive before another man's struggling. He says that he could not afterward read the newspaper they gave him, or even think about them. ". . . For some reason, my mind stopped like clockwork if I wanted to think of them and of what their lives would be, their future. . . . Even now I cannot really consider them in thought. I shrink involuntarily away. I do not know why this is."

I suggest that it was because, at that time in Switzerland, a true starlike spirit, Otto Gross, was teaching and practicing anarchism, was breaking the law in dangerous ways and suffering the retribution of society—was arrested and confined as insane soon after Lawrence reached Lerici and Frieda. I suggest that Lawrence saw himself as a compromiser, a writer, society's enter-tainer, Frieda's safe option.

In fact, Frieda had told Lawrence, when they ran away together, that he was another Otto and another Ernst Frick. She wrote this also to Frieda Gross, who told Else she thought it an odd moment for anyone else to imitate *her* fate and to model a lover on *those* examples. For in 1912, when Frieda and Lawrence arrived in Germany, Frick was under arrest in Swit-zerland on charges of anarchist conspiracy. Frieda Weekley wrote to ask if she could come to the trial, but Frieda Gross said no. Frick was discharged and returned home, only to be rearrested because other prisoners testified to his having carried a bomb. One can be certain that these events, as well as Otto's persecution by police and doctors (Frieda wrote to Munich to warn him not to cross the Swiss border, where he would certainly be arrested) and the lawsuits brought against Frieda and Frick by Hanns Gross, were all retailed by Frieda Weekley to Lawrence in those first weeks of their elope-ment.

Frieda's letters to Otto Gross have nearly all disappeared, but we do have one or two. We find her avowing love for "you-and-your-teaching," but sometimes reproaching him with not living up to it, with not being spon-taneous enough, with idealizing her. Indeed, his mind was remarkably ab-stract, as he himself acknowledged. Even to close friends he described his quarrels with Hanns Gross as Father-Son conflicts; and he tells Frieda that her sister is having an affair with a man who represents the democratic principle without ever mentioning his name.

In these same letters Frieda expresses her anger with Else for not being enthusiastic in her understanding of Gross, for not thanking God every hour for bringing "you and your teaching" across her path. "Does she then not understand the height, the beauty of the splendid newness? I am completely overawed by it sometimes—'where you stand is sacred ground—take off your shoes'—or something like that." She complains more than once that Else doesn't love her. "Is it so hard to like me—I who wish everyone well from the bottom of my heart?" And on another occasion, "We mustn't lose courage with Else, dearest. We must win." It was a very pedagogical and salvationist enterprise, their eroticism. They were going to *save* Else, which must have been hard for Else to tolerate.

But their eroticism was also, of course, what we ordinarily mean by erotic. Frieda tells Otto about her friend Madge, and her fiancé, and how she, Frieda, has liberated them both. "When you come you have to *love* her and she you. She is really my creation and I'm very fond of her and she'd do anything for me. . . ." And the fiancé, "I have won over to your way, too. They should be grateful to you, those two, and I shall, I hope, experience something nice with him." It seems clear that Frieda was creating a little Munich-Schwabing of sexual liberation around her in Nottingham. There are intimations of that, we remember, in Ursula Brangwen. It is neatly symbolic that the patron saint of the Schwabing church was Saint Ursula.

Gross's Ideas

Because of his disappointment with Freud, Gross needed ideas that would release him more completely from paternal authority. He seems to have found them partly in Nietzscheanism and partly in Anarchism, both of which were living forces in Schwabing. The first was developed mostly by the members of *die kosmische Runde*, the Cosmic Circle, which we shall describe soon; the second by Erich Mühsam, Gustav Landauer, and others of Gross's friends in the *Gruppe Tat*, or the *Aktion Gruppe*. Oscar Maria Graf describes how he met Franz Jung and Mühsam in that group around 1912 (Gross had left Munich for Ascona by then) and how they read together Landauer's *Call to Socialism* and the works of Nietzsche, Peter Kropotkin, and Max Stirner. These people were closer to political action than were the members of the Cosmic Circle, a group profoundly influenced by Bachofen and by "cosmic" ideas in general. But Gross was a revolutionary, an anarchist revolutionary, and this differentiates him from *die kosmische Runde*, as well as from Lawrence. Ludwig Klages, the member of the Cosmic Circle with whom Gross was most closely associated, had much in common with Lawrence as an ideologist. Gross was more like Landauer and Mühsam, both of whom played prominent parts in the 1918 revolution in Munich and the revolutionary government that ruled Bavaria briefly thereafter. Kurt Eisner, the Prime Minister of that government, was a friend of theirs, and he and Landauer, along with many others of their friends, were killed in the service of that revolution. Gross was in Vienna then, and although he was involved in the revolution there, he did not figure in it as prominently as he would have if he had been living in Munich. In the last year of his life, his writings were predominantly political, explicitly Communist, and appeared in such magazines as *Sowjet* and *Die Raete-Zeitung*. His Communism, however was notably anarchistic.

Gross quotes both Kropotkin and Stirner, and it seems clear that the latter in particular influenced him profoundly. Stirner envisioned the ideal society as a union of egotists in which each person would assert his own individuality forcefully. He saw the true individual as necessarily the enemy of the state, and the concept of "rights" as a fraud invented by the state. He believed not in revolution but in rebellion—individuals rising together, but as individuals, not in a mass: "Revolution aims at new arrangements; rebellion leads us no longer to let ourselves be arranged, but to arrange ourselves, and sets no glittering hopes on 'institutions.' It is not a fight against the established, since, if it prospers, the established collapses of itself. . . . Revolution commands one to make arrangements; rebellion demands that one *rise or exalt oneself*." Stirner was anti-intellectualist and antimoralist, and his writing sounds very like the voice of the later Otto Gross.

Within the anarchist movement, Gross represented that group which put most stress on sexual liberation, and on an orgiastic sexuality as the only kind that answered to anarchist principles. This led him to public conflicts with, for instance, Gustav Landauer, who was an idealist in a more ordinary sense, and who opposed psychoanalysis on the grounds that it typically led to such emancipations as homosexuality. Landauer's anarchism was more a matter of practical politics, of some buildable ideal state, and he could not accord so much primacy to personal emotional freedom. Gross's matriarchal revolution would have led to no state at all. All compulsions to work and to sublimate one's energies would be removed.

Gross had his most intense following among practitioners of the lively as well as the fine arts, but his influence was disintegrative, judged by almost every social criterion. According to more than one witness, he spread the use of narcotics among his followers, broke down their sexual and social inhibitions, freed them from their scruples of conscience, and even enabled them to kill themselves. For many years he had a profound and widespread influence on men, and even more on women, in Germany's anarcho-artistic Bohemia, and in 1919 he tried to make Communism *their* political option.

As early as 1902, Gross's friend Erich Mühsam, had lived in Friedrichshagen, an anarchist community on the outskirts of Berlin, which was also inhabited at the time by John Henry MacKay, an advocate of Stirner's brand of egotistic anarchism. Sometime in the first decade of the century Mühsam discovered Ascona, a small town on the eastern shore of the Lago Maggiore in Switzerland and the site of other newly established anarchist communities. It was to Ascona that Gross moved when he left Munich in 1910. It was by then a favorite resort for Schwabingites and for free spirits everywhere. Isadora Duncan came there in 1913 and Kropotkin at that time was spending his winters there and in nearby Locarno. Those two personalities would have been perfectly suited to play major roles in the anarchist school which Gross was then trying to establish in Ascona in order to teach students to recognize the patterns of patriarchal authoritarianism and the resultant neurotic complexes, which permeated Western civilization. When Max Brod wrote his anti-anarchist novel, *Das Grosse Wagnis*, in the disillusionment of 1919, he described an anarchist society gone wrong. He called the society Liberia and its dictator Dr. Askonas.

Kropotkin had been first invited to Ascona by Dr. Raphael Friedeberg, a Berlin anarchist and a former member of the Reichstag. In Ascona he treated his patients free of charge and housed anarchist guests, some of whom began to steal from the regular residents. Leonhard Frank's novel about Gross describes some of the thefts that were epidemic among his followers there, and other people report that they were engaged in, for instance, smuggling saccharine across the borders into Austria. Stirner in fact had celebrated crime, declaring that "A revolution never succeeds, but a mighty, reckless, shameless, conscienceless, proud *crime*, does it not rumble in distant thunders, and do you not see how the sky grows presciently silent and gloomy?" There were many who lived by crime in the individualist faction of the anarchist party then—the people who published *L'Anarchie* from 1905 to 1914. Marius Jacob and his gang operated successfully during the first five years of the century, and the Bonnot gang of neo-Stirnerites—most of whom died in gun battles with the police—began large-scale banditry in 1913.

Curt Riess says that Gross rented an empty barn and held orgies, narcotic as well as sexual, which roused general social indignation. They were, of course, sessions of purposeful self-exploration, in which people broke down their own and each other's inhibitions deliberately. The cult of Astarte, destroyed by the jealous prophets of Judea, was to be built up again. Franz Jung reports that it was the enmity of orthodox Freudians which roused the civil authorities against Gross. In any case, there was serious trouble when his mistress, Sophie Benz, killed herself with poison which he had given her.

It needs no effort to imagine how Hanns Gross felt about all this. As early as 1909, and possibly even three years earlier, Hanns was exerting pressure to get his son, whom he was supporting financially, to leave Munich, prepare for work in a university, and commit himself to medical care. Early in 1906 Otto had given poison to Fräulien Lotte Chatemmer in Ascona, and she killed herself. He did so to save her from employing some more painful means of death, and only after she had refused to come to him in Graz for psychiatric treatment. So much is certain, from his own account. Almost as certain is the fact that he would have been prosecuted were it not for the influence of his father, who forced him to undergo psychiatric treatment himself. He was diagnosed by Dr. Stekel as severely neurotic, and by C. G. Jung, later, as schizophrenic. (We learn of these diagnoses from Kurt Eissler's *Talent and Genius*, where Dr. Eissler draws a parallel between Otto Gross and Victor Tausk as fallers away from the Freudian movement—a parallel worth keeping in mind. Gross and Tausk were two of Freud's most brilliant disciples, and their twin tragic fates—Tausk killed himself in 1919—mark the tragic development of that movement.) Shortly thereafter Otto left Graz for Munich, where he began the relationships with the two von Richthofen sisters.

In Munich he was officially Assistent in Kraepelin's Psychiatric Clinic, which had been opened at the end of 1904. Emil Kraepelin was then the leading psychiatrist in the world, for in 1899 he had formulated the distinction between the two main groups of mental diseases, the Dementia Praecox group and the cyclothymic or manic-depressive group, a distinction which lies at the basis of all subsequent psychiatry. His clinic was a large and handsome building, treating between fifteen hundred and two thousand patients a year by the most modern scientific methods. It was also a teaching institution, specializing in clinical psychiatry, and a research institution, equipped for chemical and anatomical research using such advanced techniques as microphotography. But one modern development which Kraepelin was *not* in sympathy with was psychoanalysis, and he prevented its entry into his clinic "with energy and sarcasm," we are told. There was not even any provision for doctors to have private conversations with their patients.

Kraepelin was himself an embodiment of health, physical and moral, and a crusading anti-alcoholic and even anti-erotic. We are told that he *"favored"* sexual intercourse for the purposes of reproduction or of lessening appetitive tension, which is a good example of the attitude toward sex which the erotic movement attacked—the patriarchal attitude. He was notably devoid of religious or philosophical feeling, although he was devoted to nature and not above writing verses on that subject. "Kraepelin war Verstandes—und Willensmensch"—he was a creature of intellect and will-power, we are told. Freud described him as "a coarse fellow," and Ernest Jones says that he had no sensitiveness to or sympathetic insight into his patients.

Jones also tells of once having to use force to prevent Otto Gross from taking Kraepelin into court to demonstrate his ignorance of psychoanalysis, which Gross insisted was a crime in a man in his position. One powerful constituent of Gross's anger, we can assume, was the similarity between Kraepelin and Hanns Gross. Both were major manifestations of the patriarchal mode in the intellectual Germany of that time—the mode of which the greatest, though most self-divided, representative was Max Weber.

In 1908 Gross was again involved in public outcry in the Elisabeth Lang case. This nineteen-year-old daughter of a Munich sculptor had been made mentally ill by the oppression of her family, principally her father. Otto had treated her successfully, unbeknownst to her family, but she was removed from his charge and finally committed to Tübingen Psychiatric Clinic, where, he claimed, no one would be able to understand her problems because no one there had Freudian training. Her problems, he insisted, all derived from her family's oppression of her strong individuality. By means of letters to the press, he was able to effect her release.

In early March 1911 his mistress Sophie Benz committed suicide. He was responsible for her act in the sense—this is his own account—that he had refused to commit her to an institution even though he knew her mental condition to be suicidal. The two euthanasia cases involving Lotte Chatemmer and Sophie Benz were the grounds for the Austrian authorities to judge him dangerous to society in 1913; and one can guess that it was Sophie's death that forced him to leave Switzerland for Berlin at the beginning of 1913. The tragic story of his affair with Sophie seems to have made a great impact on the imagination of the artistic Bohemia of Germany; Frieda Gross says, in a letter to Else immediately after, that all Schwabing is buzzing with the story, and that the rumor has already been spread that she too has killed herself. Franz Jung described it in his barely fictionalized *Sophie* of 1915, and Leonhard Frank in his *Links, wo das Herz ist* of 1952. This affair also undoubtedly became a major part of Otto's life after he had been rejected by Frieda Weekley. And it led indirectly to his arrest. In 1913, Hans Gross had Otto arrested by the Berlin police as a dangerous psychopath (he had a certificate to that effect from C. G. Jung) and taken to Austria to be confined in an insane asylum.

Hanns had drawn up a will in 1912 which disinherited his son, on the grounds that he had long been mentally ill, and in no condition to be entrusted with money or valuables. The will describes the periods which Otto had spent in asylums and defines his mental confusion as manifesting itself in various derangements involving free love, anarchism, and the belief that it was his wife's right to have children by whomsoever she pleased. Hanns made his grandson Peter his sole heir, insisting that he was Otto's only child and implying the illegitimacy of the other three. Otto, he said, was a psychotic as well as an incurable drug addict, and he recommended that upon his own death, Otto should be taken into custody and confined in an asylum permanently.

As we have seen, Hanns changed his mind and decided that Otto's incarceration could not be postponed until his own death. In 1913 he took steps in that direction and accompanied them by a legal suit to have Frieda Gross deprived of her rights as a mother and wife. (She had become something of a propagandist for psychosexual freedom and had taken Ernst Frick to live with her.) Hanns Gross wanted Peter to be given to him and the other children to be denied the name of Gross. It was a classic case of patriarchal tyranny, the father attacking the son even in his sexual, marital, and paternal roles. It is a little paradoxical to find that it was Max Weber who exerted himself to defend the rights of the mother in that case—paradoxical that it should be he and not one of the believers in *Mutterrecht;* but only a little, because Weber was always the Brutus of patriarchy, the virtuous rebel.

The arrest of Otto Gross caused a considerable uproar—partly because he was seized in Berlin, by Prussian police, on Austrian orders. He now became a martyr as well as a prophet of the Father-Son struggle which was preoccupying so many and which figures in so much of the literary work of the Expressionists. There were articles in leading newspapers about the case, and special numbers of the little magazines, *Aktion, Revolution*, and *Kain.* In the special number of *Aktion*, Franz Jung dedicated a prose piece called "Morenga" to Otto Gross; its subject was the German colonial oppression of the Hereroes in Africa, and the parallel drawn between that situation and the one involving Otto and his father shows the ideological reverberations released by the arrest.

Jung later borrowed *Revolution*, a Munich magazine, from its editors for one edition and solicited contributions from a number of intellectuals supporting Otto and attacking Hanns. Blaise Cendrars described Otto as "un esprit des plus appréciés en France de l'Allemagne contemporaine." Ludwig Rubiner wrote that "We intellectuals, we sub-proletarians, are strong—the Professor in Graz is only anxious. . . . Our pamphlets are mightier than his alliances." And there was much play with Hann's criminal titles—"der bekannte Kriminalprofessor Hanns Gross in Graz." Franz Jung contributed a striking editorial in which he says:

> Hanns Gross is living the tragedy of the father whose genius is displaced
> by that of his son, and who becomes unproductive. Hanns Gross *has* to

work, out of the feeling that his existence is being denied, and by a man who, in contrast to Aschaffenburg [a contemporary psychiatrist], has a wonderful tenderness for youth which permeates everything, and gives everyone support. [Both men, Jung continues, have genius, and just for that reason the father must hate the son. But the son is psychically the stronger and has learned discipline from his father.] He refines the new ethic, the idea, the drive to the idea, he abhors compromise. He gives his father weapons. He will make no accommodation with normality, he turns against himself, he makes use of delirium, cocaine, opium. He destroys himself—as long as his father lives. The father, on the other hand, destroys himself by taking up these weapons. He hires as spies: detectives, landladies, porters, laundrymen, bakers, barbers, washerwomen. . . . He gorges himself on brutality, he sends his son to prison.

Hanns Gross is old. His life is fear. One must be fair.

We, who represent a considerable part of intellectual youth, want to be fair. We offer a reprieve. We are ready to intercede for Professor Hanns Gross. . . . But we will have Otto Gross back.

Jung sent a thousand copies of this number of *Revolution* to people in Graz and Vienna. The Akademische Verband für Literatur und Musik in Vienna printed ten thousand handbills with the message "Free Otto Gross" and the Vienna *Neue Freie Presse* came out against Hanns. As a result of all this pressure Otto was released, on the condition that he go into analysis with Stekel. But in a letter to *Zukunft*, February 28, 1914, Otto wrote that the *Wiener Amtsblatt* had announced that as of January 9 he was in custody of his father. He wrote begging readers to ensure that his wife Frieda be given absolute power over his children. Frieda had always feared that Hanns would do something like this, he said. Help her. These children have been born and bred in freedom. Think of their fate if they fall into my father's hands.

During the months leading up to his arrest, Gross was writing a new ethic, the manuscript of which apparently was destroyed when he was taken into custody. But a few pages from it, and some other essays, were published in *Aktion*. He also announced a forthcoming monthly, *Sigyn*, which he and Franz Jung would edit, starting in 1914, dedicated to the principles of psychoanalysis but moving out from individual problems to cultural and economic disorders, spreading the idea of the new ethic as a preliminary to realizing it in social fact.

Some of this work was in fact done in a series of publications entitled *Die Freie Strasse*, edited during and after the war by Jung and Richard Oehring. Gross contributed one number of the series, the eighth number which was dedicated to the Dadaist movement. Indeed, Jung was to become an organizer of Berlin Dada, which was more political than Zürich Dada, and through him Otto Gross supplied the movement with its ideology. Thus German Dada, including such artists as Georg Grosz, is in an important sense the intellectual heir of Otto Gross, as was, to some degree, the whole expressionist movement in Germany, particularly in those works which dealt with the revolt of sons against fathers and of wives against husbands.

In Gross's *Aktion* essays we read that the psychology of the unconscious is the philosophy of revolution. Psychoanalysis is called upon to make men capable of freedom, to create a ferment of revolt within the psyche against the dominant ego. The revaluation of all values, by which the coming time will be fulfilled, begins with Nietzsche's thought and Freud's techniques. We *can* know ourselves, and so a new ethic needs to be born, resting on the moral imperative to *really* know oneself and one's neighbors' selves. We shall then realize that what we are today is only a fragment of our full psychic potentiality. We are fragmented by conflicts which manifest themselves in our sexual lives. All of these conflicts derive from the impositions of the outside world on the individual—impositions introjected in childhood in the form of Authority. Weak characters achieve an adjustment, a seeming health, but the strong are torn apart and are in consequence regarded with horror as animals, or with awe as superior beings, or with pity as sick. Henceforth they must be recognized as the healthy ones, the front runners, the advance guard of humanity. (One may take it that he is thinking of people like Frieda Weekley.) No previous revolutions have succeeded because the revolutionaries carried Authority within their own psyches, and so the result of such revolutions was simply another patriarchal state. It is the family that is the source of Authority. Society's original sin is the enslavement of women. Today's revolutionary fights against oppression in its most elemental form, against the father and patriarchy. The coming revolution is the revolution for matriarchy.

Later Gross was to say that he made it his life work to show that as a direct effect of the existing institutions of authority, every man must be sick, and the significant man more so, in proportion to his significance. To recognize this is to demand revolution as a human hygienic necessity, and thus to demand the inward liberation of the revolutionary individual as clinical preparation. This ethic counts the claim to life of every individual as its basis and defines health as the full expansion of each person's inborn individual potentiality. Only the narrator of the Tower of Babel legend has understood humanity's psychosis—the fear that the attempt to build a tower to heaven will be punished with madness. (In a later article, in *Sowjet*, Gross identifies that tower with the true *Kultur*, which is yet to be created.)

Another essay, "The Action of the Community on the Individual," has a title that reminds one of Max Stirner, but it cites principally Nietzsche and calls Freud's work the direct continuation of Nietzsche's. The sexual effect of the individual's incorporation of the community into himself can be seen in hysterical women, who spend immense energy either in repressing sexuality or in giving it an unnatural, socially acceptable form. In men the equivalent to the sexual instinct is the aggressive, and the equivalent result of repression is pathological cowardice.

The state, Gross contends, is inherently homosexual; its hierarchical authority always lays men prone one beneath another. This secondary homosexuality, expressing the corruption of sex by power drives, is no better than marriage. Primary homosexuality, on the other hand, is an experience necessary for emotional and sexual health. To love erotically is not to feel identified with the other person, but with the third being, the relationship itself. Erotic love alone can finally overcome man's loneliness. Relationship understood as that third thing, worshipped as a supreme value, will allow the lover to combine an erotic union with an uncompromised drive to individuality. (Here Gross comes very close to Lawrence's teaching.)

After Gross's release from Troppau asylum in 1914 and his brief treatment by Stekel, he was sent, on the outbreak of war, to a children's hospital and then to a hospital for epidemic diseases in Vinkovci in the Carpathians. Apart from one or two medical publications issued from there, we hear little more of him—according to Franz Jung, his life style was comparatively conventional in those years—until he began to move in literary circles in Prague in 1917. He became the friend of Max Brod, Franz Werfel, Franz Kafka, and their friend Schreiber.

They had read Gross's essays in *Aktion*, which were for Kafka a major introduction to the theories of psychoanalysis. In 1917 Gross, together with Brod and Schreiber, planned a magazine to be called *Daimon;* it would attack cultural problems from a psychoanalytic point of view and put forward a new ethic. Kafka declared his readiness to join Gross in a battle against the world's fathers, though he was not as intimate with him as his friends were. We find in his writings from the 1920s references to Gross's theories.

But it was Franz Werfel who was most deeply impressed by and involved with Gross, both in Prague and later in Vienna. He seems to have identified Gross with the whole spirit of the revolution there in 1918. They saw a lot of each other while it was happening, but afterward, when Werfel reacted against the revolution and all radical politics, he reacted also against Gross. Gross was at his most hectic and strained in in those revolutionary months, his furthest from normal decency, both in his theories and in his life style.

It appears, from Werfel's novels and from Alma Mahler's memoirs, that she and Gross were in some sort of struggle for influence over Werfel in those days, and that, as in the last scene from *Faust*, she "saved him" from Otto. She records with disgust the dirt, disorder, and vice of the Franz Blei-Otto Gross circle in which she found Werfel. (It is interesting that Alma Mahler and Frieda Lawrence, the two great pagan goddesses of modern erotic art, were both in some sense hostile to, or turned away from, this major theorist of their erotic revolution. There was something essentially conservative—Demetrian—about both of them, and they recognized something Aphroditean in him. They carried away their lovers, both nervous little men, into protective custody, so that they could *produce*.)

After playing a part in the revolution in Vienna, Gross returned to Berlin. From there he sent the message to Frau Jaffe, asking if she would look after him if he came back to Munich. He was again writing, and his ideas were even more extremist than before. His friend Franz Jung became both a Communist and a leader of Berlin Dada, and one can understand how it was that Gross's ideas became—after his death, via Jung's mediation—an inspiration to the movement in its later phases. Club Dada in Berlin was founded in April 1918 by Jung, together with Richard Huelserbech, Raoul Haussmann, and "John Heartfield." *Die Freie Strasse*, a publication of which Gross was one of the founders, had devoted its eighth number to Dada. Now the group took over Gross's theory of the necessary opposition between the ego and the non-ego as the basis of its ideology and as a defense against the conservatism of Freudian psychology. Thus Surrealism as well as Expressionism can be thought of as artistic expressions of Gross's ideas.

In 1919 two essays by Gross appeared in *Die Erde*. One is an attack on parliamentarism in which Otto argues that a man may know whether he is a real revolutionary or a bourgeois by his answer to the question: "Do you endorse parliaments in *any* way?" The revolutionary psyche is in eternal conflict with democracy, because the latter is indissoluble from the belief in progress and the trust in the majority, who are allowed to take responsibility for every major decision. This state of affairs derives, Gross says, either from a wish that everything should remain as it is or from an unwillingness to assume responsibility. Revolution tries to bring a new idea to pass. It uses an elite to compel the masses to fight against the powerful ones of this world, the privileged of all kinds. Gross ends the essay with a quotation from the Book of Chronicles: "God said unto him: 'Thy son who comes after thee shall build my temple. Not thou shalt build my temple: because thou art a man of war.'"

The second of these essays begins with the myth of Cain, whose murder of Abel is the birth of revolutionary protest. Not hope, but dissatisfaction, is the only good thing left in a world without values. This shows behind Cain's deed, even though it welled up directly from the unconscious, Gross argues, taking a position very much like that of Max Stirner. Classical psychoanalysis depends on the status quo and will not disturb it; it justifies traditional unconsciousness by showing the "ugliness" of the "perverse" ideas in the unconscious. But by freeing the impulse to revolutionary protest we can release people from their present self-sabotage. Now that urban culture is fully developed, patriarchy and marriage (a peasant institution) are no longer justified. We are free, like men of primitive times, only at a higher level of culture. We must teach this freedom in schools; "we must teach absolutely uncompromisable opposition to every and each thing that today stands as authority, as institution, as power and morality, in the way of humanity's fulfilment."

Shortly after these essays appeared, Gross ran away from his friends, and was found too late to be saved. He died March 13, 1920, in a sanatorium in Berlin-Pankow. This was just about the time that Leopold Jessner directed his Expressionist production of *Wilhelm Tell* in Berlin. Jessner had just that year been put in charge of the official theater in Berlin and this was his first production. Its anti-militarist message, and the grotesque exaggerations of its theatrical style, provoked a riot in the theater. And in February 1920 the Expressionist film, "The Cabinet of Dr. Caligari," was released for public viewing, introducing a whole series of essays in film grotesque. Thus the spirit of Otto Gross was finding expression in German art, was gaining triumphant and public expression, at the moment of his physical death. The theme of the son's revolt against the fathers, which must always be associated with him, continued to preoccupy writers and can be said to have characterized German culture as a whole for the next decade. Among Gross's disciples in Munich, Leonhard Frank wrote a novel against fathers, and Karl Otten's friend, Walter Hasenclever, wrote the most famous of father-hate plays. I have seen it said that Hasenclever was a friend of Gross's, and certainly he visited Otten while the latter was very close to Gross. Inasmuch as Werfel also wrote anti-patriarchal fiction and drama, there was a striking conjunction of the Expressionist writers on this theme around the figure of Otto Gross. In the 1920s Arnold Bronnen's *Vatermord* succeeded to Hasenclever's *Der Sohn*, and the historical treatment of Frederick the Great's rebellion against his father was treated again and again. But Gross himself had died. And though in the realm of high culture the spirit of Schwabing was triumphing in Germany, the great days of Schwabing were over.

In these ideas, as in his fate, Otto Gross expressed Schwabing at its furthest extreme of attack on the patriarchal world. As Franz Jung put it, Gross's life unrolled like an exemplary drama before the group of artists and Bohemians who, in each of the major cities of Germany, responded to his every move, however dismissively in intention, however hostilely or treacherously in effect. He was Schwabing's culture-hero, as Weber was Heidelberg's. And he was its product as well as its hero. He represented that constituency because he grew up in it. And the part of Schwabing that had given him most was the group of men who called themselves the Cosmic Circle, *die kosmische Runde.*

Die Kosmische Runde

The Cosmic Circle was a center of ideas whose main members were Alfred Schuler, Ludwig Klages, Karl Wolfskehl, and, at times, Stefan George. These men met together in Schwabing between 1897 and 1903 to discuss a range of matters dealing with mythology, anthropology, and cultural history, out of which they developed a *Weltanschauung* in radical opposition to that of the patriarchal civilization of the West. They stood for life-values, for eroticism, for the value of myth and primitive cultures, for the superiority of instinct and intuition to the values of science, for the primacy of the female mode of being. The major outside impulse to the development of their ideas came from the Swiss scholar, J. J. Bachofen, and their ideas in turn influenced Otto Gross and ultimately D. H. Lawrence.

The best known name among them, Stefan George, was probably the least important in working out the ideas that concern us. Primarily a poet, in his hands the cosmic ideas became primarily aesthetic materials. The other members of the circle were—at least by comparison with George— anti-aesthetic, for they regarded their ideas primarily as world-changing forces. George's link with the group was at first mainly through Klages, whom he got to know in Schwabing in 1893 and whom he invited to contribute poems to *Blätter für die Kunst.* Later Wolfskehl became an enthusiastic admirer of George, and it was at Wolfskehl's house that George stayed on his visits to Munich. George's lack of fixed abode, as well as of occupation (made possible by his having a private income) was important to the image he cultivated of himself as one who lived in another dimension from the average; but it also symbolized his detachment from the Cosmic Circle, of all whom lived in Schwabing.

Wolfskehl, a Jew, was professor of German literature at the University of Munich and an enthusiastic student of myths, legends, runes, every trace of an earlier mode of culture. He was himself a rapturous poet and a Dionysiac personality, always in love, always ecstatic with enthusiasm. Klages was trained in chemistry but made his living as a graphologist and as a lecturer on character types and a theory of expression. As a young man he wrote poetry, but later he devoted himself to working out a system of philosophy which began from the ideas of the Cosmic Circle. Schuler is the hardest to define in ordinary social terms, for he did not work, wrote nothing to speak of, and pursued no subject of study. His nearest approach to a classifiable activity was the impromptu lectures he gave in people's houses on the life of ancient Rome. These evocations of the religious or sexual consciousness of the city were, of course, unsupported by evidence. In 1897 Schuler, the oldest of the group, was thirty-two; George was twenty-nine, Wolfskehl twenty-eight, and Klages twenty-five. These were their peak years of youthful vitality.

It is worth pausing to reflect on the seeming paradox that so many of the major figures of what I have called the erotic movement were not personally very erotic—or if they were, they were not lovers of women. Schuler and George were clearly homoerotic, Klages was a very stiffly masculine figure, Lawrence more a flirt than anything else. Wolfskehl and Gross were lovers of women but even so it would be easy to find a group of *opponents* of the erotic movement who were more active servants of Eros than this group as a whole. The explanation is that this movement was primarily *against* something, against patriarchal authority, industrialism, militarism, and the like. The service of Eros, and the service of Woman, were means to that end; one could be, one *had* to be, passionately committed to the end, but one did not have to be passionate about the means.

Ludwig Curtius describes both Ludwig Klages and Alfred Schuler as personalities. Klages was very handsome and eloquent—blond, blue-eyed, straight-featured—a speaker you could listen to for hours on end, with a beautiful voice. Schuler was short and thick, with a large head which was bald when he was still a young man and big bulging eyes. He could never have looked young, and was extremely attached to a pet cat. He wore a dark blue frock coat, closed to the throat like a priest, and in the rain he wore a dark cloak with a hood. He and Klages had first contacted Curtius after reading his essay on Goethe. Curtius found the two of them seated in a sacristy-like room, where Schuler immediately began to intone a prophesy, the burden of which was that Curtius belonged to the few initiates, whether he knew it or not, who are called to "see"—that is, to see through civilized and rational appearances to reality.

In sampling the Cosmic Circle's ideas, let us take Schuler first. Alfred Schuler was not a writer but a speaker, and the originality of his thought must for us now be partly just an allegation by Klages. But he did give some lectures during the war, about ancient Rome, at Klage's instigation, and these were partly taken down in note form; and these notes do yield some remarkable fragments of insight and eloquence about erotic matters and history. In them, Schuler insists that Adam and Eve together symbolize fallen man because they are two—because they are man split apart. In the healthy unfallen soul, male and female elements are mixed, he insists, echoing an argument that goes back to Plato's *Symposium*. But Schuler pushes this line of reasoning further than Plato, contending that sexual inverts are important and valuable members of society. In this he sounds like Otto Gross and the "wilder" Freudians and it is of interest that he quotes more than once from Wilhelm Fliess, the occultist inspirer of Freud.

It is for the purposes of evolution—for Schuler always an evil principle—that man has been made abnormally manly, woman abnormally womanly. This explains the false value attached to reproduction. Life is being poured outward, creating more and more, poorer and poorer beings, as the black dot, the I, is infinitely repeated, instead of becoming rich and dense. Life-values are concentrated in a few splendid individuals, Schuler argues, taking a line very much like Lawrence's. Man as Magus, purposeful and willful, the agent of evolution, is the embodiment of empty space; Christ, the "Spermatikos Logos der Stoa," is the figurehead of evolution.

Like Otto Gross, Schuler often used the myth of Babel and interpreted it to mean that a jealous God prevented men from building a tower to heaven. He also believed in city life as a positive value, as Gross did. Men can be enslaved only in the country, by means of agriculture, which ties them to the soil. The first great city was Troy, in the center of which was hidden Helena, who represented wisdom to be sure, but also eroticism, for she was the daughter of a god gone astray in the flesh. For Schuler, the story of Helen's being lured by the Trojans away from an earlier domestic life was a typical Greek lie. They just wanted to destroy the city and rape Helen themselves, being rationalist barbarians. The next great city was Alexandria, the home of the Gnostics, and some strains of thought in both Schuler and Gross are recognizably gnostic, for in these two men's thought the gnostic line coincides with the matriarchal. Gross made Cain one of his heroes, just as the early Gnostics did.

Again like Gross, Schuler hated the patriarchal society which he saw realized in republican Rome, the exemplum of virtuous patriarchy. His third great city was imperial Rome, but for the Rome of the Republic, where wife and child were totally in the power of the husband-father-master, where women could own nothing, and had no legal rights, he had nothing but contempt. His own period was late imperial Rome, which, precisely in its sexual decadence and sensual intensity, was the harbinger of a new world order. Petronius and Nero were figures in terms of whom he defined himself, and he was very keen on arranging Roman festivals, at which he sometimes appeared as Nero, sometimes in woman's costume, portraying Magna Mater herself. These festivities were the most solemn versions of the Schwabing carnival, and their orgiastic license was a religious rebellion against patriarchal virtue. Lawrence too was attracted to the idea that contemporary decadence signaled a new age, as we see in *The Sisters* and *Twilight in Italy*.

In the Epilogue I shall draw a parallel between Lawrence's and Klages's thought, which seems to me a very striking one. The table of male-female contrasts drawn up by Herman Daleski in *The Forked Flame* to explain Lawrence is very much like Klages's scheme, as reported by H. E. Schröder in *Klages: Die Jugend*. Here I shall just indicate some highlights.

Klages's masterwork, *Der Geist als Widersacher der Seele* (*The Mind The Soul's Enemy*), contains in its title the main proposition of the Lawrentian ethic and metaphysic. Soul and body are the two poles of natural life in man. Mind, which works by abstraction and logic, reifies and fixes the movements of that polarity, and so creates an artificial world of concepts, hostile to life, a system of meanings which destroys and distorts experience. The blood has much the same significance and the same importance for the *kosmische Runde* as it has for Lawrence. The *Blutleuchte*, central in Schuler's system, has much in common with Lawrence's "blood-knowledge," though in Schuler's use the idea refers primarily to the special insights of special people (and so would apply better to the "prophecies" of Hermione Roddice than to Ursula Brangwen's intuitions). In Lawrence's use, in contrast, the primary referent is normal nonrational knowledge, though of course he most often used the phrase for *important* instances of that—for blood-knowledge in conflict with rational knowledge. That difference is typical of all the other differences between Lawrence and the *kosmische Runde*, for his insights are always much more related to, and in the service of, "common sense." Thus, for example, Schuler interpreted the Black Knight in Schiller's *Jungfrau von Orleans* as a symbol of the chthonic phallus, called to life by the blood spilt in battle. The knight touches Joan to destroy her virginity and thus her powers. Both Schuler and Klages tended to be more extremist in their understanding of "blood" and sexuality than Lawrence was; Klages cited Saint Francis of Assissi's bleeding stigmata as proof of Christianity's vampirism, for in his interpretation the blood was being voluntarily drained from the body by the spirit. We are reminded once again of Lawrence's essential moderation.

In "Der Mensch und das Leben," a talk given to the Freideutsche Jugend, Klages deplored the destruction of wildlife and landscape by encroaching industrial civilization. Attacking progress and technology as such, he praised the chthonic powers, who have been driven into the underworld. "Without a doubt, we are living in the age of the waning of the soul," he announced, declaring that mind has triumphed over life. In *Goethe als Seelenforscher*, he attacks the culture of the West, which is based on thought as opposed to wisdom, and traces this rationalism to the exaggerated masculinity of the West. "The oldest wisdom of Humanity was the possession and privilege of Woman," he says, citing the Pythian oracle, the Sybils, the Valkyries, and the Swan Maidens.

Vom Kosmogonischem Eros is the major text for our purposes. In this work Klages radically distinguishes Eros from both sex and love, just as Lawrence distinguishes desire from appetite and love. Only in man do we see a death-struggle between Life and an opposite Power, which is something abstracted, independent of time and space, which separates the poles of soul and body, disembodies the soul and dispirits the body. This Power we call Mind (*Logos, Pneuma, Nous, Seele*) and it works through analytic consciousness and purposive will. Their joint aim is to create the *Ich*, the *Selbst*, which becomes an eccentric center of gravity to each man's life. From having been individuals, we become selves.

Turning to history, we see a striking likeness between Klages and Otto Gross in their joint hatred of Moses and the prophets, Plato, and Aristotle, all of whom they see equally as betrayers of soul to mind. Indeed, the initiatory rites of the new movement involved the desecration of the images of these founders of Western culture. This is particularly striking for us when we contrast it with Max Weber's self-identification with the Jewish prophets, especially with Jeremiah, and Freud's with Moses.

Prehistorical man, according to Klages, was ruled by the soul, historical man by the mind, and posthistorical man—we live in the dawn of that age—will be only a hollow mask and robot, not really alive. (In Lawrence's *Last Poems*, the name for modern man is the machine-robot.) But a terrible revenge is preparing itself in the womb of the violated earth. She will destroy all her impious children. The northern peoples of Europe have an exaggeratedly sympathetic character, and in them eroticism tends to become "emotional soul-love," which in turn leads to the "post-erotic specter of a general 'love of humanity.'" These ideas, of course, are prominent in Lawrence's thought and can be found in *Twilight in Italy*, *The Crown*, and

Fantasia of the Unconscious. Both Lawrence and Klages diagnose themselves as well as others as "exaggeratedly sympathetic" creatures, and hence as individuals who have problems with both eroticism and aggression. Just as it is themselves they diagnose as creatures of will and mind.

Klages had a deep reverence for all *Naturvölker*, as well as for the pre-Greek primitives, who lived so much better than we do. Loving and accepting death, they had no lust for immortality or for abstraction, and no use for property, dominion, and family life, all of which began when we were driven out of Paradise. He was also interested in blood-brotherhood. "The eroticism of the West stands under the sign of blood-brotherhood. The return to erotic wholeness, he insisted, must recognize the polarity of man's being: "The erotic bond is *not* a commingling; it connects the poles without transcending them." He insisted, too, on the impersonality of passion; for the more egotism there is in a lover, the more his personalty becomes idolized or divinized in the love relationship. From this arises erotic tragedy. Similarly, the more his love is characterized by desire, the more it is mere sexuality. But the more it is characterized by surrender, the closer it approaches to true eroticism. Surrender of the will is the personal aspect of impersonality. Thus "true to thee till death" willfulness announces the death-directed idealism of tragedy.

For Klages, of course, the surrender of the woman to the man was not true surrender. On the contrary, the traditional female virtues of meekness and fidelity were an assertion of selfhood—of the selfhood of the man; they indicated unambiguously the woman's acceptance of her role as the property of her man and her exaltation of him as proprietor. Goethe's Gretchen is the archetype of this sort of surrender, which is precisely why Lawrence and Frieda always criticized her as the typical heroine of the world of men. She was completely the victim, completely passive.

The surrender of the man to the woman, however, reverses this patriarchal pattern. In Lawrence's version of the world of Woman, for example, it is the women who are the sexual agents and the men who are called upon to surrender to them. "You are the Call and I am the Answer" is a typical statement from man to woman. Thus it is Anna Brangwen who undresses and caresses Will. The men are striplings, Adonises, Osirises. Even Miriam in *Sons and Lovers* runs her hands down Paul's sides appreciatively, murmuring, "How fine you are." This is a gesture which seems much more authentic when it occurs in the *Poems*, where it is attributed to Frieda, and where Lawrence expresses his resentment of her free possession of him, of her reduction of him to the role of a sexual object for herself, the Magna Mater. The resentment was, to some extent, inevitable, for it was part of the price that had to be paid for the bold reversal of the patriarchal pattern of sexuality that accompanied the new doctrine of Eros.

When one turns from Klages's erotic prescriptions to his discussion of "knowledge," one continues to find striking similarities between his thought and Lawrence's. To life the veil of Isis is a sin because it symbolizes the need to *know*; he declares: "The intellectual will to power is a crime against Life, and therefore the criminal meets Life's revengeful retaliation." This sounds very like Lawrence on Edgar Allen Poe. When one lifts the veil, what one sees is nothing, active nothing—that is to say, one sees Mind, and therein Will, the will to desubstantialize the world. This is what Gerald Crich sees when he is alone and looks at himself in the mirror. If you make Reason your ruler, this vision of nothingness will destroy you—as it had destroyed Max Weber, Klages would have noted.

The substance of the world is not material as science defines matter. The present is an arch which hovers between the past and the future—a frail and insubstantial rainbow. Thus the monuments of culture and the achievements of personality must not be laid hold of as possessions; symphonies and epic poems and love relationships will all, must all be allowed to, pass away. One must trust to the life process itself, to Life. Reason and the culture of Reason hypostatizes life by weighing, counting, measuring everything. But life is a flowing, a process immeasurable. In this argument Klages presents the metaphysic of the master strategy against Western culture in its modern phase, the metaphysic of matriarchy. D. H. Lawrence worked out his own version, with Frieda's help. He and the *komische Runde* were close allies.

The Circle was broken up at the beginning of 1904 by a quarrel between Klages and Alfred Schuler on the one hand and Stefan George and Karl Wolfskehl on the other. The ostensible cause of the quarrel was the anti-Semitic sentiments directed against Wolfskehl by Klages and Schuler. Important also must have been the transfer of the favors of the Countess zu Reventlow from Klages to Wolfskehl at the end of 1903, the growing success of George's *Blätter für die Kunst*, and the continuous increases in the size of George's band of devoted disciples. Klages and George were too similar in their leadership ambitions not to conflict with each other and resent each other bitterly. Klages accused George of stealing the ideas of the *Runde*—for which, he felt, Schuler should be chiefly credited—and turning them into exclusively aesthetic doctrines. They were intended, he insisted, to renew life as a whole.

George and Wolfskehl, it is clear, were correct in accusing Klages and Schuler of being anti-Semitic, for the two of them openly announced that the modernism they were fighting was essentially a Jewish phenomenon. Indeed, Klages persisted in his anti-Semitism even when anti-Semitism had become a practical policy of murder and mass murder. All this bears vitally if obliquely on one's feelings about Lawrence, whose ideology was so similar to theirs.

In the years before the war, the Cosmic Circle's anti-Semitism was something it was hard to take seriously. They seemed to offer guarantees, in their general social rebellion, against their ever actually misusing social power against Jews. They were Nietzcheans, not Wagnerites; in fact, everything *Parsifal* stood for was abomination to them, for in addition to being anti-Semitic they were positively anti-Christian and even antimusical and antitheatrical. Stefan George constrained his disciples to despise both music and drama. And Wagner was the official taste. The Kaiser was an enthusiastic admirer. To admire Nietzsche and not to admire Wagner seemed to demonstrate a healthy kind of interest in ideas.

What is more, there was a real and unmistakable difference between the theories of the Cosmic Circle and those of, say, Houston Chamberlain, Alfred Rosenberg, and the Nazis proper. The major symbol of the Circle's philosophy was, to be sure, blood—the power opposed to mind—but blood understood as Lawrence understood it, not as the Nazis did. For the Circle, the blood is the essential human substance, the locus of the cosmic energies in man, which are otherwise so adulterated and bastardized that they achieve no manifestation, have no effect on life. Nevertheless, writing in 1938, Marianne Weber rightly says that the prewar Schwabingites were the richest source of all those anti-Christian and antibourgeois tendencies which Germany had to deal wtih in the late thirties. They scoffed at the notion that the higher man should have to make any effort to achieve economic respectability. They scoffed at technical progress, pride in one's work, and sexual morality, because all these values and inhibitions seemed equally incompatible with the free expression of the creative mind. All that we face today, she said, was first brought into existence there by those richly gifted men. They exalted the creativity of the pagan-cosmic principle, which they saw as opposed to the life-hostile Judaeo-Christian principle. Feeling and instinct were spurred on to attack and triumph over reason and clarity of understanding.

Seven years later Alfred Weber, another champion of Heidelberg, used much the same terms to denounce the Schwabing Nietzscheans in a chapter of his *Farewell to European History* entitled "Nietzsche and the Catastrophe." "But what was happening from the points of view of life *as a whole?*" he asked. "Intellectual foci formed in various places, inwardly rich, full of the most open human relationships, capable of powerful cross-fertilization, refined, cosmopolitan in outlook. None of these foci, however, even in the cities, had the smallest relation to or the smallest influence on politics and practical life. A wall of alienation lay between. What was really going on beyond it these intellectual circles had no very clear idea for the most part. The most they did was occasionally to laugh at some of its symptoms in a smart funny paper and leave things as they were in practice. . . ."

Insofar as this was true of the *kosmische Runde*, it was so not because of their frivolity, but because of their total, uncomprising hostility to the whole of patriarchal culture. They met to discuss the prehistorical, matriarchal cultures, because they found in them the one great life-giving alternative. Indeed, the authority they most preferred to cite was not Nietzsche but Bachofen, whom no one could accuse of social brutality. Their joint reading of him was their great intellectual adventure. Klages first came across him in 1900, shut himself up alone for five weeks to study him, and emerged feeling a new man. Wolfskehl had a copy of Bachofen's *Mortuary Symbolism* bound in snakeskin and presented it ceremoniously to Klages, and so on.

Johann Jakob Bachofen was born into a patrician family in Basel, Switzerland, in 1815. His mother was only twenty when he was born and the young man grew up so devoted to her that he did not marry until he was over fifty years old. In 1848, shocked by the intellectual radicalism as well as by the violence of the revolutions that shook all of Europe in that year, he set out to reconstruct imaginatively the heritage of European culture which seemed to him in danger of being destroyed. Investigating Roman antiquities, he became interested in the traces they contained of earlier religions and cultures, which he interpreted as having been matriarchal. He published *Mortuary Symbolism* in 1859, and though it was very harshly reviewed, he continued in the same line of speculation and published his major work two years later.

Das Mutterrecht appeared in 1861, but was savagely ridiculed and neglected. In the same year Sir Henry Maine in England published his *Ancient Law*. This essentially patriarchal treatment of the same issues was what people were prepared to believe. Bachofen's great idea was that a matriarchal form of society based on "Mother-Right" had preceded the patriarchal everywhere; that there were in fact three main stages of cultural development—the tellurian, the lunar, and the solarian, the first two of which were matriarchal, the third patriarchal. The tellurian is a primitive, nomadic society which lives by hunting and foraging. Agriculture is still unknown, and there is no marriage. Its politics, if such a word is appropriate, is an undifferentiated communitarian democracy, its justice the talionic eye for an eye. Its goddess is Aphrodite and its symbols are the bitch and the swamp. Bachofen also calls this phase the Hetaerist phase because the woman's role in it is to be promiscuous and unmastered, knowing no husband or father for her children.

In the lunar phase agriculture has evolved as the basis of the economy.

A social organization has emerged capable of furthering life and love, so that the laws now are marked by special penalties attached to all injuries done to physical life, both animal and human. The greatest of all crimes is matricide. This was an especially religious culture—the central goddess is Demeter—with the religion permeating everyday life rather than being set apart. Matriarchal peoples felt the unity of all life more keenly than the peoples of subsequent cultures. The body held primacy over mind, night over day, the dead over the living. "Obedient in all things to the laws of physical existence, they fasten their eyes upon the earth, setting the chthonian powers above the powers of Uranian light."

The solarian phase is the civilized culture we know, marked by conjugal father-right, division of labor, and individual ownership of property. Its imaginative life is dominated by Apollo.

Bachofen was an evolutionist who declared his preference for the patriarchal and Apollonian virtues which triumphed in the end. But his imagination was far more engaged by, and responsive to, the matriarchal, Demetrian or Aphrodisian, virtues which had gone down to defeat. It seems clear that he needed to set under a negative sign the heretical meanings he secretly adored, just as he needed to be a scholar studying these things in order to release his imagination in response to them. Inwardly, he loved the Pelasgian civilizations he described, those that had existed before agriculture had violated the divine mother, before women were subjected to masters.

For Bachofen, all human history could be described as a conflict between the Male and Female principles. Thus he presented the victory of Octavius over Cleopatra as the historical triumph of patriarchal virility and virtue over Hetaerism, just as, in *Aaron's Rod*, Lawrence identifies the Marchesa with Cleopatra while Aaron is a kind of Antony who turns back in time to Lilly/Lawrence/Octavius. It was, then, primarily from Bachofen that the *kosmische Runde* derived their belief that in their time, as in Greece, Dionysianism could sap the life of the patriarchal state and bring back aphroditic hetaerism. Hierarchy and barriers would disappear as the reed and vine came to replace matriarchal corn and milk—not to mention patriarchal steel and blood, for as Bachofen noted explicitly, Dionysianism was irreconcilable with politics as well as with morality: "This sensualization of existence coincides everywhere with the dissolution of political organization and the decline of political life." The Thracian god Dionysos would defeat the Greek Apollo. This is what the Cosmic Circle hoped to bring about by means of the festivals which were so celebrated in Schwabing.

The adventures of Orestes in myth reflect the upheavals and struggles as paternity replaced maternity in Greek culture. Athens revered Athene, who had no mother, and Theseus, the woman-hater. In Aeschylus, Athene joins Apollo in defending Orestes against the Erinnyes. "This is a ballot for Orestes I shall cast. There is no mother anywhere who gave me birth, and, but for marriage, I am always for the male with all my heart, and strongly on my father's side." (This is the mythical statement of Else Jaffe's prefer-ence for Max Weber and his values over Otto Gross and his.) The Aphrodi-tean gods—like Otto—were hostile to marriage, which institutionalizes love for the sake of children, for the sake of productivity. In marriage, woman veils herself, subdues her claims, renounces that reign over life which is properly hers. It is another form of patriarchal agriculture. Woman is the earth, and the earth is life. Men are the leaves—they cannot generate more life. Woman is the tree. The queen bee (an image of Lawrence's for Frieda) is the Demetrian earth soul in its supreme purity. The bee-hive "symbolized the earth, its motherliness, its never-resting, artfully-formative busyness, and reflected the Demetrian world-soul in its supreme purity." And Bachofen points out that after mating, the drone mate and all other drones are killed.

There is a great deal of Lawrence's thinking in his most radical period which reminds us forcefully of the author of *Das Mutterrecht*. Let us quote a few lines from Lawrence's Forward to *Sons and Lovers* of 1913, in which he transvalues the Book of Genesis.

> The Father is the Flesh, the eternal and unquestionable, the law-giver but not the law; whereas the Son is the mouth. . . .
>
> And so the end having been chosen for the beginning, the whole chronology is upside-down: the Word created Man, and Man lay down and gave birth to Woman, whereas we know the Woman lay in travail, and gave birth to Man, who in his hour uttered his word. . . .
>
> So we take the seed as the starting point in this cycle. The woman is the Flesh. She produces all the rest of the flesh, including the intermedi-ary pieces called man. . . .
>
> So there is the Father—which should be called Mother—then the Son, who is the Utterer, and then the Word. And the Word is that of the Father which, through the Son, is tossed away. . . .
>
> And God the Father, the Inscrutable, the Unknowable, we know in the Flesh, in the Woman. She is the door for our in-going and our out-coming. In her we go back to the Father: but like the witnesses of the Transfiguration, blind and unconscious.
>
> Yea, like bees in and out of a hive, we come backwards and forwards to our woman. . . .
>
> And the bee, who is a Son, comes home to his Queen as to the Father, in service and humility, for suggestion, and renewal, and identifi-cation which is the height of his glory, for begetting. . . .

But if the man does not come home to a woman . . . if when he
enters her house, he does not become simply her man of flesh, entered
into her house as if it were her greater body, to be warmed, and restored,
and nourished, from the store the day has given them, then she shall
expel him from her house, as a drone. . . .
For in the flesh of the woman does God exact Himself.

Compare that with Bachofen's remarks in *Urreligion* (Volume II, pp. 356-59):

The mother is earlier than the son. The feminine has priority, while
masculine creativity only appears afterward as a secondary phenomenon.
Woman comes first, but man "becomes." The prime datum is the earth,
the basic maternal substance. . . . He is part of the visible but ever-
changing created world; he exists only in perishable form. Woman exists
from everlasting, self-subsistent, immutable; man, evolving, is subject to
continual decay. In the realm of the physical, therefore, the masculine
principle is of second rank, subordinate to the feminine. Herein lies the
prototype and justification of gynocracy; herein is rooted that age-old
conception of an immortal mother who unites herself with a mortal
father. She is perennially the same, but from the man the generations
multiply themselves into infinity. Ever the same Great Mother mates with
ever new men. . . .

Man then comes forth from woman by a miraculous metamorphosis
of nature, which repeats itself in the birth of every male child. . . . When
a man is born of woman's womb, the mother herself marvels at the new
apparition. For she recognizes in the form of her son, the very image of
that fecundating power to which she owes her motherhood. Her eyes
linger with delight upon his limbs. Man becomes her plaything, the goat
is her mount, the phallus her constant companion. Cybele the Mother
overshadows Attis, Virbius is dwarfed by Diana, Phaeton by Aphrodite.
Everywhere the material, feminine, natural principle has the advantage;
it takes the masculine principle, which is secondary and subsists only in
perishable form as an ever-changing epiphenomenon, into its lap, as
Demeter took the cista.

It is surely undeniable that Lawrence was working in the same direction
and the same mode of thought as Bachofen. Quite probably he never read
the *Mutterrecht,* but, because of Frieda's incarnation and enactment of the
matriarchal idea, which she had imbibed from Otto Gross, Lawrence was in
effect living Bachofen. He was enacting in practical life the female mode of
being which Bachofen had recommended so indirectly and theoretically.
That was what Klages and Wolfskehl had set out to do in 1900, but with less
luck and less success. The *kosmische Runde* described the woman it wanted
and Frieda Weekley answered the appeal, but by then the *Runde* had long

broken up and Lawrence was its heir. It was largely a coincidence that he and Frieda began their great experiment, their life together, just outside the city on which the *kosmische Runde* had set such hopes.

These ideas were the heart of intellectual Munich, of Schwabing. Here was generated the most powerful of all imaginative resistances to the patriarchal Germany of Bismarck. In this crucible were fused those ideas of the meaning of Life, of the Earth, of Woman, which inspired Otto Gross to his mission in Life, which gave Frieda Weekley her glorious identity, which gave D. H. Lawrence the informing ideas of his art. And in the crudities of this intellectual ore also lie hidden those hideous political possibilities—for there is an undeniable link between Schwabing and the Nazi ideology—which justify the revulsion of such observers as Else Jaffe and Max Weber. It is easy to sympathize with the choice that each sister made; and it is not easy to see in what way either a compromise between the two or a cool unchoosing objectivity toward these ideas would have been preferable.

Now let us place this cluster of ideas in its social setting in Munich and Schwabing.

Munich

When Otto Gross asked Frieda Weekley to leave her husband for him it was to Munich that he asked her to come. "Wouldn't you like to come to *Munich*? You like *Munich*, don't you?" It was a symbolic locale for many people then. Ernest Jones points out that is roughly halfway from Berlin to Rome—halfway from Prussian male chauvinism to the Italian female mode of being—and halfway between Paris and Vienna. Jones found the city in 1908 to be a land of youth, of romanticism, of enjoyment. "For the only time in my life," he reports, "work was subordinated to enjoyment," which he found in song and dance in the cafés of Schwabing—where the most brilliant personality he met was Otto Gross.

In 1893, the year that Ludwig Klages arrived there, the city had 390,000 inhabitants. It was thus bigger than Leipzig and twice as big as Hanover and the cities Klages knew, and yet it had less of a big-city atmosphere than either. It seemed not to belong to Bismarckian Germany, and he fell in love with it immediately. (It is significant that Klages's father had been a sergeant in the Hanoverian army and was about to marry when that army was merged with the Prussian in 1864. He resigned rather than serve Prussia, and had to put off his marriage several years. Such facts as this—and as the spoiling of the view from the Klages home by new industrial plants—are to be found in the biographical backgrounds of many of Bismarck's intellectual opponents.) It was, moreover, a *Kunststadt,* an art-city. Industry and commerce counted for very little there, but the art collections, concert halls, and theaters were famous and the parks and buildings splendidly tasteful. Finally, it stood in a Catholic peasant countryside famous for its beauty and its traditions of folk festivals and carnivals; Jones too had succembed to the charms of the village dances in the uplands of Bavaria.

A somewhat similar view is given by Ludwig Curtius, later a close friend of Alfred Weber, who arrived at Munich University as a student in 1894. He had relatives in villages nearby, and he ascribes to the country people of Bavaria a special beauty and sensuality, bright-eyed and humorous. Among these people Curtius found himself rather roughly and mockingly treated at first, but before long he was introduced into a "joyful, blossoming world" to which from then on he belonged as of right. Money and rank counted for very little with these people. They had a strong feeling for decoration, which they exercised on flowers in windows, churches, and costumes. A Russian friend to whom he showed some of their homes would not believe that they did not belong to rich people. This is the landscape Lawrence saw when he eloped with Frieda, and this richness left its mark on *Sons and Lovers* and *The Rainbow.*

The natural sensuality and humorous truthfulness of the Upper Bavarian peasant overflowed into Munich itself, and lent it a human warmth which no other of the world's big cities possessed, Curtius says. You met it already at the railroad station, in the porters in their Bavarian blue uniforms. Moreover, art was at home there, not only among the rich brewing families—the only big employers in Munich were the breweries—but among all classes. So was the intellectual life. As Herr Doktor, Curtius found that he could forget his tram pass and be forgiven, which would never have happened in Berlin, a city anyway entirely lacking in sensual charm and mystery. In his childhood, no one had talked about Berlin, always about Vienna, as a great city; and it was the Hapsburgs' portraits and the Wittelsbachs' which hung in taverns, not the Hohenzollerns'.

Moritz Julius Bonn arrived in Munich in 1906 to be Privatdozent at the university. He describes it as having never been a city but always a "court and residential town." The Upper House of the Diet was the Imperial council of the Crown of Bavaria, and on state occasions the etiquette was Spanish-Burgundian. Below that level, it was almost a classless city, however, with no very rich class. Living was cheap, and if you were invited into anyone's home, the maid went out and got you beer and sausages, and you paid her for them. Real social life went on in the beer cellars or gardens, where everyone was equal. You bought bread and cheese at the gate, the beer coming from the brewery that owned the Biergarten.

Otto, the King of Bavaria, was insane at the time, as Ludwig II had been before him. In 1910 Prince Ludwig succeeded Prince Luitpold as Regent; and in that year the thirty-seven-year-old Bonn became Principal of the new Technical College and appointed Edgar Jaffe to teach economics under him. It is interesting to compare the two men. Both were Jewish, though not close friends, and as such they stood outside as well as inside of this society. As College Principal, Bonn had to attend state occasions, and during the war, Jaffe was official financial adviser to the king. Unlike Jaffe, however, Bonn did not move in Schwabing circles. For him, Munich social life revolved around the Brentanos and the Pringsheims, one of whose daughters married Thomas Mann. John Buchan was a friend, as was James Loeb, the American millionaire. In his work, and indeed in his life as a whole, Bonn consciously modeled himself after Lujo Brentano, the urbane and socially brilliant professor of economics at Munich University; he recoiled from the tragic vehemence of Max Weber. Bonn was much more obviously than Jaffe, and less interestingly, the Jew who made good, the intellectual Jew who moved on equal terms with the most brilliant men of his city.

In prewar Munich, there was much that was of the past as well as much that was of the future. In 1913 the Regent of Bavaria was declared King. At the coronation festivities, the students marched to the palace in the Korps uniforms, half Romantic in style, half medieval, with ribbons, heavy boots, broad hats with feathers, and clanking swords, each carrying a lighted candle. Outside the palace they all doused their candles, bands began to play, and they sang "Gaudeamus Igitur." It was all so remote from the *Realpolitik* of Berlin. Bavaria had been the state most reluctant to enter Bismarck's Reich in 1871.

Under Bismarck, Munich had become a center of liberals in opposition, just as Schwabing was a center for radicals. Later, during the war years, Munich changed and the diffuse radicalism of the prewar years became overtly political. The 1918 revolution in Bavaria had broad middle-class and nationalist support largely because of local resentment against Berlin's economic policy, one result of which was that the breweries lacked barley. And because of the high losses suffered by Bavarian regiments at the front. And because of bitterness over the fact that although Bavaria was supposed to control her own army, along with her railroad and postal systems, those rights were eroded during the war with the result that Crown-Prince Rupprecht did not command the Bavarian armies in the field. But for all these middle-class grievances, the 1918 revolution was also a proletarian revolution based on elements new to Bavarian society. It began among the workers in the Krupp works, who had been brought there in 1916, and among those in the much enlarged Rapp Motor Works and Bavarian Airplane Works. And it was led by Schwabing intellectuals.

Until 1914 no one believed such a thing possible. Schwabing seemed devoted to holiday, a world of Woman and Art and Eros, determined to secede from the world of men, but not to supplant it. The country carnivals and folk festivals, celebrated by Hugo von Hofmannsthal and Thomas Mann as uniquely Bavarian, had their counterparts in the city itself, above all in the *Fasching* just before the beginning of Lent. According to Erich Mühsam, Munich had two seasons, one centering round *Fasching*, which began with the opening of the ice paths and ended with the ski season; the other centering around the *Oktoberfest,* which began when the work of the Starkbierzeit was over and ended only when people started to prepare for *Fasching.* The *Oktoberfest* was held on the Theresienwiese, a park where Edgar Jaffe and Kurt Eisner addressed the crowds in the protest meeting that turned into a revolution in 1918. It was the custom to pick up girls, known as *Faschingsbräute* and *Wiesenbräute* for the few days of the festivals. Between these two highpoints of the Munich season were also *Maibock* and *Salvator,* and, in nearby Pullach, the *Habenschadenfest,* and in Geiselgasteig the *Sommerfest.* There was in effect a year-long erotic and playful carnival, in which people of all classes, including the peasants mingled on equal terms. When Klages ascribes to the whole city the symbolic color of light blue and says that it stood under the sign of the Virgin Mother, he is making a pagan transvaluation of the Christian symbol.

Munich was, then, a symbolic city. And the heart of its symbolic meaning was the northern suburb of Schwabing. Otto Gross asked Frieda Weekley to come to him in Schwabing, begging her to wire him either at home or at the Café Stephanie, the most famous of Schwabing cafés, where he could be found at any time of the day or night. A Viennese café set down in Munich, with its thick frieze curtain behind its glass door, and its marble tables, the Stephanie had two rooms, the big one holding two billiard tables and a buffet on a low platform, the small one with chess tables set up at the window. It was open twenty-four hours a day and was full during all of them of artists and people discussing art—or revolution. It was the Reichstag of Schwabing.

Schwabing

Schwabing was primarily a center of artists. In 1892 it had been the home of the *Sezession* movement, the first split with (secession from) traditionalism in art in Germany. There was a *Sezession* exhibition there in 1898, before the one in Vienna in 1903, and the 1913 Armory Show in New York was a later version of the same thing. Fritz von Stuck, cofounder of the *Sezession*, lived in Schwabing, as did Hermann Obrist, founder of the *Jugendstil*. Matisse visited the city in 1908 and 1910, and under his influence Vasili Kandinski and Jawlensky became Fauvistes. The *Neue Künstler Vereinigung* was founded there between Matisse's two visits. Kandinski and Jawlensky had first met in Munich in 1896, both coming there from Russia to study art. They rediscovered the Bavarian folk art of painting on glass, which Fanny zu Reventlow also practiced. Kandinsky lived in Schwabing from 1897 until 1908, Paul Klee from 1898 to 1921, Franz Marc from 1904 until 1910. They were all members of the *Der Blaue Reiter* group, and Edgar Jaffe bought a painting by Marc.

What this movement opposed was the tasteless philistinism of Berlin. One of the major symbols of Wilhelmine taste was the Siegesallee, a double row of pompous and meaningless marble statues in Berlin. Another was the interference of the Kaiserin herself in matters of the theater and public morality. She changed the staging of *Salome* and prevented the opening of *Der Rosenkavalier,* for she found Strauss's eroticism too much of a threat to Wilhelmine morality. Bismarck's taste in and for the arts had been equally deplorable. The artistic instincts, for both play and mimesis, had been very minor functions of the German patriarchal mind. Naturally, then, the artists of Schwabing were nearly all serious revolutionaries.

The first Künstlerkabarett in Munich, The Eleven Executioners, opened in April 1901. The walls were hung with black, and on the stage there was a pillory, an axe, and a death's head. Three times a week a show was put on, the aim of which was always to mock the virtues of the Wilhelmine bourgeoisie. Bruno Walter played the piano, Frank Wedekind and Mühsam sang and acted, Hofmannsthal, Richard Dehmel, and Hans Thoma wrote sketches and songs. The executioners' song, sung by eleven scarlet-robed masks, became the anthem of Schwabing.

In some ways more typical was the Simplicissimus, a bar named after the Schwabing satirical journal. Kathi Kobus owned it and sang there, and Mühsam, Gross, Jaffe, and Fanny zu Reventlow often sat together there. Between 1908 and 1910 these people saw a lot of each other; in fact, there was even a tentative affair between Jaffe and Fanny, who was the spirit of Schwabing incarnated.

In the Café Stephanie another group assembled; of one of these meetings we have a record in a postcard of 1907 that happens to have survived. It has a picture of the Marienplatz on one side, and on the other the name and address of Else Jaffe in Heidelberg, to whom it was sent, bearing salutations and brief messages from Edgar Jaffe, Otto Gross, Frieda Gross, Erich Mühsam, Regina Ullmann, and Frieda Weekley, all of whom were sitting around a Café Stephanie table to write it. Regina Ullmann was a Swiss girl who four years later converted to Roman Catholicism and became—under the guidance of Rainer Maria Rilke—a writer of religious and spiritual prose. But in 1907 she was being analyzed by Otto Gross and was much under his influence. In 1908 she bore him a child. Frieda Weekley for a time thought she was pregnant by Gross, and Else Jaffe's third child, born in 1907, was Gross's son, while Frieda Gross was soon to bear a child to Ernst Frick, her husband's disciple. Thus in the group evoked by this postcard were several women bearing their lovers' children at Gross's suggestion. Regina Ullmann, five years younger than Frieda Weekley, was very unlike her, for she suffered from physical and psychological disadvantages that disabled her for any ordinary kind of happiness. She squinted and stuttered and her nose was misshapen; as a child she had been backward in school and had seen visions. Her only gifts were special ones, for spirituality. Thus Gross had created around that café table a cell, a cell of the new life, whose members were most unlike each other in everything except their faith in him.

Erich Mühsam, who knew Schwabing as well as anyone, says that when he thinks of Schwabing he thinks of "people with peculiar manners and mannerisms, but with a brilliant excitability of mind; for instance Otto Gross, the most important of Freud's successors." Mühsam's anarchist magazine *Kain* was one of those that took up Otto's cause when he was arrested in 1913. A genial as well as a brilliant man, Mühsam played a prominent part in the purely social side of Schwabing life. In Mühsam's opinion, Lotte Pritzl, who was famous for the wax dolls she modeled,—which may have suggested to Lawrence the situation of "The Captain's Doll"—organized the best *Atelierfeste* (studio parties). During *Faschingszeit* she and her friends would gather first at Edgar Jaffe's and then go perhaps to Georg Hirschfield's. Emmy Hennings, the cabaret singer, and Marietta, the famous artists' model who always stripped as she danced at around 1 A.M., were sure to be there.

Schwabing was in many ways a typical Bohemia, but it also had its intellectual and morally intense side which, as we have seen, was represented by the Cosmic Circle. Otto Gross's affair with Frieda was very much a Schwabing affair, in its sexual freedom as well as in its paradoxical morality.

Its freedom *was* moralistic, of course. Frieda Weekley could have wired Otto Gross at his home as well as at the Stephanie. There was nothing concealed about their relations, except from Frieda's English husband. Otto's wife, and Else, and Edgar, and Frieda, and Otto all knew the state of affairs between all the others. One of the major postulates of Gross's ethic, of Schwabing's as a whole, was the saving power of sexual freedom. Possessiveness and jealousy, he believed, could be overcome by the moral effort of sexual self-liberation. Chastity and fidelity, self-sacrifice and self-denial, were all moralistic corruptions of moral feeling.

But the new matriarchal morality could develop only out of the decay of the old patriarchal culture. Thus Otto Gross wrote to Frieda Weekley, "You know my belief that a new *harmony* in life can be generated only by *decadence*—and that the wonderful era we live in is destined, *as the age of decadence,* to be the womb of the great future." Alfred Schuler believed that, too, and Lawrence sometimes described his era as the end that is necessary before a new beginning can be made—"This process of death has got to be lived through"—but never quite in Gross's tone of enthusiasm. More characteristically, Lawrence stresses the possibility (and necessity) of achieving health here and now, by discarding old bad habits of feeling. He was not at ease in decadence, and it is thus fitting that he and Frieda began their life together not in Schwabing—Lawrence never lived there—but in Irschenhausen, a country village just outside Munich. In his account of the Café Pompadour in *Women in Love* Lawrence gives his judgment on such places as the Café Stephanie and the artist Loerke in that novel—Loerke is in fact the name of a Schwabing personality—represents one aspect of Munich decadence. The difference between Lawrence's attitude to Schwabing and Gross's is the difference between Demeter and Aphrodite, for Lawrence, as a creative artist, prized productivity, discipline, and order more highly than Gross. But this difference, of course, lies within the great likeness between the two, for both men were matriarchalists.

To be sure, Lawrence was not the only major writer to have repudiated Schwabing. Thomas Mann's story "At the Prophet's" is quite interesting for its picture of a quarter "where pale young geniuses, criminals of the dream, sit with folded arms and brood . . . inwardly consumed, hungry and proud. . . . Here is the end: ice, chastity, null. Here is valid no compromise, no concession, no half-way, no consideration of values. . . . Here reign defiance and iron consistency, the ego supreme amid despair, here freedom, madness, and death hold sway." What makes this interesting is the felt bad-conscience of the writer. Mann is uneasy with his subject, because he is criticizing energy and freedom of spirit—criticizing his fellow artists, fellow rebels. Schwabing in fact preferred Heinrich Mann, holding Thomas a bourgeois, who wrote for the bourgeoisie. And Franz Werfel, in *Barbara*, has Dr. Gebhart (Gross) deliver one of his brilliant but satanic monologues about freedom while a war-widow is offering her body to the men at the party one after another; and he has the speech interrupted because one of them who is a war cripple takes off his prosthesis and starts beating her with it, both of them stark naked and bloody, while the monologue continues. Mann's descriptions convey the same fears of disorder but less vividly.

But there were a thousand celebrations of Schwabing, too. It was one of the great symbolic locales of Germany, as much as Weber's Heidelberg. For our purpose, those two and Berlin were the apices of the German triangle. Berlin stood for power (patriarchal and systematic), Heidelberg for enlightenment (political and cultural), Munich for revolution primarily personal, but also political. Perhaps the best description of Schwabing comes from Klages. How well he and Gross knew each other we cannot be sure, but Ernest Jones tells us that the brilliant circle of artists and intellectuals whom he knew in Munich in 1908 revolved around Otto Gross and Ludwig Klages.

The essential Schwabing, Klages insists, was not the ordinary collection of artists, but a few significant personalities (he was thinking, of course, of the *kosmische Runde*) and several circles of young people. Nietzsche and Ibsen helped to bring certain themes to consciousness, but the great thing was that "A still unconscious change was taking place in the vitality of certain groups. . . . Schwabing was essentially the attack on the bourgeois world, in order to revolutionize it before it could complete its evil work and bring about the disasters of the present. We are dealing with a phenomenon of world-historical importance." This phenomenon was essentially an attempt to build a new life style to accord with that changed vitality; to create a new philosophy and art, a new culture in which that life style could express and reflect itself. They knew, the true Schwabingites, that socialist experimentation would not save the world. Socialism was old hat, fundamentally as patriarchal as capitalism. And they were not content to play at life, in the manner of the literati in other Bohemias. Twenty years after leaving Schwabing, Stefan George dismissed Montmartre as unworthy of comparison with it: "Here were Powers," he wrote of Schwabing, "united in the knowledge that things could not go on as they were, that mankind was ruining itself, and that no social utopia would help, but only Miracle, Action, Life." In the same vein, Klages declared that between 1893 and 1904 the fate of the world was decided in Schwabing, which was a true *Weltvorort,* a world suburb. "Here and here alone the die was cast, and the thirty years' war 1914–1945 was only the working out of fate."

Perhaps the central figure in all Schwabing was Fanny zu Reventlow. A friend of both Gross and Jaffe, she is also the only Schwabing personality besides Gross whom Frieda Lawrence mentions in her novel; at least the allusion seems to be to her. In any case, Frieda knew her and knew all about her and it seems to me likely that Frieda in many ways modeled herself on Fanny. The group at the Simplicissimus—of Fanny, Mühsam, Gross, and Jaffe— meant a great deal to the von Richthofen sisters. If we say something about Fanny zu Reventlow and her relation to Ludwig Klages and the *kosmische Runde,* we shall have sketched in the essential Schwabing which stood behind Gross.

Gräfin Franziska zu Reventlow ("die tolle Gräfin," "die tolle Fanny") was born in Husum in 1871 and died in 1918. Her dates are exactly those of Bismarck's Reich, and her life was one long protest against it. Because of their dislike of Prussia's increasing power, her family, which was aristocratic, moved to Lübeck, an independent city-republic within Germany, when Fanny was a girl. As a child she was, like Frieda von Richthofen, a tomboy and a rebel; but she clashed very violently with her mother. At twenty-one she finally ran away from home and was disowned. Her rebellions were more violent than Frieda's; she rebelled against both family and marriage. And she was more psychologically disturbed, more of a Schwabingite.

The intellectual scene of her adolescent rebellion was the Lübeck Ibsen Club, and many of the themes of her early life were Ibsenite. She acquired there the sense that adult society was a tissue of lived lies as well as the sense of suppressed and distorted sexuality everywhere. She also became sensitive to the need for the freeing of women and of artists. From the age of twenty-one, she lived in Schwabing and tried to become a painter, but in fact supported herself by writing, first translations from the French, then satirical sketches, and finally novels.

We should mention two, *Ellen Olenstjerne,* an autobiographical novel about her early rebellions, more serious and melodramatic in tone than most of her work, and *Herr Dames Aubzeichnungen*, a satirical description of *Schwabing* and its personalities, which takes as its climactic event the quarrel between Klages and Wolfskehl which broke up the Cosmic Circle.

Fanny's novels were not unsuccessful. But her essential career was made, even more than Otto Gross's, not out of the doing of particular jobs, but out of the life of Schwabing. This meant the meetings in cafés, the practice of art, the discussion of ideas, the adventures of Bohemia, the defiance of the bour- geois world, and, quite centrally, sexual freedom. She married and loved her husband, but could not remain faithful to him. The Schwabing life style was more important to her. Rainer Maria Rilke and Mühsam, Derleth and Stern, Klages and Wolfskehl were all among Fanny's admirers and lovers. But she was in search of love all her life. It seems likely that, as Klages said, her mother's early withholding of love, in punishment, had created a hunger in Fanny which nothing subsequent could satisfy. She took a great number of

lovers—she was a beautiful woman and full of high-bred charm—and on occasion sold her favors for money; yet she struck most observers as strikingly
clean and honorable in erotic matters. She had a child, whose fatherhood she
refused to divulge, and brought him up by herself, finding, from then on,
her major emotional resource in her relationship to her child.

She and her illegitimate child were exemplary figures in Schwabing.
When she began her affair with Ludwig Klages, which was the major experience in the lives of both, Adam Hentschel, one of her earlier lovers, declared
her the most significant woman of the century and Klages the most significant man. If these two joined together, he said, the world of paganism would
celebrate a revolutionary awakening, there would be a renewal of paganism
on the whole planet. (The founding of a pagan colony, a pagan island in the
world, was one of their semi-serious projects, as it was of Lawrence later.)
And it seems that Fanny herself took the cosmic ideas seriously then, despite
her later irony. She defined Schwabing as "a spiritual movement, a *niveau,*
a direction, a protest, a new cult, or rather an attempt to use old cults to
achieve new religious possibilities." Even the men she satirized in her novel
always admitted that she had understood them and what they were doing.

Klages himself called Fanny "eine heidnische Heilige," a pagan saint.
The phrase was not used loosely, for the Cosmic Circle had a fully worked
out conception of paganism. Because Christianity was, from several points of
view, the major enemy of everything it believed in, calling Fanny a pagan
saint meant that she possessed the pagan virtues, the virtues opposed to
Christian chastity, meekness, and selflessness, in the same measures as the
saints possessed their saintly virtues. The phrase reminds us of the moral
seriousness of this paganism. Fanny was a saint of sensuality, pride, power,
life-worship, and self-assertion. With her child she was a pagan Madonna,
promiscuity replacing chastity, and yet nourishing the same rich, beautiful
mother-love. She deserved a pagan version of dulia.

Fanny felt herself especially gifted for life and with life. She often per-
sonified it—as Life: "We see eye to eye, Life and I." She often felt that she
could embrace more than all the other people in the world. Though she loved
her husband, she regretfully found him not strong enough to cope with her
vitality, her "egotism" ("as he calls it"). At the same time, she was spiritually
ambitious, for there was, she noted, "always the feeling, behind everything,
that I must achieve something great. That feeling never leaves me."

Klages's description of Fanny as a "heidnische Heilige" is very similar to
the terms in which Otto Gross, who was a friend to both women, praised
Frieda. And a pagan saint is very much what Lawrence might have called her.
As with Fanny, the idea of having her children to herself was important to

Frieda; indeed, it was one of the motives for running away from Weekley. Not until a year after she left him did she realize that he would keep the children, and when she did, it was a major crisis in her life. This is why Lawrence was so upset by her concern over her children, for he knew that they were in some sense the deeper motive of her casting her lot in with him. She often complained bitterly that if she had been a prostitute she could have had her children. By not having them, she was made more dependent on Lawrence.

Klages and Fanny present an interesting parallel to Lawrence and Frieda, for all the major motifs of the former relationship were echoed in Lawrence's relation to Frieda—and, for that matter, in Otto's. That Klages and Fanny never married, that their relationship didn't last, seems to relate to the much more arid and voluntaristic character of Klage's work, especially in later years. As long as it did, he spoke of Fanny much as Lawrence did of Frieda. We are told that he made Fanny into a demi-goddess in her own eyes, revealed to her secrets of herself which she had hitherto only unconsciously known. She, who had always been in search of someone who could extend the limits of possibility for her, said of him that he was the only man with whom one could fly. For her part, she gave him a draught of Life to drink, for she was the spirit of a northern paganism incarnate. Even the discordances between Fanny and Klages derived from the same source. Though she loved the sexual act itself, Fanny would not let Klages caress her, stroke her hair or her hands, or make her something to be cared for. Essentially, she kept the erotic initiative herself, or at least would not leave it to him.

Fanny zu Reventlow's role as an emblematic character extended well beyond Schwabing—to all of Germany in fact. Marianne Weber discussed her as the representative of free love when she wrote about the different categories of love relationship. For us she is perhaps a transitional figure, rather like Lou Andreas-Salome. She began as an Ibsenish rebel against hypocrisy, as one who demanded equal rights for women—not political rights to be sure, but still rights. (This was the path that Else von Richthofen began on.) Under Klages's stimulus, she wrote her autobiographical and somewhat Ibsenish novel, *Ellen Olenstjerne*.

In the course of the 1890s, however, with the triumph of eroticism, she more or less abandoned that role as she began to place more emphasis on herself as an erotic woman and mother. But, unlike Frieda Lawrence or Alma Werfel, she never undertook a major interpretation of this new role. Perhaps she did not because the relationship with Klages failed; and that in turn has to do with her early unhappiness, for she was not made for domesticity. She was an adventuress. Her later literary work was more frivolous and satirical, more "French." And her manner, her whole personality, seem to have become aristocratic, more that of the *femme du monde,* in those late years. She became impatient with the untidier and more Bohemian aspects of Schwabing.

Some details of the publication of *Ellen Olenstjerne* illustrate the connection between different kinds of revolutionariness in Schwabing. The novel was accepted for publication by her friend Julian Marchlewski, a Polish Marxist, but in 1905, with the outbreak of the Russian Revolution, he left Munich, with the novel already set up in type, and went to St. Petersburg, where he worked beside Lenin. (Lenin himself had lived in Schwabing in 1901, along with Krupskaya and Alexander Helphand, who wrote under the penname Parvus and who was closely associated with Trotsky in the Revolution.) The Gräfin herself was not at all political, nor were any of the figures who most concern us, but revolutionaries of all kinds were welcome in Schwabing. In the Munich Revolution of 1918–1919, the paradoxes of the situation became apparent. For instance, one of the Gräfin's closer friends in her last years in Munich was Erich Mühsam, the anarchist poet, nightclub performer, political journalist, and politician. In the days of the Revolution he rose to prominence and even to power—which seemed very incongruous to those who had known him before as categorically harmless, both to his fellow Schabingites and to the solid citizens of Munich. His fellow anarchist Gustav Landauer, who was also prominent in the revolutionary government, was taken into custody by the government troops who recaptured the city, put in prison, and trampled to death. Mühsam himself might well have suffered the same fate if he had not been sent out of the city just before it was too late. Fifteen years later he was murdered by the Nazis in the Oranienburg concentration camp. He and Otto and Fanny and Edgar Jaffe were Schwabing companions in the years before 1910 and their various fates, taken together, symbolize the final fate of Schwabing.

In those years the Gräfin wanted to change her life, and was hesitating between two schemes. One was that she would become Edgar Jaffe's private secretary and at the same time be psychoanalyzed by Otto, who believed that he could free her from her compulsions and her unhappiness. The other was to go to Paris to live. In the end she chose the second option, but only briefly, moving quickly from Paris to Ascona, as we shall see. She had rejected the first scheme because it had two obvious disadvantages: in the first place, she was skeptical about psychoanalysis, and in the second place, it would lay her under obligations to Edgar, whom she liked in the abstract but not as a lover. (Witness the entry in her journal of August 9, 1908, after a night with Jaffe: "Nearly went mad and howled with disgust. Dear God, let this cup pass from me." This is, incidentally, precisely the sort of reaction to Jaffe which Lawrence attributes to Frieda in "Daughters of the Vicar.") In 1910 Jaffe asked her to go to Corfu with him, and she was tempted and would have gone—except that the trip had to include him.

Jaffe was by then informally separated from Else, who lived at Irschenhausen with the children while Edgar kept an apartment in Munich. His would-be affair with the Gräfin—he was being overambitious, overadventurous, as usual—marked the climax of his phase as a servant of Eros and the outbreak of the war irrevocably turned his thoughts back to politics. But he did not return to Heidelberg. His next few years were to make him a leader of Schwabing, a hero of the Schwabing revolution.

He had left Heidelberg in 1910, hired by the new Technological College in Munich. His chief there, Moritz Julius Bonn, described him as "a mild-mannered little man, with rather winning ways." That condescending sentence is more than anyone else ever cared to say about Edgar Jaffe. Apart from that, we have only Müller-Meininger's description of him as two-faced, and as the most hated member of Eisner's cabinet for that reason. No one at all seems to have achieved any sympathetic identification with this man who played so many remarkable roles, or rather performed so many remarkable acts, and who did so amid a group of other men—notably Weber and Lawrence—to whom so much attention has been paid.

In August 1915 he was in the administration in occupied Belgium, and it was he who proposed Max Weber for a position in which he could exert some power over the economy there. Weber had just resigned his job with the Heidelberg hospitals and he made the journey to Brussels in the hope of making a bigger contribution to the war effort. That hope was disappointed, but the episode is another example of the important ancillary role Jaffe played in Weber's career, even after the latter's affair with Else. It was in Belgium, his daughter says, that Edgar learned to hate German militarism. He soon returned to Munich, where he started a new weekly magazine of which he was editor and began a political discussion group comprised of people concerned about German policy. His co-operator in both these enterprises, Heinrich von Frauendorfer, a "dark, self-conscious man with a look of restrained passion," had been a minister of Bavaria but was driven from power by the Catholic Centrum party and—according to some observers—nourished a deep desire for revenge against the king. In 1918, Jaffe was the first man in Munich to demand the deposition of the Kaiser. And when Kurt Eisner drove out the Wittelsbach dynasty, on November 7, 1918, Jaffe became the Minister of Finance in the People's Republic of Bavaria—the only academic in the cabinet.

It was a Schwabing revolution, with Schwabing personalities taking control of the whole city of Munich, of the whole state of Bavaria. Men of ideas drove out men of business, men of speculation drove out men of practical experience, men from the world of the arts drove out men from the world of politics, men of cafés drove out men of offices. Neither Max Weber nor Else Jaffe could begin to take it seriously as a political event. Edgar Jaffe was by that time estranged from Heidelberg, abandoned by all his old gods, isolated.

His daughter remembers accompanying him to the empty royal palace when he had to decide the fate of the royal Wintergarten, on the top floor, which was consuming a lot of the city's meager coal supply. They mounted up, led by resentful royalist porters, past roomfuls of Chinese vases, gilded furniture, Greek statues, to a vast conservatory whose roof was hidden by the tropical foliage of giant trees, with a waterfall constantly splashing. They went down again into the basement to inspect what small stores of coal were left. The most promising pile turned out to be handgrenades. And finally—in some agony, for all living beauty was an object of reverence to him—the conscientious little Minister of Finance had to decree the death of all that luxuriant fertility.

He had decided, during the war, that economic individualism had always been an un-German idea, from which the heroic experiences of 1914 were saving the nation. Germans like to feel themselves part of an organic whole, each one a limb with an assigned function. Private enterprise must be subordinated to public.

Even though Jaffe had a keen appreciation for the values which the war brought to the fore in German life, he was a committed pacifist. In his pacifist enterprise he was associated with Professors F. W. Foerster and Ludwig Quidde and was in contact with American representatives in Switzerland in 1917. (Else Jaffe, like Max Weber, was militantly patriotic during the war. She hung a photograph of Hindenburg in the living room and even regretted having no son to send to her fatherland's defense.) In the same year he joined the Independent Socialist Party, and in 1918 he and Kurt Eisner, his party leader, wired George D. Herron in Geneva, whom they believed to be President Wilson's personal representative, asking for a separate peace for Bavaria, which they were in the process of leading out of the German Reich.

This was the most brilliant single achievement among all the rebellions against Bismarck and Prussia which we are recording here. And it was performed, under the inspiration of Schwabing, by the least brilliant of the personalities we are concerned with. It is typical of Edgar Jaffe's fate that he was at that time alienated from his wife and from those brilliant men to whom he had affiliated himself; and that the Bavarian Revolution which he led was crushed in a matter of months, provoking widespread reaction. It was as a part of that reaction that Nazism first took root in Bavaria. A Catholic party again took power in Munich in 1920, offering a refuge to Ludendorff and attempted to become the center of reaction for all Germany. It punished the revolutionaries savagely, and Jaffe was in extreme danger, as was Frauendorfer, who also had been a minister under Eisner. Frauendorfer committed suicide without awaiting trial and Jaffe suffered a nervous collapse in 1919 from which he never recovered. (On July 10, 1919, his wife wrote to the Staatsanwalt that he was too sick to give evidence at the Toller trial.) He died in 1921. Many of the ministers in the Schwabing regime committed suicide or died in asylums or nursing homes, even though only the most extremist, like Ernst Toller, Weber's student and friend, were ever put on trial. Of them all, Edgar Jaffe, the quietest, the most peaceable is, perhaps the most pathetic.

Ernst Frick and the Gräfin zu Reventlow had left Munich for Ascona in 1910, and Frieda Gross (Otto was now rarely with her) at about the same time. Frieda Weekley visited her there in 1911, and invited Frick to England, where she met him later that year, and in the spring of 1912, when she left England with D. H. Lawrence, she again proposed herself to Frieda Gross for a visit to Ascona.

Ascona was the Schwabing of Schwabing, where more extreme personalities, more extreme behavior, and more extreme ideas were to be found in a setting freer from big city influences. This Swiss lake resort, to which most of the anarchists went, was a village of only a thousand souls in 1899 when Henri Oedenkoven, the son of a rich Antwerp industrialist, set up there a *Naturheilstätte*, where the men wore shorts and sandals and tunics and no hat but a band round their shoulder-length hair. Shortly thereafter Karl Gräser set up another similar establishment which he called "Fort von der Zivilization." Gräser's brother became a friend of Raymond Duncan, and through this connection Isadora Duncan came to Ascona. There was modern dance, eccentric costume, long hair, sunbathing, and vegetarianism. Erich Mühsam discovered it for Schwabing, and in 1909 he recognized that Ascona contained an ideal solution to the Gräfin's financial problems—a solution which illustrates perfectly the comedy-farce style of her later life. Living in Ascona was a Baron Rechenberg, a former sailor who had fallen in love with an Italian washerwoman. The Baron wanted to inherit his family fortune so that he could endow her children, and it didn't seem to matter to him that she was happily married to someone else. In order to inherit he had to marry, so he needed someone who would marry him for a share of the money. Mühsam put the proposal to the Gräfin, and she agreed. The marriage was performed, and the father was charmed by his new daughter-in-law—until someone ex-

plained the trick to him. Some of the family money was already in the newly-
weds' hands, but that was soon lost in a bank crash; and no more was forthcoming. When war broke out in 1914 the Gräfin was planning a trip around
the world with a Chinese acrobat, serving as the target at which he threw
knives.

This was the operetta style of life from which Lawrence, for the most
part, saved Frieda. Not entirely though, for Taos, especially after Lawrence's
death, was not entirely incomparable with Ascona; and Frieda's choice of a
third husband might have appealed to the Gräfin.

The war was anathema to Fanny, as to Frieda, particularly because it
threatened to force her son into military service. She felt strongly enough
about it to disown her brother, who was a prominent chauvinist, annexation-
ist, and member of the Pan-German League, and she even went to Max Weber
for legal advice and assistance in saving her son by changing his nationality.
Presumably she had come in contact with Weber via Frieda Gross, who
moved to Ascona with her husband in 1910 and stayed on after 1913, when
Otto went to Berlin.

In 1918 Fanny zu Reventlow died in Ascona. Two years later Otto Gross
died in Berlin, from undernourishment and exposure, having eluded the
watchfulness of the friends who were looking after him, but whom he distrusted because they would not help him get supplies of drugs by violence.
Running away from them, he had hid in a warehouse and was found some
days later, in so weakened a condition that his life could not be saved. Then,
in 1921, Edgar Jaffe died in Munich, never having recovered from the nervous breakdown which he suffered when the Revolution collapsed. These
three deaths announce the death of Schwabing.

2

Max Weber and D. H. Lawrence: Berlin and Nottingham

Introduction

Max Weber and D. H. Lawrence stand for opposite things. Lawrence was not only England's greatest novelist of the twentieth century but also a bold thinker whose ideas about marriage, education, religion, and literature earned him the status of a hero of culture's protest against civilization. Weber was not only Germany's greatest academic sociologist but also a bold thinker who stands as a hero of modern liberalism because of his ideas about politics, economics, religion, and the whole range of the social sciences. Their thinking led them—and their admirers—in opposite directions, and their heroism was of opposite kinds. The differences between are, in one way or another, all represented in their opposite stances toward the erotic movement, toward eroticism.

Their circumstances were of course very different. Weber was born in 1864, Lawrence in 1885, a generation later. If Weber had been, like Lawrence, twenty-two years old in 1907, instead of forty-three, he might have responded differently to the challenge of the erotic movement. (Weber was ten years older than Else Jaffe, who was five years older than her sister Frieda, who was six years older than Lawrence. Those age differentials were part of the style of their relationships.) Moreover, whereas Weber was born into the upper middle class and close to the seat of social power, with models of that power and routes toward it available to him from early on, Lawrence was born into the lowest middle class or working class, far from social power. And Weber was born in Germany, Lawrence in England—a circumstance of which we already have seen some of the consequences.

But the interest of collocating the two men is that it is then possible to dismiss all those circumstantial differences as minor and to say that the major form taken by their opposition can be seen in their opposite *choices* of responses to eroticism—which is to say, their choices in their relations with the von Richthofen sisters. Of course, their choices did not concern only the sisters; nor were they all choices in the strict sense, for Weber was Weber before 1910, Lawrence was Lawrence before 1912. But character is always a matter of choice to some degree, of *self*-formation, and part of these men's earliest self-training had to do with choosing their erotic personalities, choosing their styles of love, their relations with their mothers, their incorporation of feminine elements into their own personalities. One chose the styles of the world of men, the other those of the world of Woman.

By tracing their erotic development, in this sense, we can see how they came to be the men they were in their relationships with the von Richthofen sisters. We also can see how each developed the unique powers of imagination which he bequeathed as a permanent legacy to the collective mind of Europe —and to us. In the case of Lawrence, at least, it seems clear that the two modes of being, the man and the imagination, influenced each other profoundly. His erotic relationship with Frieda enhanced the quality and power of his imagination and also changed its direction. In the case of Weber, we know much less, and it seems likely that the effect was less. Moreover, his love relationship was in tragic tension with his beliefs. Love strained his conscience, it did not enhance it. But because Frau Jaffe *shared* those beliefs, their joint renunciation of happiness in love reinforced him morally, just as Lawrence's achievement of happiness with Frieda reinforced him.

If the two men can be seen this way, then what leaps to the eye are certain similarities in the backgrounds to their choices. The same perspectives were painted on the backdrops against which each of the two men chose— one choosing the world of men, the other that of Woman. The major feature their backgrounds had in common concerns the structure of the families they were born into and the Oedipal conflicts from which they suffered in consequence. That conflict was a major factor in each man's life, with countless ramifications, and it helped induce other important similarities of situation, such as the similarity of type of the two girls with whom they were first involved. There are even some similarities of attitude and theory, notably in political and historical matters, which testify to an intellectual background common to both. We shall stress these shared elements, in order to make clearer the fundamental difference—the oppositeness—of the two love-choices. That opposition, between their attitudes to Eros, between each one's choice of love-partner and love-mode—climactically, between Else Jaffe and Frieda Weekley—can explain all the rest.

We shall give much more information about Weber than about Lawrence, because the former is so much less familiar a figure to the English-speaking reader. It is perhaps worth trying to fix a comparable image for him before we begin our more detailed discussion. Weber is the author of *The Protestant Ethic and the Spirit of Capitalism* of 1904, a brilliant and still controversial essay suggesting that the Protestant moral sense nourished the growth of capitalism as we know it in the West to the giant size which it has achieved here alone. Because it associates moral-spiritual phenomena with economic-historical facts, in mutual explanation, the theory of the Protestant ethic has a sardonic flavor which is typical of all Weber's work. He was an 'unmasking' intelligence, like Nietzsche, Marx, and Freud, and he focused his corrosive analyses on the whole range of current German politics, internal and external, as well as on history. He was a very powerful public speaker as well as a polemicist in newspapers and pamphlets; at various times he took on most of his academic colleagues and even the Imperial government. He tried to create an atmosphere of heroic debate in all the areas of German civilization by the force of his personal example. Of his contribution to intellectual history, we may say that he more than anybody else created modern social science and established its formidably abstract approach. And he did all this while suffering from nervous problems that would have incapacitated a lesser man—and indeed did incapacitate him for various periods of his life. A physically large man and a dominating personality annihilatingly forceful in debate, with a powerful musical voice and a full professorial beard—this is the man to set beside D. H. Lawrence in our imaginations. The slight, quick-moving, light-footed Englishman, our supreme artist-teacher of eroticism, and the heavy-fisted German, perhaps our supreme hero of liberal politics, can become for us a vivid polarity of human types.

Family Backgrounds

Max Weber was born in Erfurt, but his parents moved soon after his birth to Berlin and his education, formal and informal, was that of a Berliner. Moreover, his formative years fell in that period when just being a Berliner could be a fate in itself; when the annexation of Schleswig-Holstein, the triumph over Austria, the defeat of France, the unification of Germany, and above all the giant figure of Bismarck, the greatest statesman and personality in Europe, all combined to put intoxicating influences into the air of Berlin. The Weber family was placed so as to be able to drink in that winy atmosphere in larger measure than most.

Max Weber senior (1836–1897) was a professional politician with seats in the Reichstag, the Prussian Landestag, and the City Council of Berlin. He was a friend of all the leaders of the National Liberal Party. Bismarck himself never visited the Weber house, but his immediate subordinates did, and the conversation was in some sense always about Bismarck. Weber's friends felt themselves to be the builders—or at least the builder's mates—of modern Germany. His son Max always remembered learning of the outbreak of the war against France, at the age of six, with joyful enthusiasm; he was in Heidelberg, in his mother's family home, in the same house and room in which he was to learn of the war of 1914.

The Weber house in Charlottenburg was visited not only by party leaders like Rudolf von Bennigsen, but also by professors like Heinrich von Treitschke, Heinrich von Sybel, and Theodor Mommsen. It was moderately famous for its hospitality—it was a center—and professors were not far behind politicians as representatives of the new Germany; on Europe's intellectual map, they stood as a power in many ways comparable with the new state's political and military power. Both the "patriots" like Treitschke and the "critics" like Mommsen were, by intellectual temperament and style, figures of *power* in the intellectual world.

The professors came perhaps as much for Frau Weber (1844–1919) as for her husband. Born Helene Fallenstein, she was herself an intellectual, or a woman for intellectuals, who came from a remarkable family already rich in professors. One sister, Ida, was the wife of Hermann Baumgarten, the historian of Strasbourg; another was the wife of Adolf Hausrath, the church historian of Heidelberg and a scholar of the "higher criticism" in the tradition of D. F. Strauss; the fourth, Henrietta, was the wife of Benecke, the geologist of Strasbourg. Their father, George Friedrich Fallenstein (1790–1853), had been a remarkable man who played an enthusiastic part in Prussia's war against Napoleon, in which German national pride first leaped to life. He was a poet who made a romantic first marriage; he was nineteen and she fifteen when he proposed, and he had a mother and her family to support. When the girl's grandfather forbade the marriage, he had a nervous breakdown. They were married only a year later and lived in such great poverty that one of their children died of undernourishment. Fallenstein blamed Napoleon personally for this. Yet when he volunteered in the Prussian army against France, he paid for two comrade's equipment as well as his own. He was an idealist. In the style of the period, he gave his sons Old High-German names and cultivated an Old High-German personality style himself. His wife died after bearing several children, and four years later—by then he was working in the Prussian civil service—he married Emilia Souchay, who became the mother of the sisters just mentioned. He was a heroic soul even as a father of girls, severe and demanding, devoted to cold baths, and opposed to cakes. His daughters carried on something of his tradition in child-rearing.

The sons by his first marriage left home early, in rebellion, but the second family was close-knit. They, and their children in turn, had a life-long devotion to that big house in Heidelberg which Georg Friedrich built when he retired in 1847, and which became in the next century the home of the Max Weber circle and the scene of many brilliant intellectual occasions. For Helene's silver wedding, in 1888, her sisters had a copy made of a famous painting of the house. It showed their parents, standing on the balcony looking out across the Neckar to the Castle; with them was Georg Gottfried Gervinus, an intellectual leader of the liberal and nationalist cause and a family friend who had died seventeen years earlier. Young Max secretly hung it for her to find on the day, and she, we are told, stole away from the festivities to dream in front of it, of her youth and all her disappointed youthful hopes. That picture, as well as the house its depicts, is an important symbol in the Weber story. Max Weber's cousin Otto Baumgarten tells us that Fallenstein's grandchildren always imagined that Gervinus and Fallenstein were discussing Prussia's failure to unite Germany in 1848—their disappointment at her failure to accomplish Germany's destiny—while Frau Fallenstein, gazing out across the moonlit river, was drinking in the spiritual influences of nature. For them, then, it represented the major terms of a life-dialetic the two poles of which were nationalist politics and a spiritual religion. What is more the grouping of the figures in the picture had an even more personal and dramatic significance for the Fallenstein daughters, as we shall see.

Fallenstein's wife survived him by many years, so that she naturally played the larger part in their children's lives. Like her husband, she was intense, but she was religious where he was ethical, which caused difficulties of communication between them. Her temperament was much more fragile and 'sensitive' than his, though perhaps his kind of irritability is only the masculine equivalent of feminine sensitivity.

All four daughters (three sons died young) showed the effects of this doubly exalted heritage to some degree, but Ida and Helene seemed especially to have benefited. Both these sisters, though doubtful about Christian theology and church membership, felt called on to live moral lives of religious intensity in both the intellectual and the practical spheres. Struggle was an important word in their vocabularies. "Without struggling, struggling till you bleed, there is no true peace in life" was one of their mother's aphorisms. The lives of both professors and politicians seemed to them of very ambiguous value for their sons as well as for their husbands. The way power was used in the world of politics deeply upset them, but then so did the way power was *not* used in the world of academia, where responsibility was rarely taken. And yet both had a vivid appreciation of, and an intimate acquaintance with, both the political and the academic modes of life.

The Fallensteins had money—Souchay money—and Max Weber's family were very prosperous linen weavers in Bielefeld, seventy miles from Hanover. The Webers of Charlottenburg were upper-middle-class: not really wealthy, and not in the least aristocratic, but endowed with the privileges and anxieties of a ruling class;—which they were, in the sense of being leaders, being in possession of those ideas which are most likely to be made socially effective.

George and Lydia Lawrence of Nottingham, on the other hand, belonged just as definitely at the lower limit of the lower middle class. Mrs. Lawrence's father had been an engineer and a friend and rival of both General Booth of the Salvation Army and Jesse Boot of the great chemists' chain-stores, but her husband was a coal miner. She had been a schoolteacher and she belonged to a women's discussion group where she gave papers, but he could scarcely read or write. Unlike the Weber family, they held no responsibility for the direction in which the national culture might move. They had no power in the world of men.

The two families were therefore as different as the districts they lived in: Charlottenburg, a new, prosperous, metropolitan suburb, and Eastwood, an ugly industrial township imposed upon a village. And yet family photographs do not look altogether different. There was a generic resemblance between the two families; they were more like each other in moral style than either one was like the von Richthofens, for instance.

Frau Weber and Mrs. Lawrence, around whom the families centered, were both slender and delicate looking, but vigorous, decisive, incisive; ascetic in dress and sensual style, but lovable and loving; anxious, but humorous. Both even have the same very expressive trick of holding their heads slightly to one side, which suggests a winsome shyness as well as, perhaps, a deprecation of their own forcefulness. We know from descriptions that the charm of both was best expressed in their movements, which were notably vigorous and yet graceful. Both were "ladies" in the middle-class sense. They accepted fully all the limitations which nineteenth-century refinement imposed on the enjoying or even the feeling of sensual excitement. They accepted them so fully, in fact, that they did not feel them as limitations at all, but as the containing walls of a living cell, organically necessary to healthy life.

The fathers too were alike in being both big and handsome, giving an

impression of forcefulness, while in fact they were ineffective, morally impotent, within their family circles. They were reproached by their children—
at least by Max and David Herbert—with "taking the easy way out," "enjoying life." Theirs was in some sense an ineffective sensuality—one hears of
no sexual scandal attaching to them, as to Baron von Richthofen—but it exiled them nonetheless from the family community, and in the photographs
they look somewhat hollowed out. They have the aspect of official gods, ac-
corded a purely conventional respect by their children, at the behest of their
priestess-wives, who really direct the family pieties.

In every other respect the two men were very unlike, of course. Max
Weber senior was a very successful man, a leading citizen not only of his
city but of his country. But in Marianne Weber's account of him this
"hollowed-out" quality is unmistakable. Bismarck had emasculated the whole
National Liberal party. He was the male of Germany, and they were his
eunuchs; he wielded the power, he acted—for good and for evil—and they
enjoyed their ease. In nineteenth-century novels sensual enjoyment, even
sexual enjoyment, is the mark of "effeminacy"; and one result of such cultural
values was that Max Weber, who grew up in a situation that forced him to
respond to them, came to insist on the need for *men* in Germany to stand up
to Bismarck.

The hidden similarity between the two families is all the more striking
because of the large differences between their apparent structures. Mrs. Lawrence had openly fought her husband, defeated him, and exiled him, whereas Frau Weber suffered in silence, though an eloquent silence. But the consequences which followed from that difference, though numerous and large,
did not amount to a difference in the feeling of the more sensitive members
of the family toward their father. It is clear in Max's letters from early on
that all his feelings were focused on his mother. And in the family photograph of 1887 it is perhaps clear how alienated he is from his father—Professor Baumgarten thinks that is visible—and certainly how alienated he is
from himself. The family struggle had claimed a major victim, had inflicted
a major wound, the chief symptom of which was young Max's self-distrust
and self-contempt which made him seem then even physically coarse and
lumpish. He was in his early twenties, very unlike the forceful tragic hero of
later years, and unlike the handsome boy he had been. In the Lawrence
family group portrait, taken around 1893, David Herbert's face is too young
to be read, but of course we know how alienated he soon felt—how he could
not bear, physically, to be in his father's presence.

Frau Weber and Mrs. Lawrence were both serious women—and in the
same style of seriousness. They were interested in social problems and re-

ligion and morality, in the existential questions at the core of the social and moral sciences. In 1904 Frau Weber was made an honorary City Councillor in Berlin—the first woman to be so honored—in recognition of her work with unwed mothers, problem children, and the childbed of the poor. Her social situation, of course, gave her a scope for public activity which Mrs. Lawrence never had. But essentially the two were alike. They were not in the least aesthetes, nor serious scholars, nor women of fashion, nor stricken deer, nor pagan earth-goddesses, nor ambitious worldlings. You can put both of them in the same direction and at the same distance away from the type of Baroness von Richthofen, whom we can recognize behind Lawrence's Anna Brangwen; and of the latter's three daughters, only Else followed the two older women's style. (Max Weber remarked on her resemblance to his mother. Almost certainly so did D. H. Lawrence.) Frau Weber's favorite authors were W. E. Channing and Theodore Parker, the New England Transcendentalist Christians. We can guess pretty confidently that they, or others very like them, were also familiar to Mrs. Lawrence. Their sons both objected to that brand of enthusiastic idealism, but they also responded to it, for it was part of their ideological inheritance from their mothers.

The Webers' marriage may be said to have begun with Gervinus's attempt to seduce Helene Fallenstein. Gervinus was a professor of history and an enthusiastic worker for national unity who took part in the revolutionary Professors Parliament in 1848. He became a close friend of Georg Friedrich Fallenstein, whose daughters he tutored in history and the classics. He was a married man, much older than Helene, and a family friend, but when Helene was sixteen he tried to seduce her. This was soon after her father's death and she was severely shocked and disturbed. Very soon thereafter she visited her sister Ida, who shortly before had married the liberal and progressive historian Hermann Baumgarten. There she met her brother-in-law's equally liberal and progressive friend Max Weber, and very quickly married him.

Ida had married in the same year as her father died. She was seventeen at the time, twelve years younger than her husband, whom at first she hero-worshipped. He too had been a fighter for German national unity and was already a prominent intellectual, just like her father. But she soon became somewhat alienated from—indeed, vigorously hostile to—the academic and political world in which he lived. She was out of sympathy even with the war of 1870, on which German greatness was based. When her husband was appointed to a chair at the new university in newly conquered Strasbourg immediately after the war, she took up the mission of getting to know the

French people of the area. The German academic community as a whole felt themselves a branch of a conquering power, in much the same position as Baron von Richthofen's military administration at Metz, but Frau Baumgarten refused to see herself in that role. She became morally anti-Prussian, anti-Bismarckian. Above all, her religious interests became more predominant, more moral-social, less historical-critical; she tried to live by the teachings of the Sermon on the Mount. She became involved in the workers' movement and came to hate the "aristocratic" classicism of standard German culture. Her niece Emily Fallenstein, who later married her son Otto, gradually acquired more influence over her mind than her husband. Emily was a religious enthusiast, physically sickly, and Frau Baumgarten herself became sickly, both from the physical strain of much childbearing—three children were lost young—and from these spiritual and psychological strains.

She and her children spent their holidays in Heidelberg at the Fallenstein house, where she influenced them to be Fallensteins rather than Baumgartens —or, rather to be Souchays. She was in rebellion against what Fallenstein, and Gervinus, had stood for. In her adolescence she had been strongly influenced by Gervinus, who pushed her toward rationalism and religious skepticism. He was a follower of D. F. Strauss, whose *Leben Jesu* had launched the historiographic movement aimed at demythologizing Christ, and she had a hard struggle to win her way back to that spontaneous piety of feeling which she wanted to share with her children when she became a mother. Gervinus's two culture heroes had been Handel and Shakespeare, both of whom he interpreted in a schematically rationalist way, against which she now rebelled—again in the name of feeling. And no doubt his attempted seduction of her sister Helene must have intensified her reaction against him and what he stood for. It was a reaction against the Apollonian mind as a whole, and in her rebellion she must have identified with the picture of her mother gazing away from the two men toward Nature. So Gervinus came to stand for the academic and political type Ida Baumgarten now distrusted.

There seems no reason to doubt the genuineness of Max Weber's and Helene Fallenstein's initial love for each other, but the Gervinus incident had left a bruise in her imagination which the subsequent strains of her marriage developed into an aversion from all sexuality. (This at least was her son's interpretation.) These marital strains focused in her husband's gradual failure or refusal to accompany his wife in her wrestlings with religious and moral conscientiousness. He gradually defined for himself the role of man-of-the-world, man of common sense and common sensuality, man of effective power, participator in political alliances and friendships. How much of mortification and renunciation and defeat may have gone into his change of role we cannot say, but we know that it was a change; that earlier he too had been a reader of Channing and Parker; that it was his wife who commanded the allegiance of the children, while he was "with them" only when he took them on trips away from her; above all, that he is a very shadowy figure in the considerable bulk of biography written about the family. His character is decidedly drawn, but it is all interpretation by others, all attribution of intention. Practically no speech or gesture of his, no habitual phrase or taste, is recorded there to make a direct impact on us, even in the open conflicts between him and his eldest son. Other members of the Fallenstein family— Ida Baumgarten and her sons, for example—seem to have disliked him for his insensitivity to his wife without speculating as to its source. All the husbands of the Fallenstein sisters tended to end up isolated, having been found wanting by their wives. These few facts all seem to suggest that his role was in a sense forced upon him, enacted with no real enthusiasm of self-definition, as a way of dealing with his wife's greater vigor; that it was chosen originally, perhaps, as a way of being different from her, because in his old role he was only a paler version of the same thing, a shadow of her.

In any case, from whatever motive, he separated himself from her religious-moral interests. He spent a lot of money on enlarging their house in 1885, and on their quite "social" hospitality. It was *her* money he spent on this, and he refused to let her spend it on good works. (His income was twelve thousand Marks, hers twenty-two thousand, after 1881.) She had to go to him always with her account books, in order to get money for the household and all the while she suffered from the thought of their luxury and the poverty of so many others. And he refused to join her in her prolonged mourning and self-reproach after the deaths of two of their children in infancy. Frau Weber worked extremely hard, at household tasks as well as other things, worried endlessly over the children's moral, emotional and physical welfare, created and controlled the life of the household at every moment. Herr Weber came in when it suited him, demanded meals, talked to the friends he had brought with him, and left again. He played the part of a stupid domestic tyrant, a minor Bismarck. She suffered and the children, especially Max, suffered with her, resenting their father's behavior but also, less consciously, resenting her suffering and the burden it placed on them. But they never could deny the justice of her unspoken complaint without denying all traditional Western morality. Frieda Weekley and Otto Gross on the other hand, did deny it, and consequently refused to give conduct like Frau Weber's any moral admiration. Max Weber and Else Jaffe could only prescribe the extra virtue of reasonable resistance.

The continuity, the consubstantiality, of this domestic problem with the political one is argued at length, and quite convincingly, by Arthur Mitzman in *The Iron Cage*. One sees it all mirrored *in petto* in this passage from a letter by Max Weber to his uncle Hermann Baumgarten, of July 25, 1887, in which Max is discussing the historian Treitschke, in whom he recognized the *Pathos* and the *Ernst* of a great personality, even while hating the political principles Treitschke stood for. "It is the same as with Bismarck," Weber writes; "if the nation but knew how to handle him rightly and to value him rightly, at the right moment to resist him firmly, and then again to trust him when he deserves trust. . . ." If we alter "die Nation" to "die Mutter," we have a statement describing his parents' situation as he saw it and felt it. Other people's loyalties, most importantly Ida Baumgarten's, ran parallel to Weber's in the two spheres of German politics and Weber family life; she turned against both Bismarck and her father.

Like her sister Ida, Helene withdrew from her husband morally; and it was to Ida that she turned first, joining her in her religious and political-moral concerns. The two of them were early financial contributors to Pastor Naumann's career as a political reformer. In both families the sisters intensified their identification with the Souchay-Fallenstein heritage at the expense of their identification with their husbands. The sense of Heidelberg as the real home became, even for the children, charged with moral and emotional intensities.

Frau Baumgarten was a more extremist temperament than her sister. She really tried to live by Christian precepts of self-sacrifice. Once she took a girl into her house off the streets and it turned out that the object of her charity brought with her an infection from which one of the children died. As he grew up, Max Weber reacted against this sort of uncompromising moral passion, insisting that it was eccentric to measure every action against an ethical absolute. But he acknowledged later how much of an influence this moral sublimity had exerted on him. His aunt Ida, he said, had forced him to choose, to realize that he could give his loyalties *either* to his father *or* to his mother.

Curiously, Ida's husband also represented an important influence on Max Weber. Along with Gervinus, Treitschke, Jolly, and Sybel, Hermann Baumgarten had worked for the unification of Germany. But he came to see the dangers of Bismarck's caesaristic leadership, which he thought not even conservative in the good sense, but a threat to German culture. He hated the Chancellor's destruction of all potential rivals and the idolization of him by the mass of intellectuals; and he rebelled against Treitschke's historical glorification of the Hohenzollerns and of Prussian power—that is, against the whole intensification of the patriarchal mode. He spoke for liberalism and for the southern and western states of Germany, with an increasing bitterness and pessimism which left him intellectually isolated but which won him the respect and sympathy of his nephew Max. Though not religiously intense like his wife, he was a moral phenomenon comparable with Mommsen, an uncompromising nay-sayer in a land of complacency. Max Weber was in close touch with him between 1883 and 1893, finding in him exactly the political and intellectual integrity which his father seemed to lack. Where Max Weber Sr. praised Treitschke's monumental *German History in the Nineteenth Century* for its glorification of the Hohenzollern dynasty, Baumgarten attacked it sharply in 1883, even though doing so caused him to be shunned by his colleagues.

Baumgarten's son Otto, who became Max Weber's friend in college and who conducted his marriage ceremony, combined something of his mother's and his father's interests. A minister and friend of Pastor Naumann's, he was a Christian Socialist who had been inspired by the writing of Charles Kingsley and F. W. Robertson, Channing and Parker. He was more of a liberal than his father, who felt it to be a law of nature that Protestants must rule Catholics and that the educated must rule the uneducated. But Otto was also, increasingly as time went by, a disciplinarian and an authoritarian. He came to admire Bismarck deeply and wrote about him often; in 1918 he declared that the Allies forbidding of military conscription in Germany was the worst possible blow to the national life, because the upper classes needed that moral discipline. This Carlylean mixture of values may perhaps represent the Baumgarten mind of Max's generation. All three of these figures—as well as Emmy Baumgarten, Otto's highly spiritual sister—acted on Max's imagination as he was growing up.

For figures like these there were no equivalents in D. H. Lawrence's family. Of course we hear of uncles and of family friends who meant something to Lawrence in his formative years, but they were not people with a public role to play in the life of the English nation. Almost the only family alliance that could lead Lawrence's imagination out of its immediate environment was the fact that his aunt Ada married a German called Krenkow who became interested in Oriental studies. But Fritz Krenkow was nothing like Hermann Baumgarten, either as a figure of power in contemporary life or as an influence on his nephew. Even the intellectual circle which Lawrence got to know in Nottingham as he achieved manhood was not comparable with Weber's Berlin circle. Willie Hopkin's group, even when it was visited by the socialist lecturer Edward Carpenter, was less highly charged, because further from power, than Pastor Naumann's.

Family Influences

Like Mrs. Lawrence, Frau Weber transferred to her children, and in particular to her eldest son, the hopes, the demands, the reliance, the appeal,
which had found no response in her husband. Max, like David Herbert, was
sickly and nervous as a young boy. He had meningitis when he was four and
either recovered very slowly or at least was treated as still sick for a long time.
(Thereafter his mother never could understand how a mother could ever
spend a night away from her children.) He was for a long time afraid of the
sea, for instance, and afraid of animals. His fears and his sickliness called
forth, of course, all the more self-devotion from his mother. At school he
felt physically weak and inept, but he was phenomenally clever, though his
teachers did not think well of him because of his power of sullen resistance.
His mother, too, grieved over his "unreachableness." When the time came
for his Confirmation, she suffered from his refusal to tell her his religious
problems, thus making it impossible for her to express her own to him. She
envied her sister Ida, whose children brought their deepest problems to her
for counsel. To be sure, it was not only his mother from whom he retreated
in this way, for we have a letter Max wrote at about this time to his cousin,
Fritz Baumgarten, in which he apologizes for not sharing with Fritz his
feelings about religion. Such is, he says, his nature; he *cannot* talk to others
about the things he cares deeply about. He is aware, he admits, that this
makes him poor company.

Indeed, the most striking feature of Max's whole relationship to his
family was precisely this voluntary/involuntary refusal on his part to open
up to the constant, anxious, loving solicitations of his mother, and the consequent self-reproach on both sides. The effects of this self-reproach were far
more destructive in him, for his mother merely judged herself not "worthy"—
she had a favorite little rhyme in which the lovely *Rööschen*, the rose, was
contrasted with the humble *Mööschen*, the moss, and she was the moss. But
the boy judged himself an ugly nature, cold-blooded, resistant, inhumane.
At seventeen he left the family party in Venice, where they had been on
holiday, because he felt that he could not supply the enthusiasm for Italy
that was being *demanded* of him. An important clue to Weber's development
lies in the fact that this relationship with his mother persisted so long. She
died, still full of vitality, only just before he did. We find him confessing to
a sister when he was over fifty years old, ". . . I am a more uncommunicative
and perhaps a lonelier man than appears, and not easy to approach. That
grace Nature did not give me, and many of those whose love I once had, and
those whose love I still have, have suffered in consequence, and perhaps still

suffer." All his life he was in a state of apology, first to his mother, then to his wife.

A passage from Lawrence's "Fantasia of the Unconscious" offers itself as a comment on Weber's relation to his mother:

> Most fatal, most hateful of all things is bullying. But what is bullying? It is a desire to superimpose my own will upon another person. Sensual bullying of course is fairly easily detected. What is more dangerous is ideal bullying. Bullying people into what is ideally good for them. I embrace for example an ideal, and I seek to enact this ideal in the person of another. This is ideal bullying. A mother says that life should be all love, all delicacy and forbearance and gentleness. And she proceeds to spin a hateful sticky web of permanent forbearance, a gentleness, hushedness around her naturally passionate and hasty child. . . . It results in neurasthenia, which is largely a dislocation or collapse of the great voluntary centres, and a living a sort of half life, almost entirely from the upper centres.

One of Weber's moving analyses of his own condition begins with an image of a cripple. Writing to Ferdinand Tönnies about religion, he says that he is not himself really anti-religious, or even irreligious. "I experience myself as being, in these matters also—a cripple, a mutilated being, whose fate it is to be compelled in all honor—or else one would be perpetrating some romantic swindle—to admit that I understand what is being talked about, without—like a tree-stump, which is able to put out *buds*, again and again— without playing the part of being a whole tree."

He took the usual ways out of such difficulties. He wrote long humorous letters to his family when he was separated from them, describing things of common interest. He wrote essays on learned subjects, which he made presents of to his parents. He wrote letters of moral counsel to his brother. He developed a sentimental fondness for his sisters. Inside the family he offered all these substitutes for spontaneous relationship. Outside, he became an expert anecdotalist, joined a fraternity, drank and sang and fought duels. He became a "lustige Kumpan"—a boon companion—oddly as that sat with his deeper self.

But he never opened himself emotionally to people outside the family, never formed a deep relationship outside it. Both Emmy Baumgarten, his first love, and Marianne, his wife, were his cousins; moreover, they were both very delicate and sublimated personalities, more feminine than female—like his mother, but even more delicate. He never formed a friendship with a man older or more powerful than himself, as his mother noted and deplored. His cousin Otto was his last older friend, and this was when both were still students. He sought out relationships in which he would be the stronger—helping some comrade study for an examination, for instance. He found in his military and student life a model for a cool and unintimate, jocularly self-assertive masculinity. And later he found, outside the home, arenas within which he could operate as power incarnate—as professor, as politician, as controversialist, as Don Quixote of the law courts.

Thus he acquired power in the outer world, the world of men, even as he was aware of his weakness at home. It is in this light that we should read what he writes in "Politik als Beruf" ("Politics as a Vocation"): "Whoever involves himself with politics, that is, with the use of power and enforcement as means, he 'seals a pact' with diabolical powers." This was Weber's Faustian compact. It contrasts with Lawrence's compact for power in sexuality—for that erotic use of the flesh into which he had to force himself against so many scruples of feeling as well as of idea. Both were determined to escape a certain kind of weakness, at no matter what price, but they took opposite routes. In these two pacts, Weber represents all those who commit themselves to the world of men, Lawrence all those who commit themselves to the world of Woman. It was an ambivalent and self-dividing commitment in both men, though in intention a total one. Both came to regret the cost of what they had done. In the leadership novels,—*Aaron's Rod, Kangaroo, The Plumed Serpent*—Lawrence can be seen yearning to enter the world of men. And Weber at the end of his life shows a strong feeling for the value of other ethics besides his own.

The story of the Lawrence household and its effects on David Herbert is well known from *Sons and Lovers*. All the biographer can add is a reminder to the reader of the greater ambivalence of Lawrence's feelings in real life. His devotion to his mother was not entirely happy, easy, or natural. Some of his poems of his Croydon period, 1908–1911, while his mother was still alive, express a resentment against her which is comparable with the resentment that rings dully through Weber's dutiful devotion. In "End of Another Home Holiday," Lawrence describes his mother as "inexorable love" and "the beggar woman" who is ever at his side, frail and sad with gray bowed head:

> Why is it, the long, slow stroke of the midnight bell
> (Will it never finish the twelve?)
> Falls again and again on my heart with a heavy reproach?
>
> But when I draw the scanty cloak of silence over my eyes
> Piteous love comes peering under the hood;
> Touches the clasp with trembling fingers, and tries

> To put her ears to the painful throb of my blood;
> While her tears soak through to my breast,
> Where they burn and cauterize.

This is very much the underfeeling of Max Weber's letters, to and about his mother, only in them the feeling is "unexpressed."

Thus the division of roles was similar in the Weber and Lawrence families; to the man, sensuality and moral indifference; to the woman, responsibility and anxiety; to the children, inner conflict, Hamletism. And the division of family power was the same; to the man, its appearance; to the woman its substance. These similarities were of course part of the general pattern in Western family life at that time, but there were several such patterns. The Webers and the Lawrences belonged to the same one.

Max was the Webers' eldest son, and that fact seems to have had a profound effect on him. His wife remarks that he had as a child a strong sense of his rights as a firstborn, and his brother Alfred suffered then and all his life from feeling second best. One recalls Freud's remark about himself that a son who is preferred by his mother—Frau Weber called Max "der grosse Max"—"keeps for life the feeling of a conqueror, that confidence of success which often induces real success." To Max himself "conqueror" might have sounded ironic, but the truth in the idea stands out when we compare him with Lawrence. Max Weber was, culturally speaking, a father's son, the inheritor of his father. The generally patriarchal family structure in Germany was reinforced for his generation by achievement of their fathers' in unifying the country. (Werner Sombart, Heinrich Rickert, Robert Michels, were all also sons of "founding fathers.") Weber often spoke of the heavy fate of being an epigone, and said that the preceding generation had built "a strong house" around people like him. In comparison, Lawrence, one may say, was simply not a father's son at all; nor was he his mother's oldest or preferred son in his early years. What Max was to Frau Weber, Ernest, the oldest son who died in early manhood, was to Mrs. Lawrence. Ernest, who appears as William in *Sons and Lovers,* was more confidently masculine than David Herbert. He was good at sports as well as at school work, large, vigorous, humorously aggressive, a natural leader. David Herbert, by comparison, had a debilitatingly large element of the feminine in him. He called forth his mother's protective instincts and never offered her something to rest and rely on. In both families it was the eldest sons—Max Weber and Ernest Lawrence—who were called on to be the husbands life had denied their mothers.

This is the fundamental difference between Max Weber and D. H.

Lawrence; from it derived so many of the other differences that separated them. Max took upon himself the male role, as his culture defined it; Lawrence did not, or at least he refused certain crucial modes of "male" action. The extraordinary powers of imagination, understanding, and self-projection which both men possessed were thereafter devoted to opposite tasks. Weber was making himself into a "man," although to be sure at the same time he was critically redefining "manhood." But Lawrence was making himself into a "man-and-woman," exploring with great boldness the female mode of being, in which Weber made no significant investment. (Again, one may say that in later life both men regretted the cost of these decisions.)

All the children were called on to revenge the mother upon her husband, but this duty fell most heavily on the most sensitive and serious, upon the Hamlets of the family, Max Weber and D. H. Lawrence. The scene in *Sons and Lovers* where Paul Morel defends his mother against his father reflects real-life events. In the Weber household there was both more and less of this. Through many years of adult life in the parental home, Max did *not* defend his mother against her husband's tyranny. Because of the extensive and intensive character of academic training in Germany then, he did not escape that home until he was thirty. This prolonged dependence, under such stressful conditions, clearly prejudiced his chances of happiness and contrasts with Lawrence's early escape. We can gauge the price he paid from the troubled letters of self-defense Weber wrote to his cousin Emmy Baumgarten, explaining his inactivity in his mother's behalf.

But then, in 1897, after his marriage, he did defend her, in a terrible scene that was no less than a day of judgment on his father, which ended in Max's ordering his father out of his house. Max and his wife were then living in Heidelberg, his mother's home town. She had come on a visit, promising herself a holiday from her husband, but he insisted on accompanying her. Max reproached him for this, and for a lifetimes' brutal selfishness. The scene was shattering for all concerned. His wife and mother both begged him to stop, but in vain. Perhaps Frau Weber, like Mrs. Morel, did not want to be defended in fact but knew she had wanted it in fantasy, knew herself guilty of the scene. Perhaps, too, the son made the scene uglier than it need have been, to punish everyone, including the mother, for bringing it about. But worse was to follow. Back in Berlin, Max senior maintained a resentful silence to his wife, and seven weeks after the scene in Heidelberg he died, on a journey far from home and family, without having been reconciled to wife or son.

Max Weber's neurotic collapse began soon after the death of his father. He was incapacitated for seven years—and in some sense for the rest of his life.

Unable to lecture or hold seminars, he had to resign the position to which he had just been appointed at the University of Heidelberg; for some time he could not even read or write. So he traveled restlessly. In 1903 he went to the Riviera in January, to Italy in March and April, to Scheveningen in June, to Ostend in August, to Hamburg in September, to Holland again in October. In the South, in Italy, he was able to relax from his worse tensions, and for a time he said he would like to move permanently from Germany to the South. But that would have been, symbolically, to give up the whole "world of men" to which he had adjusted his personality, and there was too much that he valued in that. Moreover, the change would have been only symbolic, for even Lawrence, who visited the same parts of Italy as Weber in 1912–14, could not really shrug off his "English" personality there. And Lawrence was committed to that enterprise by much more hopeful motives than Weber, for he hoped to be able to come into full possession of his creative self by such an Italianization. Italy was the homeland of the matriarchal mode of being, ahistorical, cyclical paganism. It offered Lawrence every reinforcement of his creative self. But to Weber it offered only relaxation, rest; for him Italianization would have meant the loss of his creative self.

For a long time, rest was the best he could aim at. Because he could not teach or write, he could do nothing. His career was completely frustrated. He always had been a severely strained man, emotionally impotent with those nearest to him and sexually impotent with his wife. Now his impotence was total. One might perhaps say that Helene Weber and Emilia Fallenstein—Weber's mother and grandmother—had yearned for a husband like Max, who would be strongly masculine, even frighteningly powerful, but also spiritually vulnerable in relation to them, impotent against them.

The scene with his father, of course, only released forces which had built up in him dangerously before. We have a letter he wrote his wife early in their marriage, in answer to her appeal that he relax more and not work so hard. "When I finally achieved inner harmony, after years of a nasty sort of torment," he wrote, "I feared that a deep depression would follow. It has not occurred, I think, because through continual work I have not let my nerves and brain come to rest. Quite apart from the natural need to work, therefore, I am most unwilling to allow a really marked pause in my labors; I think that as long as I am not positive that I have gone past the stage of being convalescent, I can't risk allowing my present peace—which I enjoy with the feeling one gives to a really new happiness—to be transformed into enervation." After his collapse he told his wife that his old "*need* to feel submerged under a load of work is extinguished." In fact, what changed in him was that he had acquired the ability to distance himself from, and *sometimes* to escape, that need. Enjoyment, especially mindless shared enjoyment, always remained difficult for him.

But that he had always been used to. Now, in 1897, the sphere of work as well as that of love was denied him. He was delivered over to the Furies, savage in their attack. When he opened his lecture notes in 1898 and 1899, his own words swam in confusion before his eyes. When a pet cat mewed, it put him beside himself with rage. His hands trembled all the time, he could not sleep, he felt continually exhausted. And there were also the sweet Furies of his wife's love. She had wondered before if he needed her, she tells us, but now she could not doubt it. "The strong man was in constant need of her care and her presence, she had to look after him." (Marianne habitually speaks of herself as "she" and of her husband and herself as "they" in her biography of him.) He even had to acknowledge that he was morally better in this state of dependence on her, for he was now, he told her, more human. She had been right, he admitted, in saying that before his breakdown he could not have lived so completely *with* someone else as he now lived with her.

(Weber's life story, we must note, is a powerful objective correlative for Lawrence's intimations about the hollowness of the world of men—as well as for Otto Gross's theories, for that matter. Weber's life was a text on which both matriarchalists could have preached many a sermon. Lawrence did not often depict such figures or such situations as Weber's in detail, but something similar can be felt just offstage in the chapters of *Women in Love* and *Lady Chatterley's Lover* dealing with the life of intellectuals.)

In becoming totally dependent on his wife during the years his breakdown lasted, Weber had a rare opportunity to reverse the usual dependency roles, which was pleasing to one who felt that those roles had been devised by others and then assigned to him and his wife. He gave up his career completely, staying home while she went out and gave lectures, which hurt her. He revenged himself on his mother by being unable to be spoken to when she came to visit; during long evenings she had to sit opposite him and not speak to him. And he was the only one of her children not to attend her lavishly celebrated seventieth birthday. But he remained her nearest and dearest child. They were entangled together in the coils of his "shame," his inability to love.

So were he and his wife, to whom he wrote "How great this love of yours is; how it shames me; how gladly I put up with your 'uncriticalness' of me. . . . I don't know whether my own ever-ready criticalness derives from a weaker heart." Hers is the mild sunshine that melts the ice, while "the wild storm of my passionateness only manages to shake the snowflakes and the fircones from the trees," he goes on to say in a letter of 1908 in which one can see the Rochester-and-Jane-Eyre style of their expressed relationship.

It would be unnatural not to use the language of myth and psychoanalysis about such cases. And so this must, I suppose, be called an Oedipal complex. But it was not what people commonly mean by that phrase. Clearly, Max Weber felt he had wished his father's death, had caused it, and he punished himself by this neurosis. But what he felt for his mother does not fit itself plausibly to the "Freudian" pattern. Certainly Weber felt a deep temperamental sympathy with her that was rooted in preconscious experience. But the pattern of his feelings toward her seems even more determined by sentiments of moral admiration—that is, sentiments of the superego—against which both ego and id reacted with resentment. His deepest feelings toward his mother, his letters suggest, were hostile. It was *her* he wished to destroy; his father was, beside her, a trivial figure.

She demanded so many apologies and reassurances from him, as we can see, for instance, from this response of his: "What you also write, and not for the first time, about your 'inability' to do anything for our spiritual and emotional development, to be a spiritual mother also to us, I must declare with all my energy that this rests on a complete mistake, though I admit that I am co-responsible for the development of that opinion in you, through my inability, with exactly those people who are nearest to me, to appeal verbally to them and come to an understanding with them, to give myself to them in conversation cordially or even winsomely—in a word, through my 'incommunicativeness' and the charmlessness of my conversational style." It is all there, the weariness of so many protestations, the patient countering of her self-reproach with his own (which he knows to be so much bitterer), the resentful calling up of "energy" for these "declarations." He goes on to assure her of how much influence she *had* had, how difficult they all were, how different he might have been but for her influence, how she saved him from "schlechten Streiche," which his wife tells us means fornication. His mother, by her "saintly purity of being, not by anything she said," Marianne explains, ". . . had developed in him indestructible barriers against yielding to the passions."

This kind of mother-son relationship is, of course, the subject of Lawrence's first successful novel, *Sons and Lovers,* and in his own life he suffered from its effects in some of the same ways as Max Weber. This constitutes the largest single likeness between the two men. But two additional differences, one circumstantial and one essential from our point of view, need to be noted. Mrs. Lawrence died when David Herbert was twenty-six, and he had ceased to live at home long before that. But it was in the years after

Weber was twenty-six, while living at home, that he suffered most from seeing his mother mistreated by her husband. In Germany, Oedipal conflicts were likely to be stronger than in England. That is the circumstantial difference.

The essential difference was that Lawrence's Oedipus had incorporated much stronger elements of the feminine into him than Weber's had. Lawrence was in rebellion against the male mode of being of his society. He was in search of a male mode that would be defined by a predominantly matriarchal society, and because his father came to seem, as time went by, to have exemplified that, Lawrence's "Oedipus complex" was an even more complicated thing than Weber's.

Differences and Similarities

We must try here to tease out the overlapping categories for comparing the two men, some of which are a matter of class or age or nation, and some of personal development or choice. Also, continuing their biographies, we must note the similarities of type between the women with whom they were involved—similarities which surround and set off the oppositeness of their choices about *leaving* those women. That both Weber and Lawrence should ever have loved girls of the Miriam/Marianne type is connected with their Oedipal problems, and leads us to reflect further on the cultural character of that problem.

It is no coincidence that the other male with whose life story this study is concerned, Otto Gross, also suffered from a full-blown Oedipal conflict, although in his case there seems to have been a really strong father. The decades around the turn of the century were, of course, a period of particularly severe Oedipal conflicts, especially in the intensified patriarchal culture of Germany; that was why Freud had to evolve a theory to codify them. Gross's treatment of the problem was much more activist and "cultural" than Freud's, for he prescribed both personal and societal rebellion against the father. In this he was followed by the Expressionist dramatists and novelists, many of whom were under his influence. Although Lawrence's treatment of this theme was aesthetically conservative, ideologically he implied the same answer as Gross, the classical answer to patriarchy—matriarchy.

But Lawrence's attack on patriarchy was only implicit, even in his essays. It was far from being the main point of what he had to say, and it was formulated so discreetly that it could be overlooked by the reader. We see it only when we align him with Gross and Weber—with German cases. Both ideologically and personally, Lawrence made less out of his conflict with his father than Gross and Weber did out of theirs.

Nevertheless, one book about Lawrence is entitled *Oedipus in Notting-ham*. Weber, who might more justly have been called "Oedipus in Berlin," has in fact been compared rather with Orestes—because of the Furies that pursued him—and with Prometheus, the hero of suffering and achievement. In reviewing Marianne Weber's biography of her husband, Friedrich Meinecke compared the Fallensteins with the house of Tantalus: Old Georg Friedrich Fallenstein, so heroic and angry, was Tantalus, Helene was Iphigenie, the sac-rificed maiden exiled among the barbarians, and Max was Orestes, saved from the pursuit of the Furies only by the pleadings of Athene. (Else Jaffe, who came to Max Weber's rescue, was, as we have noted already, an Athene figure on many counts.) The inappropriateness of the myth is, of course, that Weber had "murdered" his father, not his mother. But I have suggested that in the realm of his wishes, in his fantasy life, the drama may have ben ambiguous. In any case, Weber's work was in important ways a rebellion against patri-archy, culturally as well as personally.

Of course, Weber did not "treat the problem" in the same sense as Gross and Lawrence did. But he was essentially a reformer, a resister, a virtuous rebel—virtuous, that is, even by the standards of the system he was rebelling against. He believed in, or stood for, a "better" patriarchy—better than he expected it ever would be. On the spectrum of human types described by Lawrence in "The Crown," Weber clearly belongs with David and Brutus, in opposition to Saul and Caesar.

Eldest sons, favorite sons, are often called, by their mothers' wills, to rebel against their fathers in the name of a better manhood. Their rebellion is a form of dutifulness. They assume the masculine virtues and build their selves upon them, while continuing to resent masculinity in other forms. Weber often said that a wife *must* resist her husband, or else she is partly guilty of his brutality towards her. This exemplifies his reformist resistance to patriarchy as a whole, a resistance very different in style from Gross's and Lawrence's. The difference derives in part from the cultures the three men belonged to.

In both Austria and England there were quite powerfully institution-alized elements of nonpatriarchal culture, which had no equivalent in Ger-many, where patriarchy met no effective resistance. In Weber's Prussia, "bet-ter manhood" was characterized only by his mother's liberal humanitarian-ism, while the figure of Bismarck, the very antithesis of her principles, stood as the symbol for the ideal of manhood as, above all, power. This Bismarck-ian version of manliness exerted its fascination over liberal professors as much as others, so that Weber was scarcely free to renounce it; he cultivated its root in himself even as he clipped its thorns.

Let us recall the anecdote of how Bismarck humiliated the Reichstag deputies by acting like an angry schoolteacher facing down pupils who had spoken out of turn. That reduction to child-status of the representatives of the people, the theoretical rulers of the nation, clearly satisfied fantasies of power in Bismarck and stimulated similar fantasies in others. (Otto Gross would point out that for "child-status" one could substitute "eunuch-status" and "woman-status" with equal truth. It was his life work to redefine manhood so that these equivalences, so ruinous to German life, should be broken.) Weber was fully aware of the dangers of power—he dedicated his political life to resisting Bismarck's influence— but he was fascinated by it.

A society in which such anecdotes are current is, as we remarked before, one obsessed by power—the power of the world of men. And Max Weber was very much of that society, both as a social personality and as a political theorist. Lawrence was not. That difference between the two is to be explained along several different lines, but one of them is the lack of an English Bismarck. There was no single great power figure in national life in England. In her unheroic way, Queen Victoria genuinely symbolized a society with "matriarchal" characteristics; they were, of course, only modifications of a fundamentally patriarchal enterprise, but they modified it enough to make it significantly different from Germany. Britain's equivalent figure to Bismarck was Gladstone, the woodcutter of Hawarden, a man of principle, a reformer, a man of ideals, a servant of Apollo. In *The White Peacock* Lawrence portrays his mother as always reading Morley's *Life of Gladstone,* and emblematically this is true. Bismarck's Germany intensified and exaggerated the patriarchal mode to which Western culture as a whole had committed itself.

Another difference, partly national, is that between the differing ideals of the life of the mind which Lawrence and Weber met at the university. This difference was only in part national, for it also derived from the two men's different positions within the class-and-culture systems of their respective countries. The English equivalent of Weber's education would not be to get a general degree at Nottingham University in the way that Lawrence did, but to go to Trinity College, Cambridge, or perhaps to the London School of Economics. But the national difference is still important; it is the difference between the ideal forms of British humanism and German *Wissenschaft.* Lawrence once said that Ernest Weekley was the only gentleman among his teachers, and even though he generally evaluated his teachers in terms of their intelligence and knowledge, the criterion of gentility might appropriately have been a major one. He never met a phenomenon of knowledge or of intellect like Theodor Mommsen, or Kuno Fischer, or Heinrich Treitschke, potentates of the academy, prodigies of learning, shapers of world-systems of thought. There was never anything seriously to challenge his assumption that the artistic imagination was superior to the philosophic mind. Whereas in Germany, Alfred Weber had ambitions to be a poet, and was in some sense fundamentally an aesthetic nature, but he became instead a man of learning, swayed by powerful example.

I do not wish to deny the importance of the two men's original genetic endowments, but those endowments seem to me to have been very similar. Both men were extraordinarily clever, extraordinarily sensitive and irritable, extraordinarily energetic. (Of course, all these terms, too, are culturally determined. The precultural, genetic endowment behind them is almost unnamable.) Almost all that we can cite as congenitally different is their looks. Weber was a big man, Lawrence a small one. Even then, the important thing is the fact that Weber thought of himself as a big man, held himself like a big man, put that idea into other people's minds, whereas Lawrence thought of himself as a small man, as physically lightweight and insignificant. But even these crucial facts took their rise from other sources besides physique. Weber was a stately tramper, Lawrence quick and light-footed. Weber had a beautiful, measured baritone voice; Lawrence's was thin, reedy, scratchy. Lawrence's eyes were, by most accounts, unusually alive and attractive; Weber's, by most accounts, were either forceful or defensive. Lawrence was a brilliant mimic, Weber a good anecdotalist. Lawrence's laugh could become a nervous giggle, but Weber was a Homeric laugher. It was these traits of behavior—traits of self-characterization which announce or betray a man's mode of belonging to the world—which made the two men's genetic endowment in physique seem so different. Weber's was a much more "manly" way than Lawrence's.

In terms of intellect as well, it is not clear that there was any large initial difference between them. Lawrence could handle conceptual knowledge very efficiently when he wanted to, and took a passionate interest in subjects like history and archeology. His book on the Etruscans may stand as proof of that. By the same token Max Weber could be sensitive to quite intricate tangles of motive and quite etiolated and exalted feelings. His letters about his Baumgarten cousins, in relation to Otto's marriage, prove that.*

* In 1885 Otto Baumgarten decided to marry Emily Fallenstein, a religious exaltee who was musical, poetic, and gifted with second sight, but sickly, eccentric, and older than himself. His father advised against the marriage, but it had his mother's enthusiastic approval. It was a story out of Dostoevski, or even more out of Lidia Ivanovna's circle in *Anna Karenina*. Weber's comments on the personalities involved show participatory understanding, even while he insists on his own healthy, normal "outsideness."

His habit of referring to himself as thick-skinned and coarse and un-
regenerate must be read as wilful role-playing, just as Lawrence's rebellion
against mind and middle-class culture, insofar as it was an implicit characterization of himself as a creature of instinct and blood-knowledge, was wilful role-playing.

Within their immediate families, both men got on well with their sisters (particularly Ada in Lawrence's case, Lili in Weber's) and badly with
one of their brothers (Alfred in Weber's case, George in Lawrence's). In Lawrence's life this hostility did not bulk large, because his path diverged from
his brother's so early, but in Weber's life the rivalry of the brothers played
an extensive and intensive part, as we shall see, just because Alfred's path
ran exactly parallel with, exactly contiguous to, Max's. The generally more
tragic atmosphere of the Webers' life has to do with this greater coherence
of the family—the way they kept coming back to Heidelberg, for instance.
But the Lawrence children were set free from entanglement in their parents'
tragedy far earlier in life and far more completely. "To be a Weber" meant
more things than "to be a Lawrence" did, because "the Webers" were a power
in the world of men. Here again, differences between the two men were in
some degree culturally determined.

Of course there were other factors. There seems to have been simply less
health and harmony in the Weber family, more tensions and tremors. For
instance, Professor Baumgarten says that Frau Weber separated Max, in his
student days, from Lili, by sending the latter out of the house, because she
feared that his affection for her was semi-incestuous. There is no record of
quite such intensity in Lawrence's affection for Ada, or at least of such dire
suspicions. The Weber family atmosphere is more reminiscent of the Criches
in *Women in Love* than of the Lawrences. But it may be that the class and
national differences here too count for something in making such fears
explicit.

In erotic matters, both men had similar problems with the girls they
first fell in love with, who were themselves similar. But they solved the problem in opposite ways, and from those two solutions issued a series of powerful consequences. Max Weber married the girl and Lawrence left her; their
lives followed opposite tracks thereafter. When I say that Weber married
her, I am referring of course to Marianne Schnitger, but, strictly speaking, the
first girl in Weber's case was his cousin Emmy Baumgarten. Their relationship
was emotionally intense from 1886 until at least 1888, but presumably there
could be no question of specifically sexual problems, because the relationship
was chaste. It seems clear that Emmy was a more extreme, a more "angelic,"
version of Marianne. She was a highly sensitive, conscientious girl, all purity
and depth of feeling, who suffered from melancholy and nervous exhaustion

and spent many months during her relationship with Max on her sickbed. She had taken very much to heart her mother's lessons in striving after perfection.

Marianne too was a nervous and hypersensitive girl, and her family on her father's side had several cases of insanity in the preceding generation. She was another Emmy—and another Miriam, if I may reverse chronology in this way—in her spiritual intensity, her intense responsiveness to ideas and ideals, her innocence, naïveté, nervousness, love of books, horror of brutality or even coarseness, her aversion from the physical. She differed from Emmy, though, in her greater practical energy—in the books she got written, for example. Her fiber must have been stronger, perhaps coarser. But the profile she turned toward the world, and toward her mirror, was very like theirs—although, seen from behind, her figure had a peasant breadth and energy.

Max and Marianne, given their experience, could have made very little of Lawrence's remark, "The woman grows downwards, like a root, towards the centre and the darkness and the origin. The man grows upwards, like the stalk, towards discovery and light and utterance." Marianne lived entirely toward the light—but that did not mean away from power and force. Her emphasis on precisely those qualities of power and force in her description of her husband's physical appearance is interesting in more than one way. The two younger Weber brothers, she says, were very handsome when she met the family. Max was not. "He is corpulent, and keeps his pear-shaped, duelling-scarred skull close-cropped. A finely drawn pair of lips stand in strange contrast to the big shapeless nose, and the dark glance often hides itself behind the down-dropping brows. No, this giant is not handsome and not youthful, but he is in every gesture a powerful *man*." This is interesting because Weber was, at least in some aspects, a strikingly handsome man. But one can see what Marianne meant in some photographs taken during the period she is speaking of, which was the period of Weber's greatest self-punishment, while he was still the pensioner of his father and had not yet come to the defense of his mother, and while he hoped at most to assert himself as undeniably, unbeautifully, there. But it is notable that she should choose to emphasize that aspect of him, when others were available. The reason presumably is that her romanticism, which was, like Max's, a patriarchal romanticism, fixed principally on *power* in a man. Jane Eyre insists on Rochester's grim and powerful masculinity, his unbeautifulness. Beauty in a man was not something Marianne Weber would care to dwell on. That would be left to Frieda von Richthofen, the representative of eroticism, who appreciated male beauty very vividly and was impatient of male power.

In this self-stylization, Max Weber followed Bismarck himself, who made his body entirely a manifestation of enormous appetites and powers—the strained and bulging eyes expressing appetites of the spirit—and not in the least an object of appetite. The best contrast would be Skrebensky in *The Rainbow,* whose figure, also a soldier's, is apprehended by Ursula (and Lawrence) in terms of delight. We see again how intimately the individual is affected by the cultural idea to which he responds—and the cultural idea represented by Weber's Marianne and Lawrence's Miriam was the opposite of that represented by Frieda von Richthofen.

Like Miriam's relation to Lawrence, Marianne's to Weber was that of a student. Immediately before their wedding, and immediately after, they were discussing books and ideas, with Max expounding, instructing, correcting her. Like Mrs. Lawrence, Frau Weber was disturbed by this and tried to shift the relationship onto another footing, but it was rooted by nature in pedagogy. Miriam and Marianne, both of whom were charming and pretty women, offered their men a very valuable appreciation. They were ready, eager, to silence their own voices completely in order to create a resonant vacuum in which the man's voice might resound the more. But they also left the sexual enterprise entirely to the men, offering themselves essentially as victims to appetite—and in both cases this had the effect of making the men impotent. They were intelligent and conscientious girls, but with quite conventional minds, essentially less interesting, even intellectually, than the von Richthofen sisters.

A letter Miriam wrote to Helen Corke in 1913 is very reminiscent of Marianne stylistically, very like her poetic prose, given the minor differences between Georgian lyricism and its German equivalent. It was written after a painful three-day visit during which both Miriam and Helen had privately realized that their friendship could not continue. Now that Lawrence had moved out of their lives, neither, and particularly Miriam, had the same sense of herself, and she could not keep up patterns which before had been natural. "I have brought back out of last week a large number of exquisite moments. Sudden aspects of the Shirley Road between the trees, of the valley beyond Purley, of that superb slope just outside the little spinney off the main road to Oxley. Then Oxley itself, sunny and sleeping, the crowded sheep-pen, the rare magic of Limpsfield in the silver dusk. These things now seem exalted and linked like beads on a chain of strange, exquisite pain, a peculiar exhaustion which still keeps the faculty of perception. I don't know how it all comes about."

In adopting this style, with the extraordinary, heartbreaking literariness of the prose, both Marianne and Miriam were trying to sing themselves to sleep, to exclude the monsters of the dark with the best lullabies of their day, the most highly recommended music—which was already old-fashioned when they acquired it, already fading back into its yellowish paper.

Both girls acknowledged the hegemony of the world of men and its powers. Their feminine values and activities were an enclave within that world, a walled garden. Both Weber and Lawrence tried to give them greater independence and separateness than they seemed willing to accept. Thus Weber wanted Marianne to become a competent Hausfrau, in order that she should have an area of expertise independent of him, "in order not to depend on my moods," he said, putting the matter plainly. There was never any question that she could be anything but dependent on him intellectually, and his life already had shown him the horrors of dependence all too vividly. When Marianne proved to be irremediably an intellectual, Max encouraged her to take up a career independent from his and to work in the Women's Movement. When Lawrence, in contrast, was unable to persuade Miriam into independence of being, into "otherness," he abandoned her. There is, by the way, a seeming paradox here, for Weber, the patriarchal man, promoted the liberation of women, whereas Lawrence, the matriarchal man, opposed it. In fact, however, there is no real paradox involved inasmuch as the Women's Liberation movement inducts women into the male mode of being, and is thus naturally a cause likely to appeal to the reformist wing of the patriarchal mind—to Heidelberg—and just as naturally the ideologists of matriarchy see it as a betrayal of the female mode.

Max's letter proposing marriage to Marianne contains some extraordinary passages of obliquity and negativeness, and deserves comparison on that score with Paul's offer to put himself in Miriam's hands at the end of *Sons and Lovers*. In a vivid image of the psychological impotence he had felt in his father's house all those years since becoming a man, he tells Marianne that he is aware she no doubt thinks that "I want to direct you toward the cool calm harbor of resignation, in which I myself have lain at anchor many years." He offers an account of himself and of "the elemental passions which Nature has planted in me; but ask my mother; I well know that her love for me, which seals my mouth, because I can never repay it, is rooted in the fact that I was in moral matters her problem child." We see there again the guilt toward his mother, and the resentment implied in his mouth being sealed, but also the strategy taken to capitalize romantically on this guilt by claiming elemental passion as its cause. "And now I ask you: have you inwardly separated yourself from me in these last days? or made the decision to do so? or are you doing so *now*? *If not, it is too late*, we are committed to each other, and I shall be hard on you and not spare you. . . ."

This is a tour de force in giving passivity the appearance of action. Nobody has taken a decision, and yet a decision has been taken. The tone is that of Rochester to Jane Eyre, or Heathcliff to Catherine. But if this was the romantic form of his relation to Marianne, the substance of that relationship is indicated by this next passage. "If you go with me, *don't* answer this. Then I shall, when I next see you, press your hand quietly, and not drop my eyes before you, and you too shall not." Everything is negative in act, portentous in significance—precisely the version of love against which the erotic movement rebelled; it is what Lawrence fled when he left Miriam. Indeed, one can admire Mrs. Lawrence more for her opposition to Miriam after seeing the effects of Frau Weber's endorsement of Emmy and Marianne. (One can also reevaluate Mrs. Morel's opposition to her husband, which has roused so much indignation, after seeing the effects on Max Weber of his mother's "acceptance" of her husband.)

The Sisters

Max Weber married Marianne Schnitger in 1893, when he was twenty-nine, and she twenty-three. The affair between D. H. Lawrence and Miriam was so indecisive and recurrent as to have no clear climax, but we can perhaps say that it was at its height in 1907, when he was twenty-two and she twenty-one. Weber, of course, was still married to Marianne then, and so there was a certain contemporaneity to the two men's experience with these women, despite the difference between their ages.

It was with the von Richthofen sisters that both Weber and Lawrence each finally found the woman he could passionately love, though not at the same moment. Weber declared himself to Else in Venice in 1910, two years before Lawrence met Frieda, but it seems that Else could not or would not betray Marianne. The event caused a revolution in Weber's life, as Professor Baumgarten puts it, but Else chose to make an alliance with his brother Alfred, a man who had long loved her but with whom Max was in bitter rivalry, always. This was a semi-public alliance, which caused Edgar great distress, but it was quite different from the proposed liaison with Max, because it did not betray Marianne and because Alfred had no wife to be betrayed. (Perhaps also it felt less immoral to Else because she did not love Alfred in any passionate way—but we do not know.) She traveled twice a year with Alfred through Italy, visiting places of historical and aesthetic interest and working with him on his sociology of culture. Max and Marianne supervised the semi-separation from Edgar, and thus the semi-alliance with

Alfred, until the strain of so many conflicting feelings became too great and Else quarreled with Max, after which she remained out of touch with him until 1917. But 1910 was nevertheless a date of the greatest significance for Max, and gave him a vision of erotic happiness. He himself compared it with that moment in Dürer's life when the artist discovered, also in Venice, the intimate dependence of all Art on living Nature. And when, in 1913, he found erotic satisfaction first, with Mina Tobler, the pianist, it seems that she was being substituted for Else.

Of what Frieda meant to Lawrence, all his work subsequent to 1912 bears witness. And because there is so much evidence about this pair, and so little about the other, we shall pay more attention to the former.

For Weber had married his "Miriam," and never left her; and Else Jaffe never left her children, and never ceased to be Frau Jaffe; whereas Lawrence left Miriam and Frieda left Ernest Weekly and her children. Clearly this was one of the great crossroads of the two lives. Perhaps if Lawrence had never met Frieda, he would have drifted back to Miriam. It seems clear that Miriam thought so, that she never gave up hope until she realized that he was living with Frieda in Germany; therewith something in the structure of her ego collapsed. And perhaps Frieda would never have left her husband but for the accident of meeting Lawrence. Though she was clearly ready to leave, she was timid in her dealings with the outside world, the world of men. Almost certainly they would not have had the courage, even together, without the inspiration of the erotic movement. It was this broader cultural movement that tipped the balance, that gave to each that extra excitement which, multiplied by mutuality, carried them together over into their great adventure. The erotic movement carried them along the road they took from the turning point formed by their mutual attachment, whereas Weber and Else resisted the movement, and thus determined the choice they made. Lawrence told Miriam when he left with Frieda that he could think of nothing but *Anna Karenina;* and his first description of Frieda was that she was "German—modern German," thinking no doubt of Strauss's *Elektra* and of those Freud-Gross theories of sexuality which she had expounded to him. That is, he saw in her from the beginning—quite ideologically, so to speak—a partner for the adventure of eroticism. And she saw the same in him. In his letters Lawrence wrote that by eloping and living together they were "making history."

Of course, Frieda also saw Lawrence not merely as a partner but also as a man who needed her help; as a man she could release from his inhibitions, and as a talent she could turn into genius. After his death, she wrote to Dorothy Brett, "Do you know how much liberating I did for Lawrence. . . . It was given to me to make him flower." And he would have agreed, as we can see from what he said and did not say about such claims on her part. She gave him sensual happiness, but she also gave him—by the same gift— a mission as a writer. She gave him her identity, her *idea*—which became his idea. She even helped him significantly with the work of translating that idea into literary terms.

Thus he wrote to Edward Garnett in 1914 that Frieda was helping him with *The Sisters* as she had with *Sons and Lovers*. "Now you will find her and me in the novel, I think, and the work is of both of us." Insofar as it was of Frieda, it was of Woman, and he regarded this as essential. He rejected the Futurists, he said, because they "progress down the purely male or intellectual or scientific line. . . . There isn't one trace of naivete in the works." We have seen, in the Foreword to *Sons and Lovers,* how explicitly he aimed at "femaleness," and in his writing of the next few years "naivete" is a prominent feature. In *A Study of Thomas Hardy* we read, "This is the desire of every man . . . that the woman of his body shall be the begetter of his whole life, that she, in her female spirit, shall beget in him his idea, his motion, himself. When a man shall look at the work of his hands, that has succeeded, and shall know that it was begotten in him by the woman of his body, then he shall know what fundamental happiness is." Clearly the reversal of the sexual roles in this is most intentional and serious—it is the whole point. Man must become passive, woman active. "Out of this final knowledge shall come his supreme art. There shall be the art which . . . knows the struggle between the two conflicting laws, and knows the final reconciliation, where both are equal, two in one, complete. This is the supreme art, which yet remains to be done. Some men have attempted it, and left us the remains of efforts. But it remains to be fully done."

We can point to the Tolstoy of *Anna Karenina* as one of the "men who have attempted it," and say that Lawrence is promising to go on from that, to complete the work of the erotic movement, although of course it was Hardy to whom Lawrence was referring primarily. In this sense, the Will-Anna chapters of *The Rainbow* are a revision—and transvaluation—of the Arabella-Jude chapters of *Jude the Obscure,* just as the Gerald-Gudrun chapters of *Women in Love* are a revision of the Anna-Vronsky chapters of *Anna Karenina.*

The relation of art to the world of Woman is made explicit in a letter written by Lawrence to A. W. McLeod in June 1914: "I think the only resourcing of art, revivifying it, is to make it more the joint work of man and woman. I think *the* one thing to do, is for men to have the courage to draw nearer to women, expose themselves to them, and be altered by them; and for women to accept and admit men."

One notices there again the passivity of the role assigned to men. They must lower their pretensions, demolish the proud fortifications of the world of men, allow Woman and Nature to act upon them. Behind these comments we can sense a general idea that the civilization men had built was dying, and indeed when Lawrence and Frieda ran away together, both of them thought that they were running away from civilization, getting rid of its traces in themselves. Frieda wanted to get out of Europe as a whole, to some uncivilized country, and Lawrence wrote, soon after the elopement, that he was losing all his little pathetic sadness and softness. The wounds inflicted on him by the world of men were healing and he was growing strong and fierce. We may translate this into terms of his literary work by saying that he was losing everything which had arrested him at the level of *Sentimental Tommy,* had threatened to make of him another J. M. Barrie. This is what Lawrence could have been without Frieda, this is what talent alone made him. She made him a genius. Compare Paul's last scene with Miriam in *Sons and Lovers* with Tommy's letter of proposal to Grizel in Barrie's *Tommy and Grizel.* The similarity of the situation is significant, as is the superiority in Lawrence's treatment—the superiority he achieved with Frieda. Or consider, in Lawrence's early fiction, the sickly-suicidal strains in *The Trespasser* and the sickly-sadistic strains in *The White Peacock.* One can see there the kind of writer Lawrence might have become if he had not had the courage to "draw nearer to" Frieda, and "be altered by" her.

The harsh side of what Frieda did for him, of her discipline, is clear in the terrible words she wrote beside the notebook draft of his poem, "My Love, My Mother": "Yes, you are free, poor devil, from the heart's home life free, lonely you shall be, you have chosen it, you chose fully! now go your way. . . . I have tried, I have fought, I have nearly killed myself in the battle to get you into connection with myself and other people, sadly I have proved to myself that I can love, but never you. . . . you cannot help me, you are a sad thing, I know your secret and your despair, I have seen you are ashamed." Harsh as it was, Lawrence accepted that discipline; it was something that both of them believed in, he as much as she. Not to face it was what they called "dodging oneself." Thus Frieda wrote to Brett, "You awful dodger, dodging yourself," and Lawrence wrote to Russell that E. M. Forster dodged himself, because the social passion and not self-realization was his ultimate desire. They felt it as their mission to introduce all their British literary friends to this discipline, and their major victim, the tragi-comic Pamela they tried to seduce, was as we shall see John Middleton Murry.

Lawrence, or Lawrence-and-Frieda, became a genius by accepting this discipline and thus entering the world of Woman, enacting in his own life the principles of the erotic movement. This is "the heart's home life" which Frieda speaks of, the "connection with other people," love. Clearly they achieved all this at the cost of extraordinary tension between them. In *Aaron's Rod* Lawrence expressed some of the sense of subordination he felt when he wrote that the woman "was the first real great source of life and being, and also of culture," whereas "the man was but the instrument and finisher." In that book, of course, Lawrence was explicitly in rebellion against Love and the world of Woman. Thus Lilly announces the end of the love mode and Jim Bricknell's craving for love is portrayed as obscene and self-destructive. But even in *Women in Love* the same idea is there: "Ursula was only too ready to knock her head on the ground before a man. But this was only when she was so certain of her man, that she could worship him as a woman worships her own infant, with a worship of perfect possession." This portrait of a Magna Mater reflects the way Lawrence saw Frieda. In a letter of December 1918 to Katherine Mansfield, he writes, "In a way, Frieda is the devouring mother. It is awfully hard, once the sex relation has gone this way, to recover. If we don't recover, we die. But Frieda says I am antediluvian in my positive attitude. I do think a woman must yield some sort of precedence to a man, and he must take his precedence. I do think men must go ahead absolutely in front of their women, without turning round to ask for permission of approval from their women. Consequently, the women must follow as it were unquestioningly. I can't help it, I do believe this. Frieda doesn't. Hence our fight." Frieda, that is, remained true to Otto Gross and to *Mutterrecht* when Lawrence rebelled against it.

Frieda's value, on the other hand, is implicit in a thousand evocations by Lawrence of the flowering *life* she brought with her. There is, for example, this reference to her in his *Hardy*: "The final aim is the flower, the fluttering singing nucleus which is a bird in spring, the magical spurt of being which is a hare all explosive with fullness of being, in the moonlight." Or this, from *The Crown*: "Yet had we listened, the hide-bound cabbage might have burst, might have opened apart, for a venturing forth of the tender, timid, ridiculous cluster of aspirations, that issue in little tips of flame, the flowers naked in eternity, naked above the staring unborn crowd of amorphous entities, the cabbages: the myriad egos." Frieda was the flower, transcendant over the democratic-citizen cabbages. It was her courage for life, not her birth, that made her an aristocrat, but it was nonetheless aristocracy, privilege, she represented, just as it was Weber who represented the rights of those cabbages. Whenever yellow flowers open in his prose—those gallant daisies and dandelions—Lawrence is thinking of Frieda. Those flowers were the fleur-de-lys of the erotic movement, and although Lawrence occasionally rebelled against that, he remained deeply loyal to it always. In a sense Lawrence was, in the early twenties, the Luther of matriarchy, a truer son of the faith than most, but a great enemy of the Church. His was the Protestantism of masculine protest. To live by the values of eroticism was a strain on him. The other women to whom he was attracted were quite un-erotic, and it is clear that some of the difficulties of his relationship with Frieda derived from the fact that it had to be predominantly erotic. He was on very friendly terms with her sister Else—Else's daughter remembers that Frieda felt some jealousy of her sister's intimacy with Lawrence—and on even more friendly terms with their mother. Mabel Dodge is no doubt right in some of what she reports as Lawrence's yearning toward herself and his desire to escape from Frieda. He often told Mabel that she seemed like a sister to him, and she offered herself as a mother; "Frieda has mothered your books long enough," she told him. "You need a new mother!" The poem "Spirits Summoned West" is perhaps Lawrence's most eloquent expression of his yearning for a sisterly relation to a woman. But all these were vel-leities. His great affirmation, which he held by to the end of his life, whatever it cost him, was the value of the erotic relationship—the value of Frieda, not of Else or Mabel.

That value was primarily an ideological value. In 1923 Frieda wrote to Koteliansky: "How little you must understand of Lawrence's books, Kot, when you can say that I am the 'Porter' in the firm! Why, my faith has been the heart of it." That is true, in a more specific sense of "heart" than is at first apparent. "And when I 'boast' about myself, I know that my religion is that I want people to *love*, genuine and whole and paradisically—*not* like Christ but including everything! And I know I can love. When you say Lawrence has loved me I have loved him a thousand times more! And to really love includes everything, intelligence and faith and sacrifice—and passion! People don't think as I do, they have such other gods, but for all that I stick to my own to the bitter end!" That was her "faith."

Many thinkers of the erotic movement subscribed to the romantic notion that works of art have to be "alive" before anything else. So important was this idea to Frieda and Lawrence that they could not admit that any dignity adhered to the "making" of a work of art or to the artist as "maker." Great-ness even in art must be always process and never fact, always becoming and never being. "If the day comes, which God forbid, that I should see Lawrence as the 'great man,' he would be a dead thing to me and it would bore me." Hence her dislike of Goethe and all "great men": "Greatness is a thing of the outer world, where I indeed am nothing and don't want to be any more! So I grant you that in the world of men Lawrence *is* and I am *not*! But *that* world is nothing to me, there's a deeper one, where life itself flows, there I am at home! And the outer world isn't my affair! All that I really want you to admit is the greater importance of the deeper world." Despite the timid, placating tone which she adopts here, as she often did, the ideas of these lines are bold. She identifies the outer world with the world of men, which is also the world of art, of *Geist,* of Heidelberg, of her sister —the world she had fled. The "deeper" world she opposes to it is clearly the world of Woman, of matriarchy, of love.

It was indeed a creed and a banner and a battle cry with her that the most important thing in the world was the ability to love, and that she had it and that other people (including Lawrence) didn't. That is why her identity was so ideological. Like other battle cries, this one too became brutal or boring through much repetition. But it was also a creed, and Lawrence subscribed to it along with her—except when he was being rebellious, of course. And it was a living faith, realized in the books that he wrote while in sympathy with her. Frieda wrote to Mabel Dodge, protesting Mabel's professed boredom with *Lady Chatterley's Lover,* ". . . don't forget that this religious (if you can call it so) approach to physical love is my feeble contribution."

Lawrence's relation to "the world of men" is exemplified in a letter from 1915 in which he discusses the war; "it is not a question of me, it is the world of men," he writes. "The world of men is dreaming, it has gone mad in its sleep, and a snake is strangling it, but it can't wake up. . . . The War finished me: it was a spear through the side of all sorrows and hopes. . . ." Lawrence's hopes, his and Frieda's whole experience, had been rooted in the belief that the world of men—of parliaments and armies and prisons and politics—was relaxing its grip. Like the inhabitants of Schwabing, they had hoped for a decadence of patriarchalism and a resurgence of matriarchal culture. But the war called all the patriarchal virtues back to life, especially the patriarchal mode of seriousness, even in those who opposed it. Hence the Lawrences' utter confusion in the face of the war experience and their inability to join conscientiously even with pacifist objectors; they felt themselves just as much at odds with Bertrand Russell as with, for instance, Max Weber, for both the pacifist and the militarist belonged equally to the world of men.

The wound which this experience inflicted on Lawrence's spirit—a wound from which he never fully recovered—is expressed in a letter of November 15, 1916, where he reflects bitterly that the war is ". . . utterly wrong, stupid, monstrous, and contemptible. . . . for me. At last I submit that I have no right to speak for anybody else, but only for my single self. . . .

And it comes to this, that the *oneness* of mankind is destroyed in me. I am I, and you are you, and all heaven and hell lies in the chasm between. Believe me, I am infinitely hurt by being thus torn off from the body of mankind, but so it is, and it is right." The belief in the "oneness of mankind" is what makes some men create the world of men around them, others the world of Woman. Without it, they live in both—which is to say, they live fully in neither. Losing that belief, Lawrence lost the world of Woman, so that after the war his novels entered the world of men. It was not until after 1925 that he began to regain the old faith.

Sons and Lovers received its final rewriting, with considerable help from Frieda in 1912–1913, and when it was published in 1913 Lawrence became unequivocally a major writer. The final changes in the story seem likely to have been made in the sections concerned with Clara Dawes. At least, Jessie Chambers ("Miriam") declared that no changes at all had been made, which is likely to mean that no changes concerned the scenes involving her, and the Morel scenes were autobiographically factual and thus would require no alterations. Clara was the invented character. By developing her, Lawrence (and Frieda) adapted the material of the novel—otherwise essentially given by experience—to a prestigious literary form, the *Bildungsroman*. The species of that genre most closely parallel to *Sons and Lovers is* Gottfried Keller's *Der Grüne Heinrich,* a four-volume semi-autobiographical work that dated from the mid-nineteenth century and was familiar to Frieda and, indeed, to the whole Weber-von Richthofen world. Keller's book is the life story of Heinrich Lee, a poor Swiss boy with a humbly loving mother and no father, who decides to become a painter. As he struggles to become an artist, he lives in a constant tension of guilt toward his mother, who sits at home and sacrifices herself for his career. He is impotent in love as in art. As an adolescent, he falls in love with Anna, a fairylike maiden, all innocence and spirituality, "out of another world," who turns pale and faints when he kisses her. (Like Lawrence's Miriam Leivers, she lives in the country, just outside Heinrich's home town.) But he is loved by Judith, a tall, strong widow of opulent sensuality who was disappointed in her marriage but who still seeks truth and love. She seduces Heinrich, in an affair that marches in step, by way of contrast, with his idealistic love for Anna. But he never loves Judith, who ruefully accepts the role of being merely a sensual object for him, even though she is a woman of pride and intellect. She wins his respect as a person, but erotically he is torn right down the middle.

This is clearly enough the fable of Paul Morel's life, to which it is much closer than are such other literary versions as the stories of Jude the Obscure or Miles Coverdale. Heinrich's love for Anna, like Paul's for Miriam, *cannot* fulfill itself sensually; that love has laws of its own, and sexual passion is a crime against them. By the same token, Heinrich's love for Judith, like Paul's for Clara, cannot fulfill itself spiritually, for equally intrinsic reasons. Heinrich, however, like Paul, does not give his sensual lover back to her husband; rather, he persuades her to abandon all claims to him voluntarily. Judith complains, "Oh, never has a man wanted to be upright and clean and pure for my sake, and yet I love truth as I love myself." Ironically, that love of truth in Judith is a part of her attraction for Heinrich, as Clara's is for Paul, and yet it arouses only esteem, which can no more flower into love, than can his reverence for Anna's princess-purity.

Keller's evaluation of the moral issues of his fable differs from Lawrence's. Heinrich explains to Judith that he belongs to Anna *morally*: he would like "to dwell with her soul in Eternity even though I should never see her again from this day onwards. For you I couldn't do all this!" In Lawrence's poem "Two Wives," the Frieda-Judith figure says to Miriam-Anna:

> Take then eternity, for what is that
> But another word, conceit and vanity!
> But do not touch this man who never yet
> Took pleasure in touching you.

These differences of moral sympathy define the change that had come over the European sensibility since Keller wrote in the 1850s. A large part of that change was a result of the triumph of the erotic movement. Keller's scheme of values, which set the two forms of love in tragic and irreconcilable opposition to each other, is essentially that of Max Weber; indeed, from 1911 to 1914—at the very time Lawrence was writing *Sons and Lovers* —Weber was conducting an affair in which he addressed the woman as Judith in allusion to the Keller novel. Heinrich Lee's dilemma was of course his, as much as it was Paul Morel's and more than it was Lawrence's, for Marianne was his fairy princess, Else Jaffe the disappointed wife with sensual experience, and he was torn down the middle by the conflict. (It was not Else Jaffe he addressed as Judith, but Mina Tobler. As we have said, however, it seems likely that Mina was the available substitute for Else then.)

There are likenesses between Clara Dawes and Else Jaffe. Clara's blondness, her melancholy gray eyes, her bruised pride, her social protest, her factory work, her failed marriage, her inability to claim happiness in love, and her willingness to be "sent back," all remind us of Else. Frieda often claimed that she had more to do with the writing of *Sons and Lovers* than any of Lawrence's other novels, which is a large claim, prompting one to wonder whether Frieda had in mind the portrait of Clara Dawes, for it was through Frieda, of course, that Lawrence met Else Jaffe.

In any case, the symbolic pattern is manifoldly suggestive. Miriam/Marianne/Anna represents the idealistic Scylla of nineteenth-century love, while Clara/Else/Judith is the "realistic" Charybdis. And Frieda/Ursula represents the saving alternative, the transcendent erotic hope which clearly can be felt in *Sons and Lovers,* buoying Lawrence up to a confident diagnosis of what was wrong with both Miriam and Clara, a confident disregard of what was wrong with Paul. That is to say that Frieda/Ursula represents the erotic movement, which was precisely a movement aimed at transcending that old tragic Scylla and Charybdis—at transcending both Miriam and Clara/Else. Again, as in her affair with Otto, Frieda triumphed over her sister by means of the talents of her lover; in Lawrence's work she was identified with life and hope.

In 1918 she herself wrote an interesting little sketch of Lawrence as a writer, which implicitly sets his work in antithesis to her sister's world. It was written for Amy Lowell to use in introducing a piece by Lawrence. "Fresh" is the key adjective of praise Frieda applies to Lawrence's work: "It is all as fresh and new as a larch in spring." *Sons and Lovers,* she says, shows the richness of life of the common people for the first time from the inside; "It is another centre from which they live. . . . The intellectual or educated can hardly conceive this form of life; by their very education they have sacrificed it." At the present moment, Frieda says, the whole world is despairing for this lost reality, this "form of life," which is, or is part of, a pre-Apollonian and prepatriarchal culture. Seen this way—which is not the way it would seem to every reader—even *Sons and Lovers* becomes an attack on Else Jaffe's world.

Meanwhile Else, like gray-eyed Athene, subscribed to the civilized world of men, subordinated herself to it. This meant mostly that she acknowledged that world's values, not that she acknowledged the superiority of individual men to herself. But it is to the point that although she was the "bossy" one, she alone among the sisters entered a relationship with a really dominant male. Lawrence was not dominant, in that environment. When Frieda's younger sister Nusch playfully sat on his knee and said, "Oh Lawrence, I love you," he looked round, frightened, for Frieda's protection. This is one family anecdote, amongst many about "poor Edgar," "poor Ernest," and so on. The only man who could not be reduced to that condition, to "poor Max," was Weber. Nusch would not have dared—would not have wanted —to sit on *his* knee. But Else understood him, because she was of his world, of the world of men. And the love between them was of that world, as that between Frieda and Lawrence never was.

This difference takes us back to those we have discussed before. Weber accepted the male role, with all its attributes of power, in a way that Lawrence never did. For him the male was seen always as an actor in the world-historical theater, and as recognizably resting from that activity when at home and engaged in personal relations. In his *Fantasia of the Unconscious* Lawrence discusses this male mode of being, arguing that it belongs to the past. Man *used to be* the doer and thinker, but "his highest moment is now the emotional moment when he gives himself up to the woman, when he forms the perfect answer for her great emotional and procreative asking. All his thinking, all his activity in the world only contributes to this great moment. . . . Man has now entered on to his negative mode. Now, his communication is in feeling, not in action." Such an idea would have seemed repugnant to Weber, and to Else Jaffe, but Lawrence in fact had no power outside his home and even inside it he felt in danger of subordination to Woman, of becoming, like Will Brangwen, "less than a man." Weber never needed to fear that, once he had secured the rather meek adoration of Marianne. (Indeed, Lawrence, too, might not have needed to fear it if he had married his Marianne.)

And outside the home, in the world of men, Weber was a figure of power. An extremely impressive public speaker, both with prepared material and as an impromptu intervener in debate, he spoke quietly, but with a musical and powerful baritone, and his sentences came to him complete and elegant. He had an inexhaustible supply of facts relevant to every issue that came up, and could modulate easily from exposition to indignation, on occasion to invective, and even to demagogic raillery. He was able to command the attention and respect of audiences of every size, even the most hostile. After his speeches men were always moved to say, "What a political leader he would have made." None of these gifts were Lawrence's. He could not, he told Bertrand Russell, tell the truth to more than twenty people at a time. Although he made plans, during the war years, to lecture on peace and on American literature, there seems every reason to suppose that he could not have done so successfully. He was impressive only face to face with one other person or two or three others. Weber, in contrast, was at his most impressive in fairly rough controversy, when he could allow himself to be cutting. In groups of two or three, we are told, he did not reveal much of himself. His purely social life occurred within the semi-public form of a salon. In the decade before the war, guests gathered in the Weber house opposite the Schloss every Sunday and Weber appeared when and as he felt like it to hold forth on the topics of the day. As a social creature Weber owed much—and gave much—to the whole town of Heidelberg; he was one of the sights of the town, a social-intellectual phenomenon which owed some of its impressiveness to the care with which his wife stage-managed these events.

Weber's Style and Setting

In order to understand Max Weber and his mode of love, one must first understand Heidelberg, the city of light, the domain of Apollo, the home of all in Germany who resisted the excesses of patriarchalism. Weber was their natural leader, although, precisely because he was a leader, he had qualities which differentiated him from those he led.

Georg Simmel wrote to Marianne Weber in 1918 that a great responsibility now rested on the *Haus Weber*: it must—that is, Max and Marianne must—reconstitute intellectual Heidelberg after the war, reconstitute "that incomparable treasure of German culture." If we allow this flowery phraseology to infect the idea with a slight unreality, we may say that *this* responsibility was particularly Marianne's. (We shall describe how she discharged it in Chapter 3.) But Simmel's point was not in the least unreal: Heidelberg indeed had a special place in Germany, and the Webers a special place in Heidelberg. It was a spiritual location—like Schwabing, a spiritual home for a German type, but a type most unlike the Schwabing type.

We have already noted that Frau Jaffe returned to Heidelberg after her husband died. Her daughter later became a student there and married one of the professors, Hans von Eckardt, a colleague and friend of Alfred Weber. Marianne Weber made her home there, and various Weber nephews and nieces lived with her from time to time. Otto Gross's son Peter was a student there in the thirties, studying under Karl Jaspers. Even Edgar Jaffe's library of economics books made its way back there from Munich, to become the foundation of the economics seminar library. Time and again we find that family members who had at least as much reason to stay away from the town returned there and made their homes there.

In 1907 Alfred Weber, for instance, left Prague and came to Heidelberg—by his own account, unwillingly. There was indeed something masochistic in his placing himself again in competition with his dominant brother, but he found so many brilliant men there that it was a "revelation to a newcomer." The intellectual life there was "intense above all because whatever happened there intellectually took place amid a strong and productive exchange of all men's powers. . . . It was fully absorbed in and permeated by the new life that had begun to develop in Germany since the turn of the century. It was intellectually and personally exciting, and also open on all sides." This was the *Heidelberger Geist*, a phrase and an idea popular at the time, and the peculiarity of this spirit, Weber says, was its skepticism about everything which gave the Wilhelmine epoch its character of banality. Heidelberg was seeking new depths of meaning. According to Gustav Radbruch, you would have to go back to the Jena of classical times to find an equivalent for Heidelberg's "unceasing discussion, that eternal conversation, that 'symphilosophizing,' . . ." as well as for the active participation of so many clever and educated women in this intellectual world. One of those women was, of course, Else Jaffe.

For Alfred Weber what Heidelberg meant above all was the decision to devote himself to the sociology of culture, the study of how cultural values interact with the forces of civilization, with politics, economics, and other social factors. He turned away from his earlier sociological concern with the location of factories and began what was to become his life work. This work was very appropriate to its place of birth and may be said to be Heidelberg's most typical expression in the second third of this century. Thus Alfred Weber, who came to Heidelberg in some rebellion against it, ended by identifying himself with it and it, yet again, with the name of Weber.

In the first third of the century Heidelberg could have been called Max Weber's town. Edgar Salin says that Berlin University drew to it all the scholars who endorsed the Wilhelmine epoch, which left the provincial universities, and notably Heidelberg, open to those who resisted it. Prominent among these resisters was Max Weber. Heidelberg "stood for" liberal Germany; at the turn of the century it was what Weimar had been a hundred years before. Indeed, it might have made more sense to have named the Weimar Republic the Heidelberg Republic. In 1908 Weber's friend Friedrich Meinecke wrote his *Weltbürgertum und Nationalstaat* (*Cosmopolitanism and the Nation State*), which traced the transition of Germany's center of gravity from Weimar to Potsdam, from Goethe to Bismarck. Meinecke gave the process a retrospective blessing, and his work came to represent the extreme effort of accommodation by the German liberal mind to the Prussian power state. But for most liberal intellectuals, the instinctive preference had always gone to Weimar. (Indeed, in 1946 Meinecke thought better of his earlier position and endorsed Weimar—which is to say Heidelberg—as against Berlin; Jacob Burckhardt and not Treitschke was now his master-historian.) Weber was both one of the centers of social and intellectual

life in the Heidelberg which was heir to the Weimar tradition and the man
who above all others carried the spirit of Heidelberg into effective political
life.

His whole appearance gave the effect of restrained power. He came
through doorways looking as if he had to bend himself to get through,
and his voice was somewhat hushed. He was described by his admirers as
a Kaiser, a *Ritter,* a duke with vassals, a giant warrior. Certainly he was a
man of stronger mind and will than most, who lived by more uncompromising truths. He had opinions on matters in every sphere of life, was a
quixotic defender of the oppressed and attacker of the unjust, often engaged in law suits, suing or being sued. Even in a drawing room he was a
semi-public character. So of course was Lawrence. Both men became myths
in their own lifetimes, and by their own wills, as well as after their deaths
and by the devotion of others. But Lawrence's myth was, in the world of men,
the myth of those hysterical quarrels with Frieda, whereas Weber's was infinitely handsomer, a matter of minority opinions and defences of the vulnerable, all of which deserved the applause of those with a public conscience.
He was sometimes compared with the Zola of *J'accuse.* The difference between Weber's musical baritone and Lawrence's squeaky giggle symbolizes
the rest.

Those who did not call Heidelberg Max Weber's town called it Stefan
George's—the town of poetry, the town of culture. Edgar Salin says that before the war it was the secret capital of the secret Germany—that is, of the
George group. "It was the spring before the First World War, that spring
of unique sweetness and sadness, which no one who was then young has
forgotten." Perhaps there is some appropriateness in associating George
with Heidelberg, leaving Schwabing to Klages, Schuler, and Wolfskehl.
Klages was not entirely wrong when he said that George was by nature
more a poetic grammarian than a poet. Certainly he was a very Hellenic, not
to say academic, poet. Heidelberg was a city of light, and both George and
Weber—paradoxical as it may seem to put them together—were manifestations of light, phenomena of mind. To George's followers Weber may have
seemed essentially dark, an enemy of the light, a servant of Power, but his
darkness was that at the core of the candle flame. He knew—he *was*—the
hollowness and the burning at the source of the light, but he still served it,
created it, sacrificed himself to it.

What Weber himself would have said about Heidelberg can be guessed
from his chapter "The Literati" in the *Religion of China,* which seems often
to bear on that academic Germany which he knew so well. Half of the
traits he lists as characterizing the Chinese literati are traits he recognized

in himself, the other half those he recognized in his colleagues. Thus he insists that their charisma was based on the skills of reading and writing exclusively, and not on any practical applications of those skills. The Chinese literati were an educational aristocracy. They achieved their success by their skill in passing academic examinations, and their success was the filling of a public office. Confucius, their master, was first of all an official and a bureaucrat, and only secondarily a teacher and a writer. It was they who created the concepts of office, duty, and "the public good"—precisely the concepts which Weber investigated repeatedly, for they were deeply interwoven with his own class and personal dilemma.

Of course, the parallels between the literati of China and Weber's own academic circles are not complete. Their language was written, not spoken, pictorial and descriptive, not logical or rhetorical, whereas Weber's language—his language as leader—was spoken, logical, and rhetorical. Their writing was characterized by "puns, euphemisms, classical allusions, a refined and literary intellectuality"; their education was what could be called "Hellenic," unconcerned with any sacred scriptures, and their politics were those of a welfare-state. By the very structure of their minds they were oriented toward peace and were the enemies of all those forces in Chinese society which lived by war.

In Weber's analysis, Taoism, which was supported by both the feudal families and the Emperor's sultanic harem, and which employed magic and mysticism, was the major enemy against which the literati had to contend, much as, in his own Germany, it was such things as the feudalism at court and the mysticism of Schwabing—both of which were certainly the enemies of Heidelberg—that Weber saw as the most dangerous forces on the scene. The Chinese literati were not interested even in natural science, much less magic. Taoism and Mahayana Buddhism, he says, appealed to the feminine, emotive mind, whereas Confucianism was very patriarchal. Thus he speaks of "the proud, masculine, rational, and sober spirit of Confucianism, similar to the mentality of the Romans." They always faced death with calm acceptance and the concept of sin was alien to them.

It is perceptibly with an ironic but affectionate admiration that Weber analyzes the Chinese literati. He makes clear the two-dimensionality of their emotional-moral life, but also their clear superiority to any of the alternatives to them as a ruling class. We can guess he had much the same attitude toward his immediate environment: impatience with the placidity and pettiness of a great deal of it, a trust that his own charisma would save him from the same weaknesses, and a readiness to fight against any revolution that aimed to substitute emotion for reason.

His own personality as we hear about it is a fact inseparable from its cultural context. Ludwig Curtius says that Heidelberg society offered or aimed at a synthesis of the *europäische Geist*—in itself something eternal, all essence—with the changing demands of the day and its current problems. An attractive freedom and equality was observed among colleagues in their common service to the highest ideals of intelligence; "aristocratic-humanistic sentiments tacitly characterized the tone." But although this republican aristocracy acknowledged no rulers, it had its *Heros Ktistes*, and that was Max Weber. Another Cromwell, he ruled over an intellectual commonwealth which took in all fields of modern knowledge. By sheer intellectual force he won their acknowledgement that he was their champion.

Naturally there was no unanimity in this opinion. Hans Driesch, the biologist, found Weber a tyrant and his circle too adoring. Carl Neumann, the art historian, said that Weber played the *Kraftmensch,* the power-figure, and went to excess in everything. But then Neumann said the same of Ernst Troeltsch, Wilhelm Windelband, and Dieterich, who were Weber's associates. Neumann thought these men "lived all of them above their pay-packet. . . . they carried on like wilder fellows than they were." The Bismarck intoxication of the period betrayed them. Neumann made the interesting point that Max became such a myth that he was known even during his lifetime as the Mythos of Heidelberg because he was a categorically Romantic figure, full of torment and struggle, whereas Kuno Fischer, another important figure on the Heidelberg scene, was categorically classical—a Thorwaldsen Christ—about whom no myth could collect.

But most people seem to have accepted Weber's personality on its own terms. There were disciples like Karl Jaspers, who was still saying in 1958, "He was the greatest German of our age. I have lived with this conviction for almost half a century." And there were sensitive and intelligent men like Gustav Radbruch, who did not dare to appraise Weber as an equal. Radbruch describes Weber's voice as a "sich selbst dämpfende Löwenstimme," (a self-suppressing lion's roar,) and says that his form and his voice were both *überlebensgross,* as if they would burst the limits assigned them were it not for severe self-restraint. This was the echo Weber got back from his environment, and it was extremely fortifying.

Weber impressed himself on others as a great personality while seeming to avoid doing so. His lecturing style has been described by Max Rheinstein, who heard him in Munich at the end of his life:

> Weber's lecturing was no reading, however, from a prepared text. All he
> brought with him into the classroom were little slips of paper upon

which he had apparently noted a few key terms of an outline. The students would thus watch the fascinating process of scholarly and artistic
creation. The words and thoughts were produced with eruptive force.
Weber spoke fast, indeed rapidly. It was not easy to follow this torrent.
But everything was presented in the most strictly elaborated systematic
order, and in the most precise verbal formulation. There were no "ahs"
or "hms," no repetitions, except where indicated by didactic considera-
tions. Everything was said in the right words and at the proper place.
The presentation was cool and objective, but behind this remoteness of
the scholar we students could feel the fire of the passion which was burning in that extraordinary man and the iron will which kept it under
control.

His brother Alfred's lecture style in contrast, was passionately aggressive,
convoluted, allusive, incomplete; all its "fire of passion" was on the surface.

Weber himself said that the cult of personality was a disease of his age,
and he genuinely opposed the call for saving truths from glamorous leaders
—a call fostered by the followers of Nietzsche and George. He declared that
there was only one way to become a personality, and that was to yield ones-
self completely to a *Sache,* a cause or a fact. *Sachlichkeit,* objectivity, was his
great moral slogan. He himself always appeared self-concealing, but he was
for that reason all the more a great personality of the kind the age worshiped. Salin writes that even the members of the George circle, though
alienated by him, had admitted the great weight of his personality: "There
was the age's ideal realized in supreme degree; personality—personality with
every edge and every sharpness, every gift and every knowledge, even with
a noble ardor and a moving sense of duty—but joyless and unhappy." They
had first been introduced to him in Rome in October 1913, and Salin remembers him then as "a giant, who trod the ground with great heavy strides,
his gaze fixed darkly inward rather than on the autumnal countryside or
on the man walking at his side—the face furrowed with grim thoughts—the
beard as it were charged with spiritual impulses and currents." There was
nothing of the artist about him, nothing of the South, nothing to indicate a
Romance heritage, as there was in George; in Weber everything was German or Slavic. On another occasion Salin compares Weber with Tertullian,
"a Titan turned with puritanical bitterness against his own nature." Com-
parisons between him and Jeremiah, or the prophets as a group, were quite
usual.

What Weber says in his *Ancient Judaism* about the prophets is bound
to strike the reader, as it did contemporaries, by its applicability to Weber
himself. They were lonely individuals who did not belong to the priestly

caste, he points out, and they imposed a severe rational control on their irrational ecstatic inspirations. Before they spoke to the people, they transformed their psychosomatic excitement, which clearly contained an element of sexual morbidity, into moral teaching. They first appeared when Solomon had sultanized the Jewish kingship, and they demanded the dismissal of the harem of foreign princesses and their priests, the removal of royal favorites from official positions, the disbanding of the standing army with its military chariots, and the dispending of the royal treasure. The great evil they foresaw was a political and cultural evil—the transformation of the Jewish state into an Egyptianized state of bondage, a liturgical state, dominated by a bureaucracy. Elijah first raised the cry against this fate.* The Jehovah celebrated by the prophets was no god of the land; the god of fertility and vegetation myths was Baal, whose priests arranged orgies where dance and alcohol were used to achieve religious ecstasy, engaged in ritual cohabitation on soil about to be ploughed, and practiced sacred harlotry. Jehovah was a mountain god, a national god, a war god. The prophets saved Israel from the kings and from Baal just as Weber was saving Germany from the feudal romanticism of Wilhelm II and the fertility myths of the Cosmic Circle in Schwabing. Weber does not shrink from pointing out that Baal always gained in popularity and power during periods of peace and prosperity, whereas Jehovah gained strength in times of war and national crisis.

This is enough to place him, in our scheme, as a "patriarchal" figure. But he belonged to the reformist wing, the Heidelberg wing, of the patriarchal party. He identified himself with the bourgeoisie; the Junkers, of whom Bismarck was the chief, were his class enemy. The Krupp-von Bohlen wedding of 1906 symbolized all that Weber hated in German politics: an alliance, sponsored by the Kaiser, between giant industry and pseudo-aristocracy.

He identified himself with the plain people, who accepted a traditional morality in sexual matters. For himself, he aimed only at the *bürgerlich* virtues. Thus he wrote to his wife that he had told Frieda Gross, "I could on occasion like a specifically 'erotic' woman well enough, as she herself must have noticed, but could never attach myself to her, or build anything on her friendship. Because I am, as has been demonstrated, no suitable friend for such women, for whom really only the 'erotic' man has any value." It seems clear that Weber is not talking about people's erotic proclivities as individuals, but about their total identities as members of the erotic movement—

---

* It is particularly interesting, in view of Otto Gross's hatred of Elijah, to see Weber associate himself with that solitary defier of Ahab and destroyer of Jezebel.

about those qualities that made Frieda's husband Otto the erotic man par excellence.

In 1906 Weber declared in a letter to Otto von Harnack that to his mind the fact "that our nation has never, in any form, undergone the discipline of hard ascetism is . . . the source of that which I find detestable in it (as in myself)." It seems that this feeling changed over the years, but still he insisted to the end on the simple, plain, average virtues as the best. He remained a representative of what Otto Gross called the democratic principle, believing only in those virtues which all men here and now can possess. One's primary moral duty is to face the facts of any situation as they really are, to live in this disenchanted world of ours, not to look for another, enchanted one. Wolfgang Mommsen said that it was Weber's life work to call the German bourgeois back to their true nature, back from the self-aristocratizing delusions induced by the Kaiser. The Germans, he said in 1918, are a *Disciplinvolk,* a nation of the disciplined. This is the characteristic note of his morality, and if it is not the morality of Potsdam, it is much less that of Schwabing. We will call it Heidelberg-reformist.

The Two Minds Compared

Weber and Lawrence chose opposite areas of knowledge to explore and opposite modes of knowledge to enact. For Lawrence it was the mode of artistic imagination and the area of personal and interpersonal relations, for Weber the modes of impersonal scientific knowledge and of political action and the areas of public facts—that is, economic and sociological facts about groups and institutions. The price each paid for his choice is obvious. Lawrence is often shrill and foolish about public facts, Weber is often dull and conventional about the inner life, even his own. Both imaginations are inauthentic outside their chosen areas of concentration. But if this is more true of them than of many other sociologist-novelist pairs one could name, it is not the result of mere stupid excess on their part. The word "inauthentic" here is simply the judgment of unheroic common sense on their respective heroic enterprises: on Lawrence's part, the attempt to reduce "public facts" to a subcategory of private life, and on Weber's part the attempt to turn all that was private and inner into sociological data. Even within their own areas there is something heroic about the operation of their imaginations, and something of self-caricature. Lawrence's version of the private life is quite fantastically private and unconditioned, with individuals wrestling against each other or themselves with no mediation by circumstances, either internal or external. (There is no such thing as an accident in his novels.) And Weber's version of public life is quite fantastically public and impersonal, with modes of legitimation and modes of dominance replacing people and events. (Consider, for example, his definition of what "friendship" means, in *Theory of Social and Economic Organization*: ". . . that we, the observers, judge that there is or has been a probability that on the basis of certain kinds of known subjective attitude of certain individuals there will result in the average case a certain specific type of action.") But these excesses are to be found in their works only in ways which coexist with a paradoxical realism and even moderation in both men, which becomes apparent when you compare their writings with those of some of their rivals. This, of course, is why we call them great minds: their excesses of interpretation are heroic, not stupid.

These differences can best be summed up by saying that Weber exemplified the Apollonian mode of mind whereas Lawrence exemplified the Demetrian. To be quite exact, we should find a goddess other than Demeter to balance against Apollo, for Demeter was the goddess of the whole matriarchal mode of being, whereas Apollo was the god of just one province of the patriarchal mode—that of the mind. Thus we can call Lawrence the novelist a Demetrian figure, but for Lawrence the essayist, the thinker, we need another word. Perhaps we can take Diotima as the patroness of the province of mind within the matriarchal mode. After all, Bachofen attached great significance to the legend of Socrates learning from Diotima, which he took to reveal the primacy of matriarchal wisdom. Diotima would then stand for a nonsystematic mental habit, almost nonconceptual, relying heavily on concrete instances, real or imagined, intuitive judgments, rightness of feeling; oriented of course toward fertility and domesticity, toward life and love, as main values; very responsive to mysteries and legends, to all that is remote and authoritative in long-gone religions and cultures. This is a legitimate use of the mind—one very appropriate to novelists and men of letters, even to literary critics—but it is clearly very different from what we call the Apollonian use of the mind.

An obvious example of the Apollonian in Weber is his employment of highly abstract categories, but the overriding feature that unmistakably puts him in this class is the fact that he was essentially a *rational* man, in a very far-reaching sense. Thus Löwith writes of the concept of the "ideal-type," which played a significant role in Weber's methodology as a crystallization in one hypothetical case of the sociological categories Weber was examining: "The ideal-type construct has at its source one particular 'illusionless' individual, who has been thrown back upon himself alone by a world become objectively meaningless and drab, and therefore is, to that extent, emphatically 'realistic.'" This illusionless individual, Weber himself, was forced, by his very illusionlessness, to create meanings for himself, to create values. He was forced to become "the human hero," the free individual responsible to no one and nothing but himself. He was what Marx called "alienated." Weber's "rationalization" is the antidote to Marx's "alienation." Rationalization is the locus of all freedom, because it challenges the metaphysical reality of *all* the orders and organizations of modern life.

The sharpest antithesis between Weber and Lawrence lies in the fact that for Weber, to act as a free person is to act purposefully. He rejected the idea—popular among his liberal friends such as Troeltsch and Meinecke—that irrational incalculability or the play impulse was the source of human freedom. Indeed, seeing that the spread of rationalization in the world was breeding irrationalism in reaction, he assigned the human hero the task of fighting this atavistic thrust. To be sure, Weber hated as well as loved rationalization; the only freedom he knew of was freedom inside the iron cage. Moreover such ambivalence, or at least *some* form of alienation, of "objectivity," always characterizes the Apollonian mind. It loves pure truth, purged of all selfishness and partiality. As Löwith points out, Weber always presented himself as a member of some section of society—as a scientist, a teacher, a philosopher—but never as a whole man. In this separation of his life spheres lay freedom; it made complete self-knowledge possible, for only by such a separation could one achieve pure objectivity. But Weber also believed that a man must commit his whole self in action inside each of these life spheres, "for nothing has any value for a man as man which he cannot do with passion." Such is Weber's strenuous and agonizing version of the Apollonian mind.

In stark contrast stands Lawrence's belief that the deepest life is never purposive, that it enters a man "from beyond" and "from behind," that one must always act as a whole man, but that at his best a man "does not belong to himself." Lawrence passionately opposed both reason and responsibility as ruling powers over a man's life. He trusted to the blood, to "the wind that blows through me," to passion. And he promised, by doing so, to act always as a whole being.

What he looked for in the things around him was their meaning, which was not just their "meaning for me," because it was life's meaning, but was still something not there the next minute or for the next person. What the Apollonian looks for is a thing's factuality—what is there for all occasions and all people, what can be counted on, what can be counted. The Apollonian mind is essentially disciplined, because it is essentially self-alienated; its main moral responsibility is to take account of everyone else's point of view and to be distributively just. That seemed to Lawrence, insofar as it was worth doing at all, not worth talking about; and the same was true of a whole cluster of virtues, like justice. Weber's patriarchalism is the mode of being of those who take responsibility for law and order, not for life and love, whereas Lawrence's mode of being was that of someone who never would be or wanted to be an administrator or a manager.

It is perhaps worth repeating that patriarchalism can be and has been challenged by a number of oppositions, not only by what we have called matriarchalism. All Western history can be read in terms of such challenges. For instance, the imaginative and moral world of Samuel Richardson is antipatriarchal; *Pamela* and *Clarissa* are protests against the domination of husbands and fathers, against wickedly glamorous aristocrats, against traditions of male initiative in sexuality. But Richardson's protest came under the sign of Virgo, and its figureheads were Pamela Andrews and Clarissa Harlowe. He and his readers rebelled against the old traditions of prerogative and power, which justified themselves by their establishment-blessed association with the will of God and the course of Nature, and by the "seed-time and harvest" pleasures which they brought with them. Such justification, Richardson implies, must no longer hold sway in men's hearts. All men and women must henceforth be considered moral beings, equal and even indistinguishable, except insofar as refinement of feeling and rectitude of conduct win advancement for this or that individual among them. Merit alone should create a human difference. To all this Fielding's *Tom Jones* was the coarsely patriarchal answer, worthy of a Junker author. Fielding's sensibility derived from the experience of a magistrate, of one who takes responsibility for law and order, not for love and life. He balances one injustice against another, recommends the old solutions to most problems, and deprecates any too subtle and too passionate investigation of moral particulars; it is the general picture which matters.

This eighteenth-century English movement of resistance to patriarchy was not unlike the Webers' nineteenth-century German reformism. Marianne Weber was an exemplary virgin who can be imaginatively associated with Clarissa Harlowe, and Max, we might say, tried to bring about in Germany a Richardsonian (and Defoian) revolution against Junker patriarchy. But it was Germany's tragedy to have missed that eighteenth-century experience of patriotic capitalism and Calvinism which modified English patriarchy, and by 1900 it was far too late to stir imaginations with a call to rebel in the name of the Virgin. Lawrence and Frieda had found the potent icon of the times; they set it up as their standard and proclaimed a rebellion which promised a real alternative to patriarchy. This was too much for Weber, who called for a mitigation, and so came to stand finally as a champion of some reformed version of the old thing. Only Lawrence's doctrine could inspire a real imaginative revolution. Hence their mutual irreconcilability.

There are, nonetheless, some striking coincidences between the two men's lists of crucial concerns. For instance, in Weber's scheme of things rationalism and charisma stood as opposite terms in one of the major polarities of historical and social development. He saw the history of Western culture as characterized, tragically, by an irreversible process of increasing rationalization, from which the only escape was offered by the irruption of charismatic individuals and the historical movements which they generated. This process of rationalization derived historically from armies and monasteries and manifested itself in the forms of Calvinism, capitalism and bureaucracy. It imposed itself by means of discipline and asceticism, with the effect of depersonalizing the individual, reifying him into a series of functions. Although this terminology is completely foreign to Lawrence, these concepts, above all this scheme of meanings, are certainly ones with which he was familiar. On this score, the difference between the two men's ideologies lies almost wholly in the schemes of action which they deduced from this diagnosis. Where Weber declares that we must endure this fate, must be broken on this wheel, Lawrence sets out to escape it, to deny discipline and asceticism, to *become* a charismatic leader, to create a center of healing faith—by means, of course, of the world of Woman. He does not try to present charismatic *men* fictionally—except in the leadership novels, and there he is not successful—but *The Rainbow, Women in Love*, and *Lady Chatterley's Lover* are full of the charismatic presence of Frieda, with powerful equivalences set up between Woman and Earth and Love and Life.

It needs no arguing that Frieda represents the opposite of discipline and asceticism, the opposite even of all vocational ethic, all *Beruf*; in fact, she pitied men because they had to waste their time doing work. But it should perhaps be pointed out that charisma in women is always likely to be different from charisma in men. In the world of Woman it expresses itself in the creation of life—in fertility, sensuality, gaiety, renewal. The charisma of the *Mutterrecht* was exemplified not only in Frieda Lawrence but also in Fanny zu Reventlow, whose ideas about unmarried motherhood were a factor in Frieda's grief over losing her children, and Lawrence's anger at her grief. She had counted on having them, and being independent of all men. In *The Plumed Serpent* we see this *Mutterrecht* charisma in Kate Leslie, where it is in conflict with the *Vaterrecht* charisma of Don Ramon, a leader of the kind

that Weber had in mind when he talked about charisma. Don Ramon's submissive wife Teresa, who is contrasted with Kate, is the perfect wife for a
charismatic man; she feeds his fire. Lawrence wants to prefer Ramon and
Teresa to Kate and Joachim, the husband who fed her flame; he wants to
prefer the patriarchal mode of leadership and love to the matriarchal. But
he cannot convince himself, and the novel ends irresolutely. *Lady Chatterley's
Lover* announces his return to the world of Woman.

There is, however, a *diagnostic* convergence of Lawrence's and Weber's
theories which becomes apparent in the following passage from Weber's
The Protestant Ethic and the Spirit of Capitalism: "Christian asceticism, at
first fleeing from the world into solitude, had already ruled the world which
it had renounced from the monastery and through the Church. But it had, on
the whole, left the naturally spontaneous character of daily life in the world
untouched. Now it strode into the marketplace of life, slammed the door of
the monastery behind it, and undertook to penetrate just that daily routine
of life with its methodicalness, to fashion it into a life in the world, but
neither of nor for this world." Lawrence and Frieda sought out all over the
world those forms of life still unspoiled by the compulsion Weber describes,
and Frieda was conscientiously triumphing over this compulsion when she
lay on her bed smoking while Lawrence and Brett built her an extension to
the ranch in New Mexico. Similarly, Otto Gross could lie in bed all day if
he felt like it, and that is what Will Brangwen cannot do but admires Anna
for doing. Lawrence, on the other hand, suffered from a compulsion to be
always working, producing, achieving, even excelling.

That Lawrence and Weber were, in many respects, on the same track is
clear in following passage, which, although written by Weber, might almost
be by Lawrence:

> An inanimate machine is mind objectified. Only this provides it with the
> power to force men into its service and to dominate their everyday work-
> ing life as completely as is actually the case in the factory. Objectified
> intelligence is also that animate machine, the bureaucratic organization,
> with its specialization of trained skills, its division of jurisdiction, its
> rules and hierarchical relations of authority. Together with the inanimate
> machine it is busy fabricating the shell of bondage which men will per-
> haps be forced to inhabit some day, as powerless as the fellahs of ancient
> Egypt.

Both Weber and Lawrence located the major historical manifestation of
bureaucratic, mechanistic rationalization in Anglo-Saxon Puritanism. Partly
for that reason, both were fascinated by the culture of white America. It is
interesting to see how similarily Benjamin Franklin is treated in Weber's

Protestant Ethic and Lawrence's *Studies in Classic American Literature*. Both men made important visits to America and wrote vivid accounts of it, Weber, typically, concentrating on the cities, Lawrence on the unpopulated land-scape. And for both, the other significant country was Russia; both learned the language and planned to go there, Weber in 1911, Lawrence after the 1917 Revolution. For Weber as well as for Lawrence, Russia was essentially the country of Tolstoy and Dostoevski, Rozanov, Shestov, and Soloviev. Weber planned to write a book about Tolstoy. For him, as for Lawrence, Tolstoy embodied the challenge of world-renunciation, a challenge which seemed much greater for having come from the creator of *Anna Karenina*. Like Gandhi later, Tolstoy offered a challenge almost equally to both the patriarchal and matriarchal modes of being.

Like America and Russia, Italy also meant the same thing to both men; it was the land of beauty, of ancient fertility, the land of the prerationalized culture. France meant by and large nothing, and England to Weber meant roughly as much as Germany did to Lawrence, a known quantity from which much had been learned but little new was now to be expected.

Their world maps, too, were much the same. Both turned away from Europe to the rest of the world, seeking explanatory alternatives. But whereas Lawrence turned most typically to the Indians of New Mexico, where some tribes have a matriarchal culture in the strict sense, or to the vanished Etrus-cans—that is, to *Naturvölker* or prehistorical peoples—Weber turned to the other great *Kulturvölker*, to China, to India, or to the ancient Jews. Both sought to illuminate the West by studying alternatives to its civilization. But where Lawrence's study always promised the hope of an escape, for at least a few people, Weber balanced advantages against disadvantages and prom-ised nothing.

It seems not too much to say that the two men lived in the same intel-lectual world, the same landscape of ideas, though the schemes of action they proposed relative to it were very different. Their feelings about many of its features, as well as their interest in them, tended also to be different. But these differences notwithstanding, Weber and Lawrence seem to have shared more of a mental perspective with each other than with, say, Virginia Woolf or T. S. Eliot.

The great difference between them in feeling, at least in their moments of highest achievement, is that Weber and Weber's world were tragic, while Lawrence's was, in intention at least, the opposite. Weber insisted that there was an intolerable but inevitable price to be paid for the achievements of the Western world. That was the implicit message of his personality as well as the explicit message of his works. For Lawrence, tragedy as much as salvation were self-dramatizing ideas—"every man his own Hamlet," as he liked to say—and the pride he took in his own development was that he had transcended them. There was much that was potentially tragic in his personal fate and in his vision of the world, but he refused to embody it. He was angry when the peasants in Mexico called him *Il Criste*; he wanted them to call him "the fox." Indeed, his life history is notably lacking in tragic events, compared with, for instance, Shelley's, with its constant melodrama of suicides, hopeless love, violence, imprisonment, and flight. Or even as compared with Bertrand Russell's.

He owed this untragicalness to Frieda, who, as he puts it in *Kangaroo,* did not "allow" people to quarrel with her. Nor did she allow them to take themselves too seriously. In Frieda's world the sun always rose again, and was a more important event as it did than anything until the next time it rose. Nothing was final but recurrence and renewal. Tragedy was the life-form appropriate to the world of men, to the world of lineal progressive moralistic history. But for Lawrence—because of Frieda—the Ship of Death always sees a spot of light growing on the horizon after having driven as far as possible into total night. This is the cyclical world of comedy, and Lawrence was in this sense the most serious of comedians, because comedy is the life-form of the world of Woman.

One of the most important principles shared by Lawrence and Weber, when they were precisely at the height of their powers, was their polytheism of values. More than simple polytheism, this polytheism of values entailed a willingness to face up to the mutual antagonism and irreconcilability of key values. Weber compared the modern situation to that of ancient paganism, with its bewilderment of creeds: "The many old gods, disenchanted and so in the form of impersonal forces, arise out of their graves, strive after power over our life, and begin again among ourselves their eternal struggle." But he takes the situation tragically. "As between values, there is no question, finally everywhere and always, of *alternatives*, but of an irreconcilable *struggle to the death*, as between 'God' and 'Devil.'" For his part, Lawrence blithely declared that he could "belong to the sweetest Christian brotherhood one day, and ride after Attila with a raw beef-steak for my saddle-cloth, to see the red cock crow over all Christendom, next day." Such polytheism is natural to the world of Woman.

But in the world of men, the world of politics, Lawrence was, on his infrequent ventures into that territory, as much Weber's vassal as Weber was his in the world of Eros. That is, when he was on Weber's terrain Lawrence fought for the same king, but with less power, less authority, less authenticity. Lawrence believed as little as Weber in the practicability of ideal democracy or in the ideality of practicable democracy. He would have liked a democracy which followed the definition Weber gave to General Ludendorff after the war: "In a democracy the people choose a leader they trust. Then he says: Now shut up and obey. Neither people nor party may counsel him." Even Ludendorff liked democracy by that definition, but the context of the remark shows the profound difference between Ludendorff and Weber and the equally profound similarity between Weber and Lawrence. For Weber said these words in an effort to persuade Ludendorff to take on the guilt of the war and give himself up to the Allies as a sacrificial victim, a scapegoat for the German nation as a whole—an idea which the general found hard to comprehend. Leadership, morally responsible to the pitch of heroism, but leadership still, was the central feature of the democracy Weber and Lawrence believed in.

Consequently, both shared a common distaste for the platitudes and half-truths of liberalism. Their relation to the standard "advanced" thinking on such subjects was similar. The *Kathedersozialisten* or academic socialists were to Weber what the Fabian Socialists were to Lawrence—the object of an early respect which turned to distaste. Both men came to feel that these two groups of older contemporaries offered self-righteous and superficial solutions, intellectually and morally slipshod, glibly rational answers to tragically irrational problems.

For them, not justice but power was the central motive of all politics. It was Weber as much as anyone who made imperialism a respectable political cause in Germany. In his Freiburg inaugural lecture in 1895 he announced that only a world mission could give Germany moral size and wake its moral energies to grapple with the tasks of internal as well as external politics. He saw the world situation always as a struggle between nations, which had effects on them comparable to the effects of struggles between individuals. "Struggle" was one of Weber's key ideas, just as it had been his mother's. He did not endorse Bismarck's *Realpolitik,* but *Idealpolitik* meant even less to him. Given the choice between "the responsibility ethic" and "the conscience ethic," he chose the former; *Kultur* and *Macht* were for him antithetical categories, and he endorsed the latter as primary in national life. Switzerland and Belgium were not really nations, he said, because they had renounced power.

A passage from Lawrence's pseudonymous *Movements in European History* makes the similarity between his attitude and Weber's apparent:

> But if men must fight their way forward, they must have a leader whom
> they all obey. . . . Europe is now again moving towards oneness, as in
> Roman days—one vast state ruled by the infinite numbers of the people—

the producers, the proletariat, the workers. . . . Germany and Russia step from one extreme to the other, from absolute monarchy such as Britain never knew, straight to the other extreme of government, government by the masses of the proletariat, strange, and as it seems, without true purpose: the masses of the working people governing themselves they know not why, except that they wish to destroy all authority, and to enjoy all an equal prosperity. . . . Therefore a great united Europe of productive working people, all materially equal, will never be able to continue and remain firm unless it unites also around some great chosen figure, some hero who can lead a great war, as well as administer a wide peace. It all depends on the will of the people. But the will of the people must concentrate in one figure, who is also supreme over the will of the people. He must be chosen, but at the same time is responsible to God alone. Here is a problem of which a stormy future will have to evolve the solution.

The style here is that of the Home University Library, the Man of Letters, the popularizer. But the ideas are those of Max Weber.

Lawrence like Weber was quite ready, in theory, to pay the price of moral carelessness, of ruthlessness, even of brutality, in exchange for vigorous leadership. On this score, both men were echoing Carlyle. Interestingly, however, both were provoked to anger by the Kaiser's conduct during the war. "I would personally take the moron by the throat and throttle him, if they would only let me get at him," Weber fumed, and Lawrence, as reported by Ernest Jones, declared: "That posturing ape, with his winged helmet, keeps telling people what a fine fellow he is, and what noble fellows they are. A real leader would not speak of himself or his followers; he would simply command: 'There is the enemy, strike.'" Although they called for leadership, the Kaiser's brand of it outraged them both. One suspects that if it had come to any hero attempting to lead *them*, they would have been found in indignant opposition.

Weber's politics, however self-contradictory, are full of understanding, reflection, and passion; they have authority. The same cannot be said for Lawrence, who, it should be noted, ventured far into these realms only when he was in rebellion against the world of Woman. Lawrence, one can say, "knew nothing about" politics, because there were profound resistances in him to such knowledge. Weber lived and moved and breathed in politics—local, national, and international—all his life. He knew the principles and the practice, intimately and objectively. He too had an antipathy to actually becoming a political leader, so that his chances of such a career along those lines never materialized. But this antipathy came into play at a point in Weber's development toward becoming such a leader far in advance of anything achieved by Lawrence.

Equivalences

Inasmuch as Lawrence never wrote about Max Weber, it is interesting to speculate on whom among his English acquaintance could be called in some sense an equivalent to Weber. The name that comes to mind is Bertrand Russell. We find in Russell as strongly as in Weber that inherited sense of public responsibility, as well as that phenomenal cleverness; and the fullness of academic aptitude combined with a determination to go beyond the academic. Weber and Russell were both born much closer to the sources of public power than Lawrence was, and their range of interests, very broad in both cases, centered on questions of public policy and philosophic theory.

"I have never been so whole-hearted or so little troubled with hesitation in any work as in the pacifist work that I did during the war. For the first time I found something to do which involved my whole nature. My previous abstract work had left my human instincts unsatisfied, and I had allowed them an occasional outlet by political speaking and writing, more particularly on free trade and votes for women. The aristocratic political tradition of the 18th and 19th centuries, which I had imbibed in childhood, had made me feel an instinctive responsibility in regard to public affairs." All this is very much what Weber might have said, and the fact that Russell was a pacifist whereas Weber was a militarist would not have seemed a crucial difference to Lawrence. The personal satisfaction both took in the public crisis brought about by the war, the way it summoned both of them to action, probably would have seemed to him more important. The difference between them was real, but so was the fact that each took the war as an occasion for attaching himself to the world of men.

The criterion of sincerity by which Lawrence condemned Russell probably would have applied with equal severity to Weber. He might have said to Weber what he said to Russell: "I believe in your inherent power for realizing the truth. But I don't believe in your will, not for a second. Your will is false and cruel. You are too full of devilish repressions to be anything but lustful and cruel." To be sure, the heroism of Russell's conduct in those years, as of Weber's, made Lawrence's conduct look pretty shabby, but this is only because the criteria of sincerity are different for the two modes of being. Russell was physically attacked and sent to prison for six months for propagating pacifism, while Weber's articles criticizing the Kaiser were suppressed and he was booed and hissed when he lectured. Lawrence, however, did nothing public, yet he complained of oppression more than either. By the standards of the world of men, Russell and Weber were heroes while Lawrence was merely contemptible. But by the standards of the world of Woman, Russell and Weber were hollow suits of armor, clanking around in heroic postures, while Lawrence was the great truth-teller who refused to get involved in false heroics.

If we look for an equivalent of Weber upon whose work, as distinct from his beliefs and actions, Lawrence passed judgment, we find Thomas Mann, who has more than once been called the equivalent in literature of what Weber was in sociology. Mann was the other great ironic German of that period, with the same massive weight of learning as Weber and the same tendency to erect elaborate and abstract structures. The opposite of *naiv* in the Schillerian sense, both men handled the world through an alienating conceptual mechanism. In contrast with most intellectuals and artists of their time, both were culturally middle-class and conservative, holding by the old traditions of German *Kultur*. In Lawrence's essay on *Death in Venice,* which seems to be the first thing written about Mann in English, he is, naturally, out of sympathy with the book and its author, though respectful: "Thomas Mann seems to me the last sick sufferer from the complaint of Flaubert. The latter stood away from life as from a leprosy." He finds Mann's immense burden of consciousness and artistic conscientiousness unprofitable, and he repudiates the book's death-directedness. Mann's work is "banal" and "stale" and his formalism, which makes form triumphant over life itself, is, Lawrence feels, already outdated. The spirit of the times, Lawrence sensed already, was with him rather than Mann: "But Thomas Mann is old—and we are young. Germany does not feel very young to me." The essay, which was written in 1913, closes with this declaration, in which the editorial "we" can be taken to include Frieda. Lawrence repudiates Mann in the name of his and Frieda's common cause, their great enterprise of life-renewal. Something similar he would surely have said about Weber's "Wissenschaft als Beruf" ("Science as a Vocation").

Weber and Lawrence did not know each other at all, and each knew too little about the other to constitute an influence. In the case of Weber, there is no call for surprise about this. He no doubt never read a word by Lawrence and heard about him only as the writer with whom Else's sister had eloped. In the case of Lawrence, who lived on ten years after Weber's death and who must have heard much from Frieda about this impressive personality, it is much odder. Frieda specialized in being impressed by impressive men, and any man with whom Else was in love would be of prime interest to her. But we must remind ourselves how even odder is Lawrence's neglect in his fiction of Otto Gross. Of course, the prime mechanism we must predicate to explain all such cases of neglect is not at all odd. It is that of the artistic conscience. Lawrence knew which subjects he could write about well, and which would disturb his tact and spoil his taste. It is clear enough when that happens in his work, and also clear how rarely it does happen. He had a very active artistic conscience, though it was not the sort of thing he talked about much. Such talk belonged too much to the world of *Geist*.

I don't think, therefore, that anything he wrote is "about" Max Weber. But there are one of two minor portraits of men of power in his work, which are rather interesting in this connection. Insofar as all of Lawrence's experience was closely interrelated, these portraits indirectly refer to Weber. The Promethean type appears in *The Rainbow* in Alfred Brangwen, Tom's eldest brother. He is a man in deep rebellion against his own fate, which compels him to design lace patterns on a graph paper of tiny squares, with intense exactitude, while by nature he needs to design boldly. He is cruel to himself, and to others, in consequence. His marriage is a mistake, and in later years he takes a mistress, an intellectual and emancipated woman, who appreciates his mind. Tom Brangwen admires both his brother and the woman, though he finds her too cold for his own taste. Most important is Tom's sense that his brother is more of a *man* than he is—in his saturnine solitude—just because Tom belongs to Lydia and to marriage and to the world of life.

Another such figure is glimpsed in "The Captain's Doll" in the figure of the Herr Regierungsrat, whom Hannele nearly marries. A large, sardonic, frightening personality, not attractive but impressive, he suggests nothing so much as a small-town Bismarck. The Regierungsrat, an intellectual like Alfred Brangwen, is physically gross and psychologically tragic, but he exerts the same fearful fascination on Hannele that some women felt for Max Weber. But such particular coincidences are only useful as indicating a general—and quite fleeting—likeness. The Regierungsrat is related to Kangaroo, the most charismatic of Lawrence's political leaders, and that portrait too gives us hints of what Lawrence would have said about Weber.

One last figure, furthest of all from Weber himself, and yet still suggestive of Lawrence's attitude to men of power, is the portrait of Dr. Mitchell in *The Lost Girl*. The humiliation of Dr. Mitchell by Alvina is a comic version of the triumph of women over "dominant" men. If Lawrence had met Weber, he would have had a keen eye for his foibles of self-projection, for the falsities of some of his power and passion, and for his reliance on winning other people's awe and admiration—for the hollowness of the personal life behind the terrific facade. No doubt Frieda saw all this for herself.

In the only instance in which Lawrence treated the themes of Weber's life on a large fictional scale, it seems very unlikely that he was thinking of Weber specifically. I am referring to Gerald Crich in *Women in Love*, and many of his qualities derive from his being cast in the role of Lawrence's "Other Man"—blonde, plump, and desirable—an image surely incompatible with that of Weber. But *for us* some aspects of Gerald are nevertheless imaginatively evocative of Weber. Most important are the themes of the Crich family life. Here Lawrence for once treated the life of the upper middle class, the Weber class, exemplified by a family who have made a fortune out of modern industry and who are close to all the forms of power of modern civilization. In Mr. Crich he gives us the Christian industrialist, whose moral life is an attempt to atone for the luxury and the power he has so effortfully achieved. In Mrs. Crich he gives us the defeated contrary impulse to live out morally the motives of pride and passion. In the Weber family, to be sure, the roles were differently divided, with the wife anxiously Christian, the husband determined to enjoy the good things with which the culture rewarded their efforts. But the themes are the same. So are the conflicts and their destructive effects on the children.

Both are "unlucky" families. Gerald Crich shot his brother when a child, Diana drowns and drowns her fiancé with her, Winifred is "peculiar." The Weber family too was very inharmonious. Lili committed suicide, Alfred and Karl never married, and all the sons were hostile to their exemplary mother during their adolescence. The relationship between Max and Alfred was especially destructive.

What is more, Gerald's position as eldest son—eldest son of the whole culture, symbolically—the man with every gift except that of faith in life, is very like Max's. He is the world of men incarnate. It is Gerald's inability to believe in erotic marriage which leads him to his love affair with Gudrun, and so to his death. The great turning point in his life is the scene at the Water Party, when he is called back into action, command, and effectiveness, back into the world of men and the world of death, just when he was beginning for the first time in his life to relax, to sleep, to love, to heal. That scene has, I am sure, some symbolic reference to the effect on the whole culture of the outbreak of war in 1914, which shattered so completely Lawrence's hopes for a new world which was being born out of the relaxation of the old one. And in Max Weber's life too, we have a vivid example of much the same phenomenon. The war called him back to full effectiveness after seventeen years of psychic trouble. He put on uniform and took charge of nine hospitals in the neighborhood of Heidelberg, organizing them, working, dealing with people and problems, *happy,* twelve hours a day. "The lion got one whiff of blood and leaped to life," as his colleague, Carl Neumann, put it. Like Gerald, he took command in the world of men, and the world of death, at the moment of crisis.

Gerald's death in the blinding snows and the icy winds of the Alps, symbolic of the extreme of abstraction to which the scientific Western mind tends, suits Max Weber even better than Gerald Crich the industrialist. "It was pure organic disintegration and pure mechanical organization. This is the first and finest state of chaos," Lawrence says of Gerald and the mines. It is also what Klages and Erich von Kahler said about Weber and his sociology, and there were expressions of this attitude even in the obituary notices in 1920. Thus Ernst Correll wrote in *Die Hochschule* that Weber's mass of specialized knowledge made one ask, "What use is all this?" No one could ever employ it all. Weber was the last of his kind, the last of the great specialists in Western science. Correll concludes, "In this sense I say—with respect—that the greatest representative of knowledge in our times has led knowledge up to a peak and even to the edge from which it must come down." This specialization and disenchantment of knowledge could be so destructive that it actually was in one case explicitly connected with suicide. Walter Theodor Cleve says that Weber's "rationalism" found many victims: "Alfred Seidel perhaps was destroyed by the 'intellectualization of man in a disenchanted world.' In his last letter, before he hanged himself, he writes: 'The only thing to do is to annihilate myself. It is the beginning of the great despair of Western culture, as it set in with Schopenhauer and Max Weber.' " Weber himself lived on intimate terms with the thought of death. He was deeply in sympathy with those who killed themselves among his own family and acquaintance, and his own death seemed to some who knew him to be as voluntary as Gerald's, a self-release from the torments of a life envenomed by revengeful Eros. "Not summer's bloom lies ahead of us," he said in 'Politik als Beruf,' "but rather a polar night of icy darkness and hardness, no matter which group may triumph externally now."

We have, of course, no corresponding hints of what Weber might have said about Lawrence. The nearest thing is something that corresponds, rather, to Lawrence's comments on Russell. Weber had much to do with Otto Gross, though indirectly more than directly. He knew Emil Kraepelin, whose Assistent Gross was in Munich; he knew of course Edgar Jaffe and Fanny zu Reventlow and Erich Mühsam; and it was Weber's friend Hans Gruhle who found Gross dying in 1920. He became a friend of Frieda Gross, and in the course of Hanns Gross's law suit against her, which lasted many years, Weber must have reflected often on the tragedy of Otto's life. Above all, he had been made the godfather of Peter Jaffe, and this seems to have been a very significant relationship for him, and significant in his and Else's approach to each other.

Thus in 1917, when she first saw him again, in Munich, after their estrangement, he wrote her this letter, about the boy, who had died in that month two years before.

Munich, 30, X, 1917

DEAR ELSE,

I only wanted to say that I thought of the child and indeed always think of him, the more his no longer being on earth becomes an everyday fact. I stayed, hoping to get to his little grave, but I see that both the early and the late trains are so awkwardly timed that I wouldn't be able to catch the only train to Heidelberg that would let me find Marianne still awake. So I must celebrate a (belated) All Souls' Day for him in my thoughts.

YOUR MAX

And in another letter, a month later, he said, "The dream child, with his silence and his access in himself to knowledge, was somehow connected for me —I couldn't say how or why—with faded dreams of a child of my own." Otto Gross's child had become his, by a spiritual paternity of adoption, and had made him a co-parent with Else. In 1919, after the suicide of his sister Lili, the memory of Otto Gross's child seems still to have been bound up with his love for Else and with his wistful affirmation of love and happiness. "The date reminds me that you too—something that had slipped my mind—have a memorial day, my darling—then a ray of the sun of love comes out, the sun that lives and works deep hidden in the hearts of men, broken up into innumerable rays. I think with deep love and thankfulness of this child, who time and again took us by the hand and led us to each other, brand new and in such loveliness—he gave me the young mother, who shelters and cherishes me, now that the old one's true and faithful eyes no longer can manage it."*

In some measure Max Weber owed the emotional richness of his last years to Peter Jaffe, and so to Otto Gross, and it seems likely that he was conscious of that. But the only document we have is Weber's 1907 letter rejecting the essay Gross submitted to the *Archiv.* It is an outright rejection, rough and contemptuous, but in the following years Weber moved a long way toward sympathy. In 1919 he wrote to Frieda Gross that he still sympathized with her mission in life, her cause, which by then was, like Otto's, erotic emancipation. But of course Weber still held by his own values of objective realism, of all-around responsibility, so he could never have gone far toward theirs. Indeed, a recurrent theme of his late speeches and essays was the deplorable cult of "experience" and of "religion" among intellectuals, which suggests that the philosophical substructure of the movement aimed at erotic emancipation was still detestable to him, and that Lawrence's writing would

* Professor Baumgarten says, "When he fell in love most passionately, most liberatedly, and most fully, it was for him a perplexingly new and yet old experience, because it was rooted in his familial affections. 'My mother, my sister, my unutterable happiness.'"

have been so too. Weber never ceased calling for objectivity and realism above all else.

Moreover, Marianne Weber's books express essentially Max's opinions, and they are nearly all directed against free love and against "the opinions fashionable in certain medical circles that one's health will suffer unless the sexual drive is satisfied." That is to say, Marianne Weber's books, essays, and lectures were a defense of society against the attacks of Otto Gross. This is the nearest thing to outright controversy between two of our principals, and one may say that those essays and lectures were directed against Lawrence too, insofar as he stood with Gross.

Weber also dealt with modern poetry and poetic "prophecy," as they were found in the person of Stefan George. He had conversations with George and was treated as an honorable enemy by the poet's followers. Although George was quite unlike Lawrence—more like Yeats—in personality and doctrine, from Weber's point of view they probably would have seemed like they belonged together. In a speech at the first meeting of the German Sociologists, in 1910, Weber put the George disciples and the Freud disciples side by side (together with race theorists) as modern groups who were developing into sects. He pointed out the semi-divine quality attributed to George by his followers and the secrecy of the Freudians about the ethic they were developing from their specialized knowledge. His larger point was the inappropriateness of deriving an ethic from a science, from *Wissenschaft,* and so his remarks apply to Gross and not to Freud. Implicitly, though, he was condemning both groups, and all men like Gross, for introducing religiosity into the disenchanted modern world where religion had no natural roots or functions. Presumably he would have said the same about Lawrence.

Reactions and Interactions

In 1919 Max Weber took a post at Munich University, his first regular appointment since the one at Heidelberg which he had had to resign because of his breakdown. He was there thrown into the company of Else Jaffe, whose lover he had already become. He visited her in Ludwigshöhe, the country house she had moved to after leaving Irschenhausen. It was in the winter of 1918–19, the first winter after the war, the season of Lili's suicide, the season of the Eisner tragedy, that they meant most to each other, and the language of his letters to her is full of the imagery of the times. Thus, on February 1, 1919, "Quite deeply entrenched barricades and entanglements are erected through the fate one makes oneself. . . . Enormous piles of rubble, from innumerable shattered images of gods—and idols—avenues of life lie uncompleted and abandoned and collapsed houses in which I sought shelter and did not find it . . . across the earth-choked gates bars are bolted so that neither a man's gaze nor—let's say his committed desire—can reach beyond them." And he conjoins his feelings for her with his feelings about the moment in history. "There is very little love in the world, Else—a cold wind —people who love each other must be very good to each other nowadays." And he says that men must live away from God, in loneliness, but toward him. "In fact, one can't live toward God in the daytime, one can only seek out that other Tristan-land*—and then die toward Him, when it is the time and He wants it—He will be a Shylock about it, we can see that clearly, *He* chooses the time. And those laws which even the Tristan-land (let him who dares call it Satan's land) dares not impugn, which make sure that we take account of every second, they exist. . . . Above all, I can live toward only one person in truth, and that I can and must do that is the last and decisive necessity in my life, loftier and stronger than any god."

In Else's "Retrospect," which she wrote probably in July 1920, just after he died, she cites many instances of his preoccupation with death and defeat during their time together, of which the most moving is perhaps this. "Then also his remarks about how well Alfred had arranged everything when Lili died, and that it had been like that when his father died, that others had happened to do what should have been his task. I asked him if he had ever lived through a death. 'No, oddly enough, never yet.' And I said, Not death, nor birth, nor the War, nor power—as if Fate had drawn a veil between him and the reality of things—was that perhaps his star? And he stared straight ahead and whispered a few words like 'Yes, that's the way it is.' "

Marianne Weber had been elected a member of the Badenian Parliament when women first got the vote in 1919, and so she could not come to live with him in Munich. It is clear from some of the letters between them that she was worried about the stability of their marriage. She apologizes in one of them for having complained about the amount of time Max spent with Else; she says she understands that he needs some things which only Else can give him. In effect, she says she is willing to share him.

Marianne wanted to adopt the four children left by Lili, who committed suicide when her husband died, feeling herself to be an unfit mother for them. Although Max had doubts about his own fitness to be a father, he wanted to give Marianne the experience of motherhood. The passage that follows, from one of her letters, speaks for itself:

* Another quotation will make this phrase clearer. "What death is, who can say? Only as much as Tristan, 'it is the dark land of night, out of which my mother brought me.' "

You have my deepest gratitude for these sweet and blessed letters. I shall keep them as a costly gift. And don't worry about our future. I will think everything over carefully. But without your blessed power, without the life-breath you breath, no, the poor children, perhaps I wouldn't have the courage to tear them loose from the Oso [their school]. For I know well enough what my nature can do and what it can't; it *can't* manage whatever the moment demands, as Else so incomparably can, but it *can* manage patience, tenderness, loving understanding, and conscientiousness in care—and I hope also sunny cheerfulness. . . . But you will be our life's sun. . . . The sun burns one often and often hides itself behind dark clouds, but one knows it is there and will give happiness when the right moment comes. Yes, indeed, what a stupid idea, as if I could live entirely or partly in Oso with the children. You silly boy. Only you can separate me from yourself—and only if I suspect that the grace has left me to somehow make you happy. Then perhaps I could find the pride and the strength to separate myself from you. . . . *You* shall have a home, that is the main thing.

It is clear there that she both knows and does not know that he wants to leave her; that she is telling him that he will have to send her away, and that there is nothing else in life for her. From all we know of him, of his obligations to her and his lack of "obligations to himself," or lack of courage for happiness, as Lawrence would say, we can see how intolerable a dilemma this put him in. She also wrote to Frau Jaffe, renouncing all claim to exclusive possession of her husband, which must have made any thought of dispossessing her even harder. The situation was of a type popular with satirical writers of the decade to come, with epigoni of the erotic movement.

Weber's sudden illness and death in June 1920 seemed a tragedy for Germany even while it was happening. To everyone of the Heidelberg party it seemed that the only man among them who might have made reason prevail in politics had disappeared just at the moment when the traditional safeguards against disaster were breaking down. And he had not merely disappeared, he had been destroyed. He died in the presence of his wife and Frau Jaffe, both of whom had joined in caring for him at the end, and it seemed, to those intimate with the whole situation, that his divided love for the two was tearing him apart. In moments of delirium he would call for Else, and if the nurse brought Marianne instead, he would send her away angrily. It was an agonizing and embittering death, despite the elements of harmony and nobility which made it tragic. In its private aspect as well as its public, it corresponded to the agony of German culture as a whole. It played its part, among other such events, in stamping the character of sardonic bitterness on the German psyche of the twenties. The hopefulness of 1910, the hopes of renewal, of the erotic movement, seemed very remote. The spirit of Otto Gross, embodied in the Expressionist movement and Dada, triumphed for a time, but it was a triumph incompatible with the spirit of Max Weber. The Aphroditean sexuality and destructive social cynicism of Germany after 1918, which may fairly be associated with Gross, were inimical to the needs of the parliamentary democracy set up by the friends and followers of Max Weber. And even the spirit of Otto Gross did not triumph long.

In is interesting to find that the reaction against Expressionism in Germany in the 1920s took as its slogan "Die neue Sachlichkeit," the new objectivity. This reaction is usually dated around 1925, the year of Carl Zuckmayer's *Der fröhliche Weinberg*, a play in this new "objective" style, and quite unlike his earlier Expressionist *Kreuzweg*. So it was Weber's moral slogan which was taken up by that movement in the arts which opposed and conquered Gross's movement. Another example of *die neue Sachlichkeit* was Franz Werfel's *Verdi* of 1924, a novel in which the composer is portrayed as a long tormented man made impotent by his fascination with Wagner, who appears as a sick genius. Only when Verdi throws of Wagner's influence can he go on to that triumphant creation of cool objective health, *Otello*. Werfel too had been an Expressionist, and, as we shall see, in Werfel's personal life it was Otto Gross who played the part of the sick genius. The change from Expressionism to Objectivity in the middle of the twenties may therefore be seen generally as the victory of Weber's values, or at least as the defeat of Gross's. If it was a victory for Weber, it was just as short-lived as Gross's had been, for of course the shadow of Hitler was already visible.

Moreover, historians draw a parallel between these events in the history of the arts and a change in political tendency halfway through the decade. Peter Gay speaks of a "Revenge of the Father" motif as characterizing the period, symbolized by the election of Hindenburg as President in 1925 and enacted by the reactionary propaganda issued by Alfred Hugenberg through his press and film empire. Though the historical subject of Frederick the Great's revolt against his father continued to be the subject of literary and dramatic works, this was the period of Joachim von der Goltz's *Vater und Sohn,* a patriarchal treatment in its sympathies. The earlier spirit of the twenties, which Gay describes as characterized by a "Revolt of the Son," clearly had been Gross's, and Lawrence had an equivalent period of popularity in England as an emancipator. Lawrence's period of popularity was longer than Gross's, largely because British political conditions were less threatening than German, but it too was cut short by a new political realism.

Let us remind ourselves of the very different moods in the lives of our principals between 1910 and 1912. In 1910, in Venice, Max Weber and Else

Jaffe began a love relationship; in 1912, first in Nottingham and then outside Munich, D. H. Lawrence and Frieda Weekley began theirs. These were the crucial years in the erotic movement. In 1910 Lou Andreas-Salome published her book, *Das Erotik;* two years later she was in Munich with Viktor Tausk, the Freudian analyst who committed suicide in 1919. In the same years, Alma Mahler was at the height of her stormy affair with Oskar Kokoschka, which also took place partly in Munich. And in 1912, finally, Frieda Weekley sent to the husband she had left the letters of Otto Gross, in explanation of why she had had to leave him. The *Zeitgeist* was Eros.

Of course, the older spirit persisted. In 1911, a great exhibition was held in Berlin on the theme of "Die Frau in Haus und Beruf" (The Woman at Home and at Work). Active in organizing the exhibition was Elly Heuss-Knapp, who had published a book on the Women's movement in 1910. Her great inspiration in her feminist work was Frau Stadtrat Weber, Max Weber's mother. Elly Heuss-Knapp was the daughter of Professor Knapp, one of the Kathedersozialisten, and the wife of Theodor Heuss, a political disciple and lieutenant of Friedrich Naumann, the liberal reformer and friend of Max Weber. Their marriage ceremony was performed by Albert Schweitzer. Clearly then, liberal-reformist Germany was still active in those years. (Indeed, inasmuch as Theodore Heuss became President of West Germany, in which role he tried, into the 1960s, to act in the spirit of Max Weber, we may say that it is still active, despite all its setbacks.)

In 1910 Else Jaffe gave a talk on the work of a factory inspector to a conference on the conditions of factory work for women. She ackowledged, however, that the spirit of the times had changed; ten or fifteen years before, everyone, especially young people, had been interested in "the social question" above all others. But now, "The social question is no longer *the* question, it has become one of many; . . . broader cultural ideas captivate our minds, and, especially when we feel the supreme value of aesthetic things, we succumb to the temptation to keep our distance from that which is unbeautiful and full of tormenting problems." She concluded, of course, "But just there we women should be on the scene," but her continued involvement with social problems is far less striking than the extent to which she had been affected by the erotic movement.

All Heidelberg was affected by it in those years.

We may take as an expression of the mood that came to consciousness around 1910—the mood symbolized in *Women in Love* by Gerald's relaxation at the Water Party—an essay by Alfred Weber. Published in 1912, it was the text of a talk he gave in Prague the preceding year. Alfred was, of course, a close friend of Else and Edgar Jaffe, and to some extent of Frieda and Lawrence. By and large, his thought was very deeply influenced by his brother Max's, for Alfred was dependent on him all his life. Nevertheless at this point in time he committed himself to a line of thought largely opposed to his brother's. This essay, therefore, testifies to the power of the erotic movement at that moment.

Speaking of the late Roman portraits on view in museums, Weber says that they claim the attention of his contemporaries because their melancholy and brutalized faces portray his own era too. We have, he argues, more energy than late Antiquity had, but no more faith in life. Thus we feel a big discrepancy between our *Wollen* and our *Können*. Our *Kosmos* has become inhuman and we have been through too many movements, the most recent one being the Women's Movement. Nevertheless, a faith in life is nowadays not only necessary but possible.

Causal-rational thinking had made religion impossible in the nineteenth century, he goes on to say, but now, thanks to Bergson, it is again possible. Now we can again go beyond causal categories of rationalism and the brute struggle for existence. We can worship Being and *das Lebendige selber,* Life itself. But our new religion cannot be a revived and revised Christianity, for Christianity is hostile to life. It does not tell us what to do with our love, our ambition, our power drive, even our mother-love. At least since the Reformation, where Protestantism has held sway, the power of sex has been broken and life energy has been perverted into work, savings, asceticism, and capitalism. Nature has been *entgöttlicht,* desacralized, and work has been made sacred in its place. A life really derived from otherworldly religion must necessarily uproot man at the very source of his *Gestaltung,* his formation, must deprive action, before it is performed, of its charm and beauty, must deprive desire, before it is felt, of its warmth. It is thus, as victims of Christianity, that we come to have feelings like those of late Antiquity.

It is only putting the same thing a different way to say that our mood of world-weariness derives from the dismally maladjusted mechanisms of our intellectual, bureaucratic, and ethical lives. There is a death-rigid shell or armor over all life, Alfred says, referring to what his brother had described in *The Protestant Ethic* as "a steel-hard casing." This shell takes the form of outer mechanisms and rational schemas, so that, in desperation, intellectuals turn to Buddhism or theosophy. The masses, though, are still *lebenspositiv,* on the side of life, but only for so long as they do not get what they keep asking for.

Nevertheless, Alfred asserts, he is confident that we will find *das Lebendige,* the Living. We know now that there is no Man, but various men, no one Life, but the manifold of living things, no one Good or Great, but many values. This knowledge will lead us not to a wilful grasping at life, but to an acknowledgement of an inner necessity—something alien to all wilfulness—which will allow law to form spontaneously. Such a life will be hard, for it is far easier to follow the line of given norms, but it can be achieved. If we are to accomplish this, we must feel that such a mode of life is already existent somewhere, as a center "which is the home of our being and our nature." Religion is the faith to create this in our lives. Ours must be a religion that creates life. It will bear the symbol not only of the cross but also of the beacon, "which we will let flame up to heaven in thanks for the beauty of existence."

It is easy to recognize in Weber's speech, which we have just summarized, the major themes of both the *kosmische Runde* and Lawrence's writings. Like Lawrence and the members of the Cosmic Circle, Alfred Weber was, in his own way, expressing the erotic movement.

But that mood was not to prevail. The war shattered it, and before faith in life could gather strength, the rise of Nazism shattered it again, first in Germany and then in England and finally in America. Lawrence and Frieda had spent the war years in England, in great misery as far as all public events were concerned. Frieda kept in touch with her family by writing to Frieda Gross in Switzerland, and though for the most part her anger at the war was quite extra-national, still some of her loyalties were different from Lawrence's. Even in their private lives they were under great tension, for Lawrence had come to rebel against the world of Woman, in which Frieda was so much more dominating a personality than he. As soon as they could after the war, they left England, Frieda for Germany and he for Italy. They came together again in Italy and spent the next few years there, but for the rest of Lawrence's life they were continually on the move. From Italy they went to Ceylon, from there to Australia, and from there to New Mexico and Mexico. The excitements of traveling, and the fact that Lawrence's work was again becoming popular—at least among intellectuals—gave them some sense of happiness and achievement.

For Else Jaffe and Marianne Weber the situation was grimmer. The incomes of both families were destroyed by the war and the financial crises that followed on it—so much so that Lawrence had to send money to Else and to her mother. Both Else and Marianne returned to Heidelberg after the deaths of their husbands in Munich, Frau Weber in 1921, Frau Jaffe in 1925. Alfred Weber was waiting for Else there, but even with his support it was a terrible thing, having to live in the ruins of her Germany and the monstrous shade of the new state all through the 1920s and 1930s. Her experience, public and private, was to be more "German" than Frieda's. In a sense it was to answer to that sardonic style she had early adopted in defense against life, since it called for a great deal of "realism" and "objectivity." In very different ways, both sisters could have felt that history had corroborated them.

Max Weber died in Else's presence, Lawrence in Frieda's. But Else was there only as a friend of the family, for Marianne was the widow. This is emblematic of all the differences between the sisters' relationships. There was so much of renunciation and dissimulation between Else and Weber, so much of open drama between Frieda and Lawrence. What is more, Else's dissimulation was not only a matter of keeping up appearances, for she also had to be best friend to Marianne Weber during thirty-four years of the latter's quite public widowhood. What sardonic bitterness, what grim self-discipline this must have involved. It seems certain that during all that time she never told Marianne what had passed between her and Max. For even longer she lived with Alfred Weber and never told him.

Fate seemed to have driven her, despite all her energy and courage, into positions of shame, so that bitterness was mixed with all her suffering. Both her major love affairs were things she could not publicly, or even privately, acknowledge. She was ashamed of the relationship with Otto Gross because it had been a betrayal of all she had learned from the Webers, all the realism and responsibility she had deliberately espoused for herself. She was ashamed of her relationship with Max Weber because it had been a betrayal of Marianne and of marriage. And her closeness to Marianne and Alfred over so many subsequent years kept those shames from sleeping.

Weber's love letters were hidden away for over fifty years, and the only public manifestations of his love for Else were in the parentheses or the footnotes of his scientific essays. For instance, in the hypothetical examples in the essay, "Ethical Neutrality," published in *Logos* in 1917, Weber analyzes the proposition, offered about a man's relation with a woman, "At first our relationship was only a passion but now it represents a value." He points out that according to Kantian values this "passion" meant using another person as a means to one's own end, and so was evil. But, he goes on argue, there are differences between the values native to the ethical and the nonethical spheres of experience. Eroticism permits or prescribes the use of another to one's own ends:

> But the negative predicate can be regarded as a degradation of what is most genuine and most intrinsic in life, of the only, or at any rate the royal road away from the impersonal or supra-personal "value" mechanism, away from enslavement to the lifeless routines of everyday existence and from the pretentiousness of unrealities handed down from on high.

... [This is] a sphere claiming its own "immanent" worth in the most extreme sense of the word. Its claim to this worth could not be invalidated by demonstrating its hostility or indifference to everything sacred or good, to every ethical or aesthetic law, and to every evaluation in terms of culture or personality. Rather its worth might be said to derive just from this hostility or indifference. Whatever may be our attitude towards this claim, it is still not demonstrable or "refutable" with the means afforded by any "science."

Primarily this argument demonstrates Weber's familiarity with, his ease with, the thought of the erotic movement, the thought of Klages and of Gross. But to some degree, perhaps, it may echo his own experience of love.

Almost certainly that experience is echoed in the amplifications of one chapter of the *Religionssoziologie* (Sociology of Religion) from which we already have quoted. Weber wrote Chapter 2 in 1911, rewrote it in 1916, giving it the title "Zwischenbetrachtung," and rewrote it again in 1920. Each time the sexual and aesthetic spheres of experience received more extensive and more sympathetic treatment. In 1964 Professor Baumgarten, drawing our attention to the character of these amplifications, tells us that he was given the manuscript of the last rewriting by Frau Jaffe, in whose keeping it had remained for nearly fifty years. He also says that the history of these amplifications began in 1908 when Weber asked Else, on a walk to Heidelberg Castle, "But you wouldn't say that any *value* could be embodied in eroticism?" To which she replied "But certainly—beauty!" At which Weber fell silent and thoughtful. It was a new idea to him. And later he associated beauty with eroticism in his essay. This is the best example of how Weber's work improved in richness, during his last few years.

Eroticism occurs, we are told in this essay, wherever love "collides with the unavoidably ascetic trait of the vocational specialist type of man." In such a case, once man is emancipated from the old, simple, and organic cycle of the peasant, love outside marriage can come to seem the only tie still linking him to the natural fountain of all life. Thus there comes a joyful triumph over rationalism and all ethical or religious salvationism. The sexual desire of the relationship becomes its glory. "This boundless giving of oneself is as radical as possible in its opposition to all functionality, rationality, and generality. . . . The lover realizes himself to be rooted in the kernel of the truly living, which is externally inaccessible to any rational endeavour. He knows himself to be freed from the cold skeleton hands of rational order, just as completely as from the banality of everyday routine." The deadly earnestness of this eroticism is as unlike the love of chivalry as the love of a mature man is unlike the passionate enthusiasm of youth, Weber says, in a passage in which, perhaps, he is contrasting his feelings for Else with those for Marianne. But inner-worldly asceticism—with which he always associated himself, his wife, and Else—cannot accept anything but the rationally regulated marriage:

> From a purely inner-worldly point of view, only the linkage of marriage with the thought of ethical responsibility for one another—hence with a category heterogeneous to the purely erotic sphere—can carry the senti-ment that something unique and supreme might be embodied in mar-riage; that it might be the transformation of a love which is conscious of responsibility through all the nuances of the organic life-process, "up to the pianissimo of old age"; and the mutual granting of oneself to another and the becoming indebted to each other (in Goethe's sense). Rarely does life grant such value in pure form. He to whom it is given may speak of fate's fortune and grace—not of his own "merit."

There is something very moving, even heartbreaking, about those sen-tences when one puts them into relation to the lives behind them. And yet how meager a tribute they are, compared with *The Rainbow, Women in Love,* and *Lady Chatterley's Lover.* Above all, how hidden from everyone. In 1954, when Marianne Weber died, Else Jaffe, deeply moved, wrote a letter to Frieda in which she said things about her own life which Frieda took to be an admission of this long-hidden relationship. Frieda had guessed the crux of the story without ever being told, and she wrote back regretting that this great love was lost to the world and consoling her with the observation that the books written about herself and Lawrence had never understood them. Else, it seems clear, had not intended to betray as much as she had. If she replied at all, she did not tell Frieda about the hidden letters, which would tell the world about "this great love." (She was then eighty and Frieda sev-enty-five.) But soon after this exchange of letters with her sister she gave Weber's letters to Professor Baumgarten, to be published after her death.

This hiddenness had many consequences. Max Weber had offered him-self as a kind of hero of truth—which was precisely how Karl Jaspers had taken him. Around the personality of Weber, Jaspers built that existentialist moralism which had such great effect among German students in the 1920s and again after the Second World War. Jaspers helped build up a myth of Max Weber. He counseled the widow to destroy Weber's account of his neu-rotic symptoms as well as one of the last letters Weber wrote, on the Jews in Germany; because publication would have injured his image. More privately, when Marianne asked Jaspers what he thought had been the re-lationship between her husband and Frau Jaffe, he replied that among all the possibilities, of one thing they could be certain: "Max Weber war die Wahrheit selber"—was truth itself. That seems to have been too strong even for Marianne Weber, who replied, "Let us hope that you are right." In fact, Jaspers was not right, and his moral philosophy was founded on a false faith.

In other words, Weber's life was, in one important aspect, hypocritical. His love story is a Victorian drama of renunciation and of involuntary, ethically noble hypocrisy. We must not forget, however, that this corresponds, in Lawrence's case, to the more twentieth century hypocrisy, the erotic movement hypocrisy, of sexual heroics in a drama of fulfilment. It seems likely that in those late years when he was most publicly the prophet of sexual fulfilment, Lawrence himself was sexually passive. He got himself into the position of having to claim more sexual prowess, more masculine desire, than he had, whereas Max Weber had to claim the opposite. Otto Gross, in contrast to both, was guilty of neither hypocrisy. But his innocence was related to the unworldliness, the "unreasonableness," which made both von Richthofen sisters reject him. Both Lawrence and Weber were concerned to build up, rebuild, the world—and within the world, to build up and rebuild marriages for themselves—and it was to such men that these sisters awarded themselves.

·

Part Two

The Annals of the Century, 1870-1970

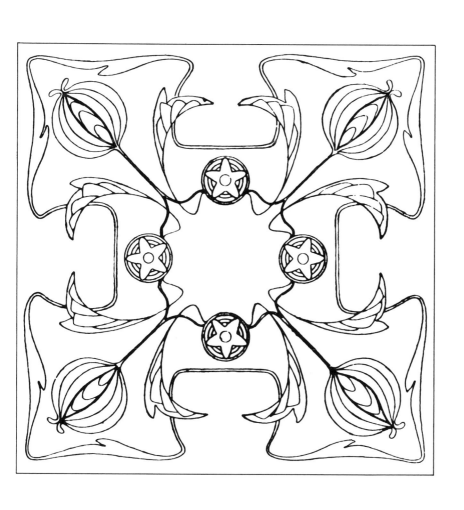

I take the facts of public life mostly from Neville Williams's *Chronology of the Modern World* (*London*, 1966) with a few additions and corrections.

1870–1880

In this decade we record only births in the category of personal life; the rest must be events of the public life.

In 1870 the Franco-Prussian War broke out in July. In September Napoleon III capitulated at Sedan, two days later France became a republic, and two weeks after that the Prussians encircled Paris and began to besiege it. On October 27 Metz—which was to be the von Richthofens' home—surrendered to the Prussian army. On October 28 Strasbourg—which was to be Baumgartens' home—also surrendered. Badenia joined the North German Confederation, which meant she submitted to Prussia's leadership.

In this year Richard Wagner's *Die Walküre* and Fyodor Dostoevski's *House of the Dead* were published. Vladimir Ilich Ulyanov, who later became Nikolai Lenin, and Rosa Luxemburg were born. Charles Dickens and Alexandre Dumas died.

Defense estimates, in millions of pounds sterling, were: Britain, 23.4; France, 22; Russia, 22; Germany, 10.8; Italy, 7.8. John D. Rockefeller founded Standard Oil.

Baron von Richthofen was wounded in the war and invalided out of the army. Marianne Schnitger, Max Weber's future wife, was born. (Max Weber himself was born in 1864, and his brother Alfred in 1868. Of the von Richthofen husbands, Max von Schreibershofen was born in 1864, Ernest Weekley in 1865, Edgar Jaffe in 1866.)

In 1871 France surrendered to Germany and Wilhelm I of Prussia was proclaimed German Emperor. Germany adopted the gold standard. In Paris the Commune was set up in March and destroyed in May.

In this year Charles Darwin's *Descent of Man* and Friedrich Nietzsche's *Birth of Tragedy* were published. Fanny zu Reventlow was born. So were Marcel Proust and Paul Valéry, Theodore Dreiser and Stephen Crane, Friedrich Ebert and Karl Liebknecht.

The population of Germany was now 41 million; of the United States, 39 million; of France, 36.1 million; of Japan, 33 million; of Britain, 26 million.

In 1872 compulsory military service was introduced in France and Japan. Bakunin was expelled from the International at the Hague. In Germany the *Verein für Sozialpolitik* was founded by the Kathedersozialisten, the academic and anti-Marxist socialists, who included Adolf Wagner, Lujo Brentano, Gustav Schmoller, and Georg Friedrich Knapp.

This was the year of Duse's debut, and of the founding of Strasbourg University. Giuseppi Mazzini died; Bertrand Russell and Sergei Diaghilev were born.

In 1873 the Germans evacuated France. James Clerk-Maxwell's *Treatise on Electricity and Magnetism*, Herbert Spencer's *Study of Sociology*, and Walter Pater's *Studies in the History of the Renaissance* were published. Arthur Rimbaud's *Une Saison en Enfer* and Leo Tolstoy's *Anna Karenina* presaged the erotic movement. (*Tristan und Isolde*, 1865, *Madame Bovary*, 1857: the erotic joy—sexual pleasure becoming the source of health and creativity—is greater in each successive work, though always denied before the end.)
John Stuart Mill died, Sergei Rachmaninoff was born.

In 1874 military conscription was introduced in Russia. Britain annexed the Fiji islands and France "protected" Annam. There was an attempt on Bismarck's life. Wagner's *Götterdämmerung* and Modest Moussorgsky's *Boris Godunov* were performed. The first Impressionist Exhibition was held in Paris. Britain was overtaken by Germany, France, and the United States in industrial production. Winston Churchill and Robert Frost, Gertrude Stein and Arnold Schönberg, were born. Else von Richthofen was born.

In 1875 George and Lydia Lawrence were married. Albert Schweitzer and Rainer Maria Rilke were born. German Marxists and Lassalleans united in the Gotha programme. Mark Twain's *Tom Sawyer* and Mary Baker Eddy's *Science and Health* were published. The military strength of Russia was 3,360,000; of France, 412,000; of Germany, 2,800,000; of Britain, 113,649.

In 1876 Alexander Graham Bell invented the telephone and Thomas A. Edison invented the phonograph. The Bayreuth Festspielhaus opened with the first performance of *The Ring*. Mikhail Bakunin and George Sand died. Konrad Adenauer and Pablo Casals were born. Frieda Schloffer was born in Graz.

In 1877 Britain annexed the Transvaal and Queen Victoria was proclaimed Empress of India. A caucus was active for the first time in British national elections; machine politics were born. War broke out in the Balkans between Russia and Turkey. Otto Gross was born. Max Weber, thirteen years old, wrote two precociously learned essays in celebration of Germanism.

In 1878 there were attempts on the lives of both Bismarck and the Kaiser, and as a result some laws against the Socialists were passed, forbidding them to have public meetings and publication. Henrich von Treitschke began to protest against the growth of Jewish power in Germany. *The Return of the Native* was published, and General Booth founded the Salvation Army.

In 1879 Britain went to war with the Zulus. Henry George's *Progress and Poverty* and Henrik Ibsen's *The Doll's House* were published. Alsace and Lorraine were declared parts of the German Reich. Frieda von Richthofen, Alma Schindler, and Mabel Ganson were born. So were Paul Klee, E. M. Forster, and Albert Einstein. So were Iosif Dzhugashvili and Lev Bronstein, who were later to become Joseph Stalin and Leon Trotsky.

1880–1890

In this decade the personalities of our German protagonists began to shape themselves by crucial decisions.

In 1880 Dostoevski published *The Brothers Karamazov*. Gustave Flaubert and George Eliot died. Oswald Spengler was born. Edison made the first practical electric light and Andrew Carnegie opened the first large steel furnace. In Britain the first girl's high schools were opened.

In 1881 Thomas Carlyle, Benjamin Disraeli, Dostoevski, and Moussorgsky died. Béla Bartok and Pablo Picasso were born. Ibsen's *Ghosts* was published. There were pogroms in Russia. The population of London was 3.3 million; of Paris, 2.2 million; of New York, 1.2 million; of Berlin, 1.1 million; of Vienna, 1 million; of St. Petersburg, 600,000.

In 1882 France and Britain established dual control of Egypt. The first hydroelectric plant was built, in Wisconsin. There were 2500 agrarian outrages in Ireland, and ten thousand families were evicted. This was the year of the Phoenix Park murders. The Married Women's Property Act was passed in England.

Nietzsche's *Die Fröhliche Wissenschaft* and Wagner's *Parsifal* were published, as were Ibsen's *An Enemy of the People* and Oscar Wilde's *Lectures on the Decorative Arts,* which expounded the aesthetic creed.

Charles Darwin and Ralph Waldo Emerson, Henry Wadsworth Longfellow and Anthony Trollope died; Virginia Woolf and James Joyce, Igor Stravinsky and Georges Braque were born. Giuseppe Garibaldi died, Franklin D. Roosevelt was born.

Max Weber went to Heidelberg University to study jurisprudence, joined his father's old student fraternity, and became friends with Otto Baumgarten. Johanna von Richthofen was born.

In 1883 Bismarck introduced state sickness insurance schemes, and the first skyscraper was built in Chicago. Nietzsche published *Also Sprach Zarathusthra* and Hermann Baumgarten his sharp attack on Treitschke. Max Weber did his first period of military service near Strasbourg and became close friends with his uncle. Wagner and Marx died, Benito Mussolini and John Maynard Keynes were born; Ivan Turgenev died, Walter Gropius and Karl Jaspers were born.

In 1884 the Fabian Society was founded, Sir Hiram Stevens Maxim invented the machine gun and cocaine was first used as an anesthetic. Peter Kropotkin published *Parolas d'un Révolté* and Friedrich Engels published *The Origins of the Family;* Twain published *Huckleberry Finn* and Ibsen published *The Wild Duck*. Max Weber became a section leader in the army. Regina Ullmann was born.

In 1885 Germany annexed Tanganyika and Zanzibar, joining the other powers in imperialism; also the Bismarck Archipelago and Northern New Guinea. Britain "protected" Southern New Guinea and Northern Bechuanaland, occupied Port Hamilton, Korea, and began war with Burma. Louis Pasteur cured hydrophobia. Gottlieb Daimler invented an internal combustion engine. Volume 2 of *Das Kapital* was published. Tolstoy published *My Religion* and *The Power of Darkness*. Victor Hugo died and Ezra Pound was born. Max Weber studied at Berlin University, under Treitschke, Theodor Mommsen, and others. David Herbert Lawrence was born, his parents' fourth child.

In 1886 Britain annexed Upper Burma. William E. Gladstone introduced a bill for giving Ireland Home Rule. In Chicago there were "anarchist" riots in Haymarket Square. Baron Richard von Krafft-Ebing published *Psychopathia Sexualis,* and Nietzsche *Beyond Good and Evil*. Franz Liszt died, Oskar Kokoschka was born. Max Weber took his law exams in Gottingen. (From 1885 to 1893 he lived in his parents' home in Berlin-Charlottenburg.)

In 1887 Max Weber did his second period of service as an officer—in Strasbourg—and was in love with his cousin Emmy. In Berlin he got to know a reformist group of young economists, theologians, and political theorists. J. J. Bachofen died.

In 1888 Wilhelm I died; his son Friedrich reigned only ninety-nine days; Wilhelm II succeeded. Vincent van Gogh painted *Sunflowers* and Richard Strauss composed *Don Juan*. The Kodak camera and the pneumatic tire were invented. Matthew Arnold died, T. S. Eliot was born; so were Katherine Mansfield and T. E. Lawrence.

In Germany the *Archiv für soziale Gesetzgebung und Statistik* appeared, the organ of the Kathedersozialisten, later to be bought by Edgar Jaffe and edited by Max Weber. In this year the latter became a member of the Kathedersozialisten's *Verien für Sozialpolitik* (hereafter called the *Verein*). He did his third major period of military service, in East Prussia.

The United States produced 31.8 percent of world production; Britain, 17.8 percent; Germany, 13.8 percent; France, 10.7 percent; Russia, 8.1 percent; Austria, 5.6 percent; Italy 2.7 percent.

In 1889 the Dock Strike in Britain announced the new militancy of unskilled workers, whose unions could not provide pensions, and who therefore demanded state provision. There were important strikes in the Ruhr also. The British South Africa Company, headed by Sir Cecil Rhodes, was granted a royal charter which allowed for expansion at the expense of the Transvaal. George Bernard Shaw published *Fabian Essays* and Henri Bergson *Les Données Immédiates de la Conscience*. William Butler Yeats published *The Wanderings of Oisin* and Maurice Maeterlinck *Serres Chaudes*. John Middleton Murry was born. Charles Chaplin and Adolf Hitler were born. Max Weber finished his thesis at Berlin University on the history of the commercial organizations of the Middle Ages, having learned Spanish and Italian in order to document the study.

1890–1900

This was the decade of marriages; by 1901 only Else von Richthofen remained uncommitted, and hers was to be the most unfortunate match of all.

In 1890 Bismarck was dismissed by Wilhelm II, and Max Weber began to publish reviews of books on medieval commerce. Sherman's Anti-Trust Law was passed in America, and in England an act was passed controlling working-class housing. The first underground railway was built, under the Thames, and the first corridor trains were used.

William Morris founded the Kelmscott Press. Sir James Frazer published *The Golden Bough* and William James his *Principles of Psychology*. Rimbaud and von Gogh died, as did Gottfried Keller and Cardinal Newman. Charles de Gaulle and Vyacheslav Molotov were born.

In the Reichstag elections Max Weber voted for the first time, as a free-conservative. He attended the first *Sozial-evangelisch* Congress, made contact with Pastor Naumann, Paul Göhre, and Otto von Harnack, the Christian reformers, and was commissioned to participate in the Verein's Farm Worker inquiry. He contributed articles to the *Christliche Welt*.

In 1891 the Katanga Company was founded by Leopold of Belgium to exploit Congo copper. The Pan-German League, advocate of German expansion, was founded. The German Socialist party adopted a Marxist program at its Erfurt conference. The Papal Encyclical on social-political matters, *Rerum Novarum,* appeared.

James Russell Lowell and Herman Melville died; Paul Gauguin went to

Tahiti; Franz Wedekind published *Spring's Awakening,* Thomas Hardy, *Tess of the d'Urbervilles,* and Wilde, *Dorian Gray.*

The population of the United States was 65 million; of Germany, 49.4 million; of Japan, 40.7 million; of France, 38.3 million; of Britain, 33 million.

In 1892 there was the Homestead Battle of strikers against Pinkerton police in America; Alexander Berkman tried (with Emma Goldman's help) to assassinate Henry Frick, the man who brought in the Pinkertons, and was sent to prison for fourteen years.

Walt Whitman and Alfred Tennyson died. Max Weber finished his report on the farm workers for the Verein and delivered it orally, with great success. In the *Christliche Welt* he defended Göhre, a pastor who had worked in a factory, against attacks by ecclesiastics. And in the fall he got engaged to Marianne Schnitger, who had come to live in the Weber house that spring.

In 1893 the British Independent Labour Party was founded under Keir Hardie. In Germany a new military bill increased the size of the army. England and Germany agreed on their respective rights in Nigeria and the Cameroons. The Third International Socialist Workers Congress met in Zurich.

Moisei Ostrogorski published his *Organizational Forms of the Parties in Modern Democracy.* Hanns Gross published his *Handbook for Investigating Magistrates.* Jan Sibelius composed his Karelia suite. Pyotr Ilich Tchaikovsky and Charles Gounod and Guy de Maupassant died. Ernst Toller was born.

Max Weber was appointed professor at Freiburg, and was commissioned by the Sozial-evangelisch Congress to conduct a second inquiry into East Prussian social conditions. In the fall he married. He published ten times, on academic matters—mostly reviews—and on the social political problems of East Prussia.

In 1894 the Turkish Sultan began to massacre the Armenians. The French Premier was assassinated by an Italian anarchist; in Italy new laws suppressed all anarchist and socialist organizations. Britain "protected" Uganda.

Engels brought out Vol. 3 of *Das Kapital.* Naumann published *What Does Christian-Socialist Mean? The Yellow Book* appeared, with Aubrey Beardsley as art editor. Claude Debussy composed *L'Après-Midi d'un Faune.* Walter Pater and Herman von Helmholtz died, Nikita Khrushchev and Aldous Huxley were born.

Max Weber did his final period of military service in the spring, and in the fall began to lecture at Freiburg. He met Else von Richthofen, then teaching school there. He reported the results of his farmworkers' inquiry to the Sozial-evangelisch Congress, and his conclusions, being hostile to the interest of the big landowners, split the Congress by alienating the conservatives. Thirteen publications are listed for him this year, including his brilliant pamphlet explaining the stock exchange, written for Naumann's *Worker's Library.*

In 1895 Captain Alfred Dreyfus was convicted of treason by a court-martial in camera and imprisoned on Devil's Island, French Guiana. An anti-Semite was elected Mayor of Vienna. The Jameson Raid took place, which was defeated by the Boers. Oscar Wilde was found guilty in court of homosexuality. Wilhelm Röntgen discovered X-rays. Sigmund Freud published *Studies in Hysteria* and launched the psychoanalytic movement. Gustav Mahler composed his second symphony. Huxley and Engels died. Ernest Weekley published the first of his many schoolbooks of French grammar and passages for reading.

In 1896 the Kaiser sent President Kruger a congratulatory telegram on the failure of the Jameson Raid and Rhodes resigned at Cape Town. Britain decided to reconquer the Sudan in order to protect the Nile from the French. Gladstone's last speech exhorted Britain to act unilaterally to stop the Turkish massacre of the Armenians. Bismarck published the secret Russo-German Treaty of 1887. Anton Chekhov published *The Seagull* and Hardy *Jude the Obscure.* Strauss composed "Thus Spake Zarathustra" and Alfred Harmsworth founded *The Daily Mail,* the first twentieth-century-style British newspaper.

Max Weber was offered a chair at Heidelberg. He attended more than one congress, made speeches at them and elsewhere, and published articles.

In 1897 Jacob Burckhardt and Johannes Brahms died, Wilhelm Reich was born. The Kaiser repeated demands for laws to check the growth of revolutionary movements. Hanns Gross published *Criminal Psychology* and Havelock Ellis *The Psychology of Sex.* During the next few years there was extreme public interest in psychopathology. In July Max Weber attacked his father for his treatment of his mother, and in August his father died. Frieda von Richthofen met Ernest Weekley, and Alfred Weber began publishing, in *Schmollers Jahrbuch,* parts of his dissertation, which he finished this year.

In 1898 Emile Zola published *J'Accuse* about the Dreyfus case, and was imprisoned. Bismarck published his *Reflections and Memoirs.* The Spanish-American War took place. The Curies discovered radium and polonium, and Ferdinand von Zeppelin built an airship. Gladstone and Bismarck died. Naumann ran for the Reichstag but failed. Max Weber took part in a protest meeting, organized by Naumann and Otto Baumgarten, on behalf of the striking dockworkers of Hamburg. The Kaiser, as King of Prussia, started disciplinary proceedings against Baumgarten, as Prussian professor. In the spring Weber had to go to a sanatorium on the lake of Geneva for his nerves. He published only one article this year. D. H. Lawrence won a scholarship to Nottingham Boys' High School.

In 1899 the Boer War began and the Hague Conference on International Peace was held. There was a split in the German Socialist Party between the revisionists led by Eduard Bernstein and the orthodox Marxists led by Karl

Kautsky. Frieda von Richthofen married Ernest Weekley. Max Weber took leave from his job on health grounds for the summer semester, but had another break-down as soon as he tried to teach in the fall. In the winter he offered to resign. Alfred Weber published twice in the Publications of the Verein.

1900–1910

The events, both private and public, now begin to come thick and fast. Hopes were high and talents were brilliant. In the private lives, too, it was the decade of giving birth.

In 1900 the very patriarchal German Civil code came into effect. The Boxer rising in China and the Ashanti rising in Africa were suppressed. Max Planck elaborated the quantum theory, Gregor Mendel's work on heredity was rediscov-ered, and the Browning revolver was invented. Nietzsche died.

Freud published *The Interpretation of Dreams,* and Bergson *On Laughter.* Paul Cézanne, Claude Monet, Pierre Auguste Renoir, Henri Toulouse-Lautrec all painted canvases that became famous. Giacomo Puccini composed *Tosca* and Sibelius *Finlandia.* Naumann published *Demokratie und Kaisertum,* Rosa Luxem-burg *Sozialreform oder Revolution.*

In search of health, Max Weber went to Urach in the Alps, in July, to Corsica in the fall and winter. One small publication. Alfred Weber gave his inaugural address at Berlin, which was published the following year. Johanna von Richt-hofen and Mabel Ganson married. Frieda Weekley bore her first child, a boy. Else von Richthofen became a factory inspector (exact date unkown). Lenin came to live in Schwabing, to edit *Iskra* and *Zarja.* He lived there two years, under assumed names, first got to know Rosa Luxemburg there, and returned for short periods in 1907 and 1913.

In 1901 Queen Victoria died and President William McKinley was assassi-nated by the anarchist Leon Czolgosz; Emma Goldman was suspected of inciting him. There were strikes and anarchist outrages in Belgium, the French miners voted for a general strike, and the Italian Socialists extended their political in-fluence by means of strikes. In Russia the Social Revolutionary Party was orga-nized. From England Guglielmo Marconi sent wireless telegraphy messages across the Atlantic. Giuseppe Verdi died, André Malraux was born, Thomas Mann pub-lished *Buddenbrooks.*

In March Max Weber was in Rome, then traveled in southern Italy, spent the summer in Switzerland, and returned to Rome for the fall and winter. He announced a course of lectures in Heidelberg for the summer semester of 1902, which again had to be canceled.

Johanna von Schreibershofen and Mabel Evans bore children, and Else von Richthofen's doctoral thesis was accepted at Heidelberg. Otto Gross published *Compendium der Pharmako-Therapie für Polikliniker und junge Artzte;* at least, this book *seems* to be by our Otto Gross. He certainly published articles, this year and next, in his father's *Archiv für Kriminolgie.*

D. H. Lawrence's brother Ernest (the William of *Sons and Lovers*) died. Lawrence met Jessie Chambers, Miriam. He took a job with a manufacturer of surgical appliances, but left after a serious attack of pneumonia.

In 1902 the Boer War ended and the Education Act made the British government responsible for secondary education. Hormones were discovered and research work began on the pituitary gland.

At Easter Max Weber went to Florence, from where he again offered his resignation to the university. In April he returned to Heidelberg. He began to write his methodological study of Roscher and Knies's work, and did a review for the *Archiv für Soziale Gesetzgebung.* Alfred Weber published twice, both times on the current political situation.

Elsa Weekley and Hadu von Schreibershofen were born. Frieda Weekley edited Schiller's *Ballads* for Blackie's Little German Classics series. Else and Edgar Jaffe were married. D. H. Lawrence became an uncertificated teacher at Eastwood. Otto Gross published *Die cerebrale Sekundärfunktion.*

In 1903 the British completed their conquest of Northern Nigeria, the Krupp Works at Essen were built, and Britain and France began their Entente Cordiale. The Wright brothers made the first airplane flight. Otto Weininger published *Sex and Character,* a patriarchal theory of sexual identities.

Mommsen and Herbert Spencer died. Eric Blair (George Orwell) and Evelyn Waugh were born. This was the year of Max Weber's six journeys abroad, but he did finish the first part of his study of Roscher and Knies, and the logical problems of economics. He was made honorary professor, with no rights in the promotion of colleagues and no right to speak at faculty meetings. Otto Gross married Frieda Schloffer at Graz, and Else Jaffe bore her first child.

The United States produced 88.7 million barrels of petroleum oil, which was 49 percent of world production; Russia produced 80.5 million barrels.

In 1904 the Entente Cordiale became established. The Russian minister Vyacheslav Pleve was murdered by Sasonow, a social revolutionary, in July. In England a World Union for Women's Suffrage was founded. The first photoelectric cell and the first ultraviolet lamp were made.

Max Weber went to America for the St. Louis Exhibition, and took over the *Archiv für Sozialwissenshaft und Sozialpolitik.* Under its old title, *Archiv für Soziale Gesetzgebung,* it had been the organ of the Kathedersozialisten. He repudiated their political bias and demanded a severer *Wertfreiheit.* He published three essays in the *Archiv* in 1903 (From now on this abbreviation for his *Archiv für Sozialwissenschaft und Sozialpolitik* will be used.), and another in a similar journal, and his St. Louis lecture was also a massive piece of work. Edgar Jaffe's dissertation on English banking was accepted at Heidelberg, and Barbara Weekley was born. In this year Romain Rolland began publishing *Jean-Christophe,* which continued until 1912 and was the great success of the prewar liberal sensibility.

In 1905 there was an insurrection in the Congo and a revolution in Russia. The Tsar promised a constitution. Lenin and Trotsky returned to Russia. The German Socialist Party declared their sympathy with the Russian workers. The Kaiser visited Tangiers and provoked the first Morocco crisis. Lenin published *Two Tactics in the Democratic Revolution* and Einstein his first theory of relativity. George Santayana published *The Life of Reason* and Wilhelm Dilthey *Experience and Poetry.* Henri Matisse and Picasso both painted canvases that became famous, and the Matisse group took the name Les Fauves. In Dresden the Die Brücke group of painters was formed. Arthur Koestler and C. P. Snow were born.

Max Weber learned Russian (in three months) in order to follow the events of the Revolution in Russian newspapers. He welcomed the Revolution in the hope that it would lead to a liberalizing of the Tsarist regime. He published three times in the *Archiv.* The first essay, in two parts, was "Die protestantische Ethik und der 'Geist' des Kapitalismus." Else gave birth to Marianne. Hanns Gross returned to Graz.

It is sometimes said that there was a generation of 1905, of men who became twenty-one around that year (D. H. Lawrence turned twenty-one in 1906); this group is said to be characterized by its anti-rationalism. There were the Georgianer in Germany; the followers of Gabriele D' Annunzio in Italy; and in France the Bergsonists, plus the quite different followers of Auguste Barrès and Charles Maurras, and famous converts to Catholicism like Jacques Maritain and Paul Claudel. Among our texts, Alfred Weber's essay of 1912, "Religion und Kultur," expresses this mood best.

In 1906 there was a liberal landslide in the British general elections. In France Dreyfus was acquitted. In Russia the first Duma was dissolved soon after it had been elected, and Pyotr Stolypin became Prime Minister. Ibsen and Cézanne died, Samuel Beckett was born.

Max Weber attended the meeting of the Socialist Party in Mannheim, which was preoccupied with the problem of the general strike, and found the atmosphere petit-bourgeois. He exhorted Naumann to make the new Reichstag election an occasion to campaign openly against the Kaiser. He wrote two essays on the Russian Revolution and compared the Kaiser's rule to Tsarist autocracy. He took part in several debates, his contributions to which appeared in print later, and wrote for the *Frankfurter Zeitung* for the first time.

Emma Goldman began editing her magazine, *Mother Earth*. Frieda Weekley edited Bechstein's *Märchen* for Blackie's Little German Classics Series. D. H. Lawrence began his courses at University College, Nottingham. Otto Gross gave poison to a young woman named Chatemmer, for her to kill herself, and then left Graz for Munich. Both Else Jaffe and Frieda Weekley visited the Grosses there, and both began affairs with Otto.

In 1907 the second Duma was dissolved and some of its delegates, including Trotsky, were sent to Siberia. Lenin fled abroad. The third Duma was elected by a much narrower franchise, and Stolypin began a regime of repression. In the new elections in Germany, Naumann finally entered the Reichstag. There was a Peace Conference at the Hague, an Anarchistic conference at Amsterdam, attended by Emma Goldman, and a Neuro-Psychiatric conference in the same city, probably attended by Frieda Weekley and certainly by Otto Gross. William James's *Pragmatism* and Bergson's *Creative Evolution* were published, and so were *The Education of Henry Adams*, Rilke's *Neue Gedichte,* and Strauss's *Elektra.* (Lawrence and Alice Dax saw a performance of the latter in London, and he was excited to the point of making love to her. Strauss's operas carried the erotic gospel to Alma Mahler too.) Francis Thompson died, and W. H. Auden was born.

Marianne Weber published *Ehefrau und Mutter in der Rechtsentwicklung,* dedicated to her mother-in-law. Otto Gross submitted to Weber's *Archiv* the essay on the liberation of women which occasioned Weber's annihilating letter of rejection. At a meeting of the *Verein für Sozialpolitik,* Weber sharply attacked both the Kaiser and the Social Democrats. In his Heidelberg home there were many social-intellectual occasions, attended by Friedrich Gundolf, Karl and Gertrud Jaspers, Werner Sombart, Georg Simmel, Gertrud Bäumler, Minna Tobler, Emil Lask, and Robert Michels, among others. In bohemian Schwabing and provincial Eastwood, Gross and Lawrence also led active social lives.

Alfred Weber came to Heidelberg to teach. Wolfgang Peter was born to the Grosses. Gross published *Das Freud'sche Ideogenitätsmoment.* Else Jaffe gave birth to Peter.

In 1908 there were protests against the undemocratic electoral system in Prussia, and international criticism of the new law allowing Prussia to resettle its Polish workers in West Prussia. There were meetings in Heidelberg of both the National Liberal Party and International Philosophical Congress. Working conditions for German women and youth in factories were regulated.

Marc Chagall and Maurice Utrillo were painting. E. M. Forster published *A Room With a View,* and Arnold Bennett *The Old Wives Tale,* both of which helped establish the novelist's options for Lawrence.

Max Weber studied the psycho-physics of work at his cousin's linen factory in Oerlinghausen. He took part in the National Liberals' meeting and attacked colleagues who were resisting parliamentarism. He also attacked, in the *Frank-*

furter Zeitung, the way German universities refused promotion to Social Democrats. He published eight times a year, all substantial pieces, either in scholarly
learning or in moral passion.

A Psychoanalytic Congress was held at Salzburg and attended by both Otto
and Frieda Gross (she too was deeply involved in the liberation movement).
Freud reproved Gross for his extra-medical concerns.

D. H. Lawrence took a post as schoolmaster at Croydon, where he met Helen
Corke.

In 1909 old-age pensions were awarded to all British subjects over seventy.
Austria annexed Bosnia and Herzegovina. There were more demonstrations all
over Germany against the Prussian franchise. The model-T Ford was built.
Mahler composed his Ninth Symphony and Diaghilev took his ballet to Paris
for the first time. Lenin published *Materialism and Empiric Criticism,* and Helene
Lange *Die Frauenbewegung in ihren modernen Problemen.* William James
published *A Pluralistic Universe* and Bergson *Time and Free Will, Matter and
Memory.* Kokoschka painted *Princess Montesquieu-Rohan* and Frank Lloyd
Wright built Robie House, Chicago. H. G. Wells published *Tono-Bungay* and
André Gide *La Porte Étroite.*

Max Weber took part in the Vienna meeting of the Verein für Sozialpolitik,
and argued against Gustav Schmoller's propaganda for increasing the bureaucracy's power of control over working conditions. He published an important
study of the agriculture of antiquity in *Handwörterbuch der Staatswissenschaften,*
which is in effect a study of the decline of antiquity. He collaborated on it with
M. I. Rostovtzeff, whose later work derives from this. He also published a number
of articles in the *Archiv.*

Alfred Weber published his *Über den Standort der Industrien,* Part I.
Through Jessie Chambers's initiative, D. H. Lawrence had his first poems published in *The English Review,* and met Ford Madox Ford and his friends. Gross
published *Über psychopathische Minderwertigkeiten;* from this point on, he published little that was orthodox psychiatry, or even unorthodox. His essays are political or cultural, and revolutionary.

Else Jaffe gave birth to Hans.

1910–1920

In the first four and a half years of this decade the brilliant singing of hope, rebellion, and talent mounted to a climax; and then came the shattering breakdown
of the war, and the resurgence of the patriarchal mind. This is the decade most
crammed with facts for us to note, facts of the public life and of the private lives
we are following. The two fullnesses coincide partly because these were significant
people.

In 1910 Germany's machine tool industry overtook Britain's. Among Weber's friends, Naumann founded the *Fortschrittliche Volkspartei,* and Gertrud Baümler became president of the *Bund deutscher Frauenvereine* at its Heidelberg meeting, a post she held until 1919. Else Jaffe gave a talk on the effect of factory work on women, from the point of view of a factory inspector. The first German Sociologists' Meeting was held in Frankfurt, and the Sociological Society was founded under Weber's leadership. He gave a report there. He also won two lawsuits which he had initiated, one against a journalist and the other against a colleague, on points of public and professional morality.

This was the year he and Marianne moved into his grandfather's house on the Ziegelhäuserlandstrasse. Ernst Troeltsch took the top floor. Stefan George came there for discussions, as did Georg Lukács and Ernst Bloch, in addition to those previously named. In the spring the Webers and the Jaffes went to Italy together. Marianne returned to Heidelberg alone, and in Venice Max declared himself in love with Else. He published two pieces in the *Archiv,* relative to his "Protestant Ethic," and his vigorous and aggressive interventions in the meetings of the Verein für Sozialpolitik in Vienna the year before were published.

Roger Fry arranged the first Post-Impressionist Exhibition in London. The Futurist Manifesto was drawn up. Bertrand Russell and Alfred North Whitehead published their *Principia Mathematica,* and Marie Curie her *Treatise on Radiography.* Albert Schweitzer published *The Quest for the Historical Jesus,* and Igor Stravinsky composed *Fire Bird.* E. M. Forster published *Howard's End,* and D. H. Lawrence's *White Peacock* (published next year) was put into his mother's hands before she died (December 9). Lou Andreas-Salome published *Die Erotik,* and Edgar Jaffe the second edition of *Das Englische Bankwesen.* Tolstoy died, as did Florence Nightingale, Mark Twain, William James.

In 1911 there was a dock strike in London and a railway strike across England. Italy conquered Tripoli. David Lloyd George introduced National Health Insurance. At the fourth meeting of university teachers, Max Weber attacked the dictatorial methods of the previous Prussian minister of education, Althoff, and also the corporate constitution of the commercial colleges, thereby generating a heated debate in the press. He was also prominent in a controversy in which he attacked a chauvinist-militarist speaker at Freiburg University, taking on the Freiburg faculty as a whole in the debate. Schönberg's manual of harmony expounded the twelve-tone scale, and Vasili Kandinski and Franz Marc founded *Der blaue Reiter* in Munich. Alban Berg, Schönberg, and Anton von Webern as well as painters were associated with this group, which remained a center of modernist art until the war broke out. Gropius built the Fagus Factory, Mahler composed *Das Lied von der Erde,* and Rilke published the *Duino Elegies.* Emma Goldman published *Anarchism and Other Lectures.*

Weber's publications included several debate speeches—on technology and culture, on racialism, on natural law and naturalism, among others, at the Frankfurt Sociologists' meeting of 1910. Alfred Weber published in *Archiv* on his *Standortslehre*. Lawrence, after publishing *The White Peacock*, fell ill in November and had to give up teaching. Middleton Murry began publishing *Rhythm*. Mahler died.

In 1912 the Prime Minister of Russia, Stolypin, was assassinated. The Bolsheviks separated from the Mensheviks. Lenin became editor of *Pravda* and got to know Stalin. The Balkan War began. In Germany the elections to the Reichstag gave the majority to the Socialists. Rosa Luxemburg published *Die Akkumulation des Kapitals*. Freud was one of the founding members (with Einstein, Mach, and Popper) of the Society for Positivistic Philosophy in Berlin. A coal strike began in Derbyshire and spread across England. In America Eugene Debs won 900,000 votes as Socialist candidate for President. Troeltsch published *Die Soziallehren der christlichen Kirchen und Gruppen*, which followed up Weber's insights, and Hanns Gross opened his Kriminologisches Institut in Graz. *Der blaue Reiter* held its second exhibition in Munich. Kandinski published *Über das geistige in der Kunst*, one of the great manifestoes of modernism in all the arts. Schönberg composed *Pierrot Lunaire*. Marcel Duchamp painted *Nude Descending a Staircase* and Lawrence published *The Trespassers*. August Strindberg died and Tennessee Williams was born.

At the second German Sociologists' meeting in Berlin, Weber expounded his value-free concept of nationalism. He and the left wing of the Verein planned a demonstration on the theme of progress in social legislation, and when the attempt failed because of differences of opinion, he sent out a circular letter urging more such attempts.

Alfred Weber published three times, including "Religion und Kultur." D. H. Lawrence published poems and stories. In April he met Frieda Weekley, and in May they eloped to Metz together, where her father was celebrating his Jubilee year. Then they went separately to Munich and lived in Irschenhausen until August, when they began walking across the Alps to Italy, passing the winter in Gargnano. Alma Mahler was having a stormy affair with Kokoschka (they attended Diaghilev's ballet together in Vienna), and Lou Andreas-Salome with Viktor Tausk. Mabel Dodge returned from Italy to New York, and met John Reed. Jane Addams was busy at the organization of the Progressive Party in Chicago. It was this year Otto Gross allowed his mistress Sophie Benz to kill herself in Switzerland. Ernest Weekley published *The Romance of Words*.

In 1913 the Reichstag considerably increased the army's size. Russia declared war on Bulgaria. Henry Ford introduced the conveyor belt system of progressive assembly. Niels Bohr made discoveries in the structure of the atom. Edmund Husserl published *Phenomenology* and Freud *Totem and Taboo*. Thomas Mann published *Tod in Venedig* and Proust *Du Côté de chez Swann*. D. H. Lawrence published *Sons and Lovers* and Stravinsky composed *The Rite of Spring*. "Look-

ing back upon it now," said Mabel Luhan in 1936, "it seems as though everywhere, in that year of 1913, barriers went down and people reached each other
who had never been in touch before." She mentions Gertrude Stein's writing,
the interest in telepathy and the fourth dimension, *Boris Godunov* at the Metropolitan Opera, the Russian dancers and actors in Europe, the wearing of turbans
and trousers by women. The words of the day, says Van Wyck Brooks, were
"renascence" (Edna St. Vincent Millay's poem of that name appeared in 1912) and
"creative"—there was creative writing, creative thinking, even creative criticism.
Mabel Dodge had promoted the Armoury Show of Post-Impressionist Art, and then
she and Reed and others organized the Paterson Pageant in Madison Square
Garden with the letters "I.W.W." in red lights ten feet high on the tower, two
thousand people on the stage together, and fifteen hundred spectators, to commemorate the strike of the silk mill workers for an eight hour day.

Karl Jaspers published his *Allgemeine Psychopathologie,* which alluded to
Weber as a major modern thinker, Max Scheler his *Zur Phänomenologie der
Sympathiegefühle,* and Stalin his *Marxism and the National Question.*

Max Weber's publications were again either aggressive and moralistic speeches
in debate or assertions of the sciences' freedom from values. Alfred Weber published
a program for essays on the sociology of culture and an essay on bureaucratization.
Otto Gross moved to Berlin and published revolutionary articles in *Aktion.*

The Jugendbewegung held a mass meeting on the Hohen Meissner, and
Alfred Weber and Ludwig Klages were among the speakers. Jane Addams went
to Budapest as delegate to the Women's Suffrage Association.

Lawrence and Frieda spent April to June in Irschenhausen, went to England
for the summer (where they met the Murrys), then back to Italy (Lerici) separately, Lawrence walking through Switzerland alone in September. On November
9 Otto Gross was arrested in Berlin, taken to the Austrian border, handed over
to the Austrian police, and confined in Troppau Asylum as insane, on his father's
orders.

In 1914 the First World War broke out, in which it is estimated that 10
million people died and 20 million were wounded. Britain lost almost 1 million
dead and 2 million wounded; Germany, 1.8 million dead and 4.2 million wounded.
The cost has been estimated as £8 billion. On July 26, a very beautiful day in
Heidelberg, everyone assembled at Weber's house for the usual Sunday tea, and he
prophesied a long war. The next Sunday he appeared in military uniform, out-
raging Lukács and Bloch. D. H. Lawrence was on a walking tour in the Lake
District when war broke out—he was playing with the idea of Rananim—and the
news of war first stunned and then shattered his spirit.

The army strengths at the time of mobilization were 4.2 million for Germany,
3.7 million for France, 1.2 million for Russia, 800,000 for Austria, 700,000 for
Britain. At the battle of Tannenberg, where 100,000 Russian prisoners were
taken, Hermann Schäfer, Weber's brother-in-law, was killed.

The Canadian Pacific Railway was completed and the Panama Canal opened.
James Joyce published *The Dubliners* and D. H. Lawrence *The Prussian
Officer,* and *The Widowing of Mrs. Holroyd.* Margaret Sanger's magazine, *Woman Rebel,* began to appear in New York. Otto Gross published "Über Destruktionssymbolik" in a psychoanalytic journal edited by Wolfgang Stekel, who was
analyzing him. Ernest Weekley published *The Romance of Names.*

Max Weber had traveled in Italy in the spring, among the Northern lakes,
with their colonies of Utopian idealists, anarchists, and so forth—like what Lawrence planned as Rananim. Weber wrote to his mother for her seventieth birthday
from Ascona; he was the only child not at the Berlin celebrations. In Ascona he
helped Frieda Gross defend her maternal rights against Hanns Gross. Later he
helped Fanny zu Reventlow save her son from military service. But when war
broke out he turned all his energies to war work. Unable to fight, he took on the
organization of nine hospitals around Heidelberg. He published the first part of
Wirtschaft und Gesellschaft, which was planned to be his contribution to *Grundriss der Sozialökonomick,* the giant survey by many hands which was never
finished, but of which nearly all his subsequent works were intended to be
chapters.

In 1915 Italy entered the war, the Germans used gas on the Western front,
there were U-boat attacks on British ships and Zeppelin attacks on London. Duchamp painted *The Bride Stripped Bare by her Bachelors* and Albert Einstein put
forward his general theory of relativity. D. H. Lawrence published *The Rainbow,*
dedicated to Else von Richthofen (he wanted the dedication, Zu Else, printed in
Gothic type); the book was suppressed in November as obscene.

In July, 1,347 representatives of German intellectual life signed a very aggressive declaration of war aims drawn up by two Berlin professors, Seeberg and
Schäfer. One hundred forty-one personalities, including Weber, made a counter
declaration.

Karl Weber and Emil Lask, a friend of Weber's died in battle. Weber tried to
get war employment in Brussels, and then in Berlin, where he wanted to work on
winning the Poles over to friendship with Germany. Frustrated both times, he
turned to his sociology of religion again. Alfred Weber published *Gedanken zur
deutschen Sendung.*

Baron von Richthofen died. Frieda and Lawrence got to know Bertrand
Russell and Lady Ottoline Morell. They spent the last part of the year in Cornwall.

In 1916 the war spread further, Italy declaring war on Germany, Turkey on
Russia, Germany on Portugal. The Battle of Verdun was fought. In England
Lloyd George formed a Coalition Government, conscription began, and the
South Wales coalfields were taken over by the government because of strikes.
The Easter Rebellion broke out in Dublin; the Dada movement began in Zurich.
James Joyce published *Portrait of the Artist as a Young Man,* and D. H. Lawrence

Amores and *Twilight in Italy.* Lord Kitchener and Henry James died, Harold Wilson and Edward Heath were born.

Max Weber was involved in public debates about pacifism in *Die Frau,* and in Naumann's Working Committee on Central Europe, which tried to work out a customs and economic union for the Central European countries. This was frustrated by official resistance. He wrote a paper against U-boat warfare which he sent to the party leaders, the ministry for foreign affairs, and elsewhere. He published "Between Two Laws" in *Die Frau* on the incompatibility of the Tolstoyan Christian ethic with responsible political behavior. He also published work on Confucianism and Taoism and the very important *Zwischenbetrachtung* which accompanied the latter, discussing the relation of religion to art, to eroticism, to charisma. He also published his study of Hinduism and Buddhism, all to be parts of his sociology of religion for the *Grundriss.* And he gave a speech on Germany's position among the world powers which was censored before it could be printed. Bertrand Russell gave the lectures which he had planned together with Lawrence, and was sent to jail as a pacifist.

Murray published his worshipful book on Dostoevski—which Lawrence hated—and co-translated Kuprin and Shestov. Lawrence finished *Women in Love* and cooperated and quarreled with Russell. Also with the Murrys. Edgar Jaffe began publishing his weekly magazine on European political and economic affairs. And Ernest Weekley published *Surnames.*

In 1917 Revolution broke out in Russia in March. The Tsar abdicated on the 15th and Aleksandr Kerensky led a constitutional government. In November Lenin, Trotsky, and Grigori Zinoviev led the Bolsheviks to set up a Soviet Republic.

In January Germany had resumed unlimited U-boat warfare, and in April America declared war against her. The same month the Kaiser promised electoral reform after the war. The shortage of food led to riots in Berlin, and there was trouble in the German fleet.

Weber published in the *Frankfurter Zeitung* his plans for Poland; also an attack on the new law of entail (which helped create aristocratic estates); also comments on electoral reform. These articles attracted a lot of attention and brought the censor down on the paper. In a Munich paper he launched a sharp attack on Alfred von Tirpitz's *Vaterlandspartei.* He took part in a Heidelberg meeting of the *Fortschrittliche Volkspartei,* and sent Haussmann proposals for a new national constitution. In May and October he took part in the Lauenstein meetings, where he met Ernst Toller, Erich Mühsam, and other socialist-pacifist types, who were often at his house thereafter. Out of his twenty publications listed for the year, besides those named, there was a piece on Russian constitutionalism; an essay on value-freedom in the social sciences; a book on Ancient Judea; an essay on the Pharisees; and an essay on democracy and the franchise in Germany, defending parliamentarism.

In Ireland there were Sinn Fein riots in Dublin. In Switzerland George D. Herron published *Woodrow Wilson and the World's Peace,* which led people to believe that Herron represented the American government; and in December he sent to Ambassador Sharp in Paris a report of peace proposals he had received from two German professors, one of them probably Edgar Jaffe. In Paris Pablo Picasso designed sets and costumes for Diaghilev's *Parade,* which Guillaume Apollinaire described as "surrealist" in the first recorded use of that word. C. G. Jung published *The Unconscious.* T. S. Eliot published *Prufrock and Other Observations,* and D. H. Lawrence *Look, We Have Come Through.*

Lawrence was medically examined in June 1917 but found unfit for military service. In October he and Frieda were expelled from Cornwall under suspicion of spying for the Germans. Mabel Sterne moved from New York City to Taos. Otto Gross was moving in the literary circles of Prague.

In 1918 Soviet Russia signed the Treaty of Brest-Litovsk with Germany. In July the Tsar and his family were shot. British and French troops intervened in the Civil War in Russia.

In January President Wilson outlined his Fourteen Point program for peace. In August the German High Command decided that Germany could not hope any longer to defeat the enemy, and in September that she could not fight any longer. On October 3 Prince Max von Baden, a liberal, became Chancellor. On November 3 the sailors mutinied at Kiel; on the 4th Max Weber gave his famous speech in Munich, warning against revolution; on the 5th there were strikes all over Germany; on the 7th Kurt Eisner set up a workers' and soldiers' council in Munich, and the King fled; on the 8th Eisner set up a separate Bavarian republic, with Edgar Jaffe as Minister of Finance. On the 9th the Kaiser abdicated, Ebert became Chancellor, and Liebknecht proclaimed Germany a socialist republic. And on the 11th the Armistice was signed and the Kaiser fled into Holland. On the 17th Eisner gave a concert in Munich at which he recited his hymn "To the Revolution" to music, with Bruno Walter conducting, a concert repeated twice more. On the 30th all German women were given the right to vote; in the next elections Marianne Weber was elected first woman member of the Badenian parliament.

Max Weber had gone to Vienna to teach the summer semester. (Otto Gross was also in Vienna, playing a prominent part in revolutionary plotting.) After the military collapse, Weber told Naumann to persuade the Kaiser to abdicate immediately. (Jaffe was the first man in Munich publicly to demand the Kaiser's abdication.) On November 4 Weber spoke in Munich against "peace at any price" and was met with such an angry reception that for the first time he could not complete his speech. He was speaking against revolution in the presence of all who were planning it, and it was his own students—Eugen Levine among others— who shouted him down. In Heidelberg he was made a member of the workers' and soldiers' council and dominated several meetings.

Alfred Weber, Erich Koch-Weser, and Naumann founded a Deutsche Demokratische Partei, and Max, after some hesitations, made a series of powerful speeches on its behalf. One was published as a special supplement to the *Frankfurter Zeitung*. He was spontaneously nominated as a Reichstag candidate for Frankfurt, but later, at the national conference, was put far down the list of party candidates and had no chance of election. He was proposed as Secretary for the Interior in the new Cabinet on November 15. This fell through, but he was the only non-official member of the commission for the new constitution. He published more essays on the need for parliamentarism in the *Frankfurter Zeitung* and gave a lecture on Socialism in Vienna which was printed as a pamphlet.

In England the influenza epidemic reached dangerous proportions. D. H. Lawrence was seriously ill with it at the beginning of 1919. In September 1918, in Derbyshire, he had another medical examination. He published *New Poems* and the first version of *Studies in Classic American Literature,* in the *English Review*. Murray published his *Poems 1917–18* and *The Critic in Judgment*. Russell published *Mysticism and Logic* and Lytton Strachey *Eminent Victorians*. Spengler published the first part of *Der Untergang des Abendlandes,* and Diaghilev came to London. Paul Klee painted his abstract *Gartenplan* and Blok published his revolutionary "The Twelve." Fanny zu Reventlow died in Ascona.

In 1919 there was a general strike in Berlin and the Spartacists made a revolution. On January 15 Rosa Luxemburg and Karl Liebknecht were murdered by right-wing officers. On February 21 Kurt Eisner was assassinated. (Heinrich Mann spoke at his funeral, March 3.) His second minister, Auer, was seriously wounded. On April 7 a *Räteregierung,* a soviet regime, was set up in Munich (Edgar Jaffe did not take office) with Toller and Mühsam, Landauer, and Niekisch in power. On April 8 a Rote Garde was created by arming the people. On April 13 the regime of six days earlier was replaced by one which was more closely oriented to the Communist Party and headed by Levien and Levine. This was overthrown by troops from the German army. Landauer was trampled to death and Levine shot, and a brutal right-wing repression began. Edgar Jaffe had a nervous breakdown. On July 10 Else wrote to the authorities on his behalf that he was too sick to come and bear witness in Toller's trial. Von Frauensdorfer shot himself and other people who had been involved in the revolutionary government entered insane asylums.

In February the newly elected *Nationalversammlung* met in Weimar and in July adopted the Weimar Constitution. Ebert became *Reichspräsident*. In May Weber went to Versailles as a member of the German delegation there. In June the Peace Treaty was signed. He then visited Ludendorff and asked him to give himself as a scapegoat to the Allies. The Deutsche Arbeiterpartei (later the N.S.D.A.P.—the Nazis) was founded in Munich, and among its first members was Adolf Hitler. Mussolini founded the Fascist party in Italy. The Communist Third International was founded.

In Britain the War Cabinet was dissolved and the first woman M.P. was elected. In Italy Gabriele D'Annunzio and his army of irregulars seized Fiume. In America, Emma Goldman and Alexander Berkman were deported, by J. Edgar Hoover's doing. Theodore Roosevelt and Andrew Carnegie died.

John Maynard Keynes published *The Economic Consequences of the Peace,* and Luigi Pirandello *Six Characters in Search of an Author.* Hermann Hesse published *Demian* and Proust volume 2 of *À la Recherche du Temps Perdu.* All were great successes. (The contrast in success between Proust's first and second volumes is increased by the concurrent fall from fame of *Jean-Christophe.*) Walter Gropius founded the Bauhaus School of Design, Buildings, and Crafts in Weimar. D. H. Lawrence published *Bay: A Book of Poems;* Otto Gross published some revolutionary essays in *Die Erde, Sowjet,* and *Das Forum,* as well as "Über den inneren Konflikte," three essays in sexual theory.

In this year Max Weber's mother died, and also his political friend and ally, Friedrich Naumann. He began the year with speeches for the D.D.P., given in several cities, and was again sought as a member of the Reichstag—for Heidelberg, this time. To students in Munich he gave his famous lectures, "Wissenschaft als Beruf" and "Politik als Beruf." He opposed the peace settlement as unfair, and was a member of a Heidelberg Union which fought against Germany's assuming the moral blame for the war. At the end of June he moved to Munich and began a lecture series which was later published as his *General Economic History.*

D. H. Lawrence had been seriously ill with influenza, but in October Frieda left for Germany and Lawrence soon after for Italy—to Florence, via Turin. Reunited there, they went to Sicily and Capri. Otto Gross left Vienna at the beginning of the year for Berlin—probably secretly. From there he sent a message to Else Jaffe in Munich asking if she would look after him if he came to her. In November he grew angry with the friends who were caring for him, because they would procure him no more drugs, ran away and hid in a warehouse. When he was found, starving, it was already too late to save his life.

1920–1930

This is the decade of deaths. Otto Gross's happened only just before and Lawrence's only just after. The culture lay in something like death-throes too. But both Weber's and Lawrence's publications were numerous and weighty.

In 1920 the Treaty of Versailles came into effect in January and the League of Nations came into being. Left-wing demonstrators in Berlin were fired on and forty-two were killed. In March there was a right-wing Kapp Putsch. In Munich Hitler announced his Twenty-five Point Program at the first mass-meeting of the Deutsche Arbeiterpartei in the Hofbrauhaus. In the elections Weber's servant girl voted for Hitler. In America women were given the vote and the sale of alcoholic beverages was forbidden. The first public broadcasting stations were opened in Britain and the United States.

Jung published his *Psychological Types,* which owed much to Otto Gross, and there was a Dadaist exhibition at Köln, at which the spectators were invited to smash the exhibits. Franz Kafka published *The Country Doctor* and D. H. Lawrence *The Lost Girl* and the play *Touch and Go.* There was also a private edition of *Women in Love* in New York. T. S. Eliot published *The Sacred Wood,* the book of criticism which includes "Tradition and the Individual Talent," the *locus classicus* of Eliot's belief in artistic impersonality and hence of his opposition to Lawrence and Murry.

Max Weber rebuked the Munich students in January for demanding a reprieve for Arco, Eisner's right-wing assassin; in consequence, the Korps students demonstrated outside his house. His lectures were howled down. His sister Lili committed suicide in April, leaving four children whom Marianne wanted to adopt. Max was working on his collected essays on the sociology of religion when he caught cold and died on the 14th of June.

These essays on which he had been working at the time of his death appeared in three volumes, 1920–1921. His book-length essay on *The City* appeared in the *Archiv* at this time. Karl Jaspers gave a remarkable address in celebration of Weber at Heidelberg. Alfred Weber published his *Prinzipelles zur Kultursoziologie,* also in the *Archiv.* Murry published *Aspects of Literature.* Lawrence spent most of the year in Italy and in Sicily. He got a letter from Mabel Luhan, inviting him to Taos, and liked the sound of the place.

In 1921 appeared *Movements in European History,* the history book Lawrence wrote under a pseudonym, and also *Sea and Sardinia, Tortoises,* and *Psychoanalysis and the Unconscious.* Aldous Huxley published *Crome Yellow,* one of his earliest satirical novels. Ernest Weekley published *An Etymological Dictionary of Modern English,* the first of his many dictionaries. Edgar Jaffe died in Munich, never having recovered from the nervous breakdown brought on by the failure of the 1918 revolution.

The first volume of Weber's *Economy and Society* appeared, as did his book on *The Rational and Social Foundations of Music.* Marianne edited the first volume of his *Collected Political Writings.*

In January Lawrence and Frieda made the trip to Sardinia described in the book published in December.

In 1922 Walther Rathenau, the liberal-idealist Foreign Secretary of Germany, a rich Jew, was murdered. In India Gandhi was sentenced to six years imprisonment for civil disobedience. In Italy Mussolini marched on Rome and formed a Fascist government. In England the Lloyd George Coalition fell, and the Conservatives returned to power. Niels Bohr described his theory of the circuits of electrons within the atom.

T. S. Eliot published "The Waste Land" and James Joyce *Ulysses.* Ludwig Wittgenstein published *Tractatus Logico-Philosophicus* and Rilke *Sonette an Orpheus*; Katherine Mansfield published *The Garden Party* and D. H. Lawrence *Aaron's Rod.* In America he also published *Fantasia of the Unconscious* and *England, My England.* He left Sicily for Ceylon and then Australia. By the end of the year he was in Taos, New Mexico. Murry published *Countries of the Mind* and *The Problem of Style,* two collections of his best criticism. Ernest Weekley published the third edition of *The Romance of Words.* Marcel Proust died. So did Alexander Graham Bell and Alfred Harmsworth.

In 1923 the Soviet Union was established. The Ruhr was occupied by French troops (not for the first time) because reparation payments had not been made. In July the cost of living in Germany was 39,000 times its prewar level. On October 11, one pound sterling was worth ten million marks; on November 15 one American dollar was worth 2.5 billion marks. The rentier class in Germany (including the Webers and Jaffes) had their incomes destroyed. Alfred Weber published *Die Not der geistigen Arbeiter,* which drew attention to the economic plight of the cultured classes and predicted dire consequences for the nation. Martial law was enforced in Germany. In November Hitler attempted a *coup d'état* in Munich but failed. Ernst Troeltsch died, and so did Katherine Mansfield. Murry began to publish *The Adelphi,* to carry Lawrence's message. Weber's *General Economic History* was published by students from their lecture notes, commissioned and guided by Marianne.

D. H. Lawrence published *Kangaroo;* and *Studies in Classic American Literature;* a translation of Verga's *Maestro Don Gesualdo;* an Introduction to Maurice Magnus's *Memoirs of the Foreign Legion; Birds, Beasts, and Flowers;* and the novellas "The Fox," "The Captain's Doll," "The Ladybird." In March the Lawrences left New Mexico for Mexico City. In August Frieda sailed to England from New York, but Lawrence went back to Mexico until November. They had been quarreling bitterly. In England he asked Dorothy Brett and Murry to come to Taos to found a colony.

Anita von Schreibershofen married and Johanna von Schreibershofen divorced to marry Emil Krug (1870–1944), a bank director for Mendelssohn and Weber in Berlin.

In 1924 Hitler was sentenced to five years imprisonment but released in December. In the Reichstag elections, Nationalists and Communists won seats away from moderates. In Britain the first Labour Government was elected. E. M. Forster published *Passage to India* and Thomas Mann *Der Zauberberg* (*The Magic Mountain*). D. H. Lawrence published, together with Molly Skinner, *The Boy in the Bush.* Murry published *Discoveries, The Necessity of Art, To the Unknown God,* and *The Voyage.* F. R. Leavis finished his Ph. D. dissertation at Cambridge, "The Relationship of Journalism to Literature." Ernest Weekley published *A Concise Etymological Dictionary of Modern English*. Lenin and Woodrow Wilson died, as did Eleonora Duse and Joseph Conrad.

Two volumes of Weber's essays, one on social-economic history, another on sociology and social legislation, appeared under Marianne's editing. Alfred Weber published *Deutschland und die europäische Kulturkrise, Wissenschaft und soziale Struktur*, and an attack on Spengler.

In 1925 Trotsky lost his struggle with Stalin for control of the Communist Party. Hindenberg became President of Germany. The Bauhaus moved to Dessau because of local hostility in Weimar. Adolf Hitler published *Mein Kampf*. Part I. Virginia Woolf published *Mrs. Dalloway*. D. H. Lawrence published "St. Mawr," "The Princess," and "Reflections on the Death of a Porcupine." He had been seriously ill with malaria at Oaxaca, where he had been working on his novel about Mexico. In September he and Frieda returned to Europe. Murry published *Keats and Shakespeare*, one of his manifestoes of literary patriotism. Alfred Weber published *Die Krise des modernen Staatsgedanken in Europa*, and Talcott Parsons went to Heidelberg to study sociology, having come to hear of Max Weber. Karl Jaspers discussed Weber as a philosopher in *Psychologie der Weltanschauungen*.

In 1926 there was a General Strike in England, May 3–12. Kafka published *The Castle*, D. H. Lawrence *The Plumed Serpent, and* T. E. Lawrence *The Seven Pillars of Wisdom*. Murry published a *Life of Jesus*, and Marianne *Max Weber, Ein Lebensbild*. Else Jaffe translated "The Fox," which was published as "Der Fuchs." (She also translated *The Plumed Serpent* but could not get it published.) The population of Russia was 148 million; of the United States, 115 million; of Japan, 85 million; of Germany, 64 million; of Britain, 45 million; of France, 41 million; of Italy, 40 million.

In 1927 Trotsky was expelled from the Communist Party by Stalin. Hitler published *Mein Kampf*, Part II, and Kemal Atatürk published *The New Turkey*. The German economic system collapsed on Black Friday. Martin Heidegger published *Sein und Zeit*, Russell *The Analysis of Matter*, and Werner Heisenberg his paper on the uncertainty principle. Ernest Hemingway published *Men Without Women*, and George Antheil composed *a ballet mécanique*, with all the sounds made by modern machines. T. E. Lawrence wrote *Revolt in the Desert*, and D. H. Lawrence *Mornings in Mexico*. Lawrence was living in Italy, though he made visits to England and Germany. He went on a walking tour of the Etruscan tombs and did some painting. Max Weber's *General Economic History* was translated into English and published in America. Alfred Weber published *Ideen zur Staats und Kultursoziologie*, Murry published *The Evolution of an Intellectual*, and Ernest Weekley published *Words, Ancient and Modern*.

In 1928 the first Five Year Plan began in Russia, and complete equality of suffrage was given to women in Britain. Penicillin was discovered and a Geiger-counter was built. Yeats published *The Tower*, Virginia Woolf published *Orlando*, and Aldous Huxley published *Point Counter-Point*, a satical novel in which Lawrence appeared as a figure of health. Lawrence himself published *Lady Chatterley's Lover*. This was the third version of the novel and was privately printed in Florence; it could not be sold publicly because it was judged obscene. He also published another translation of Verga, his *Collected Poems*, and "The Woman Who Rode Away." Else Jaffe translated the last as "Die Frau, die davon tritt." Murry edited Katherine Mansfield's *Letters*. Talcott Parsons' thesis, " 'Capitalism' in Recent German Literature: Sombart and Weber," was published in *The Journal of Political Economy*. Thomas Hardy and the Earl of Asquith died.

In 1929 the Wall Street Stock Exchange crashed. Trotsky was expelled from the Soviet Union by Stalin. Einstein published his *Unitary Field Theory*. The second Surrealist Manifesto was published, and the Museum of Modern Art opened in New York. In England an exhibition of D. H. Lawrence's paintings was held in London, which was raided and closed by the police in July. (Murry published *God: An Introduction to the Science of Metabiology*. This was a book which he said "should have been written" by "a man of fundamentally religious genius like D. H. Lawrence.") Lawrence spent the winter at Bandol, writing poetry and short articles. He published *The Paintings of D. H. Lawrence, Pansies*, and *Pornography and Obscenity*. Else Jaffe translated a French book on American foreign policy. Ernest Weekley published *The English Language*. Georges Clemenceau and Gustav Stresemann died, as did Diaghilev and Hugo von Hofmannsthal.

1930–1940

In this decade both Weber and Lawrence began to sink out of the general view. For different reasons, they were both out of tune with the times.

In 1930 a Nazi, Wilhelm Frick, became minister of state in Thuringia. In German elections the Socialists won 143 seats, the Communists 77, the Nazis 107. In India, Gandhi opened another civil disobedience campaign. José Ortega y Gasset published *The Revolt of the Masses*, F. R. Leavis *Mass Civilization and Minority Culture*, Jaspers *Die Geistige Situation der Zeit* and Freud *Civilization and its Discontents*. T. S. Eliot published "Ash-Wednesday" and D. H. Lawrence "Love Among the Haystacks" and "The Virgin and the Gypsy." He also published *Nettles*, "A Propos of Lady Chatterley's Lover," and *Assorted Articles*. Evelyn Waugh published *Vile Bodies* and John Cowper Powys *In Defense of Sensuality*.

Talcott Parsons translated *The Protestant Ethic and the Spirit of Capitalism*, and it was published with a Foreword by R. H. Tawney. Both F. R. Leavis and Stephen Potter published volumes entitled *D. H. Lawrence*. Murry edited Keats and Katherine Mansfield. Ernest Weekley published *Adjectives and Other Words*.

D. H. Lawrence entered Ad Astra sanatorium in Vence on February 6, and moved out to the Villa Robemond only the day before he died, on March 2. Later in the year Frau von Richthofen also died. Frieda took Murry as a lover.

In 1931 the bankruptcy of the Kredit-Anstalt in Austria began the financial collapse of all Central Europe. All German banks were closed until August 1. Britain abandoned the gold standard, and the value of the pound fell from $4.86 to $3.49. There was a budget deficiency of £100 million. Hitler made an alliance which secured the Nazis the support of the great magnate, Hugenberg. Ernest O. Lawrence devised the cyclotron. Sergei Rachmaninov's music was forbidden in the Soviet Union as decadent. D. H. Lawrence's "The Man Who Died" and *Apocalypse* were published. Murry published *Son of Woman* and Ada Lawrence Clarke *Young Lorenzo*. Alfred Weber published *Das Ende der Demokratie?* and "Wie das deutsche Volk fühlt!" Ernest Weekley published *Cruelty to Words*. Anna Pavlova and Nellie Melba died, as did Thomas Edison and Arnold Bennett.

In 1932 the Nazis won 230 seats in the Reichstag, the Socialists 133, the Center 97 and the Communists 89. The Japanese occupied Shanghai. Oswald Mosely founded the British Union of Fascists. Louis-Ferdinand Céline published *Voyage au bout de la nuit,* and Jaspers *Max Weber: Politiker, Forscher, Philosoph.* Karl Löwith published an important article in the *Archiv,* "Max Weber und Karl Marx." Wilhelm Reich published "The Masochistic Character," which Freud said had been written in the service of the Communist Party.

D. H. Lawrence's *Letters* were published, with an important introduction by Aldous Huxley; also Lawrence's *Last Poems, Etruscan Places,* and "The Lovely Lady." Frieda went back to Taos. F. R. Leavis founded *Scrutiny* and wrote reviews of books about Lawrence, attacking Eliot's treatment of him. He also published *New Bearings in English Poetry* and *How to Teach Reading: A Primer for Ezra Pound.* Catherine Carswell published *Savage Pilgrimage* and Mabel Luhan *Lorenzo in Taos.* Murry published *The Necessity of Communism* and *The Fallacy of Economics.* Ernest Weekley published *Words and Names.*

In 1933 Hitler became Chancellor of Germany, with Hermann Göring, Wilhelm Frick, and Franz von Papen in his cabinet. The Nazis engineered a fire in the Reichstag and blamed the Communists for it. Hitler was given dictatorial powers, to last until April 1937. The persecution of German Jews began. Kandinski and Klee left Germany. Alfred Weber pulled down the Swastika when it was hoisted over his Institute in Heidelberg, and resigned his professorship. The union of undergraduates at Oxford University resolved that they would not fight for king or country. Reich published *The Mass Psychology of Facism,* was expelled from the German Psychoanalytic Society, and driven out of Germany and in effect out of the Communist Party. America repealed Prohibition. Trotsky published his *History of the Russian Revolution* and Malraux *La Condition Hu-*

maine. T. S. Eliot published *After Strange Gods: A Primer of Modern Heresy,* which contains his major attack on Lawrence, and Leavis published *For Continuity,* which contains two essays in praise of Lawrence. Murry published a *Life of Katherine Mansfield,* a book on Blake, and *Reminiscences of D. H. Lawrence.* For *The Wanderer,* a little magazine he began that year, he wrote three remarkably Lawrentian essays "On Marriage." Dorothy Brett published *Lawrence and Brett,* Helen Corke *Lawrence and Apocalypse.* John Galsworthy and Stefan George died.

In 1934 there was a general strike in France and riots in Paris. A plebiscite confirmed Hitler in power in Germany. The assassination of Sergei Kirov led to a purge of the Communist Party in Russia. Mikhail Sholokhov published *And Quiet Flows the Don,* and D. H. Lawrence's "A Modern Lover" and "A Collier's Friday Night" appeared. Frieda Lawrence published *Not I, But the Wind . . .* Alexander von Schelting published *Die Wissenschaftslehre Max Webers,* and F. R. Leavis "Mr. Eliot, Mr. Wyndham Lewis and Lawrence" in *Determinations.* Sir Edward Elgar and Frederick Delius died.

In 1935 the Saar was restored to Germany, which was once again beginning an expansionist policy. Italy invaded Abyssinia. Germany reintroduced compulsory military service. Murry published *Marxism* and *Between Two Worlds,* his autobiography. "E. T." (Jessie Chambers) published *D. H. Lawrence: A Personal Record.* Alfred Weber published *Kulturgeschichte als Kultursoziologie,* dedicated to Else Jaffe, and Talcott Parsons defended Max Weber against H. M. Robertson. The ashes of D. H. Lawrence were brought from France to Taos and interred in a shrine. Ernest Weekley published *Something About Words.* T. E. Lawrence and Alban Berg died.

In 1936 Léon Blum founded a Popular Front ministry in France, and a forty-hour working week was instituted there. France, Switzerland, and Holland abandoned the gold standard, and Italy devalued the lira. Chiang Kai-shek declared war on Japan. Germany and Italy acknowledged Franco's government in Spain. The Spanish Civil War broke out. George Orwell and Emma Goldman went to Barcelona, their sympathies with the Anarchists.

The volume of unpublished work by Lawrence, *Phoenix,* was edited by Edward D. Macdonald. A volume of Max Weber's letters, *Jugendbriefe 1876–1893* was edited by Marianne Weber. Murry edited Katherine Mansfield's *Journal,* and introduced E. T.'s book in America.

In 1937 the Japanese captured Peking, Shanghai, and Nanking. Lord Halifax went to Germany to appease Hitler over the Sudeten problem. The Nazis held an exhibition of "decadent art" in Munich and dismissed Jaspers from his post at Heidelberg University. Murry published *The Necessity of Pacifism.* Jean-

Paul Sartre published *La Nausée* and Martin Buber *I and Thou*. Orwell published *The Road to Wigan Pier*. Else Jaffe translated, and edited, *Not I, But the Wind ...* as *Nur der Wind ...* F. R. Leavis reviewed *Phoenix* and Talcott Parsons published *The Structure of Social Action*, his study of Weber together with Emile Durkheim, Vilfredo Pareto, and Alfred Marshall.

In 1938 Germany annexed Austria and at a conference in Munich Neville Chamberlain and Edouard Daladier agreed to transfer Sudetenland to Germany, in return for a guarantee of Czechoslovakia's frontiers. Murry published *The Pledge of Peace, Peace at Christmas,* and *Heaven—and Earth*. Talcott Parsons published "The Role of Theory in Social Research" in the *American Sociological Review.*

In 1939 Italy invaded Albania, Franco captured Barcelona, Germany invaded and conquered Poland. Britain and France declared war on Germany. In this war only 250,000 British soldiers were killed and 280,000 wounded. But Germany lost 3 million dead or missing and 1 million wounded. Marianne (Jaffe) von Eckardt evacuated 250 German Jewish children to a Quaker camp in England and then returned to Nazi Heidelberg. Murry published *In Defence of Democracy* and *The Price of Leadership*. Joyce published *Finnegans Wake* and Ernest Weekley *Jack and Jill*.

Sigmund Freud died, as did Havelock Ellis, Ford Madox Ford, and Ernst Toller (by his own hand).

1940–1950

In this decade of war few people thought much about either Lawrence or Weber.

In 1940 Germany invaded Denmark and Norway. Germany, Italy, and Japan signed ten-year economic and military pacts. There were heavy air raids on Britain. Winston Churchill became Prime Minister of England. France fell, and half was occupied by the Germans. (Alma Mahler, already a refugee from Austria, fled from France into Spain and finally to America.) The British army was evacuated from Dunkirk. The Battle of Britain began. In one month 160,000 tons of British shipping were sunk. Murry published *Democracy and War, The Brotherhood of Peace,* and *The Betrayal of Christ by the Churches*. Trotsky was assassinated in Mexico. Chamberlain and Emma Goldman died.

In 1941 German troops under General Erwin Rommel crossed from Italy into North Africa, despite British attempts to stop them. Germany invaded Russia, conquered much of it, and began the siege of Leningrad. The Japanese bombed Pearl Harbor. Britain and America declared war on Japan. America declared war on Germany and Italy. British pacifists, including Murry, organized a

People's Convention to stop the war. The Manhattan Project of atomic bomb research began in Chicago and Los Alamos. Joyce and Virginia Woolf died, as did Bergson and Frazer and Sombart.

In 1942 Singapore fell to the Japanese. The V–2 rocket was launched by the Germans. The Battle of El Alamein took place in North Africa. Enrico Fermi split the atom. E. H. Carr published *The Conditions of Peace,* which was used, in secret translation, by Germans intriguing against Hitler as the basis of their plans for a separate peace with the West; among these Germans was Eduard Baumgarten. Murry published *The Dilemma of Christianity,* and Parsons "Max Weber and the Contemporary Political Crisis."

In 1943 the Allies began saturation bombing of German cities. Italy surrendered. Russia won the Battle of Stalingrad and recaptured two thirds of the territory lost to the Germans. The Third International was dissolved. The French National Committee of Liberation was formed, including Charles de Gaulle. The *Frankfurter Zeitung* was suppressed by Hitler. Alfred Weber published *Das Tragische und die Geschichte.* Aram Khatchaturian composed his "Ode to Stalin" and Sartre published *L'Être et le Néant.* F. R. Leavis published *Education and the University: A Sketch for an "English School."*

In 1944 the siege of Leningrad was raised and the Germans were driven from Russia. The Allies landed in Normandy and de Gaulle entered Paris. The first V–2 rockets fell in England. T. S. Eliot published "The Four Quartets" and Sir William Beveridge published *Full Employment in a Free Society,* a plan for postwar England which employed the techniques of social science and was later followed by the Labour Government. Murry published *Adam and Eve: An Essay Towards a New and Better Society.* His "plan" was a proposal to save Western culture by propagating Lawrence's doctrine of sexual tenderness—"the regeneration of generation."

In 1945 the Russians reached Berlin in April. On the 28th Mussolini was killed. On the 30th Hitler killed himself. On May 8, Germany surrendered. On August 6, America dropped the atomic bomb on Hiroshima and Japan surrendered. War-crime trials began in Nuremberg. Russia estimated that 20 million of its citizens, military and civilian, were dead. It is estimated that 5 million Jews, of 6.5 million living in Europe in 1939, had been killed by 1945.

George Orwell published *Animal Farm.* Karl Jaspers and Alfred Weber published, in *Die Wandlung* (a new magazine they began), essays dedicated to giving Germany a new political idea of itself. Besides Mussolini and Hitler, Roosevelt and Lloyd George, Valéry and Bartók died.

In 1946 the United Nations held its first General Assembly. The population of China was 455 million; of India, 311 million; of Russia, 194 million; of the United States, 140 million; of Japan, 73 million; of West Germany, 48 million; of

Britain, 46 million. The *Viking Portable D. H. Lawrence* was published, and *From Max Weber: Essays in Sociology,* edited by H. H. Gerth and C. Wright Mills; both were major means by which the American public came in contact with these authors. Talcott Parsons (with A. M. Henderson) translated *Theory of Social and Economic Organization,* for which he wrote an introduction. Alfred Weber published *Freier Sozialismus,* a program for a new political party, with A. Mitscherlich; and *Abschied von der bisherigen Geschichte: Überwindung des Nihilismus? Jasper* published *Die Schuldfrage,* his lectures on German war-guilt. Keynes, Wells, and Gertrude Stein died.

In 1947 Alfred Weber's last mentioned book was translated into English as *Farewell to European History.* (He was now, as a leader of the new Germany approved by the Allies, an international figure.) He wrote several political essays and gave lectures on the new kind of free, non-Marxist socialism he was proposing. Jaspers published *Von der Wahrheit,* of which one part (translated as *Tragedy Is Not Enough*) relates to Alfred Weber's work on tragedy.

In 1948 the city of Berlin was blockaded by the Russians. There was a Communist coup in Czechoslovakia. The railways were nationalized in England. Gandhi was assassinated. Alfred Weber again contributed essays (he was now eighty) to the "Schriftenreihe der Aktiongruppe Heidelberg zur Demokratie und zum freien Sozialismus." Murry published *The Free Society* and *The Challenge of Schweitzer.* D. H. Lawrence's *Letters to Bertrand Russell* were published. Leavis published *The Great Tradition,* his book on the British novel which used Lawrence as a touchstone; and Eric Bentley brought out a volume of selections from *Scrutiny* in America.

In 1949 Alfred Weber published, in the fourth volume of *Die Wandlung,* "Haben Wir Deutschen Seit 1945 Versagt?" and other essays on contemporary politics. A Federal Republic was set up in Bonn. Theodor Heuss was elected President and Konrad Adenauer Chancellor. A Communist Republic was set up in China. Britain devalued the pound. Orwell published *1984,* and Simone de Beauvoir *Le Deuxième Sexe.* Max Weber's *Methodology of the Social Sciences* was translated by Edward Shils and Henry Finch. F. R. Leavis published an essay on Lawrence and Bloomsbury.

1950–1960

In this decade several of the principal figures in this story died. But Lawrence and Weber began to come alive again in the minds of others.

In 1950 war broke out in Korea, involving America and China. The first series of riots provoked by racial policy broke out in Johannesburg. Russia manufactured an atomic bomb. Arthur Koestler and others wrote essays in repudiation of their previous Marxist faith, collected in a volume called *The God That Failed.* F. R. Leavis published two essays under the general heading "The Novel as Dramatic Poem," one on "St. Mawr," and one on *Women in Love.* Weber's "Social Causes of the Decay of Ancient Civilization" was translated for *The Journal of General Education,* and his "Hindu Social System" for the Sociologists Club Bulletin of the University of Minnesota. The Festreden for Alfred Weber's eightieth birthday were published in the official papers of Heidelberg University. George Orwell and George Bernard Shaw died.

In 1951 Weber's *Religion of China* was translated, and in Germany his works began reappearing with scholarly editing by Johannes Winckelmann. F. R. Leavis published two more essays on *Women in Love,* and one on T. S. Eliot and Lawrence. Alfred Weber brought out a new edition of *Kulturgeschichte als Kultursoziologie,* and edited a new volume of culture sociology. Murry published *The Conquest of Death;* Gide and Schönberg died.

In 1952 Britain produced an atomic bomb and America exploded a hydrogen bomb. Dwight D. Eisenhower was elected President of the United States. Doris Lessing published *Martha Quest.* Weber's "Ancient Judaism" was translated. F. R. Leavis published three essays on *The Rainbow.* Murry published *Community Farm.* Ernest Weekley published a new edition of a dictionary and *The English Language,* with a chapter on American English by an American.

In 1953 an armistice was signed in Korea. Stalin died and Nikita Khrushchev rose to power. Russia exploded a hydrogen bomb. There were widespread strikes in France and a rising in East Berlin. Senator Joseph McCarthy accused many American intellectuals and officials of having been Communists and of being therefore untrustworthy. Karl Jaspers's *Tragedy is Not Enough* was published in English. Marianne Weber died.

In 1954 Alfred Weber was nominated for the Presidency of West Germany by the Communist Party, but Heuss was again elected. France and Germany signed a cultural and economic agreement. Britain, France, Russia, and America agreed to end the occupation of Germany, and a nine-power agreement on European unity was signed. McCarthy was reproved by a Senate subcommittee. There was concern about radioactive wastes and about the link between cancer and cigarette smoking.

Max Weber's *Law in Economy and Society* was translated by Edward A. Shils and Max Rheinstein. F. R. Leavis published an essay on "The Captain's Doll." Murry reissued *Son of Woman* with a new introduction. Ernest Weekley died.

The von Richthofen matriarchy, Else, the Baroness, Frieda.

Frieda Weekley.

Else Jaffe.

The two husbands, Ernest Weekley and Edgar Jaffe.

"The Lover"

This is Otto Gross (1877–1919) as a boy, in the only known photograph. The brilliant only child of Prof. Dr. Hanns Gross, the founder of the science of criminology in Austria, we see young Otto here encased in plush, still his father's prize possession. As he grew up, he was subjected to severe pressures by his brutally domineering father. As a very young man, Otto assisted in his father's criminological research as a medical expert, but he soon rebelled, becoming a Freudian psychoanalyst and then going beyond Freud to encourage his patients to rebel against their fathers and against all patriarchal values. By 1906, when he met the von Richthofen sisters, Otto Gross had become the spirit of Bohemia, of anarchy, and of sexual revolution.

D. H. Lawrence.

Max Weber.

The Lawrence family. Left to right, Ada, Emily, Mrs. Lawrence, George, Bert (D. H.), Ernest, Mr. Lawrence.

The Weber family. Left to right, Arthur, Klara, Alfred, Lili, Frau Weber, Karl, Herr Weber, Max.

Besides the psychological parallels between the two mothers, the two fathers, and the two eldest sons (defenders of the mothers against the fathers), there were also similarities between the two youngest daughters, Lili Weber and Ada Lawrence, to whom Max and Bert were emotionally close, and between the two handsomest boys, Arthur Weber and George Lawrence (renamed "Arthur" in *Sons and Lovers*), who were the least strenuous and difficult, the most conventional of the sons.

Frieda Gross and child.

Else Jaffe and child.

Both children were called Peter, both were born in 1907, both were engendered by Otto Gross. In the two mothers' continuing friendship, their ideological sisterhood, Gross saw his *Welt-Frühling*.

Frieda Weekley and child.

Alma Mahler and child.

The two great Demeters of twentieth-century art, luxuriant in life and love and life-giving.

Alfred Weber, the other man in Else Jaffe's life

John Middleton Murry, one of the other men in Frieda Lawrence's life.

Mabel Luhan, the spirit of Taos.

Marianne Weber, the spirit of Heidelberg.

Jessie Chambers, the schoolteacher whom Lawrence left for Frieda.

Isadora Duncan was another Frieda, but in term of the dance.

Lou Andreas-Salomé,
intellectual and seductress.

mma Goldman, revolutionary
and mother-figure.

J. M. Murry and F. R. Leavis, whose books
reflect the development of Lawrence's heritage.

Karl Jaspers and Talcott Parsons, whose work marked two stages in the
development of Weber's heritage.

Wilhelm Reich, whose books carried into the
1940s and 1950s, and to America, the same
message as Gross had delivered before the
First World War in Germany.

In 1955 Italy, France, and West Germany agreed on European unity; West Germany entered NATO. Samuel Beckett published *Waiting for Godot* and Vladimir Nabokov *Lolita*. Alfred Weber published several essays, including the autobiographical "Die Jugend und das deutsche Schicksal." Leavis published *D. H. Lawrence: Novelist*. Albert Einstein and Thomas Mann died.

In 1956 there was a rising against the communist regime in Hungary, and Britain failed to cow Gamal Abdul Nasser in the Suez crisis. The Aldermaston marches of protest against the military uses of atomic energy began. The neutrino and anti-neutron were discovered. More of Max Weber's work was reissued under Winckelmann's editorship. Frieda Ravagli died in Taos.

In 1957 Belgium, France, Italy, Luxemburg, the Netherlands, and West Germany formed the Common Market and Euratom. German atomic physicists refused to cooperate in the production or testing of atomic weapons. The International Atomic Energy Commission came into existence. Russia launched

Sputnik I, which circled the globe every ninety-five minutes. Murry published *Love, Freedom and Society,* on D. H. Lawrence and Albert Schweitzer. Murry died. Wilhelm Reich died, in prison.

In 1958 there were racial disturbances in Nottingham and Notting Hill. The United States Supreme Court ordered Little Rock High School in Arkansas to admit black students. De Gaulle became President of France. The Beatnik movement spread from America to Britain. A thousand electronic computers were in use in America, 160 in all Europe.

Boris Pasternak published *Dr. Zhivago,* and Wittgenstein's *Blue Book* and *Brown Book* appeared. Weber's books on the city, on music, and on the religion of India were translated. Talcott Parsons published an essay on "Authority, Legitimation, and Political Action" in *Authority,* edited by C. J. Friedrich. Alfred Weber died.

In 1959 Battista was driven out of Cuba and Fidel Castro became Premier. The first atomic submarines were launched. The United Nations voted not to admit Communist China and condemned South Africa for its apartheid policies. Norman Mailer published *Advertisements for Myself,* and C. P. Snow "The Two Cultures and the Scientific Revolution." Leavis published "Romantic and Heretic?", an essay on Lawrence. Wolfgang Mommsen published *Max Weber und die deutsche Politik 1890–1920*. This book attacked Weber as a politician obsessed with power. Snow's book attacked that "literary" hostility to science and technology of which Lawrence was a prime representative.

1960–1970

This was a decade of political assassinations and of mass demonstrations of a cultural-revolutionary kind. Max Weber became identified as ideologist of the older generation, while Lawrence became popular among the young.

In 1960 John F. Kennedy was elected President. There was a crisis in the Congo.

In 1961 Patrice Lumumba was killed in the Congo. Dag Hammarskjöld also died there. Adolf Eichmann was found guilty in Israel of crimes against the Jewish people. Yuri Gagarin orbited in space. Carl Gustav Jung died and so did Ernest Hemingway, an apparent suicide. Parsons and others edited a collection, *Theories of Society,* in which a chapter taken from Weber was given great importance. In England *Lady Chatterley's Lover* was judged not obscene. Leavis wrote essays on that novel and a volume of essays on *The Social Theories of Talcott Parsons* was published in America. Regina Ullmann died.

In 1962 Russia and Cuba signed a trade pact. America blockaded Cuba, fearing a build-up of Russian arms there. Eichmann was hanged in Jerusalem. The second Vatican Council began. America had two hundred atomic reactors in operation, Britain and Russia thirty-nine each. Doris Lessing published *The Golden Notebook,* and Alexander Solzhenitsyn *One Day in the Life of Ivan Denisovitch.* Leavis gave his lecture at Cambridge attacking Snow and using Lawrence against him.

In 1963 President Kennedy was assassinated. Britain was refused entry into the Common Market. Martial law was imposed in South Vietnam. Rachel Carson drew attention to man's poisoning of his environment in *Silent Spring.* Günther Grass published *The Tin Drum* and Rolf Hochhuth *The Deputy.* Parsons wrote an introduction to a translation of Weber's *Sociology of Religion,* among other things defending him from current political stigmatization as a conservative. Leavis published *Two Cultures,* his attack on Snow, and an attack on scholarship about Lawrence.

In 1964 there was a Civil Rights March on Washington, and President Lyndon B. Johnson signed the Civil Rights Act. Khrushchev fell from power in Russia. China exploded an atomic bomb. There were race riots in Harlem and heavy fighting in Vietnam. For the centenary of Max Weber's birth there were elaborate intellectual celebrations at Heidelberg. The German Sociologists devoted their fifteenth meeting to him, April 28–30. Parsons and Herbert Marcuse, Raymond Aron and Wolfgang Mommsen gave the main addresses, taking very different attitudes to Weber and provoking violent reactions from a student audience mostly hostile to him. The place of honor on the platform was given to Frau Jaffe. Parsons's lecture praised Weber for having transcended ideology.

In 1965 there were race riots in the Watts district of Los Angeles. Malcolm X was assassinated. American troops were authorized to engage in offensive operations in Vietnam. Project Camelot was set up. Nine African states broke off relations with Britain because she did not use force against racist Rhodesia. Parsons published "Max Weber 1964" in the *American Sociological Review*. Winston Churchill, T. S. Eliot, Le Corbusier, and Albert Schweitzer died.

In 1966 Sinyafsky and Daniel were sentenced to prison in Russia for subversive writings. Jaspers published *Aspekte des Bundesrepublik* an attack on the politics of Bonn, and a warning against feebleness of democratic life in Germany.

In 1967 there was a Six Day War in the Middle East. Britain devalued sterling again. Biafra broke away from Nigeria. There were mercenary-led rebellions in the Congo. There was a cultural revolution in China and a march on the Pentagon. William Mitchell published *Sociological Analysis and Politics: The Theories of Talcott Parsons*. Konrad Adenauer and Krupp von Bohlen died.

In 1968 Robert F. Kennedy and Reverend Martin Luther King, Jr. were assassinated. President Johnson announced he would not run again for office. Senator Eugene McCarthy campaigned for the Presidential nomination as a youth candidate. In Paris there was a revolution in May, of which the dominant student leader was Danny Cohn-Bendit. In Berlin, the S.D.S. leader Rudi Dutschke was severely wounded by a would-be assassin, and there were widespread riots in Germany, led by students. In Czechoslovakia the liberal regime was overthrown by the use of Russian force.

In 1969 there was another big march on Washington. Leavis published *English Literature in our Time and the University,* a series of lectures he had given in 1967 in which he defined Lawrence as "The Necessary Opposite." Émile Delavenay published *D. H. Lawrence: L'Homme et la genèse de son Oeuvre,* an anti-Leavisite and anti-Lawrentian view of Lawrence. Eisenhower died. So did Gropius and Jaspers, Osbert Sitwell and Leonard Woolf.

In 1970 four students were killed at Kent State University when state troopers fired on a group of protesters, and widespread student strikes followed in America. There was a D. H. Lawrence Festival in Taos to commemorate the fortieth anniversary of his death. Bitter opposition arose among the speakers, as at the Weber celebrations, but the student audience was mostly enthusiastic for Lawrence. But in the new Women's Liberation Movement he was attacked. Kate Millett in *Sexual Politics* and Germaine Greer in *The Female Eunuch* followed Otto Gross rather than Lawrence. Alvin W. Gouldner in *The Coming Crisis of Western Sociology* attacked Parsons for making sociology serve the status quo.

Heinrich Brüning and Édouard Daladier, statesmen from the Hitler period, died. So did Aleksandr Kerensky from the Russian Revolution of 1917 and Charles de Gaulle from postwar France. The United Arab Republic's Gamal Abdul Nasser, Indonesia's Sukarno, and Portugal's Antonio Salazar died. E. M. Forster and Bertrand Russell died.

Else Jaffe lived on.

Part Three

Consequences, 1930–1970

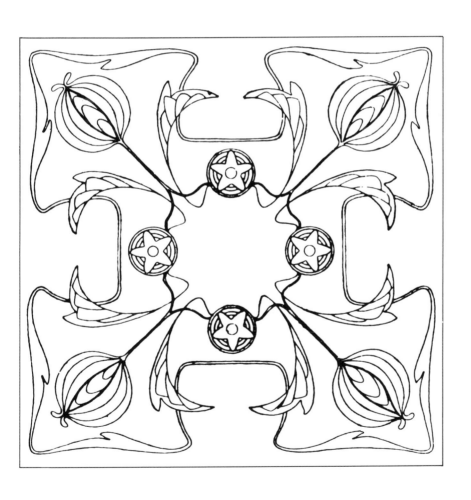

3

The Sisters: Their Lives
Continued and Compared

In 1930, both the sisters still had half their adult lives to live, half their diverging curves of adventure to complete. And "diverging curves" remained an appropriate figure. Though they were both "settling down" in these years, they were not drawing closer to the average or to each other, in spirit any more than in place. Robert Lucas, in his biography of Frieda, tells an anecdote which indirectly shows how the distances and differences between them were likely to grow broader now that Lawrence was gone. Soon after he died in Vence, Frieda became very worried about the health of her daughter Barbara, who came to stay with her there. The girl was depressed and irritable to the point of psychic sickness, physically feverish and enfeebled and prone to fainting. Frieda decided that the doctors were not helping the cause, and devised a sexual remedy; she sent a young Italian stonemason to make love to Barbara as she lay sick in bed. This stonemason, named Nicola, was one of the workmen she was employing to carve the phoenix on Lawrence's gravestone at Vence, and the whole incident is so like and unlike Lawrence's own faith in sex that it is bound to make us reflect on the differences between their two "uses" of eroticism. After all, sending such a man to such a girl's bed is just what Lawrence had done imaginatively, in *The Virgin and the Gypsy*, which was written just before he died and was after all, *about* Barbara. But that was a work of the imagination, a work of art. One feels that Lawrence would not have done what Frieda did, or allowed her to do it. But why not? Out of some sort of prudence or tact, surely, not out of principle. Else's response to the news makes that clearer. Frieda told her sisters what she had done, when they all met at their mother's deathbed in November of that year, and Dr. Lucas says that Else was shocked into declaring that *her* daughter should have died rather than be cured that way. There is a clear difference of principle here, and it was one that was bound to get sharper now that Frieda did not have Lawrence to restrain her. But that difference did not express itself so much in the form of conflict in the years to come. Their lives curved away from each other, and we must bring them together under the rubric of contrast—broad, not detailed, contrast.

In the second halves of their life spans, the sisters lived less adventurously and eventfully than before, and we shall not report in detail what happened to them during those years. We are interested rather in the ideological implications of the life style which each had chosen and which answered, however "naturally," to her beliefs. They had each chosen a settled pattern of living and an environment, which we shall characterize by describing two leading personalities in each case, a man and a woman who stood close to each sister. The word used in the Weber circle for the phenomenon which we are concerned with was "constellation"; Alfred Weber made much use of the term in his sociology of culture to show how people and values significantly group themselves and interrelate; and Else Jaffe used the term to describe her own life course, by speaking of the Weber-Heidelberg constellation, "in which my star also stands." By characterizing these various constellations, we hope also to characterize the sisters' ideas and values, which they continued to serve as before, though in a less "heroic" style.

After the deaths of Max Weber and Edgar Jaffe, Else went back to Heidelberg, and eventually went to live with Alfred Weber. After the death of D. H. Lawrence, Frieda went back to Taos and took to live with her Angelo Ravagli. Ravagli had owned the Villa Mirenda, which Frieda and Lawrence had rented often between 1925 and 1928. She bought him out of the Italian army, where he had been a captain, and he separated from his wife, a schoolteacher, and went away with Frieda to New Mexico. She wanted, she said later, to see what he would make of the Rockies and what the Rockies would make of him. Officially her business partner, in reality he had no head for business or for any official matters. He worked on the ranch and painted. He was, it seems, a sensitive, honorable, and original man, temperamentally authentic, but not in the least an intellectual. Nor was he in the least a man of blood and iron. He was somewhat the same type as Baron von Richthofen—to Anglo-Saxon eyes, an anomaly as an army officer. Frieda had found her father again, in a man considerably younger than herself.

Alfred Weber was a professor, who became a *Herr Geheimrat*, head of the Institute of Sociology in Heidelberg, subject of two *Festschriften*, author of over two hundred and ninety books and articles, a sociologist of culture, an intellectual of intellectuals.

Alfred Weber and Angelo Ravagli were very unlike each other; and yet, seen in relation to the sisters, they show a certain similarity. Both could be said to be more managable versions of their predecessors—more limited, less impressive, less imaginatively challenging. And both allowed the women to enact the roles they had chosen for themselves more comfortably or at least more satisfyingly than was possible with those predecessors. By reading for Alfred Weber and reporting on books, by reading aloud to him, by translating for him from French and English, by simplifying his style in German, by traveling with him to art museums, churches, castles, in Italy—in all these ways Else was able to serve *Geist*. In dedicating his *Kulturgeschichte als Kultursoziologie* to her, he paid tribute to all that activity and work. Living and working with him, she continued to be an active part of Hedelberg. He was of a harsh and difficult temperament, not generally sociable, and jealous even of her children's claims on her. But she seems to have found satisfaction in half-sacrificing herself to him, and through him to *Geist*.

Frieda assertively did not want to sacrifice herself and seems to have found in her companion a true servant of Magna Mater and priest of her own mysteries. In 1970, in a newspaper interview, Ravagli was reported as brooding over a complete illustrated series of *Immortal Women of the World* and saying, "Women, women. All my life I love women. Now I'm too old. Tutto finito." Frieda's letters and memoirs show her sometimes lamenting his lack of interest in ideas and exercising protective responsibility and authority over him in worldly and financial matters, on occasion even finding him loyal to the world of men—he insisted, to her dismay, that the experience of fighting in the Great War had been something great. But by and large he gave her what she wanted. Living with him, she continued to be a part of the Taos enterprise, as her sister was part of Heidelberg.

Both sisters, however, also continued to "live with" the great men who had played such decisive and disruptive parts in their lives. In "The Border Line" Lawrence had predicted just such a divided future for Frieda after his death. The business affairs in which Captain Ravagli was officially supposed to be Frieda's partner were mostly those of the D. H. Lawrence estate. Even the purely financial aspects of that estate became large and complex over the years, because of reprint rights, film rights, dramatizations, collected and selected editions, as well as the posthumous volumes which appeared all through the thirties. His reputation among literary critics was an even more living presence, first as his life and works were interpreted and evaluated by those who had known him personally—notably the books by John Middle-

ton Murry, Mabel Luhan, Dorothy Brett, Catherine Carswell, Frieda herself—and later as he became the subject of studies by professional critics and
scholars. Who Lawrence really was, what he really said, which of the things
that happened after his death he would have approved, these questions continued to stir up passions of admiration and anger throughout Frieda's lifetime, and a large proportion of the people who came to see her must have
had something to say about them. It was understandable that Captain
Ravagli often felt that he had heard enough about Lawrence.

There was just as much ferment in Germany about Max Weber, but
Else Jaffe was not the official widow; moreover, Marianne Weber very much
was that. "Max Weber's desk is now my altar," she writes in her *Lebenserinnerungen*, describing the first decade after his death. She went back to
Munich for anniversaries of his death, and her prose about those occasions—
written at the time, no doubt, but printed in 1948—is full of tears. Some of
her exclamations are addressed to Else Jaffe and give us glimpses of the relations between the two women. Daily, weekly, monthly, she says, they
evoked Max Weber's presence to each other—his manner of speech, his
clothes, all the details of his being. Speaking of those drowning tears, she
says, "You, Else, then sealed off their source for me." We are prompted to
see Frau Jaffe yet again in her life offering supportive reassurance to a self-
dramatizer, but this time the lock-gates of ironic awareness and self-denial
must have narrowed the stream of sympathy dangerously. The sympathy
was there nonetheless, apparently. Marianne and Else remained loyal to each
other through another thirty-five years, and loyal to each other's silences.

Marianne and Alfred Weber will be interesting figures for us to place in
the background of our main grouping of principals, both because they literally and factually constituted so much of Else's environment, her constellation, her Heidelberg, and because they symbolically represent roads not taken
by Frieda, by Lawrence, by Otto Gross.

Marianne

Marianne's mother had been a Weber by birth, a niece of Max's father. She
made an unfortunate marriage at nineteen and died at twenty-four. The
marriage was unfortunate in that her husband had soon shown himself
insanely jealous and suspicious. While Marianne was living with her grandmother and aunts, effectively an orphan, she saw two of her father's brothers
become completely insane and have to be institutionalized. These early experiences no doubt predisposed her to melancholy and nervousness, and per-

haps also to that aversion from all ugliness and brutality which was so strong in her as to be a kind of unrealism. Whatever its source, she certainly had a fairy princess quality of being unacquainted with evil, which she kept all her life long. This called forth from some protective chivalry and from others contempt and hostility, just as it did with Princess figures in Lawrence's novels. (Miriam in *Sons and Lovers* was sometimes known as the Princess, and the story of that title deals, in sexual terms, with this quality of artificial, though quite genuine, innocence.) It is this quality that reminds us, as we noted in Section 2, of the Anna in Gottfried Keller's *Der Grüne Heinrich*.

As a "mind," however, measured in terms of average contemporary opinion, Marianne Weber was a bold radical. She had loved her schooldays and her schoolteachers, and she rebelled against the middle-class domesticity of Bielefeld, the Westphalian city where she spent her childhood, when she returned there. She needed the life of the mind. She decided to train for a profession and her family agreed to let her go to Berlin to live with the Max Webers in order to find one. This was in 1892, when such a move was a bold step for a young girl. She was encouraged in her ambitions by Helene Weber, for whom she conceived a great admiration. Her first book, *Ehefrau*, in 1907, was dedicated to Helene. It was Helene she loved before Max, and that relationship in a sense set the pattern for the second, the marital, love. (Marianne was all her life a girl capable of "crushes"—which is to say she was all her life a girl.) Helene had known Marianne's mother, who had gone to school in Heidelberg and had been made welcome at the Fallenstein house there. Marianne's life, also, therefore, was in a sense a "return to Heidelberg."

She and Max were married in 1893. Her book makes it clear that she offered him total devotion, a kind of worship, from the time of their first meetings. She was intelligent enough to appreciate his strengths, too innocent to recognize his weaknesses, ardent enough to devote her life to him, meek enough to like being the weaker. It was a match made in Heaven—or Heidelberg, as Lawrence might have said. Although not literally a match made by Max's mother, who had had other plans for both of them, once Helene got used to the idea she could not but be delighted to see her two favorites complementing each other. Marianne's devotion immensely fortified Max, and he on his part was willing and able to give her that which she *thought* she wanted—an intellectual career and intellectual freedom—no ordinary marital subordination or domestic drudgery. That he could not give her his desire, nor she him her desirableness, was a tragedy; but perhaps no more of a tragedy than was bound to occur one way or another because of the wounds inflicted on them early in life. Both Max and Marianne were prizes by the conventional standards of the marriage market. She was a very pretty woman in a piquantly schoolgirlish style, small and dainty, always simply and neatly dressed, with large, dark, and eloquent eyes set in irregular features, and a voice that remained young and silvery after her hair turned gray. Joined together, they made a handsome and impressive couple, exempt from criticism. Moreover, they were really devoted to each other.

He soon received his first major appointment, at Freiburg in 1895. It was there that both of them, but at first particularly Marianne, became close friends with Else von Richthofen. Else was four years younger than Marianne and may have been grateful and admiring in those first years of the friendship, for the two girls had the same ambitions, which were at that time then shared, or at least actively pursued, by few women. Moreover, Marianne was an intelligent and industrious student, her temperament quite ardently submissive to, responsive to, the disciplines of *Wissenschaft*. Possibly she may have "done better" than Else in the university courses they took together. But Else's was the stronger mind, more independent, more variable, more mature, with a greater range of experience and a greater capacity for sardonic judgment. Else often shocked Marianne, and Marianne enjoyed it. Else had early learned to take the measure of men and institutions which Marianne had to be taught to criticize, and then could criticize only by rote. On the other hand, it was Marianne who went ahead and wrote books, had a career in politics, and became a leader of the Women's Movement. Else's skepticism and melancholy prevented her from acting in the world of men—to which of course the Women's Movement belonged—as much as from believing in the world of Woman. She lived on the borders and on the sidelines. She *served*.

Marianne completed and published her book on marriage and the legal position of women through the ages in 1907, the year of the affair between Gross and Frieda and Else, the year of Gross's sudden impact on Heidelberg. At the same time she also began to give lectures on marriage and to write essays on the different forms of love relationship, the decay of morals, the differences between the sexes, and so on. She became a major spokesman for Heidelberg—for liberalism—on these issues. She was their David—except that, dressed in the giant armor of Max's arguments, she looked like Goliath —against Gross.

In her "Sexual-ethische Prinzipienfragen" of 1907, she declares it absurd to judge marital arrangements by the criterion of perfect happiness, fulfilment, or harmony; a general harmony between what is natural and what ought to be has never existed anywhere. Conflict is our unavoidable fate, wherever men strive for spiritual and moral culture. "A man can be greater than his guilt only if he takes that guilt as a great and serious matter," she writes. Then, sounding even more like Max, she adds, "A moral norm is no more to be deduced from what the average man does, than a scientific truth from what he believes." Nowadays, she points out, we see around us a sexual-ethical skepticism, which derives partly from a sense of the beauty and nobility of the erotic, but partly also from the desire, prevalent in contemporary medical circles, to treat sex as a matter of hygiene. We must of course reform the marriage laws and eliminate patriarchal tyranny, but we also must agree that a great passion can exist only in an erotic relationship which at least believes in its own permanence. Of course, a man's nobility is not disproved by his failing to achieve what he has earnestly striven after, and we must admit that we are living in a period of great sexual tension. However, marriages cannot be lightly dissolved, no matter how great the mutual frustration of husband and wife. Children need two parents. (One must think of Else Jaffe reading these arguments, and indeed of these ideas being hammered out in discussions of and with her.) Moreover, sexual desire is not necessarily and of itself noble, Marianne continues. It often happens that ". . . every unfettering of the sexual passions means a brutalizing of the feelings, and that it is the woman who has to pay the price of that brutality." Women must learn a calling, a *Beruf*, in order to gain the education in dignity and self-reliance which comes with that. "German mothers should educate their daughters to spiritual and economic independence, but also to demand high ethical standards of the men who woo them." They must deny love and respect to those who claim a right to sexual gratification on hygienic grounds. (We do not know if Frieda read this, but it is quite likely that it was recommended to her while she was wrestling with the question of whether to leave Weekley.) The central formula is pure Heidelberg: "Not, then, a substitute *for* marriage, but a reform *of* marriage."

Marianne insisted in that essay that prostitution exists among primitive peoples. Three years earlier she had discussed the whole theory of *Mutterrecht*, "because so many people treat it as a kind of Paradise Lost." This earlier essay was written before Gross was known in Heidelberg, so it was intended as an attack on the theories of Engels or of the *kosmische Runde*. In it, she argues that one can still find *Mutterrecht* existing today—wherever a man cannot or will not give his woman the rank of wife. Of course, we must resist the excesses of *Vaterrecht,* but that has been a necessary stage in the development of individualism, and there is no historical evidence for the much-loved theory that men invented monogamy for their own advantage in order to have heirs and thus achieve a kind of immortality. Here again, then, Marianne recommends resistance to the evils of one policy but not the following of its opposite.

In "Die Frau und die objective Kultur" of 1913, she speaks quite eloquently about the dangers of *Beruf*: "We see today how often the man active in his calling gets submerged in the prosaic—not in the great sense of sacrificing himself for something greater, but in such a way that his human substance is slowly consumed away through the inescapable excess of daily demands by his business, which has ceased to be his creation and servant and become his master." Women must realize what *Beruf* means before eagerly claiming a vocation. And even when they do, they must still discharge their old and opposite duty. A wife must stand between a man's ideals and his self-dissatisfaction: "His disharmony she must counter with her harmony, his specialization with her wholeness, his submission to the objective with her submission to the living." This is a prescription which fits the Weber relationships, between Max and Marianne, between Alfred and Else. Otto Gross and Frieda, on the other hand, believed that men should renounce the domination by *Beruf*, rather than that women should soften its impact upon them.

In "Authority and Autonomy in Marriage," an essay written in 1909, Marianne insists that women too now feel the need to work with men, to build together with them, in the suprapersonal world of culture. This is the drive that sends Ursula Brangwen out into the "Widening Circles" of *The Rainbow*, a drive felt by both Else and Frieda von Richthofen. But in Frieda it was soon supplanted, or transformed, under Otto Gross's tutelage. And the world followed Frieda. Thus in "The Personality Change in the Woman Student," an essay written eight years later, Marianne admits that things are no longer as they were. Women students used to be militant about their rights and to dress soberly, in almost masculine style. Now they are ultra-feminine and seek love above all things. We have now the "romantic type" of woman student who longs to be touched by Eros more than anything else, and is explicit about matters which used to be left unmentioned. Thus Marianne Weber records the impact of the erotic movement. She warns that, because love always means more to a woman than to a man, this new eroticism, this opening of oneself toward Eros, is dangerous for women.

As long as Max was alive, Marianne was his spokeswoman. His ideas and even his phrases are discernible in her work. But her real talent was for modestly impressionistic accounts of men and ideas. When her subject is impressive enough to challenge her skills (as it is in her biography of her husband, *Max Weber, ein Lebensbild*) the transparent medium she creates is a genuine achievement. But as a judge of ideas or men, as an assimilator of experience, she is negligible. Women like Frieda (not to mention men like Gross) must have seen in Marianne's career striking proof that the world of men would call "significant" and "serious" only those women who never dared to be anything of themselves, of their female selves, women who agreed to be always pupils in the world of men. But Marianne too represented something, *was* what she was so intensely as to become a living idea. She was all feminine—not female—winsomeness, an incarnate occasion for chivalry—and yet clear-minded, hard-working, self-subordinated to the social purpose.

But it was not only such bold spirits as Gross who were irritated by Marianne. She was protected by powerful personalities like her husband, and by social conventions, from real contact with much of "life"—that is, from challenges which others had to meet. What is more, she tended to take on airs of authority which provoked the resentment of the young. At Frau Professor Rickert's sixtieth birthday party in the 1920s, where speeches had been deprecated and were otherwise avoided, Marianne nevertheless felt moved to rise and address the group about love and the Frau Professor as an incarnation of love; Frau Rickert, painfully blushing, found herself transformed, finally, into one of those *Ewig-Weibliche* great lovers who fluttered round Faust's soul on its way up to God. Other guests were indignant. And at her regular gatherings of intellectuals, Marianne would sweetly remind, one by one, all the ladies who had forgotten to remove their hats that it would be much nicer for everyone if they did so. She was a dainty tyrant in her small sweet way.

Her Sunday teas were a center of Heidelberg intellectual life right through the Nazi era and into the war, from 1924 to 1944, although under the Nazis they stopped temporarily and then resumed, but as a more private occasion, with fewer students attending. But they were still intellectual occasions, and during the Nazi years it was there, rather than within the university, that the traditions of the old Heidelberg were best preserved. A lecture was given and discussion followed. Jaspers and Alfred Weber spoke there, as did Ludwig Curtius, Friedrich Gundolf, Thomas Mann, and Martin Dibelius. Marianne was keeping alive—the implications of sickness are not inappropriate—the old Webers' Heidelberg in the new Germany.

But young people after 1918 were especially irritated by her role as authority on love and sexuality, subjects of which her demeanor proclaimed to them her ignorance. *Die Ideale der Geschlechtergemeinschaft* was published in 1929, the year Lawrence's "A Propos of *Lady Chatterley's Lover*" was written; both essays defend marriage in a rather "modernized traditional" way. Lawrence was becoming more conservative as Marianne was becoming more liberal. But her essay looks extremely feeble beside his. In such matters, and others, Heidelberg was not able to move with the times. It no longer represented the new thought of Europe.

One particular manifestation of Heidelberg's general weakness was the fact that not even Alfred Weber, who knew Lawrence, nor Else Jaffe, who translated his work into German, was able to appreciate him. By their criteria, he was not a writer or a thinker to take seriously. They cherished essentially older—essentially old-fashioned—models of intelligence and seriousness. Thus Lawrence wrote to Else in 1929 that he would not send her *Lady Chatterley's Lover* because he knew that she belonged "to the opposite direction in things of this sort." She would call the book "satanisch," whereas he himself felt that ". . . Lucifer is brighter now than tarnished Michael or shabby Gabriel. . . . Yes, I am all for Lucifer, who is really the Morning Star. . . . I agree with you in a sense, that I am with the anti-Christ. Only I am not anti-life." Frau Jaffe admits that she did not then believe in Lawrence's genius and knew at the time that they belonged to hostile worlds. In an interview in 1967 she said, "I admired and respected and was very fond of Lawrence. But I must say quite honestly that I didn't feel as such his extreme importance. Now more. I shouldn't say now, but *later* more. Because I did come from an intellectual world, so that my standards for judging were different, somewhat different." Indeed, she still finds his books wordy and the dialogue bad. She took Frieda more seriously than Lawrence, but not as an intellectual. She translated Frieda's *Not I But the Wind* into German soon after it appeared in English, but she made several changes, not only omitting whole letters but also altering sentences to make them more discreet or correct. She was, she admits, used to editing and correcting Frieda because she had done so all her life. It must of course have been galling to her that she should have to serve Frieda, even in the realm of books.

It is typical that both Alfred and Marianne Weber were always much concerned about the duty of the educated class in the community to give a moral lead which the lower classes should follow, though they often refuse to do so. Alfred Weber's disciples and sympathizers are often to be found discussing questions like "Have Americans a culture of their own?" Alfred and his followers were much concerned about elites and the training of national leaders. Their idea of culture was rooted in privilege as well as in responsibility, and their idea of its nourishment was traditional—the best that has been thought and said, and the great works of art of the past. The last great men, said Weber, were Goethe and Beethoven. In the nineteenth century only destructive geniuses like Nietzsche were possible. This ideology or sensibility is very appropriate to its place of origin, of course, a place steeped in cultural privilege. "Have Americans a culture of their own?" is a very Heidelberg question.

But Marianne Weber had an intellectual career of her own after Max died, which she carried on in addition to her efforts at preserving the prewar tradition. She set to work to collect her husband's papers immediately after his death, and the bulk of his published work appeared under her editing during the twenties. Then came her largest book, *Max Weber, ein Lebensbild,* published 1926, in which she made much of their marriage. The self-praise is not crass, but the Webers appear in the book as an exemplary married couple for liberal Germany. At the same time she allied herself with Karl Jaspers, who was building his existentialist moralism out of his sense of Max Weber. Jaspers helped Marianne in many ways and often spoke on the subject of Max Weber at her house.

Then, during the late twenties, Marianne had a friendship with Peter Wust, a Catholic philosopher of religion who, though married, found in her an inspiring Virgin Mother. "Dear little mother Marianne," he wrote her, "hold your dear pure woman's hands protectingly over my ever endangered life." Wust was a small, nervous, insecure man, with intense, troubled, and spiritual eyes, embarrassed on all "social" occasions, rather like the curé de campagne in Georges Bemanos's celebrated novel. He was a friend of Max Scheler's, the Catholic Nietzsche, but also of Henri Brémond, Jacques Maritain, and Paul Claudel, all spokesmen for a current of thought in many ways critical of and hostile to Max Weber, who was taken to be a champion of secularized and fragmented Western rationalism. Walter Theodor Cleve, who, as we saw in Chapter 2, blamed Weber for Alfred Seidel's suicide, was a disciple of Wust. Marianne Weber's turning to Wust no doubt owed something to her greater sympathy with world-renouncing religion in the years of Germany's collapse.

Predictably enough, however, she did not care to see her image reflected exactly as she projected it, at least in eyes so like her own, however fervent the accompanying feeling. She was more comfortable with larger, stronger, fatherly men, and gradually let the relationship with Wust lapse. But he seems to have been the second man in her life, comparable with Alfred Weber in Else's or Middleton Murry (briefly) in Frieda's. It was an intense relationship while it lasted. His comments on finding himself in Max Weber's house, making love—most spiritually—to Max Weber's wife (he read her the Marienbad elegy and cherished the memory in subsequent letters), are very country-mouse in style. But already his very first letter to her was extraordinarily passionate, intimate, flattering, self-abasing, even though they had only just met. Both Lawrence and Weber would have felt the same impatience with his whole performance, and one can apply to it some of Lawrence's harshest comments on Murry. Even Marianne, though dedicated to the death of all impatience and all harshness, and though not unlike Wust in her own behavior, showed some uneasiness.

In the 1930s Marianne was involved with another religious enterprise.

She joined Die Köngener, a religious Youth Movement whose members wore gay unconventional clothes and danced and made music together, but whose purpose was nothing less than to rescue Christianity, or to rescue a living faith *from* Christianity for Germany. They held Work Weeks, in which representatives of various viewpoints came and spoke, and discussions followed. Marianne spoke on love and marriage. C. G. Jung and Martin Buber and Gertrud Baümler came, and a Nazi, a Communist, a Roman Catholic. Marianne sometimes spoke as the representative of old-fashioned individualism. In 1933 Jakob Wilhelm Hauer, the leader, joined with Graf Ernst zu Reventlow, Fanny's brother, to head the Study Group on German Belief and the League of Free Believers, with Nazi blessing. Both were organizations trying to save the working classes from communism. Most Köngener refused to enter these organizations and remained under the leadership of the second in command, Rudi Daur, a minister.*

Marianne first attended the group's meetings in 1930 and they continued until 1940, but Hitler was not to be stopped nor the problems of Germany solved by such means. Nevertheless, Marianne was making her contribution, doing her bit for the public weal. She was still "a remarkable woman." While Frieda Lawrence, in Taos, scarcely read a newspaper, Marianne Weber was still active in the world of men. And in the forties she was still a figure in Heidelberg intellectual life. Soon after the first American troops entered the town in 1945, she was visited by former students of Talcott Parsons at Harvard, and she sat late into the night with them, discussing such large historical issues as German war-guilt. In 1946 she published her most ambitious book, *Erfülltes Leben*, a work of homespun philosophizing and moralizing which had failed to find a publisher during the war. Soon she began preparing her *Lebenserinnerungen* for publication.

Else Jaffe remained her friend. In 1930, the year of Lawrence's death, came Marianne's sixtieth birthday and intellectual Heidelberg celebrated her *Altersfest*. Jaspers gave a speech again about Max Weber, and among the lavish celebrations was a skit about her acted by her friends and family, in which Marianne was portrayed as a Prioress who gets elected the world's first female Pope. Else Jaffe acted the part of Marianne. The various ironies must have made a thick brew. In 1940, for the second *Altersfest,* this time in Bavaria, Else again attended and recited verses she had written for the occasion. And in 1954, as Marianne lay sick for the last time, at eighty-four, it was Else's hand she held and Else's name she whispered as she died. Their fates had indeed been profoundly intertwined. Marianne had in some

* Hauer's "German religion" was discussed by T. S. Eliot in 1939 as one of the major modern heresies.

sense cheated Else of her happiness. No wonder that the latter was so deeply moved—moved to the point of indiscretion for once—when she wrote to Frieda Lawrence about that death. It was a "Christian," a religious feeling for Marianne which she expressed: "You know how close, how mysteriously close, was the bond between us—no, not was, but *is*—but still, the separation is profoundly significant. I have always been clear, that when Marianne died, then the constellation in which my star also stands would sink below the horizon." She meant, of course, the Weber-Heidelberg constellation. Alfred Weber was still alive, but perhaps—there are other hints to make one think this—perhaps Frau Jaffe's strongest *feelings* went toward women. Marianne's death was one of the climaxes of her later life.

Alfred

The other major event of Else's old age must have been the death of Alfred Weber, in 1958, at the age of ninety, though the intense discretion shrouding their relationship forbids our asserting much about it. Else von Richthofen first met Max Weber's short, handsome, excitable, irritable brother in Berlin before 1900, when she was studying there. He had begun his intellectual career by studying art history, but he was, when she met him, following very much in Max's footsteps—as she herself was. He had written a thesis on the sweating system in the confectionery industry, which derived from work he had done for the *Verein für Sozialpolitik*. In 1900 he gave his Inaugural Address at Berlin University on the economic problems of home industry. In 1909 he published his *Industrielle Standorts-theorie* on the siting of factories, which has been accepted as an important contribution to economic theory. It was translated into English and consulted in Russia by Bolshevik planners. But even by the time it was in print he was turning to sociology, again like Max, but with a characteristic concentration on the problem of the fine arts and high culture in general. He was more aesthetic than Max, in general taste and temperament, as well as in his style of self-expression.

In Berlin he had worked in close contact with Gustav Schmoller, the academic socialist, in his economic work, and one of his teachers at Bonn had been Karl Lamprecht, who was then introducing a new historiography which stressed the conflict between the political and the cultural interest, and which investigated the socioeconomic substructure of cultural history. In his *Moderne Geschichtewissenschaft* (1905) and *Einführung in das historische Denken* (1913) Lamprecht tried to show the sociopsychological development of man *inside* the large social units and called for a study of the economic conditions favorable to intellectual development. Inasmuch as these are themes of Alfred Weber's later work, we may see his work as in part a response to Lamprecht's stimulus. But the antirationalist, antipositivist spirit of the times affected him even more through its expression in philosophy and the arts. Bergson's antitheses of Reason to Intuition, of Space to Time, of Matter to Life, strongly influenced many of Weber's world in the prewar years, even among sociologists, who were in some sense committed to "science." (At least, Max Weber insisted that they were.) Georg Simmel as well as Alfred Weber spoke of the immanence of the transcendent in vital processes. Graf Hermann von Keyserling, Max Scheler, and Oswald Spengler all were influenced by *Lebensphilosophie*, but the idea of devising a sociology of culture, a positivistic study of the categorically free spirit of life, was a response to the division in himself characteristic of Alfred Weber in particular.

It seems to be true that he was in love with Else von Richthofen from before 1900, but that there was no question of marriage. (She got engaged in 1900, briefly, but it was to someone else.) Soon thereafter Alfred went on a trip to Hawaii, and after he returned was appointed to Prague University. He was there only three years, but when he came to Heidelberg in 1907— that fateful year in our story—he gave himself out a changed man, a rebel against his mother's teachings, who symbolized his apartness by living at the other end of town from Max and Marianne. Perhaps his main motive for doing this was to get away from "der grosse Max," for it seems clear that the dominant theme of his life was the cruel and crippling competition with that preferred sibling. (When Max lay delirious in 1920, he grasped at a glass of milk, muttering, "Give it to me quickly, or Alfred will suck it all away." Everything, even Else von Richthofen, became an object of competition between them.) In fact, Max had recommended Simmel for the post that Alfred finally got, which must have reinforced the "personal" motive for keeping apart from him.

But it is also true that Alfred had acquired a new *Weltanschauung* while he was in Prague. He had gone over much more completely than Max ever did to the ideas of *Lebensphilosophie*, using the term loosely to cover all the schools of "life values" then current in advanced circles, particularly in Austria. He had become a favorite teacher and friend to Max Brod and his friends in Prague, who made up the Jewish literary circle which Otto Gross was to frequent, and to influence, a decade later. In his autobiography, Brod gives us one of the rare descriptions of Alfred (he also portrayed him as Professor Westertag in his novel, *Jugend im Nebel*). Alfred was, Brod says, of middle size but strongly built, with a powerful step and jerky movements. His face was full, even sumptuous, with its red cheeks, dark brown beard, sharp-cut features, and small but sparkling eyes deep-set above the cheeks. He was, though not big and blond, a very German type, dark, nervous, irritable, always pulling together his disordered faculties in order to achieve something intellectually significant. Brod spread the word of this phenomenon—he compared him with Schopenhauer and Dehmel—among his friends and made Alfred's lectures fashionable in Prague intellectual circles.

One gets some sense of Alfred's speaking style from one of his lecture-essays of 1926, "Der Deutsche in geistigen Europa." Addressing the intellectual representatives of the various European countries at an international conference, he presents what Germany has to offer the rest of Europe as a vision of youth, seen by a generation reared on Nietzsche, but not nihilist, a generation full of potential faith and not really represented by the cynical art of their times. These are no blond beasts, though they are the opposite of mentalized humanity or footnote-stuffed scholars. He contrasts them with more conventional manifestations of the spiritual life, and appeals for generosity from the representatives of other countries. "But why should they not mean something spiritual to us? Why should we not?"—he rises to a crescendo of rhetorical questions—"Why finally should we not rise above this low tide of vulgarity? The true virtue of a spiritual aristocracy is a mutual admiration—let that be our posture. Let us make each other no empty compliments. But let us look each other in the eye. . . . Messieurs les Anglais, tirez les premiers . . . [etc.]" Clearly, Alfred Weber was a self-exciting speaker.

In Heidelberg before the war, his home became a center for the George disciples there. These people were essentially hostile to Max Weber, so that the two brothers moved in circles that were largely separate. Erich von Kahler, the George disciple who wrote the major attack on Max's "Wissenschaft als Beruf," had been a student of Alfred. In these years Alfred began his close relationship with Else Jaffe, who was, of course, intimate with Max and Marianne. He rented a house near Frau Jaffe's in Irschenhausen—the house lived in by Lawrence and Frieda in 1912—and took long trips with her through Italy.

He did not go over to *Lebensphilosophie* wholeheartedly. Involuntarily, he remained loyal also to his brother's opposite values. He was deeply committed to political action in the conventional sense, a commitment which was alien to his "aesthetic" friends. In Prague he was a friend of Thomáš Masaryk, the Czech philosopher-statesman, and in Heidelberg of Friedrich Ebert, the future President of the Reich. He had been deeply impressed by

Theodor Mommsen, after whom he modeled himself in some respects, and
the motto of his life might well have been the pessimistic stoicism of this
passage from Mommsen's testament, a passage he often cited: "I believe that
with the best part of me I have always been an *animal politicum,* and
wanted to be a citizen. That is not possible in our nation, where an individual, even the best of individuals, does not rise above servile service and
political idolatry." Like Max, Alfred was always deeply drawn to and at the
same time repelled by the image of Bismarck. About ninety of his publications deal with political issues current at the time of writing. Bismarck himself recurs as a subject in Alfred's writings more often than he does in
Max's.

Nevertheless, around 1909 Alfred was talking about German destiny in
cultural terms that were assertively *not* political in the conventional sense. In
"Der Kulturtypus und seine Wandlung" he said that the great period in
German history came around 1800, when educated Germans of the Goethean
generation were displaying great depths and complexities of being. By contrast, the 1848 type had no inner conflicts; everything in them was exterior-
ized and politicized. In turn, their values were reversed in their successors,
the type created by Bismarck, in whom realism and opportunism replaced
idealism and liberalism. Thus there came into being the physically and
psychically crew-cut, the "kurzgeschorene," the energetically organizing
"realist" of the new Germany. Even *this* type, Alfred pointed out, had some
feeling for community values, but nowadays we have only the tradesman of
life, and his opposite counterpart, the aesthete.

In "Der Beamte" of 1910 he analyzed bureaucracy as the giant force that
poisoned everything. Presenting the statistics of its growth at the lower levels
of the economy which we gave in Chapter 1, he deplored the current seduction of the upper classes into the ranks of officialdom. Their exchange of
freedom for comfort and security was all the more lamentable because they
were the nation's *Kulturträger.* The only escape from this domination by
bureaucracy must lie in our escaping from rationalization as a whole. So our
new criterion must be the individual person. Things must be held valuable
insofar as they serve the individual and his personal life, and no further. For
this reason we don't want communism, however dissatisfied we are with
capitalism. What we want is to keep our faith in freedom, to keep our limbs
supple and the soil prepared, ready for the future dance.

Here we recognize the same ideas as in the *Religion und Kultur* essay
of 1912, and we see again how close to Lawrence—or at least to Edward
Carpenter—he then was. His political concerns, and the whole half of his
nature which followed Max, seemed to have no relation to all this. His

chariot was drawn by two very different horses, striving to go in different directions, and both, at this point in his life, were spirited steeds. This conflict of directions was something recurrent in his life, but at different times it was more or less profitable.

The outbreak of war recalled him to realism and patriotism and the patriarchal virtues; although a version of realism and patriarchalism that was, to some degree shaped by the principles of *Lebensphilosophie*. Germany is going to be a warrior nation for a long time yet, he declared in *Gedanken zur deutschen Sendung* in 1915, dismissing French and English liberalism— *Ratio and Rationalismus* are the banners of the Allies—and announcing that the significant opponent, from whom Germany might learn something valuable, was Russia, with her barbaric, sensual-mystical freedom from the tyranny of reason. He often quotes Dostoevski. The English gentleman type must no longer dominate the world. The war has introduced a new era, just as the Revolution of 1789 did. The age of democracy is over now. By virtue of its robust *Urnatur*, its closeness to the "pristine and eternal Sources," Germany alone among European nations had seen through the false idealism of "democracy." Weber's ideas and tone are very like those of Thomas Mann's contemporary writings on the war. Mann's essay on Frederick the Great was published in the same series, in fact. (Max Weber was contemptuous of this set of ideas—the "German ideas of 1914," as they are called. He held by his skeptical faith in parliamentary democracy.)

After the war Alfred Weber confessed the weakness of his and his friends' wartime position. Their criticism of democracy had been too external and too aesthetic. He had interpreted democracy to be all machinery, a political fraud perpetrated by capitalism. He and his friends had not seen its soul, its development of man's consciousness. Thus they could not create what they had wanted, a post-democratic national faith. "It was not to be found. We must have failed in the necessary closeness to life," he concluded. Life was still the supreme value, we see, but now it was explicitly combined with orthodox political concerns, which have, nonetheless, no temperamental affinity with it. The philosophy Weber gradually shaped for himself was essentially eclectic; in terms of temperament as well as in terms of ideology it was full of incompatibilities. Its total form expressed no organic life within.

Alfred moved in the circle of Prince Max von Baden, a leading liberal who served as the last Chancellor under Wilhelm II, and he took some part in the founding of a new party in 1918, as we have seen. But he soon withdrew, for he was not of a suitable temperament for active participation in politics. He devoted himself to his sociology of culture, which was an attempt to do justice to both the aesthetic and the societal aspects of works of art—to understand, for instance, Michelangelo's David both in the splendor of beauty which lifts it above its rivals and also in that similarity of origin which roots it among them. He tried to arouse Europe's consciousness of its cultural heritage to a pitch of intensity we usually associate with a political faith. This was his version of keeping Heidelberg's mission alive.

In order to bring Weber's culture sociology into line with our scheme of ideas in this book, one may note that it assimilates *Lebensphilosophie* values to an Apollonian (or academic) mode of study. This accounts for the haunting similarity between his work—its mood or point of view—and Leavis's (which we shall discuss later), despite the great difference between what the two men got from Lawrence. Clearly Weber, like Leavis, was deeply inspired by the values of *Lebensphilosophie*—including even their manifestation in aestheticism and eroticism—which they were confident could save contemporary Europe from dessicated rationalism and cultural lifelessness. At the same time he, again like Leavis, was a university teacher by profession and a cultural conservative by temperament, and hence most averse from the more flamboyant and experimental forms of aestheticism and eroticism. (Heidelberg was named Cambridge's *Partnerstadt* after the war, its German counterpart, and both are indeed the same kind of city.) Weber and Leavis both built elites of cultural leadership, saving remnants, by means of a moral and intellectual discipline which was exercised in the name of *Lebensphilosophie* but very unlike it in spirit. Weber seems to have been less successful than Leavis, in what he wrote as well as in his immediate environment, but he is not without interest.

He distinguished culture from civilization, assigning the former to the realm of pure value, of purposeless and absolute splendor. He also distinguished both culture and civilization from the political movements of conquest and colonization, mechanization and other manifestations of patriarchal domination. He attempted to interpret cultural history in terms of the three models of man which have been used by the three successive phases of culture in the world. He saw the present cultural crisis in terms of the suppression of the third man, Promethean man, the moral-temperamental model which has served Western civilization since the Greeks—that is, since the Promethean man himself superseded the magical, mythical, fertility-worshiping culture of the second phase. This third type, Promethean man, was, Weber thought, being superseded by a fourth, whom we can see exemplified in the bureaucratic robots of totalitarian states.

Alfred's theory was that there are three processes going on in history. There is the socializing process, determined by the will-to-life, the natural-vital will. There is the civilizing process, determined by the will to a pleasant

life, the rational-utilitarian will. And there is the cultural movement, determined by the will to a free life, the ideal-transcendental will. The first is
exemplified in the migration of peoples, the second in the discovery of
atomic fission, and the third in the creation of a symphony.

Of course, these three life areas are always interrelated and affect each
other mutually. The fact that Athens and Florence were busy market towns
affected their cultural creativity, and vice versa. But the heights and depths
in the culture movement are unpredictable and incomparable one with
another. It is a wave movement, determined vertically by an ideal goal which
is never attained. Culture therefore must be free. Its life is threatened by any
close involvement with nature, or with the world—concepts which are other
names for the other two life areas. When culture is excessively involved with
nature, we get totemism, magic, myth—the second man's culture. (This is
not unlike what Bachofen called matriarchal culture.) When culture is excessively involved with the world, with civilization, we get the rigidities of
Egypt and China, which are indeed versions of the third man's culture, but
only at a primary stage. (This primary stage corresponds roughly—though
Weber does not say this—to what we have called Prussianism or extreme
patriarchalism.) Only in Greece and our Western culture which followed
from Greece do we get that secondary state of the third man which is what
we usually mean by "culture." In primitive history, the three life areas are
so closely connected that culture is encapsulated. In recent history, again as
in Egypt before, the state has interfered too much for cultural health. The
state can at best *protect* culture, but culture can *develop* only under its own
direction, which is to say, the direction of great individuals: "genius calls to
genius."

Implicit in this theory is the need for imaginative men to separate themselves both from nature and from civilization. Also implicit is the belief that
what makes life worth living, historically as well as individually, are great
works of art and great artists. In order to get the works of art, we must
cultivate some spiritual relation to the transcendent, but this must be an
aesthetic spirituality. Europe's real spiritual history, says Weber, has not been
a matter of dogma, but of the faith of great individuals—most typically, of
great poets. In periods of culture crisis, such as Weber's world was passing
through, that history lapses, technicians come to stand as high as priests and
poets, and the result is seen in the proliferation of split personalities, like our
atom-bomb scientists, and of pathological personalities, like our totalitarian
bureaucrats and our modern masses. The theory's ultimate hero is Goethe.
Its imaginative locus is Weimar or Heidelberg.

Alfred Weber's *Kulturgeschichte als Kultursoziologie,* dedicated to Else

Jaffe, was written between 1931 and 1934, in defense of all the old cultural values which Weber saw being overwhelmed by destruction—in Germany by the Nazis, in Russia by the Bolsheviks, and everywhere by the rise of the masses. For Alfred Weber, culture is inseparably connected with an elite class; he insists that Athenian culture depended on the slave system, and that all culture as we know it derived from the dominance of the *Reitervölker*. Because of its content, the book had to be published in Holland. It is worth noting that in it the primitive cultures are treated in only eleven of four hundred and seventy-nine pages. We on the New Planet which modern technology has created are again suffering from the primitives' *Daseinangst*, which culture proper banishes, Weber contends; we have gone beyond culture proper. But despite this insight, almost all of his creative interest is focused on that culture of the past, the third man's culture.

In *Das Tragische und die Geschichte*, his most sustained discussion of a single topic, he studies the sociology of Greek tragedy. Greek art was always for Weber the supreme achievement and yardstick of Western culture. Although this book was printed in Germany, the general public was forbidden to buy it. This was 1943, and Weber was well known as an anti-Nazi.

These are the works on which he spent his life, and with which Else Jaffe helped him so much. In sum, they amount to Alfred and Else's translation of Heidelberg into contemporary ideological terms. They are less lively than his early essays of 1910. Perhaps nothing in and of Heidelberg could be so lively after the war; the university's great period was definitely over, and liberal Germany had been dealt a mortal blow. Moreover, Alfred Weber was not the man to formulate and carry through large conceptual schemes. He was a fragmentary person, full of stops and starts—the sort of public speaker who never completes his sentences. He claimed that all cultural and artistic life derived from "tensions," and he was himself "temperamental," which usually means that the temperament is to some degree inauthentic—perhaps an involuntary imitation of Max's. To most people who knew him superficially, like members of the von Richthofen family, he seemed "a typical German professor," dictatorial in his opinions, boring, jealous, difficult, eccentric. To academic colleagues he seemed always in opposition, always up in arms, rather ineffectual. But the one or two who knew him well called him extremely vulnerable and self-doubtful.

He was an uneasy soul, always in quest, whose only friend in Heidelberg in his later years was Ludwig Curtius. He had hated to leave Prague for Wilhelmine Germany—"so sure of itself, so healthy." All true vitality comes from inner conflict, he declared; he was himself full of such conflict, and his feeling went all to such figures in the culture of the past. "These spiritually lonely great men stand there like lighthouses, pointing out the path we seek," he wrote. There are many hints that the manifold competition between him and his brother Max was deeply destructive on both sides. Certainly Alfred suffered from being overshadowed by Max. Did Else Jaffe's self-sacrificing devotion to him derive in part from guilt at the way *she* had distorted the temperament of a younger sibling? In addition, of course, to the fact that she knew him to be both intelligent and brave. In 1933 Alfred Weber personally climbed the roof of his Sociology Institute in Heidelberg and pulled down the swastika when students first hoisted it there. All through the Nazi era he was openly, if passively, hostile to the regime, with the consequence that in 1945 he was treated by the Americans with enthusiastic reverence, and consulted about many projects of reconstruction of the German universities and German politics.

As in 1918, again in 1945 he helped launch a new political party, with a doctrine and a program of Free Socialism, which was to lead the new Germany into the paths of parliamentary democracy. For this potential party he wrote several pamphlets, even though he was nearly eighty years old, and lent all his energy as well as his prestige to the enterprise. It comes as no surprise to hear that the American authorities, "named" him the Nestor of sociologists and the Grand Old Man of Heidelberg.

These titles seemed unintentionally mocking of Alfred Weber, and their effect on him was unfortunate. He became a political philosopher and a Nazi-hunter, capitalizing on his past virtue, without having anything new to say; as a sociologist his reputation in inner professional circles remained significantly lower than it was with the political authorities. Some of his students called him Minimax, in reference to his brother, and he always sat with his back to the bust of Max Weber when he had to lecture in the room where it stood. He was still, in his eighties, a younger brother. As he had written in 1915, "[I]t is never a matter of indifference, whether someone is a first-born or a second-born child—not indifferent his whole life long, and not indifferent for what he makes out of himself. . . ."

In 1954 Weber's name was proposed by the Communist Party as a candidate for the Presidency of West Germany. Max Reimann, leader of the West German Communist Party, declared that Theodor Heuss's election as President would be a disaster and proposed Weber. In East Germany the propaganda machine took up the idea and Alfred Weber's name was for a time much touted. In fact he got ten Communist and two Social Democrat votes, against Heuss's 871, in the Federal Assembly. It must have seemed another sardonic irony to Else Jaffe and Frieda Lawrence that this man, at this point and by these means, should be nominated for President. They could look back forty years, over two world wars, to the Alfred Weber of before 1914 and compare him with the other men in their lives. Weber, of course, had no responsibility for his candidacy, no chance, and in fact no desire to win. He said he considered it a bad joke, for he was famous for his anti-communism. The proposal was simply the Communist Party's satiric comment on the type of men—their age, their antecedents, their ideology—who were likely to get elected. It used Weber to caricature Heuss.

But there was an extra twist of irony. Heuss was a great admirer of Max Weber, and while he was in office wrote yet another essay about Max, which he sent to Alfred. In reply Alfred expressed a cool surprise that people were still interested in so outdated a figure, so romantic a political philosopher. Alfred was then nearly ninety, but the passing of time never saved him from being Max's younger brother, from being identified, whether in honor or in anger, with what Max stood for. In 1968, when the centenary of his birth occurred, the University of Heidelberg celebrated it with minimal observances which contrasted strikingly with the stormy but large-scale Max Weber celebrations of four years before. Frau Jaffe was almost alone in expressing indignation at this slight.

This, then, was the man with whom she spent most of her life, in whom she invested most of her energies. He was, one disciple says, a man with no private life, an intellectual who had dedicated himself to the nation's welfare. Certainly he was full of nervous oddities. He could not bear it if anyone was in the room above the room in which he slept, and so he permanently rented the apartment over his own (he lived for half a century in the same house in Heidelberg) and was forced to rent hotel rooms above his own whenever he stayed in hotels. When he and Frau Jaffe found a hotel on their travels, they would have to drive on if the room above theirs had been rented. Frieda's letters to her mother contain some indignant complaints against Else's subjection to his deeply neurotic whims. And there were more serious eccentricities, like his never marrying Else, which left her in serious financial straits from which the pension of a professor's widow would have saved her.

As we have pointed out, there are similarities between some of Weber's ideas and some of Lawrence's. He was not nearly so opposite to Lawrence as Max Weber was. But the differences were still much more striking than the likenesses. It is Alfred's world, the world of culture, which Lawrence evokes in this stanza of "Dreams Old and Nascent":

> My world is a painted fresco, where coloured shapes
> Of old, ineffectual lives linger blurred and warm;

> An endless tapestry the world has woven shapes
> The halls of my life, compelling my soul to conform.

Behind the culture-dream one senses always thick stone walls. Lawrence always felt uncomfortable and out of place in Heidelberg, as he did in Cambridge. He had committed himself to an opposite temperamental discipline, and his pulses ran out of rhythm with the occasions when he had lunch with Alfred and his friend Professor Curtius. Lawrence, following Frieda, was struggling to make his life out of the second kind of dream, of the two he contrasts in this poem:

> For the proper dream-stuff is molten and moving mysteriously,
> And the bodies of men and women are molten matter of dreams
> That stir with a stir that is cosmic, as ever, invisibly
> The heart of the live world pulses, and the blood of the live world teems.

Alfred Weber too was a poet, though an unpublished one. His last, work, written just before he died, "Wolken-Vision vom Heiligenberg," is a Goethean, God-in-Nature vision dealing with the experience of the transcendent, which he came to believe was the only thing that could save Western man as a whole from metaphysical despair and, ultimately, moral ruin. Considered out of context, what he had to say on this matter often sounded quite like what Lawrence said in his more conservative phases.* But the same concepts mean something quite different when put in the context of, on the one hand, Weber's and Else's turning away from civilization toward culture, and on the other, Lawrence's and Frieda's turning away from culture toward life.

In some ways, Alfred Weber is well defined by pointing to the connection between him and the German Youth Movement, the *Jugendbewegung*. Involved in it early, both he and Klages addressed the *Freideutschen* group within the movement at the huge meeting on the Hohen Meissner in 1913. The *Wandervögel* movement, as it was first called, had been founded in 1901 by Karl Fischer, in reaction against modern capitalist corruption; it fought alcohol, smoking, pornography, all big-city immorality, with weapons of body culture, natural leadership, group wanderings, folk songs, and folk dances. The movement spread rapidly and widely in Wilhelmine Germany, and in 1914 Alfred Weber again spoke on behalf of the *Freideutschen*, this time defending against attacks in the Bavarian Parliament, where deputies had been disturbed by the movement's pacifism. (The 1913 meeting had been called partly as a pacifist protest against the chauvinistic festivities ar-

* See the passage quoted in Chapter 4, p. 335.

ranged throughout Germany for the centenary of the Battle of Leipzig.)
Weber was able to speak reassuringly of the movement's healthy vigor and
passionate patriotism—and, indeed, within a few months he and they were
fighting for Germany with great enthusiasm. The *Jugendbewegung,* with
its romantic love of nature, its "healthy" clothing, its "clean" youth-and-
maiden eroticism, is recognizably a reflection of *Lebensphilosophie.* But it
was the mild, middle-class, moralizing reflection appropriate to Heidelberg
and Alfred Weber, the expression on a larger than usual scale of something
to be found in other countries among the children of professors. It lacked
the forcefulness of feeling, the adult realism, the "organic" vitality which
Lawrence's, Gross's, and Max Weber's ideas possessed, but it expressed
Alfred Weber perfectly. And it was Alfred Weber's Heidelberg which was
Else Jaffe's background for the second half of her life.

Jack

In Frieda's life there was no real equivalent to Alfred Weber. She did not
commit herself to anyone—certainly not in Else's sense of "serving." The
man with whom she lived, Angelo Ravagli, more or less illiterate in English
through all his years in Taos, could hardly have been less like Weber. But
she did have a brief affair, and an enduring relationship, with John Middleton Murry. Murry, seen in relation to Lawrence, was not unlike Alfred
Weber, seen in relation to Max. It was the relation of a younger to an older
brother, competitive, tormented, mutually destructive, and yet creative. And
in both cases the relationship between the men was expressed, to some
degree, via the women. If Frieda had gone to live with Murry in 1930, her
life might have been quite parallel with her sister's during the next twenty-
six years. By not doing so, however, she generated an even more interesting
divergence of their life lines.

Murry differed from Alfred Weber in much the same way that Frieda
differed from Else. He had Frieda's impulsive individualism, which tended
to cut him free from institutional connections, her emotional salvation-seek-
ing, her radical naïveté. He was a star in her constellation, not in the sense
that they were colleagues or neighbors, but in the sense that he was her kind
of man.

It is worth giving some details of Murry's early career, because they
throw light on Lawrence's own career and on several of this book's themes.
He went to Christ's Hospital in 1901, when he was eleven. One of the first
six scholarship boys—that is, working-class boys—to be admitted to this four-

hundred year old boys' school, he told his classmates that his father was in the Indian Civil Service. In fact Mr. Murry was a low-grade clerk in Somerset House who worked at night in a bank for extra money. Jack was, involuntarily and unhappily, an imposter. Apparently lethargic in class, involuntarily resistant, he nevertheless wrote home sophisticated and humorous letters, as if he were happy. His parents "accepted" this upward class shift for him, and his alienation from them.

"I had been the average sensitive little boy, unexpectedly put through the education of a 'gentleman,'" Murry says in *Reminiscences of D. H. Lawrence*, but the effects seem to have been more drastic than that suggests. His naked mind, his intellect, seems to have become his center of psychic gravity, so that he had to use his personal charm to make contact with people. In 1908 he went up to Oxford, and began to spend his vacations not with his parents but at a farmhouse at Stow-on-the-Wold, making the Peacheys, these Cotsweld farmers with whom he stayed, his family. For Christmas 1910 he went to Paris, where he fell in with *Fauvisme* and Post-Impressionism. Captivated by this more exciting world, he dropped both Oxonianism and the Peacheys. He decided that as soon as he had his degree he would spend a year and a half at the Sorbonne studying under Bergson, another year and a half in Germany, and then become a journalist. His temperament was, and remained, extremely labile.

What Paris meant to him was primarily the religion of art—art as expressing a new wholeness of the personality, in which the intellect was merely instrumental. Bergsonism, Syndicalism, Debussy, Mahler, Picasso, Derain—these were the names and the ideas which filled his mind. To put his development in the terms we have been using throughout this study, we may say that he joined the crusade against the nineteenth-century patriarchal sensibility; but he entered not the erotic but the aesthetic wing, which is usually called Modernism or *Symbolisme* and which was distinct from the erotic wing and yet a first cousin to it within the *Lebensphilosophie* family. With a characteristic enterprisingness, he immediately started to plan a magazine which would propagate the new art and in fact brought out a few members. Its title, *Rhythm*, referred to the idea that true art is that way of life which resists mechanical uniformities, and that the artist is a man who must manifest his self-discipline in a life-rhythm. Edited by Murry and Michael Sadleir while they were still undergraduates, the magazine began to appear in 1911, and was distributed in Paris, New York, and Munich— the cities of art. But its main function was to be to bring the new aestheticism—which meant also sexual freedom—to England. Murry had, naturally enough, begun an affair in Paris that Christmas.

In 1912 he began living with Katherine Mansfield, the short-story writer. Slightly older than Murry, she had had a much more varied erotic career than he including a nonmarriage, a miscarriage, and an abortion. She had nearly adopted a child, intending to bring it up without a father. She wanted to be a free woman, but even more she wanted to be an artist in prose. Thus she had some of the characteristics of the hetaera, but she was more the type of Sue Bridehead or Lou Salome than of Fanny zu Reventlow or Frieda von Richthofen.

That same year he read *The Brothers Karamazov* in Constance Garnett's translation and wrote a review in which he compared it, in its significance for the next age of British writing, with "the most epoch-making translations of the past." He put it on a level with North's *Plutarch*, as opening up a new world to his contemporaries, a new way of writing and of feeling. His own *Dostoevsky*, which followed four years later, was the most emotional and mystical, the most "Russian," of all the books written about that author. It was neither biography nor criticism, Murry declared, but a religious exegesis of the great man's life and works. In fact, it was a late item in a succession of such exegeses written by the Russian "Decadents" (all followers of Dostoevski), a line begun by Rozanov in 1890 and continued by Merezhkovsky, whose *Death of the Gods* was translated into English in 1901. On the English literary scene the most extreme example of this type of exegesis was to be Murry's own *Son of Woman*, about Lawrence. The writing of that book was a conscious act of betrayal, for Lawrence had hated Murry's *Dostoevsky,* and Dostoevski himself, and all the Russian "Decadents" he had read. He had struggled against Murry's tendency to see their relationship in "Dostoevskian" terms, with Lawrence cast as the tormented religious *exalté* and Murry as his loving but doubting disciple. Both men described that kind of relationship as a Jesus-and-Judas sort of affair, for Dostoevski and his "Decadent" followers had redirected attention to the Gospel story, read now as a Russian novel. But whereas Lawrence struggled to escape the former role, Murry struggled to force it on him, even at the price of himself playing Judas—although, of course, a Dostoevskian Judas. Through Dostoevski, Murry was hoping to escape the impoverishment of life in which, as an "intellectual," he felt trapped. His enthusiasm for the Russians was shared by Katherine Mansfield, who stood together with Dostoevski on the opposite side of Murry from Frieda and Lawrence. Both spiritual-religious and life values had entered his life at the same moment, and he was chronically torn between the two.

Frieda and Lawrence first met Katherine and Murry in 1913, when the latter were editing *Rhythm* and the former had just come back from Italy.

Both couples were unmarried lovers and this coincidence, as well as Murry's lower-class origins, gave them the feeling they were all allies in the same great adventure and rebellion. Soon Murry grew to admire Lawrence's work enormously, and Lawrence hoped that his new friend would also become his prophet as a literary critic. "I am *sure* you are the best critic in England," he wrote to him in encouragement. Murry was four years younger than Lawrence and ten years younger that Frieda, who, so much more alien to him in every way, gradually came to represent the greater challenge. Her splendor simply could not be assimilated to any Dostoevski-Jesus model of humiliated suffering, as Lawrence's could. In Frieda, Murry met Lawrence's doctrine incarnate and untranslatable, met Woman trumphant.

Having grown up between his mother, his aunt, and his grandmother in a very feminine world, he was a born rebel against the world of men. But he did not, in those days, believe in Woman. Perhaps he never accepted, never fully understood, the erotic movement. We shall say more about that later on, but here we shall only point out the difference in style between the love relationships in which Murry and Lawrence were involved. Katherine and Murry made a religion out of love. "Lo, I have made love all my religion" is a line out of one of his poems, and Katherine Mansfield, struggling to express herself against him, quoted it and asked him who wrote it, so deep and unconscious was their unanimity. But it was a rather conventional and sentimental religion. They had the word "lovers" always in their mouths, and often applied it to themselves. They "played the role" of lovers in a sense that Lawrence and Frieda did not; one might say that Lawrence and Frieda were inventing their drama as they went along, whereas Murry and Katherine were assimilating themselves to a well-established literary convention of love—a gay, lyric-tenor version of the Romantic convention. One can hear that reliance on convention in a certain complacency of Katherine's "In spite of all, in spite of all, no two lovers walked the earth more happily than we." There was no such tone between Lawrence and Frieda, or if there was, it was not central to their relationship. They wanted something more nakedly honest, more deeply original, more free from conventional guarantees. They wanted something more than "love." But of course they were delighted to ally themselves with two such gifted and attractive people in a common rebellion against convention, stupidity, ugliness, dreariness, death. The four were very happy together at first, and perhaps one may say that in all the Lawrences' life together they found no couple to share their struggle as fully.

But there were always disturbing elements in their relationship, arising largely from what Lawrence called a lack of seriousness in Murry, a deliberate immaturity, which he located most seriously in Murry's relationship with Katherine. As Murry puts it in his *Reminiscences of D. H. Lawrence,* "In this vital matter of the relation between a man and a woman, I stood at the absolutely opposite pole to Lawrence. . . . He wanted me to prove on my pulses a love experience like his own. That would have meant denying Katherine Mansfield and myself." Katherine was, to use a term Murry applied to her slightly later, a girl and not a woman. Moreover, in their relationship—to use *her* terms this time—Katherine played the masculine role. As a lover, Jack was a boy, for his manly intensities went into his Dostoevskian relationships. To Lawrence this seemed a very serious shirking of the main issue of their cause; Murry was shirking the discipline which Frieda had imposed on Lawrence, the discipline of eroticism, the rooting of one's identity in one's manhood, without which the rest of their lives, from the appreciation of nature to the practice of poetry, must wither at the root.* Lawrence tried to save him from this shirking of his manhood, exhorting him to change his relationship with Katherine and inviting him to enter a *Blutbrüderschaft* relationship with himself. But his pleas were of no avail, for what Murry had in mind for them was the Dostoevski-disciple relationship, which was what Murry understood a spiritually intense relationship between men to be. His writing of *Dostoevsky* coincided with Lawrence's offer, and the conjunction gives us the two men at the crossroads.

But insofar as Murry seemed ready to submit, eager to learn, he became Lawrence's younger brother, the only one Lawrence ever had, though he had so many sisters. The role of older brother was not an easy one for him to enact. He was, after all, palpably younger than Frieda in the central, identity-conferring relationship of his life, and with Murry he tended to hector, to overbear, for he lacked natural authority. For his part, Murry, though he was always seeking a master, was skilled in evading real self-commitment.

By all accounts, Murry was a figure of ambiguity, who gave many people the idea that he would betray, but at the same time he was very intelligent, very talented, and very attractive. He had the intelligence to understand what Lawrence asked him to. His talents were, as Lawrence said, primarily for criticism, but of the largest and most ideological kind. His *Problem of Style* contains some of the best "classical" criticism of its

* Manhood is very important in the religion of Demeter, and is not a matter merely of sexual performance, as it is to Aphroditeans. It is a cultural and moral identity as much as a sexual one, though it is not, as it is to patriarchal sexologists, primarily and monumentally moral. To Demetrians, manhood and womanhood are the anode and cathode of life in the service of more life, of life in the service of love and growth, delight and fertility, creativity and adventure.

time, and even his most wildly emotional writing has something interesting to say. His attractiveness is best captured by Lawrence in "Jimmy and the Desperate Woman":

> He was editor of a highclass, rather highbrow, rather successful magazine, and his rather personal, very candid editorials brought him shoals, swarms, hosts of admiring acquaintances. Realize that he was handsome, and could be extraordinarily "nice," when he liked, and was really very clever, in his own critical way, and you see how many chances he had of being adored and protected.
>
> In the first place his good looks, the fine, clean lines of his face, like the face of the laughing faun in one of the faun's unlaughing, moody moments. The long, clean, beautiful dark-grey eyes with long lashes, and the thick black brows. In his mocking moments, when he seemed most himself, it was a pure Pan face, with thick black eyebrows cocked up, and grey eyes with a sardonic goaty gleam and nose and mouth curling with satire. That was Jimmy at his best. In the opinion of his men friends. . . . In the opinion of his women friends, he was a fascinating little man with a profound understanding of life and the capacity really to understand a woman and to make a woman feel a queen; which of course was to make a woman feel her *real* self. . . .

This is a description of a potential Adonis, a stripling lover for Magna Mater. But Jimmy's own idea of himself, we are told, is as a martyred Saint Sebastian. He refused his erotic movement identity.

As Murry puts it, he had been chosen to be the friend who understood, and chosen precisely because he stood in such opposition to Lawrence in the crucial matter of love. He then admits that he refused to understand. This was true, as we shall see, in the literal sense that he kept professing himself "bewildered" by what Lawrence said. But what he means in *Reminiscences* is that he refused to acknowledge their opposition, and refused to challenge Lawrence with the truth about himself. "I loved an ideal Lawrence. I had not the courage to love the real one: that is my failure." This "truth" about Lawrence Murry did not speak until he wrote *Son of Woman* in 1930, after Lawrence's death. He shrank from the necessary conflict. "My true function in this friendship was not only to be destroyed, but to destroy. To use Blake's language, we had to annihilate each other's Selfhood. . . . I am speaking esoterically, for those who have ears to hear. To destroy Lawrence was not to annihilate him—as though it were possible to annihilate the starry genius of our time—but to shatter with strong hands the core of Selfhood in him that his marvellous identity might be free. . . . Those who understand this story—perchance only one living soul—will understand that the writing of *Son of Woman* was my final act of self-liberation; my complete entry into my own identity . . . it is the holocaust of my personality." The one living soul addressed must have been Frieda, for his struggle with Lawrence was a struggle with and about Frieda.

He was thinking of himself again as Judas when he wrote the passage just quoted. In his last interview with Lawrence, in 1925, he had outlined to him a theory of Judas as "the one friend who understood." According to this theory, Judas had understood Jesus as no other disciple did, had understood the enormous strain and risk involved in proclaiming oneself the Saviour of Mankind, and had killed himself after the Crucifixion not because of any betrayal—that was a story invented later by others—but out of suffering and despair. (Four years before, in *Aaron's Rod*, Lawrence had portrayed himself listening to a treacherous "friend" expounding such a theory of Judas with enthusiasm. Murry in 1925 seems to have been echoing Lawrence's own printed words.) Lawrence listened in silence, Murry tells us, and then declared his impatience with all this emotion about Jesus and his sufferings. The obsession with that theme was unprofitable as well as unattractive. Nevertheless, in the years that followed Lawrence wrote often about Christ (in "The Risen Lord," "The Escaped Cock," "The Man Who Died")—but never about Jesus, the man of sorrows, always about the resurrected lord of life, the Easter morning hero of eroticism. It is a catholic, pagan, Christianity he endorses, as in *A Propos of Lady Chatterley's Lover*. And when he wrote about "the Russians," it was angrily; for instance, in his review of Rozanov's *Solitaria* in 1927, where he declares his detestation of all these "whelps from Dostoevsky's kennel" for their morbid wallowing in adoration of Jesus—an adoration which expresses a strong desire to drag him down and spit upon him. In other words, he identifies them all as Judases. Lawrence had repudiated the disciple relationship, connecting it with the Judas complex, as early as *Women in Love* or even *Sons and Lovers*. Lawrence had always felt threatened by the tendency to treat him as a religious *exalté*. Both "Miriam" and "Hermione" are depicted as pushing him into that role, and in both cases the character Lawrence modeled after himself is shown fearing that they will thus deprive him of his normality, his virility, his erotic movement identity. Of course, they were a threat only because "Jesus" in fact was a shadow identity of his; indeed, Lawrence often spoke of people around him as his Magdalens or his John the Baptists. Nevertheless, as an emotional identity it was something he mostly rejected and repressed. Frieda saved him from it, by giving him an erotic identity. Whereas Murry, as we shall see, forced it on him, explicitly and in print as well as privately.

Let us briefly trace the history of his relation to the Lawrences. During the war years the relations between the two men became very strained, and they did not meet again until 1923, when Lawrence returned from New Mexico the first time. Murry had got an O.B.E. for his work at the War Office between 1917 and 1920, and he became editor of *The Athenaeum* in 1919, where he published George Santayana's *Soliloquies in England* and Paul Valery's *La Crise de l'Esprit* as well as T. S. Eliot and some of the Bloomsbury people. He had new friends, many of them people very unlike the Lawrences. There can be no doubt about Murry's intelligence, sophistication of taste, and originality of mind. But it is striking that these qualities did not alienate him from the sources of official favor as Lawrence's equivalent virtues did him. Thus in 1921 Murry lectured at Oxford at the invitation of Sir Walter A. Raleigh. He got literary fund grants via Edmund Gosse and Thomas Hardy, and was offered chairs of literature in the early twenties. In 1923 he became editor of *The Adelphi*, a magazine which he proposed to make into a platform for Lawrence, for he had been overwhelmed by reading *Fantasia of the Unconscious*, which he published serially in his magazine. The book had explained to him, he felt, what had gone wrong between himself and Katherine, who had just that year died. His spiritual love had *caused* her tuberculosis, he came to feel. Lawrence had been right and Dostoevski wrong.

However, there were soon problems between the two men again. Frieda had returned from Taos before Lawrence, and had traveled with Murry to Germany, where he was going to consult a psychiatrist on behalf of T. S. Eliot's wife. On the journey she offered Murry an erotic relationship with herself. (This is a neat example of the different ways in which Lawrence and Frieda were effective. His book and her love offer both made a big impact on Murry, and both impacts had a very similar tendency, pushing him in the same direction. Is it possible that Frieda's offer was an act of competition, because Murry was showing himself so devoutly admiring of Lawrence?) Lawrence sensed that this had happened, and his relationship with Murry was full of the idea of "betrayal," even while he was inviting him to come to Taos with them to start a colony there. This tragi-comedy episode culminated in the "Last Supper" given Lawrence by friends at the Café Royal, at which Lawrence collapsed drunk. He had said to Murry, "Do not betray me," and Murry put his arm round him and said, "I love you, Lorenzo, but I won't promise not to betray you." This was the moment at which both acted out the Jesus-Judas roles most explicitly, and it is significant that Lawrence was drunk and not in full control of himself. The idea of Murry's joining the new colony was pursued further, but came to noth-

ing. Murry reverted in his love life to his old Romanticism. He married
Violet le Maistre a month after the Lawrences and Dorothy Brett sailed for
New Mexico. (Violet was very like Katherine Mansfield in looks and talents,
having consciously made herself so. When she discovered that she had
tuberculosis, she cried, "Oh, I'm so *glad*! I wanted this to happen. . . . You see,
Golly, I wanted you to love me as much as you loved Katherine—and how
could you, without this?") He said later that he did not go to Taos because
he knew that he would have become Frieda's lover there, and this would
have destroyed Lawrence. The betrayal he spoke of at the dinner presumably
would have involved this—and also, we gather, his "revealing" that Lawrence was sexually inadequate despite his theoretical eroticism.

Murry thought he knew who Lawrence really was, and Frieda and
Lawrence knew who Murry really was, as we saw in the description of him
as an Adonis figure in Lawrence's "Jimmy." In 1923 Frieda presumably
meant to offer Murry the kind of manhood, the kind of erotic movement
discipline which she had conferred upon Lawrence. And Murry slowly,
fragmentarily, accepted. He yielded, with qualifications and reservations.
When Lawrence died, in 1930, Murry became Frieda's lover, briefly. (Barbara Barr remembers his stay with Frieda in Vence as being about three
weeks long.) And he already had come to accept Frieda's and Lawrence's
teaching. Though he had declined her offer of 1923, he thought about it a
great deal afterward, and in some sense his later life was an attempt to apply
their doctrine. His second wife, Violet, was, like Katherine Mansfield, a
"girl," but after her death he married a "woman." At least this was his own
formulation of the event. In the journal he began on the day he finished
Son of Woman—in the year of his affair with Frieda and the last year of
Violet's life—he wrote: "Probably I couldn't love anyone but a girl. Katherine was a girl. I don't know what a Woman is: and never shall. Not that
I have avoided Woman. It is simply that I can't see, can't make contact with,
Woman. . . . Not in my destiny. In my destiny only Love and the inevitable
disaster of Love." The terms of this self-analysis are orthodox erotic thinking.
And so, predictably enough, he changed his "destiny." Violet died on March
30, 1931, and in May he married Betty Cockayne, a healthy, sensual, spontaneous, jealous, fierce thirty-five-year-old, unintellectual and unspiritual.
"This looks like being my baptism into direct knowledge of the Female—
the thing that I have always eluded," he wrote in September of that year.
He was marrying a version of Frieda. It turned out an even worse experience
for him than Lawrence had predicted it would be, in "Jimmy" and in "The
Border Line."

What Murry said about Lawrence in his books will be discussed in

Chapter 4, insofar as it was literary criticism or ideology. But it was also part of his relationship with Frieda, and that part belongs here. He wrote *Son of Woman*, which "revealed" that Lawrence was no sensual superman but a nervous and spiritual creature, perversely pretending to be animal. And then *Reminiscences*, which describes the Café Royal supper, and his seeing "Lawrence's secret," though he does not quite name that secret. (What he "saw" that night, we can only assume, was that Lawrence was sexually impotent.) This was his long-heralded Judas act, both betraying and exalting his hero. It does not seem to have offended or upset Frieda. What she saw, perhaps, was that finally, after Lawrence's death, first by giving himself as her lover and then by attacking Lawrence openly, with masculine courage, Jack was accepting the challenge to become their kind of man. Of course, by the same act, he was insisting that Lawrence was *his* kind of man—a Dostoevski figure whose deepest aspiration was to a Christian spirituality. He claimed Lawrence for Jesus at the same moment as he himself submitted to Pan. (Lurid as Murry's account sounds, I cannot see that it exaggerates the facts. And the relationship between Max and Alfred Weber would prob-ably sound no less lurid, if the whole truth were ever told. We get different kinds of insight into different parts of our story. On Frau Jaffe's side of the family, everyone was discreet. It was only Frieda who inspired these con-fessional lovers, responding to their power as much as to their plight even though she herself was so different. She said in a letter after Lawrence's death that Murry is "the only one I am afraid of.")

Frieda was certainly seriously attracted to Murry, although in the end she took Angelo Ravagli and he took Betty Cockayne. But in 1932, *after* his marriage to Betty, Frieda remarked in a letter that perhaps Murry might come out to the Taos ranch for six months to help her write her book about Lawrence. If he had become her third husband the result certainly would have been a very remarkable book—perhaps the beginning of a truly Lawren-tian criticism.

In fact, of course, Frieda and he did not see each other for over twenty years and lost contact even by letter. During that time, her inspiring influence was poured out on other men, among whom we might mention Aldous Huxley as a case very parallel to Murry's. Like Murry, Huxley at first had fought off Lawrence's influence, satirizing him in an early short story, and then had become his disciple, portraying Lawrence and Frieda quite ador-ingly in *Point Counterpoint*. In *Eyeless in Gaza*, his novel of 1936, he drew the character of John Beavis from Frieda's accounts of Ernest Weekley, as Dr. Lucas tells us. In 1937 he spent four months at her ranch writing *Ends and Means*. In 1955 he drew Frieda again as Katy, the goddess, in his story and play *The Genius and the Goddess.* Both Murry and Huxley were quite unlike Frieda, and both felt they had much to learn from her. It is only the directly erotic relations between her and Murry which make the latter the more appropriate figure for this chapter to concentate on.

In 1931 he had bought the Old Rectory at Larling in Norfolk, which had a big walled garden and a meadow, and which he hoped to make a self-supporting economic unit. He took up carpentry and gardening and beekeeping and getting to know nature—all done in the spirit of Lawrence. But in the same year he read D. H. Tawney's *Equality,* and then *Das Kapital,* and became a Marxist Communist, which Frieda, who came to visit him at Larling, could not approve. Murry joined the Independent Labour Party for the time and attended several summer schools of social-ism. In 1935 he found the Adelphi Centre at Langham, near Colchester, which was designed to be a self-supporting socialist community of about twelve men and women. It was equipped with a guesthouse and conference center for discussions of socialism, and Murray compared it with St. Bene-dict's Monte Cassino. In 1937 he was converted to pacifism and to Christian Communism, away from Marxism. The twists and turns of his ideological career—and his public enterprises—were too many to be charted, but he did remain a leader of the pacifist movement through the war. When the war was over, he, like Alfred Weber, wrote pamphlets and drew up programs for the regeneration of his country and the salvation of Europe's endangered culture.

In the late 1940s he resumed his correspondence with Frieda, asking her what she now thought about himself and Lawrence as lovers. Frieda replied gushingly but with a discreet vagueness. It was a distasteful exchange, at least his side of it. He refers in it to "The Borderline," the story Lawrence wrote in which he predicted that Murry and Frieda would marry after his own death. The story is certainly an ugly revenge fantasy, in which the ghost of Lawrence returns and cuckolds and kills his successor. But in life, and in his letters to Frieda, Murry attempted much the same thing, only covering it up with sweetness. He asked Frieda to write a "love-autobiog-raphy" which "seems to me so terribly important," and one of his motives undoubtedly was his hope of being awarded higher marks than Lorenzo therein. He continued to treat her as a love-goddess, flattering her, which is just what Lawrence accused "Philip" of in "The Borderline." But Jack had never been fully her Adonis, and some of the effects of his failure of com-mitment are visible in his intellectual instability, his inconsequence, his provinciality, compared with Lawrence.

Murry took up a number of extremist ideological positions—communist,

Christian, pacifist—but all were in some measure counteracted by a quite different, an incompatible, sensibility. This sensibility was sometimes "classical," in the T. S. Eliot sense, sometimes merely that of the man of letters, but at its best and most intense it was controlled by Keats and Shakespeare as well as by a zodiacal sign. By propagating that sensibility, he, like Lawrence, preached a rebellion against the patriarchal virtues and the patriarchal system. But Murry's rebellion, compared with Lawrence's, was hopelessly eclectic. The creed and the gospel of Murry's religion are emblazoned with the word Love, but in addition to the matriarchal meaning of that slogan, in addition to what Frieda Lawrence meant by love, Murry always preached a highly spiritual love, derived from Dostoevski and not from Lawrence. And his behavior was as extremist as his creed was eclectic.

This extremism was the source of his power over the Lawrences, as well as of their final disapproval of him. Frieda was always fascinated by emotional extremism, perhaps because she herself was never quite as bold as she wanted to be, and Lawrence found Murry's "Russian" behavior quite impossible, for his English Erasmianism joined his matriarchal life-values to forbid it. But Murry thought he was by his performance honoring an Englishness also, the Englishness of Keats, Blake, and Shakespeare, which had become overlaid by rationalism and convention in the course of the nineteenth century. What Murry rebelled against, in short, was the English temperament as characterized by Leslie Stephen's idea of John Bull. His attempt to bring about a renewal of Englishness *à la Russe* was his chief contribution to the life of the mind, and it had something in common, ideologically, with Lawrence's contribution; but it is inferior, in some final sense. Murry's certainly great intelligence and fine taste were not successfully integrated into this performance or made use of in it. It was an eclectic performance of love, an *eccentric* performance, in the etymological sense of the term. Its tendency was centrifugal, its only center being Murry's personality, the winsome, faunlike Narcissus of British intellectual life, which easily degenerated into too much mere winsomeness, if not self-prostitution. In any event, there was altogether too much self-dramatizing about Murry to give stability, to permit him to be a source of faith for others—just as, in his relationship with Frieda, he could not give her the stability that Lawrence could.

In 1957, the last year of his life, in his last book, Murry again wrote about Lawrence, setting him this time in contrast with Albert Schweitzer, treating them as the two polar types of religious feeling in our age. "It is the best I have written about him," he told Frieda. He described Lawrence as a great genius, far above himself, but a man incapable of love, a man who

preached hatred and sensuality as higher truths because of his own incapacity, a man of less than normal, as well as more than normal, powers.

In 1955, in *Einführung in die Soziologie,* Alfred Weber had written his
final treatment of Max's work, and he, like Murry, could not achieve the
generosity of appreciation at which he aimed. "It is always a pleasure to
speak of intellectual and moral greatness," he began, "even when this presents itself divided and split up, like a mountain range full of abysses." Max's
theoretical work was, he wrote, profoundly "conditioned" by the date of its
writing, so long ago now, and was in any case a highly personal solution to
the problems it considered, pursued along just one line of evaluation. By
now it has become, he concluded, in part dangerous in its effect on sociology
as a living science, and as a whole perhaps unfortunate.

The younger brother role—literal in Alfred's case, symbolic in Murry's—
thus proved to be destructive to both Jack and Alfred. The genius of the
older brothers exacted its price from them. But they made their contribution, a not insignificant contribution, to the history of ideas in their times, and
the character of their work is strikingly parallel with, congruent with, the
character of their relationship with the von Richthofen sisters. What Jack
was to Frieda, he was to English literature; and what Alfred was to Else—
so far as we can know what that was—he was to German sociology.

Mabel

When Frieda took Angelo Ravagli to live with her, she was also in a sense
going to live with Mabel Luhan; to live in Taos was to live in Mabeltown,
as Lawrence once called that village. Mabel figures as an important star in
Frieda's constellation, for Frieda rooted herself in Taos, in all it stood for, as
determinedly as her sister did in Heidelberg.

Mabel Ganson was born in Buffalo, New York, in the same year as
Frieda and she married and bore a child at about the same time Frieda did.
But she was left a widow soon after, and married an architect, Edwin
Dodge, with whom she went to live in Florence. Her first marrage she de-
scribes as having been one of the very few things that happened to her. The
second, like the third and fourth, she made happen.

She was a woman of very strong will power, though her appearance and
immediate personality belied her deeper nature. Short and plump, round-
faced, comely, and notably quiet in voice and manner, her behavior combined with her personality in a familiar New York paradox. She was not a
brilliant talker, a wit, or a monologuist. Her power was exerted rather as a

listener, drawing out other people, and her comments were sympathetic and sober rather than vivid. But her actual behavior, in both public and private relationships, was ruthless, restless, and often destructive.

Her parents had been unhappy together, like Frieda's. Her mother, strong and beautiful, defeated three husbands in succession. Her father was an angry, irritable, and weak man whom Mabel joined her mother in despising. She developed specifically female powers; she could always talk to a man about his work, his own subject, better than he could, but work, as an ethic, she declared that she never understood, and institutions were always unreal to her; "I have always hated machinery and policemen," she declared. The creative power in life she identified with Woman: "I wonder, I really do, if any woman can ever do anything that is not drawn out of her by the man. It seems to me that the function of the male principle is to give impetus to the feminine life." That is clearly very like what Lawrence said during the first years of his life with Frieda, during the first flush of the erotic movement.

Mabel worshiped nature and repudiated civilization. She stood for the unconscious. Hutchins Hapgood wrote to her that he too dreamed of achieving "one unselfconscious moment—one moment of full cosmic sympathy. But I never had had even *one* moment. I see the thing you seem to have, but do not feel it. I want it only with my imagination, not with my temperament." Commenting on her pregnancy, Mabel observed that nature "lets us play and wander and lose ourselves psychologically to the God who is the Father of the psyche, but when *she* [nature] wants us, she summons us firmly and like a kind, firm mother says: 'Now, no more nonsense. Time to get down to the real job . . .' And I can truly say that in those weeks, blessed without the dream of loving or of being loved, without the friction of wills or appetites, I lived more deeply and more truly than I have ever lived before. . . . I believe I would give up all of the psychological life for the nine months of the biological claim."

This she wrote in the 1930s, when she was in alliance with Lawrence and Frieda. It had not been her faith before, perhaps, 1910—certainly not when she married Bostonian Edwin Dodge around 1902 and launched into the aesthetic movement.

Her career as Mabel Dodge was an attempt to make a life out of the pursuit of beauty, primarily the beauty of the past, as manifested in works of art. It was an attempt to live an aesthetic life. She devoted her extraordinary energies to decorating a beautiful house in Tuscany, the Villa Curonia, and to entertaining aesthetic people there. She became a friend of Gertrude Stein and Eleonora Duse and the Berensons and many people out of the world of Henry James. It is worth noting that in this period of her life her sexual interests, as divulged in her autobiography, were mostly lesbian.

But in 1911 she and her husband—whose kindness and facetiousness had quickly come to irritate her, much as Ernest Weekley's did Frieda—returned to New York, to categorically ugly America, where Mabel began a new career by becoming involved with the 1913 exhibition of modern art at the Armory. She wrote an appreciation of Gertrude Stein, comparing her use of language with Picasso's use of paint, and worked hard to make the show a success. In this second career she took upon herself the sponsorship of modern thought in America. In order to pursue this aim, the *Zeitgeist* persuaded her, somewhat incongruously, to adopt the role of Magna Mater.

Lincoln Steffens, one of her friends in that period, supposedly said to her, "You have a centralizing, magnetic social faculty. You attract, stimulate, and soothe people, and men like to sit with you and talk to themselves! You make them think more fluently, and they feel enhanced. . . . Have Evenings." And in fact she ran a very successful salon, at which men of political as well as aesthetic ideas, some of which were revolutionary, met to talk. From that developed the Madison Square Garden pageant in support of the Paterson silk mills strike. In the course of her work on the pageant she took John Reed as a lover. At this point her career became quite similar to Frieda's—and, as we shall see, to Alma Mahler's. She now became a queen of heterosexual love and a Magna Mater.

She was significantly older than Reed. He was the boy-lover, ardent but impatient, the stripling; but he was also full of political enthusiasms. And she, as she describes the relationship, was the love-goddess, experienced, skeptical, gentle, entangling, a Venus to his Adonis. Reed was eager to read the newspapers each morning and then be off to do something; Mabel boasted that she "never read the news in all my life." He modeled himself, however unconsciously, on Richard Harding Davis, as did other writer-journalists of that period, including Frank Norris, Stephen Crane, and Jack London. Davis is described by Van Wyck Brooks as "one of those magnetic types . . . who establish patterns of living for others of their kind." This is, of course, just what Frieda, Fanny zu Reventlow, and Mabel herself did, but his was a countertype to theirs. Morally a lightweight, the dashing young war reporter typified the version of patriarchal man current amid the decadence of the imperialist nineties. There were plenty of examples of the type in England, both in real life and in fiction—Kipling and Stevenson, for example—but in America it was lived out more intensely. (Hemingway was to be its major representative.)

Between John Reed and Mabel Dodge there raged a conflict *in petto* of patriarchal and matriarchal life principles within a love affair, which his subsequent career makes patricularly symbolic. He became the great celebrant of the Bolshevik revolution, and its great American hero, buried in the Kremlin, while she who said she *wanted* to be his mother, lived in Taos with the Indians, following the creed of D. H. Lawrence. When she took Reed to her villa in Italy in 1913, he was most impressed by how much *men* had *done*, and he only wished he had been there while it was being done, in order to take active part. This annoyed her. It "went contrary to her life-flow." She wanted him to admire nature, the nonhuman and the recurrent, to appreciate the beautiful. When the war broke out, he went off eagerly as a war correspondent and was enthusiastic about the war experience, something she could not sympathize with.

She wrote an article for *The Masses* called "The Secret of War"—and the secret is that men enjoy it. She described history as the study of the behavior of men turning somersaults in a vacuum. By the time Reed went to Russia, to describe the revolution there in *Ten Days That Shook the World*, she had lost all interest in him. She had taken up Maurice Sterne, a Russian Jewish painter whom she was determined to make into a sculptor. She had returned to the world of art.

The war meant nothing to her, and her comments on politics—as had been true even in the days of her involvement with radicals, the days of the Paterson strike and the Tannenbaum trial—were very naïve. She was turning toward beauty again, though she needed now to place it in a different ideological context, for the old aestheticism was outworn. Unfortunately, Sterne proved to be no help in her search for a new ideology.

From 1913 to 1920 she was a great friend of Elisabeth Duncan, Isadora's sister, who trained the girls with whom Isadora danced. She and her manager, Max Mertz, had trained one group of children in Darmstadt, and Isadora appropriated them for her own performances. In 1915 Elisabeth brought a second generation of her students with her to America and started a school in Groton, with financial support from Mabel Dodge. The insistently Greek quality of all the Duncans' dancing, of the brother Raymond's sandals and of Isadora's tunics, were flamboyant signs of the erotic movement. In her association with all this, Mabel was unconsciously moving toward Lawrence. (Isadora herself appears on the edge of our story more than once —for instance, in Schwabing and Ascona, where she may have known Otto Gross—but the nearest thing to a documented relationship between her and one of our principals is this connection between her sister and Mabel Sterne.)

Soon after Mabel married Sterne she sent him to the Southwest and he wrote back that she could find her lifework among the Indians. She moved to Taos in 1917 and soon had persuaded John Collier to come there for a year in order to work for and with Indians politically. In 1920 she began writing to D. H. Lawrence, urging him to come too. She had decided that he was the one man living who could capture in writing the landscape, the feel of the place, the life and culture of the Indians, above all the hope for the world which was incarnate there. For she believed that the white man's era was over, and hoped that the Indians would be the world's masters. She had found a new lover in a Pueblo Indian, Tony Luhan, and sent Maurice Sterne away. Tony taught her, she believed, to love as the Indians love and to overcome her anxious and nervous egotism, to be in harmony with nature and life. "This time it was as though a gentle organic growth was taking place, and actually in my heart I felt small, imperceptible movements, like tiny leaves unfurling; a wonderful evenness marked my days and nights so that waking or sleeping I felt a sweet balance that was delicate and strong."

By and large one may say that Lawrence and Frieda found in Taos what Mabel had promised them they would. It *was* the place they had been looking for, the effective antithesis of the city and of civilization. Frieda made it a reproach to Mabel's book about Lawrence that it didn't take account of the great change which Taos had made in him, the fulfilment he had achieved there. "Knowing the Indians changed us all, into a deeper realization and connection with the earth," she wrote. "He could never have written *Lady Chatterley* if he had not known Taos." Lawrence himself said that it was New Mexico which finally liberated him from the inherited inhibitions of Christianity. Indeed, Frieda never left the place, once she was installed there after Lawrence's death.

Mabel Luhan was able to be right, in their terms, about Taos, because she too was a participant in the erotic movement. But she was wrong, in the sense that she personally spoiled the place for them, just because she was not sufficiently in the movement, not sufficiently redeemed by Eros from her old mischief-making, power-seeking ways. She had been a wicked skeptic in the world of men, and had carved out a piratical career for herself, preying on society's legal shipping; and even though she "believed in" the world of Woman, the old habits of skepticism and wickedness persisted, for they brought too much enjoyment to be given up. Thus she wrote that she never gave up her chronic habit of being "indiscreet."

> Everybody says I tell everything, my own and everybody's secrets, and it's true. I cannot, to this day, resist that peculiar urge to tell what is not really mine to tell. . . . But I don't know that I feel particularly sorry any more. The less secrets the better—of my own or anybody else's. Need anyone *ever feel ashamed*? I doubt it.

In contrast, Frieda was very discreet, which was a symptom of the larger fact that there was nothing destructive about her.

Above all, Mabel was, compared with Frieda, an inferior priestess of the erotic mysteries. Thus, she tried to take Lawrence from Frieda without having any sexual feeling for him and therefore without any true erotic feeling. She offered him instead a spiritual relationship, which is to say that she betrayed everything they stood for. And her grotesque misinterpretation of Frieda as a merely carnal, merely sexual being, makes one doubt if she ever knew the meaning of the creed she proclaimed. But of course such a willful woman knows something one minute and does not know it the next. Frieda said—a typical locution—that she was "bored by" Mabel's machinations, and although this may sound too lofty to be plausible, it is true that with all Frieda's flightiness, she did not throw herself at other men merely in order to make trouble, nor did she do so without the sanction of an erotic attraction. This is the root of all honor within her system of morality, and when it came to honor, Frieda was an aristocrat compared with Mabel. She was a superior priestess of the erotic mysteries, and that is the ultimate reason why Lawrence could never really hesitate between the two women.

Mabel's marriage with Tony Luhan, however, was one of the most striking cases of the erotic movement's ideal of marriage. Clearly it went in the same direction as, but further than, Frieda's marriage with Ravagli. Perhaps it went further even than Frieda's marriage with Lawrence—that is, further in the direction that Lawrence himself preached to Frieda, and that Klages preached to Fanny zu Reventlow. Not that Tony was a stripling lover; clearly he was the father-figure Mabel needed. So their relationship does not answer perfectly to the Magna Mater pattern. But that pattern is only one, though the major one, among the *Gestalten* of the erotic movement. The essential criterion is the moral-psychological *effects* of each patterning of the sexual relationship, and in the case of Mabel and Tony the effects were the best possible by Lawrentian standards. Between the Luhans the similarity of minds, the competition of personalities, the mutuality of nerves was at its minimum. The man had the maximum of otherness, of dignity, of separateness.

Taos, then, we may see as an Antipodes to Heidelberg in marriage styles as in so much else. It was not unlike Ascona, for the same forces were at work in both places. It is no accident that the anarchist university which Otto Gross planned to found in Ascona found its exactly contemporary parallel in Mabel Dodge's New York, in the Ferrer School, where "constructive anarchism" was taught by her friends of the war years. Courses were given by Emma Goldman and Alexander Berkman, painting was taught by Robert

Henri and George Bellowes. Elizabeth Gurley Flynn lectured on the Paterson strike, at which she had been arrested. Louis Levine and André Triton lectured on syndicalism; Guitérrez on Mexico; Clarence Darrow on Voltaire, Edwin Markham on poetry. In fact, Lawrence had planned to run a school in America when he first thought of founding a community there, and such a school would have had to have much in common with Gross's and with the Ferrer.

In Ascona in these years Frieda Gross was still living with her four children in great poverty. Ernst Frick had left her for Margaretta de Fellerer, the photographer, a much younger woman, who also lived in Ascona. Margaretta, who had a private income, became a threat to the Frieda-Frick relationship as early as 1920, though they continued to live together, unhappily, for several years after that. Frick's father had suffered from melancholia and his sister from paranoia, and his own personality seems to have had the pathos, and the charm, of an invalid's. Though he lived to be seventy-two, he had the appeal always of one not long for this world, someone to be protected. He did no work, he didn't even paint. Max Weber saw him as a would-be Tolstoyan saint while Frick described himself as a moralist—an anarchist moralist, of course. He is described by those who knew him as a natural gentleman, the purity of whose motives was not to be doubted, but who lived out of touch with reality. In part, he lived in a world of conspiratorial fantasy. He went to jail before the 1914 war for his part in a plot to free some men from the Zurich prison—a part which his friends thought was probably minimal, but which he proudly amplified to the judge. In the 1930s he felt that he was on the fringe of vast plots and counterplots aimed at exploding the bourgeois world. After his death— Frieda Gross died before he did—Margaretta de Fellerer took the surviving children to live with her. Peter, Otto Gross's only child by Frieda, died still young, of the tuberculosis he had long suffered from, a very gifted but troubled boy. He had learned Russian by himself from books, but failed exams which more ordinary students passed. He suffered from crises of identity and took cocaine like his father. His sisters too lived unhappy lives. One committed suicide. Gross's Ascona did not turn out to be the Promised Land. Frieda's Taos did not aim so high and did not fail so badly.

But as the women at Taos aged, the colony increasingly became a center of Ladies in Retirement. In Frieda's correspondence with Dorothy Brett and Mabel Luhan there is a great deal about embroidery and gardening and recipes, a great deal of gossip, and a marked absence of *men*—not only of men who represent the world of men, but also of first-class men by matriarchal standards. It reminds one of nothing so much as a superannuated girls' school, and Mary McCarthy's comments about her old school seem apposite: "The tinkling of this girlish operetta, with its clink-clink of changing friendships, its plot of smuggled letters, notes passed from desk to desk, secrets." Thus Frieda to Mabel: "A nice friend you have been to me, you nasty thing. I can never be fond of you any more, and I tell everybody what I think of you, but they all know and think less of you than I do." And Frieda to Brett: "Brett, I am tired of our old hate and your spite and your melodramatic imagination about me—I have done with it and you—You'll never change and realize how ungrateful you have been towards my generosity. But you always were a silly owl. Frieda Lawrence." Though later, of course: "Brett, my dear, well our correspondence goes on flowing. I have never written to anybody so regularly except when I was in love or to my mother."

The absurd drama of the interment of Lawrence's ashes is the largest single example of the decay of Taos. In 1935 Angelo Ravagli brought the ashes back from France, losing them twice on the way, and Frieda planned a ceremony for their interment on the ranch in a chapel which Ravagli had built. But Mabel persuaded some friends that Frieda intended to exploit Lawrence, and that he would have preferred to have his ashes scattered to the free winds of heaven. So a plot was hatched to steal them and so scatter them. It failed, but Frieda found out and was much upset. Everyone became passionately involved, and the event certainly had some relation to important issues. But primarily it meant a degradation of those issues to the level of trivial comedy. In all the events of Taos life from then on, it is hard to feel that the hope of world regeneration was being enacted there. It ceased to be a world of Woman and became a world of women.

Mabel Luhan went back to New York City in the winter of 1939, where she opened a salon and attempted to revive the glories of her past. This time her stars were such men as Thornton Wilder, and Dr. A. A. Brill, the psychoanalyst. If the salon had thrived, a new phase in her life might have started and Taos and Tony Luhan might have sunk into the background, like so many previous episodes. But the salon did not thrive, and she returned to Taos in the spring of 1940. Seven years later she published *Taos and Its Artists*, including Dorothy Brett, Maurice Sterne, and Angelo Ravagli, and wrote a novel about Taos. She remained there until her death in 1962. Occasionally she made news, but after the war she was always treated very satirically by national magazines like *Time*, *Newsweek*, and *The New Yorker*. Her name was a joke; her day was definitively over.

Frieda gradually became much more like her mother—a change that had been perceptible even before Lawrence's death. She became another Anna

Brangwen rather than an Ursula, if we recall the contrast Lawrence made between them at the time of Ursula's adolescence. The girl's tentativeness, her rush of sympathetic response, her unbounded spiritual aspirations were replaced by the woman's heartiness, confidence, and realism. "I am a lucky one," Frieda wrote to Mabel in 1929. "The Lord has made me rich inside." And in her *Memoirs* she noted, "I am on the best of terms with the universe. If you are a woman, you can think as you please. . . . Being women, we are allowed to love everything." Most characteristic, perhaps, were her injunction to herself, "I won't let my blood turn sour," and her often repeated affirmation, "I know I can love." There are moments when one can believe Mabel Luhan's story of Lawrence telling her that no one could know how awful it was to have "that woman's" hand on one when one was sick. But of course this change was only partial, for Frieda was always Frieda and her life was always a spiritual adventure. In her *Memoirs*, she says, "I believe I had what few women have, a real destiny."

The sisters met once after the war. Frau Jaffe came to America to visit her children and flew to Albuquerque, where Frieda met her. Frau Krug, the youngest sister, went to stay in Taos with Frieda for quite a long time, but Frieda wrote in a letter that a long visit from Else would not do—"she is too bossy." Nevertheless, they wrote to each other warmly and had a high respect for each other—at least when they were at a distance. In letters to her mother, Frieda had more than once defended Else as "being after all someone" (*jemand*) and as therefore deserving the extra care in handling which in effect she demanded. They recognized each other as queens of rival countries of the mind.

The drama of their past conflicts, moreover, continued as long as they lived. Frieda told her daughter Barbara that Else and Marianne Weber had between them *killed* Max Weber. Else's "spirituality" had demanded the sacrifice of real love, and her lover had been torn apart between his passion for her and his loyalty to his wife. On the occasion of Marianne Weber's death, as we have seen, the sisters exchanged letters which inadvertently exposed what they had silently agreed to suppress—Frieda's knowledge of Else's love affair. Perhaps because Frieda took it for granted that their love would never be made known to the world, her sister shortly thereafter gave the letters to Eduard Baumgarten, Max and Alfred's nephew, to publish, at least in part, after her death. (Max had told her, half seriously, to have them preserved for posterity.) The occasion of her handing them over was full of historical ironies. Alfred Weber was still alive, a hero of the intellectual resistance to Nazism. The nephew had loyalties to both his uncles, so that Else and Marianne Weber subjected him to irreconcilable claims, for to be loyal to the one uncle was to be disloyal to the other. Moreover, Max and Alfred Weber stood for different political options, so that Baumgarten's choice between them was related to crucial political choices he had to make. In fact, merely reading the letters was an event in his life. Thus the drama of those old commitments, and their political and historical connections, continued to unfold into the 1950s and the 1960s. When Arthur Mitzman went to Heidelberg to work on *The Iron Cage*, the book on Max Weber he published in 1968, Frau Jaffe told him much that she had not told before, and gave him the underlined copy of Goethe's Hafiz love poems which Weber had given her. But she did not want him to print what she had revealed. So much had still to be kept secret, from members of the family, just because it had been secret so long. In 1971, when Frau Jaffe knew I was coming to see her, she told Professor Baumgarten, "If you tell him anything, seven years in Hell." Heidelberg had become a hive of secrets, just as Taos had become a hive of scandals.

So much for both environments and constellations. But by going further afield, outside the range of people the sisters knew socially, we can define their identities more clearly yet.

Alma

Alma Schindler was born in 1879, the same year as both Frieda and Mabel. But she was born in Vienna, in a milieu of painters, poets, and composers, in the very seedbed of the erotic movement and of modern art. She became a much more complete version of the love-goddess than Mabel Dodge. She resembled Frieda Lawrence quite strikingly in the major features of her temperament and career, but born as she was the daughter of a leading Viennese painter, and educated by first-class practitioners of several fine arts, she chose her first husband much more appropriately—though no more successfully in terms of marital happiness.

It seems to have been after marriage, in her case too, that she began to take her erotic career, her erotic destiny, with full seriousness. This was the result both of the disappointments of her marriage and of the fact that the ideas of the erotic movement—often embodied in declarations of love from brilliant men—became much more vivid to her in the years after 1905. In her autobiography she often quotes from her Diary of those years passages which show her familiarity with those ideas: "The subconscious is the link between all matter; it is the immortality of the daemons. Consciousness is critique, life, movement, the outside world," and so on.

She married Gustav Mahler in 1902, when he was already famous as the director of the Vienna State Opera and as a composer. She was determined to make her career among great artists, but Mahler died in 1911. The following year she began that tempestuous affair with Kokoschka—that "three year battle of love," as she calls it—which was, of all her relationships with which we are concerned, the one most parallel to that between Frieda and Lawrence. "You are the Woman and I am the Artist," Kokoschka wrote to her, using the language of the erotic movement. "I must have you for my wife soon, or else my great talent will perish miserably. You must revive me at night like a magic potion; I know it is so." But, as that language suggests, he was not prepared to *worship* Magna Mater. He wanted, as she put it, to keep the upper hand over her, which she would not endure. He tried to dictate Alma's dress and to change her upper-class ways. Their relationship became a stormier version of the battle between Mabel Dodge and John Reed, or between Frieda and Lawrence, or between Fanny and Klages. Kokoschka was seven years younger than Alma, and thus a year younger than Lawrence. He painted her in his lithographs for *Der Gefesselte Kolumbus* of 1913, and in "Die Windsbraut," his most important painting of that year and a triumph of Expressionism in art. These works can be compared with Lawrence's portraits of Frieda in *The Sisters*, and Maurice Sterne's "Portraits of Mabel Dodge," also contemporaneous. Each of these artists celebrated his mistress with great splendor, even though they all battled to turn their mistresses into wives.

In 1912 and 1913, when Lawrence and Frieda were at Wolfsrathausen, outside Munich, Alma and Kokoschka were often in that city, as was Lou Salome, who conducted some of the episodes of her affair with Viktor Tausk there. The air of Munich then must have been highly charged emotionally and imaginatively. But of course it was not only Munich. There was Vienna, too, and in 1912 Kokoschka and Alma attended the Russian Ballet on its first trip there; later employing the talents of Diaghilev, Stravinsky, Picasso, and Cocteau, the ballet was a powerful force within the erotic movement. So was Isadora Duncan's dancing. And these same years, we must note, were those of Mabel Dodge's affair with John Reed.

Lawrence and Frieda, Alma and Kokoschka, Mabel and Reed—these were all erotic movement affairs in which the woman was Magna Mater. Paradoxically, even Alma's first marriage answered to that pattern in some degree. Freud once told Mahler, when he worried about being older than his wife, that Alma loved him *because* of his age and frailty and the intensity of his mental life, because he was not himself an erotic or "masculine" figure. She agreed that it was a man like her father she was always seeking—

a short, slight, sensitive, temperamental man. "I too always looked for a small, slight man, who had wisdom and spiritual superiority, since this was what I had known and loved in my father." Kokoschka was too big and powerful for her, just as her early lover, Max Burckhard, had been. Burckhard was a great sailor and mountaineer who had lived among brigands in Sicily, an anti-Christian preacher of Nietzschean ideas, as well as judge, poet, theater director, novelist, playwright, and lover of women. "As a man, though, he was not my type . . . his ardor sickened me . . . his strong masculinity. . . ." She did not like men who were too masculine. Nor did Frieda. After her mistaken experiment of marrying Walter Gropius, Alma picked Franz Werfel, who clearly belonged to the same "spiritual" type as her first husband.

These affairs, like Frieda's, carried within them the hope of regenerating society as a whole by regenerating its great talents. Alma identified herself strongly with life, and often triumphed over the men who loved her, because they were identified merely with mind. Thus she writes about her brief love affair with Hans Pfitzner: "There you have the great artists, I thought. Dilettanti of life, each one of them. Everything flows into their work. Life won't give them the right echo because they're calling wrong." And in 1911 she wrote to Joseph Fraenkel, another of her Jewish lovers: "The fate that parts us is the divergence of our own souls. Every fiber of my heart draws me back into true life, while you are striving for consummate dematerialization. . . . When it comes to living you're a miserable failure. At best, men like you are put between book-covers, closed, pressed, and devoured in unrecognizable form by future generations. But such men never *live*. Today I know the eternal source of all strength. It is in nature, in the earth, in people who don't hesitate to cast away their existence for the sake of an idea. They are the ones who can *love*." This is the essential creed of the erotic movement, written at its peak. She accused even Kokoschka of not being interested in *living*; "We lived for his work alone," she complained. All this is very like Frieda, who once said she had been married to Lawrence's *work*, and who described a man's poems as bearing the same relation to his life as a goat's droppings do to its life. At the same time, Alma—like Frieda—was devoted to art and artists and the life of art. Her formula of self-justification at the end of her autobiography is that she has held the stirrups of some of the horsemen of light of our time, and has known the works of genius in our time before they left the hands of their creators.

One can see in several of her diary entries how immediately she converted a love relationship into an artistic partnership. Thus in 1918: "A glorious night! Werfel was with me. . . . He is the resolving chord of my life. . . . Beside me, he told me his idea for a play, 'Mirrorman.' I like it enormously and will not rest until he finishes it. I will invite him into my house at Breitenstein, make everything warm and cosy for him." (It is interesting that Alma should have been enthusiastic about *Mirrorman,* because it is another work in which Werfel depicted—and repudiated— Otto Gross's ideas.) Alma and Frieda justified the paradox of their evaluations of art—its being both very important and very unimportant to them—by preferring that kind of art in which life is more important than mind. But because ordinary experience offers occasions for *achieving* Life, the occasions represented by Lawrence's gamekeepers and gipsies, art must always be a minor option, and it must always be a paradox for people with principles such as they held to love it so much. In fact, however, they were in love with mind as much as with life, but their principles disguised that. And their principles were to their advantage, to the advantage of their erotic identities. For them, to represent life *vis-à-vis* mind was to hold a perpetual advantage over their artist-lovers. Lawrence wrote to Murry soon after they met how he hated the fact that most people—everyone but Frieda—thought him "a queer fish who can write." He struggled his whole life to escape any such classification, as a mere writing machine, a mere sensibility, or a mere intelligence. It was Frieda who could grant him—and could, if she wished, deny him—the status of being a fully alive man.

Alma Mahler is particularly interesting to us because her relations with Jewish intellectuals throw light on others of her sisterhood. Gustav Mahler was one of twelve children in a Jewish family, a small man like Edgar Jaffe, and though handsome and fiery, also melancholy like Jaffe. "A Christian Jew, he paid the penalty," Alma says, adding that "I, a Christian pagan, got off scott-free." Mahler found beauty only in suffering, she says, and he wanted her to be ugly and sorrowful. Much older than she, and successful before their marriage, he set out to dominate her, forbidding her to go on with her composing when they were married. She carried round with her the songs she had composed "as if they were a coffin": "I buried my dream and perhaps it was for the best. It has been my privilege to give my creative gifts another life in minds greater than my own. And yet the iron had entered my soul and the wound has never healed." Thus her first Jewish husband, by his asceticism, exemplified one aspect of what was for her the Jewish character; but the second was much more satisfactory. With Werfel, ten years her junior, she finally achieved the full Magna Mater relationship. He told her she was a genius, as Lawrence told Frieda and Klages told

Fanny. When he died she wrote, "I lost my sweet man-child." In Werfel she had found a boy-lover who would not try to dominate her and with whom she could achieve a perfect sexual mutuality. "The similarity between us was incredible. He found a word for it: 'panerotic.' It was true. I did not need the consummation; I felt its ecstasy in everything," she wrote, describing precisely what Cipriano teaches Kate in *The Plumed Serpent*. But Alma was interested in more than personal gratification, and her feeling for Jews derived from several sources.

Her friend Ida Dehmel's diary for 1905 contains the entry: "Mahler is the first Jew, except my father, to impress me as a man—one who doesn't, to put it crudely, strike me as impotent. I am glad that such a beautiful, proud, strong, Christian girl has married him." Alma was glad, too, and for more than personal reasons. She, like Frieda, always took pride in granting sensitive and self-doubtful men their potency. And the men were always either literally Jews or symbolically so—that is, they were artists. Around the time of her marriage to Werfel in 1929 she writes, "I could not live without Jews—after all, I live with them constantly—but they often make me want to burst with anger. Why can we never be happy, never content to enjoy what we have? Why do we keep seeking 'the other'?" These are the two aspects of the Jew for her: the delicate, sensitive man on whom she can confer masculinity—and therewith artistic as well as sexual potency; and the morally intense and troubled soul who achieves greatness but rejects happiness. In the other Magna Mater cases we have been considering, the relationship is not so centrally with literal Jews as it is with Alma; but the artist figure is, after all, very like the Jew. Magna Mater and the Jew embrace at the core of the modernist movement.

Before Werfel, Alma was married briefly to Walter Gropius. Handsome, honorable, and admirable, Gropius could not play the part of a lover of Magna Mater, for he did not need to be made a man. With his Protestant background and Prussian schooling, he was already a prodigy of work, strength, planning, and achievement; his feeling for art was collective and political. In 1913 he was discovering the beauty of the American grain silos, and after declaring that "We want an architecture adapted to our world of machines," he went on to invent the architecture of the modern factory. This idea must have been anathema to Alma and Frieda. What is more, he was a pedagogic organizer of the arts, who differed from the other great architects of his time—Mies, Wright, Le Corbusier—just by his belief in cooperation in creativity. The Bauhaus organization, and the Bauhaus collective style, are typical of his career and his temperament in many ways. He illustrates vividly how talent in the arts, and specifically modernist talent, can be found in temperaments alien to the erotic movement. He is the artist as non-Jew, the artist as a man in no need of Magna Mater. It is no wonder that in 1915 Alma, who only recently had married Gropius, decided to fall in love with Werfel. She made the decision, she tells us, one day as she sat in their carriage, waiting for her husband and reading Werfel's *Einander*, the book of poems which made him the leader of the Expressionist movement in literature. Here was a talent which needed her.

Like Frieda Lawrence, Alma Mahler was politically conservative. Just as Harriet Somers, in *Kangaroo*, "didn't believe in revolutions—they were *vieux jeu*, out of date," so Alma deprecated all organized attempts to change the structure of social life. Hostile to the 1918 revolution in Vienna, which she described as both ludicrous and gruesome, she drew Werfel away from his revolutionary involvement. Living with her, Werfel came to believe that any primacy granted to politics enslaves the spirit, but in 1917 or 1918 he had been arrested for high treason and he was very active in communist conspiracy at the time. When Alma visited him during his revolutionist phase, she "felt that the room reeked of vices" and that "no immortal works could be created there." It was the reek of Otto Gross she sensed, the reek of Hetaerist revolution, for Werfel's cause was Otto Gross's version of communism and he was very much under Gross's influence then. But he accepted Alma's offer of herself and her comfortable house and nonrevolutionary art, and when he wrote about Gross in his fiction thereafter it was from a deeply alienated point of view. Besides *Barbara*, *The Black Mass*, and *Mirrorman* there is a short novel, *Not the Murderer* (the last three all written between 1918 and 1920), in all of which Werfel depicts Otto Gross or his ideas and condemns them, under Alma's influence. Alma was, like Frieda, a conservative political influence on modern art.

Also like Frieda, she had strong "spiritual" yearnings as unfullfiled alternatives to her actual career. She wrote to Annie Besant in India, proposing herself as a student to learn Sanskrit from her; and later she planned to go to work with Gandhi. But, again like Frieda, she seems to have been doomed to caricature herself in her writings. So many of her sentences sound foolishly sentimental or self-congratulatory that one dismisses the whole person as negligible until one reminds oneself how much she meant to men of first-class intelligence. And she meant so much because she embodied so important an idea so successfully. Alma Mahler and Frieda Lawrence— along with many minor versions of the same idea—were important forces in the creation of modern art and thought.

Isadora

Among the major forces was Isadora Duncan. Born in 1878, she was raised by her mother, a music teacher who read poetry to her children and brought them all up to the artistic life after her father deserted the family. Mrs. Duncan also read them Robert Ingersoll's essays in atheistic rationalism, and Isadora remained devoted to him and to the great German evolutionist Ernst Haeckel, a fact which may remind us of Anna Brangwen's rationalism in matters of religion, which can seem in puzzling contrast to her intuitive emotionalism. Even as a child in this matriarchal home, Isadora decided against marriage, which she saw as a kind of slavery, but for motherhood.

She danced as a child in pantomime, but made her debut in her own kind of dancing in London in 1900, dancing in Botticelli costume to Mendelssohn's spring music. She expressed her joy in beauty by sequences of "Greek" movements which defied the tightly drilled modes of dancing then fashionable. She went on to Berlin and Budapest, but it was in Munich in 1902-3, Otto Gross's Munich, that she first won serious recognition. Munich was then, she tells us, a veritable beehive of artistic and intellectual activities. She danced privately for Erich Mühsam and his friends, for she was indeed a part of the same movement of liberation as they. Her eroticism was joyful, triumphalist, ideological, pedagogical. Her politics could be seen in her dance version of the Marseillaise and the *Marche Slav,* but in a sense all her dancing was political. Choreographically, it was all a revolutionary protest again classical ballet, a demonstration against what she called "the dance—form of kings." Above all, she represented the female wing of the liberation movement, and so was particularly at home in Munich. "If my art is symbolic of any one thing," she often said, "it is symbolic of the freedom of woman and her emancipation from the hidebound conventions. . . ." It was Frieda's kind of emancipation she spoke for, not Else's—Alma Mahler's, not Marianne Weber's. Her dancing was a public manifestation of the freedom Frieda and Alma enacted in their personal lives.

The young people in Munich immediately recognized the religious eroticism of her dancing, which had puzzled or passed by her American audiences. She tells us how she had told the American impresario Augustin Daly, "I have seen the ideal figure of youthful America dancing over the top of the Rockies." Her German audiences understood that, but all the American producers had told her that her dancing might suit a church, but certainly not a theater, even though from early on her tunics were transparent or semi-transparent. But in Germany the students called her "die göttliche, heilige Isadora." Germany became her spiritual home, for it taught her "der Heiligtum des Gedankes," the sanctity of a solemn eroticism. Indeed, her love of Greece and Greek antiquities, and the museum character of her art in general, had something very "German" about it. In Berlin she danced to a full orchestral rendering of Beethoven's Seventh Symphony, and in Bayreuth to Wagner. The students, she recounts, often harnessed themselves to her carriage and pulled her in triumph through the streets after seeing her performance. She was the figurehead of their liberation movement.

If, as we said, Isadora's career was a public and theatrical rendering of the same themes as Frieda and Alma rendered privately and domestically, it was perhaps a somewhat extravagant and unreal version, with its crowds of dancing children, its insistent eroticism, its flamboyant public defiance of society, its public exhibition of her naked body, its succession of young lovers, and through all this its moral intention to save the world by returning it to healthy and beautiful sensuality. (Isadora had always at the back of her mind the idea of a *school*.) In her private life, too, the parallels with Frieda and Alma are quite striking. Her first lover, whom she calls Romeo, was too masculine for her, too "manly" in style. He stopped being Romeo, she says, and turned into Mark Antony, wanting her to be merely his wife. What is more, he hurt her physically by the ardor of his love-making, and for some years after that she avoided physical love. From then on her preferred lovers were always intellectual men, and quite often, it seems, impotent. She describes herself as a "cérébrale." Two of those with whom she had intense affairs without sexual intimacy were of some importance in the erotic and aesthetic movements: Hermann Bahr, the Austrian literary scholar, friend of Hofmannsthal, and patron of Freudianism and Expressionism; and Henry von Thode, the husband of Daniela von Bülow and professor of art history at Heidelberg. Gordon Craig, her first great love, was also an important figure in those movements, but like Kokoschka he would not play Adonis, the stripling lover, to her Venus. Her last famous lover, the Russian poet Sergei Esenin, was many years younger than she. When she describes Gordon Selfridge, a late romantic interest, she says that he was her first contact with a man of action. "[H]e might almost have been of another sex," she writes, "for I suppose all my lovers had been decidedly feminine . . . artists and dreamers." This is all very like Frieda and Alma, and there are dozens of small similarities, insignificant in themselves but building up the whole. Like them, she deplored the modern cult of feminine slimness; like them, she despised the haggard beauty that comes from pain and self-denial. Frieda danced in the nude, or semi-nude, until she reached a relatively advanced age—her letters often coyly boast of it— as, of course Anna, Gudrun, and Connie, do. Indeed, even Ursula's vision of the horses in *The Rainbow* is a fictional version of a Duncan dance. And what Isadora says about her erotic career as a whole sounds very like both Frieda and Alma. "I was once the timid prey, then the aggressive Bacchante, but now I close over my lover as the sea over a bold swimmer, enclosing, swirling, encircling him in waves of cloud and fire. . . . I am now grown to a full-blown rose whose fleshly petals close with violence on their prey." This is the career of the Frieda figure from Ursula to Connie.

Isadora's lover in 1912, that year of Eros, was Gabriele D'Annunzio, and the conjunction of him, Isadora, and Eleanora Duse is an illuminating one for our inquiry. D'Annunzio demands comparison with Lawrence, both as poet of eroticism and as a would-be political adventurer. He courted Isadora, she tells us, with speeches in which he identified her with Nature. "Oh, Isadora, it is only possible to be alone with you in Nature. All other women destroy the landscape, you alone become part of it. You are part of the trees, the sky, you are the dominating goddess of Nature." This identification of women and Nature and Love and Earth was an integral part of the rhetoric of the erotic movement, though not all nature was equally Nature, any more than all women were Woman.

At the time of her involvement with D'Annunzio she was already a friend of the great actress Eleanora Duse, an abandoned mistress of D'Annunzio and a woman who was *not* to be identified with Nature. Isadora gives us an interesting sketch of that nineteenth-century *femme fatale*, who represented the pre-erotic-movement woman with a destiny. Like Frieda, Alma, and Isadora, Duse was also a woman with an *erotic* destiny, but hers was a different eroticism, all yearning, grief, and unrequital, and her personality style was very different. D'Annunzio's abandonment of her and his courtship of Isadora mirrors a movement of the times. Isadora describes Duse as Dante's Beatrice reincarnate and clearly sees her as a type opposite to her own—all suffering and prophecy and grandeur. This was a confrontation of types like that between Ottoline Morell and Frieda over Lawrence, between Ursula Brangwen and Hermione Roddice. Hermione was a Duse of the private and domestic stage.

Emma

In New York in 1912, someone says, there were three arch-symbols of the New Woman, Isadora Duncan, Mabel Dodge, and Emma Goldman. The last of the three had the least in common with Frieda Lawrence, but she is worth considering briefly, for the sake of some enlightening contrasts.

Emma was born in Lithuania in 1869 to a Jewish family. It was her mother's second marriage and an unhappy one. Protected from her father by older half-sisters—by a world of women—Emma always retained some hostility to men. She passed the examination required to enter a German gymnasium in Königsberg, but was denied the needed certificate of character by her religion teacher. The family moved to St. Petersburg in 1881, and after six months more of schooling, she went to work in a corset factory. She read Nikolai Chernyshefski's revolutionary novel *What Is to Be Done?* and modeled herself on its heroine, Vera Pavlovna. Indeed, she kept this enthusiasm for Chernyshefski and this identification all her life. Like Vera Pavlovna, she was to set up a cooperative sewing shop, to enter a companionate marriage, and to live the life of a revolutionary. Alexander Berkman, her principal companion in America and, afterward, in Europe and Russia, modeled himself on Chernyshefski's hero, the revolutionary Rakhmetov. These facts, of course, highlight the enormous mass of differences between herself and the three love-goddesses. Emma Goldman was essentially a political woman and a political revolutionary; she participated in the world of men.

She helped Berkman plan his attempted assassination of Carnegie Steel president Henry Frick. She walked the streets as a prostitute to get money to buy him the revolver he used. After the deed, when the influential German-American anarchist Johann Most said that Berkman must be a crank, Emma horse-whipped him. She was always under police suspicion when something was bombed, like the Los Angeles *Times* building in 1910, a Lexington Avenue apartment building in 1914, the San Francisco Preparedness Day procession in 1916. All this is a far cry from Frieda and Alma and Isadora. However, Emma Goldman's politics were anarchist, Kropotkin-anarchist, and when she arrived in Soviet Russia in 1920, deported from America, she was soon disillusioned by the loss of individual liberty there. For her, revolution was primarily a matter of personal emancipation.

She was, moreover, not exclusively political. In 1916 she was arrested for propagating birth control, for she was a prominent sexual rebel, too, and had been touched by the erotic movement. She had been in Vienna in 1895—when Lou Andreas-Salome was there—and had heard Freud lecture, and had read Nietzsche and Ibsen at the same time. She herself lectured on Whitman, stressing his bisexuality. She believed, as Otto Gross did, that sexual possessiveness could be overcome, and she took as lovers men younger and more fragile than herself; in her private life she was another Magna Mater figure. Moreover, she did not believe that the vote for women would change anything important, or that Jane Addams or Ida Tarbell were the pioneers of any female freedom she cared about. "The great movement of *true* emancipation has not met with a great race of women who would look liberty in the face. Their narrow, Puritanical vision banished man, as a disturber and doubtful character, out of their emotional life," she wrote. In such remarks as these one sees what Emma Goldman had in common with Frieda and Alma and Isadora, what she might have admired in them; indeed, if those three had had any serious politics, it would have been Emma Goldman's. Perhaps they couldn't have, in that they were committedly nonpolitical, but still Emma Goldman, despite all her violence and her commitment to public and political issues, was nearer to them in life-purpose than she was to Jane Addams. Had she been younger when she first encountered the erotic movement, she might have resembled the others yet more.

Her temperament was in some ways similar. She took a strong interest in literature, particularly in the drama, and she was a propagandist for sexual and imaginative liberation, for rebellion as well as for revolution. She differed from Kropotkin in nothing so much as in her powerful concern for the problems of sexuality, which meant little to him. In fact, her position is close to that of Otto Gross, and her political activities in defense of that position should make us reflect on the nonpoliticism of the other women.

In 1906 she began to edit *Mother Earth*, an anarchist magazine whose title symbolizes the close connections between anarchism and matriarchal ideas. It was to have been named, in honor of Whitman, *The Open Road*, and inasmuch as that was the phrase from Whitman most dear and most meaningful to Lawrence, we are reminded of how sympathetic to him much of this anarchism was. It was the political movement closest to his own ideas, except in his "leadership" phase. *Mother Earth* was published for nine years, with the readership fluctuating between 3,500 and 10,000. It presented reprints from Tolstoy, Dostoevski, and Gorky, Emerson, Whitman, and Thoreau, plus new pieces by Floyd Dell, Ben Hecht, and other contemporary radicals. There was, however, no literary experimentation in its pages, as in Margaret Anderson's *Little Review*, and no great poet was first published there, a fact which marks the limits of Emma Goldman's commitment to literature and the predominance of the political in her. One symbolic anecdote about the relations between art and politics in her life has it that in 1914 Ben Reitman, her lover, was distracted from his work for the magazine and for the anarchist cause by reading *Sons and Lovers*; the novel opened up to him his whole relationship to his mother, who was staying with him and Emma at the time. So preoccupied did he become with his personal life as a result of reading Lawrence's novel, so neglectful of his anarchist duties, that Emma lost her temper and threw both him and his mother out of her house. Art was dangerous to politics.

Throughout her long relationship with Reitman she had played the mother role, and in this it was characteristic of all her love relationships. If she was like Frieda and Alma in this way, however, she was unlike them in being more dominant than her lovers in her and their public activities. As a public performer she was more like Isadora Duncan, and she was often described as the finest woman speaker in America. She was not limited to the private sphere and to personal relationships.

Lou

Lou Andreas-Salome was more like the first three than like Emma Goldman in the number of brilliant men among her lovers. But in more important matters she is to be related to a different model of the woman with a destiny. She throws light on them primarily by her differentness.

She was significantly older than the women we have been discussing, being eight years older than Emma Goldman, and the first part of her career was cast in a significantly different mold. As a girl, she kept a photograph of the student revolutionary, Vera Zasulitch, in her desk, and her own ambitions were strenuously intellectual and masculine. She clearly wanted to enter the world of men. It seems likely that she was genuinely embarrassed by the sexual importunities of her early admirers, Hendrik Gillot, Nietzsche, and Paul Ree. When she married, she lived with her husband entirely without sexual intercourse. He had children by the housekeeper Marie, who was herself devoted to Lou, but he remained in love with his wife. There is much in her career to remind us of the student heroines of Hardy and Ibsen. Sue Bridehead in particular is a novelistic treatment of the themes of Lou's early life.

But the second phase of her life was shaped by the ideas of the erotic movement, and was quite different in consequence. The Great War, for instance, seems to have been quite unreal to her, just as it was to the other erotic women, though it loomed so large in the world of men. And she opposed the Bolshevik Revolution in Russia, putting all her faith for the country's regeneration in the peasants. She had changed. Her clothes, her hair, her whole appearance and body had become much more feminine. Because in 1895, when Frieda, Alma, and Mabel were sixteen, Lou fell in love in Vienna. It seems likely that this was an ideological act, and the particular object of her affections was unimportant, but his name was in fact Richard

Beer-Hofmann. He was a poet who aimed at recreating myths—specifically Jewish myths—and he belonged to a circle of poets with a similar interest in the primitive and the irrational, a circle Lou tried to join. She then became the mistress of Dr. Pineles, a Viennese doctor who was already one of Freud's seminar members. In other words, she moved in circles where interest in sexuality, eroticism, and myth ran high, circles with ideas comparable to those of the *kosmische Runde*, then at the height of its development. (It is worth pointing out that four of the key figures in Lou's erotic life were Jews—Ree, Pineles, Beer-Hofmann, and Freud himself.) She had a number of affairs, in which she seems to have been coldly, and briefly, passionate, keeping as Magna Mater, the erotic initiative in "masculine" style, like Fanny zu Reventlow. When she was over forty she seems to have decided to bear a child, but she later changed her mind and secured an abortion. (In 1902 nearly all the women we have mentioned were pregnant—Else, Frieda, and Johanna von Richthofen, Mabel, Lou, and Alma.) And in 1897 she became the mistress of Ranier Maria Rilke, living with him in Wolfrats-hausen, where Else owned the house in which Frieda and Lawrence spent their honeymoon. He was twenty-two and she was thirty-six. He wrote to her describing Fanny zu Reventlow's joy in her illegitimate son Rolf and urging Lou to bear a child herself in order to become another such pagan madonna.

In her relationship with Rilke Lou clearly played the same role as Frieda played to Lawrence and Alma to Franz Werfel, the role of earth-mother or love-goddess. She taught him how to achieve a direct and natural relation to the outside world, the world of nature. She showed him how to escape the artificialities of art, the whimsical sentimentalities of his early verse. She disciplined him, in many of the same ways as Frieda was to discipline Law-rence. But she would not marry him. More like Mabel than like Frieda or Alma, she wanted her independence, and she was not quite at ease in the role of love-goddess. It was an idea to her. We hear of her declaring, with radiant blue eyes, "The reception of the semen is for me the height of ecstasy." Like Mabel Luhan, she had got the idea, and she knew how to live it out for a few hours or a few weeks at a time, but she could not manage it on the scale of the other two. It is presumably no accident that Mabel and Lou are also much the cleverest of the four, and the best writers. In 1910, in the heyday of the erotic movement, Lou wrote a book called *Die Erotik*, at Martin Buber's invitation. It is the book of a high priestess of Eros, we are told; the tone is incantatory and the diction sibyllic.

Else's Sisterhood

It is not so easy to find prominent figures whom we can compare to Frau Jaffe, as we compared Mabel Luhan, Alma Mahler, Isadora Duncan, Emma Goldman, and Lou Andreas-Salome to Frieda. To be comparable with Else, such figures would have to have been discreet, and to have spent much of their energy in seeming to the public eye, quite ordinary. What is more, because she herself was so discreet, little has been written about her, by herself or by others, and we know infinitely less about her than about Frieda. Perhaps when the Max Weber correspondence is published we shall be able to "place" her more exactly or more fruitfully. But it is possible even now to say something suggestive.

Like Lou Andreas-Salome, Else Jaffe began her life as an aspirant to the masculine world of mind, of *Geist*, and then encountered this new idea of the mind which required of women that they create a world of their own, a world of Woman. For a short time, as we have seen, she responded to the teachings of Otto Gross, and she may have been sincere in telling him that she was carrying them out by starting an affair with her "democratic" lover. But Gross was right when he wrote Frieda that such an affair, with such a man, must be implicitly hostile to everything he and she stood for. Else could never have become a citizen of the world of Woman; her radical loyalties went to the world of men, to the world of Apollo, to that liberal-critical-reformist mind which was in some sense doomed when she first met it. Being born out of her time, according to the rhythm of the history of ideas, she was doomed to guess wrong again and again, to back the wrong ideological horse to win the intellectual stakes; to guess wrong about Otto, about Lawrence, about Alfred. Ironically, it was scatterbrained Frieda who was in tune with the times.

Figures appropriate for comparison with Else might be sought among those women who devoted themselves to social and intellectual causes, like Jane Addams and Florence Kelley in America. Max Weber visited Hull House when he came to Chicago, and he described Florence Kelley to his mother as the most impressive American he had met during the whole of his visit. She was perhaps the American most like both his mother and Frau Jaffe. "A passionate Socialist, she revealed the evils of the system to us," he wrote.

Born in Philadelphia in 1859, Florence Kelley graduated from Cornell in 1882. She became the first woman factory inspector of Illinois, serving in that capacity from 1893 to 1897; she was a resident of Hull House from 1891 to 1899, at which point she left Chicago to found the Henry Street Settlement in New York. Over the course of her career she stimulated much socially protective legislation and served as general secretary of the National Consumers League for thirty-three years, from 1899 to 1932. Else Jaffe cited her with great respect in her paper on women factory inspectors in 1910.

Jane Addams, about whom we know more, consciously rejected culture, of the kind that Mabel Dodge theatricalized in Florence and Alfred Weber and Else Jaffe sociologized in Heidelberg. It was too merely feminine for her. Like Lou Andreas-Salome, Jane Addams had worshiped her father, morally as well as emotionally; she entered his world, the world of good men, and never rebelled against it. At college, Port Royal had been her ideal. Later she devoted herself to social work. In addition to the settlement house she set up in Chicago in 1889, she was involved in innumerable good works. She campaigned for the Progressive Party in the Dakotas, Iowa, Oklahoma, Colorado, Kansas, and Missouri; in 1912 she played a part in the organization of the party at its convention in Chicago, trying to get it to declare itself against war. In 1913 she went as delegate to the International Suffragist Alliance in Budapest. Like Lou Andreas-Salome, she made a pilgrimage to Tolstoy, but there could be no question in her life of an erotic-movement phase.

In the cathedral described in Vachel Lindsay's *Golden Book of Springfield* of 1920, Miss Addams was celebrated as a living saint—beside Emerson and Lincoln. In 1931 she received the Nobel Prize for Peace. A career such as hers may have been briefly a dream of Else Jaffe's, who deeply respected such achievements, but the evidence suggests that Else did not herself aspire to sanctity. She never could bring herself to a world-redeeming faith in any *porro unum necessarium.*

Certain features of her career suggest a comparison rather with Beatrice Webb. Born Beatrice Potter in 1858, the future Mrs. Webb grew up as the next youngest and the most intellectual of nine girls, who together formed a formidable sisterhood in upper-middle-class London. Despite her social rebellions, and her insistence on going her own paths, she remained emotionally attached to her family, which meant to her sisters. Like Else von Richthofen, she grew up devoted to her father and got on badly with her mother; at one time or another most of her acquaintances remarked on the "masculine" character of her personality. Again like Else von Richthofen, she was a beautiful woman, with a similar style of aristocratic and rather ascetic beauty, slender, erect, and proud. She remained a spinster until after her sisters were married. Then, in 1892, by which time she had made herself a name as a sociologist, or social observer, she married Sidney Webb, who was as short and thick as she was tall and slender. It is indeed in her marriage that she most resembles Else Jaffe.

Like Edgar, Sidney was strikingly ineligible, with his thick glasses, expressionless face, unhealthy skin, and husky whispering voice. Both men wore pince-nez and small beads, had disproportionately big heads and big noses. Whether or not a Jew, Sidney seemed very much a Cockney among Beatrice's friends, in his voice and manner, or lack of manner. Webb and Edgar Jaffe seem to have had much the same virtues and talents—primarily their extraordinary industry and intellectual efficiency combined with extraordinary selflessness and subordination of their own egotistic emotional claims. It is said of Sidney that he could memorize a whole page with one reading. Shaw saw in him the perfect collaborator, the perfect complement to his own more brilliant qualities—and so did Beatrice Potter. But, as long as social or sexual criteria were being invoked, Sidney was, like Edgar, a contemptible figure, and Beatrice did not mitigate this.

The Webbs and the Jaffes were both couples in which the man and the woman were "partners," and the similarity or complementarity of mental endowment and social purpose had to outweigh a striking incompatibility of personality and physique. (Lawrence's and Frieda's judgment of Else and Edgar, in "Daughters of the Vicar" can be read as applying to the Webbs, too.) The similarity between the Webbs and the Jaffes is heightened by the fact that both partnerships were sociological in their interests, but whereas the Webbs worked together with great success and to tremendous effect, the Jaffes seem to have written nothing together. The Webbs produced *The History of Trade Unionism* soon after they were married, *The Prevention of Destitution* in 1911, *The Constitution for the Socialist Commonwealth of Great Britain* in 1920, and *Soviet Communism* in 1924, to mention only a few of the more famous titles.

The also exerted great influence in the London County Council, the Labour Party, the Fabian Society, and in the pages of *The New Statesman*. They brought some sensible pressure to bear toward achieving a major change both in the structure of British civilization and in the opinions of British culture. Presumably, the Webbs' greater effectiveness had something to do with their greater "human" eccentricity. Beatrice appears in many memoirs by people who knew her as something of a monster, whereas Else is mentioned only discreetly and as discreet. The two women seem to have had some similarity of endowment—a fundamental melancholy of temperament, and a consequent investment of energy in book-learning and clarity of thought and expression. But Beatrice, from childhood on more extremist than Else, seems to have settled for satisfying what Lawrence calls "the social passion" at the cost of everything else. She bore no children—children made up so much of Else Jaffe's life—and she took no lover. She even gave up her theatrical, musical, and artistic interests when she married, devoting

herself completely to work in one direction. Before her marriage, relationships with brilliant men—notably Herbert Spencer and Joseph Chamberlain
—had been an important part of her life, and although she continued to
know such men afterward,—most notably Shaw and H. G. Wells—her relations with them were sexually and socially eccentric. She dealt with them
as if she were "the Webbs." Beatrice Webb was to Else Jaffe as Isadora
Duncan was to Frieda Lawrence—a poster version, perhaps even a cartoon,
compared to an intimate portrait.

The group with which Else can best be associated seems finally to be the
one she may well have taken as something of a model, the group of brilliant
German women around whom the Romantic movement crystallized at the
beginning of the nineteenth century. I mean Dorothea and Caroline Schlegel,
Rachel Levin, and Henriette Herz, all of whom made themselves the centers
of intellectual circles, and of whom all, except for Caroline Schlegel were
Jewish and Berliners. Their variously managed renunciations of their Jewish
heritage and their late love relationships with brilliant non-Jewish men
dramatized their decisive and risky conversions to the creed of Apollo and
the style of Athene. It was a risky conversion for women then, but they carried it through in cautious style, refusing to be bluestockings, refusing to
lecture and even to engage in anything more than minor writing projects.
They served, though in no posture of humility, the values of the mind. They
read, they took notes, they criticized, they wrote short articles on subjects
all over the range of literature and the arts, philosophy and politics. But they
let their men friends take the credit, publicly, for their ideas.

They were concerned about the position of women in their culture and
fought against "male chauvinism," but their style of fighting was neither
that of the militantly organized movement, like the Suffragettes, nor that of
Magna Mater individualists, like Frieda and Alma. They represented a
middle road, reformist and liberal, the style of Athene. Though they resisted, and resented, the crasser forms of patriarchal authority, they subscribed joyfully to the best values of the world of men—that intellectual and
imaginative province ruled by Apollo.

It is generally symbolic of their position, and also a particular link with
Else Jaffe, that they were early enthusiasts for Goethe's work. Sometimes
Caroline, sometimes Rahel, is credited with first establishing his reputation
as the supreme poet and recognizing his infinite superiority over Schiller. The
two of them, and Dorothea as well, established this doctrine of taste as a fact
in their various circles, and because their circles were made up of men of
influence, their position became an important watershed in the history of
German literature, and in Goethe's life. This matter is important in under-

standing them, as it is in understanding Else, because the worship of Goethe is always the worship of Apollo.

It is best to associate Else with the group as a whole, because in one feature or another she differs from each of them as individuals. But of them all it is perhaps Dorothea she most resembles. Dorothea was born in 1764, the daughter of Moses Mendelssohn, the Jewish philosopher and friend of Lessing, a man famous as the exemplary Jew who won tolerance for his race by himself practicing every Christian virtue. She grew up therefore in an intellectual and highly ethical house. Although she was devoted to her father, she nevertheless married young an intellectual banker, Simon Veit, whom she never loved but with whom she stayed until she met Friedrich Schlegel at Henriette Herz's salon. She was older than Schlegel and far from beautiful, but she offered him such passionate understanding and self-sacrificial tenderness that he loved her, and she left her husband and went with him, as his mistress, to live in Jena, with his brother Wilhelm and his wife Caroline and the other Romantics.

Caroline, perhaps the more brilliant of the two women intellectually as well as socially, was also devoted to the home-making and salon-making arts of womanhood. She too did not compete with men in the public sphere, and she let her husband take the credit for her ideas, her critical judgments, her learning. Both women were devoted to the life of the mind, but practiced it privately. Dorothea was, however, more melancholy and moralistic than Caroline, whom she was shocked to see gradually giving her love to Friedrich Schelling. Dorothea's love for Schlegel was all the more wifely for her not being married to him, and she had devoted herself to his welfare maternally, if not slavishly. He was a difficult and unsatisfactory husband and she had to put up with much personal neglect and still offer him every intellectual encouragement. It seems to have been because of her that his more imaginative and aesthetic interest in Catholicism was brought to the point of conversion (for both of them) and then marriage. Thus she exerted a powerful influence on his career, but from a humble and "wifely" position.

The likeness between her and Else Jaffe is not in their marriages or in their lives as a whole—after all, Else's Schlegel was Otto Gross, and she *refused* to run off with him—but in their intellectual careers. Like other women in the Romantic group, Dorothea Schlegel expressed herself mainly through her talk with, and her listening to, more famous people. Like Frau Jaffe, she did not publish under her own name. She did write a novel, *Florentin*, which was actually published under her husband's name. But for the most part her intellectual work was like Frau Jaffe's, more typically translation. Dorothea translated old French and German romances and

Mme. de Stael's *Corinne*. This last act of service was particularly ironic, because the Schlegel brothers spent months at the brilliant Frenchwoman's court, while Dorothea was left to cope with practical problems in Cologne. (One might compare *Corinne* with *The Plumed Serpent,* and say that Dorothea stood in the same relation to Mme. de Stael as Else Jaffe did to Lawrence and Frieda.) Like Else Jaffe with Alfred Weber, Dorothea Schlegel discussed with Friedrich all the religious, philosophic, and poetic ideas which preoccupied him, but which he found difficult to bring to clear utterance. Above all, she expressed herself in her family life, devoting great care to the education of her sons by her first husband. She was essentially a maternal woman, but not in the least Magna Mater. Hers was the maternity of self-sacrifice.

The alignment of Else Jaffe with Dorothea Schlegel is doubly interesting because the latter must have been in George Eliot's mind when she created Dorothea Brooke, the heroine of *Middlemarch*. Of course, she herself was what was mostly in her mind, but the name Dorothea must have sounded right because of the "great-hearted" and self-sacrificial resonances which Dorothea Schlegel's life had given it. Casaubon was Dorothea Brooke's Veit, Ladislaw her Schlegel. Dorothea herself stands as the supreme embodiment in fiction of those Victorian attitudes to love, marriage, womanhood, and the life of the mind against which Lawrence was reacting. Ursula Brangwen is his answer to Dorothea Brooke.* Which is to say that Frieda was a living antithesis to that Victorian icon of womanhood, that liberal idea served by both Dorothea Schlegel and Else Jaffe. Again the sisters' antithesis, their ideological antagonism, re-emerges. There are important differences between Else and the two Dorotheas; the former was a drier, sharper, more pre-shrunk personality, more averse to self-dramatization. But she is, by virtue of her idea, one of that sisterhood, against which Frieda rebelled when she joined the sisterhood of Alma Mahler, Isadora Duncan, Mabel Luhan.

* This will be discussed further in the Epilogue.

❦ 4 ❦

Weber and Lawrence: Their Lives Transmitted and Transformed

Let us remind ourselves, to begin with, of the crucial fact that Lawrence and Weber were enemies. There was an ideological war between them far more acute than anything between the two sisters. Lawrence has a poem, "The Revolutionary," a declaration of war against his enemies, which could appropriately have been addressed to Heidelberg, and to the Webers in person. It begins,

> Look at them standing there in authority,
> The pale-faces,
> As if it could have any effect any more.
>
> Pale-face authority,
> Caryatids,
> Pillars of white bronze standing rigid, lest the skies fall.
>
> What a job they've got to keep it up.
> Their poor, idealist foreheads naked capitals
> To the entablature of clouded heaven.

This poem was first published in January 1921, so we may perhaps take it to have been written about the time of Weber's death—certainly after the post-war revolution. Lawrence attacks pale-faced idealism in the name of darkness.

> To me, all faces are dark,
> All lips are dusky and valved. . . .
>
> To me, men are palpable, invisible nearnesses in the dark
> Sending out magnetic vibrations of warning, pitch-dark throbs of
> > invitation,

But you, pale faces,
You are painful, harsh-surfaced pillars that give off nothing except
                                                        rigidity,
And I jut against you if I try to move, for you are everywhere, and
                                                        I am blind,
Sightless among all your visuality,
You staring caryatids.

See if I don't bring you down, and all your high opinion,
And all your ponderous, roofed-in erection of right and wrong,
Your particular heavens,
With a smash.

The poem is a declaration of attack, and a boast that he will destroy his
enemy. It ends,

See if I am not Lord of the dark and moving hosts
Before I die.

But when Lawrence died, in 1930, he was not that. He had kept faith, he
could be called in some sense triumphant, but he was not Lord of Hosts. The
issue between him and Weber remained to be decided, remained to be fought
out—as, over the next forty years, it was fought out by their lieutenants.

But of course Weber and Lawrence were not only each other's enemies.
Their heritages could be developed in many different directions, and sometimes Weber's heirs even found themselves the allies of Lawrence's. But a
fundamental hostility was always latent and it became overt toward the end
of the century we have marked out for study, as we shall see now as we study
their heirs.

Their Reputations

When Weber died in 1920 his death was reported as a national event; it was
taken by many Germans as a national tragedy. Lujo Brentano wrote that "a
cry of grief has gone up not merely from his pupils. . . . [There is] the feeling
that Germany has lost one of her best men and at a moment when she most
needed him." Ernst Troeltsch declared that Weber was "one of the few great
men of present-day Germany, one of the very few personalities really in the
class of genius whom I have met in my life." Gertrud Baümler wrote, "our
gods have deserted us," and "Why was he not our leader?" Friedrich Mein-

ecke compared his personality in his late years to the late self-portraits of Rembrandt, and Joseph A. Schumpeter declared him the one teacher of freedom, forceful freedom, in German culture.

All these tributes came from men of achievement and experience among his contemporaries, in some cases from his rivals. Younger people stressed the daemonic side of him. Thus Theodor Heuss, the future President of West Germany, began his obituary notice of Weber: "For older people and specialized scholars he was an economist or whatever; for us young people meeting him meant the experience of a daemonic personality. He had power over men, the power of destructive anger, of objective clarity, attractive grace; all his utterances were suggestive, endowed with "charisma," with the grace of inborn leadership. And there was also an ascetic severity in him, a tragic renunciation, a bitterness, which put the passions of the subjective will and feeling under the law of necessity." Perhaps a dozen obituary tributes by young people are preserved in recently published collections, and all of them corroborate what Heuss said. I will cite only Karl Loewenstein's. He spoke of the daemonic power of a personality designed on a more than human scale: "in the dimensions of his being he was of Bismarck's class. It was his tragedy that he had to attack Bismarck's work." Loewenstein wrote this account for the *Berliner Tageblatt* in June 1920. Forty-four years later he gave an address in honor of Weber at the Munich University celebrations of the centenary of his birth. He described his first meeting with Weber, when the latter had put the whole field of music into a sociological perspective. "It was a turning point in my life," Loewenstein notes. "From that moment on I belonged to him, I had become his vassal." He reproduced notes taken forty-five years before, describing Weber as a public speaker: "If he is thoughtful, his face contracts like the sky before a storm. The appearance is manly, something elemental, often even something titanic is in it. He speaks freely with that bronze-ringing voice, in a wonderfully masterful German, each word in perfect relation to its companions, and yet the whole seems spontaneous. His volcanic temperament is always breaking through."

It is clear enough what a revitalization and reinforcement of the male image the young man was getting from Weber. Nearly fifty years later, at the end of Professor Loewenstein's own career, the impression remained as powerful as ever. He described Weber as he looked after death, transfigured, imperial, and said that the photograph of the dead face had hung above his study desk for all the intervening decades. Professor Baumgarten, too, told me that Weber alone among the men he had known as a boy had continued to seem as much older than himself as he was when they first met; though Baumgarten is now older than Weber ever became, he still has the sense of being somehow younger than his uncle, for he never caught up with that exemplar of adult manhood. This is what we mean by speaking of Weber as a hero of the patriarchal mind, and it has its significance for political as well as personal life.

In *Max Weber's Political Ideas in the Perspective of Our Time,* Professor Loewenstein traces the relationship between Weber's ideas and the subsequent political history of Germany. Weber offered Germany, he thinks, a chance to repudiate that "German" idea which had proved so dangerous. Tragically, this chance was not really taken up until 1945. Weber had insisted on the need to break the hegemony of Prussia, for instance, but only a tentative break was achieved under the Weimar constitution. After the war it finally was carried to completion in contemporary West Germany. What is more, although he foresaw the difficulties of federalism, he had recommended a federalist structure, and this too was finally adopted. Thus Germany's subsequent history *corroborates* Weber. Though the tone of Professor Loewenstein's discourse is academic, in affect he is expounding a prophet. Nearly fifty years after Weber's death, he quarrels with his authority only over minor points— for instance, he reproves him for applying the category "Caesarism" to Bismarck ("a man rather of his own stamp") instead of reserving it for the two Napoleons. Loewenstein implies that Weber was, even posthumously, the Bismarck of the twentieth-century Germany, or the nearest thing to another Bismarck which that Germany had. He has been, purely by virtue of his ideas and personality, her master-manager. This is the implicit message of Loewenstein's study, a book published as recently as 1966.

Lawrence's death, on the other hand, although in some sense a world event that received wide coverage, was closer to being merely a news item. Janet Flanner, writing about it for *The New Yorker,* blended misinformation with ill-judged condescension—"among other eccentricities, he had a fancy for removing his clothes and climbing mulberry trees"—in a way that could hardly have been used about Max Weber. (This is the way people talked about Otto Gross and his ideas.) Weber's success and Lawrence's differed in quality; one recalls the distinction which Sir Clifford Chatterley drew in reflecting on his own merely literary success: it is only men of action who are really taken seriously.

There were, however, serious tributes, notably the defense of Lawrence sent by E. M. Forster to *The Nation* and *Athenaeum,* March 29, 1930. In the same year Richard Aldington wrote in *Everyman* that Lawrence was a genius who "gives you direct contact with his own mind and with the earth and with human life; and so—to our eternal shame—we called in the police spies and the military and lawyers and saw to it that he was exasperated and hound-

ed into exile and bitter rage. I think England owes Lawrence an apology."
(Again, one cannot but recall Otto Gross, and wonder what kind of apology
would be appropriate to him. The police, the military, and the lawyers
came much closer to Otto than to Lorenzo, for in his case they all were embodied in his father.)

Murry wrote in *The Times Literary Supplement*: "Lawrence was the
most remarkable and most lovable man I have ever known. Contact with
him was immediate, intimate, and rich. A radiance of warm life streamed
from him. When he was gay, and he was often gay—my dominant memory
of him is of a blithe and joyful man—he seemed to spread a sensuous en-
chantment about him." Rolf Gardiner ascribed Lawrence's power to "the
dark, fecund forces of Nottinghamshire which threshed through his earlier
books," while Frieda connected him finally with the Mediterranean, "which
he loved so much." This was the characteristic note struck: while Weber had
promised leadership, had promised to create order, Lawrence promised life,
sensuous gaiety, contact with the earth—which is to say, the antithesis to order
and leadership.

There were young men and women who knew Lawrence in his last
years and were inspired by him as personally as Professor Loewenstein and
Professor Baumgarten were by Weber—young men and women like Gardiner,
Rhys Jones, Brewster Ghiselin, and Barbara Weekley. The equivalents of
Heuss and Jaspers were perhaps Aldous Huxley and John Middleton Murry,
men who promised to "make something of" Lawrence in the second half of
their careers, just as Heuss and Jaspers promised to make something of the
heritage of Weber. And of course they did, all four of them, in varying ways.

Both Weber and Lawrence died prematurely and suddenly and in both
cases the deaths were followed by a spate of publications, of books both by
and about them. This lasted six or seven years, after which the sharpest
attention of serious people turned away from them and they became of prime
interest only to a pious cult—with the notable exceptions of Jaspers and
Leavis, whose works have an intensity which scarcely permits them to be put
in that class. With the coming of the Nazi regime in Germany and the war
in England, both their reputations paled into "irrelevance." Indeed, Lawrence
was sometimes blamed for the rise of the Nazis. Eric Bentley's *A Century of
Hero-Worship* (1944) and William York Tindall's *D. H. Lawrence and
Susan His Cow* (1939) mark the nadir of his reputation, as much by the
factual inaccuracy and the condescension of tone they think they can get
away with as by the violence of their attacks on him. An equivalent criticism
of Weber during the war—by J. P. Mayer—was infinitely more respectful.

After the war, however, each of them gradually became, over roughly the same period, the essential foundations of massive structures of ideas and sentiments which came to characterize a whole academic discipline; indeed, it is not too much to say that each became a province of a national culture. Lawrence in England and Weber in America were names given to ideas which shaped the worlds of a generation of sociology and literature students, ideas which formed their personal intellectual styles, which is to say their styles in more than intellectual matters.

In 1945 Marianne Weber commissioned Eduard Baumgarten to re-present Max Weber to a new generation who did not know him, even in Germany. But nineteen years later Baumgarten was able to write that by then Weber's influence in America had made him a world classic, alongside Marx, Freud, and Nietzsche. Robert Merton's *Social Structure and Social Theory* has far more references to Weber in its second edition of 1957 than in the first of 1949, and it would be easy to find histories of literature in which the numbers of pages devoted to Lawrence increased over the same period. The decade from 1950 to 1960 might be designated the period of the two men's highest effectiveness, when interest and imitation among intellectuals was at its peak, although among students Lawrence has been even more popular since. But in the sixties trouble loomed for both men, and even more for the disciples who had shaped their work into the "ideas" I spoke of.

As symbolic events marking the climaxes of their reputations and the coming of trouble, we might designate the 1964 Weber centenary celebrations at Heidelberg, which were also the fifteenth meeting of the German Sociologists Association, and the 1970 Lawrence Festival at Taos. Both generated intense feeling and elaborate thinking, which were in both cases not exclusively scholarly and not exclusively admiring of their subjects.

At Heidelberg there were a thousand participants, three days of discussion, bitter dissension, and dissatisfied conclusions. Talcott Parsons spoke first, praising Weber as the founder of objective sociology. He was answered by Jurgen Habermas, who, to the applause of students, "envied" the ease with which Parsons could credit Weber with having transcended ideological conflict. In Germany, Habermas said, Weber had to be seen ideologically. He had to be seen as one of those who had brought in the Führer state and as the predecessor of the Nazi ideologist Carl Schmitt. Then Raymond Aron spoke, and described Weber as a power-oriented man, both in politics and in sociology. Then Wolfgang Mommsen took the same line, using terms like "chauvinistic" and "imperialistic" and names like Nietzsche, Hobbes, and Machiavelli. Herbert Marcuse, who was received with the greatest enthusiasm by the students, even disputed the value of Weber's main categories, and supplied alternative Marxist analyses. Other established scholars of course defended Weber, especially the Americans, but the occasion was marked by the attack rather than the defense.

The Lawrence Festival was not planned or conducted on the same scale, but it contained representatives of several countries and most attitudes toward Lawrence. F. R. Leavis was not himself present, but his spirit was represented by Keith Sagar. The significant opposition to the Leavisite position came not only from David Garnett, representing Bloomsbury, and Émile Delavenay, representing scholarship, but also from Robert Bly, who wanted to "use" Lawrence, to make him "relevant," and from Taylor Stoehr, who was assertively unimpressed by Lawrence, whom he found "uptight about sex." These two represented new directions for modern youth, for whom Lawrence in one case figured as important, in the other didn't, but for both of whom the traditional Leavisite Lawrence no longer counted. The young people there in possession of the new ideas could respond only to a Lawrence whom they could identify as "the first hippie"—a figure, it was clear, they would not long be able to reconcile with what he wrote.

It seemed clear at Taos, as it had at Heidelberg, that Lawrence like Weber was about to be returned to the shelf, relegated to the classics, installed among the great dead. But despite this relative decline in the sixties, on the whole we can say that Lawrence and Weber were granted an intense posthumous life which still affects all of us. In this section we want to trace that life, in the form it took in two disciples in each case, John Middleton Murry and F. R. Leavis for Lawrence, Karl Jaspers and Talcott Parsons for Weber. From where we stand at the moment, it is clear that Talcott Parsons and F. R. Leavis have been more important, but in the first posthumous decades it was Jaspers and Murry, the two disciples who had known the great men personally, who consoled and supported the widows, and who explicitly offered to make the dead men's *personalities* into parts of their idea, who were the more active and effective. In some sense—though in very different senses—both Jaspers and Murry sentimentalized and mythified their heroes.

It is no mere coincidence that in the sixties even as the reputations of Weber and Lawrence suffered severe setbacks, the renewed interest in Dada and Expressionism, and the intense response to Jean Genet, Norman O. Brown, R. D. Laing, and Timothy Leary announced the renaissance of Otto Gross's "idea." (Leary and Laing together are a contemporary equivalent for him, both in career and in ideology.) The renewed enthusiasm for Wilhelm Reich's sexual theories was also in effect an enthusiasm for Gross's. There is no evidence that Reich knew Gross, but he carried into the later decades of our century much the same mission as Gross first conceived; both rooted psychic health in political revolution and vice versa. Reich began to be active just when Gross perforce fell silent. Reich's theory of the orgasm, theory of character, and theory of character analysis are all ideas with equivalents among Gross's, while his theory of matriarchy (especially important in his *The Mass Psychology of Fascism* and *The Sexual Revolution*) is exactly the same. Like Gross, he believed that both personal and social life *must* have a pure original form, in which conflict is absent and to which we *can* return. This is an *a priori* principle of theirs, and no doubt related to their naïve scientism. Like Gross, too, Reich was rejected by both Freudians and Marxists of the orthodox kind when he tried to unite them. Between 1929 and 1935 he wrote six books that tried to combine the truths of both ideologies, to transform each one by means of the other. But in 1932 Freud declared that Reich's "The Masochistic Character" had been written in the service of the Communist Party, and in 1933 *The Mass Psychology of Fascism* was declared a liability to the psychoanalytic movement and he was expelled from it—despite the fact that the Austrian Communist Party had closed down Reich's socialist sexual-hygiene clinics in 1930 and the German Communist Party forbade the distribution of books from his publishing house in 1932. With that, Reich left Germany, soon left Europe, and gradually left politics. Like Gross, he was too idealist for political action. He came to America in 1939, set up his private institute in Maine in 1942 and died in prison in 1957, the year after Frieda Lawrence. Reich, like Frieda, found America much more sympathetic—in both senses of the word—than Europe (one can imagine that Gross might have felt that too). In the 1960s, under the sponsorship of Paul Goodman, Norman Mailer, and Susan Sontag, his ideas came to seem peculiarly American. In a sense, then, Gross too has lived on into our times. But because this was not a case of influence so much of as coincidence of cultural factors, we shall not study it in the same detail.

Although we are constructing our pattern out of thinkers, we recognize that it would be possible to build other patterns. We could ask who was D. H. Lawrence's inheritor as a novelist (I should answer Doris Lessing) and who was Weber's inheritor as a politician (my answer would be Heuss if we think of who learned from Weber, but de Gaulle if we think of who accomplished something remarkable in the Weberian style*). But by constructing such patterns we would lose the chance to parallel and contrast, so we will confine ourselves to their intellectual heirs.

In addition to paralleling the two, we want also to indicate the curve of each posthumous life, taken as an influence on others, an idea of our times, an archetype of intellectual activity. For many people of my generation, Law-

---

* Both Wolfgang Mommsen and Raymond Aron present the argument connecting Weber with de Gaulle.

rence was a way of thinking and feeling that redeemed the times, redeemed England. By identifying myself with him, I could feel in the right relation to my country and my culture. I could repudiate oppressive claims on me for admiration and loyalty (to certain authors, certain institutions, certain modes of being and manners) and could give my admiration and loyalty where *I* chose, in self-definition. I acquired heroes, and enemies, of whom I could feel proud. I had them by the grace of Lawrence; which is to say, by the grace of Lawrence-and-Leavis. And it seems to have been the case for some Germans that Weber offered *them* a similar principle of simultaneously personal and impersonal self-creation. But Weber offered also, in the hands of Parsons, a principle of pure understanding, a clarification precedent to action on any problem anywhere; not a principle of self-creation but of escape from self. Weber and Lawrence alike offered something of the first importance to a whole generation of intellectuals who came to consciousness after the Second World War. For a decade or two before that, they had been only great men of the past, and there are signs that that is what they will be again.

Jaspers

Let us first get some sense of Jaspers's career and personality independent of their connections with Weber—though those connections will keep obtruding themselves, because they are vital to any sense of the man. Jaspers admired Weber tremendously and studied him passionately from early on.

Born in 1883, Karl Jaspers took his M.D. from Heidelberg in 1909, when he was twenty-six, which must have been about the same time that he began to attend the Webers' Sunday afternoon salon. He was nineteen years younger than Weber, of the next generation. He then became an Assistent in Psychiatry at Heidelberg, and his first publications drew on his medical experience. Although he gradually advanced toward the borderline between psychiatry and philosophy, and finally crossed it, his early work has continued to have an effect. His *General Psychopathology* of 1913 had its seventh edition in German in 1959 and was translated into English in 1963 for the Manchester University Department of Psychiatry. Professor Anderson introduced the volume as the major text of the "Heidelberg school," and therefore of that phenomenological psychiatry which, with its sober, scientific, and pluralistic approach still offers the best alternative to the psychodynamics of the Freudians and their most effective opposition. Even in this new psychiatric context, the label "Heidelberg" still clearly stands for what Weber stood for in sociology, and Jaspers in fact used some of Weber's ideas as early as the first edition of his book. (He also cited Otto Gross's work, describing it as "Freudian.")

As time passed Jaspers became suspicious of science, and especially of modern man's trust in science. He felt that both Freudian psychology and Marxian economics expressed a retreat from man's full freedom and responsibility. But he also distrusted reason itself, or at least rationalism; he said that philosophy began where reason ended. We must *live* philosophy, for all philosophical problems are personal problems. At the same time, he was much concerned with contemporary politics and with the threat to moral culture posed by the institutions developed by twentieth-century civilization. These concerns taken together were the inspiration of his Existentialism. Despite a style, of language and of thought, which rival philosophies called prolix, melodramatic, and imprecise, he imposed his Existentialism on at least one generation of Germans as the moral philosophy of the age.

From childhood on, Jaspers suffered from bronchiectasis with cardiac decompensation, and he always expected to die in his early thirties, he tells us, of pyemia. Because of this condition, which made any fatigue, and hence any exertion, dangerous to his health, he lived a retired life, which led other people to think him very aloof. He had few friends until he met Ernst Mayer, when he was twenty-four, and then Mayer's sister Gertrud, whom Jaspers married in 1910. They came from a Jewish family, very studious, serious, pious, introspective. Ernst Mayer, a doctor like Jaspers, was himself disposed to depression and even to mental illness (one sister of his was institutionalized, and Gertrud became a psychiatric nurse), but he made himself an ardent disciple of Jaspers's philosophy and contributed a great deal of detailed criticism and suggestion to the latter's great work, *Philosophie*—right up to the day of its publication. So did Gertrud. The devoted, self-subordinating attention which the brother and sister paid to Jaspers, the latter in turn paid to Max Weber. They were all in love with greatness, which was to them moral greatness, and something to be associated with sickness rather than with health.

Jaspers's personality is vividly though critically described in Hermann Glockner's *Heidelberger Bilderbuch* of 1969. Glockner saw Jaspers first in 1919, as the latter strode onto the podium to lecture, tall, thin, arrogant-seeming, glancing at no one. His narrow face hung "as if on hinges; the sloping shoulders and the bowed-forward posture gave the still youthful body a lanky look, like a not-quite-open penknife." He wore a very neat suit and his long dark hair was combed straight back from the long pale face; the small tired eyes gazed far away, unfocused for those near him; he had a powerful brow and a weak lower face; a very earnest and unsmiling lecturer, altogether. He made philosophy blend into psychiatry, and for him the greatest moments of both kinds of knowledge were to be found together, in men like Kierkegaard.

Broaching Hegel in seminar, Jaspers admitted that he himself did not understand the Hegelian system fully, nor did he care to. Academic philosophy did not interest him. He saw *The Phenomenology of Mind* as an intellectual quarry, out of which he could hew the *Weltanschauungen* which did interest him, the living thoughts that characterize living men. He attacked the "modern scholasticism," the dead book-learning, of university philosophy in Germany. He spoke always out of his moral discontent, critical and severe. It was the depths of human evil, something behind what most philosophers deal with, which held Jaspers's attention always, Glockner says. He lived in, as he talked about, life's *Grenzsituationen*—the front lines of life. Even his bodily life was one of pain. He could glance at a companion only briefly in those days; he would knit his brows in effort, then open his eyes wide to stare at someone he wanted to look at. Later he overcame this tic, but at the price of making his face permanently stiff and masklike.

Gertrud Jaspers, whom Glockner also got to know, was a colorless figure until she spoke, which she did eagerly, intensely, and unstoppably; she was also a highly personal interrogator of others. More overtly moralistic than her husband, an extremely neat, competent, and frugal housekeeper, she also participated in his intellectual career in a very intense and partisan way. The two of them together, along with her brother, Ernst, when he was present, made up a party, dedicated servants to a cause which took up all their time and energy. They were forever in judgment, dissecting the personalities about them, and condemning most (including Glockner) as "an aesthete" or "frivolous" or "worldly." All this made a powerful contrast with what other professors at Heidelberg were then offering—a contrast like that made by Leavis at Cambridge, where Lawrence, just like Weber, was being made the sanction of intellectual severity. By 1929, and again in the 1950s, Jaspers was, with Heidegger, the philosopher of the hour in Germany. Glockner blames Jaspers for much of the tendentiousness of modern German literature.

Jaspers got the chair of philosophy at Heidelberg in 1922, just after Weber's death, and by his own account he took the direction of his life work from that event. He says in his *Philosophic Autobiography* of 1956, "My task became clear to me. Max Weber was dead. It seemed to me that the philosophy of the academicians was not really philosophy. . . . [My task was to be] to bear witness to philosophy, to direct attention to the great philosophers, to try to stop confusion, and to encourage in our youth the interest in real philosophy." That was the enterprise of the Jaspers party, which Glockner described from outside, and in that enterprise Max Weber played the role of the exemplary hero. (Change "philosophy" to "literature" in that quotation. and "Weber" to "Lawrence," and the enterprise is Leavis's.)

Ernst Moritz Manasse has said that Jaspers's thinking derives from his personal communication with Weber, a communication which was only enriched by his intellectual relation to the works of Kant, Kierkegaard, and Nietzsche. The last three gave him the conceptual tools to analyze his relation to Weber, but Weber had "repeated" those men's lives in his own being, doing, and suffering. According to Manasse, all his life long Jaspers played Plato to Weber's Socrates. Manasse makes this point in "Jaspers's Relation to Max Weber," an essay which Jaspers himself seemed to endorse; at least he received it very graciously. Manasse goes on to say that Weber was present in Jaspers's work even when not named; he was the original behind the "new type" described in *Psychologie der Weltanschauungen,* the daemonic or enthusiastic type, who lives in ultimate situations and has a grasp of the infinite, the type who both embodies objectivity and exceeds it by acts of self-commitment. What is more, Manasse argues, in Volume II of Jaspers's *Philo- sophie* the secret standard by which Jaspers judges all the possibilities discussed is in fact Weber's philosophic *Existenz.* And in Volume III again some general philosophic principles are detectably related to Jaspers's idea of Weber's "absolute negation" and his "failure"—the kind of failure necessary to all transcendence.

Jaspers gave his first speech specifically on Weber, which is really a remarkable philosophic essay, at Weber's *Trauerfeier,* the ceremony of mourning arranged by the Heidelberg students on July 17, 1920. (He already had cited Weber as a great modern thinker in his *General Psychopathology;* and Marianne Weber had written to Max in 1916 that Jaspers had built a theory of him as "a new type, who has the power—despite complete disillusionment —to contain and build on both monstrous tensions in himself and the contradictions of the outer world.") The speech was severely moralistic in tone. The only way really to honor a man like Weber, Jaspers declared, is oneself to work for "the actualization of what he has made potential, each to set to work on his own small part. . . ." Max Weber was *the* philosopher of our time, though to learn to see him as such is precisely one of the tasks he has bequeathed us. He was fragmentary, both in publication and in political action. He created no synthesis. He even split knowledge off from values. But the passion *for* values was incomparably alive in him. He has given the idea of a philosopher its contemporary meaning: "The philosopher is representative; what the epoch is, he is in substantial form. . . . We have seen in Max Weber an existential philosopher in the flesh. . . . He enacted in his broad spirit the fate of our times. . . . The Humanity (*Makroanthropos*) of our world stood personally before us in him." Weber was opposed to all philosophic systems, from Hegel to Windelband, for he believed that man cannot grasp the whole or an absolute. But Weber himself, by enthusiastically grasping fragments, made philosophic *Existenz* palpable to others. "It was not the vehemence merely of a temperament, but the vehemence of an idea . . . the Spirit was in him . . . unrestrainable life . . . daemonic."

But, Jaspers continues, Weber was opposed to any search for individuality. Freedom to him was merely the medium in which the suprapersonal might grow. He actively sought out his own limits, in order to avoid posturing as a prophet. He himself acknowledged no prophets, recommended none to others. He recommended only rigorous honesty. "All is naught before God, but it is our nature to make meanings, to fulfill tasks, else we are nothing worth." Today many are imaginatively fleeing the present as something dese-crated, or at least desacralized, but Max Weber gives the present to us instinct with that greatness, for good and evil, which we might otherwise attribute to the past alone.

Jaspers's lecture was a truly remarkable statement, still gripping when read today. Jean Paumen took it up as late as 1955 and expounded it as a leading text of existentialism. And of course it aroused a good deal of attention at the time. Heinrich Rickert, Professor of Philosophy at Heidelberg, took ex-ception to it. According to the account given by Jaspers in his *Philosophic Autobiography,* Rickert told him that not only was the speech philosophic nonsense, repugnant to the spirit of Weber, but Weber himself, though a great man in other ways, was philosophically childish. According to Jaspers, Rickert went on to describe Weber as being up to his death philosophically just one of his own, Rickert's, pupils. It seems likely that Jaspers's account is exaggerated—he was always a myth-maker—but there *was* a fierce, life-long quarrel between Rickert and him, and Max Weber was the cause and symbol of that quarrel. Rickert was a highly competent neo-Kantian, the last in the succession of great academic philosophers at Heidelberg. He had been a friend of Weber's, indeed an admirer, but he was not prepared to see all his own values swept aside in the institution of some new idolatry Jaspers was building. An anti-academic academician and a philosopher opposed to philo-sophic-system, Jaspers's deepest sympathies went to sick genius—to Strind-berg and Nietzsche, to van Gogh and Kiekegaard. These were his prophets, and he found their spirit embodied in his own place and time in Max Weber.

Rickert seems to have been a man determined to be comfortable in his own life, and to interpret his place and time in comfortable terms. He kept his rigor for his philosophy, and moved into it as from one world into another.

In having several worlds he was more like Weber than Jaspers was, for Jaspers tried to transfuse everything with the same moral and intellectual rigor. But of course Jaspers was right in pointing to the enormous difference between Weber and Rickert; the separation of worlds for Weber was not a convenience, a means to comfort, but a drama and a struggle, in which the intensest feelings of self-determination were involved. Jaspers was right not only to point to the difference, but to call it crucial. His way of treating Weber made the latter uniquely "relevant" (our contemporary use of the word is entirely appropriate) and made Rickert irrelevant, a figure out of Wilhemine academia with nothing to say to postwar Germany. Rickert did everything in his power —he was an expert academic politician—to prevent Jaspers from getting the second chair of philosophy at Heidelberg, always opposed his candidates within the department, and spread the word that Jaspers had never been and never would be a philosopher, but was merely a belated Romantic. Even Rickert's occasional courtesies betrayed the same hostility. He congratulated Jaspers on his *Nietzsche* by calling it, "if you don't object to the word, a *scholarly* book."

In 1932 Jaspers published a long essay, *Max Weber as Politician, Scientist, Philosopher,* which had been written in order to remind Germany, in that time of crisis, of her true voice. "He [Weber] was the modern man, who veils nothing from himself, who in this integrity finds the motive power of his life, and allows himself no escape into despair." Introducing the postwar reissue of the book, Jaspers says, "In Germany, in the years before the First World War, Max Weber was for many the man who embodied human greatness, whom they believed, by whom they oriented themselves, and above all whom they loved with the love that elevates us and causes what is authentic in us to grow." It is obvious how ill at ease Jaspers must have been in Wilhelmine Germany, and how grateful therefore to Weber; Jaspers was, in a simpler sense than Weber, a spirit in contradiction to his times; in *Die Geistige Situation der Zeit,* published in 1931, he deplored the general leveling down of culture and called for a campaign to save the minority of the best. He admitted his hostility to progress, to machines, and to the masses. All his enthusiasm went to that which could not succeed here and now. Every kind of philistine complacency was abhorrent to him. Weber, said Jaspers, stood supremely for the meaning of failure in our time—the failure of both German culture and Western civilization—and an aura of failure clung about him personally. Such failure is triumph. With the lucidity of an unconditional being, Weber could help other men come into possession of their own being through him.

Nineteen thirty-two was also the year of Jaspers's three-volume magnum opus, *Philosophie,* which systematically set forth his Existentialism. He defined *Existenz* as the experience of life's *Grenzsituationen,* including suffering, guilt, struggle, and death; and entailing the freedom to choose and the possibility of communicating. What this meant in terms of an actual life was exemplified, of course, by Max Weber. In 1937 Jaspers was dismissed from his teaching post by the Nazis, both because of his political opinions and because his wife was Jewish. As long as the Nazis were in power, the Jaspers lived a very retired life in Heidelberg. He devoted those years to the study of the Bible—the same years that Alfred Weber devoted to Greek tragedy. In 1945 he was reinstated by the Allies and delivered the inaugural address at the reopening of the medical school at Heidelberg. He contributed essays to *Die Wandlung,* the magazine in which Weber and others tried to define a new politics for Germany after the war. Jaspers was much concerned that Germans should admit their guilt for the war and purify themselves.

In 1946 he published *Die Schuldfrage* and was made an honorary senator of the university. Two years later he was offered a chair at Basel, where he spent the rest of his life. He continued to cite Max Weber as the hero of our time, and a hero with a message for Germany in particular. Indeed, he continued to deliver that message himself. Like Alfred Weber, he wrote on the philosophic-moral themes of history and tragedy, but he also wrote articles and broadcast talks on political issues of the day. He criticized the Bonn Republic from the point of view of Heidelberg, stirring up a great deal of controversy in the process. He was still living in the spirit of Max Weber.

In 1956, in his *Philosophic Autobiography,* Jaspers declared, "When Max Weber died, it was to me as if the world changed. The great man, who had justified and given life to the world for my consciousness, was no longer there. . . . Max Weber had been the authority who never pronounced judgment, never relieved one of responsibility, but gave one courage. . . . Now it was as if the court of appeal had disappeared, in which lay the absolutely reliable, not directly expressible, authority of reasonable discussion. . . ." And in reissuing his 1932 essay in 1958, Jaspers said, "He was the greatest German of our age. I have lived with this conviction for almost half a century."

In the same year, 1958, the year in which Jaspers was given the German Peace Prize, to crown his career, a new edition of Weber's *Gesammelte Politische Schriften* appeared. Theodor Heuss, then President of West Germany, wrote an Introduction for it, prompting Jaspers to send Heuss a rather severe letter. Indeed, a number of people wrote to Heuss about that Introduction, including T. W. Adorno, who attacked the doctrine of *Wertfreiheit,* and Weber with it. Weber was no longer an intellectual hero for the avant-garde. But Jaspers, fervently loyal, claimed that Heuss should have aligned Weber, not with ordinary politicians, but with Cromwell, Bismarck, and Caesar. "Max Weber seems to me, if one may ever say any such thing, one sent by Fate, in order that through him might be tested what German politicians are, and that they might be reminded what they could be. The Germans did not recognize this." Even today Weber is the German mentor, Jaspers insisted; he alone could awaken Germany's feeling for the seriousness of power and for the ethics of political thought. Jaspers scolds President Heuss for not having challenged present-day Germany harshly enough in his presentation of Weber.

Clearly, Jaspers "made a lot out of" Weber, and it is not surprising to find that he also contributed to his mythification in other ways. He advised Marianne Weber to suppress bits of information which might have damaged the image. One of Weber's last letters was on the number of Jews in the Reichstag commission examining the German army's war record. Weber thought it unwise to have so many Jews on that commission, because of the right-wing reaction it would provoke, and his language in saying so was allegedly anti-Semitic. Jasper also assured Marianne that Weber could not have been unfaithful to her with Frau Jaffe, even though this was not his only infidelity. Most notably of all, Jaspers advised Marianne to destroy Weber's own account of his neurotic symptoms, written for psychiatric analysis; apparently a remarkable document, the only part which has been recorded is that his sleeplessness was related to his fear of uncontrolled ejaculations, a fear which, if we remember his impotence with Marianne, is very poignant. Ever a moralist, Jaspers had also in this case a political motive, in that he feared the Nazis would seize the documents.

Ludwig Curtius's account of Jaspers at Heidelberg confirms Glockner's. He describes Jaspers's intellectual style as clinical, and his personal life as monastic in its exact regulatedness. Gertrud Jaspers, he says, was known as "das Flämmchen," the little flame, for her eagerness. Curtius felt that Jaspers was a modern saint, but that his ideas would lead one logically to another Geneva and another Calvinism, which Curtius found not to his taste. Alfred Weber, a friend of Curtius, may be supposed to have held a sharper version of the same opinion. He seems to have felt no personal sympathy for Jaspers, though they were the two spiritual leaders of Heidelberg after the war. Alfred still held by some *Lebensphilosophie* ideas, and he could be no priest of a religion in which Max was a major saint.

Nevertheless, Alfred Weber and Karl Jaspers worked together to renew Germany from her sources, to redeem the hideous past, to make dominant those traits in the national character—the Heidelberg traits—which had long been recessive. It is a striking fact to reflect on, those four people in Heidelberg—Alfred and Marianne Weber, Else Jaffe, and Jaspers—living through the Nazi regime, the war, the reconstruction of Germany, the fifties and in the case of Jaspers and Frau Jaffe, the sixties too, still thinking of Max Weber. They worked for Germany and for culture during those forty, fifty, years after Weber's death and always referred the big questions to that remembered judgment. Jaspers says that in a crisis he and his wife would always ask, "What would Max Weber have said?" Alfred's *feelings*, of course, must have been very unlike Jaspers's, but still all four *thought* of Max Weber in their work for Germany and for civilization; and their work counted, for they were Heidelberg. When we turn to Lawrence, there is a partial equivalent in the women who lived on in Taos—Mabel Luhan, Dorothy Brett, and Frieda herself—all of whom in some sense remained in love with Lawrence. But none of them was working for America. Whereas Leavis and Murry worked for England in terms of what Lawrence had said and been, and Eliot and Russell worked against that. But we do not have the four of them together in that dramatically concentrated focus of a single town. There was no English Heidelberg.

It is clear enough what a manifold use, what a profound inspiration, Jaspers made of Max Weber, and how unlike it was to the use which Talcott Parsons was to make of him. And it will already have occurred to the reader, no doubt, how similar Jaspers and his "party" were, in moral temperament, to F. R. Leavis. Leavis took his life task from Lawrence and in his name quarreled bitterly with his academic colleagues at Cambridge. And constructed out of Lawrence's life and work a moralistic philosophy which intoxicated generations of students, just as Jaspers did with Weber. That Calvinist party member's intensity, and the anti-academic academician's career were very fully developed in both. Leavis is much more like Jaspers than Murry was.

Murry

Nevertheless, I think it is enlightening to see Jaspers as a figure whose discipleship to Weber parallels Murry's discipleship, to set the Judas figure against the John of Patmos. Moreover, Murry's work parallels Jaspers's chronologically. His major book on Lawrence appeared in 1931, just after Lawrence's death, just as Jaspers's *Trauerfeier* speech followed Weber's death. It was an equally remarkable work, though very different. In *Son of Woman* Murry told the story of Lawrence's life with many parallels to the New Testament. He told it with intense sympathetic participation and seriousness. But a major point of his diagnosis is Lawrence's sexual abnormality—his near-impotence and near-homosexuality, and his desperate need to deceive the world and himself about those tendencies. "This man, we feel, has no business with sex at all. He is born to be a saint. . . . What genuine and unhesitating passion there was in Lawrence's life before his mother's death went to a man, not a woman." Indeed, one of the implicit messages of the book is that Lawrence was in love with Murry himself. (If course, similar messages are implicit in other of Murry's books, and about other people. He was the Great Beloved of English letters.) Thus Lawrence, as Murry sees it, perversely made himself into an anti-type of Jesus, in rebellion against his own fate. Murry's interpretation of Lawrence's work therefore climaxes with "The Man Who Died," because in that story Lawrence finally imagined himself in Jesus's position, and gave us his reinterpretation of the Resurrection. Although Murry later came to accept Lawrence's teaching as more than perversity, he repeated this diagnosis of the man again in 1954, when he wrote a new introduction to *Son of Woman.* But still Lawrence was for Murry, in words Jaspers might have used about Weber, *the* genius of our times; "through Lawrence we learn to know ourselves, in a way which men have never known themselves before."

Murry's treatment of Lawrence, in his articles of reminiscence as well as in his book, roused great excitement and, among Lawrence's friends and disciples, great anger. Catherine Carswell wrote her own reminiscences of Lawrence, under the title *The Savage Pilgrimage,* and made Murry the villain of the story. She attacked many things in the "Reminiscences of D. H. Lawrence" which Murry published in *The Adelphi,* accusing him even of misrepresenting facts. Murry in turn accused her of the same, and was able to prove his points. The publishers of *Savage Pilgrimage* withdrew the book after two thousand copies had been sold, and Murry brought out *Reminiscenses of D. H. Lawrence* as a book. It contained the *Adelphi* articles, plus a refutation of Mrs. Carswell's objections to them as long as the articles themselves, plus a highly emotional essay explaining why he had had to "destroy" Lawrence in *Son of Woman,* plus all his reviews of Lawrence's books (to prove that he had not attacked him during his lifetime). The effect, of course, was to intensify the superficial and scandalous excitement surrounding Lawrence thus, in a sense, justifying T. S. Eliot's attitude of disapproval and distaste. At the same time Murry was on a fellowship from the University of Liverpool to write a book about Blake and was also about to write on Keats. His career as a critic and scholar seemed to be established. But at a deeper level it had been broken by his encounter with Lawrence, for he was about to begin his experiments with building communes and with spiritual leadership. After Lawrence, Murry could not be content to be even the best of literary critics. He had to be a hero.

Perhaps one should say that the encounter with Dostoevski had sum-

moned Murry away from mere criticism long before. His 1916 book on Dostoevski was iconoclastic and "religious" enough in style. But he had returned
from that adventure. His *The Problem of Style* in 1921 was a retreat to classical criticism which owed a great deal to Eliot's *The Sacred Wood*. Murry was
again a man of letters, in the new style of severe intellectuality. But after
1931 his major energies went into changing the forms of *life,* not into appreci-
ating literature. By then Lawrence had displaced Dostoevski, who plays a
much diminished part in Murry's subsequent writings, as the representative
of more-than-literature. Murry's life style became Lawrentian. He married
no more consumptives, he lived on a farm and preached Eros and marriage.
He played Judas to nobody else. He had the right to claim, in *Reminiscences,*
that in writing *Son of Woman* he had shattered his old identity and received
the truth that Lawrence had to give him.

We have already discussed that change of identity and his conversion to
Lawrence, insofar as they affected his relation to Frieda and his love-life—
that is, his private self. Here we are concerned with his public relation to
Lawrence, as critic.

Even granting the equivocal nature of the Judas relationship, one is
struck by anomalies and sometimes evasions in Murry's early treatment of
Lawrence. He did not write about Lawrence (or about Dostoevski) as a
writer—that is, as a novelist or a poet. This is striking because he wrote about
Katherine Mansfield as a model stylist and fictionist as well as a letter-writer
and personality. He wrote about her in the same terms as he wrote about
Keats; indeed, he explicitly identified them. As early as 1921, while she was
still alive, he was quoting passages of her work as models. But not Lawrence.
He referred to Lawrence exclusively as a spiritual explorer, and so, while honoring him highly, he avoided certain confrontations with him, excluded him
from areas where Murry took himself with professional seriousness, such as
literary criticism. (In *God*, a book published in 1929, Murry described Lawrence as "a man of fundamentally religious genius." The book itself, he said
"should have been written by Lawrence," but was not because Lawrence refused to acknowledge his own kinship to Jesus, his deep Dostoevskian preoccupation with Christ.) Murry's treatment of Lawrence in his writing is
quite parallel with his way of dealing with Lawrence in their face-to-face encounters. He often declared himself bewildered and amazed by what Lawrence said about, for instance, Murry's relations with Katherine. Lawrence, he
tells us, had intuitions, and moral principles, which were entirely beyond
Murry's comprehension; and he says this about pronouncements on Lawrence's part which do not seem to us very hard to understand. We cannot but
suppose that Murry did not *want* to understand many of the things Lawrence

said to him. He offered him that extravagant deference as a substitute for listening.

It was the same when he wrote about him. Even in book reviews Murry wrote about Lawrence as a personal friend, but also as "something more than human." The first tone was flirtatious. In his review of *Lady Chatterley's Lover*, for example, he reproaches Lawrence for identifying all "touch" with sex. "Do I not touch Mr. Lawrence at this moment through his book, even though he hides himself within? Veritably touch him, and closer than by laying my hand upon his arm." The second tone is exalted and awe-struck. In *God*, for example, he says, "Whereas I am in no danger of discovering that I am like the founder of Christianity, D. H. Lawrence veritably is." (Murry published several times on Jesus between 1925 and 1929, while he was also writing about Lawrence.) The effect of combining the two tones was to reduce all his affirmations of Lawrence to the status of personal effusions, although Murry did mean what he said, despite the flawed ambiguity of his kind of sincerity. Indeed, he had nearly laid his hands, as the title of his 1931 work suggests, on the largest single truth about Lawrence. Following our pattern, we may suggest that Jaspers saw Weber as a *Son of Man,* an embodiment of spirit and justice, whereas Murry saw Lawrence as a *Son of Woman,* except that he did not see him as an embodiment of love and fertility. He did not see the crucial thing because he made the phrase mean mainly son of Mrs. Morel, sufferer from Oedipal conflicts.

There was a lot which Murry did not see about Lawrence, could not see because he had never understood the erotic movement, never adequately confronted eroticism. Because he built for himself a religion of love, he was of course profoundly responsive to, excited by, what Lawrence and Frieda said, and did, and were. But, as he himself said often, he never understood them; not because of any intellectual difficulty in the doctrine, obviously, but because his own imaginative energies were committed to an opposite enterprise. Even later he fought Lawrence off. In *Adam and Eve* in 1944 he says, "For years and years it seemed to me that, so far as all the evidences went, Lawrence had been right and I wrong. And yet, somewhere in the depths of my soul, I could not surrender. If I were to have admitted what Lawrence and circumstances were conspiring to wring from me, my inmost core of integrity would have dissolved." Self-annihilation yes, self-violation no. His truths and Lawrence's were still antipodal.

However, Murry's writings and lectures were effective in their way as propaganda for Lawrence. He was a popular serious writer. A lot of people outside the cultural establishment—working-class audiences, particularly Nonconformist and Catholic in the north of England—responded to his "religious" sincerity, his anti-intellectual and anti-aesthetic emotionality. His Prospectus for *The Adelphi* in 1923 said: "We are sick of 'Art' " and promised that the magazine would publish no reviews and nothing highbrow. Even during the Second World War his books sold in thousands, though his reputation was then at its lowest with both the official establishment and the literary avant-garde. He never had a national position equivalent to Jaspers's to put at Lawrence's disposal, although in 1934 Rayner Heppenstall tried to make him into England's intellectual leader with his *Middleton Murry: A Study in Excellent Normality*. But Heppenstall weighs less as a disciple than Jaspers's disciple, Hannah Arendt. Nevertheless, Murry did have influence. His writing helped to make Lawrence a big figure in British culture in a way that he was not, for instance, in American culture. This is in some sense the measure of Murry's achievement. I myself first came to Lawrence through Murry, not through Leavis.

This meant that I came to Lawrence the personality or the legend, Lawrence the friend of Murry. It was left to Leavis to enforce a disciplined encounter with Lawrence's work. But still I gathered from Murry that Lawrence was a remarkable *mind,* someone to collocate with, say, Blake. Murry elaborated his theory of marriage with the help of quotations from Blake and Lawrence. His actual practice in marriage, which he made public, also owed much to Lawrence. He had first chosen Betty Cockayne to be his wife, as we have seen, on the Lawrentian grounds that she was a Woman. And we also find him, after long quarreling, attempting an erotic reconciliation with her, "in fulfillment of D. H. Lawrence," and deciding to beget a child upon her and call it David in his honor—which he did. Murry made Lawrence potent to others by the way in which he allowed Lawrence to act upon his own life, much as Jaspers did for Weber in his much more austere style.

Just as Weber changed Jaspers's life by forcing him to take power politics and nationalism seriously—Jaspers's family had hated Prussia and Bismarck's Reich, and he grew up anti-political—so Lawrence changed Murry by forcing him to take sex and sensual love seriously. These reactions were representative, for Weber had the same effect upon Friedrich Naumann and Lawrence had the same effect upon Aldous Huxley. In the end, Jaspers combined Weber's new teaching with other, more orthodox spiritual doctrine, just as Murry combined Lawrence's. By the end of a long life free from inner conflict, Jaspers came to be quite synoptic in his wisdom. At least this is what Eduard Baumgarten said in an interesting essay of 1956, in which he accused Jaspers of thus betraying his professed allegiance to Weber. Baumgarten is Weber's nephew and another of his intellectual heirs, so that his reproach to Jaspers can be compared with Murry's and Huxley's mutual reproaches à propos the Lawrence heritage. Baumgarten argues that a hidden center to Jaspers's thought was a contrast drawn between Kant and Goethe and decided in Kant's favor, because Kant, like Jaspers, believed in Radical Evil. But, Baumgarten insists, this preoccupation with Radical Evil was alien to the spirit of Weber, who, given that contrast, would not have simply preferred Kant. (The equivalent reproach to Murry might point to his frequent contrasting of Shakespeare with Milton and his preference of Shakespeare because of his "submission to life.")

But of course there was a difference between the two disciples. Unlike Jaspers, Murry never went in for rigid probity in his own life, nor did he ascribe it, or any equivalent, to his hero. It is typical that whereas Jaspers suppressed the evidence of Weber's sexual problems, Murry exaggerated the evidence for Lawrence's. *Son of Woman*, his equivalent for Jaspers's obituary praise of Weber, was for most readers an *attack* on Lawrence. The sacrificial victim and the knife are entirely appropriate to each other, said T. S. Eliot, and Murry himself acknowledged the publication of this book to be the act of a Judas. He was, indeed, essentially equivocal about Lawrence. But he lived in crisis as much as Jaspers himself; for he was all spiritual-moral intensity. And he was devoted to Lawrence and Lawrence's ideas—but in a dialectical way. One could apply to him vis-à-vis Lawrence the formula Ernst Manasse applied to Jaspers vis-à-vis Weber and say that at least his later thought all derived from his "encounter with" Lawrence.

Some of the difference between Murry and Jaspers derived simply from the different modes of being which their heroes had espoused. Weber had stood for the morality of man as citizen, the morality of the public life, though he traced that inward, of course, to the core of conscience and understanding. Lawrence had stood for the morality of man as lover, for the private life, though he traced that to the mind and conscience. Murry's sincerity, even toward Lawrence's ideas, was that of a lover, whereas Jaspers's was that of a priest.

His persona as the-critic-as-lover was something that Murry got from his Russian masters rather than from Lawrence. I have pointed out that his *Dostoevsky* belonged to the line of interpretive criticism begun by Rozanov in 1890 with his *Legend of the Grand Inquisitor* and that Lawrence's most vehement attacks on the "Russian" mind and its Judas-mysticism occur in his essays on Rozanov. This becomes doubly interesting when we study the pattern of Rozanov's personal relation to Dostoevski for Rozanov, like Murry, was a critic-as-lover. He admired Dostoevski and identified with him to an abnormal degree. In fact he married the older man's ex-mistress in order, he said, to become intimate with his spirit. This woman, moreover, Apollinaria

Suslova, was not only Dostoevski's mistress but also his model for Polina in
The Gambler, Aglaia in *The Idiot,* Grushenka in *The Brothers Karamazov*—
for most of his haughty, violent, destructive women. She held the position
in Dostoevski's work which Frieda held in Lawrence's. Rozanov married her
in 1880, the year before Dostoevski died. He was younger than she, and a
much less powerful personality, and she used him very badly. The resemblance between his behavior and Murry's must have been very striking to
Lawrence, at least after 1923, when he became aware of Frieda's attraction
to Murry. We can take his Murry stories, "The Borderline" and "Jimmy and
the Desperate Woman," as proof of his imaginative preoccupation with the
future relations between Murry and Frieda. Though Lawrence refused the
role of Jesus, he certainly saw Murry then as betraying him with Frieda,
and therefore—inasmuch as Murry was protesting extravagant devotion to
Lawrence at the same time—as a kind of Judas, a fake kind, who "worked
up" his own treachery and excited himself with the thought of his spiritual
enormity. But then all Judases were like that to Lawrence. His view of the
matter only reinforced Murry's determination to see him as Jesus, the betrayed saint, to turn him into another tortured and humiliated Dostoevski,
instead of the laughing and bearded centaur which Lawrence liked to present
himself as.

To see Lawrence this way was a betrayal, but an exaltation too, for Murry,
for it revealed in Lawrence that divided innermost self in which he resembled
the great Russians. It revealed his greatness. (To Murry, we may note, the true
hero of *Crime and Punishment* was Svidrigailov. All great souls were deeply
divided against themselves and suffered greatly; they necessarily sacrificed
their normality and got betrayed.) The Judas theme and Jesus's inviting of his
own betrayal had fascinated intellectuals all over Europe around the turn of
the century. Nietzsche and Ibsen had written about such themes before, and
there was much about it in the French and German literature of the first
decade of the century. But it was in some sense a specially "Russian" subject,
as Nietzsche had pointed out in *Anti-Christ,* because it brought together so
many of the themes of Dostoevski's work and that of his Decadent heirs—
primarily the interaction of spirituality and sensuality, humility and pride,
adoration and betrayal. Andreyev's *Judas* of 1907 was one of the most brilliant
treatments. Murry made himself into England's "Russian." Jaspers in contrast,
never played a "Russian" role in real life, although, to be sure, his sensibility
was Dostoevskian in some ways.

Murry's behavior, his frequent autobiographies, his conversions, his can-
did and intimate editorials, his highly public marriage experiences, his mystical cult of Katherine Mansfield after her death, his religious musings, were all

a performance of this "Russian" temperament. The word "performance" seems right because of the element of the factitious, of the self-displaying, of the unscrupulous, which accompanied his undeniable sincerity and courage. He was performing for English readers a version of that temperament which took intellectual Europe by storm at the turn of the century—that mixture of passionate ebullience and mystical meekness, of sensuality, emotionalism, and spirituality, which the West met as for the first time in the novels and tracts of Tolstoy, Dostoevski, Chekhov, Gorki, Shestov, Rozanov, and the other figures of the Russian renaissance. These writers were known as "the spiritual realists," to contrast their works with the "sensual realism" of French literature, and they were Murry's great alternative to the Man of Letters before he yielded to Lawrence. They were his escape from "being an intellectual" or "belonging to the privileged class."

In behaving in the "Russian" way, Murry therefore felt himself, though mistakenly, to be in alliance with Lawrence. This did not change totally in 1931, when he "came over" to Lawrence, but his opinions, the contents of his books, did change. In this he differed from Jaspers, whose devotion to Weber seems to have flowed on smoothly, only deepening with time, whereas in Murry's case 1931 marks a watershed in his treatment of Lawrence. Of course, Murry was not consistent in the change he underwent; his treatment of Keats, for instance, continued to express the former Murry even after 1931; in writing about Keats he continued to celebrate Love.

Murry's religion of love was, insofar as it was sexual rather than Dostoevski-spiritual, a version of the old Romantic religion, in which love and suffering and beauty were profoundly interrelated and gave birth to each other. This is, of course, exactly the idea of love which the erotic movement set out to destroy and replace. As far as Murry was concerned the major historical hero of the religion of love was Keats. (Its major contemporary heroes were himself and Katherine Mansfield.) In the four editions of *Studies in Keats* which he published between 1930 and 1955, Murry recited the story of Keats's torturing passion for Fanny Brawne, of his death from consumption, and of the composition of his great poetry, insisting all the while on the relations between all three processes. To be sure, he did not say they *caused* each other. By then Murry stood for "health"—especially when he was thinking about society rather than literature—and he never admitted that disease was necessary to beauty, art, and love. But he brought all three very close to each other and made an emotional unity out of them. It was Lawrence's denunciation of this connection, in Murry and Katherine, which bore down so hard on him, and which he alternately assented to and fought off all his life.

Now Keats *is* an appropriate hero for anti-patriarchal rebels, as his nineteenth-century reputation makes clear. To men of strictly patriarchal values, Keats's virtues will seem weakness, effeminacy, sensuality, self-indulgence. But the rebellion of which he is the hero will be no more matriarchal than the rebellion of which Clarissa Harlowe is the heroine. Murry had committed himself to the Romantic rebellion against patriarchy, which was imaginatively as out of date as Max Weber's.

He identified himself, his size, his looks, his class origins, his life story, with Keats. The wonderful spirit that died in Rome was reborn in London eighty years later. Even more, he appropriated Keats and his story. He identified Keats also with Katherine Mansfield (and to a lesser extent with his second wife, Violet le Maistre) because of her tuberculosis and her achievement as a writer. In the paragraph quoted below, taken from the "Fanny Brawne" essay in *Keats,* he alludes not only to his own experiences of the death of a loved one, but also to his own immediate remarriages, in a way that would be clear to the initiated reader:

> Nothing more powerfully prepares a man's instinctive and unconscious nature for passionate love than prolonged contact with hopeless illness in a loved one. The deep unconscious being reacts away from the menace of death and the pain of beholding its approach. The consciousness may strive to suppress this motion as callous and heartless, but the motion persists. The instinctive being turns away from physical death and seeks to be renewed by plunging into the instinctive life of which passionate physical love is the consummation, and longs for this renewal most desperately in the extremity of its own suffering for the dying one. The inordinate demand of unavailing spiritual love on the man's nature creates a void in the total being that craves replenishment in love of a woman.

That last sentence will remind us of Lawrence, and of the powerful effect which *Aaron's Rod* and *Fantasia of the Unconscious* had on Murry in 1921 and 1923. He acknowledged, by such responses, that Lawrence had much to teach him about such matters. But his dominant strategy was to avoid the challenge of eroticism by aligning Lawrence with Dostoevski-Jesus, as a *spiritual* teacher, while he, Murry, played the role of the lover. Lawrence's scorn for "love," his emphasis on the conflicts within the erotic relationship, on the cruelty and anger, the naked sensuality, above all on the impersonality of passion, were taken by Murry to show that Lawrence was as far from "ordinary love" as Jesus, though in the opposite direction. They both deserved reverence, but he, Murry, was the normal man, who had to work out his destiny in terms of love, applying their doctrines insofar as he found them useful. Past this point Murry would not go on yielding to Lawrence, except for occasional moments of enthusiasm.

However, after 1931 Murry did take seriously—though not steadily or whole—the ideas which conceptualized Lawrence's interpretation of life. In his magazine *The Wanderer* which he began in 1933, he published three essays "On Marriage," beginning in the second issue, which reproduce Lawrence's teachings with great intelligence and sympathy. "The work of Lawrence without his marriage is quite unimaginable," he says. "Driven by his daimon, he entered on his marriage; driven by his daimon, he gave his marriage to the world. We were best to look at it. . . . No one can know what he ought about marriage in these days without knowing about Lawrence; and no one can know what he ought about Lawrence without knowing about marriage." He points out how Frieda refused to acknowledge "the man's world" and demanded deference from Lawrence because of her femaleness. There is no denying that Murry quite clearly saw Lawrence's relation to matriarchy.

He continued this line of thought in *Adam and Eve,* published in 1944. This "essay towards a new and better society" is perhaps Murry's major effort to make use of Lawrence's achievement societally, as a way to save England. It can be compared with Jaspers's 1932 essay on Weber, for England's crisis did indeed come much later. In Part 2, "On the Religion of the Individual," Murry begins by contrasting Lawrence with Aldous Huxley as alternative spiritual explorers. He contrasts *Fantasia of the Unconscious* with *Grey Eminence,* individual sex-fulfilment with individual self-annihilation, mysticism of the flesh with mysticism of the spirit. He flatly rejects the second alternative in each case, and by so doing implies his disaffiliation from Dostoevski. "I have never tried to live by Huxley. . . . In one matter—which is the substantial theme of this book—I have always been quite certain that I knew better than he did: namely, about the nature of love. Lawrence is quite a different kettle of fish. Him I have tried to live by; and from him I have learned very much indeed, in the sense that a substantial part of the pattern and fabric of my life derives from him." Murry tells us that when he took the plunge into sensual love he was following Lawrence. "And I discovered, on my pulses, that he was wrong." Wrong because one can, one must, *combine* sex-fulfilment with such Christian virtues as gentleness. Only by an *inclusive* tenderness can we save civilization. He insisted that he could combine the truths of eroticism with those spiritual-religious truths which Lawrence had thought incompatible with them.

This is a cruder version of the way Jaspers, if we may believe Eduard Baumgarten, combined Weber with Kant. Each disciple came to take liberties with his master's heritage, although each was deeply reverent of it. Murry and Jaspers made their masters live on—Weber in German minds, Lawrence in English—as great heroes. To extend the pattern of comparison, both disciples met antagonists, of course, and in both cases they were former friends of the great man. Georg Lukács, who had been before the war a friend of Max Weber's, later became his and Jaspers's enemy. Lukács became a Marxist Communist during the war, and was made Kommissar of Education in his native Hungary in 1918. From then on his career was made within the Communist movement, where he became, as he was until his death in 1972, the movement's leading literary critic and theoretician. As such he had to render judgment on Max Weber and Jaspers.

In 1934, in Moscow, he acknowledged his sins of revisionism and blamed Weber, together with Georg Simmel and Max Scheler, for having led him astray. In *Die Zerstörung der Vernunft* (*The Destruction of Reason*) of 1952, he bracketed Jaspers with Heidegger as "the Ash-Wednesday of parasitic subjectivism" and dealt with Weber under the heading "German Sociology of the Imperialistic Period." He reproached Weber with the betrayal of reason, charging that Weber had falsely justified capitalism by identifying it with rationality, though he had also replaced causal with analogous explanations—for instance, in drawing an analogy between the modern state and capitalist enterprise, instead of investigating the cause and effect relationship between the two. This was because he was reacting against Marx, against reason itself, and so had to be anti-rational, Lukács explained. Consequently, his sociology synthesized all the elements of anti-socialist thought and made a system out of them. (Lukács also dealt, much more contemptuously, with Alfred Weber, another former friend.)

Marxist thought has continued to be hostile to Weber, as we shall see. It is interesting to see him criticized from a still more rationalist point of view, as well as from the more predictable vitalist or "matriarchal" position. (Erich von Kahler began that second line of attack as early as 1920, with *Der Beruf von Wissenschaft,* a rejection of everything in Weber's idea of science and scholarship.) In the case of Lawrence, an ideological equivalent of the Marxist attack on Weber would be, perhaps, the anti-Lawrentianism of Norman O. Brown. But a more all-around equivalent to Lukács, including similar biographical elements, is offered by Bertrand Russell, who had been an admirer and in some sense a disciple of Lawrence's early in the war, just as Lukács was of Weber. In 1916 an accusing letter from Lawrence was enough to bring Russell to the point of suicide. But he turned against Lawrence with great contempt later, declaring that Lawrence was "a positive force for evil." His "mystical philosophy of 'blood' " had always seemed to Russell "frankly rubbish, and I reject it vehemently, though I did not then know it led straight to Auschwitz." In retrospect, he declared, he did not think Lawrence's ideas had any merit whatever: "The world between the wars was attracted to madness. Of this attraction Nazism was the most emphatic expression. Lawrence was a suitable exponent of this cult of insanity." Russell may be said to belong to that "Bloomsbury-rationalist" side to British culture, which has supplied a hostility to Lawrence as consistent as the Marxists have to Weber. He and T. S. Eliot have stood against Lawrence the way that Lukács and George have stood against Weber.

Murry and Jaspers were very unlike figures, and the coincidences between their careers as disciples are not profoundly meaningful. That they published on Lawrence and Weber up to 1932, and gradually thereafter devoted themselves to other matters until after the war; that Murry began corresponding with Frieda Lawrence again in 1946, and Jaspers began lecturing again in Heidelberg in 1945; and that both published on their heroes again 1957-8—these are coincidences which illustrate the general trend of the times, rather than anything unique to these two men. But in Murry's last book, *Love, Freedom, and Society,* which is half about Lawrence, half about Albert Schweitzer, he derived some of his inspiration from Jaspers, whom he had met in Geneva and admired, and whose *Tragedy is not enough* he had read on on his way to developing an interest in Existentialism. He projected this new interest back onto Lawrence, so that in his 1954 essay on Lawrence he could say that England need not look to the Continent for instruction in existentialist thinking: "Lawrence is the thing itself." Indeed, Murry's Lawrence *was*—in some way always had been—an existentialist. Murry's most painfully spiritual and Jaspers-like side had always been turned toward Lawrence. It was the "Russian" side of both disciples which most modulated their master's personalities and teachings in transmission.

Although, in this last book, Murry cites Jaspers (and Simone Weil) in the course of contrasting Lawrence with Schweitzer, he reminds us of Alfred Weber as much as Jaspers—mostly because of his strong sense of the doom of European culture (the threat of the bomb) and his treatment of communism as the new, great, and deadly social religion, but also because of his general vague *Lebensphilosphie.* Thus Lawrence's prime disciple ended up in a position not too far from those of Weber's prime disciple and his brother. Certainly there was no war between them of the kind promised in Lawrence's poem, "The Revolutionary." But the secondary and major disciples remained far apart from each other. It is to them we must now turn.

In that last book, Murry spent a lot of energy arguing against Leavis, who by 1957 had completely ousted him from the position of being Lawrence's main defender and expounder. He objected particularly to the contrast Leavis drew between *St. Mawr* and Eliot's *The Cocktail Party*, for the purpose of annihilating the latter. By that time, Murry was Eliot's ideological as well as personal friend. He may have aligned himself with Lawrence, and against Eliot, in his theory of marriage, but it was, unlike Leavis's, a friendly opposition he directed against Eliot on this score. His own attitude toward Lawrence was, always, very humble: "we ordinary folk . . . a person of ordinary faculties cannot . . ." But he flatly declared Lawrence incapable of love, the force on which Murry had come to pin all his hopes. Above all, he still did not deal with Lawrence as a writer, and consequently, he could not deal with Leavis on his own ground. Like Jaspers, he was concerned with his hero's meaning, or essence, not his work. It was left to Leavis to interpret Lawrence through his achievement as a writer, his contribution to literature, just as it was left to Parsons to interpret Weber through his achievement as a sociologist, his contribution to sociology.

Moreover, along with Leavis's and Parsons's concentration on their heroes' *work* went an ideological purification. The secondary disciples were in some sense purer than the primary, and they made something purer out of their heroes. Jaspers's Weber was not so Apollonian as Parsons's was to be. Jaspers's Weber was a hero of spiritual torment who only just managed to contain his inner dissensions and still offer leadership—a sort of Gladstonian Kierkegaard. Similarly, Murry's Lawrence was not so Demetrian as Leavis's was to be. Murry's Lawrence was also a hero of spiritual torment, but one who perversely denied his own spirituality—a sort of Jesus *manqué*. The secondary disciples had to slough off this "Russian" romanticism in order to set the true spirit of the masters free. In Parsons's hands, Weber more completely than before represented the male principle, the patriarchal world of order and management; and in Leavis's hands, Lawrence more completely represented the matriarchal world of life-values, fertility, health.

Thus, although in the 1950s Jaspers and Murry found sizable audiences to listen to their heroes' messages about the spiritual crisis in England, in Germany, in all Europe, Parsons and Leavis offered more authoritative interpretations. The development of Weber's and Lawrence's heritages from the time of their deaths until now generally has been in this direction, making them embody the opposing principles of being, the male and the female, more fully and purely, and the corresponding antithetic principles of mind, symbolized by Apollo and Diotima. (Diotima is the patron of Leavis's own thinking as a literary critic, a man of ideas, whereas Demeter represents Lawrence's world as an imaginative novelist.) It is precisely because we have been under the spell of Apollo and Demeter without realizing it that Bachofen's scheme of ideas seems so illuminating now.

Of course, not everyone has been under those spells. We can remind ourselves of that by reading the autobiography of Franz Jung who, as Otto Gross's major disciple, occupies a position roughly parallel to that of Jaspers and Murry. His autobiography is entitled *Der Weg Nach Unten* (*The Way Down*) and was reviewed in the *Times Literary Supplement* under the heading of "The Alienated Self." The reviewer took the book as significant and the author as representative, concluding that the book commemorated a life of incorrigible isolation, bitterness, and maladjustment. Jung "could have been the German Céline," except that even his belief in Nihilism had been destroyed. At the time of Gross's death, Jung had become a successful Spartacist orator and agent in the German revolution of 1918; indeed, he once captured a telegraph office for his party. In 1920 he was smuggled aboard a ship off Hamburg and persuaded the sailors to take it to Murmansk and present it to Soviet Russia. In 1921 he returned to Russia and worked there three years, with tractors in agriculture, in charge of a match factory, in charge of a machine and tool factory. He left Russia as a stowaway and spent the next few years in Germany, writing plays and serving as a financial and business editor for a number of papers. At some point in the twenties he collected a number of Gross's late essays, added an essay about Gross, and put them together in a book called *Von Geschlechter Not zur Sozialen Katastrophe,* (*From Sexual Deprivation to the Social Catastrophe*). He tried to find a publisher for it, but in vain. He also helped finance Brecht's *Mahagonny*. Everywhere he made his mark, but nowhere could he find fulfillment in what he did. Despite his vigorous commitment to the cause of revolution, he ended up—he died in 1963—with "atrophied energies," in "agonized indifference." As he himself said, the single individual, isolated, cannot defend himself against a corrupt and hostile society, and cannot even develop enough resistance to feel himself in communion with other victims. This was alienation at a pitch which makes Jaspers and Murry seem, by contrast, comfortably adjusted to their respective societies. And one might evoke for a moment also the memory of Wilhelm Reich, dying in 1957 in an American prison. But we must pass on to the secondary disciples of the other two men. We will describe each disciple's career in relation to Weber and Lawrence, and then examine what each took from his master, how they institutionalized it, and what confrontations it involved them in.

Leavis

F. R. Leavis was born in 1895 in Cambridge and attended the Perse School there, where Henry Caldwell Cook, the author of *The Play Way,* was a teacher of English. Cook taught literature by the Play Way, which meant largely by means of creative participation in ceremonies, pageants, and dramatizations; his literary and cultural taste lay in the direction of a Merrie England, William Morris, sort of ruralism. He did not arrive at the Perse until 1911, and thus may not have affected Leavis directly, but he represents the educational ethos which seems to have left perceptible traces on the critic. From the Perse School Leavis went to Emmanuel College, Cambridge, and read first history and then English. He took his B.A. in 1924. A combative personality, he provoked enemies and was not made a university lecturer when others of his generation were. Not till 1936 did he get a college Fellowship and a university Assistant Lectureship. Soon he came to lead a movement against the Cambridge Establishment. His home became a social center for young people with at least some literary-ideological tastes in common, among which the most important came to be an enthusiasm for D. H. Lawrence.

Leavis published a pamphlet on Lawrence in 1930, but this was a professedly *critical* essay, and its tone was very unlike what we now think of as the Leavis tone about Lawrence. He begins by asserting that Lawrence was a genius, but he defines genius by using the phrasing of Eliot's essay on Blake. Moreover, while praising E. M. Forster's generous letter to *The Nation* in defense of Lawrence, Leavis "at risk of being included in Mr. Forster's 'highbrows whom he bored,'" admits to finding Lawrence's later fiction "hard to read through." (He gradually comes to include nearly all the fiction under that rubric "hard to read through," and says that the verse is rarely poetry.) In this pamphlet Leavis calls *The Lost Girl* Lawrence's best novel and *Lady Chatterley's Lover* an artistic success: "So far as artistic success can validate his teaching, *Lady Chatterley's Lover* does so." Most striking of all, he then reflects that in order to accept *Lady Chatterley's Lover,* we should have to give up both Jane Austen and *Passage to India,* and the implication seems to be that the sacrifice would be too great. In other words Leavis identifies himself with the literary intelligentsia of the time and its "classical" sensibility; he calls Lawrence a Romantic, and indicates how alien he himself finds Romanticism and the Romantic type. His movement from that position to his position in 1970 has been a 180-degree swing of attitude. This self-reversal, this intellectual journey, is a result of the education he has accepted from Lawrence, an education he has in turn enforced on England.

He has accepted much from Lawrence, in the process rejecting much from Eliot which at first seemed authoritative. Probably the two changes were independent and autonomous, though they also interacted and intensified each other. Leavis tells us that Eliot wrote to congratulate him on *Mass Civi-*

lization and Minority Culture (1930), and asked him to write a pamphlet for *Criterion* but then rejected what Leavis wrote, which was a savage attack on the procedures of contemporary reviewing and literary cliques. Leavis took Eliot's rejection of the pamphlet as proof of his cowardice in dealing with issues on which the Establishment needed to be attacked, as a declaration of his willingness to live at peace with fools and knaves in power. Lawrence's "Romanticism" must have seemed attractive to Leavis partly by contrast with such classical composure.

Still, in 1932, when Leavis began to edit his critical quarterly *Scrutiny,* his first essay in the first number makes a rather "classical" reference to Lawrence: "Lawrence was a 'prophet', but it is only because he was an artist of genius that his prophecy matters. . . . His gift lay, not in thinking, but in experiencing. . . ." The point was, of course, to dismiss some of Murry's claims for Lawrence, and even more, Murry's claims for himself as a critic. *"Son of Woman* is another book about Mr. Middleton Murry," Leavis announced, expressing his determination to dissociate himself from Murry and from that autobiographical criticism which sloppily mixed ideas and experience together with that which properly occupies the literary critic.

Already in the second issue, however making reference to Lawrence's letters, Leavis changes his tone. He says that the man was greater than his art, a statement whose implications contradict saying that his prophecy matters only because of his art. And in the third issue, defending Lawrence against Eliot's attacks, Leavis lays his primary stress on the former's *sanity*. Lawrence is, in his letters, "normal, central and sane to the point of genius, exquisitely but surely poised and with a rare capacity for personal relations." These shifts of emphasis derive from a paradox, or a tension between different aims, within Leavis's criticism as a whole. He is still determined not to discuss writers for their contemporary "message"—or for that academic equivalent, their place in intellectual history. He owes (and acknowledges) a great debt to Eliot, who saved him from Murry's sort of sloppiness. But at the same time he is now determined not to discuss writers in terms of the purely formal properties of their works and not to depersonalize the artist, as Eliot did. Lawrence became the test case in working out this policy. And Lawrence's letters, giving the reader access to that normality of his which Leavis prized so highly, were the key text. The most important effect of this shift in critical attitude is on Leavis's evaluation of Lawrence, whom he now found not only a great writer, but a validation of the "normal" and the touchstone for all other critical judgments—the touchstone of a great tradition. Lawrence was a test case because his artistic work embodied strengths which Eliot's creative work lacked, and which Eliot, even as a critic, resisted and rejected.

One might put it that Lawrence—and Leavis—derived from their De-
metrianism a moral stiffening which Eliot lacked. They had many cultural
enemies in common with him, enemies who represented one facet or another
of modern culture, but to Leavis it seemed that Eliot was too ready to compromise with some aspects of our civilization. Like some other literary intellectuals, Charles Williams and C. S. Lewis, T. E. Lawrence and Joyce Cary,
for example, Eliot was too "Oxonian," too ready to play the games of academe
and of high society and of elite superiority. (The *Festschrift* Symposia for Eliot
certainly support this diagnosis.) This weakness derived, unconsciously, from
his inability to believe in any alternative to the world he saw around him,
the world of men. Lawrence's letters convinced Leavis that he had found such
an alternative, had both envisioned it and realized it in his life—in his "rare
capacity for personal relations." Only the Demetrian or matriarchal faith
could give one such a vision, could enable one to create for oneself a world
of love and life, instead of a world of law and order. Lawrence and Leavis—
the latter partly by the grace of Lawrence—felt that they had found a life-
medium to root themselves in, which was out of the world but not in retreat
from it, a position in advance of the patriarchal world and exultantly at war
with it. Eliot simply did not believe in their position.

In his review of *Son of Woman* in *The Criterion* for July 1931, Eliot had
spoken of what it revealed about Lawrence as "an appalling narrative of spiritual pride, nourished by ignorance. . . . Such complacent egotism can only
come from a very sick soul. . . ." He went on to connect Lawrence with
Leavis—covertly. "Had he become a don at Cambridge his ignorance
might have had frightful consequences for himself and for the world,
'rotten and rotting others.'" Here Eliot maliciously pointed to Leavis's identification of himself with Lawrence, something which has, both in fact and in
fancy—that is, in other people's mistaken understanding of that identification
—been an important feature of literary culture in England ever since.

An equally important feature, however, has been that Leavis identified
with Eliot also, or at least apprenticed himself to him, used an Eliot-like rigor
of analysis to expound Lawrence. Accepting the doctrine that literary criticism, to be modern, had to accept some "classical" rigor, Leavis opted for
an approach which is the critical equivalent of Eliot's poetic and Henry
James's fictional professionalism. Murry, in contrast, largely because of Lawrence's influence on him, defined himself as "Romantic," and declined to
invest that passion in the "science" of criticism which Eliot and Leavis invested. He showed, in *The Problem of Style,* that he *could* follow in the footsteps of *The Sacred Wood,* but in effect he chose not to. He said, at the end
of *Countries of the Mind,* "The function of criticism is, therefore, primarily

the function of literature itself, to provide a means of self-expression for the critic." Even while assigning a moral function to criticism, he also described it as an art whose function is to give delight. This is the looseness to which Leavis had to find an alternative. His critical method turned out—for reasons we shall examine—to be the way to win Lawrence acknowledgement as *the* modern British author, not Murry's ostensibly more modernist linking of Lawrence with Dostoevski and with Jesus Christ.

As Malcolm Bradbury points out, there had been a "classical" revolution in critical method in the first twenty years of this century, parallel with that in the creative arts. The period was noted for a passion for criticism which expressed itself first in the proliferation of avant-garde little magazines addressed to a bohemian-intellectual audience. But after 1920 this new criticism tried to consolidate its position and establish an orthodoxy of taste among the general educated public. The three great reviews of the 1920s, Bradbury says, were Eliot's *The Criterion*, Edgell Rickword's *Calendar of Modern Letters*, which was in some sense a model for Leavis's *Scrutiny*, and Murry's *The Adelphi*. Of the four magazines named, all but the last were in some sense "classical." The superiority of the "classical" mode of art and sensibility over its opposite had been made familiar by Eliot, and by T. E. Hulme, notably in his *Speculations*, published posthumously in 1924. We can describe "classical" criticism as the kind which makes criticism a mode of knowledge as rigorous as any science. It is the antithesis of all vague "poetic" enthusiasms and all connoisseurship of personal taste. Bertram Higgins wrote in the *Calendar* that "the characteristics of a healthy criticism are always 'classic,' tending towards an ever greater rigidity of principle, organizations more explicit, and the canalization of the wide, shallow stream of taste."

Leavis also was determined to make criticism into a rigorous mode of knowledge. Murry's self-indulgent and self-dramatizing romanticism was repellent to him. But he discovered in the process that he would have to modify his "classicism" as he came to recognize more and more fully the size— and the significance—of Lawrence's achievement. The crucial representative of classicism in England was T. S. Eliot, who not only was hostile to Lawrence personally, but stood explicitly for an opposite life-principle, the principle we have called Apollonian. Eliot found his way to the specifically twentieth-century version of Apollonianism—Weber's version—and applied it to literature with great authority. In *The Sacred Wood* of 1920, he expounds the same doctrine as Max Weber in "Politik als Beruf" and "Wissenschaft als Beruf," which were published the same year and which had similar enemies in mind. The most famous essay in the Eliot volume, "Tradition and the Individual Talent," could have perfectly well have been entitled *Dichtung als*

Beruf, for it is all about the poet's need to escape from personality and emotion, just as Weber's essays are about the politician's and the scholar's need for such an escape. "The progress of an artist is a continual self-sacrifice, a continual extinction of personality," Eliot wrote, "[T]he more perfect the artist, the more completely separate in him will be the man who suffers and the mind which creates. . . . Poetry is not a turning loose of emotion, but an escape from emotion; it is not the expression of personality, but an escape from personality. . . . The emotion of art is impersonal. And the poet cannot reach this impersonality without surrendering himself wholly to the work to be done."

This is the quintessence of Weberism, of Apollonianism. Eliot insists on our seeing the poet's mind as a chemical retort in which "feelings" enter into new combinations "of themselves." The life-adventure of the poet is of no importance: his artistic career is all that matters. Such teaching was of course diametrically opposed to everything that Lawrence stood for and precluded any enthusiastic response to his work, so that Leavis was forced to make a series of choices of loyalty, in order to build a criticism which could honorably claim to relate to both men. Leavis made those commitments of loyalty, and built that criticism, but it took him time. It has been his life's work.

Leavis continued to discuss Lawrence throughout the 1930s and 1940s, but above all in those years he used him as a touchstone by which to measure what was wrong with Eliot, Wyndham Lewis, Bloomsbury, Murry, and so forth. It is not too much to say that he measured contemporary writing as a whole, both critical and creative writing, by its bearing on Lawrence, without ever discussing one of his novels at length. It was in the 1950s that he began to publish essays of full-scale analysis of Lawrence's novels, leading up to the appearance of *D. H. Lawrence: Novelist* in 1955. He continued to use Lawrence, as before, as a touchstone. As late as 1969, in *The State of English Literature Now and the University,* he devoted several pages to a discussion of Lawrence's criticism of *Hamlet* (the passage occurs in *Twilight in Italy*), making it an example of that kind of criticism which is really valuable and contrasting it with Eliot on *Hamlet.* The title of that chapter, "The Necessary Opposite: Lawrence," refers to Lawrence's oppositeness not only to Eliot but also to the professional literary mind. The phrase could also stand as an explanatory comment on Leavis's own career. He and Lawrence are inseparable as ideas, as forces in our minds.

Parsons

The equivalent to Leavis in the history of Weber's reputation has been Talcott Parsons. He was born in 1902, the son of a Congregational minister who was also an English professor and a college president. He graduated from Amherst in 1924, spent two years at the universities of London and Heidelberg, where he first made acquaintance with Weber's work, and then returned to America as an instructor, first at Amherst, then at Harvard. Ever since 1927, which is roughly when Leavis's academic career began, Parsons has been teaching at Harvard, so that both Cambridges have seen the birth of "movements" and the training of devoted intellectual emissaries. From Cambridge, England, "Lawrentians" have gone out into the world to spread the light they received there, from Cambridge, Massachusetts, "Weberians." Leavis's disciples and Parsons's disciples have been prominent features of their respective professional worlds and of the larger cultural scene.

But Parsons has had a smoother academic career than Leavis, as was to be expected. Though he met with opposition early on, he became Chairman of the Department of Sociology in 1944 and first Chairman of the Department of Social Relations in 1946. What is more, he has been closer to the sources of power of the greater society. He was officially consulted on questions of American policy toward Germany after the war, for example. He has been an officer of the American Sociological Association, and his allies and former pupils, between them, have been the controlling forces there for many years. He can be said to represent or embody the American sociological establishment, and as such he has become a figurehead for all those social scientists whom Noam Chomsky called the New Mandarins and accused of complicity in the misuse of American power in the Vietnam War and elsewhere. Chomsky does not name Parsons, but for radicals in social science, Parsons is the mandarin *par excellence*. For this reason he has shared the odium of, for example, Project Camelot, the 1965 scandal in social science. (The Special Operations Research Office, sponsored by the U. S. Army, offered $4.6 million just to begin financial sociological research into left-wing insurrections in Chile, their causes, and ways to defeat them. This is the archetypal scandal of sociological "complicity.") There is no reason to associate Parsons personally with this project, but as the figurehead of his whole generation of social scientists, and of the functionalists in particular, he has acquired guilt by association. This, I think, gives the resonance his image has among young radicals today.

Parsons was born thirty-eight years after Weber, in another country, and only heard about Weber after his death, whereas Leavis is only ten years

younger than Lawrence and has known many of the same people Lawrence
knew both as friends and enemies. There is no tincture of Leavis-like identification in Parsons's treatment of Weber, or, so far as one can see, in his feeling for him. That would not be to be expected even if Parsons were of the
same age and nation as Weber, for his temperament, personal and intellectual—the very thing he has taken over from Weber, legitimately or illegiti-
mately—is cool, objective, Apollonian.

He has insisted in fact that he feels *less* kinship to Weber than to his other
teachers, because Weber's work had the character of a breakthrough and followed from a breakdown. Parsons claims that he feels more fellowship with
Durkheim and Freud, whose work followed a more "logical," step by step
development. They are his "paramount role-models," whereas Weber was
"of Luther's type." I would argue that in Freud's case there is as much sign
of revolution as of evolution in his intellectual development, and that Weber's
case is one of extraordinarily hard work and prodigies of self-discipline. So I
cannot see the opposition Parsons claims to see. But the significant thing in
Parsons's statement is his resolutely Erasmian sense of himself, his repudiation
of everything Faustian, his *Sachlichkeit*—which was, after all, the virtue
which Max Weber most inculcated and, in his fashion, exemplified.

Like Leavis, Parsons has changed his mind over the decades. His 1935
paper "The Place of Ultimate Values in Sociology" is an attack on behaviorism, and his key term in *The Structure of Social Action* is "action," chosen
to contrast with "behavior" by stressing the voluntary component and to dissociate his theory from behaviorism. But he has said since then that this theory
did not take account of the insights afforded by psychoanalysis and anthropology. His massive impact on American sociology began in 1951, it is often
said, with the publication of *The Social System*, and the key term became
"system." Although this book was accompanied in the same year by *Towards
a General Theory of Action*, and followed two years later by *Working Papers
in the Theory of Action*, in effect "action" had been displaced by "system" as
the dominant model of Parsons's sociology. Moreover, during the 1950s Parsons gradually abandoned Weber's principle of "Verstehen" in sociology,
which limited the subjects of inquiry to actions reasonable enough to be "understood," and developed in its place the laws of "equilibrium" which applied
to subhuman activity as well as to human.

The catchword "system" perhaps seemed magical in those years because
of the contemporary development of cybernetics and the computer; and so
"system" theory became the obligatory body of theory for American sociology
students. So at least says Robert W. Friedrichs, in *A Sociology of Sociology*,
published in 1970. Other popular ideas of the time stressed "equilibrium" and

"system," and Parsons gradually assimilated Weber into a more and more Apollonian theory of society. In 1970 he wrote a personal history for *Daedalus,* in which he described two of his recent books as "in the spirit of Max Weber," but his 1968 Preface to *Structure* says that his theory has now developed to a point where it owes more to Durkheim than to Weber, because it was Durkheim who was the more concerned of the two with the integrated sociocultural *system*. Thus Parsons has moved away from Weber, or past him, during the period when Leavis was moving toward Lawrence. But still, Parsons has become more Apollonian, just as Leavis has become more Demetrian.

Studying under Edgar Salin at Heidelberg in the 1930s—he also took a seminar in Kant from Jaspers while he was there—Parsons wrote a thesis on Weber's, Marx's, Brentano's and Sombart's theories of capitalism, and his first big book, *The Structure of Social Action* (1937), put Weber together with Durkheim, Vilfredo Pareto, and Alfred Marshall, to show how the theories of all four converge toward a single theory of social action. This approach has been typical of all his subsequent work, which has combined other people with Weber. (Leavis on the other hand, has set Lawrence in opposition to others, pointing out how light they weigh in the scales against him.) Parsons has never appropriated Weber, or dramatized himself in relation to him or to anybody else. It is a far from trivial emblem that some of Parsons's work on behalf of Weber in America has been translation, that humblest of services, and that several of his books have been written in cooperation with others. Indeed, he is to be identified with Weber almost as much for all those translations and introductions as for his theoretical development of the ideas; he has "linked his name with" Weber's.

Thus he has not been so concerned as Leavis to deal with his hero's enemies, any more than with his own, though he did write an article answering H. M. Robertson's criticisms of Weber's theory of capitalism. He is not an attacker. It is rather that Parsons himself has been attacked, and with increasing frequency over the last ten years. These attacks have come mostly from radical students of sociology, but at the 1964 conference at Heidelberg he was confronted by Herbert Marcuse. Parsons's lecture had been titled "Evaluation and Objectivity in the Social Sciences" and had defended Weber's doctrine of *Wertfreiheit*, as meaning the freedom for a scientist to pursue those values to which he must, as a scientist, be committed. This differentiation between a scientist's values and those of other people results from the development of science as a social subsystem. Science can be, must be, objective, even in its study of the most subjectively felt values. Weber's work centered first in the study of law—material to which Marx's categories had proved, he thought, ill-adapted—then was applied to politics, then to economics, and finally to religion. For Weber had seen that sociology's main focus must be on the normative control of interests and on the conditions necessary for successful control of this kind. How do men's passions and appetites get transformed into societally useful motives? Parsons summed up Weber's achievement by saying that Weber had built the heritage of humanistic historical scholarship into the canons of an analytical and empirical social science at a far higher level than was ever before achieved.

Marcuse's lecture was entitled "Industrialism and Capitalism in the Works of Max Weber." In it Marcuse blamed Weber for treating industrialism and capitalism as though they were the historical fate of the Western world and the contemporary fate of his Germany. *Something* like what we have was inevitable, Weber seemed to be saying, according to Marcuse; *some* form of domination was thus made to be an ultimate reality. Who will rule was the only question to be decided. But Weber's "fate," Marcuse contended, is merely the acceptance of the existent. Weber had identified his own work with the historical mission of the bourgeoisie and had accepted the alliance with the forces of repression. The rationality of his "rationalism" is profoundly suspect: "The 'formally most rational' mode of capital accounting is the one into which man and his 'purposes' enter only as variables in the calculation of the chances of gain and profit," said Marcuse. Politically, "The Weberian conception of reason ends in irrational *charisma.*" And *Wertfreiheit* means that science is free to accept any values imposed upon it from outside, whereas in fact the mission of science is to question and examine these very values: "Accusation is the function of true science." Marcuse was the speaker most applauded by the student audience—and most attacked by other people on the platform. He and Parsons were the two ideological extremes of the conference.

In Leavis's case the big confrontations over Lawrence came much earlier, in the 1930s. In recent years he has had to waste his shot not on attackers of Lawrence but on unworthy admirers, would-be comrades like Harry T. Moore. In *After Strange Gods* Eliot wrote of "the alarming strain of cruelty" in Lawrence, of "the effects of decadence" visible in him, and even of "diabolical influences." He found a lack of *any* moral or social sense, any conscience, in all the relations between Lawrence's men and women. Thus whereas Joyce is ethically orthodox even when he is rebelling against the church, Lawrence is almost perfectly heretical in his ethics, having inherited no training and no tradition. Eliot distinguished three aspects of Lawrence: the ridiculous, well treated by Wyndham Lewis; the undeniably keen intuition; and the sexual morbidity. *Lady Chatterley's Lover* is the work of a very sick man indeed, Eliot concludes.

Earlier Eliot had written, in *La Nouvelle Revue Française*—and Leavis had denounced him for it—that Lawrence "écrit d'extrêmement mal. . . . Quand ses personnages font l'amour . . . non seulement ils perdent toutes les aménités, raffinements et grâces élaborés afin de rendre l'amour *support-able* [Leavis's italics] mais ils semblent remonter le cours de l'évolution . . . jusqu'à quelque hideux accouplement de protoplasme." The long Eliot-Leavis quarrel over Lawrence was really a quarrel over the meaning of civilization, over culture and its relation to nature. By and large, Eliot was wrong and Leavis was right, and there is no occasion, now at least, for anyone else to join in.

But it is interesting, for a moment, to try to place Eliot against the background we have been building. His quarrel with Lawrence was a quarrel with eroticism, and it involved him in destructive paradoxes, pushed him to absurd extremes just because he was a modernist poet. I have said that aestheticism and eroticism were first cousins in the family of *Lebensphilosophie,* but it was quite possible, though very stressful, to embrace the one passionately and to reject the other. When aestheticism quarrels with eroticism in this way, we get the "classical" phenomenon which Eliot represents more vividly than anyone else in English. He was aesthetically bound to reject Milton for Shakespeare, as much as Leavis and Murry, but he has never offered Shakespeare the total devotion which they offered, because Shakespeare is an artist-hero of eroticism. It was Shakespeare's verbal techniques and talents Eliot loved, not his "philosophy." He has preferred Dante, as a type of the serious artist, and Jonson, as a dramatist. This pattern of preferences is so marked in him that one might think it proved a disconnection between modernist aestheticism and *Lebensphilosophie.* There is much in Eliot, not to mention his friends T. E. Hulme and Wyndham Lewis, which may be characterized as anti-life. They share a style of realism that reminds us of Max Weber. But when one comes to Eliot's theory of culture, one is struck by how much he has in common with Murry, Leavis, and Lawrence, with how important culture is to him, how similar is the role it plays for him and for them, and how much it is the antagonist to civilization. One realizes how much he, as much as they, believes (at the level of cultural theory) in life-values.

At the level of aesthetic practice, of course, his poetry and plays are "anaphrodisiac," and his preferences among writers are sharply hostile to eroticism and its *Lebensphilosophie* values of intuition, impulse, and emotionality. Most crucially, he has been sharply hostile to Hardy and Lawrence, and much of Leavis's career has been devoted to attacks on him for that reason. But the crucial engagements between them on that issue occurred in the 1930s. A public confrontation on the level of the Heidelberg conference occurred for Leavis in the 1960s, but it was not with Eliot.

But before examining that confrontation, we must first define in more detail just what Leavis inherited from Lawrence, and Parsons from Weber—how they selected what they took, how they combined it with material from other sources, and how they omitted other things.

Heritages

What was the essential heritage for Leavis? We can sum it up in the slogan "life-values." What he found in Lawrence was reverence for life expressed with moral and imaginative authenticity in a thousand ways—some aesthetic, some moral, some domestic, and so on. Moreover, this reverence for life had the authentication of genius behind it. Lawrence was clearly—at least it was clear to Leavis's critical sense—a great modern novelist, with an imaginative daring and originality that ranked him with the other great modernist writers. But he was also, uniquely, sane and normal. One should recall Leavis's early phrase about him: "sane to the point of genius." The connection between the two key words is itself a key. Thus in his remarks on the *Letters* he says that Lawrence "makes it possible to cherish some faith in the future of humanity." In the same connection he sets Lawrence in opposition to Surrealism and quotes Lawrence: "Thank God, I'm not free, any more than a rooted tree is free." If we take Surrealism as a literary expression of the spirit of Otto Gross, this comment stands as Demeter's reproach to Aphrodite. Leavis's hero is the Lawrence who set himself in opposition to Gross, and to a great deal of the radical experimentalism and libertarianism then current in the arts. Eliot was, in one half of him, much more experimental than either of them. In other words, the normality, centrality, and sanity which Leavis recognized with such relief in the letters of this man of genius were the normality, centrality, and sanity of matriarchal and Demetrian culture.

These qualities stood in opposition to both the Hetaerism of Gross and the Apollonianism of, for instance, the classicizing side of Eliot. In fact, in that same essay on the *Letters*, Leavis names Lawrence the greatest critic of "classicism." Of course Apollo and his brother gods find a much more sinister expression than classicism in the whole structure of politics and militarism and everything that Leavis calls "civilization." It has been his conviction that the relations of culture and civilization should embody a hostility, and his objection to Bloomsbury's version of "civilization" was precisely that it was no more than a frivolous surface gilding of the iron facts, a velvet glove dilettantism of the arts and social elegancies. In other words, for him civili-

zation is patriarchal and culture matriarchal, when it really deserves the name
of culture.

In finding this significance powerfully embodied in Lawrence, Leavis
was clearly right. On the other hand, there are other Lawrences. It is even
a valid, though trivial, criticism of Leavis to say that he gave scant recognition
to those other sides of Lawrence. But it is more important here to recognize,
without complaint, that he did not deal with Lawrence the sick man, Lawrence the modernist, Lawrence the political theorist, or Lawrence the neo-
Nietzschean. We can have no complaint, because in order to do the valuable
thing he did do with Lawrence, it was at least natural, perhaps necessary, that
he should *not* do these other things.

What has the Weber heritage meant to Parsons? A solution to the problem of order. That has always been for him the key problem in the theory of
society and social action. Hobbes first raised the question of how the natural
state of war of each against all could be so governed that the use of its most
efficient means, force and fraud, could be limited. Out of this question is born
the theory of the social contract. Locke and his followers developed the theory
one way, Marx and his followers another. Weber's and Parsons's work is a "scientific" and "value-free" investigation of that problem. If it is value-free, however, it is nonetheless essentially value-oriented. It focuses on those social
norms which create order. The utilitarian-positivistic tradition of social action
theory came to an end with Herbert Spencer. *The Structure of Social Action*
attempted to create a successor to that tradition, in what Parsons calls the
voluntaristic theory of action, on which Weber, Durkheim, Pareto, and
Marshall all converge.

It is even clearer about Parsons than about Leavis that he neglected important elements in the total phenomenon of his master. He left aside Weber
the political commentator and critic, the potential political leader. He left
aside Weber as a figure produced by and responding to all the conditions of
German culture. He left aside Jaspers's Weber, the existentialist hero. Again
like Leavis, Parsons had a perfect right to leave aside these aspects of Weber,
but we need to remind ourselves of the character of his selection. By recognizing that, we can understand and evaluate the process out of which Weber
emerges as a hero of Parsons's Apollonian sociology.

In order to understand clearly what Leavis took from Lawrence and Parsons from Weber, one must know first what each was being offered by other
comparable figures, and second what Leavis's and Parsons's contemporaries
managed to "inherit" that was different in character.

In the case of Leavis, it seems clear that he was independently responsive
to a number of other writers who offered something culturally comparable

to Lawrence, like Thomas Hardy and George Eliot, and John Bunyan, Richard Jefferies and George Bourne, and to cognate cultural activities, from folk-dancing and the survival of local crafts in rural England to the arts and social forms of primitive societies. (George Bourne's *Wheelwright's Shop* received much attention in *Scrutiny*.) All these phenomena represent the world of Woman. But Leavis was equally responsive to something almost opposite in character, the highly elaborated "conscience" art of New England, as expressed in the works of Henry James and T. S. Eliot and in the cognate European irony of Joseph Conrad. (A blending of the two lines can be seen in the work of T. F. Powys, of whom Leavis long thought very highly.) Putting the matter *very* crudely, one might say that the life-values ideology so strongly to be felt beneath the pattern of his preferences owes more to the former, and that his critical-analytical method owes more to the latter, though his highly idiosyncratic prose style is a rope made up of both strands intertwined.

Meanwhile, his contemporaries in Bloomsbury responded to Gide and Proust more than to Lawrence, or any other modern writer, to judge by the evidence of their own imaginative work. Their taste and style can be called in a general and loose sense "French"—that is, if one is looking for those features of their taste and style which differentiate them from Leavis. Leavis has made a point of preferring Richardson to Proust, and George Eliot to Flaubert, and Arnold to Sainte-Beuve. (Bloomsbury had a good deal in common with Leavis, a good deal which made them his comrades, however incongruously, in a common enterprise. Indeed, Leavis has shown that he appreciates Virginia Woolf, Forster, Eliot, and Joyce, although his attitude toward them could not be called generous.) Nor did he respond much to Hemingway, Faulkner, and Fitzgerald. The Americans, as much as the French, were felt to have nothing to put into the scales against Lawrence. And while Leavis read the Russian novelists, especially Tolstoy, with great attention and responsiveness, he avoided discussing them at length.

His taste, particularly as expressed in the pattern of subjects he chose to write whole essays about, was assertively English, with his life-values, his reverence for life, focusing on the idea of health. In this he was like Murry, with his celebratory books about Keats and Shakespeare and Blake, and his hostility to the anti-life cynicism of Swift. (Murry even made Katherine Mansfield into a Shakespearian Rose of England.) There is a marked vitalistic nationalism about the two men's tastes, which is especially striking if they are compared with, say, T. S. Eliot. (Eliot's *theory* of culture, on the other hand, is not so different from theirs.) Consequently, they can be aligned, in a large loose fashion, with John Cowper Powys, G. Wilson Knight, Herbert

Read, perhaps Henry Williamson, all of whom endorsed mystical darkness
and blood-knowledge. But Leavis and Murry, along with the others, also can
be aligned with such pure common sense as George Orwell's. In all these
men there is a Hardyesque sense of "the English soil," a distrust of cosmopolitanism, and a positive, a valuable, provincialism. It is—most notably in Leavis
and Orwell—a noble version of that conservative provincialism—implicitly Demetrian—which characterized all British culture between the two wars. Indeed, it has not been supplanted yet. One sees the same thing in Richard Hog-
gart and Raymond Williams.

   Culture and Environment: The Training of Critical Awareness, which
Leavis and Denys Thompson published in 1933, is still a good example of
what he stands for in terms of cultural taste. Reissued, in its ninth impression,
in 1962, the book is an attempt to arm the people, intellectually, to defend
their old culture against the encroachments of civilization. There is much on
"standardization" and "leveling down," and chapters on "Advertising, Fiction,
and the Currency of National Life, and "The Loss of the Organic Community," while "tradition" is contrasted with "substitute-living." These phrases
are resonant with the moral earnestness and historical desperateness which
people call "Puritan" in Leavis. We are told that men nowadays are "exposed
to the competing exploitation of the cheapest emotional responses" in films,
newspapers, advertising, publicity, and cheap fiction, which offer "satisfaction at the lowest level . . . the most immediate pleasures, got with the least
effort." Education therefore must teach awareness of the general process of
civilization as it spreads its domain, and of the immediate cultural environment.

   In a healthy state of culture we could leave the citizen to be formed unconsciously by his environment, but given the culture we have, Leavis argues,
a critical habit of consciousness must be systematically inculcated. The dramatic significance of Leavis's work lies precisely in this attempt to create a
conscious substitute for something, irretrievably lost, which was essentially unconscious: ". . . it is on literary tradition that the office of maintaining continuity must rest. But literary education, we must not forget, is to a great
extent a substitute. What we have lost is the organic community with the
living culture it embodied." Folk songs and dances, Cotswold cottages,
and handicraft products were all expressions of an art of life, "an adjustment,
growing out of immemorial experience, to the natural environment and the
rhythm of the year." In hidden parts of the country, speech is still an art. The
literary taste that follows from this general sensibility can be seen in Leavis's
assertion that *Pilgrim's Progress* is the supreme expression of the old English
people and that Bourne's *Wheelwright's Shop* will one day be recognized as

an English classic. But Leavis also had a taste for all that T. S. Eliot represents as a poet; and at that height of bold aesthetic experiment only D.H. Lawrence both expressed and represented these "natural" and "organic" values.

Turning to Talcott Parsons, we already have mentioned the other three men whose theories he combined with Weber's in *The Structure of Social Action*. Of those three, Marshall counted for least, and if his name were replaced by that of Freud, we should have a much more vivid summary of Parsons's *Weltanschauung*, which grew out of Weber, Durkheim, Pareto, and Freud. In the book's second edition of 1949 he regretted the omission. He had become acquainted with Freud's work too late to include it, but Freud's thinking is, he says, "a development which, in spite of the differences of his starting points and empirical concerns, must be regarded as a vital part of the same general movement of thought." It offered another kind of rationality, another kind of normativeness, to add to the religious, the political, and the other kinds of rationality explored by modern sociology. (Parsons has always been as interested as Leavis in values, or norms, but his interest has focused on the process of their internalization, not on the propagation of the right ones.) Elton Mayo had told him to study Freud when he began working in a hospital to research his study of the medical profession. (Parsons decided to do a sociological study of one of the professions for the very characteristic reason that the social structure of the professions seemed to elude Marxist "class" analysis.) In 1946 he entered psychoanalytic training as a Class C candidate at Boston Psychoanalytic Institute, and thereafter Freud was a major intellectual influence which he combined with Weber.

The general position, or complex of allegiances, to which Parsons belongs within American intellectual culture—the equivalent of what in Leavis's case I crudely called "Merrie England"—I would define in terms of Germanizing sociology and post-Christian social management. To take the latter aspect of the complex first, Alvin Gouldner found by poll in 1964 that twenty-seven percent of American sociologists had entertained serious thoughts of becoming clergymen at some point in their careers, and the proportion was highest among the Functionalists—those who follow Parsons's theories. Many of those who were not themselves ministers were sons of the manse. In Parsons's case it was his father who was a social gospel minister, but Albion Small himself had been a minister, and Dewey's work at Hull House and his school-teaching were at least quasi- or semi-ministerial.

Parsons himself, who belongs to a later generation than Small and Dewey and to a Harvard world of which they were never a part, we tend to associate with the professions rather than the ministry, but still with people in management of society. As William Mitchell has pointed out, Parsons has written about the professions but not about blue- or white-collar workers, about leaders but not the led, about propagandists but not the propagandized, about doctors but not patients.

There is a conservative and managerial pessimism about many of his opinions: "The possibility [of equality], however, has never been very closely approached in any known large-scale social system. . . . Some set of norms governing relations of superiority is an inherent need of stable social systems. . . . [T]here must be an important part played by discipline and authority . . . ," and so on. His politics, Mitchell says, have been shaped by his contacts with and admiration for the Eastern elite—the Achesons, the Harrimans, the Roosevelts—regardless of political party. This sympathy with management is a product of his concern for normative order. He has always shown a special sympathy with religion, as Durkheim did, because of its function as a source of social order. Indeed, he himself has remarked on the close historical connection between sociology and the ministry in America, noting that social gospel ministers became interested in social welfare generally and thus in sociology.

What I called the Germanizing aspect of the complex cooperated with its social management aspect, for the homeland of American sociology was the Germany of Stocker and Wagner, Schmoller and Brentano—the anti-Marxist academic socialists among whom Weber began. (Albion Small, chairman of the sociology department at Chicago in its great period, studied under Roscher, Schmoller, and Wagner from 1879 to 1881.) Their influence became powerful first in Wisconsin, through the work of Richard Ely, who came back to America with a Heidelberg Ph.D. in 1880. His ideas about society, formed with those of Robert M. La Follette, influenced the Progressive Party via Theodore Roosevelt, and ultimately Woodrow Wilson, Franklin Delano Roosevelt, and the New Deal.

In addition to this activist strain in German sociology, there was also an emphasis on *Wissenschaft*. Germany was the breeder of polymaths like Weber himself, and American sociology, following this lead, became a science, full of methodological machinery, in the style of German scholarship. The St. Louis Fair Conference of 1904, in which Weber and Troeltsch took part, is a good example of the spread of Germanic influence in American scholarship. No fewer than 308 people presented major papers there, of whom 202 were Americans, 49 were Germans, 21 were English, and 17 were French; and of the non-Germans, 106 had had German training. Of the professors of chemistry, eighty percent were German or German-trained; of history, fifty-three percent; of social science, fifty percent. (John Dewey, Woodrow Wilson, Frederick Jackson Turner, and J. H. Robinson all spoke there.) In the new science of sociology there were no significant British models to offer an alternative to the German style. The new subject remained German in style until it became Midwestern. It was characterized by the pursuance of massive "research" and great intensification of the "scientific" character of university work.

This Germanic sociology established itself first at the University of Chicago. In the Midwest social problems of a new size were demanding solution, the traditions of the old humanism were less established, there was a greater readiness to investigate society scientifically, there was a more democratic intellectual attitude that found everyday phenomena worthy of scholarly investigation, and there were a lot of German émigrés or German descendants.

This is the background against which to place Parsons, and it is implicitly as Apollonian, though democratic, as Leavis's is Diotiman. To be sure, he was not himself a Midwesterner, and he was of a later generation than Dewey, Small, Ely and Park. Perhaps the influences that somewhat differentiate him from them are best typified in the figure of L. J. Henderson, who played a significant part in the writing of *The Structure of Social Action,* and who was a notably patriarchal but also "aristocratic" mind. Henderson (1878–1942) went to Harvard Medical School, became a biochemist at Strasbourg, and returned to teach at Harvard. He studied neutrality regulations in animal organisms and devised a mathematical formula for expressing the acid-base equilibrium. His *Blood* of 1928 applied homeostatic concepts to the description of blood. He and Walter Cannon, another physical scientist much read by social scientists, worked out the idea of the body's having an internal environment, and, of dynamic equilibrium as the condition characterizing all life. This dynamic equilibrium is the life sciences' version of the equilibrium so important to engineers. It is manifested in the way in which an organism makes compensatory adjustments in response to danger—e.g., the blood clots faster, blood vessels contract. Thus the organism maintains its total equilibrium by changing that of its parts.

In 1928 Henderson read Pareto, and from then on Pareto seems to have been his major intellectual inspiration. (Pareto too was interested in equilibrium; he wrote his thesis in 1870 on the mathematical theory of equilibrium in elastic solids, and his pessimistic theory of society made much use of this model.) Henderson lectured (Sociology 23 at Harvard) on "the social system," something he defined by transferring Pareto's engineering ideas of "system" into biochemical terms, and then assimilating society to that.

Henderson was a man of power at Harvard, a friend of President Eliot, and a close friend of President Lowell. He got the Society of Fellows founded in 1933 and, always a passionate and overbearing discussant himself, became first chairman of the Senior Fellows. Intellectually and politically he was a pragmatic conservative. His great medical hero was Hippocrates, whose *vix mediatrix naturae* was a complex of homeostatic forces. He classed Hippocrates with Walpole, Bismarck, Richelieu, and Cavour, as opposed to Hegel, Mill, and Marx: "I fear the 'intellectuals,' the sentimentalists, and the uplifters—to me they are all one—even as I do the politicians and the profiteers." He moved always with men of power, both in the National Academy of Science and in the business world. It was his idea that the social sciences could be of help to men of affairs, men of the world. He was essentially a citizen of the world of men. In 1927 he became the first director of the Fatigue Laboratory at the Harvard Business School, and he influenced the famous sociological work done at the Hawthorne Plant of Western Electric.

Henderson was, particularly in his immediate social personality and impact on others, rather like Max Weber. Both were men of power who enforced, if not their own opinions, at least their standards of what is reasonable and what is interesting on everyone with whom they discussed these matters. Moreover, they were seriously interested in power as something manifested everywhere in society, and their theories bare the imprint, the character, of that interest. Weber's admiration for Alfred Hugenberg parallels Henderson's admiration for his friend Chester I. Barnard, the president of New Jersey Bell Telephone. Henderson's action on Parsons, which came at a crucial point in the latter's intellectual life, is therefore likely to have reinforced and extended Weber's influence, and to have made Parsons significantly more Weberian, especially in contrast with the earlier Midwestern sociologists.

Henderson first introduced Parsons to Pareto, and then went over *The Structure of Social Action* with him, revising it chapter by chapter, for a three-month period which Parsons describes as one of the most significant experiences of his life. They differed politically—and probably enough to let one say that Parsons was and is a liberal to Henderson's conservative—but what they had in common was more important, and that was an Apollonian interest in the problems of social management. Henderson felt that Willard Gibbs had shown that this is a world of systems, primarily physico-chemical systems and that better explanations for all phenomena could be got from mutual dependence, equilibrating effects, and other systems concepts, than from cause-and-effect propositions. Explanations in terms of mutual dependence and equilibrating effect imply that all systems tend to maintain stable patterns of activity and interactivity as a kind of dynamic equilibrium to which they return—*of their own accord*—after undergoing a shock such as, in the case of a human society, a revolution.

Such an approach lies at the heart of Parsons's work and the work of other Functionalist social scientists. George C. Homans, William F. Whyte, and Crane Brinton are said to owe a lot to Henderson. Equilibrium is the key word. Marshall's economics was built partly on an equilibrium model, Dewey defined knowledge as a state of equilibrium achieved by that doubt-inquiry function we call thought, and Freud's theory of personality is, Cynthia Russett points out, essentially homeostatic.

The use of an equilibrium model, Russett adds, prohibits thinking in terms of revolutionary change, and the social comments of Parsons and Cannon, not to mention Pareto and Henderson, bear her out. Parsons was the great ideological enemy of C. Wright Mills, sociology's radical, and in 1956 he wrote a hostile review of Mills's *The Power Elite*. His conservatism is temperamental. There is an anecdote to the effect that at Heidelberg in 1964, Parsons declared himself glad to be leaving there for Moscow, where people know what life is really like. He had been listening to the Utopist attacks on Weber, including Marcuse's, and finally exclaimed in disgust that all this talk was utterly unrealistic—don't these people know that life is always unhappy, and things can never be *much* better than they are? However inexact the letter of the anecdote may be, its spirit is surely true to the self-disciplining "realism" at the core of Parsons's thinking. It is this realism that makes him a true son of Weber, and even of Pareto, despite his genuine liberalism, and despite his "American" optimism which strikes one at first.

As a result of his contact with Henderson and Pareto, the latter of whom was deeply influenced by Machiavelli, Parsons acquired that highly unAmerican conservatism, that highly "male" amoralism, which bears the mark of Ares as much as of Apollo. But in Parsons's mind this partriarchal virility has lost much of its virulence by being combined with other influences. It is Durkheim, that orderly mind and orderly personality dedicated to building up order, dynamic moral order, *solidarité,* in the decadent Third Republic, with whom Parsons can best be paralleled. Indeed, perhaps the thing that marks Parsons off from his contemporaries and compatriots within his ideological group—as Leavis's response to Lawrence marked him off from, say Bloomsbury—was his use of four foreigners, Marshall, Pareto, Durkheim, and Weber, from four different countries—that is, his cosmopolitanism. Where Leavis has been a provincializing and nationalizing force in his country's intellectual life, Parsons has been a cosmopolitanizing one. He is, however, not in the least a "man of the world," for his cosmopolitanism for the most part has been simply the most striking instance of his consensualism, his Apollonianism.

Institutionalizations

One feature common to these two men's careers is of special interest here because of the pattern we are drawing. I am referring to the academic institutionalization of their subject matters. Both English literature and sociology have become major subjects of study at universities only during these men's lifetimes, both fields having undergone considerable shaping by the beliefs and actions of these men. (In the case of English study, these remarks do not apply so well outside Leavis's own university and England in general, and in both cases they describe local situations quite accurately and larger circles perhaps less so.) Leavis and Parsons, in short, have made Lawrence and Weber count for something in these institutions and systems of thought. Because of this process of institutionalization, those two men's imaginations—in some ways so remote from us now—have come to be effective forces in British and American society since the Second World War. The academic worlds of England and America, and the cultural worlds affected by them, have been profoundly responsive to Weber and Lawrence, and those worlds dispose of a great deal of power. They have a large population, many publications, many jobs, some status in the larger society, and they spend a lot of money. What is more, outside the academic world the effects of this institutionalization have been felt by thousands, indeed millions, of individuals. The kind of novel that gets written and read, the kind of movie that gets made and watched, on the one hand; the kind of welfare systems set up and the kind of industrial management promoted, on the other; "close reading" and *Scrutiny,* "plant sociology" and Project Camelot—all these derive to some degree from these remote sources. The world we now live in has been shaped, in many ways, by Weber and Lawrence. Of course, the *effects* of Weber and Lawrence, as mediated through these institutions and through the interpretations of Parsons and Leavis, are sometimes in comic or sad contrast with their initial *intentions.*

The English Tripos was established at Cambridge in 1917, and only in 1926 did new regulations make it possible (or at least attractive) to take a degree entirely in English. In that year also Old English was moved out of the English Tripos, and assigned to departments of archeology and anthropology. These facts, plus the recruitment of faculty during the war and just after, when the normal processes of training had been interrupted, made it possible for the English Tripos to make "a fresh start," to be notably different and modern, compared, for instance, with Oxford's equivalent. A paper was required in Practical Criticism and one in comparative literature, but there were no compulsory papers in language or in pre-Chaucerian literature.

It is interesting to learn, from E. M. W. Tillyard's account, that the Tripos developed partly in opposition to German philological scholarship. Breuer, the first professor of German at Cambridge, and his cousin Braunholtz, Reader in Romance Philology, were close allies and formidable scholars, opposed to any Tripos in English, and doubly opposed to any versions of such a scheme, which would diminish the importance of philology. But Chadwick, a professor of Anglo-Saxon who had heard Brandl lecture in Berlin on phonetic changes in Middle English, had decided that this was no subject for undergraduates. During the war the German professors were effectively muzzled, and the idea of English studies they represented—interpreting *Beowulf* as a Teutonic *Odyssey*, for example—was in disrepute. Indo-Germanic philology was at that time associated with Wagner and Teutonic doctrines of race superiority, and was, in addition, an intellectual discipline of formidable difficulty. The intellectual discipline was Apollonian, although the cultural content definitely was not. The English Tripos rebelled against both the style and the content in the name of liberal English humanitarianism. It rebelled, intellectually, against what Weber represented; like Erich von Kahler, it objected, morally and emotionally, to the cruel subordination of personality demanded by such a concept of learning.

The Tripos was, then, liberal. We may take Tillyard's word for it, and his own mind as representing it. At Cambridge, he writes, "There was to be no distinction between a good short story written yesterday and a Petrarchan sonnet of the age of Elizabeth; and the learner had the right to sport in every glade and green pasture." The student of English must never treat facts "as an end in themselves; he must ever subordinate them to ideas. And those ideas must be his own. . . ." Tillyard's liberalism was, of course, a reaction against the illiberal way in which he had been taught the Classics.

As one would expect, this liberalism was more or less asking to be supplanted by some more rigorous idea. Otherwise it was going to fall into either the sloppy emotionalism of a Murry or the trivial mildness of a Tillyard. The first rigorous idea applied to the field was I. A. Richard's method of close reading and reasoning about words, in the manner of G. E. Moore in philosophy, combined with physiological and psychological explanations of poetic effects. Tillyard takes 1929, the year Richards's *Practical Criticism*, as the climax of Cambridge liberalism, but soon Richards moved off in other directions.

The second rigorous idea, which proved much more uncomfortable for the rest of the English faculty, was Leavis's. *Scrutiny* was founded in 1932. Tillyard adds that by 1930 boys who already had been taught the new Cambridge ideas at school began arriving at the university. To them Leavis alone among the dons could offer, as it were, a second act in which the pitch of moral and intellectual emotion rose adequately. I have said that Leavis's methodological roots were in Eliot, but it would be equally true to say that they were in Richards. But the crucial element in Leavis's development was what he supplied himself: the passionately held *Weltanschauung* in which life-values were dominant, and the aggressive and dogmatic moralism which made quite small points of tone, inference, and allusion major determinants of position and occasions for moral judgment of a highly personal and yet total kind. Lawrence, we remember, "makes it possible to cherish some faith in the future of humanity," and every author was likely to be judged by some such criterion, and every critic by his attitude to some such author.

Leavis has always been implicitly hostile to institutions, like most people whose values are matriarchal. But his hostility is not theoretical, and therefore not total. He believes in the idea of a university. He has often asserted that he and his friends represent the true Cambridge—temporarily usurped by the unworthy—and the true English Tripos. I think he would even call a true Cambridge the natural place for Lawrence's teachings to be critically expounded, and therefore Lawrence's appropriate institutional home. He has shaped his critical essays to be acts of teaching in the most literal and institutional sense. And in his "Retrospect," written when *Scrutiny* finally stopped publication in 1953, he says that the magazine was "the product, the triumphant justifying achievement, of the English Tripos."

The teaching of English literature was, then, the first level of institutionalization for Leavis's point of view—unless one regards the social and intellectual life of the home which he and his wife established in Cambridge even before they had teaching jobs there as that. Their home certainly was a center, an institution of sorts; indeed, it was the nucleus round which the new Cambridge grew. Leavisism was further institutionalized in the choice of contributors to *Scrutiny,* the choice of subjects to be written about—not only literary subjects, but also educational ones—and the aggressive and highly committed manner of discourse common to all contributors. All this was Leavis. And Lawrence figured prominently in the criteria of all these choices, as well as in the magazine's pantheon of great writers. *Scrutiny*'s predecessor as a critical quarterly, *The Calendar of Modern Letters,* had had the same manner, but a somewhat different set of standards. The *Calendar* was more assertively "classical," in opposition to Murry's romanticism, and although it published Lawrence, its critical tone about him was severe. For instance, we read: "Thus it is possible to say that the criticism in Mr. Eliot's *Sacred Wood* not only is a more valuable work than Mr. Lawrence's latest novel, but takes precedence of it, makes it obsolete." It was *Scrutiny*'s task to

reverse this evaluation while maintaining the scrupulous exactitude and in-
direction of the phrasing, the manner.

The next level of institutionalization is that of the party loyalties within
the academic world, the positions held by Leavisites in universities and teachers' training colleges. This factor is not easy to specify without a lot of detail,
but it is now generally accepted that a great many of Leavis's pupils, unable
to get positions in England, went to teach in Commonwealth universities (a
famous example is D. J. Enright in Singapore) or in Extra-Mural courses or
the Workers Educational Association. Raymond Williams is the most famous
example of the latter. From these positions many have since moved inside the
universities of England, as the system expanded in the 1960s and as Leavis
came to prevail intellectually. (*Culture and Environment,* a book co-authored
in 1933 by Leavis and Denys Thompson, was, its authors said, designed for use
in teachers' training colleges as well as in schools and had derived partly
from W. E. A. experience.) But it seems still to be true that the characteristic
centers of influence of Leavis's disciples are the teachers' training colleges.
This is to be expected, both because of Leavis's passionate interest in education, school and classroom education, as the field of the battle between culture
and civilization. It is so also because the teachers' colleges are less meeting
places for ideas in the largest sense—ideas deriving from many cultures—and
more places where the charge of intellectual provincialism is not so crucial.
For them, Lawrence as interpreted by Leavis is an irreplaceable value. Thus
an elaborate institutional machinery, superintended by F. R. Leavis, conducts
Lawrence's ideas through the whole land of England.

Sociology first became institutionalized in America at the University of
Chicago. (Institutionalization in this field covers more than it does in English
studies, for the least institutionalized teaching of sociology is perhaps more
so than the most institutionalized teaching of English; nevertheless, if the
habits and characteristics of both disciplines are kept in mind, these generalizations seem fair.) From early on, both the president and the professors at
Chicago were determined to make the university a center of research, although empirical sociology began only after Robert Park, who had been a
journalist as well as secretary to Booker T. Washington, joined the staff. Up
to then, German sociology had been speculative and "idealistic," although
some work, notably by Weber, had been done in questionnaire surveys.

As early as the first decade of the twentieth century, Chicago began to
train its students in conducting surveys. The muckrakers' survey reports were
studied in class, and Florence Kelley and John Commons served as advisers
to the very first one done, a study of Pittsburgh in 1907. (The connection, via
them, of the survey technique with the social reformism of Hull House is no
accident.) After the First World War, Park and W. T. Thomas, another Chi-

cago sociologist, were given many commissions by foundations and city councils to study aspects of society. A professional world also grew up around sociology at Chicago. Dissertations done in the department were published in the Chicago Sociological Series, and the *American Journal of Sociology* became a Chicago organ. Regular summer institutes of the Society for Sociological Research became important meeting places for people and ideas, and jobs opened up at universities through the Midwest and Northwest. Chicago, Wisconsin, and Michigan were the great pioneers, followed closely by Indiana, Iowa, Nebraska, and Illinois. Unlike the elite Eastern schools, these universities had no patrician humanist traditions; they sprang directly from Enlightenment ideas. So did American sociology. Park believed that the spread of sociological knowledge would advance progress, justice, and reform.

In England, it is interesting to note, sociology never flourished; for a long time not even taught at Oxford and Cambridge, it grew only outside the universities, and consequently without the necessary institutional support, in pockets of Benthamite-Utilitarianism. Leavis, in the early numbers of *Scrutiny,* regretted the lack of sociology at English universities and praised American studies like the Lynds' *Middletown.* Conversely, although the study of English literature certainly flourished in America, there was no equivalent to the Leavisite blend of intense literariness with sociocultural relevance, nor to the aggressive-moralist Leavisite manner. The nearest equivalent seems to have been the comparatively uninstitutionalized New York Jewish style, to be found in *Partisan Review* and *Commentary.*

Chicago lost its pre-eminence when Park withdrew to go to Fisk. The center of American sociology then moved east, to Harvard and even more to Columbia. At the latter university, Robert Merton's and Paul Lazarsfeld's work at the Bureau of Applied Social Research formalized research techniques and avoided commitment to any particular *Weltanschauung* by sticking to middle-range theory. Parsons, however, stood for something different. He has always stood for grand theory, and that is the great use he has made of Weber. The only American sociologist of note who has never presented any body of empirical research in a paper, Parsons is undeniably the theorist of sociology.

Edward Shils, the source for much of the information in this sketch of the institutionalization of American sociology, says that Parsons has been the only one of Weber's followers who extended his master's ideas. In Germany, Karl Mannheim almost alone taught Weber, but Mannheim's career was broken by the Nazis. Parsons, however, located Weber's central ideas and developed them further, although, Shils contends, he has not institutionalized his sociology as efficiently as Merton has his.

Alvin Gouldner we shall note, disagrees with Shils's account. Gouldner feels that Parsons's system is by far dominant system of American sociological theory, and that it owes this position in no small part to its institutional origins. Functionalism is clearly the product of Harvard, thrives in this insulated university situation, and thus has managerial positions to offer its successful students. Parsons's students, such as Robert Merton, Kingsley Davis, Robin Williams, and Wilbert Moore, have been the officers of the American Sociological Association, and he himself was editor of one of its journals. The Harvard sociology department was founded only in 1931, during the Depression, when sociologists seemed especially called on to explain the social situation. Although they were a clean-handed group compared with economists, they were more socially "relevant" than any other academics, and thus appeared glamorous to students. Moreover, from the beginning, Parsons personally was able to offer his very able students an incomplete system within which each could work out something of his own, in striking contrast to the "complete" systems of Marx and of Pitirim Sorokin, who was then chairman of the department.

To the intellectual advantages attached to studying sociology at Harvard were joined material ones. Gouldner points out that in two generations America has trained a cadre of full-time specialists in sociology at least two or three times larger than that in all the countries of Europe. According to a poll he conducted in 1964, eighty percent of American sociologists were Functionalists to some degree. Both C. Wright Mills and Parsons have noted that we are living in an era of sociology. The Federal Government spent $118 million on social science in 1962, $139 million in 1963, and $200 million in 1964. That is a seventy percent increase in two years. In Belgium the increase was from $2.9 milion to $4.8 million in the same period. No wonder that in 1964 the Weber centenary was the occasion for conflicts of opinion about the direction the subject was taking.

Parsons, says Gouldner, has been the most intellectually relevant of American sociologists and has touched on more of the really important problems than any of the others. But, Gouldner contends, he is a metaphysician more than anything else, and his "unmistakable" metaphysical conviction is that social systems are organic wholes, that the world is one, and that its oneness is its most vital character. His categories triumph not when tested for their predictive power, but when they are found applicable to many levels of things and ideas at the same time, thus unifying or revealing a unity. The manifold conceptual categories which Parsons invents (excessive from every other point of view) are all ports of access to that wholeness. He is not interested in individualities. His description of human behavior begins with group values. It ignores behavior deriving from, for instance, internal conflict and competition, and neglects the latent identities of individuals—e.g., the sexual identities. His Functionalism continues nineteenth-century Positivism's stress on moral order while ignoring its stress on technological progress. Even more Apollonian than Positivism, Functionalism implies that the problems of social order can be solved without reference to economic or technological questions. Parsons is a purer Positivist, a later, American, Durkheim or Comte, with the same taxonomic zeal and the same assumption of the nonrationality of human behavior.

Gouldner concedes that Parsons has communicated better than anyone the image of a whole social system, and because this image legitimatizes sociologists in their work, it is a very potent thing to control. He adds that Parsons has won this power largely through the force of his conceptualizing rhetoric, not through any actual proofs or explanations. (This is a reproach often made to Leavis also, although of course Leavis's rhetoric is quite different.) Parsons's style is notably conceptual and notably obscure, largely because he is so eager to present us with so many things at the same time, and cannot deal with anything thoroughly. Besides, he seems to feel that none of the parts matter anyway, compared with the reality-conferring whole. In this feeling, Functionalism parallels Platonism as well as Positivism, for Platonic philosophy and Functionalist sociology, Gouldner says, have similar infrastructures of domain assumptions and sentiments. For both, men are raw material, redeemed only by belonging to God or to Society; by themselves they are essentially appetitive, and their insatiability is the source of all the evil in the world. Platonism and Functionalism are both body-mind dualisms which operate entirely in the realm of mind and reject the body completely; they fear love and prefer friendship, they fear death and seek an immortality of the mind. They are concerned with order, not freedom or fulfilment. Dirt and evil and disorder have no ideal form, and so are mere absences. In other words, both are Apollonian.

It is of course gratifying for our argument that one of Gouldner's major categories for Parsons and his sociology should be Apollonian: "To seek order . . . expresses an Apollonian vision of a social world composed of firmly boundaried social objects, each demarcated and separated from and setting limits upon the other . . . continuity, cumulation, codification, convergence, the joyless prescriptions of a structuralizing methodology that is the fit counterpart of an Apollonian vision of society." Convergence, says Gouldner, is an Americanized version of Hegelian *Geist,* the academic counterpart of wartime and coldwartime solidarity, the sign of the professionalization and institutionalization of sociology. Thus Parsons in America, like Leavis in England, set up an elaborate machinery for conducting his master's ideas to crucial points of social effectiveness.

Confrontations

Gouldner's *The Coming Crisis of Western Sociology* came out in 1970, the last year of the century we are considering, and announced a rebellion against Parsons and Functionalism. Gouldner admires Weber and sees him as a Romantic figure, and his own book is a rebellion against everything that "classical" Western sociology has become. (Similarly, Dennis Wrong, who also has his quarrel with Parsons, sees Weber as very unlike Parsons. Wrong calls Weber "the only truly great man we sociologists have a clear right to claim as one of our own"; but he aligns him with Freud and Orwell among his own intellectual heroes, and indeed the three men do have important things in common. Parsons seems to him a much narrower figure, and narrowing in his effects.) Gouldner's rebellion derives from his conviction that nowadays Functionalist sociology increases the control power of the Federal Administration. Classical sociologists, led by the Functionalists, have become the market researchers of the Welfare State and the agents of the new managerialism. Because Gouldner sees the Welfare State as merely the home front of the Warfare State, all attempts to serve the one and not the other appear to him to be self-deceiving. He describes with sympathy the shadow meetings held by the radical students' Sociological Liberation Front at the 1968 meeting of the American Sociological Association. These meetings culminated in a protest speech at the plenary session in which the Secretary of Health, Education, and Welfare, the featured speaker of the evening, was attacked as a military officer who coordinated the war against the people, and all classical sociologists were denounced as Uncle Toms, collaborators, Quislings. In that same year the German sociologist Jurgen Habermas, who had been the hero of the students in 1964 when he criticized Parsons at Heidelberg, was himself attacked by students demonstrating at Frankfurt. Radicalism had become something more extreme. The students now spoke sometimes with the voice of Marx, sometimes with that of Otto Gross, but in any case against classical sociology, against everything with any taint of classicism or objectivity. With them, Weber's position as a politician is equally in disrepute. His enemies have become today's heroes, and vice versa. In 1969 Sebastian Haffner's book on the 1918 revolution in Munich—Edgar Jaffe's revolution, previously dismissed, as Weber dismissed it, as something foolish if not wicked—made Kurt Eisner into a revolutionary hero of German history. It said that Germany today is still sick because it still suffers from the betrayal of that revolution; *Die Verratene Revolution* (*The Revolution Betrayed*) is the book's title. The implication of this historical interpretation is that Edgar Jaffe, not Max Weber, knew what Germany needed in 1918. The revolutionary has come to seem *prima facie* authoritative, and the established to seem suspect. Gouldner's prediction that Russian sociology is now ready to turn Functionalist, that behind the Iron Curtain Parsons is now the object of the greatest interest and respect, only tends to confirm the students' convictions.

In Leavis's case there have been no such demonstrations, no such student anger, and, so far as I know, no book like Gouldner's. Leavis has presented himself always as a passionate protester against the establishment, and never as an Apollonian. He has been a figure like C. Wright Mills, Parsons's passionate opponent. Leavis has been a Demetrian or Diotiman *radical,* just as Weber was an Apollonian *radical.* The recent criticism of Leavis in books comparable with Gouldner's—for instance, in John Gross's *Rise and Fall of the Man of Letters*—has been a continuation of the old feuds. Among the student population, however, he is going out of fashion and is subjected to hostile analysis of the same two kinds as are directed at Parsons—that is, doctrinaire Marxist and Otto Gross-libertarian.

The difference between Leavis and Parsons is expressed even in their appearance. Leavis so intensely dramatic, so disheveled and burning-eyed, so hollow-cheeked and husky-tenored, burning up vital energy before your eyes and refusing material nourishment; Parsons so short and solid and anonymous, neatly bald-headed and ginger-moustached, a steady-voiced expert, a boffin, a technical colonel or major in mufti, backroom boss of the new mandarins. Paradoxically, though, it is Parsons who writes so freely of himself and his intellectual autobiography, whereas Leavis austerely refuses the merely personal role.

The big confrontation in this decade for Leavis was only indirectly related to Lawrence, and yet it exemplified perfectly the categories this book is concerned to establish. I am referring to his celebrated battle with C. P. Snow over science and the two cultures. Snow is essentially a representative of the patriarchal and managerial level of our society. He stands for science, technology, industry, politics, and institutions, and all his novels are about institutions and life as it is lived in institutions, about moral problems as they arise in institutions. This has a good deal to do with why Leavis thinks him a crying scandal as a novelist. For Leavis, culture and the arts, being matriarchal, should be always somehow engaged in attacking patriarchal civilization. For Snow to reproach literary men with a hostility to science, with an ignorance of science which amounted to a lack of full participation in modern civilization, struck Leavis as both a typical absurdity and a sinister cynicism.

Lawrence entered Leavis's argument at several points—as a great novelist whom Snow failed even to acknowledge, never mind to measure up to. More importantly, Leavis associated Snow as a personality with Sir Joshua Mattheson, a character in *Women in Love,* with Bertrand Russell, the original from whom Lawrence drew his character, and with H. G. Wells. Leavis charged that none of these men live, to use Lawrence's phrase, "on the spot where they are." They live, to use Snow's phrase, "in the social hope." These two slogans, which Leavis juxtaposes dramatically, epitomize the contrast between the Diotiman and the Apollonian moralities; the former judges people by their "realized" affirmations, the life-values they unconsciously embody; the latter judges them by those social enterprises in which they consciously invest parts of their energies. The absoluteness with which Leavis identifies literature with the Demetrian option is striking. Snow, he repeats, asking the reader to take his words literally, "doesn't know what literature is." Because, for Leavis, literature is a means consecrated to a certain kind of meaning, a certain range of values, and no others.*

> In coming to terms with great literature [Leavis writes] we discover what at bottom we really believe. What for—what ultimately for? what do men live by—the questions work and tell at what I can only call a religious depth of thought and feeling. Perhaps, with my eye on the adjective, I may just recall for you Tom Brangwen, watching by the fold in lambing-time under the night sky: "He knew he did not belong to himself."

It is indeed a whole perspective of religion—Lawrentian and Demetrian religion—which Leavis opens up in those sentences. He invoked it also in his 1964 essay on Bunyan, when he said that this is the true religion—as opposed to the theology—of *Pilgrim's Progress.* On that occasion he quoted the whole sentence from *The Rainbow:* "But during the long February nights with the ewes in labour, looking out from the shelter into the flashing stars, he knew he did not belong to himself." Leavis ascribes a "change-defying validity" to this religion, which stretches across centuries and is common to Bunyan, Lawrence, and himself.

It is worth noting the similarity between the Lawrence image Leavis uses here and the following passage from Alfred Weber's *Farewell to Euro-*

---

* I myself joined in the two cultures controversy, and the limitations of my analysis, which I felt obscurely at the time, derived from my unconsciously identifying the arts and literature with matriarchal culture, much as Leavis did. Like him, I saw with surprise that in fact there are novelists, like Snow, who represent the patriarchal world of "civilization," but although that seemed to me an anomaly, unlike Leavis I found this phenomenon and these novelists interesting for that very reason. I did not then use the term "matriarchal culture" or understand the idea fully, but what I wrote in *Science and the Shabby Curate of Poetry* is really all a section of this argument.

pean History in which Weber invokes "the powers reigning in the invisible and unlocated background":

> And when, on a clear, starry night our visible cosmos unveils before us, when we can imagine, sensing in its nature and configuration the presence of a sublime will, that our Milky Way is built up by something other than the foci of forces made accessible to us by mathematics, or the vectors of motion and light velocities and electromagnetic fields and world lines which physics establishes. This "something other" may only echo in us like a bell-note.

Clearly this is the same *Lebensphilosophie* idea as Lawrence's, though a different temperament lay behind this expression of it. At moments like this the diverging lines pursued by the two sisters' lives come together, and we see a certain conservatism common to all the ideas we associate with them.

Snow is not a figure to remind one of Max Weber, but he is rather like Parsons; he represents in other walks of life—of the life of the mind—the same qualities. "The contented moralist," one of Gouldner's phrases for Parsons, catches exactly the tone of Leavis's revulsion from Snow. We may associate both Snow and Parsons with the world of industrial management; both see the modern world as characterized by problems of the sort one finds there, and both accept the same sort of solutions to these problems. Other sociologists, in contrast, repudiate the Functionalist solutions, and people like Leavis repudiate the very problems, or at least ignore the significance attributed to them.

Let us take an example of those problems. The subdiscipline of Functionalist sociology which has aroused most indignation is perhaps plant sociology, the study of industrial relations in factories. The plant sociologist, we are told, sees the factory manager as the creator of a stable social organism, not as, for instance, the class enemy of the worker. He assumes that the individual is always an integral member of some social whole at a preconscious level of sentiment and thus removes "political" problems from the sphere of politics, of conscious deliberation and free choice. Clark Kerr and Lloyd H. Fisher claim that plant sociology sets the idea that society is tribalized in opposition to universalist rationalism, sets the diversity of cultures in opposition to the unity of men, sets organic analogies in opposition to mechanical models, sets function in opposition to purpose. It asks how a group works, not what it works at. The plant is taken to be the new social unit, which replaces the church, the guild, and the community, all of which have been dissolved by industrialism. The worker is thus seen as motivated in his work by "sentiments" rather than by reason. Sociology "scientifically" undermines the political passions.

The three sociologists who are most closely associated with plant sociology are Elton Mayo, William F. Whyte, and George C. Homans, but Mayo is a Functionalist, inspired by Pareto and Durkheim in particular, and it is generally agreed that Parsons's own principles, if applied to such material, would work out to similar results, so that plant sociology can be taken as essentially a Parsonian offshoot. In 1958, just a year after the appearance of the Kerr and Fisher essay just referred to, Ralf Dahrendorf also attacked Parsons's "Platonism" and called for a sociology derived from a conflict model of society, a sociology that would see societies as held together by constraint rather than by consensus.* According to Dahrendorf, Parsons—and Weber—can be held responsible for the repressive political neutralism of our managers.

The important thing, of course, is to realize the character which Functionalism bears within sociology, as well as the cultural character of all sociology *vis-à-vis* literature. It is a character with which we may fairly associate both Parsons and Snow. The two cultures controversy therefore can be seen as the most significant recent British clash between the Apollonian and the Demetrian principles. (The followers of Otto Gross's principle stood by, despising both antagonists.) I would suggest that in most countries today one will find such clashes between these two principles—these three, counting Gross, for Gross's heritage is now being worked out intellectually by Norman O. Brown, and more practically by R. D. Laing. Its institutionalization is a matter of hippie groups, its confrontations are with the police.

But it is perhaps worth remembering—especially by those among my readers who will react against the patriarchal option—that Weber's principles lead one to take an interest in Gandhi whereas Lawrence's do not. It is students of Weber who are likely to study such phenomena sympathetically, not disciples of Lawrence. In 1950, Professor Wilhelm E. Mühlmann, author of *Max Weber und die rationale Soziologie*, wrote a book called *Gandhi*, which he tells he was able to do only by using Weber's categories. The patriarchal mind *is* concerned with and sympathetic to such moral and religious phenomena as Gandhi—or the late Tolstoy, for that matter—whereas the matriarchal mind is profoundly embarrassed by them. During the war, Weber wrote, in "Between Two Laws":

---

* Leavis also uses organic models of society, we should note, but he implies that *contemporary* societies—his own Cambridge, for example—are held together by constraints, and so his organicism, applying itself only to the ideal past, does not feel effectively conservative.

The life of all those who receive only 1¢ of rent which others have to pay directly or indirectly, who own something or consume a product which is imbued with the sweat of labour of others rather than his own, all these lives are dependent upon the pitiless economic struggle for existence which is devoid of love—a struggle which bourgeois phraseology calls "peaceful cultural work." . . . The attitude of the Gospel towards all this is absolutely clear. It is opposed not only to war, which is not mentioned specifically, but ultimately to all laws of society to the extent to which it represents earthly culture, beauty, dignity, honour and greatness of men.

It is the intense sympathy with the ascetic position that is interesting here, and equally so is the fact that Lawrence was not sympathetic, was not interested. (Of course, there are hints that Lawrence was interested and sympathetic to some extent—how could he not be?—but what he wrote is not based on this interest and sympathy, which are alien to the formed opinions of his formed Demetrian self. The Apollonian mind, just by virtue of its self-alienation, enters more easily into positions hostile to itself.) In the same way, Professor Baumgarten is writing a book about Hitler using Weber's categories, and one is forced to reflect that Lawrence's categories would not help one *there,* nor lead one to struggle with the problem.

All this is, I realize, a far cry from the personal intensities of Lawrence and Weber. If the two parties and principles I speak of "derive from" those two figures, the correspondences are not one-to-one. Lawrence, for instance, was at times highly ambivalent about matriarchal values, and Weber—to be understood as a whole—must be understood in many other terms besides "patriarchal." Certainly Leavis and Parsons are not *personally* to be called matriarchal or patriarchal, for the designations apply to them only as leaders of these two parties and as representatives of these two categories. It is quite typical, moreover, that in his comments on Frieda Lawrence Leavis has been more hostile than not, and certainly has not treated her as the source of what he regards as valuable in Lawrence. In his essay on *Anna Karenina* he describes Frieda as an "amoral German aristocrat." He attributes a certain lack of understanding of the domestic life discernible in Lawrence's later fiction to the Lawrences' rootless way of life. Implicitly, he blames Frieda for the weaknesses in Lawrence's work, rather than praising her for its strengths. But one sees that to attack Frieda for these reasons is only to celebrate the Demetrian principle the more fully, to find even her an unworthy representative of it. Just so, Leavis finds *Lady Chatterley's Lover* unworthy of Lawrence himself, because it expresses no faith in, or understanding of, marriage. Leavis sees in Frieda Otto Gross's woman, and it is the Hetaerist principle which he attacks in her. This may serve—Parsons's revulsion from the more Faustian manifestations of Weber's virility of mind would do just as well—to illustrate the many qualifications, concessions, and counterarguments which one would have to enter into in order to adjust the general categories to these figures perfectly. I have taken it for granted that the reader can see the sense—the limited sense—in which Parsons and Leavis—and Lawrence and Weber, for that matter—represent these principles personally.

Nevertheless, as representatives of their disciples and their disciplines, in literary studies and in sociology, Leavis and Parsons surely *are* to be seen as matriarchalist and patriarchalist. Leavis's disciples, more than any other critics of literature, are likely to hold implicitly by the Demetrian values of growth and fertility, of authenticity in personal relations and personal feelings. Indeed, all students of literature are more likely than sociologists to hold by those values. Conversely, Parsons's disciples more than other sociologists are likely implicitly to believe in the values of objectivity and administrative justice and the virtues and skills needed to make a large institution work. This is the way I would now define the "two cultures" and the conflict between them. It is a conflict, one may say, between Lawrence and Weber—between their two ways of using the mind.

But now, perhaps, I would not be impelled to write a book on such a subject. The decade since I did has seemed to mark the passing away of certain urgencies, the blurring of certain alignments, the dimming out of certain allegiances. A century has ended. Weber and Lawrence, and the posthumous life they were granted in the doctrine of their disciples, have died. Their images are shrinking back to the dimensions of two great but mortal men, fit companions of the two sisters. Their faces now seem more human than mythical, remote now from the institutional machinery and doctrinal rigors invented in their name to save civilization.

All the further from these matters of academic style and domain assumptions must seem the two interviews I began by describing, with Frieda Lawrence and Else Jaffe. But the connection is there. Frieda's face has been the unseen heraldic sign on the flyleaf of hundreds of works in the modernist and irrationalist tradition, and Else's pure and classical features, or those of someone just like her, may be said to have inspired as many works of reason and scholarship; think of Frau Jaffe sitting in the place of honor at the 1964 Max Weber celebrations at Heidelberg. Each was a face that launched a thousand ships.

Epilogue

What New Light Does This Throw on Lawrence's Work?

How much light a new lamp throws can best be measured by switching off the old one, which I am not willing to do. I think the light thrown by Leavis's—and Herman Daleski's—criticism brings out what is most valuable in Lawrence's achievement as an artist. Here I would merely extend and elaborate their judgments, insofar as the evaluation of individual works goes. My emphasis is on Lawrence's imaginative context, the context in which it is imaginatively most profitable to set his work as a whole. There my propositions amount to a major counter-suggestion, substantially modifying traditional practice. But in matters of evaluative judgment or even interpretation of individual works, my argument may not make a great deal of difference.

Perhaps it is worth summarizing that argument's tendencies here, and to do so I shall divide them into three ways Lawrence and his work were affected by this context: the mass of Lawrence's imaginative experience and fictional ideas supplied by the von Richthofen milieu in which I include all his contacts with German culture; the effect of living with Frieda—that is, of living in an outpost of Munich-Schwabing; and the extent of Frieda's co-authorship of his books.

THE EFFECT OF THE VON RICHTHOFEN MILIEU

The first of these categories supplies most in the way of detailed interpretive suggestion. It has not been generally appreciated, I think, how completely Lawrence submerged himself in the von Richthofen milieu when he ran away with Frieda. He left England for the first time, went to a country where he could scarcely make himself understood, and entered a familial world socially and educationally superior to his own. Else and Nusch and the Baron and Baroness von Richthofen were all in different ways—but also in the same way—formidable people, and Frieda was not only older than he, but also far more experienced in the erotic life to which he was committing himself. In addition, Lawrence had no money and they lived at first in houses lent them by Else's friends, in a country-

side where he did not even know the names of the flowers, and where he must
have seemed, or felt he seemed, to the people he met on walks a very odd fish.
"Alone and exposed and out of the world," is one of his phrases for himself
abroad. In the sketches written in those first few months ("A Chapel in the
Mountains," for example) there is always a suggestion that Frieda might have
come there with another lover—"Why did I choose *you?*" she cries—whereas for
Lawrence there were no alternatives.

Moreover, if one studies Lawrence's movements from April 1912 to June
1914, one will be struck by how much time he spent encountering *other* von
Richthofens or their friends, living in their houses, accepting their hospitality.
They were as important a part of Lawrence and Frieda's environment as their
English visitors, like David Garnett. Indeed, they may have been more important
in relation to Lawrence's creative work, for the Germans—Edgar and Else Jaffe,
for example—had played major parts in the drama of Frieda's developing identity
and fate, which was so much the inspiration of *The Sisters* and the short stories
of the period. During those months, Lawrence was absorbing Frieda's life into
himself—her ideological and experiential dowry, which remained all his life his
major imaginative capital—and he absorbed it from the von Richthofen milieu as
well as from her.

I have suggested that *Sons and Lovers* owed something to his experience
in that milieu. He began rewriting it September 7, 1912, four months after
their elopement, and its final form seems clearly to owe much both to the inspiration which Frieda's feeling for Else may have given to the figure of Clara and to
the external form given to the Clara episode. Indeed, the form of the whole
novel, as I have said already, strikingly resembles the first version of Gottfried
Keller's *Der Grüne Heinrich,* the version that ended with the death of Heinrich's
mother, a novel with a very high reputation among people like the Webers and
Jaffes in those years. The main themes and the structure of *Sons and Lovers* are
very like Keller's, though the values and the texture are not. (The texture Lawrence surely learned from Tolstoy, and it is this quality that realizes so marvelously
the life-values Lawrence was celebrating.) Keller was a much more essayistic
novelist, in the tradition of the *Bildungsroman,* than Lawrence ever let himself
be. Any "rational dryness" clearly would have been a disgrace to a novelist of the
erotic movement. In *Sons and Lovers* the autobiographical and reminiscent nature
of the material helped him escape that danger, but even later on, when he had
different material to shape, Lawrence's *Bildungsromanen* defied their own form.

There is one striking example of this. It seems not to have been noticed how
perfectly *Aaron's Rod* follows the rules of the *Bildungsroman.* Like Wilhelm
Meister himself, Aaron Sisson is met first as he leaves his comfortable bourgeois
home and sets out on picaresque adventures which lead him to make fundamental
life-choices. He moves into social circles very different from those he has known,
all of which are in one way or another more sophisticated than his native one.
In a series of developments which parallel the career of Wilhelm Meister, he

wanders from the Midlands to London, earns his living with his flute in a theater, has an affair with a member of a Bohemian set there, meets a mystic teacher, a Magus, falls gravely ill, goes abroad for the first time, stays in Novara with a plutocrat, goes on to Milan and Florence, encountering along the way a gallery of vividly depicted rebels against ordinariness. The essence of Aaron's character, as of Wilhelm's, is naïveté of a shrewd and sophisticated sort. And in each encounter the other person exerts pressure on him to move in some new direction.

Lawrence wrote this book in a state of opposition to Frieda, and without her usual cooperation; he was trying to free herself from the world of Woman, but unsure if he could, and in certain ways the book lacks self-confidence, and therewith formal completeness. Most clearly, for instance, Lawrence could not "believe in" his Magus, Lilly, or in Aaron's final submission to him, and so the climax of the story becomes an anticlimax. In itself, this is a formally interesting effect, and an artistically valid one, but as part of the total design it is a blur, which is perhaps why the form has gone unrecognized. Also, of course, the novel is not large enough or weighty enough—again a result of the author's lack of self-confidence—to suggest a comparison with Wilhelm Meister. And yet Part I of Goethe's novel surely did supply Lawrence with his pattern, either directly or via the *Bildungsroman* tradition. Of course, Lawrence avoided the high seriousness and the essayistic effect we find in Keller and Thomas Mann, and that is presumably why *Aaron's Rod* was not recognized for what it was, whereas *The Magic Mountain,* published three years later, was. In structural terms, Lawrence's book is in fact closer than Mann's to the tradition in which both were working. Julian Moynahan has called it a Russian novel in English, but actually it is German. One of the things Lawrence got from the von Richthofen milieu was the skill to write German novels in English—to extend the British tradition in fiction by introducing German elements.

The major work in which the lives of the von Richthofen circle, as distinct from their literature, comes to expression is *The Sisters,* the novel about Frieda which eventually split into *The Rainbow* and *Women in Love.* This, too, bears the traces of having been originally a *Bildungsroman,* but a woman's *Bildungsroman.* If we consider only the material dealing with Ursula's life, from her first meeting with Skrebensky to her final departure for Italy with Birkin, leaving Gudrun in the Alps, we can see her as another Aaron Sisson, or another Wilhelm Meister, with all the differences attributable to the fact that she is a woman. She tests men principally as lovers, and finally rejects the whole world of men in the name of Eros.

As the novel got rewritten and expanded, the prehistory of the Brangwen sisters, the lives of earlier generations of their family, came to take on more and more importance, till in the version we now have almost the whole first novel is preliminary to the main action. This obscures the original design. The material of *The Rainbow* is all thematically relevant, in that it presents various cases of matriarchy, but Lawrence's treatment is so much less ideological than, say, Klages's, so much to be emblemized by "the world of Woman" and not by "*Mutterrecht,*" that one can miss that point. The early material tends to seem merely historical, or "religio-poetico-historical." But if one reimagines the original design, with the preliminary material foreshortened, it becomes clear that it was a *Bildungsroman* of and for women, in which all the men were experimental material, on trial. Gerald Crich clearly sums up all the others, sums up the whole world of men, the army, the mines, exploring the primitive world, capitalism, and so forth. It is all summed up in him in order to be condemned as death-directed, and the available feminine counterbalances to his world, represented by Maggie Schofield, Hermione, Minette, and even Gudrun, only complement him. They do not constitute a world of Woman.

Only Ursula, when in conjunction with Birkin, offers a salvation. Only her forcefulness, when directed and controlled by his intelligence, is a great force for life. This is why the destructive aspects of that forcefulness, manifested in her relationship with Skrebensky, are not condemned, for it is the force of life itself that destroys Skrebensky, who, all hollowed out as he is, is the enemy of life. By passively yielding to his army career—to the world of men—Skrebensky has betrayed the life within him, in an adolescent way that foreshadows Gerald Crich's more final and tragic self-betrayal. Ursula is plainly possessed, in those moments in the moonlight, by a daimonic force beyond good and evil. Involuntarily, she becomes Magna Mater and he becomes a stripling lover, an Adonis, to be loved and cast aside, used up, exhausted. Only Birkin can transform Ursula from an Aphroditean or Hetaerist goddess into a Demetrian goddess, a source of law as well as of life. (Only Lawrence, putting the matter in more homely terms, could persuade Frieda to cook and sew and wash and keep house.) When she accepts his teaching, her education, her *Bildung,* is complete.

Not only in form and ideas, but also in more direct and tangible ways the material here is clearly von Richthofen-German. Will and Anna Brangwen are inwardly the Baron and Baroness von Richthofen, without major alteration of trait or relationship. (The external circumstances of their lives seem to be those of the family of his first fiancée, Louie Burrows.) Ursula and Gudrun represent the three sisters, Ursula being a composite of Else and Frieda, Gundrun being essentially a portrait of Nusch inspired by Frieda's feelings about her, although other traits—most notably things taken from Katherine Mansfield—got grafted onto Gudrun later in the writing. Much of the relationship of the child Ursula to her father comes from Frieda's experience, as her *Memoirs* reveal, and much of Ursula's adolescent experience is taken from Else's life—her struggle to teach and to study, for instance. (*The Rainbow* is dedicated "To Else," and the central character was called Ella in an early version.) The novel was, in short, the *Bildungsroman* of the von Richthofen sisters.

Lawrence wrote to Sally Hopkin in 1913 that he was writing something that would do more for women than the suffrage, and he clearly intended *The Sisters* to show—and to show sympathetically—women struggling against and bursting

out of the confines of their traditional roles. But of course he did not want to
show them finding fulfillment in the world of men. Ella/Ursula was to be Frieda
even more than she was Else. She was to go into and through the world of men,
but out the other side, into a higher form of what I have called the world of
Woman. There, ideally, she would achieve a life so splendid that it would compel
men also into admiring emulation, and so, to some degree, save the world just
as much as suffrage claimed it was going to. Lawrence's novels intended to do all
this, and in a sense they did it.

It is toward precisely such a project of world salvation that Ursula and Birkin
turn at the end of *Women in Love.* Birkin knows by intelligence what she knows
by the blood, and they are partners. They go down from the Alps, where Gerald,
the best of "manly" men, has died, into Italy, the land of fertility and fruitfulness,
the land of flowers, which is also, historically or prehistorically, the land of the
Virgin Mother. They are moving away from both England and Germany, which
have engaged themselves fully in the twentieth-century madness of civilization.
In the total whiteness of the snows Ursula had suddenly remembered, "as if by
a miracle . . . that away beyond, below her, lay the dark fruitful earth, that towards the south there were stretches of land dark with orange trees and
cypress. . . ." That dark fruitful earth is Woman. She and Birkin take the "great
Imperial road leading south to Italy."

In interpreting this image we should remind ourselves not so much of the
Bildungsroman form as of Bachofen's idea scheme, which was also a part of
Frieda's ideological dowry, part of the von Richthofen intellectual milieu. The
meaning of Italy and the distinction between the true and the false Italy were for
Lawrence exactly what they were for Bachofen. *Twilight in Italy* begins by de-
scribing that "great Imperial road" and by attributing Germany's lust for world
dominion to its inheritance of Roman imperialism via the Holy Roman Empire.
Like Bachofen, Lawrence always associated Prussia with Rome, hating both. In
Etruscan Places, he too pointed out Mommsen's blindness to the Etruscans in his
history of Rome; a Prussian historian naturally would identify himself with
Rome, but the Etruscans were the true Italy. (Lawrence's first allusion to the
Etruscans seems to occur in his poem "Cypresses," which was published in October
1923. In 1922 he had received, from Else Jaffe, a copy of Klages's *Vom Kosmogonischem Eros,* which is full of references to Bachofen and his ideas; but even
before he knew about the Etruscans, Lawrence had created in his imagination
an "Italy"—the antithesis to his "Germany"—which stood for Etruscan qualities.)

In *My Life in Retrospect,* Bachofen evokes the poignant beauty of the Etruscan tombs, in their utter remoteness and forlornness. "Everything was dissolved
in mist and fog by the Hyperboreans [Mommsen and Niebuhr], who believed in
their self-conceit that the great epochs of the ancient world could permanently be
reduced to the petty proportions of their own minds," he complains. Mommsen
and Niebuhr, being Prussians, worshiped Rome. Similarly, in *Etruscan Places*
Lawrence says, "Because a fool kills a nightingale with a stone, is he therefore

greater than the nightingale? Because the Roman took the life out of the Etruscan, was he therefore greater than the Etruscan? Not he! Rome fell, and the Roman phenomenon with it. Italy today is far more Etruscan in pulse than Roman: and will always be so. The Etruscan element is like the grass of the field and the sprouting of the corn: it will always be so."

Let us now apply this information to our interpretation of the descent into Italy at the end of *The Sisters*. Ursula is going to find in Italy an ancient, pre-patriarchal mode of being which, now that it is crystallized in the modern, post-patriarchal teachings of Rupert Birkin, will revolutionize the world in a nonpolitical way. These "Italian" or "Etruscan" teachings are nothing else than orthodox *Lebensphilosophie* eroticism; they impose moral and metaphysical disciplines on love, as we see in Klages's letters to Fanny zu Reventlow and Lawrence's to Frieda, but they promise also to save the lovers thereby from domination by the world of men.

Moreover, in *Women in Love* Lawrence insists that there is a stream of destruction as well as a stream of life, and neither ever halts. Bachofen had said that Typhon, the stream of destruction, must be let flow; it may be deflected, but it must never be destroyed. Everything is dual and polar, from the stream of historical tendency down to individual lives. This duality is symbolized by that contrastive black-and-whiteness of the eggs in the tomb paintings which first intrigued Bachofen in the columbaria of the Villa Pamphili. Those colors also are to be associated with the sexes, the blackness being female-material, the whiteness male-ideal. Male power is to be associated either with water or with light, female power with the earth or with the sun. This is another part of the "Etruscan" wisdom which Birkin rediscovered for himself.

Lawrence himself discovered these ideas embodied in the landscapes to which Frieda led him. The descriptions of the Brangwens and their farm in *The Rainbow* are very like some descriptions of the Bavarian landscape round Munich in *Twilight in Italy*. Indeed, even today the Bavarian landscape and the physical type of the farmers of the region is recognizable as belonging to the imaginative universe of *The Rainbow*. (There is even, as in the novel, a railway line prominently cutting across the little road to Irschenhausen.) The Alpine descriptions at the end of *Women in Love* also come from that early experience. Moreover, it is clear from *Twilight in Italy* that the two geographical symbols were originally closely linked, forming a single unit of two antithetical parts. The Alpine crucifix which Gerald sees before he dies and the mumming plays of Cossethay both appear on the same page in *Twilight,* where they are presented as features of Bavarian life. The life of the farm is opposed to that of the mountains explicitly: "Everything is of the blood, of the senses. There is no mind. The mind is a suffusion of physical heat, it is not separated, it is kept submerged. At the same time, always, overhead, there is the eternal, negative radiance of the snows. Beneath is life, the hot jet of the blood playing elaborately. But above is the radiance of changeless not-being. And life passes away into this changeless radiance . . . the radiant cold which waits to receive back again all that which has passed for the moment into being." In *The Rainbow* the farm life contrasts only with what the vicar and the squire represent; the transcendence of the mountains never appears until the end of *Women in Love*. But the basic movement of the myth begins in the Marsh Farm, Cossethay, and ends on the Alpine peaks whence Birkin and Ursula are descending into Italy and the new life.

These Bavarian mountains, like all mountains for Lawrence, stood under the sign of Prometheus and Jehovah, patriarchal heroes and gods, the enemies of Eros and Dionysos, who belong to Italy. The mountains threaten madness and destruction. In this connection one should think not only of the nineteenth-century idealism of Arnold, Wordsworth, and Leslie Stephen, but of Berchtesgaden. It is, above all, the idealism of "progress" which is being evoked. One can think also of Cape Kennedy—man leaping and soaring away, off the face of the earth, from the soil in which things grow, the soil found in Italy. The effects on the individual of this leaping and soaring into the bright purity of mountain air is the baking and glazing of the sun-kissed skin, the glittering brightness of eye and tooth, the surcharged energy of muscular development, which remove one from ordinary human limits. We can think of the *Wandervoegel* and also the *Hitlerjugend,* perhaps. Lawrence's word is "übermenschlich."

Twilight in Italy is a valuable source book for *The Sisters,* in its definition of the symbolic meanings of the landscapes and in its many adumbrations of the characters and incidents of the later work. The writing about crucifixes in Chapter 1 corresponds to Will Brangwen's carvings and his "dark" mystical attraction to death. (This writing hints at Miriam's and Hermione's Lawrence, the Lawrence who would have become predominant if Frieda had abandoned him.) The figure of Anthony Schofield in *The Rainbow* is clearly derived from the man Lawrence calls "Il Duro" in *Twilight in Italy*. The married boy who buys the Birkins' chair in *Women in Love* is there as Pietro, the boy Tom Brangwen as Giovanni, his mother as Maria, the adult Tom as Paolo—all momentarily but recognizably. Even the image of the rainbow is foreshadowed in the "twilight" of the earlier book's title, a neutral mingling of light and dark that is the antithesis of the rainbow's luminosity.

As for Lawrence's intellectual history, his place in the history of ideas, one finds in *Twilight* one of his rare explicit references to Nietzsche and the latter's relation to the erotic movement:* "And now, when Northern Europe is turning back on its own Christianity, denying it all, the Italians are struggling with might and main against the sensuous spirit which still dominates them. When Northern Europe, whether it hates Nietzsche or not, is crying out for the Dionysiac ecstasy, practicing on itself the Dionysiac ecstasy, Southern Europe is breaking free from Dionysos, from the triumphal affirmation of life over death, immortality

---

* Nietzsche borrowed his Apollonian-Dionysian contrast from Bachofen but made no use of the rest of Bachofen's scheme; indeed, Nietzsche was as powerful an influence on the *kosmische Runde* as his predecessor.

through procreation." It is typical of Lawrence's treatment of such themes that there is a dialectical hint here of sympathy with the counter-erotic movement. All through *Twilight in Italy* he applies Nietzsche's and Bachofen's ideas to the life he sees around him. What is more, the long and fascinating excursus on *Hamlet* cannot have been written without some inner reference to the equivalent in *Wilhelm Meister*. Thus *Twilight in Italy* can be read as a philosophic diary of the first months with Frieda in the von Richthofen milieu. To contrast it with *Sea and Sardinia* is to see how differently Lawrence could write, particularly about himself. In the later book, written in rebellion against Woman, he is the typical Erasmian Englishman, as the Maurice Magnus Introduction makes clear.

Lawrence's great works are, then, more "German" than his lesser productions, a fact which provokes speculation about the fecundating effect of intercourse with a foreign culture. The Germanisms in *Women in Love* are innumerable, but the most important for us is the connection sketched between Gerald and Bismarck. This is most powerfully symbolized in the rabbit Bismarck, around whom one chapter is built. This animal's savagery, wickedness, blood-lust, and cruelty draw Gerald into equal savagery in his determination to subdue it, and so provide the occasion for his and Gudrun's compact of corrupt love. Symbolically, their mutually destructive love derives from this assenting participation in Bismarckian *Blutlust.* But there are other, more discursive hints at that connection. Gudrun believes that Gerald's powers can "solve the problems of the day, the problem of industrialism in the modern world." He already had worked a revolution in the mines, and if he went into politics at her prompting, "he would clear up the great muddle of labour and industry. . . . He would be a Napoleon of peace, or a Bismarck—and she the woman behind him. She had read Bismarck's letters, and had been deeply moved by them." Another Bismarck, who might solve the problems of the day, clear up the great muddle of labor and industry, was what Max Weber's friends saw in him, and Gerald, we are told, had attended German universities and studied sociology there, had learned the new science of society.

In the fiction written immediately after *The Sisters* there is less evidence, in formal, ideological, and experiential terms, of the von Richthofen influence, except insofar as the Munich revolution lies behind *Kangaroo.* This absence had something to do with Lawrence's rebellion against Frieda in these years. But he never fully renounced the material he drew from her, anymore than he renounced her inspiration. His rebellion was only partial, and loyalty as well as resentment is reflected in the portraits of Harriet Somers and Kate Leslie. There exists an earlier version of *The Plumed Serpent* in which Kate's background is filled in, and it is the von Richthofen background, described with some of the old sympathy. Kate's mother in this version is on excellent terms with the Lawrence figure (Kate's first, now dead, husband). She understands him because she was

> tolerant and so sensible in her old age. She understood her daughter Kate, too, for she herself was of a wilful, downright nature. But Lady Fitzpatrick had

always loved the framework of society, as a setting. She loved it still. It was always a kind of game to her, to be Lady Fitzpatrick and have generals and lords for her friends. . . . Sir Anthony, her husband, Kate's father, had been rather scandalous. . . . [She was] really a rough-handed woman. Kate had hated her mother's heavy hand, as a child, and her mother's rough, caustic, humorous nature. She had loved the subtle, untrustworthy Sir Anthony.

Moreover, it is quite clear that the relation between Connie and her sister in *Lady Chatterley's Lover* is modeled on that between the von Richthofens. Else Jaffe is clearly reflected in Hilda, who suddenly married a man ten years older than herself, who writes philosophical essays and has a job in the government; she lives, we are told, in a circle of "the real intelligent power in the nation"; and she is ever ready to protect Connie from husband or lover when they are difficult. Lawrence seems to have been acutely aware, in his last years, of the closeness of that relationship and of the way in which husbands and lovers were external to the circuit of feeling and power which united the sisters and their mother. In fact, the last five years of his life were spent more deeply immersed in a von Richthofen world than any other period since 1914. Thus the matriarchal theme, handled now in a somewhat resentful spirit, continued to be associated with the von Richthofens even to the end of his life.

In addition, there are several short stories that make use of von Richthofen material—for instance, "Once," about an adventure of Nusch's or Frieda's, and "The Mortal Coil," about the Baron. The latter material was used again in the brilliant first half of "The Captain's Doll," where Nusch also appears again; and the second half uses the Alps in the same way as they are used in *Women in Love*. The doll itself clearly has German origins. Lotte Prizl, who was Edgar Jaffe's friend in Munich, made such dolls, and in 1918 or 1919, just before Lawrence wrote the story, Kokoschka had a life-size model of Alma Mahler made and took it with him to the theater. "New Eve and Old Adam" is a story about Frieda. Like the play *The Fight for Barbara*, it shows the Frieda of the honeymoon period in a much more critical, though not derogatory, light than *The Sisters*. This is Ursula Brangwen seen from a point of view critical of the erotic movement, a point of view that takes into consideration the cost to others of a heroic career in that style. "The Daughters of the Vicar" and its treatment of Else have already been discussed in these pages—though I must return to it in the next section.

Perhaps the largest critical generalization one is incited to make about this profusion of connections is that Lawrence displayed a great deal of skill in adapting German material to British settings and superficies—in adjusting the von Richthofens' characters to, for instance, the Burrows' circumstances, in order to create the Brangwens of *The Rainbow*. This process is very striking, for instance, in *Kangaroo*, where the figure of Harriet Somers, though so vividly a portrait of Frieda, also often sounds exactly like Mrs. Morel. In other words, Lawrence has found a way to modulate imperceptibly between the mid-European aristocrat and the lower middle-class English lady. Perhaps it is Mrs. Morel rather than Mrs. Lawrence who sounds like Frieda—that is, perhaps even in *Sons and Lovers* there has been some broadening of the scope of the original figure, some redemption of his mother from a narrowness of moralism which would have made her less suited to her function in the novel. Almost certainly Lawrence's very happy relationship with the Baroness von Richthofen must have increased his confidence that all over the world and at every social level there were such women radiating life-force and struggling with "weaker" husbands—the confidence in this general diagnosis which is expressed in the very title of the work, *Sons and Lovers*.

Thus in *Kangaroo* Lawrence achieves a brilliant compromise which is untrue to neither original by the standards of realism. Clearly, he had a much larger task of adaptation in creating Mrs. Brangwen out of Anna von Richthofen, and the more one thinks about all this, the more imaginative energy one sees must have gone into these feats of adaptation. This was the energy not only of bold conceptions, with which Lawrence is easily credited, but of patient small-stitch embroidery, of taste and tact. In other words, to approach Lawrence from the point of view of his use of von Richthofen materials and forms is to see him as a very delicate artist, adapting non-British material to British appearances with the skills of a virtuoso.

But Lawrence wanted, I think, to be felt as a powerful artist rather than as a delicate one, and one of the benefits he derived from the von Richthofen milieu was that it helped him seem original by providing him with a store of fictional material quite unlike what his contemporaries in England had to draw on. This is not to say that, for instance, E. M. Forster had not met anyone like Nusch, but that in evaluating and responding to Lawrence he and the whole circle of British writers whom Lawrence knew could not check on the use Lawrence made of such material as Nusch—his blending of the German with the English—could not compare the original with the portrait. Although Lawrence *did* in fact draw from living models, habitually, he did not offer the results as portraits. To have his characters checked for "accuracy of portrayal" tended to reduce them to something like "satires," in the narrow sense. Lawrence did not want to be a satirist, a typical form of that "merely literary" identity ("a queer fish who can write") from which Frieda saved him. He wanted to be a prophet. In his major novels he escaped the satirist's role, partly by using von Richthofen materials. The works of fiction he wrote without grace of Frieda's participation, like *Aaron's Rod, were* satires and were not major; and the English parts of *Women in Love* were *taken* as satire, which blunted the book's impact.

An even more important value of Frieda's Germanness for Lawrence was that it intensified her "otherness," which he valued so highly for giving him an escape from self-consciousness and nervous-mental mutuality. She was "other" in very profound ways, but also in the very prosaic sense that she belonged to a different country and a different social class and spoke a different language. Frieda had elementary problems of communication when she dealt with ideas in part because of that self-caricaturing mental inefficiency we have described already, but also because of her Germanness, and those problems enhanced her "blood-consciousness." She knew far more than she could ever say, for prosaic as well as poetic reasons. Of course the essential meaning of blood-consciousness is something quite different, is what Lawrence describes, but these circumstantial meanings were not without their effect. If Lawrence had met the ideas of the erotic movement "in English"—as he did, to some degree, before he met Frieda, by reading Edward Carpenter—he would have got much less from them. He would have met them conceptually, known them mentally, as most of us do. But he had the luck to meet them in the flesh, the conceptually inarticulate flesh of Frieda Weekley, which was yet translucent to the glow of a passionate idea, a glorious identity, burning within.

THE EFFECT OF LIVING IN SCHWABING

The second proposition—that to live with Frieda was to live always in an outpost of Schwabing—helps primarily in understanding Lawrence's ideas. It helps by giving them something like an extra dimension of solidity, an extra set of connections, which make them more of an ideology. Without those connections one can of course read Lawrence unideologically, as Leavis does. And inasmuch as Leavis expounds Lawrence so well, we are reminded that this extra dimension is not necessarily to understanding him. But inasmuch as Leavis also reads him semi-prophetically, we know that an ideological commitment is there for him, too, although an unspoken one. The difference between reading Lawrence within the Schwabing context and without it is the difference between using a term like *Vaterrecht* and using a term like "the world of men." The latter invokes no ideology. But when you read Lawrence in the company of the Schwabing writers, you find that there is an ideological structure beneath him. You find that the Etruscans meant more to Lawrence than he explicitly makes of them in *Etruscan Places,* that they lie at the source of Bachofen's *Mutterrecht* theory, that the equivalences Lawrence draws between the patriarchal Romans and the Prussians (and the Fascists) are the same as those Bachofen drew, and that those equivalences therefore have ideological implications which one can follow out in Bachofen. You realize that the Cornish are, for Lawrence, a British equivalent of the Etruscans, and thus some of the implications of his treatment of the Cornish character become clearer.*

Within his major fiction, moreover, this proposition calls for, and explains, the cardinal distinction between the matriarchal novels, *The Sisters* and *The Lost*

---

* On the other hand—perhaps the warning should be given here—my terms have been chosen to give order to the conjunction of Lawrence, Weber, and Gross. They are not so well adapted to exploring Lawrence's world itself. Except for *Kangaroo,* none of his novels use "the world of men" as a major category, and other terms would serve one better.

Girl (the latter a much lighter-weight effort), and the patriarchal leadership novels, *Aaron's Rod, Kangaroo,* and *The Plumed Serpent.* (*Lady Chatterley's Lover* was a return to the old faith, despite Lawrence's sympathy with Clifford's struggle to be a man in the world of men, and to escape Connie.) Within his non-fiction, one can say, perhaps, that the major essays (*Twilight in Italy* and *The Crown* and *Thomas Hardy*) belong to the Schwabing phase of his thinking where-as the later articles do not, although even where he is being explicitly anti-mat-riarchal he still retains many Schwabing traits. Thus it is interesting that in Law-rence's leadership novels, particularly in *Aaron's Rod,* he presents himself as a leader of rather the same sort as George and Klages. Aaron's self-poisoning re-lationship with the Marchesa can be paralled with Gundolf's marriage, which George forbade him. And in *The Plumed Serpent* Don Ramon's politics are Schwabing politics, which accounts for their resemblance to Hitler's a passing resemblance which should not lead us to imagine any equivalence between Hitler and Lawrence, who was the most unpolitical of men.

Among Schwabing thinkers it was Ludwig Klages and Alfred Schuler whose systems of thought are most parallel with Lawrence's. Klages says, in the Preface to the fourth edition of *Die Grundlagen der Charakterkunde* (*The Foun-dations of Characterology*), that the book is based on lectures given in Munich between 1905 and 1907, and both the dates and the content make it extremely likely that Otto Gross and/or Frieda Weekley attended them or heard them discussed. In these lectures Klages proposes a psychology opposed to atomic and experimental sensationalism. For Klages the soul must be studied as a whole, as an image. It is like a cell, he argues, modeling his psychology on vitalistic or Goethean biology, much as Lawrence did. The real psychologists are Goethe, Jean Paul, and Novalis, and the great man is Nietzsche, "the great piercer of souls and knower of spirits." Like Nietzsche, Klages believed that an envy of life (*res-sentiment*) lies at the root of every moral judgment, and that atrophy of instinct manifests itself as idealism.

His characterology is a typology of attitudes and structural forms to be found in different egos. Most men live in a middle segment of a range which runs from total repression of the spirit, in primitive peoples who are dominated by the body and its appetites, to total repression of the body, in the ascetic orders of re-demptive religions. (The reader of *Women in Love* is reminded of what is rep-resented by the two symbols of the African statuette and the crucifix among the snows, the two big signs of death for Gerald.)

Klages did a research degree in chemistry. (In fact, he worked on the syn-thesis of methone, the industrial use of synthesized biochemicals being a very characteristic example of the applied science in which Bismarck's Germany excelled.) He distrusted the empiricism and positivism of his science and com-plained about the way vitalists like Oken and Schelling were being neglected. Seventy-five percent of scientific "discoveries" are insignificant, he declared, and eventually he came to hate the whole mode of scientific knowledge. (One can see in Klages the connection between Goethe's science and Lawrence's.) Science as the West knows it is a major manifestation of the Apollonian mind.

Like Lawrence—and Goethe—Klages lived a very intense life in relation to the elements and felt that most people live far too much in the merely social world of human beings. He made it a great point against Wolfskehl—and all Jews—that he had said, "People are my landscape." Also like Lawrence, but in this case unlike Goethe, he was not responsive to mountains. His elements were sunsets, rain, stormy winds, and above all the ocean, the Dionysian sea. In "Mensch und Erde" (1913), he deplores the destruction of wildlife and landscape, and sounds very like Lawrence in his primitive reverence for the soil and his attack on progress and technology. He deplores the triumph of Prometheus and the solar myth heroes over the chthonic powers who have been driven underground.

Also like Lawrence, Klages exhorted lovers to turn their feelings away from each other and toward that third thing, the relationship between them, which was so much more important. Neither love nor sex was important to him, but only Eros, a force which entered men and acted in them. Lawrence expands the same doctrine in *The Rainbow:* "Between two people," Lydia tells Anna, "the love itself is the important thing, and that is neither you nor him. It is a third thing you must create."

In some significant sense, both Lawrence and Klages, along with Alfred Schuler and other members of the Schwabing circle, were anti-sexual and anti-love moralists. They were austere, both personally and ideologically. But they were also anti-Christian worshipers of Pan, anti-ascetic devotees of Magna Mater. They belonged, imaginatively, to the primitive past. They hated machinery, militarism, and imperialism—though not conflict or even killing; they hated organized politics as the West knows it. A savage contempt for democracy, rationalism, and liberalism was common to Lawrence, Klages, and Schuler, and so was the prophecy of the world disaster which would follow from contemporary democratic, rational, and liberal policies.

A passage like this by Lawrence, from "The Novel," could have been written by any one of the three of them: "It's the oldest Pan-mystery. God is the flame-life in all the universe, multifarious flames, all colours and beauties and pains and sombernesses. For sex is so much more than phallic." Or this from "Him With His Tail in His Mouth": "that which is good, and moral, is that which brings into us a stronger, deeper flow of life and life-energy." Or this, from "Blessed Are the Powerful": "strength must come to a man 'from beyond.' Life comes 'from behind.'" Or this from "Aristocracy": "Sun is always sun beyond sun beyond sun. Otherwise it goes stale. . . . The children of the sun shall be lords of the earth." Lawrence wrote these words in New Mexico; he and Frieda had made Taos into an outpost of Schwabing.

There were, of course, important differences of opinion between Schwabingites. Klages, like Lawrence, thought the modern psychoanalytical idea of the unconscious a caricature, because it is really a projection downward of the conscious mind's *idea* of an unconscious. He insisted on the need for mythical and mystical concepts to describe and understand the unconscious. This anti-scientific tendency separated both Lawrence and Klages from Otto Gross, and it is so significant a separation that Gross's work—at least his written work—has finally quite a different feeling from theirs, even though so many of his practical recommendations for conduct were similar to theirs, and even though in some purely conceptual sense his *Weltanschauung* was very like theirs.

Otto Gross's influence may be seen, perhaps, in Lawrence's use of Biblical themes and images, which becomes striking in the Foreword to *Sons and Lovers,* in *The Rainbow,* and in *Twilight in Italy*—in other words, in work written soon after his elopement with Frieda. We know that Otto made much use of transvalued Biblical myth in conversation as well as in essays. This sort of material does not appear in Lawrence's work much before the elopement. But when Ursula listens in church to the reading from Genesis—her favorite book of the Bible, as it was Otto's, according to Werfel—she finds herself reinterpreting it: "After all, how big was the Flood? Perhaps a few dryads and fauns had just run into the hills and the further valleys and woods, frightened, but most had gone on blithely unaware of any flood at all, unless the nymphs should tell them. . . . Ursula wished that she had been a nymph. She would have laughed through the windows of the ark, and flicked drops of the flood at Noah, before she drifted away to people who were less important in their Proprietor and their Flood." This is one of those passages in *The Rainbow* where one is most aware of the presence of Frieda as co-author. We knew from her *Memoirs* that she had played this game of reinterpreting the Bible with Otto, and almost certainly she did so with Lawrence, too.

What is more, the freedom of Lawrence's imagination—though not of his expression—to deal with homosexuality may have owed something to Otto's teachings. Further, the anti-authoritarianism and anti-domesticity of these novels, the repudiation of both fathers, Crich and Brangwen, are louder than what we hear in Lawrence's other novels—except of course in the case of Walter Morel, but then *Sons and Lovers* was strongly influenced by Frieda, and thus by Gross. Finally, the conception of Gerald's character is a psychoanalytic conception to a degree that is not true of other Lawrentian persons—except insofar as Paul Morel is seen Oedipally, which again derived from Otto Gross's ideas. Gerald's relation to his father and mother, the family drama there, the murder of his younger brother by accident, his relations to women—all the main lines of his character correspond more vividly to those of a psychological case study than do those of any other character in *Women in Love* or in any of the other novels. Typically, the major figures in Lawrence's fiction are seen as self-determining, not as products of psychological and sociological factors. We know, too, that Gross had a strong sense of who Max Weber was and what was wrong with him—that he was a master-slave of the world of men, a blind, bound Samson.* Thus we find many

---

* After studying a sample of Weber's handwriting, Klages once declared that Max Weber was a man whose instincts were twisted. Weber acknowledged to Else Jaffe—probably the person who had given Klages the sample—that this analysis was very accurate.

promptings to connect the drawing of Gerald Crich with Gross as well as with Weber. Because he was a presence in Frieda's mind, Gross also influenced Lawrence, but other Schwabingites were more congenial to him personally.

A most important part of Klages's teaching was the antithesis he set up between desire and will. Of course it parallels that other antithesis—also to be found in Lawrence—between soul and mind, and the more familiar one between life and consciousness. Although these distinctions are familiar ones, in Klages's hands, as in Lawrence's, they become the foundation for large developments of thought. Thus Klages teaches that images are the ultimate reality, of which things are the conceptual deposit, and that in the pursuit of our desires we experience images, whereas in wilful action we experience only ourselves. To desire belongs bodily need and the satisfying image; to will belongs motive and aim. Desire moves toward the appropriate image; will moves only toward itself. Desire forms part of an overall pattern and rhythm; will does not. The movement of desire is pathic, that of behavior is reactive. Desires are manifold, the will is singular.

In "Heidnische Feuerzeichen," written between 1900 and 1913, Klages expresses his disdain for consciousness, which was, he insisted, always effect and never cause, and therefore unreal. Because our feelings are nearly always conscious feelings, he warns us against attributing too much importance to them. The realities of life are images, not feelings. In connection with this, he also attacks Christian asceticism, arguing that satisfied desire is the necessary substructure of all cosmic radiance. Prometheus and Heracles prefigure Christianity, Klages said; they herald the destruction of the earth and the automatization of man.

Blood is the site of all orgiastic experience, and consciousness is its enemy. Life is flow. Logic is ordered darkness, mystery is rhythmic light. Christianity is a war against moral sleeping and dreaming, although in dreams both health and truth are to be found. ("Christ never fell from the Cross as Odin did from the Tree of Night, a ripened fruit and a fertile seed," Alfred Schuler said, using a very Lawrentian image. Schuler's lectures during the war said much that Lawrence's lectures would have said if they had been delivered—if we may judge by "The Crown.") Action, work, and system all belong to the mind, not to the soul. Of course the artist must have something of mind in him, in order to produce, but he must be rooted in soul. Woman and poet are closely related. Bachofen had pointed out that decisive moments in female life, much more than in male life, are bound up with a flow of blood and a change of blood. Menstruation, deflowering, conception, child-bearing, nursing—these are the experiences that are reflected in the Schwabing and Lawrentian doctrine of the blood. (Clearly this is quite a different doctrine of the blood from that associated with Nazism or other kinds of racism.) These men tried to know with their blood rather than with their minds, to know as woman knows, in order to defend their integrity against the domination of Apollo and Ares. The poet, they taught, gives a voice to woman's intuitions and aspirations. Woman embodies the peaceful inside of life, man the active outside. Heroes and tragedies, from Prometheus to Bonaparte, are all phantasms of the mind. And Constantine, Charlemagne, and Cromwell, the *organizers* of society (Max Weber presumably represents the same principle in the intellectual sphere), are the outcasts of life. They are the instruments of Jahweh—personally powerless, they revenge themselves on those who are powerful with life.

Klages was far more anti-Semitic than Lawrence and saw in the Jew the embodiment of mind and will. At his best he distinguished between this idea and the literal Jew, and insofar as this is the case one could say that his enemy is not really an ethnic group but rather the type of objective and categorizing scholar best represented by Max Weber. Unfortunately, he did not try to be at what we call his best very often or very strenuously. Thus we get: "The Jew is the vampire of mankind, *collecting* the fragments of the broken urn of Paganism." The activity being attacked here is Weber's, but the word "Jew" is introduced distortingly. In Klages's works, the doctrine of the blood was not only the politically innocent thing it was in Bachofen, for at times it came close to being what Houston Chamberlain and Alfred Rosenberg made of it.

In *Movements in European History*, his school history book of 1921, Lawrence is very reminiscent of Klages in his emphasis on physiognomy and racial character, and also in his implicit preference for paganism over both Jewish and Christian morality, which he defines much as Klages does: "The pagans had no preaching, no praying, no talk about sin or salvation, no service at all. . . ." Instead, they had gay processions, the dancers going in front, dancing for the gods. "But it was all part of the active, actual, everyday, normal life—not something apart. In the country the peasant people loved to take flowers, or a little cake, or a gift, to the shrine of some nymph by the fountain, to the god Pan among the trees, to Priapus in the orchard, to some fauns or nymphs in a cave. . . . It simply pleased the people to visit these little sacred places." The Jews stand in sharp contrast: "And only the God of the Jews was a jealous God. Only the Jews showed their hatred and horror of this free and easy pagan worship. . . . [L]ooking on with black hatred and horror, [they] could not refrain from breaking out into fury, trying to stone to death these hated idolators and their idols."* Lawrence goes on to attack both Jews and Christians, for Lawrence, like both Nietzsche and Otto Gross, sees Christianity as a religion of slaves: ". . . these quiet, silent Christians, with their distant manners and humble bearing and their patient looks of reproach, and their air of secret power."

Tracing these connections with Schwabing further, we find that in his discussion of Savonarola Lawrence sounds quite like Schuler. After praising the gay and exquisite cities of the Renaissance, and praising Boccaccio above Dante, he attacks the puritan reformer and the people of Florence: Savonarola "filled them with a wicked madness of destruction, and an ugly lust for exciting events. . . . Truth, beauty, happiness, wisdom, these meant nothing to such fanatics." What

---

* In a passage such as this, Lawrence gives us a quick sketch of what Otto Gross, as depicted in Franz Werfel's *Black Mass,* conjured up with hallucinatory vividness.

is more, the achievement of national unity and freedom in both Germany and Italy turns out, in his analysis, to have been merely a caricature of true freedom, that "beautiful, flexible freedom of human men and women. . . . In the modern republic there was no superiority of one man over another, except the superiority of the money-maker. . . . And so Italy was made modern Italy. Fretfulness, irritation, and nothing in life except money." Particularly in discussing Italy Lawrence shows his resentment at the way in which politics spoils life:

> And in this way the movement for liberty began in Italy. Now, when so much is accomplished and achieved, we cannot help regretting that ever the deep religious spirit in man tacked itself on to politics . . . politics, at last, works out to nothing more than a mere arranging of the material conditions of life. . . . You can't save mankind by politics. Liberty isn't salvation. We must have liberty. But having liberty, we have only got food to eat. . . .

In this book Lawrence sounds more like Klages than at other times. He also sounds less impressive than at other times. This is because the exigencies of his task compel him to spell out ideas which would be, if he were creating freely, only scaffolding and springboards for images of individual action and characterization, images of which he was a great more convinced than of the ideas. Klages said that things themselves are the conceptual deposit of images, are what our minds make of those transcendent realities; certainly in the life of the mind, for many artists, including Lawrence, ideas about history are a conceptual deposit of imaginative insights about individuals.

But they are also supportive structures, deliberately acquired to justify one in seeing what one wants to see, in feeling and doing what one wants, and not scrupulously tested for other consequences. Once again we realize how much tact guided Lawrence in his usual choice of subjects to write about and modes to write in.

In the matter of love, Klages teaches that cosmic or pagan man does not love somebody else. He burns in his own erotic flame. Thus there can be no such thing as unhappy love for a pagan. (Lawrence, too, takes no interest in unrequited love and like Klages turns away from the intensities of *Tristan und Isolde, Anna Karenina,* and the whole tragic love genre. He felt that these feelings were based on implicitly falsifying images.) Indeed, both men placed a heavy emphasis on the inevitability, and the valuableness, of being alone even within the most intimate relationship. Thus Lawrence says, "The magic and the dynamism of life rests on otherness. . . . But the central fulfillment, for a man, is that he possess his own soul in strength within him, deep and alone." What these statements give as doctrine is treated fictionally in *St. Mawr.*

If a man will accept his isolation, he may meet the forces of nature as forces, as supra-personal persons. Schuler saw the sun as Omphalos, the golden Phallus, neither male nor female, but more than both, spreading its power in a golden swastika, and in the same vein both Lawrence and Klages emphasized the value of the nonhuman. Both were practical lovers and appreciators of trees and clouds and animal life, and also theorists of the value of these things as foci for our general orientation in life. Man was originally as elemental as Nature itself, they felt, and must therefore find a way to return to being so, a way to escape the dehydrating effects of civilization.

Both men were interested primarily in primitive peoples, especially those who had built their cultures before Greek rationalism became dominant. It was culture in the sense appropriate to such people that seemed to them the essential thing, not culture as it describes the superstructure or the structure of civilized life. The arts were to be regarded as exuberances of life, not to be treated too technically. In some sense, then, both Lawrence and Klages were anti-aesthetes. Lawrence observes in *Mornings in Mexico* that Indians dance toward no spectator, only toward each other, the participants, because in their religion there is no one overpowering God; and he makes us feel that this is better. Theater was a form toward which he was essentially hostile. So were Klages and Schuler. The art forms within Western culture of which all three could most approve were the folk song and folk dance, but it was the even more "primitive" arts like Indian tribal dances that they loved. This was Schwabing taste, even when worked out in Mexico.

The most important thing to say about all these ideas is that they were denied as well as affirmed by Lawrence; that there was a debate about these matters going on at the core of his imagination. I have emphasized the affirmation because I think it "came first" in every sense, and because it has been neglected by most criticism, and because it remains the final thrust of his work. But also true and important are the denials. Perhaps the classical statement of the debate in idea form comes in *Fantasia of the Unconscious*:

> Was man, the eternal protagonist, born of woman, from her womb of fathomless emotion? Or was woman, with her deep womb of emotion, born from the rib of active man, the first created? Man, the doer, the knower, the original in *being,* is he lord of life? Or is woman, the great Mother, who bore us from the womb of love, is she the supreme Goddess? This is the question of all time.

Lawrence's answer is that man is primary, but only by a hair's breadth:

> Assert sex as the predominant fulfillment, and you get the collapse of living purpose in man. You get anarchy. Assert *purposiveness* as the one supreme and pure activity of life, and you drift into barren sterility . . . [but] you have got to keep your sexual fulfilment even then subordinate . . . by a hair's breadth only: but still, by that hair's breadth subordinate.

This is clearly not so much a solution of the problem as the breaking off of a debate over it. You can follow the debate in fictional form, between Richard Lovat Somers and Harriet, in *Kangaroo*.

But that debate went on all the time. Even as early as *Twilight in Italy,* even as he celebrates Italy as the great saving antithesis to England, he both criticizes it and detaches specifically himself from it, defines his own image in opposition to its worship of the sensual mysteries. "I was pale and clear and evanescent like the light" while the Italians were "dark and close and constant like the shadow." When he thinks of London and the great cities of Europe, they seem meaningless: "The kingdoms of the world had no significance: what could one do but wander about?" But he is quite clear in his rejection of Italy and her Aphrodite worship also. "The phallus will never serve us as a Godhead: because we do not believe in it: no Northern race does." And he even says, "I thought of England, the great mass of London, and the black fuming, laborious Midlands and north-country. It seemed horrible. And yet it was better than the padrone, this old, monkey-like cunning of fatality. It is better to go forward into error than to stay fixed inextricably in the past." And in his reflections on England we see what Lawrence's purposive social work is to be: "to build her knowledge into a great structure of truth. There it lay, vast masses of rough-hewn knowledge, vast masses of machines and appliances, vast masses of ideas and methods, and nothing done with it. . . ." Doing something with it was precisely what he meant to do, and in the name of that he claimed male primacy over the female. It was an ideal which Max Weber shared with him.

In the fiction which I have called matriarchal, however, such an idea remains of minor importance, and the major statements are clearly hostile to the world of men and to the ideals of social purpose which that world proposes. In this fiction, there is a third alternative to "anarchic sexuality" on the one hand and "sterile purposiveness" on the other. These, after all, are recognizably the Hetaerist and the Apollonian modes of being, and the third alternative is the Demetrian. Thus Ursula Brangwen, under Birkin's influence, becomes a source of law as well as love, a source of creation. Whenever Lawrence is fully in possession of that alternative he does not incline to the "male chauvinism" of the comments just quoted. In his matriarchal fiction the world of men is depicted as being irredeemably alien and hostile to his overriding message. In *Women in Love,* for example, even Gerald sums up Birkin thus: "Birkin was delightful, a wonderful spirit, but after all not to be taken seriously, not quite to be counted as a man among men." In *The Rainbow* we are told that the minds of the Brangwen women turned from the farm to where "men moved dominant and creative," but the whole point of that novel, and its successor, is that this is an illusion. The farm life described in the first chapter is the female mode of being, even though it is the men who most completely belong to it. In Lawrence's eyes, any peasant-agricultural or tribal-primitive life is female; it is the Promethean or Apollonian energies of manly men that begin "progress" and "civilization." When the Brangwen women get into the world of men, they find that men do not in fact move dominant and creative there. This is the ideological tension of *The Sisters,* and of Lawrence's whole life. In *The Sisters* that tension is resolved by the faith in a renewed reign of Demeter. But in Lawrence's life that faith sometimes failed, and the tension then threatened to destroy him. For he then had to believe in some reform of institutions and ideology which he could design (to believe in the world of men) at least enough to keep a sense of his own mission and purpose and achievement, and thus to win himself a firm ideological masculinity. Without this, to live with a powerful ego like Frieda became intolerable slavery. And yet, living with Frieda, everything he got from her forbade him to believe in the world of men. It is out of this dilemma that he speaks in *Fantasia of the Unconscious.*

The clearest matriarchal image of the conflict between the world of men and the world of Woman is the contrast between Lydia Brangwen's two marriages:

> She loved both her husbands. To one she had been a naked little girl-bride, running to serve him. The other she loved out of fulfillment, because he was good and had given her being, because he had served her honourably, and become her man, one with her. . . . During her first marriage, she had not existed, except through him, he was the substance and she the shadow running at his feet. . . . In her heart she felt a vague tenderness and pity for her husband, who had been her lord. He was so wrong when he died. She could not bear it, that he had never lived, never really become himself.

This comes from no debate, obviously. The issue is resolved. The first husband, a political-patriotic hero—his career as Lawrence gives it sounds somewhat like Max Weber's—is simply *wrong.* This is written in full faith in Demeter, in the world of Woman.

At the end of *The Rainbow,* Ursula's dream of a circle of threatening horses, which she escapes, surely must mean, in the context of the novel, the world of men. By a Freudian interpretation, of course, it *must* mean male sexuality, but this is a good example of the limitations of such interpretations of Lawrence. Ursula is not afraid of male sexuality. Everything in the novel's action has shown us that. What she is afraid of, as her mother was before her, is the world of institutions and public events, the world of the school, the army, the war, the police, the factory. These are what surround and threaten Ursula symbolically, and these are what she is destined triumphantly to elude. It is not until after *Women in Love*—notably in *Aaron's Rod*—that we get strong counter statements, hostile to women.

The Plumed Serpent, although artistically unbalanced, paradoxically contains one of the most complex and equally balanced statements of this debate. Though we see Don Ramon, Don Cipriano, and all Mexico through the eyes of Kate Leslie, it is made clear that her account of things is to be trusted only up to a certain point. She represents the subtlest and finest feminine perception of modern Europe, but no more; she falls short of Don Ramon's vision. Her limitations are pointed out again and again: "She was alone, as usual. It occurred to her that she alone willed this aloneness. She could not relax and be with these people. She always had to recoil upon her own individuality, as a cat does. . . . Suddenly she saw herself as men often saw her: the great cat, with its spasms of voluptuousness and its lifelong lustful enjoyment of its own isolated, isolated individuality." It is clear that this egotism causes her negative judgments on what is going on: "She was a woman. He was a man, and—and—and therefore not quite real. Not quite true to life. . . . Her sensitive, desirous self belonged to Ramon and Cipriano: the other, hard and finished, accomplished, belonging to her mother, her children, England, her whole past. . . . In it, she was an individual and her own mistress." In Ramon and Teresa, Kate is brought face to face with a sexual relationship which is opposite in type to the ones she knows, ones in which she, as a woman, is always triumphant and unassailable: "Kate watched in wonder. She herself had known men who made her feel a queen, who made her feel as if the sky rested on her bosom and her head was among the stars. She knew what it was to rise grander and grander, till she filled the universe with her womanhood. Now she saw the opposite taking place. Ramon as sultan . . . now the power of the world was passing from the blue-eyed men, who made queens of their women, to the black." The blue-eyed men are the group to which her husband Joachim, and therefore Lawrence, belong. (In the Houghton Library version of the novel, the husband, there called Desmond Burns, bears the same relation to his mother-in-law as Lawrence had to his.) Joachim dies because Kate did not devote her life to him: "Joachim, letting himself be bled to death for people who would profit nothing by his sacrifice, he had been the opposite extreme. The black and magnificent pride of will which comes out of the volcanic earth of Mexico had been unknown to him. He was one of the white, self-sacrificing gods. Hence her bitterness." But as we have seen, Kate failed him, by not being a Teresa.

And yet, despite all these bitter criticisms of Kate, her doubts about the adventure to which Don Ramon invites her remain the novel's final statement about it all: "When Cipriano said: *Man that is man is more than man,* he seemed to be driving the male significance to its utmost, and beyond, with a sort of dogmatism. It seemed to her all terrible *will,* the exertion of pure, awful will. . . . Yet surely he and she were more than two currents between which the Morning Star flashed? Surely she had one tiny Morning Star inside her, which was herself, her own very soul and star-self? . . . Was the individual an illusion? Man, any man, every man, by himself just a fragment, knowing no Morning Star? . . . 'Still!' said Kate, 'It still seems to me that it would be better for each one to keep her own soul, and be responsible for it.' This remains the final statement of the novel. Lawrence cannot get beyond Frieda.

The polarity of blood versus spirit, of eagle versus dove and tiger versus lamb, was one in which Frieda and Lawrence believed. Indeed, she endorsed both poles, which meant above all that she would claim her right to be eagle and tiger from time to time. However, Lawrence and she were also much concerned about a different polarity, the polarity between individualism and leadership, between man and manifestation. The crossing of these polarities defined their position. Faced with this second polarization of values, Frieda—though interested in both extremes—endorsed exclusively the former. Lawrence tried to endorse the latter also, for the latter was necessary for action in the world of men. But as we have seen, he could not, finally, endorse Ramon.

In *Lady Chatterley's Lover,* the basic attitude to the heroine is the reverse.

Lawrence had come round to, or submitted to, Frieda. Connie Chatterley is not to be condemned or even judged by the reader, but to be consulted as the criterion by which everything and everyone else is judged. What makes Mellors superior to Clifford is his recognition of and response to Connie's dishonored femaleness. That is the supreme value and the supreme test. In every other way, Mellors is in ignoble retreat before life, but because in this way he is noble, he is the novel's hero. He is a hero of the world of Woman; as Daleski puts it in *The Forked Flame*, Mellors has a preponderantly "female" character and his phallic conscious-ness is in service of the female principle.

Yet even here there is evidence of Lawrence's imaginative sympathy with Clifford and his resentment of Connie. We are told that Clifford "realized now that the bitch-goddess of success had two main appetites: one for flattery, adulation, stroking and tickling, such as writers and artists gave her; but the other a grimmer appetite for meat and bones. . . ." Lawrence, too, was a writer, and wanted to be something more effective than that. "Mrs. Bolton tempted Clifford to enter this other fight. She made a man of him as Connie never did. . . ." He began to work on modernizing the mines. "Connie kept him apart, and made him sensitive and conscious of himself and his own states. Mrs. Bolton made him aware only of outside things. Inwardly he began to go soft as pulp. But outwardly he began to be effective." With his shadow self, Lawrence wanted to be effective, to escape the world of Woman, the world of art:

> He had been gradually dying, with Connie, in the isolated private life of the artist and the conscious being. . . . [The colliery] gave him a sense of power, power. He was doing something: and he was *going* to do something. He was going to win, to win: not as he had won with his stories, mere publicity, amid a whole sapping of energy and malice. But a man's victory. . . . And he felt triumphant. He had at last got out of himself. He had fulfilled his life-long secret yearning to get out of himself. Art had not done it for him. Art had only made it worse. But now, now he had done it.

Frieda declared that Lawrence had identified with Clifford as well as with Mellors, and these passages make it clear that there is in this novel something of the same resentment against his own fate—that is, against her—as was expressed in *The Plumed Serpent*. But of course there is no question that it is only Law-rence's shadow self that identified with Clifford, that the hero of *Lady Chatter-ley's Lover* is Mellors, that Clifford belongs with Maurice Magnus as an exemplar of the dreadful fate from which Frieda had saved Lawrence; had saved him—as the diagnoses of both Clifford and Magnus show—precisely by her power as Woman. This is why Connie is the source of all value in the novel, for Lawrence's values, although he rebels against them more irritably at some times than at others, are always clearly and strongly matriarchal and erotic—the values of *Lebensphilosphie*.

Approaching Lawrence from this point of view, then, the light falls differently in that we see him as a part of a European movement, and not as a purely British phenomenon. We again admire the skill and tact with which he adapted these ideas—ideas about marriage in particular—to his British heritage and gave them a more conservative cast. And we notice that he gave them also an anti-ideological cast; he spoke of the world of men rather than of *Vaterrecht*. In his essays Lawrence was ideologically bold and brilliant, but he did not aim at consistency, at constructing a system, in any ordinary sense, and in his fiction he quite notably obscured his ideology, lowered its profile. In doing so he was of course being true to his ideology, which was hostile to abstract conceptual systems and preferred powerful images. It was an ideology which demanded to be expressed by the artistic imagination rather than by the philosophic reason. In referring contemptuously to his own "pollyanalytics," in writing them so dashingly and mockingly, Lawrence was being truer to blood-knowledge than Klages was in all fifteen hundred pages of *Der Geist als Widersache der Seele*.

But Lawrence was not merely adapting German ideas in the way that he adapted German narrative elements and characters material in his fiction. His ideas were his own, as much as anybody's ever are. He was quite capable of "thinking for himself" and no doubt merely found that Klages, for instance, had been proceeding along the same lines as himself. (Else sent him Klages's *Vom Kosmogonischen Eros* in 1922.) But it is nevertheless extremely important to a thinker to know that other people are thinking along similar lines, and this knowledge inevitably has a marked effect. He may want not to know in detail the exact terms of their thinking, but he is given great encouragement by the general fact and feeling of their cooperation. It was one of Frieda's great gifts to Lawrence that she was extremely sensitive to men's directions of thought, even unconscious thought. Her expression was muddled, but her reaction was strong, and Lawrence found that her intuition was usually right. By the same token she could be cruelly insensitive to a man and his ideas when they seemed to her lifeless or insignificant. Lawrence complained about this insensitivity, but it was simply the obverse side of her extraordinary sensitivity; she created powerful interference against ideas she found devoid of life and powerful amplification of everything favorable to "life" as defined by the tenets of *Lebensphilosophie*.

It is interesting, for a moment, to compare Frieda with Dorothea Brooke. George Eliot made her heroine also a symbol of protest against German *Wissenschaft* and protest in the name of life-values. But Dorothea represents the nineteenth-century mode of such protest, Frieda the twentieth-century mode. Essentially, the nineteenth century had merely continued that Richardsonian protest which one might call liberal and reformist, but which was in some sense passive, under the sign of Virgo. Thus Jane Eyre recapitulates Pamela Andrews. (Both Else Jaffe and Marianne Weber, we have seen in earlier sections of this book, belonged to this mode.) Dorothea suffers but does not fight back, does not even run away from her husband; she pities his suffering, everyone's suffering, more than her own. But Frieda fights back, runs away, asserts joy, refuses tragedy. Of course, she too suffered and pitied, just as, of course, Dorothea asserted herself and rejoiced. Nevertheless, the dominant modes of feeling we must associate with each of them are antithetical. Dorothea represented nineteenth-century British liberal humanism, sanctified by a sorrowing ethical religiosity. This is precisely what Miriam represented to Lawrence in his early years, for even before he ever saw Frieda Weekley he explicitly associated Miriam's love for him with Jane Eyre's way of loving, and explicitly demanded Anna Karenina's way instead. In Frieda he finally met the great alternative, the twentieth-century joyful protest in the name of life—the Schwabing protest.

THE EFFECT OF FRIEDA'S CO-AUTHORSHIP

The idea of Frieda as co-author of certain of Lawrence's works invites us to see Lawrence as that particular kind of genius who achieves his extraordinary and quite personal force as a writer by allowing in important ways a woman to take over his mind. Ernest Weekley had not allowed Frieda that, but neither would most sensitive and creative men have. But with Lawrence, I think, Frieda is to be co-credited with the moral-artistic success of his work. What such a formula means is perhaps best made clear by evoking a few contrasts. There seems no reason to suppose that T. S. Eliot's poetic success is to be credited to either of his wives; nor that Nora Joyce can be credited with even the Molly Bloom sequence of *Ulysses*. But Frieda guided as well as inspired Lawrence's writing. She livingly demonstrated the values which Lawrence himself could possess only imaginatively; she supported him in the processes of creation, remaining patiently passive, and yet passionately responsive to the act of writing. Sometimes, moreover, she was a participant in the imagining or reimagining of fictional scenes, and was always appreciative and critical of what was finally produced.

We may add that neither Tolstoy nor Proust had the kinds of talent that could allow a woman to take over their minds. It required that a man such as Lawrence find such a woman as Frieda Weekley before the formula could work. It is not just "a woman" who can take over such a mind; it must be "Woman." This is why the enterprise has sounded so ludicrous (except where it has sounded odious) to those who have glimpsed what was going on.

If one compares *The White Peacock* or *The Trespasser* with *Sons and Lovers,* or, to focus the contrast more sharply, if one compares the treatment of the character who stands as the author's surrogate in the early novels (and in "A Modern Lover" and "The Shades of Spring") with the treatment of Paul Morel, then one sees how much Frieda did for Lawrence artistically. She was, by all accounts, deeply involved in the final writing of *Sons and Lovers,* and the writing there is immensely improved over Lawrence's early work, as judged by the most pure and severe of aesthetic standards. In *The White Peacock* Lettie is a Hardy heroine, Nethermere is a Hardy location, and the endless flirting reminds one of *Jude the Obscure,* except where an inept fashionableness reminds one of Marie Corelli. The author is trying out roles in a somewhat embarrassing way, unsure of who he is or what he wants to say. In *The Trespasser* one is in the familiar world of free spirits, beauty-lovers who stifle in suburban squalor—the world of Wells and Barrie and Bennett, with daringly French episodes of sensuality. Thus Cecil Byrne in *The Trespasser*, like Cyril (nicknamed Sybil) Beardsall in *The White Peacock*, had been essentially an acolyte of a woman, a man whose male identity is in doubt. The writing, too, was in doubt of its own integrity. The contrast with *Sons and Lovers* is immense. Frieda had saved Lawrence from artistic as well as sexual impotence, and by the same act of grace; for Lawrence, for most writers then, the two things necessarily went together. Literature was moving with the erotic movement. They had to write about erotic subjects, and therefore they needed some *total* immersion in eroticism. They needed that baptism of fire in passion which Paul Morel told Miriam he had to leave her to get, but would come back to her after he did get. They needed, simply as writers, some assurance that they had had the whole thing, and could tell the truth about their own experience, unafraid that what other men said derived from their having gone further. Without that act of grace, what would Lawrence have become? A working-class E. M. Forster? A modernist Edward Carpenter?

Can one not say that Lawrence's genius as a modernist artist "derived from" the fullness with which he encountered Frieda and underwent the Magna Mater experience? He implies such a theory himself when he says in *Fantasia of the Unconscious* that some men always accord women primacy and "creative positivity":

> And in certain periods, such as the present, the majority of men concur in regarding woman as the source of life, the first term in creation. . . . Man's highest moment is now the emotional moment when he gives himself up to the woman, when he forms the perfect answer for her great emotional and procreative asking. . . . He begins to have as many feelings—nay, more than a woman. . . . Man begins to show strong signs of the peculiarly strong passive sex desire, the desire to be taken, which is considered characteristic of woman.

If this was the hidden truth of that cultural moment, then the creative artist would be called on to explore it by acting out that part fully. Murry clearly did not answer that challenge fully, nor did any of the other major creative minds of the epoch, such as Eliot, Mann, Gide, or Proust. Is there not, we must ask, some evidence that the weaknesses of each one can be explained in terms of his not meeting that challenge? Is it not possible that genius in modernist art emerges from talent when the artist undergoes what Lawrence called the baptism of fire in passion—specifically, the Magna Mater passion?

There is surely a meaningful poignancy in the coincidence of our chronology, that in 1917 Lawrence published *Look, We Have Come Through,* and Eliot published *Prufrock,* which might have been subtitled *Look, We Have Not Come Through Because People Like Us Just Don't.* Or that in 1913, when Lawrence was writing *The Rainbow,* he was reading *Death in Venice.* In the same year, Lawrence published *Sons and Lovers* and Proust the first volume of *À La Re-*

cherche du Temps Perdu, in both of which a wounded son, coining his personal bitterness into aesthetic sweetness, pays tribute to a marvelous mother, to that all-beneficent life-source that has emasculated him. But Lawrence's book is strong with the faith that he has been saved, that the problem was resolvable, whereas Proust's is strong in other ways. Forster and Virginia Woolf, Bloomsbury in general, England in general, paid verbal homage to Eros, but had no touch of his fire in themselves. Among would-be Lawrentian essayists, Murry already has been contrasted with Lawrence, and you could make much the same points with regard to Huxley. Even Joyce, as Stephen Dedalus, wrote the stiff, dead, blighted prose of one cast out by Magna Mater, the source of life, although as Bloom he celebrated her mysteries with marvelously poetic blasphemy. All of this proves primarily that Lawrence's was a different *kind* of achievement from the achievements of these other writers. But secondarily—because they all did want to celebrate Eros, because they all did take their places in the erotic movement—it means that Lawrence's achievement was in a major mode and theirs was in a minor. From this it follows that a certain degree of comparison, and a consequent recognition of superiority in Lawrence, is appropriate. Because Lawrence underwent the baptism of fire in passion with Frieda and they did not, he wrote better. He ceased to be a talent and became a genius.

The big problem with such a theory is the case of Franz Werfel. There we have a man of phenomenal talent conjoined with a wonderful Magna Mater figure, but genius did not result. Of course, cultural theories are like alchemical experiments; when one has followed all the instructions one has only made the signs propitious for the desired event; one has not, as in chemistry, compelled it to occur. There is no question of the laws of cultural theory having scientific exactitude, no hope of making them cover every case. What is more, one can see major differences between Werfel and Lawrence in Lawrence's much sharper mind and firmer identity, a mind and identity which are *not* to be credited to Frieda, of which she was *not* co-author. Moreover, one sees in Alma Mahler less of that troubled tentativeness which marked Frieda's early years, when she felt always wrong and suffered from Else. It is this that made her susceptible to Lawrence's authority in ways which Alma probably was not susceptible to anyone's (after Gustav Mahler). This susceptibility balanced Frieda's self-confidence, whereas Alma's self-confidence was unmitigated; it cannot be good for a woman *always* to be known as "the most beautiful woman in Vienna." Indeed, as Frieda settled down confidently into being herself—a fairly conventional self now, much like her mother's, and not susceptible to criticism because no longer aiming as high—Lawrence began to show signs of losing the battle for his finest creativity. There is a touch of Werfel's sort of blatancy about his later work, as we have said, and if he had lived as long as the other man there is no telling how like him he might have become.

However, in what he did write, the greatness owed much to Frieda. Even after she had saved him, and saved his novel about his mother, he still needed her support all along the way. There are plentiful assertions of this dependence, from his side too, in letters and in poems, but they have been taken to refer exclusively to personal and psychosexual matters. However, if one compares the writing of *The Plumed Serpent* with that of *Lady Chatterley's Lover,* it becomes clear that only when he wrote in sympathy with Frieda, with Woman, could he achieve that lambent, plasmic *life* in his prose which was his best individual gift and an essential part of his best syntheses. The plan of *The Plumed Serpent* calls for the reader to pass beyond Kate's sympathies—because she cannot stretch them sufficiently—out into the mysterious new world ruled by Don Ramon. But in fact Lawrence himself cannot pass beyond Kate/Frieda's sympathies, and Don Ramon's hymns and processions remain mechanical devices and projections.

Nowadays, because of the pressure of the Women's Liberation movement, we are bound to ask ourselves if the women of Frieda's sisterhood were victims of their situation as women. The first thing that occurs to one to say is that they disposed of so much power that the word "unliberated" seems too much of a paradox. Frieda Lawrence, for instance, clearly was an unliberated woman, in the sense which the current movement gives to that term. She thought of herself as woman-and-not-man, she never attempted to enter the world of men or to compete with men on their terms. She composed her identity and her fate out of "womanly" materials. And the price she paid is certainly evident in what I have called her self-caricaturing of her own mind. But surely even more evident is the sense of power and fulfillment she had, and the meaningful rebellion she directed against many of the world's institutions. By her standards, and Lawrence's, to be a woman-and-not-a-man was not inferior to being a man-and-not-a-woman; it was if anything superior. "Unliberated" is surely so inappropriate to so many features of her life, or Alma Mahler's, as to be simply inapplicable.

This, then, is the kind of author Lawrence was, a co-author. He was Frieda's secretary, and not only Frieda's. Before he had known Mabel Luhan a week, they had begun to write together a novel based on *her* life experiences—though Frieda put a stop to that. And this is only part of a pattern. As soon as he ran away with Frieda he began to write *The Sisters,* which turned into two great novels, based closely on her life-story and her development. *The Trespassers,* of course, was based entirely on Helen Corke's experiences, and *The Boy in the Bush* on Mollie Skinner's. Even *The White Peacock* is built around the figure of his sister, toward whom the narrator plays an ambiguously recessive and "feminine" role. And *Sons and Lovers* is built around his mother. Indeed, the only novels not built around a woman are the leadership novels, the novels of rebellion against his fate, and it is generally agreed that in those novels Lawrence's talent shows itself comparatively crippled, lacking a completeness it elsewhere commands. Lawrence was a novelist of the world of Woman in this sense too.

How Do We Know All This?

The relationship between Frieda Weekley and Otto Gross was no secret, even when I first began to think about this subject. Frieda translates some passages from his letters to her in her *Memoirs,* and the editor identifies the pseudonym she gives him. That the letters still existed—such of them as Freida had kept—was not so generally known but still was no secret, although the illegibility of the documents perhaps lent them something of that character. I was lucky enough to find that Lois Madison Hoffmann had deciphered and translated them shortly before I went to Texas to study them. This was a great help to me.

In that correspondence is found the information about Else Jaffe's affair with Otto Gross, which might otherwise have been unsuspected, although there is unpublished Weber correspondence which touches on it. It is striking how discreetly those affairs were conducted, considering the atmosphere of Schwabing then. Of course, the sisters were not "of Schwabing," in the sense that Fanny zu Reventlow or Marietta or Emmy Hennings were. Frieda and Else were alike in that. They led private lives as well as public, and their affairs with Otto Gross fell in the former category. Those private lives were kept very separate from their public involvements, and were contemplated only in private. They *kept* their correspondence with Otto Gross—and with others—"kept it to themselves." Such letters were documents, but not public documents. Frieda kept her letters from Otto privately for over fifty years, long after everything to do with Lawrence was published, although, as I have mentioned already, she did send them to Ernest Weekley in self-justification when she left him in 1912. And Else kept her letters from Max Weber even longer.

Also published in Frieda's *Memoirs and Correspondence* is her letter to Else of 1954 which refers to the latter's "great love." There are also one or two family letters, between Frieda and her mother, which refer, though rather unclearly, to Weber as the man Else loved. This "secret," which really was kept as such for half a century, is betrayed in two books of the last few years, Arthur Mitzman's *The Iron Cage* and Eduard Baumgarten's *Max Weber: Werk und Person.* Each, taken independently, is so guarded in its indiscretion that it can only rouse a suspicion. But taken together they lead one unmistakably to the truth. Of course, Frau Jaffe firmly, though dispassionately, denied the story; one of her favorite proverbs, I was told, was "Tell a lie and stick to it." Coming from her, this bit of wisdom, which she offers as British, though it is new to me, certainly has a lot of resonance. But on my trip to Germany I saw and heard much that confirmed this or that detail of my hypothesis, though no one even in the family knew, and only one or two suspected the whole story.

Apart from that, I've gathered my information in the ordinary ways. I've read the books by and about Weber, Lawrence, and the other figures who appear in these pages. I've inquired in state and town archives in Germany and Austria, I've read unpublished letters and manuscripts in university libraries (Harvard, Yale, and Texas), and I've had correspondence or interviews with several people, of whom I most particularly and warmly thank Frau von Eckardt and Professor Baumgarten.

But I mean the title of this section to suggest two other ideas. With what degree of certainty do I know these things? And with what kind of response are you invited to meet them? To take the first one first, some of the connections I draw and some of the motivations I ascribe have much more of the status of facts than others. The facts of Lawrence's and Weber's life are well established; of course, those "facts" are what a consensus has determined to be so, and have only a consensual stability, but they have as much stability as any propositions in our field; and that there are unpublished letters from Weber to Else Jaffe is a very simple kind of new fact. In contrast, almost everything dealing with the emotions of Else Jaffe's life is not established, because of the extreme discretion she observed about herself and imposed on her friends. In the case of Otto Gross, there is obviously a great deal more written by him than by Else, and from these works we can derive a good number of "facts"; but on the other hand, practically nothing was written *about* him, except as a character in novels. He was excluded from the world of public honor, and therefore also from that of carefully objective interpretation—those worlds into which Weber and Lawrence were so early welcomed. Gross was relegated to the world of private fantasy—indeed, to the world of nightmare. In his case, I have reported that part of what the novelists said which was closely supported by factual sources, and repeated by more than one of them. And I have indicated the nature of my certainty. As in Frau Jaffe's case, I have used such forms as "may," "perhaps," and "probably."

However, I have taken liberties of interpretation. Where the evidence is insufficient for certainty either way, or where I feel confident of my intuition, or where the points have no large significance for my main argument, I assert things without giving all the pros and cons of the preceding arguments. Moreover, I often suggest, for instance, that people should think of Else, and of Frieda's feeling about Else, when they read the Mary and Massy episodes of "Daughters of the Vicar." This, clearly, is not a fact at all; it is a suggestion. This is even more true of the passages in which I involve Max Weber's imaginative presence in *Women in Love*. I trust I have made it clear that *Lawrence* was not thinking of Weber, so far as I know, but I see Weber when I think about the novel because I find that it clarifies a great deal about the book to do so.

Thus, even if I am absolved from the charge of deceiving, I still may be accused of wasting people's time. It is against the decorum of scholarship to ask people to entertain uncertain propositions, unless their truth is, by future experiment, ascertainable; to entertain them is after all to invest imaginative energy in them. That is why I raise my second question. With what kind of response do I invite you to meet these propositions? I intend my answer to this question to justify both my putting these propositions to you and the minor liberties of interpretation which I have taken along the way.

IMAGINATIVE CONTEXT

The key word in my answer is "imaginative." How do we know all this? We know it imaginatively. I want you to meet these "facts" as elements in the imaginative context of D. H. Lawrence, a context which is a vital part of our imagination. It seems to me that the study of literature, nowadays, badly needs to be set back inside a new and living context of that kind—not a history-of-ideas context, but a context of the history of sensibility or imagination. The difference between the two kinds of history consists not so much in the latter's dealing with image clusters rather than logical systems, as in the kind of connection each type of history establishes between its component elements, and between them and the rest of life. For instance, the careers of Frieda, Alma, or Mabel as Magna Mater do not belong in a history of ideas because they are a matter of behavior, sexual behavior; imaginative history, imaginative life, precipitates ideas from time to time, but, for the most part, by its very nature it holds them in solution. What is more, those careers were not history in any ordinary sense because they were so private in scope, so deprived of significant numbers or organizational consequences. But they are important to any history of the imagination, for they made a big difference to the way other people imagined, and even enacted, their own sexual lives. We can know this only by using our imaginations. Thus all my major categories—like the cities of Heidelberg and Munich and all the things I label the "erotic movement," "matriarchy," even *"Lebensphilosophie"*—were treated here as imaginative history, even where they were quite susceptible to the methodology of the history of ideas. This is the context within which Lawrence must be encountered.

But first a few definitions—which paradoxically must be given rather in the style of the history of ideas. *Lebensphilosophie* is the largest and loosest of these categories, and I used it to refer to everything that stressed life-values in that period, from 1870 on; everything that stressed the value and power of the unconscious, of the emotional, of the spontaneous, of the primitive, of the original, of the organic, of the fertile; plus everything that analytically depreciated the opposite values, with their emphasis on rigid moral and epistemological systems, traditional certainties and imperatives. Thus figures like William James and Henri Bergson represented *Lebensphilosophie* as well as figures like Lawrence and Klages.

Among the many ideas and groups included in the *Lebensphilosophie* category, there is one with more profile, a more unified identity, and this I have called the erotic movement. This includes Lawrence and Klages, Frieda Lawrence, Alma Mahler, and Isadora Duncan, to name only the most salient cases, but it excludes Bergson and James. I have defined this movement as characterized conceptually by its finding the supreme life-value in erotic love, by its naming love the supreme locus of the unconscious, the emotional, the spontaneous, the primitive, the original, the organic, and the fertile. Despite this conceptual definition, however, its activities were primarily imaginative rather than conceptual, as is to be expected. A *logician* of the erotic movement, like Klages, is a living self-contradiction; the members of the movement more typically created literary, musical, and visual images in celebration of love and life.

One rather extremist wing of the erotic movement adopted as its ideological slogan the term *Mutterrecht*. This group included Otto Gross as well as Schuler and Klages, although if we described this group broadly as "the celebrants of the world of Woman" and did not make some ideological attack on patriarchy a criterion of membership, then it would include far more people and be far less extremist in character. Most novelists, most artists of all kinds, are to some degree celebrants of the world of Woman. (I have pointed out that most of the time Lawrence writes as if he belonged to that larger group, which is to say that he can be understood perfectly well by being read that way.)

Then, within that *Mutterrecht* group, at one of the centers common to all these circles or ellipses, we can distinguish some individuals who exemplified either by their behavior their imagination, or their beliefs the Magna Mater pattern of erotic relationship, with the woman a priestess, or a goddess, of love and fertility, the man a stripling lover or a priest of her mysteries. This subgroup includes Lawrence but not Klages, Isadora Duncan with Sergei Esenin but not with Gordon Selfridge, Mabel Dodge with John Reed but not with Tony Luhan.

These ideological concepts and these realities—that is, the people who held these beliefs or followed these patterns of behaviour—can be quite independent of each other, for a man or a woman might belong to one of the groups and not to any of the others. But when they coexist they seem to be concentric in intensity. At least as far as the imaginative arts are concerned, it seems that there was a kind of ultimacy of commitment to the erotic movement, and even to the various values of *Lebensphilosophie*, which could be achieved only by entering into the Magna Mater relationship. Thus I have suggested that with a number of modern artists an important clue to their identity and their achievement is the degree to which they realized themselves within that pattern of relationship.

This is the sort of material that makes up Lawrence's context. But how does such knowledge *work*? *How* does one know Lawrence in his imaginative context? Imaginative context is to be known by establishing imaginative connections, by seeing A (some feature of a novelist's work, for instance) as being alternative to B (the way another novelist treated that subject), as being illustrative of C, as being twin to D, and so on. To control this field of connection we have to rely on our sense of imaginative relevance, our sense that one connection is worth making and another is not. The term imaginative relevance is modeled on Leavis's "critical relevance" and it is a major principle by which literary study—and the other humanities—should be guided. Indeed, it always is so guided, but most often un-self-consciously. We always have a strong sense of which connections it is worth drawing, or permissible to draw, between, say, a character in a novel and people outside the novel, such as the novelist himself, or a friend of his, or a public figure of the time. Our connections are likely to be much freer in that personal and private speculation which constitutes our "experience" of the novel than in our public writing and discussion, but even in private we do control our response by reference to a sense of what is relevant. But that sense varies with periods of literary history. We have just ended a period in which the primary and characteristic emphasis was laid on narrowing the range of permissible connections, concentrating on "the words of the page." We now need to place our major books and authors in a new field of connection where we will see, in the form of similarities, contrasts and other forms of connection, striking and significant truths jump to the eye.

Lawrence has been seen up to now almost exclusively in a British context. This context was of course appropriate, and also useful in bringing out the points Lawrence wanted to make as well as those he thought not worth making. It brought his works into a humanist connection, relating them to history and politics, without derogating from their integrity as literary works of art. And implicity, this context, without admitting what it was doing, dramatized the meanings of the stories and poems it dealt with; it made Birkin and Hermione culture heroes and villains by linking them up with the actual contemporary cultural scene. Above all, this contextual criticism of Lawrence allowed the critics to talk about, to denounce and illuminate, in thunder and lightning, the whole contemporary more-than-literary world without ceasing to talk about Lawrence as a writer. I have no quarrel with that in principle. But in practice the usefulness of that particular context is exhausted, its fruitfulness has become sterility, its behavior, its habits have become mechanical and an oppression to the imagination. It is time to stop seeing Lawrence as an alternative to Aldous Huxley and John Middleton Murry, or to T. S. Eliot and Virginia Woolf, and time to start seeing him as alternative to Max Weber and Otto Gross. If Lawrence is to remain a source of life for us, he must be put in a new imaginative context.

I have put him into a number of them, which perhaps can be thought of as concentric: the contrast with Weber; the connection with Klages and Schwabing; the whole German scene, including Gross; the history of the century, including the work of Parsons and Leavis; and, largest of all, Bachofen's scheme of the patriarchal and matriarchal principles and their various subdivisions. This is the largest because it offers the possibility of illuminating the whole history of culture. Such schemes *can* only be known imaginatively, so in this sense too, in this sense above all, I "know all this" imaginatively.

The simplest single example of what I am trying to do in this book is the connection which I propose between Lawrence and Weber. The biographical and factual content of this connection is less important than the ideological and imaginative, but there is no need to set these two kinds of content in opposition to each other. The factual content is the skeletal structure which supports the ideological, and the whole is the imaginative context which the two men create for each other.

This use of mutual context—here primarily one of contrasts—is nothing new. We used to think of Dickens and Thackeray that way. And the method has in fact been applied to Lawrence, and quite recently, by old-fashioned writers such as Murry, who contrasts Lawrence with Schweitzer in *Love, Freedom, and Society,* and Rees, who contrasts him with Simone Weil in *Brave Men.* But in both of those cases there was no biographical connection between the two people being contrasted, and biographical connection contributes a valuable skeletal or sinewy element in such contrasts. Moreover, neither Murry nor Rees was writing at the top of his form in those books. They were out of sympathy with the literary ethos of their times and could only hark back to faded old models. Among contemporary studies I can think of only George Steiner's *Tolstoy or Dostoevski* as following this method of contrastive context. Applying this technique to Weber and Lawrence offers the extra stimulation that each of the figures represents a different field of knowledge and a different mode of imagination.

But the field of connection—always to be controlled, of course, by the principle of relevance—contains more than contrastive context. It contains, for instance, parallelism or similarity. The most important case of that here is the similarity between Lawrence's ideas and those of Klages and Schuler. The way in which the second two developed their matriarchal ideas in reaction against the sudden monstrous patriarchalization of Germany by Bismarck at the end of the nineteenth century throws light on Lawrence, for when his work is looked at in isolation, it does not seem to *demand* explanation in terms of "the world of men." What is more, behind Klages and Schuler stood Munich-Schwabing, the kind of locus for those matriarchal ideas for which the English scene provided no parallel. Hence we are able to draw in a more detailed background for Lawrence than in the contrast with Weber.

On the other hand, the differences between Lawrence and the Schwabingites with whom he can be compared are also important. Lawrence, for example, would not live in Schwabing; he and Frieda stayed in Irschenhausen, a village outside. Further, neither Klages nor Schuler ever entered into a Magna Mater relationship; nor did Stefan George or Wolfskehl; in fact, Schuler and George seem never to have attempted an erotic relationship with any woman, for Schuler's imagination was stirred only by the Duse-type of Elizabeth of Austria. Above all, there is the remarkable rigidification or masculinization of Klages's ideas after the failure of his relationship with Fanny zu Reventlow; the ideology remained matriarchal, but the systematization, its *spirit,* became patriarchal. No doubt in consequence, Klages's political stances were much more sinister than Lawrence's—for instance, in the matter of anti-Semitism. Thus the principle of similarity includes—as it always does—dissimilarity.

It is neither contrast nor similarity which primarily determines the interest we take in Otto Gross. Nor is it primarily the way he foreshadows striking ideas and personalities of our own time. We make the connection between him and both Lawrence and Weber because he represents a vivid life-option, a tragic fate, which challenges the options they chose. It is again a kind of context which he and they create for each other—all connection is context, of course—but this is the context of challenge rather than the many-sided equality of contrast which operates between Weber and Lawrence.

The figure of Hanns Gross, taken together with that of Bismarck, gives us the idea of German patriarchy in its most powerful manifestations, the servants of Ares; it symbolizes all the new ways in which, at the end of the nineteenth century, patriarchal realism of thought and dominance of action extended themselves literally all over the globe and all over the educated imagination. Echoes of the elder Gross's work, of its cultural significance, reach the general reader today in police-detective novels. For instance, Georges Simenon's Inspector Maigret consults Gross's *Criminal Investigation* as an authority in his work of catching criminals; and it is no accident that Maigret is in every way a vivid minor emblem of the patriarchal mode of being. H. R. F. Keating's Indian detective, Inspector Ghote, also consults Gross's *Criminal Investigation* as an authority—in fact, as Authority. In the second case, the book symbolizes the whole "system" of Western civilization to which the Indian aspires but which he cannot achieve for himself, whereas Maigret is at home with Gross, is himself another Gross. In Keating's myth, we see a nonpatriarchal culture bowing before a symbol of the patriarchal and trying to imitate it. In Simenon's myth we feel almost nostalgic about that same symbol, because the West now takes the patriarchal discipline for granted, or rebels frivolously against it. In both we see Gross's place in the structure of European culture, and the roaring tides that overwhelm other cultures as a result of its expansion. Police-detective fiction is, as a genre, patriarchal.

In Hanns Gross's son we see the most extreme reaction against those values. In Otto's life the meaning of these abstractions becomes concrete; patriarchalism means at its most extreme, a son being put in prison by his father, being officially declared insane, even having his children taken away from him and their mother and made into his father's children. Less vividly, but still importantly, these ideas are relevant to Weber and to Lawrence. There were no such events in Max Weber's life, and he was a different person in consequence; that is important. But it is also important that Weber's *myth*, his feeling for what life is like, nevertheless featured such conflicts, such choices, such events—less centrally and dramatically than Otto Gross's myth did, but still significantly. The same is true of D. H. Lawrence, who was clearly enough anti-patriarchalist, but whom we need to see in the context of Germany and imperialist expansion if we are to understand what "anti-patriarchalist" means.

When we extend our perspective in time to cover the century between 1870 and 1970, we see our main figures and their works in relation to different problems. In this larger context, for instance, we must take account both of anti-Semitism and of Nazism. Both Lawrence and Weber were ready to think in racial terms about individuals on occasion, and though this usually led them to *prefer* Jews to others, sometimes—on account of some traits—they disliked them. In Weber's case, the balance seems to have inclined toward his liking and admiring them; in Lawrence's case—if we go by his expressed opinions, or rather, his use of the word "Jew"—we might want to call him anti-Semitic. However, I think that the record of his relations with men like Koteliansky suggests that such remarks—which are all trivial, in both thought and feeling—did not express anything passionate in him. They were a by-product of his matriarchalism. He saw in the Jew what Klages saw in him: the metropolitan mind, rootless, disintegrated. and disintegrating, incarnate skepticism, represented, at a high intellectual level. by Freud, Marx, and Einstein. (Curiously, just as good an example of what Lawrence and Klages hated in the Jew could have been seen in Prussian Max Weber.) At the end of the nineteenth century, as System extended its hold to grip more and more of life, to expropriate more and more of the "instinctive" and "organic," Jews seemed to many thinkers the ubiquitous emissaries of the patriarchal mind, scurrying like ants all over the face of the earth, making fortunes in finance capitalism, or intellectually dominating the world by means of theoretical physics, psychoanalysis, economics, or sociology, "the Jewish science." (No doubt Edgar Jaffe was one of those who seemed to illustrate and confirm this idea.)

The figure of Kangaroo represents something different, of course. But Kangaroo's idea is a voluntaristic reversal of this "Jewishness." He offers everyone and everything love, but it is a wilful love, no more rooted in nature, in the world of animals and plants, in his own instincts, or in the habits of *personal* eroticism than is the critical skepticism he is reacting against. Kangaroo is just as rootless, and therefore just as "Jewish," as Freud, Marx, and Einstein.

Klages's idea of Jewishness was crude enough for him to declare, even in 1940, that the secret history of the nineteenth century was the Jewish conspiracy and that in the twentieth century the Jews were the wire-pullers of World War I, and the wage-masters of the Russian Revolution. He admitted, of course, that not every Jew has the Jewish character, and that not only Jews have it. But the Jew is the Golem, a mock-man with no feelings of his own, because he has no roots. (He says this while discussing Wolfskehl, who he claims stole Schuler's ideas and gave them to George, who in turn trivialized them into literature. Thus the matriarchal idea, which should have saved the world, was cheated of its destiny by the intervention of Jews and *littérateurs*.) This clearly is anti-Semitism. Schuler, in his lectures on Ancient Rome, turned even the life of Nero into an anti-Semitic myth, the Semite being seen, along with the Stoic and the Christian, as the representatives of patriarchal Mind, of evolution. Nero was a mother's son, like Schuler himself, for Nero was a hero of his. How, then, did Nero come to perform mother- and brother-murder? The blame lies in part with Poppaea, who was Jewish, Schuler explains; and even more with Seneca, Nero's tutor, who was a Stoic. Seneca morally separated mother from son, thus drying up the bonds of nature between them. The "Zentrale von Evolution" compelled Nero to kill, and decreed, too, the persecution of the Christians, which so much aided their cause in the long run. The blood they gave in martyrdom nourished the poison-tree seeds of their life-hating Church. Schuler describes Nero's death as a mirror image of Christ's, with three women again weeping for the dying hero. As in a mirror, this tragedy was the reverse of the Christian one in all its values.

As this example makes clear, anti-Semitism of this sort was not in the least Christian. It was, indeed, anti-Christian, hostile to the whole moral tradition of the West. It is alleged (by Willy Haas and Hans Boehringer) that Hitler heard Schuler's lectures in Munich in 1922 and was one of Schuler's circle of initiates. Whether or not this is true, it is clear that Munich-Schwabing was the birth-place of Nazism, both geographically and intellectually. Hitler, Hess, Röhm, and Rosenberg all lived in Schwabing, and the irrationalism we have described there provided a congenial atmosphere and nourishment for the ideology they developed. The Nazis too were in their way an anti-Apollonian and anti-patriarchal party. Moritz Julius Bonn tells a story which illustrates the anti-Prussian—which is to say, anti-patriarchal—character of the Nazis. In 1933, just before he fled Germany, he stood with Hitler and Goebbels on a reviewing stand. As the last of the impeccably goose-stepping Prussian regiments passed out of sight and the first Nazi Brown Shirts appeared, merely shambling along, it seemed, when one contrasted them to the Prussians, he felt the birth of a new age. A new spirit had taken control. A different element of the German character held the hegemony. Apollo had gone down before Dionysos. The more patriarchal manifestations of Germany—its science, its bureaucracy, its army—became tools in the hands of these anti-patriarchal mystagogues—which was precisely what Max Weber had often warned against.

There was a remarkable book of 1931, Georg Fuch's *Sturm und Drang in München,* which treats Schwabing—Schuler's and Klages's Schwabing—as the source of the Nazi regeneration of Germany. In Schwabing the secret Germany first rebelled against official Germany. Fuchs begins by comparing Youth's salute to Bismarck in Schwabing in 1892 with its adoration of Hitler in 1931, and his basic myth is that Bismarck's Germany was betrayed by Wilhelm II, and that after military defeat it slumped into Jewish decadence (symbolized by Franz Wedekind), until Bismarck's true successor emerged in the person of Adolf Hitler. Jewish decadence he sees as in natural alliance with blandly liberal and bourgeois conventionalism, for he claims Hitler to be the inheritor of the *Jugendbewegung,* which rebelled against both equally. By using the phrase "Sturm und Drang," Fuchs means to parallel Klages, Schuler, George, the *kosmische Runde,* with Goethe and his friends in 1790. Their Rousseau was Nietzsche, or even more Bachofen. From him they learned to believe in a world where "divine newborn children of an undoomed human race should reign, men who should triumph in their full amoral splendor over decadent mankind." Fanny zu Reventlow, a Nazi Mother *avant la lettre,* is the book's heroine, and its enemy is bureaucratized Soviet Russia, the machine state. Thus the blood-knowledge of *Mutterrecht* was being made politically effective by Hitler, who was saving Germany from being controlled by dried-up middle-class rationalists (like Max Weber, we might add).

Julius Langbehn's *Rembrandt als Erzieher,* of 1890, an enormously popular book in its day, had described German fate in terms of the same alternatives Fuchs depicts, the same historical dialectic. Though he was grossly nationalistic, Langbehn despised Berlin as lacking in grandeur, as "unteroffizierisch." He called for a new birth of the great Germany from within, by means of art and in defiance of the machine and of industrialization. He believed in irrationalism ("das Rembrandtisches Helldunkel") and adored Bismarck, a giant-hero of irrationalism and intuitiveness. In Langbehn's historical scheme, Bismarck was aligned with Luther in opposition to the rationalist Erasmus and the hated Mommsen, Bismarck's critic. Langbehn spoke particularly to artists. He influenced Schwabing through the *Heimatskunstbewegung*—people who believed that healthy art must have its roots in the soil—and the Worpswede group of artists, to which Clara Rilke belonged. (She and Rainer Maria Rilke both lived in Schwabing, and his *Sonette an Orpheus* are said to owe much of their mythology to Schuler.) Langbehn's call for the birth of a new Germany was answered in Schwabing, and Fuchs, who was a lifelong Schwabingite, thought that Nazism was its political equivalent as late as 1931.

All this is a far cry from D. H. Lawrence. But among Frieda Lawrence's unpublished papers in Texas there are notes for an essay on *Mein Kampf.* The notes are undated, but she says this book was published "a few years ago" and has passed unnoticed—which lets us date it approximately—and that it has given masses of people a new impetus in life, and is good writing. She quotes a few paragraphs and then beaks off—there are several such uncompleted projects for essays among her papers—but clearly she intended to recommend and defend the book. Frieda was, of course even more naïve about politics than Lawrence, and even less of a Nazi. Nevertheless, it is not surprising that she liked *Mein Kampf,* whereas it would be surprising if she had liked something comparable by Lenin. Max Weber would, I think, say that both Frieda's essay and *The Plumed Serpent* represent a real political danger, although even as representations they are politically as well as artistically trivial. Of course, Weber's enemies say that it was he who "brought on" Hitler, by his demand for charismatic leadership and his contempt for so much of democratic politics. To be sure, anyone who has heard Weber's voice inside his formulas knows that he didn't mean anything even remotely like Nazism; but the events of World War II, and of the Nazi Reich, should resound in one's mind as one reads both Lawrence and Weber—and Otto Gross as well.

We must not forget, however, that the mythology of German anti-Semitism was not exclusively the product of the matriarchalists. It was as much the work of the patriarchal mind, though for them the Jew was characterized in a seemingly opposite way, because he was identified with modernist art. This patriarchalist characterization of the Jew contradicts the matriarchalist version insofar as men like Klages and Lawrence had called Jews "uncreative" and "unerotic." But the opposition here is not substantial because in modernist art the artist often can be described as analytical and even skeptical and "destructive" as much as creative, for much of his work is indeed an attack on those naïve faiths which keep life going. This sort of modernism is particularly destructive of faith in social institutions, like marriage, and a certain kind of destructive satire often has been associated with Jews—by Lawrence, among others. We saw how, in Alma Mahler's life, Werfel's Jewish skepticism offered her much more than Gropius's Prussian straightforwardness. Werfel's art work, which could be called both analytic and synthetic, both sentimental and cynical, was half of what attracted her to him. Of course, Lawrence himself wrote some brilliantly satirical attacks on marriage and Nature and all his own enthusiasms. On the whole, however, it is his distinction among modernist authors that so much of his work is not such an attack, is "affirmative," in this sense, is "rooted in the soil." It seems demonstrable that he owed the achievement of that character to his relationship with Frieda, for if he is not unique in being affirmative—for there are several Dionysian-Aphroditean affirmations among the modernists—one is hard put to find a parallel to him as a Demetrian affirmer among men of passionate intelligence. (In the lower ranks of intelligence, to be sure, it is easy enough to find parallels.) This is why he assumes such importance in the value scheme of F. R. Leavis.

Such affirmations are also to be found in Jewish writers, of course. Nevertheless, in this very special sense of anti-Semitic, Lawrence is an anti-Semitic author, for he intended to be the opposite of the "Jewish" analytic-critical-sentimental intelligence. And he does think in racial terms, he does accept the most brutal of politics. We cannot feel easy about Lawrence in relation to such issues.

Finally, the Schwabing circles with which Lawrence associated should be understood within the framework of Bachofen's anthropology. Such understanding is imaginative knowledge in the profoundest sense. As Bachofen himself put it, the critical historical method cannot lead us to understand the largest things: "one can only understand antiquity by reassuming antique health of soul." Even Max Weber would not disagree that there is an imaginative mode of knowledge. He would insist on adding only that it be distinguished from a scientific mode of knowledge. Weber himself deduced from that distinction the right and the need to banish the imagination from the center of "public" intellectual life, but that need and right seem to most of us today to derive rather from the pathos of his own dilemma. He had to enact the crucifixion of his self-alienation, and this was the creed which "justified" that. Judged by the criteria of real knowledge, nothing that is imaginatively or emotionally potent is ever *known*; it is always a construct of our fancy in part, and we must forever disillusion ourselves. We all have to enact or live out that self-discipline to some degree, and Weber's proud self-crucifixion is profoundly moving and noble. But it has no more power to compel imitation than Lawrence's deliberately spontaneous rages or his prophetic poses. We are free to understand both on our own terms—imaginative terms, if we so wish, and are capable of them.

To understand the world in Bachofen's terms is particularly useful today in distinguishing between different kinds of revolutionariness. Broadly speaking, the contemporary movements are matriarchal rather than patriarchal. The patriarchal revolutionary is typified by the member of a severely organized Communist cell, of the sort out of which the Bolshevik party grew and which one can find described in Doris Lessing's work. This is an organized equivalent of Max Weber's intellectual world. Today's revolutionaries, typically, are rebelling against system of any kind, or at least on any large scale. They want to renew life from its roots in the soil and in personal relations. This formula however, applies to both the Hetaerist and the Demetrian models of matriarchy, and it is interesting to see how the revolutionary movement today divides itself according to their two different interpretations of that formula; and why the two divisions are implicitly at odds with each other. The most flamboyant kinds of revolutionaries clearly follow the Hetaerist interpretation and include members of Gay Liberation and Women's Liberation. They are, from our point of view, followers of Otto Gross. But there are those who believe in a renewed "family" life in retirement, sometimes on the scale of a community, and these are Demetrian followers of Lawrence.

Both are to be seen quite prominently on our campuses and on the streets of our inner cities. Otto's followers are the wilder types, the stutterers, the drug addicts, the disheveled and unkempt, the "dangerous cases," dangerous to others and themselves as measured by the standards of even the most liberal of societies. Lawrence's followers may resemble him as much as Otto's followers resemble Otto, but they tend to look more like the images he constructed for our edification. For instance, in a late article he exclaimed how different things would be if only twelve young men would walk down Picadilly wearing tight scarlet trousers. Well, that has happened; the habit of that happening has formed. And the erotic Christ image, which he suggested for us in "The Man Who Died," is to be met with on every campus lawn—the noble purity and gravity of the dark-eyed face, the perfumed dark ringlets out of a nineteenth-century icon, but below it the rich ripe brown body, offered to the world, the sacred garden in which this face blossoms. Not only is this to be found, it imposes itself; as much as anything, it dominates and characterizes the campus, makes those lawns and porticoes its locus. Otto and Lorenzo have had their say; what they asked for has come to pass, as much as—to invoke the appropriate criterion of societal enactment—as much as what Max Weber asked for.

Within patriarchal religion Bachofen distinguished three stages, the Sunchild, the Dionysian, and the Apollonian. It was on the first of these that Klages and Schuler fixed their hopes, and perhaps their dreams were realized in the *Jugendbewegung*. The sun-child for them was essentially male and self-loving, Castor and Pollux in one. George's Maximin was an example. But the idea is not necessarily sinister. The equivalents today are those golden children of the middle class and academia, who, though laden with every gift patriarchal society has to offer, decline to cooperate with it, and who are to be seen trooping along in their thousands, and their hundreds of thousands, to Woodstock, radiant in their own beauty and innocence. What they can offer—beyond that spectacle—to the rest of the world is not so easy to see. Within our cast of characters, the only *Sonnenkinder* seem to be Frieda and Fanny; *they* had the gift of radiant innocence, recreating life anew each day from within themselves. But it was only through Lawrence—and therefore through a *different* mode of being—that Frieda was able to mean anything to the world. Indeed, Bachofen says that though the radiant son, the *Sonnenkind,* promises to deliver men from the maternal darkness to the light, he is himself still governed by his mother. He knows no father, no patriarchal principle. True deliverance occurs only in the Dionysiac phase, when the sun is in the zenith.

It is puzzling to find Dionysos, the main opponent of Apollo, associated with so much light. Perhaps it helps to remember Otto Gross's self-identification with the sun. This is a semi-tropical blazing sun, Lawrence's golden lion of the skies, Schuler's Omphalos, whose overbearing dazzling flaminess melts away all the civilized bonds and blocks in men's minds, returns them to primal being. The Dionysiac stage is prominent enough in modern life, as may be seen in what goes on theatrically and musically at events like Woodstock. As Bachofen points out, this stage is very closely connected to the Hetaerist stage of matriarchy, and often leads people to revert to that type of primitivism. (Acccording to him, such a reversion happened to whole cultures in Asia and Africa.) Dionysos is for Bachofen essentially a woman's god, but he is the enemy of Demetrian matriarchy. He is hostile to marriage, and even to children insofar as they are taken to be the aim and justification of marriage. He is hostile even to agriculture. His life is ecstasy. At Argos the chief festival of Aphrodite was called Hysteria, because swine were sacrificed to her there. There was also a Festival of Wantonness at Argos at which everyone was transvestite and the priests of Aphrodite were often homosexual or castrated. Lais was murdered at such a festival in Thessaly, and violence is associated with them often. The myth tells us that the rational King Peleus, spying on a festival as a critical observer, was so excited as to assume costume himself, only to be torn to pieces by his similarly ecstatic mother, who mistook him for a lion.

The Apollonian stage we have already identified with Heidelberg. Its glamour as an achievement we must apprehend in the careers of Max Weber and Stefan George, in order to see how effortful an achievement it can be. In our current situation, where the Apollonian option seems so lacking in interest and drama, so identified with the ready-made, the mode into which one drops when one lacks courage for anything better, these men repay study. Their pathos, their strainful self-alienation,⋅ and their institutional equivalent in the perfect instrumentality of the German army and the German bureaucracy under Wilhelm II and Hitler—all this is obvious enough. But that Max Weber should have been the greatest analyst of all this and the prophet of the doom that was to follow from it, *and yet lived out that doom in his own life,* that is not obvious and deserves careful reflection. It is the fragility of the Apollonian order that today needs to be stressed.

When the solidity of the patriarchal world becomes transparent to young people's eyes, it will begin to live again for them as a value.

Bachofen had a strong sense of the fragility of Apollo's reign over men's minds, much as he rejoiced in that reign. Apollo being free from any bond with woman, he says, his familial line, his succession, is spiritual and adoptive, and so he is immune from death. But history teaches us that mankind owes the reign of Apollo to the Roman imperium and its laws, to the patriarchal world and its institutions. Wherever Apollo unsupported clashed with Dionysos, the latter triumphed. Apollo needs the support of the other Olympians, including Ares. It was Dionysos who won the worship of the Ptolemies. They were the children of Alexander the Great and inherited his world, which was ordered by Apollo. But Alexander was only a child of the sun and thus not fully a patriarchal figure, and the sun at its zenith melted down the rational convictions of his heirs. In their hands, in Hellenic Egypt, the Apollonian culture of Greece succumbed to Dionysiac luxury and orgy. Only Rome stood firm, by the strength of systematic Roman law and the rigidly disciplined Roman legions; and only thus could Octavian defeat Cleopatra and establish Apollo's kingdom. This gives us a historical vignette of the three stages of patriarchalism. According to this scheme Max Weber appears as a Roman redivivus, a son of Apollo, trying to bring his brothers back into alliance with, into control of, the followers of an Ares out of control, but seeing his best friends turned against him by the seductions of Dionysos, so that the whole patriarchal order slid down into ruin.

Above all, it is Bachofen's scheme itself which repays study. It is remarkable that his work, and Klages's should have remained so hidden from the English-speaking reader. In the Bollingen Series volume of Bachofen published in 1967, almost the only thing by him in English, we are told that he was rediscovered by a group of young people centered round Stefan George in Munich in the 1920s. It is not often you find, in such a scholarly work, so many misstatements gathered together in one sentence, and it shows the extent to which scholars are unaware of Klages and the others. I myself have only dabbled in both Klages and Bachofen, but I found—as it seemed to me—enough to illuminate whole landscapes of earlier knowledge.*

If we turn from the positive principle of imaginative connection to the

---

* I should perhaps say a word here about the connection between these ideas and those other terms I used in *Cities of Light and Sons of the Morning:* Faustian, Erasmian. Calvinist. My present terms describe just the same sort of reality—that is, temperamental types which can and do become ideological ideals and hence models for self-formation. The two sets of terms are mutually hostile, in the sense that each, as a set, interlocks and covers every possibility, so that every class of phenomenon becomes a subcategory or a combination of the original three. But they can, and should, be used in combination. nevertheless. Max Weber was Apollonian and Faustian, D. H. Lawrence was Demetrian and Faustian. As I shall point out, Edward Carpenter was ideologically a matriarchalist but temperamentally an Erasmian. The two sets of terms can be thought of as differing the way two profiles of a mountain taken from different vantage points do.

complementary negative principle of imaginative relevance, we find that the most striking application of the latter is the exclusion of the third von Richthofen sister, Johanna. I decided that the mass of extra material which I should have to include, in order to give her anything like equal treatment, would *prevent* the important connections being made; most importantly, it would blur the contrasts between Frieda and Else. But it is not for the negative applications of imaginative context that I expect to be reproached. In what sense, people will ask, do all these positive connections throw light, evaluative or interpretive light, on Lawrence's *work*? I have tried to answer that question specifically in the first section of the Epilogue, but the more general answer is simply that studying Lawrence's *work*, given the implications of such an emphasis, is not the most fruitful way to approach Lawrence these days. We need to let our minds play with the total phenomenon of Lawrence, the career, the personality, the ideas, the techniques, trying them out in different combinations. Only by this play will we discover our true seriousness about him. The old seriousness, carried by rigorous close reading, will not lead us any deeper into ourselves or into him. (In the case of Weber, of course, I have made no claims to throw new light on his works, which I understand only in the most undergraduate way. Or rather, I have made no claim to demonstrate that new light. Implicitly I do believe that seeing Weber in this context brings out a new profile to his intellectual personality, and thus must lead eventually to a better understanding of what he said about particular issues.)

This play of our minds over the total phenomenon, which must seem wanton to many, in fact would *be* wanton if it were not controlled by the criterion of relevance. For example, interpreting individual works of art, I invited you think of Else Jaffe behind "Clara" and "Mary," of Mabel Luhan behind "Ethel Cane," of Marianne Weber behind "the Princess." I invited you to think of Weber's sociology behind the icy abstract Alps where Gerald died—though it would be relevant also, but not *as* relevant, to think of Einstein, who was working out the general theory of relativity in Switzerland in just those years when Lawrence was obsessed by the Alps as a symbol. But it would not be relevant to think of, say, Calvin's theology; that connection would not be worth making.

That is perhaps as much as one can say. Though the principle of imaginative relevance operates by means of rational criteria, it consults so many of them in such a zigzag fashion, following a sequence that varies so much from case to case, that each decision is unpredictable, unrepeatable, in the loose sense "intuitive." Like "critical relevance," like most other such principles, its operations can be rationalized after the fact, but only in such a way that future decisions, except for minor ones within well-known categories, cannot be foreseen. It is a practical principle, an art, to be learned only by being practiced.

To sum up my ideas about imaginative knowledge, I invite you to know all the things I have talked about in this book in terms of the three emblematic figures: Weber, dominating a crowded convention hall from the podium, encased in solid black broadcloth and starched wing collar; Lawrence, digging in the garden in his loose linen jacket, expertly inserting the blade of the spade, deftly stooping and inserting the young plant; Gross, leaping up from his café table to greet a friend, seating him or her beside him, fixing that look of question and understanding on her face. Gross unkempt and gap-toothed, bloodstained, needle-scarred, amid the cigarette smoke and the international newspapers of a big city café at two in the morning; Lawrence quick, concentrated, birdlike, self-completed in the silence of the vast sunlit space between him and the Rockies; Weber, self-scornfully correct in dress, brutally charismatic in speech, amid the sentimental ineptitudes and the rhetorical vaguenesses of the other speakers. In terms of these three emblematic figures we can know all these books and ideologies and policies—and our own reality too.

A Couple of Challenges

Let me conclude by contrasting my method with that of a recent, more ortho-dox study of Lawrence, and then by citing a case in which my method is as risky as it ever is. In *D. H. Lawrence and Edward Carpenter* Émile Delavenay shows what striking similarities there are between the ideas of these two men, and the mass of evidence he brings convinces me at least that Lawrence probably first met those ideas in Carpenter's books. I say probably because there can be no proof of such a proposition. The multiplicity and the ambiguities of human communi-cation are too great to allow it. And suppose we *knew* (which we don't quite) that Lawrence heard of these ideas from Willy Hopkin, and that Hopkin had been reading Carpenter, what would that prove? It is just as likely that Lawrence also came by these ideas by some unrecorded, unknown means—hearing them from Miriam, say, who had been reading something quite different and unpopu-lar at the time, which she may even have got wrong, and which we will never know she read anyway. Moreover, we would not accept such evidence as "ex-plaining" the ideas of a much more ordinary man, and the protean aptitude of a mind like Lawrence's makes such attributions practically impossible. The fact that he met these ideas in Carpenter's work would not mean that he "got them from" Carpenter. But I think that he *probably* met these ideas in Carpenter, and I find that interesting. The degree to which such ideas were generally current in Eng-land at that time—the degree to which Lawrence was "typical"—it is good to keep this in mind. However, for me to put in that "probably" is to take out the value of my assent from M. Delavenay's point of view, for the whole excitement of his argument derives from its proving something important about Lawrence; the reader must, he feels, say yes or no to it, and that must commit him to something important: either Lawrence stole his ideas from Carpenter or he was original. But that is a false dilemma, and the only resolution that makes any sense to me there, the "probably" resolution, does not lead toward any important decision. Carpenter was a popularizer of ideas—of those *Lebensphilosophie* ideas which meant so much to Lawrence, and which Lawrence made mean so much to us—

but whether Carpenter or somebody else first put those ideas into Lawrence's hands really doesn't matter. The evidence, to my eye, suggests that Carpenter would have been an improbable sponsor for them, the wrong man, from Lawrence's point of view, to receive them from. Carpenter was the kind of man Lawrence was determined not to be, the kind Frieda saved him from being. *That* was his basic importance to Lawrence.

Carpenter was born into a genteel family, had several sisters who found themselves doomed to lives of frustration, was a clever nervous boy who took orders in the Church of England in 1870 but found himself sexually maladjusted and suffered a nervous breakdown. He read Whitman and took a long convalescent holiday in Italy in 1893—an immersion in "primitive paganism" such as had become traditional for upper-class Englishmen then—and returned reconciled to his own homosexuality. He resigned from the church in 1874 and began teaching University Extension courses. In 1882 he bought a cottage in Derbyshire and lived there until 1922, lecturing and writing on literary-philosophical-political themes, all anti-patriarchal. He became an expert popularizer of ideas because his temperament, as distinct from his ideology, was Erasmian, and not at all anarchist-revolutionary. He was a gentle man, clear of mind, just and equable. He was the perfect Home University Library writer and Workers Educational Association lecturer. But what Lawrence wanted was to become a powerful man, profound of vision, angry and loving. The style of *The Rainbow* is the opposite of the Home University Library style: "D. H. Lawrence" was to be the opposite of "Edward Carpenter." E. M. Forster tells us that Carpenter was in some sense the sponsor, or inspirer, of his gentle homosexual novel *Maurice*. The distance between *Maurice* and *The Rainbow* measures the misdirection of M. Delavenay's argument.

What is more, the fact that this is so illustrates the conflict between my method and M. Delavenay's. With my sense of Lawrence, and my sense of imaginative relevance, Carpenter could only have meant one thing to Lawrence—the threat Lawrence felt of being condemned to impotent gentility, to belletristic philosophizing in a cottage—and the conjunction of the two men can only mean that to us. With M. Delavenay's sense of Lawrence, and his sense of scholarly relevance, Carpenter must be the hidden source of Lawrence's ideas.

Another point. I have agreed that in some unimportant sense of the word "source," Carpenter may well have been one of Lawrence's "sources" before Lawrence left England. But it is most unlikely that—as M. Delavenay suggests—the recrudescence of *Lebensphilosophie* ideas in Lawrence's work in 1913 was due to his rereading of Carpenter, to his happening on some second-hand copy in a Lerici bookstore. Frieda was surely Lawrence's source of those ideas in 1913. She was incomparably more important to Lawrence than Carpenter *as a source of ideas*. Frieda was a living idea. As long as scholarship ignores such facts as that, and thinks that one set of conceptual words can derive only from some other such set, it is wrestling itself into a hammer lock.

Someone may object that M. Delavenay's scholarship is of a narrow kind, and that there are many alternatives to it besides what I propose. This is true. The critical work done on Lawrence in English has been mostly much broader in its scope. It has related Lawrence to the class-cultural geography of England, and to the moral-imaginative alternatives for the educated men among whom he took his place. Nevertheless, as I have argued, that broader work too is at the end of its power to stimulate our imaginations. We need a fresh start. And to make that fresh start we need to remind ourselves in a radical way of what imagination is and what knowledge is in these matters of literary study. M. Delavenay's work, which has its own freshness in the context of Lawrence studies, provides a useful reference point.

The risky case of interpretation is that of "The Daughters of the Vicar," and of my reading of the Mary-and-Massy episode in connection with Else and Edgar Jaffe. The risk derives from two facts: that Lawrence wrote a story called "Two Marriages," presumably the first version of this story, in 1911, before he had met Frieda or Else; and that a different version of "Daughters," called "Two Marriages," was published in 1934 and is not substantially different from the one we know in its treatment of the Mary-Massy theme. If the 1911 and the 1934 versions are the same, then Lawrence wrote that episode without thinking of Else and Edgar Jaffe.

My own assumption is that the 1934 version was written in 1912 or 1913 and that it incorporated into its treatment of that episode Lawrence's new experience of the Jaffes; but I have no evidence to make this decision more than an assumption. I did not assert, in the early part of the Epilogue, that he definitely *was* thinking of them. But by my method I asked you to respond imaginatively as if he were. My justification is that if he wasn't it doesn't matter, for the imaginative connection between the story and those people is still valuable for us to make. We are still right to put the facts of Else's marriage into conjunction with the description of Mary's; this is the *kind* of thing Lawrence was talking about, whether or not it was this particular thing. The factual link may prove weak, but the imaginative connection will still hold good. On the other hand, if I *knew* that the factual biographical connection did not exist, I should not ask the reader to make that imaginative connection. But I am ready to go beyond what I know—not in defiance of what I know—in the name of imagination. It is for the reader to judge, both of the principle and of its present application.

Bibliography

This is a very selective bibliography, with a very limited function: to give the reader a first start in pursuing for himself the subject of each section in turn. It offers to name one or two important sources not named in the text, and to fully specify those only incompletely identified. It does not repeat information given in the text or in the Annals, so it can only be used as a supplement.

Chapter 1

J. J. Bachofen, *Myth, Religion, and Mother Right*. Princeton, 1964.

J. R. Becher, *Abschied*. Berlin, 1960.

M. J. Bonn, *Wandering Scholar*. London, 1949.

Ludwig Curtius, *Deutsche und Antike Welt*. Stuttgart, 1950.

Leonhardt Frank, *Links, Wo Das Herz Ist*. 1952.

Peter Gay, *Weimar Culture*. London, 1969.

Hermann Glockner, *Heidelberger Bilderbuch*. Bonn, 1969.

Otto Gross, "Die Affektlage der Ablehnung," *Monatschrift für Psychiatrie und Neurologie*, XII, 1902.

——, "Über Vorstellungszerfall," ibid., XI, 1902.

——, "Zur Phylogenese der Ethik," *Archiv für Kriminalistik und Archeologie*, IX, 1902.

——, "Paralyse," *Neurologisches Centralblatt*, XXII, 1903.

——, "Beitrag zur Pathologie des Negativismus," *Psychiatrische Wochenschrift*, V, 1903.

——, "Zur Nomenclatur des Dementia Conjunctiva," *Neurologisches Central-blatt*, XXVIII (twice), 1904.

——, "Über Bewusstseinszerfall," *Monatschrift für Psychiatrie und Neurologie*, XV, 1904.

——, "Zur Differentialdiagnostik," *Psychiatrische Wochenschrift*, VI, 1904.

——, "Elterngewalt," *Zukunft*, Bd 78, 1908.

——, "Zur Überwindung der Kulturellen Krise," *Aktion*, 1913.

——, "Die Psychoanalyse oder wir Kliniker," the same.

——, "Die Einwirkung der Allgemenheit auf das Individuum," the same.

——, "Anmerkungen zu einer neuen Ethik," the same.

——, "Notiz über Beziehungen," the same.

——, "Brief," *Zukunft*, February 28, 1914.

——, "Über Destruktionssymbolik," *Zentralblatt für Psychoanalyse und Psychotherapie*, IV, 1914.

——, *Vom Konflikt des Eigenen and Fremden*, Verlag Freie Strasse, Berlin, 1916.

——, "Über den Inneren Konflikte," *Abhandlungen aus dem Gebiet der Sexualforschung*, II, 1919.

——, "Zum Parlamentarismus," *Die Erde*, 1919.

——, "Protest und Moral im Unbewussten," the same.

——, "Orientierung der Geistigen," *Sowjet*, 1919.

——, "Die kommunistische Grundidee in der Paradiessymbolik," the same.
(A more complete list of Gross's psychological publications can be found in Hall and Co.'s *Author Index to the Psychological Index* of 1960. But readers should bear in mind that more than one Otto Gross was writing on such topics in those years.)

Ernest Jones, *Free Associations*. London, 1959.

Franz Jung, *Sophie*. Berlin, 1915.

——, *Der Weg Nach Unten*. Neuwied am Rhein, 1961.

Ludwig Klages, *Der Mensch und das Leben*. Jena, 1940.

——, *Goethe als Seelenforscher*. J. A. Barth, 1932.

——, *Vom kosmogonischem Eros*. Bonn, 1963.

Frieda Lawrence, *Memoirs and Correspondence*. New York, 1964.

Robert Lucas, *Frieda von Richthofen*. Munich, 1972.

Erich Mühsam, *Namen und Menschen*. Leipzig, 1949.

Karl Otten, *Wurzeln*. Damrstadt, 1963.

——, *Ego und Eros*. Stuttgart, 1963.

——, *Prüfung zur Reife*. Leipzig, 1928.

Talcott Parsons, "Democracy and Social Structure in Pre-Nazi Germany," *Essays in Sociological Theory*. Free Press, 1954.

Fanny zu Reventlow, *Ellen Olenstjerne*. Munich, 1903.

——, *Herr Dames Aufzeichnungen*. Munich, 1913.

Max Rheinstein, *Max Weber on Law in Economy and Society*. Harvard, 1954.

Curt Riess, *Ascona*. Zurich, 1964.

H. E. Schröder, *Klages: Die Jugend*. Bonn, 1966.

Wilhelm Stekel, "In Memoriam," *Psyche and Eros*. New York, 1920.

R. H. Tawney, "Introduction" to Max Weber's *Protestantism and the Spirit of Capitalism*, trans. Talcott Parsons. London, 1930.

A. J. P. Taylor, *Bismarck*. London, 1955.

Alfred Weber, *Deutschland und die europäische Kulturkrise*. Berlin, 1924.

——, *Ideen zur Staats- und Kultursoziologie*. Karlsruhe, 1927.

Marianne Weber, *Die Frauen und die Liebe*. Leipzig, 1936.

Chapter 2

Eduard Baumgarten, *Max Weber: Werk und Person*. Tübingen, 1964.
Otto Baumgarten, *Meine Lebensgeschichte,* Tübingen, 1929.
W. T. Cleve, *Wege einer Freundschaft: Briefwechsel Peter Wust-Marianne Weber*. Heidelberg, 1951.
Helen Corke, *D. H. Lawrence's Princess*. London 1951.
Ludwig Curtius, *Deutsche und Antike Welt*. Stuttgart, 1950.
Kyklos XI, Alfred Weber zum Gedächtnis, 1958.
Karl Löwith, "Max Weber und Karl Marx," *Archiv für Sozialwissenschaft und Sozialpolitik*. Heidelberg, 1932.
Arthur Mitzman, *The Iron Cage*. New York, 1970.
Wolfgang Mommsen, *Max Weber und die Deutsche Politik 1890–1920*. Tübingen, 1959.
Harry T. Moore, *The Intelligent Heart*. London, 1955.
Edward Nehls, ed., *The Composite Biography of D. H. Lawrence*. University of Wisconsin Press, 1957–59.
Gustav Radbruch, *Der Innere Weg*. Stuttgart, 1951.
Edgar Salin, *Um Stefan George*. Küpper, 1948.
Alfred Weber, "Die Jugend und das Deutsche Schicksal," *Wegweiser,* 1955.
Marianne Weber, *Max Weber: Ein Lebensbild*. Heidelberg, 1927.

Chapter 3

Max Brod, *Streitbares Leben*. Munich, 1960.
Richard Drinnan, *Rebel in Paradise*. Chicago, 1961.
Isadora Duncan, *My Life*. New York, 1927.
Mabel Luhan, *Intimate Memories,* London, 1935— (4 volumes).
———, *Lorenzo in Taos*. London, 1933.
Alma Mahler, *Gustav Mahler*. New York, 1946.
———, *And the Bridge is Love*. New York, 1958.
John Middleton Murry, *Between Two Worlds*. London, 1935.
H. F. Peters, *My Sister, My Spouse*. New York, 1962.
Mrs. Sidgwick, *Caroline and Her Friends*. London, 1889.

Chapter 4

Malcolm Bradbury, "Introduction" to *Little Review Anthology*. Portland Oregon, 1966.
Karl Jaspers, *Max Weber*. Heidelberg, 1920.
———, "Max Weber as Politician, Scientist, Philosopher," in *Three Essays*. New York, 1964.
———, "Philosophic Autobiography," in *The Philosophy of Karl Jaspers,* ed. P. A. Schilpp. New York, 1957.

Frank Lea, *John Middleton Murry.* London, 1959.

Talcott Parsons, "Unity and Diversity in Modern Intellectual Disciplines," *Daedalus,* 1965.

———, "On Building Social Science Theory: A Personal History," *Daedalus,* 1970.

C. E. Russett, *The Concept of Equilibrium in American Social Thought.* New Haven, 1966.

Edward Shils, "Tradition, Ecology, and Institution in the History of Sociology," *Daedalus,* 1970.

E. M. W. Tillyard, *The Muse Unchained.* London, 1958.

Max Weber, *Jugendbriefe.* Tübingen, 1936.

Max Weber zum Gedächtnis, ed. R. *König,* J. Winckelmann. Westdeutsche Verlag, 1963.

Max Weber und die Soziologie Heute, ed. O. Stammer, Tübingen, 1964.

Max Weber: Gedächtnisschrift, ed. K. Engisch, B. Pfister, J. Winckelmann. Berlin, 1966.

Epilogue

Émile Delavenay, *D. H. Lawrence and Edward Carpenter.* London, 1971.

Ludwig Klages, *Rhythmen und Runen aus dem Nachlass.* Barth, 1944.

———, *Der Geist als Widersache der Seele.* Munich, 1954.

Alfred Schuler, *Dichtungen.* Hamburg, 1930.

———, *Fragmente und Vorträge aus dem Nachlass.* Leipzig, 1940.

Index